HEALTH SECURITY
AND GOVERNANCE

HEALTH SECURITY AND GOVERNANCE

Critical Concepts in Military, Strategic, and Security Studies

Edited by
Nicholas Thomas

Volume III
Global Health Governance – Politics, Institutions and Ethics

Routledge
Taylor & Francis Group

LONDON AND NEW YORK

First published 2013
by Routledge
2 Park Square, Milton Park, Abingdon, Oxon OX14 4RN

Simultaneously published in the USA and Canada
by Routledge
711 Third Avenue, New York, NY 10017

Routledge is an imprint of the Taylor & Francis Group, an informa business

British Library Cataloguing in Publication Data
A catalogue record for this book is available from the British Library

Library of Congress Cataloging in Publication Data
Health security and governance : critical concepts in military, strategic, and security studies / edited by Nicholas Thomas.
  p. ; cm. – (Critical concepts in military, strategic, and security studies)
  Includes bibliographical references and index.
  ISBN 978-0-415-67104-0 (set : alk. paper) – ISBN 978-0-415-67105-7 (v. 1 : alk. paper) – ISBN 978-0-415-67107-1 (v. 2 : alk. paper) – ISBN 978-0-415-67108-8 (v. 3 : alk. paper) – ISBN 978-0-415-67109-5 (v. 4 : alk. paper)
  I. Thomas, Nicholas, 1970– II. Series: Critical concepts in military, strategic, and security studies.
  [DNLM: 1. Health Policy. 2. Communicable Diseases, Emerging. 3. Human Rights. 4. Security Measures. 5. World Health. WA 530.1]
  LC classification not assigned
  362.1–dc23
                                                                    2011051203

ISBN: 978-0-415-67104-0 (Set)
ISBN: 978-0-415-67108-8 (Volume III)

Typeset in 10/12pt Times NR MT
by Graphicraft Limited, Hong Kong

Publisher's Note
References within each chapter are as they appear in the original complete work

Printed and bound in Great Britain by the MPG Books Group

CONTENTS

CONTENTS

CONTENTS

CONTENTS

ACKNOWLEDGEMENTS

The publishers would like to thank the following for permission to reprint their material:

American Medical Association for permission to reprint Alexandra M. Stern and Howard Markel, 'International Efforts to Control Infectious Diseases, 1851 to the Present', *Journal of the American Medical Association*, (Vol. 292, No. 12, 2004), pp. 1474–9.

Cambridge University Press for permission to reprint Mark Harrison, 'Disease, Diplomacy and International Commerce: The Origins of International Sanitary Regulation in the Nineteenth Century', *Journal of Global History*, (Vol. 1, No. 2, 2006), pp. 197–217.

Oxford University Press for permission to reprint Ilona Kickbusch, 'New Players for a New Era: Responding to the Global Public Health Challenges', *Journal of Public Health Medicine*, (Vol. 19, No. 2, 1997), pp. 171–8.

Lynne Rienner Publishers for permission to reprint Kelley Lee and Richard Dodgson, 'Globalization and Cholera: Implications for Global Governance,' *Global Governance*, (Vol. 6, No. 2, 2000), pp. 213–36.

Wiley for permission to reprint Allyn L. Taylor, 'Governing the Globalization of Public Health', *Journal of Law, Medicine & Ethics*, (Vol. 32, No. 3, September 2004), pp. 500–8.

The Sheridon Press for permission to reprint Derek Yach and Douglas Bettcher, 'The Globalization of Public Health, I: Threats and Opportunities', *American Journal of Public Health*, (Vol. 88, No. 5, 1998), pp. 735–44.

Lynne Rienner Publishers for permission to reprint Caroline Thomas and Martin Weber. 'The Politics of Global Health Governance: Whatever Happened to "Health for All by the Year 2000"?', *Global Governance*, (Vol. 10, No. 2, 2004), pp. 187–205.

Elsevier for permission to reprint T. J. Downs and H. J. Larson, 'Achieving Millennium Development Goals for Health: Building Understanding, Trust and Capacity to Respond', *Health Policy*, (Vol. 83, 2007), pp. 144–61.

Elsevier for permission to reprint 'Who Runs Global Health?', *The Lancet*, (Vol. 373, No. 9681, 20 June 2009), p. 2083.

The American Association for the Advancement of Science for permission to reprint Jon Cohen, 'The New World of Global Health', *Science*, (Vol. 311, No. 5758, 13 January 2006), pp. 162–7.

Elsevier for permission to reprint Kent Buse and Gill Walt. 'Role Conflict? The World Bank and the World's Health', *Social Science Medicine*, (Vol. 50, No. 2, January 2000), pp. 177–9.

The Sheridon Press for permission to reprint Jennifer Ruger, 'The Changing Role of the World Bank in Global Health', *American Journal of Public Health*, (Vol. 95, No. 1, 2005), pp. 60–70.

Wiley for permission to reprint Daniele Archibugi and Kim Bizzarri, 'The Global Governance of Communicable Diseases: The Case for Vaccine R&D', *Law & Policy*, (Vol. 27, No. 1, 2005), pp. 33–51.

World Health Organization for permission to reprint Roy Widdus, 'Public–Private Partnerships for Health: Their Main Targets, their Diversity, and their Future Directions', *Bulletin of the World Health Organization*, (Vol. 79, No. 8, 2001), pp. 713–20.

World Health Organization for permission to reprint Kent Buse and Gill Walt. 'Global Public–Private Partnerships: Part II – What are the Health Issues for Global Governance?', *Bulletin of the World Health Organization*, (Vol. 78, No. 5, 2000), pp. 699–709.

Indian Journal of Medical Ethics for permission to reprint Augustine D. Asante and Anthony B. Zwi, 'Public-Private Partnerships and Global Health Equity: Prospects and Challenges', *Indian Journal of Medical Ethics*, (Vol. 4, No. 4, October–December 2007), pp. 176–80.

Elsevier for permission to reprint Nirmala Ravishankar, Paul Gubbins, Rebecca J. Cooley, Katherine Leach-Kemon, Catherine M. Michaud, Dean T. Jamison and Christopher J. L. Murray. 'Financing of Global Health: Tracking Development Assistance for Health from 1990 to 2007', *The Lancet*, (Vol. 373, No. 9681, 20 June 2009), pp. 2113–24.

Oxford University Press for permission to reprint David McCoy, Sudeep Chand, and Devi Sridhar. 'Global Health Funding: How Much, Where it Comes From and Where it Goes', *Health Policy and Planning*, (Vol. 24, 1 July 2009), pp. 407–17.

Lynne Rienner Publishers for permission to reprint Garrett Brown, 'Multi-sectoralism, Participation, and Stakeholder Effectiveness: Increasing the role of Nonstate Actors in the Global Fund to Fight AIDS, Tuberculosis and Malaria', *Global Governance*, (Vol. 15, No. 2, April–June 2009), pp. 169–77.

Oxford University Press for permission to reprint András Miklós, 'Public Health and the Rights of States', *Public Health Ethics*, (Vol. 2, No. 2, 2009), pp. 158–70.

Elizabeth M. Prescott for permission to reprint Elizabeth M. Prescott, 'The Politics of Disease: Governance and Emerging Infections,' *Global Health Governance*, (Vol. 1, No. 1, January 2007), pp. 1–8.

Oxford University Press for permission to reprint Stefan Elbe, 'Haggling over Viruses: The Downside Risks of Securitizing Infectious Disease', *Health Policy and Planning*, (Vol. 25, No. 6, November 2010), pp. 476–85.

Oxford University Press for permission to reprint Simon Rushton, 'AIDS and International Security in the United Nations System', *Health Policy and Planning*, (Vol. 25, No. 6, November 2010), pp. 495–504.

Oxford University Press for permission to reprint Philippe Calain, 'Exploring the International Arena of Global Public Health Surveillance,' *Health Policy and Planning*, (Vol. 22, 2007), pp. 2–12.

American Medical Association for permission to reprint J. L. Sturtevant, A. Anema, J. S. Brownstein, 'The New International Health Regulations: Considerations for Global Health Surveillance', *Disaster Medicine and Public Health Preparedness*, (Vol. 1, No. 1, 2007), pp. 117–21.

The Sheridon Press for permission to reprint Theodore M. Brown, Marcos Cueto, and Elizabeth Fee, 'The World Health Organization and the Transition from "International" to "Global" Public Health', *American Journal of Public Health*, (Vol. 96, No. 1, January 2006), pp. 62–72.

Springer for permission to reprint Giok Ling Ooi and Kai Hong Phua. 'SARS in Singapore—Challenges of a Global Health Threat to Local Institutions', *Natural Hazards*, (Vol. 48, 2009), pp. 317–27.

Wiley for permission to reprint Andrew Green, 'The Role of Non-Governmental Organizations and the Private Sector in the Provision of Health Care in Developing Countries', *International Journal of Health Planning and Management*, (Vol. 2, No. 1, January/March 1987), pp. 37–58.

Elsevier for permission to reprint Cathal Doyle and Preeti Patel, 'Civil Society Organisations and Global Health Initiatives: Problems of Legitimacy', *Social Science & Medicine*, (Vol. 66, No. 9, 2008), pp. 1928–38.

Oxford University Press for permission to reprint Lucy Gilson, Priti Dave Sen, Shirin Mohammed and Phare Mujinja, 'The Potential of Health Sector Non-Governmental Organizations: Policy Options', *Health Policy and Planning*, (Vol. 9, No. 1, 1994), pp. 14–24.

Taylor & Francis for permission to reprint Christer Jönsson and Peter Söderholm, 'IGO–NGO Relations and HIV/AIDS: Innovation or Stalemate?', *Third World Quarterly*, (Vol. 16, No. 3, 1995), pp. 459–76.

The Sheridon Press for permission to reprint Mark J. DeHaven, Irby B. Hunter, Laura Wilder, James W. Walton and Jarett Berry. 'Health Programs in Faith-Based Organizations: Are They Effective?', *American Journal of Public Health*, (Vol. 94, No. 6, June 2004), pp. 1030–6.

Massachusetts Medical Society for permission to reprint Susan Okie, 'Global Health—The Gates–Buffett Effect', *New England Journal of Medicine*, (Vol. 355, No. 11, 2006), pp. 1084–8.

Nature Publishing Company for permission to reprint Weiss, Robin A. and Anthony J. McMichael. 'Social and Environmental Risk Factors in the Emergence of Infectious Diseases', *Nature Medicine*, (Vol. 10, No. 12, December 2004), pp. S70–S6.

A. J. McMichael for permission to reprint A. J. McMichael, 'Environmental and Social Influences on Emerging Infectious Diseases: Past, Present and Future', *Philosophical Transactions of the Royal Society of London B Biological Science*, (Vol. 359, No. 1447, 29 July 2004), pp. 1049–58.

Disclaimer

The publishers have made every effort to contact authors/copyright holders of works reprinted in *Health Security and Governance (Critical Concepts in Military, Strategic and Security Studies)*. This has not been possible in every case, however, and we would welcome correspondence from those individuals/companies whom we have been unable to trace.

INTRODUCTION
Unhealthy governance

Nicholas Thomas

Whether naturally occurring or intentionally inflicted, microbial agents can cause illness, disability, and death in individuals while disrupting entire populations, economies, and governments. In the highly interconnected and readily traversed 'global village' of our time, one nation's problem soon becomes every nation's problem as geographical and political boundaries offer trivial impediments to such threats.[1]

To be successful, the securitization of infectious diseases requires the mobilization of resources, actors and institutions. In the past such resources were coordinated at the national level. Later, as an international community devoted to public health began to emerge (particularly after the Second World War), global actors could add their resources to those of states. But these actors were limited by the sovereign concerns of the afflicted states, and when states did not request or want outside assistance international organizations could not interfere. The threats posed by SARS and H5N1 highlighted the shortcomings of this system. Any system that only recognized the interests of states could not respond to an infectious disease outbreak in a timely manner, as states were not the repository of all knowledge and resources. Nor could states be guaranteed not to act in a self-interested manner, placing their domestic concerns above regional or international obligations. What was needed was a more pluralistic health order; one that was inclusive rather than exclusive and held the potential to coordinate an array of actors to respond to outbreaks within and across national boundaries.

While sovereign interests still weigh on such transarchical responses to infectious diseases, the contemporary health order is now far more open than at the start of the century. What this indicates is that the governance of health threats has begun to change. An increasing number of states are now more willing to cooperate with international actors – not just state-centric bodies such as the World Bank or the World Health Organization, but also major foundations and pharmaceutical companies as well as international

1

civil society organizations. Sovereign borders – all too easily perforated by diseases – are becoming more open to cooperation.

It is the purpose of this volume to identify how the actors and institutions now involved in global and transarchical health governance operate, and to explore how the different epistemic communities relate to each other. This introduction will briefly outline key issues and processes in health governance before moving on to chart how infectious diseases emerge through governance failures. These two sections are designed to develop the contextual foundation for the rest of the volume.

Governance and health

No ideal, singular method of global health governance exists, so multilevel governance is inevitable and necessary.[2]

Governance is a problematic concept. Its utilization has grown over the last two decades until it stands in danger of meaning all things to all people. Originally located within the nation-state, it has since expanded to the global and – most recently – regional levels. Roseneau describes governance as encompassing 'the activities of government, but it also includes any actors who resort to command mechanisms to make demands, frame goals, issue directives, and pursue policies'.[3] According to Marks and Hooghe, these activities and the authority that underpins the decision-making mechanisms can be taken either within 'general purpose' jurisdictions – at the 'international, national, regional, meso, local' levels – or within 'specialized jurisdictions' that operate across these five levels, according to a given issue.[4]

At the domestic level there are numerous ways in which the term governance is used. Krahmann states that

> [At the] national and sub-national levels, the term governance is used primarily in four ways. The first treats governance as a generic category synonymous with the concepts of political system or state structure . . . The second usage concerns the reform of public administration since the 1980s. It refers mainly to the devolution of political authority from national administrative agencies to subnational bodies . . . The third use regards the governance of particular policy sectors . . . And the final usage concerns the analysis of corporate governance.[5]

Weiss suggests a further eight ways the term is used, of which the following is arguably the most relevant: 'The concept of governance refers to the complex set of values, norms, processes and institutions by which society manages its development and resolves conflict, formally and informally.'[6]

In his book on the globalization of diseases, Fidler describes a transitional world order where states – in addressing issues of health governance – are

2

moving from a Westphalian to a post-Westphalian order. Fidler characterized the Westphalian health order as 'a particular governance structure and process through which states would address the international spread of infectious diseases'.[7] Citing the series of Sanitary Conventions adopted or negotiated since 1851, Fidler concludes that such agreements represent 'the problem of the cross-border transmission of infectious diseases [being] slotted directly into the structure and principles of Westphalian governance'.[8]

Fidler suggests that – by examining the behaviour of WHO and related bodies – it is possible to identify a post-Cold War shift towards a post-Westphalian health order. This new order is characterized by the dissolution of the traditional domestic and international categories that were, in turn, an outcome of the clear policy recognition (led by the United States) that not only does the spread of infectious diseases not respect national boundaries but that their spread represents a clear challenge to all countries.[9] As was noted in the previous section, this was not a new insight. What was new, however, were the institutional and normative shifts that now accompanied this recognition.

This 'de-Westphalianization' of health reached a peak between mid-2005 and mid-2007, with the revision and subsequent implementation of the new WHO International Health Regulations (IHR). Under the new regime the ability of states to block information transfer was lessened, while WHO was given greater scope to utilize non-state information in developing its official position. Member states are now also required 'to respond to the WHO's request for verification of information, irrespective of its source or origins'.[10] This allows civil society groups and private sector organizations to pass information to WHO, which it can then act upon – instead of waiting for states to provide formal notification. As a result, WHO members have far less scope for self-interested action than was previously the case; although many still return to expressing sovereign rights when it suits them to do so.

In the developing world, however, it remains questionable as to what extent the de-Westphalianization of global health is adhered to by states. Numerous studies have shown that an abiding characteristic of the regional order in Asia, Africa, and South America is the retention of sovereignty – both as an intrinsic operating principle of a state's foreign policy as well as a reactive domestic policy against territorial incursions. Hence, even when a state is pre-disposed towards a de-Westphalian system – and even when it may engage at the global level in such processes – the realities of the accompanying regional order means that a largely Westphalian orientation prevails domestically and regionally. One good example of this was seen in Indonesia, when Health Minister Supari placed national sovereignty over the sharing of virus samples. Thailand also put its sovereign economic interests ahead of its international health obligations by initially choosing not to reveal its outbreak of H5N1. Nonetheless, even in the case of Indonesia, there is a degree of cooperation proceeding, if not on a multilateral basis then on a bilateral basis. Thus, in considering why a state chooses to securitize health threats, it is necessary to balance its

3

domestic constraints against its international obligations. When domestic costs outweigh international benefits then a Westphalian response can be expected. When the potential costs and benefits are more mixed or when the benefits are more recognisable there is more scope for de-Westphalian actions as suggested by Fidler.

Sources of unhealthy governance

The question that then arises is how do health governance shortcomings lead to the spread of infectious diseases? This can be ultimately answered as a failure – at some level or levels – of the host nation-state, which if left unchecked can spill over into other states. The need to address such potential failures is the main reason why the revised IHR require states to undertake 'core capacity requirements for surveillance and response' in the event of an infectious disease outbreak.[11] Colebatch and Larmour identify three sectors where such failures can occur: the bureaucracy, the market and the community.[12] Bureaucratic failure occurs when time constraints and information requirements do not meet the needs of a particular case. This may be compounded by conflicting requirements between the central authorities and those implementing the policies at 'street level'. This failure may be also arise when different organizational units have conflicting goals.[13] Market failure occurs when an information gap is present or when externalities are generated. The market can also fail when the goods (in this case public health) are controlled by a narrower group of people than those immediately threatened[14] Community failure can transpire when individuals' overlapping needs and identities cause them to not 'pull in the same direction', thus destabilizing the nation-state.[15]

Therefore, when considering where threats emerge to challenge state security and given that it is failures in one or more sectors that create vulnerabilities, this approach provides a model from which the origins of security threats could be ascertained. Further, in a transnational setting, the identification of a threat emanating from a failed sector could assist in the identification of sectors most at risk in other states. Colebatch and Larmour concluded that the resolution of a failure generally requires support from, at least, the two other sectors, if not in addition to the remaining capacity from the failed sector. In other words, a market failure could require the combined resources of the bureaucratic and community sectors, and may even require market resources from other parts of the sector, if it is to be successfully overcome.

When translating this model into a developing world setting a number of issues immediately arise. First is the role of the state. As noted earlier, governance theory is an explicitly pluralist model, where numerous actors can mobilize a variety of powers and/or resources to engage with – and realize – a particular policy outcome. Not all states in the global south welcome or willingly recognize such a governance model. Many states in this hemisphere remain illiberal or authoritarian, where domestic policy-making powers are largely centralized within the state. To the extent that the state may engage with non-state actors to address an issue of concern, the flow of information and power is top-down and ends when the issue is dealt with, instead of building up capacity for future challenges. As *The Lancet* noted in May 2007, overcoming political obstacles – rather than just financial obstacles – is 'a far more daunting task'.[16] This creates an expectation gap when dealing with outbreaks on a global scale when the different perceptions between states in the global north and south intersect.

The second issue is the role of the civil society – in terms of its internal capacity/capacities, its relations with the state and market actors and its transnational networks. As Gilson *et al.* noted, civil society organizations offer states alternative capacities in providing public health goods; although the authors also observed that frequently there has to be higher levels of trust between the organizations and the state if the partnership is to work effectively.[17] At the global level, Doyle and Patel suggested that there is a similar legitimacy issue if such partnerships (this time between the state and international civil society organizations) are not managed with respect to the needs of both the supplying organization and the state. However, the authors concluded that civil society organizations can and do play a significant role in global health initiatives.[18] Beyond supply and demand actors and institutions, there is also the role that transnational social flows play in spreading diseases over borders. As Wilson stated, 'The current world circumstances juxtapose people, parasites, plants, animals, and chemicals in a way that precludes timely adaptation. The combination of movement at many levels and profound change in the physical environment can lead to unanticipated diseases spread by multiple channels.'[19]

The third issue is the role of markets – in terms of private sector organizations and economic capacities. Private sector health groups via their research and development capacities, their specialization in the sector and their economic leverage can play a significant role in supporting global and transnational responses to infectious diseases. However, the key question with such actors is the imperative behind their behaviour. For most, the imperative is usually profit-driven. This can create a mismatch in expectations and cost sharing when it comes to resolving disease outbreaks. As Wilson *et al.* noted, the expectation of profit can alter the intended results of cooperation, particularly in the case of vaccine development and distribution. The authors concluded that 'the expected transfers of biological data may result in a country losing financial benefits that could be derived from the development and sale of a vaccine developed from the data. Also, there are no guarantees that a country will be provided with an adequate amount of the vaccine to administer to its population.'[20]

Straddling the market and civil society sectors are the major foundations whose economic and policy strengths enable them to develop programmes, empower local health organizations and attract state support. But the presence of these bodies also presents a challenge to other parts of the global health architecture as more actors can end up competing for the same amount of resources, leading to competition rather than cooperation.[21]

All of these issues suggest that if failures of governance can lead to infectious disease outbreaks then resolving them by improving global and national health governance will equally reduce the threat posed by outbreaks of infectious diseases. However, with so many actors operating at different levels, what is still missing is a clear articulation of a global health architecture – one where all the actors and institutions have defined roles and rules, and where the behaviour of new players will support rather than detract from efforts to prevent and resolve health threats.

Conclusions

In the contemporary world there is a pressing need for cooperation to prevent the spread of infectious diseases and other health threats around the world; yet, all too frequently, sovereign interests clash with the needs of the international community. As the chapters in this volume highlight despite such limitations there is an emergent health order at the global level, one whose structure is akin to that needed for the successful securitization of diseases. This could suggest that twinning governance approaches with securitization objectives may be an effective way forward in dealing with the threat posed by infectious diseases – locally, transnationally and on a global scale.

Notes

1 Mark Smolinski, Margaret Hamburg and Joshua Lederman (eds) *Microbial Threats to Health: Emergence, Detection, and Response*, Washington DC: National Academies Press, 2003, p. xvii.
2 Lance Gable, 'The proliferation of human rights in global health governance', *Journal of Law, Medicine & Ethics* 35(4) (2007): 534–44, at 541.
3 James Roseneau, *Along the Domestic-Foreign Frontier: Exploring Governance in a Turbulent World*, Cambridge: Cambridge University Press, 1997, p. 145.
4 Gary Marks and Liesbet Hooghe, 'Contrasting visions of multi-level governance', in Ian Bache and Matthew Flinders (eds) *Multi-level Governance*, Oxford: Oxford University Press, 2004, pp. 15–30.
5 Elke Krahmann, 'National, regional, and global governance: one phenomenon or many?', *Global Governance* 9(3) (2003): 324–5.
6 Thomas Weiss, 'Governance, good governance and global governance: conceptual and actual challenges', in Rorden Wilkinson (ed.) *The Global Governance Reader*, Abingdon: Routledge, 2005, p. 70.
7 David P. Fidler, *SARS, Governance and the Globalization of Disease*, Basingstoke: Palgrave Macmillan, 2004, p. 27.
8 Ibid., p. 29.
9 Ibid., pp. 43–4.
10 Sanjit Bagchi, 'WHO regulations to prevent the spread of diseases', *Canadian Medical Association Journal*, 177(5) (2007): 447–8, at 448.

11 For more information, see *International Health Regulations* (2005) at http://www. who.int/csr/ihr/en/
12 Hal Colebatch and Peter Larmour, *Market, Bureaucracy and Community*, London: Pluto Press, 1993, pp. 28–39.
13 Ibid., pp. 33–4.
14 Ibid., pp. 29–33.
15 Ibid., p. 35.
16 'International Health Regulations: The Challenges Ahead', *Lancet* 369 (2007): 1763.
17 Lucy Gilson, Priti Dave Sen, Shirin Mohammed and Phare Mujinja, 'The potential of health sector non-governmental organizations: policy options', *Health Policy and Planning* 9(1) (1994): 14–24 (Chapter 88 in this volume).
18 Cathal Doyle and Preeti Patel, 'Civil society organisations and global health initiatives: problems of legitimacy', *Social Science and Medicine* 66(9) (2008): 1928–38 (Chapter 87 in this volume).
19 Mary Wilson, 'Travel and the emergence of infectious diseases', *Emerging Infectious Diseases* 1(2) (1995): 39–46, at 45 (Chapter 93 in this volume).
20 Kumanan Wilson, Barbara von Tigerstrom and Christopher McDougall, 'Protecting global health security through the International Health Regulations: requirements and challenges', *Canadian Medical Association Journal* 179(1) (2008): 44–8, at 46.
21 Nirmala Ravishankar, Paul Gubbins, Rebecca J. Cooley, Katherine Leach-Kemon, Catherine M. Michaud, Dean T. Jamison and Christopher J. L. Murray, 'Financing of global health: tracking development assistance for health from 1990 to 2007', *Lancet* 373(9681) (2009): 2113–24 (Chapter 71 in this volume).

Part 10

GLOBALIZATION OF GLOBAL HEALTH

INTERNATIONAL EFFORTS TO CONTROL INFECTIOUS DISEASES, 1851 TO THE PRESENT

Alexandra Minna Stern and Howard Markel

Source: *Journal of the American Medical Association*, 292:12 (2004), 1474–9.

Many 21st-century observers explain international efforts to control infectious diseases as a function of globalization and recent transformations in international commerce, transportation, and human migration. However, these contemporary global health initiatives can be more fully understood by also exploring the origins of international health organizations and regulations, which were initially dedicated exclusively to stemming the tide of infectious epidemics. This article reviews 3 eras of international approaches to controlling infectious diseases (1851–1881, 1881–1945, and 1945 to the present) and concludes by assessing how nations have a strong fiscal and humanitarian incentive to invest in infectious disease control programs and infrastructures in and beyond their own borders.

Recent history has shown that, despite claims of conquest, infectious diseases are far from a relic of the past. According to the World Health Organization (WHO), every 60 minutes, 1500 people die of an infectious disease.[1,2] Not only have old epidemics, such as tuberculosis, malaria, and measles, recrudesced but also newly emerging diseases, such as West Nile fever, Ebola fever, and severe acute respiratory syndrome (SARS), have appeared around the world and demand new interventions and strategies. In addition, for the past 2 decades AIDS has killed and debilitated millions of people and exposed the limits of scientific knowledge and its therapeutic applications.[3]

Throughout the past few decades especially, framing approaches to controlling newly emerging and reemerging infectious diseases in terms of globalization and modern transformations in international commerce, transportation, and human migration has become commonplace.[4–6] There is certainly a great deal of truth to such assertions. For example, the outbreak and containment of SARS in the spring of 2003 was facilitated by new global technologies such as transoceanic air travel (which can allow microorganisms to travel from country to country and provide them with a propitious environment to incubate and spread) and the Internet (which greatly enhances the potential for epidemiologic surveillance and rapid communication between distant laboratories). However, we argue that it would be a mistake to view today's approaches to controlling infectious diseases solely through the window of the past few decades. We illuminate a more extended history by exploring the origins of international efforts to combat infectious diseases, and concomitantly promote health, during the past 150 years.

This historical survey illustrates the extent to which national interests, political or cultural beliefs, scientific debates, and financial concerns have hindered and helped the world's ability to confront and quell infectious diseases. Tracking international responses to infectious diseases during the past century and a half, from cholera in the 19th century to SARS in the 21st, underscores that triumphal narratives of human and medical progress are misplaced. Sadly, the lack of authority to enforce coordinated responses to epidemic outbreaks around the world and a weak system of incentives for public health investment have limited the capacity of international health organizations since their inception. We review 3 eras of international approaches to controlling infectious diseases (1851–1881, 1881–1945, and 1945 to the present) and conclude by suggesting why strong incentives are needed to encourage nations to invest in health programs and infrastructures in and beyond their own borders.

Setting the stage: the first International Sanitary Conferences, 1851–1881

As people began to travel and trade, the microorganisms and infectious diseases they harbored traveled with them. For example, the spread of bubonic plague epidemics during the Middle Ages was linked to human migration patterns and the resulting development of quarantine laws.[7] The mere threat of an impending plague visitation typically prompted the closure of entire ports and cities to foreign travelers and goods.[8] In the 15th century, along with plans for colonization and evangelization, Spanish conquerors imported microbial diseases such as smallpox and measles that decimated native populations in the Americas.[9] After the boundaries of modern nation-states began to crystallize in the 18th and 19th centuries, improving global health became integral to national welfare and international diplomacy.[10,11] Many leaders of nation-states began to accept that controlling the spread of infectious diseases from one nation to another required international solutions and organized international conventions and draft covenants, almost all of which related to quarantine regulations.[12] Conflicts frequently arose as nations sought to balance territorial sovereignty and economic interests with the need for transparent and universally applied health protections.

Cholera, which ravaged Asia and Europe in successive waves in the early to mid-19th century, inspired physicians and politicians to convene the first International Sanitary Conference in 1851.[13,14] Representatives from 11 European countries met in Paris to formulate a utopian quarantine policy capable of simultaneously curtailing the transnational importation of diseases and upholding the imperatives of trade and commerce. The practical results of this gathering were limited because scientific disagreement about disease etiologies, coupled with the mercantilist prerogatives of participating nations to protect their boundaries and commerce, stymied the elaboration of mutually acceptable measures.[14] Nonetheless, this inaugural conference was instrumental to the formation of the first international network of scientists and policy makers devoted to the global control of infectious diseases and should be recognized as the cornerstone of today's multinational health organizations.

From 1851 to 1900, 10 international sanitary conferences were held, with each successive meeting drawing more delegates.[14] These meetings focused exclusively on the containment of epidemics, and their specific agendas varied, depending on whatever disease outbreak (cholera, plague, or yellow fever) was most urgent. As Howard-Jones[14] has pointed out, these gatherings provide a window onto a transitional moment in modern medicine when the previously stark lines between contagionist and anticontagionist doctrine were becoming increasingly blurred. The same disease agent could in one afternoon session be referred to as a germ, miasm, animalcule, zymotic poison, microphyte, seed, fungus, or virus.[14,15] In their search to ascertain how germs were transmitted, delegates formulated intricate, if convoluted with hindsight, theories. For example, one of the most prominent participants at these meetings, the German scientist Max Von Pettenkofer, can be most aptly described as a "contingent contagionist."[14,15] He maintained that cholera was spread through contaminated groundwater, a theory that combined persuasive elements from various models of disease causation.[16] Whatever theory they endorsed, however, delegates sought to formulate transnational quarantine procedures and mechanisms. Nonetheless, divergent theories and the belief that noxious elements in the environment were responsible for disease or that particular ailments were geographically specific often militated against consensus.

Decades before the articulation and demonstration of germ theory, these meetings presaged many of the organizational structures of contemporary public health administration that are taken for granted today. They encouraged the formation of national health agencies with designated delegates who were dispatched to international meetings and shared findings upon returning home. More important, they set the stage for the eventual establishment of standardized definitions of quarantine and systems of information gathering and disease surveillance. Despite intellectual, personal, political, cultural, and linguistic differences, delegates demonstrated a shared commitment to continue to reassess critical health issues against the backdrop of rapidly changing scientific theories and discoveries. For example, it is easy to forget that the public health methods often endorsed before the germ theory era, although inspired by sanitarian concepts such as cleaning up the streets and purifying the food and water supply, had a salubrious effect on health indicators and reduced endemic and epidemic diseases.[17,18] Indeed, these are proven measures that have the advantage of targeting many social and structural conditions that can give rise to disease and could benefit many developing countries today.

During this era, international health endeavors were propelled by technologic developments, such as the telegraph, telephone, and typewriter, as well as new modes of transportation, particularly the railroad and steamship lines. However, there was a negative underside to this period of scientific and technologic change because some of the most spectacular medical and scientific gains of the 19th century were frequently enmeshed with colonialism and imperialism.[19,20] Africa, Asia, and the Caribbean often served as laboratories for experimentation and human and animal subject research that today we would find disturbing. For example, European missions were sent to Egypt and India to investigate cholera; the plague bacillus was isolated in Hong Kong, independently, by a Frenchman and a Japanese bacteriologist; and the insect-vector transmission theory of yellow fever was confirmed in the wake of the US military occupation of Cuba and the Panama Canal.[20-24] Today, we all benefit from these medical discoveries. But we should not forget that they were made during the zenith of European and US colonialism and were one part of a constellation of interventions aimed, at least in part, at improving the health and productivity of laboring populations and enhancing commercial and territorial dominion.

The advent of germ theory and the rise of bacteriology, 1881–1945

Not surprisingly, the emphasis of the international sanitary conferences was determined by the most deadly infectious disease of the day. The first 4 meetings in 1851, 1859, 1866, and 1874, for example, concentrated almost exclusively on cholera, the great infectious scourge of the 19th century.[14,25] At the 1881 conference held in Washington, DC, on the other hand, US delegates brought attention to yellow fever because it had broken out in epidemic proportions in the Mississippi River Valley 3 years earlier.[14,26,27]

By the 1890s, delegates had built functional working relationships and increasingly shared the same scientific and legal vocabulary, and, as a result, substantive consensus on international sanitary and quarantine regulations began to emerge.[13,14,28] As more and more delegates accepted the germ theory of infectious disease, they were more likely to agree on rudimentary measures for containment and control. Hence it was at the 1892 meeting that the first International Sanitary Convention, dealing exclusively with cholera, which had just appeared in pandemic proportions, was signed.[13,14] Five years later, at the 10th International Sanitary Conference, a similar convention focused on plague was drafted and signed. Plague was of particular concern that year, given the recent outbreaks in India and the announcement that Alexandre Yersin, a Swiss bacteriologist and protégé of Louis Pasteur, had identified its etiologic agent.[14]

Even if the international sanitary conferences, which were held until the eve of World War II (1938), resulted in relatively few long-lasting agreements and conventions, they influenced international health in myriad ways. First and foremost, they served as forums in which the latest findings about bacteriology were announced and deliberated.[10,11,13,14] As scientific luminaries such as Louis Pasteur, Robert Koch, Carlos Finlay, and many others shared their revolutionary discoveries about the leading infectious killers of the day, delegates initiated the formulation of a modern, scientifically informed, international canon of quarantine regulations, medical inspection of travelers and goods, disease surveillance methods, and disease classification.[13,14,28,29] In many cases, these new techniques of infectious disease control were codified into national law and informed the missions of regional and service organizations. In the United States, for example, medical inspection, quarantine, and laboratory standardization went hand in hand with the gradual federalization of public health, away from local and state entities to the US Public Health Service (USPHS).[30] Indeed, it is only against the background of medical internationalism that we can begin to understand the elaboration of USPHS regulations on immigrant inspection, quarantine, and vaccination during the early 20th century.[31]

In 1902, greater hemispheric cooperation, particularly with respect to yellow fever, led to the creation of the Pan American Sanitary Bureau (now called the Pan American Health Organization, or PAHO), which soon became a model for transnational health promotion and information sharing.[32-35] Across the Atlantic Ocean, the Office International d'Hygiène Publique (OIHP), based in Paris, was founded in 1907 to collect and disseminate data about infectious diseases to strengthen quarantine and other global public health regulations.[13,14] The OIHP functioned chiefly as an international information clearinghouse and by World War I was systematizing the latest findings on malaria, typhoid, hookworm, tuberculosis, and other health threats.

After World War I, the League of Nations formed a Health Committee in which individual US physicians participated, but not the United States at large because of the decision by the US Senate not to ratify membership in the league.[13,14] However, despite friction and redundancy between the League of Nations Health Committee and the OIHP, the 2 organizations collaborated to launch international health studies and encourage demonstration projects in afflicted regions of the world and were pivotal to the elaboration of modern international disease classifications. Alongside the health campaigns of the International Labor Organization and the International Red Cross, the Pan American Sanitary Bureau, the OIHP, and the league's Health Committee began to broaden the international health portfolio to consider maternal and infant health, nutrition, housing, physical education, narcotic trade and addiction, and occupational health.[13,14,36,37] Their work was substantially complemented by the International Health Board of the Rockefeller Foundation, which sponsored projects targeting many tropical diseases, especially malaria and hookworm, in countries such as China, Brazil, and Mexico.[38] These organizations concentrated on the control of infectious diseases, and health officers undertook their eradication and prevention efforts with vigorous determination.

During the construction of the Panama Canal from 1904 to 1914, for example, US physicians and scientists took far-reaching measures to eliminate any source of standing water where mosquitoes could breed.[22-24] Although the US public health efforts in the Canal Zone were stunningly effective in quelling yellow fever through mosquito eradication, this success came at the cost of neglecting more mundane but just as deadly maladies such as pneumonia and diarrheal diseases, a pattern that has frequently been repeated in the decades since.[39]

Furthermore, during this era, infectious disease interventions sometimes converged with distorted assumptions about race, ethnicity, and class that reflected and perpetuated inequities in health status and access. In the United States, for example, particular immigrants were often viewed as the vectors of particular diseases even as bacteriology continued to demonstrate that microbes were the most egalitarian of living beings when it came to finding a host to infect.[40,41]

Despite these problems, however, by the 1930s the reforms and campaigns promoted by international, national, and local health agencies, along with new technologic and scientific developments, were reshaping the international health landscape.[10,11] Even before the introduction of antibiotics and the development of many vaccines we take for granted today, the worst scourges of the past, such as tuberculosis, bubonic plague, and cholera, began to diminish around the world. This trend only intensified with the emergence of penicillin and the mass production of a host of antibiotics. In the aftermath of World War II, as the brutalities that took place in the Nazi death camps began to be widely reported, nations collectively pledged to prevent such human brutality in the future. This humanitarian movement led to an unprecedented degree of international cooperation that would be harshly tested by the vicissitudes of politics, the global economy, and a wide spectrum of deadly, chronic, and debilitating diseases.

The WHO: a new definition of health, 1945 to the present

When the United Nations Conference was convened in San Francisco in 1945, delegates unanimously concurred that a single global health organization should be founded and recognized as an essential component of the postwar international system.[42,43] Toward this end, members of the Pan American Sanitary Bureau, OIHP, the league's Health Committee, and a few additional organizations were entrusted with drafting a constitution for the proposed WHO. WHO's constitution was signed the following year at a conference in New York City and ratified in 1948, and shortly thereafter, WHO's premier body, the World Health Assembly, gathered for its inaugural meeting in Geneva.[44] Its charge was to foster and coordinate public health campaigns across the world, in large part by spearheading cooperation between nations and fomenting national health agencies.[42-45] Moreover, WHO's mission was guided by a new definition of health, which was now seen not just as the amelioration of disease but also, more positively and broadly, as the promotion of universal physical, mental, and social well-being.[42-45] This redefinition was facilitated by the medical advances of the past century, as well as an explicit emphasis on human rights, which acquired heightened meaning after world-wide recognition of the horrors of the Holocaust.[46] Individual and collective health was now considered by representatives of the United Nations to be "fundamental to the attainment of peace and security."[45]

WHO subsumed its predecessor organizations to become the world's officially sanctioned public health organization. WHO established 6 semiautonomous regional offices, taking its cue from the USPHS, which had long maintained geographic district offices.[47] PAHO was incorporated under WHO's umbrella in 1949, followed by offices for Europe, the western Pacific, Africa, the eastern Mediterranean, and Southeast Asia.[42,43] Recognizing the necessity to combat infectious diseases, in 1951 WHO adopted a revised version of the International Sanitary Regulations first approved at the 1892 international sanitary conference. However, this set of regulations was originally created specifically to control cholera, plague, and yellow fever and still remains in effect today, demonstrating the degree to which present approaches to controlling infectious diseases are rooted in and potentially constrained by their 19th-century antecedents.[48]

During its early years, WHO had high hopes of using the latest biomedical techniques and advances in the quest to eradicate infectious diseases and improve basic health indices. Its initial major campaigns included the containment of yaws, which, thanks to penicillin, was spectacularly achieved and transformed the lives of millions of afflicted children, particularly in Africa and the Caribbean. Emboldened by the success of this "magic bullet" approach and perhaps too much faith in microbiological or pharmacologic solutions, rather than combining these efforts with programs of broad social interventions, WHO spent its first 2 decades launching similar disease-specific campaigns, principally targeting tuberculosis, malaria, and smallpox.[49]

One of WHO's greatest triumphs was the smallpox eradication drive that culminated with the last naturally occurring case in Somalia in 1977.[49] But these efforts also demonstrated the crucial role that local health workers play in any treatment or vaccination program. Similar efforts to contain malaria demonstrated just how socially complex the task of mosquito control could be. Hence it was the experiences among WHO scientists, community health organizers, and the local populations that helped to generate awareness of the dire need for improved health infrastructure, culturally sensitive public health campaigns, and the availability of primary medical care.[49,50] Along these lines, by the 1970s postwar optimism had faded and was gradually replaced by an awareness that the eradication of specific diseases would translate into few if any gains in regions that lacked sewage systems, potable water, adequate food, health clinics, and rudimentary knowledge of illness and treatment, to name but a few crucial positive contributors to a population's general health. For example, after the famine in Biafra and its disastrous aftermath during the early 1970s, dissatisfaction with the failure of WHO and the International Red Cross to address the structural and political precipitants of health catastrophes prompted a group of French physicians to found Médecins San Frontières (Doctors Without Borders).[51]

Eager to move beyond the limits of disease-specific approaches, WHO consciously shifted its course in 1977, when the World Health Assembly resolved that "the main social target of governments and WHO in the coming decades should be the attainment by all the citizens of the world by the year 2000 of a level of health that will permit them to lead a socially and economically productive life."[50] The following year, delegates from 134 countries, 67 United Nations organizations, specialized agencies, and nongovernmental organizations gathered in Alma-Ata, in present-day Kazakhstan. There, Dr Halfdan T. Mahler, WHO's director-general, challenged participants to address the social, economic, and cultural problems that produced and reinforced the marked discrepancies "between the health 'haves' and 'have-nots'" around the world.[50] At this historic meeting, delegates—many from African nations that had recently gained their independence through anticolonial struggles—pronounced their commitment to creating a health-for-all value system and working toward making access to health care a reality for everyone.[50,52]

Since the Alma-Ata summit, WHO's achievements, particularly immunization of children in third world countries, have been clouded by the difficulty of the dual goal of diminishing specific infectious diseases and delivering basic health services to impoverished areas. WHO's mission has also been hindered by bureaucratic logjams, geopolitical tensions, internecine religious and ethnic warfare, and ongoing if not worsening economic disparities between the developed and developing world.[1,3,4,53]

Conclusion: future investments in the international battle against infectious diseases

In the 19th century, international health conferences and the drafting of quarantine and sanitary conventions produced the first set of global strategies and regulations for combating infectious diseases. By the 20th century, these gatherings had played a central role in the standardization of disease classification and surveillance methods. However, rifts and rivalries between nations too eager to blame foreigners for disease or hesitant to implement a quarantine on their own shores because of lost commerce and tourism often undermined the efficacy and relevance of international health provisions. Moreover, since their inception in the mid-1800s, international health organizations have lacked the supranational power to require nations to follow internationally mandated health conventions.[48] In the case of WHO, for example, many would argue that acting as the global medical police contradicts its charter and commitment to the protection and promotion of human and civil rights.

Given the rise of newly emerging and emerging infectious diseases and that it is unlikely that WHO will possess such unilateral authority in the near future, we must identify incentives to encourage substantial investments in the battle against infectious diseases and work as a global community toward achieving health as defined by WHO in 1946. Nothing less than a cooperative partnership of nations, health care professionals, medical researchers, public health specialists, and concerned corporations and individuals will suffice.[1,6] Much more can be done to prevent and treat many infectious diseases, provided nations are prepared to make the necessary financial and social commitments to the task.[54] Tens of thousands of dedicated health workers affiliated with WHO and other global health organizations have been working toward such goals for decades now, but in our shrinking world all health practitioners and policy makers must view international health as a local concern, which necessitates an umbrella approach that involves philanthropic organizations; economic foundations; nongovernmental organizations; national, regional, and local medical societies; academic institutions; service organizations; and citizens. As concerned health care professionals, we can put the movement of globalization to good use in the battle against infectious diseases. Specifically, with the rise of global markets where people, goods, services, and information now flow routinely and swiftly across regional and national borders, there is a greater need for transparency and accountability not only in economic matters but also in terms of infectious disease control. Indeed, this is one of the historical lessons of the SARS epidemic of 2003.

In September 2000, the United Nations held a Millennium Summit in which leaders of 180 nations set several goals for promoting the health of all the world's citizens by 2015. Among these were controlling epidemic diseases, reducing the world's childhood mortality rate by 66% and the mortality rate of women during childbearing by 75%, reversing the global spread of AIDS, and halving the proportion of people in the world who have no access to safe drinking water or adequate food and whose income is less than $1 a day.[55]

Columbia University economist Jeffrey Sachs was asked to develop a Commission on Macroeconomics and Health for the United Nations to begin accomplishing these noble and lifesaving aims. The commission's 3 core findings were elegantly simple, though hardly simplistic. First, the massive amount of disease burden in the world's poorest nations poses a huge threat to global wealth and security. Second, millions of impoverished people around the world die of preventable and treatable infectious diseases because they lack access to basic medical care and sanitation. And third, we have the ability and technology to save millions of lives each year if only the wealthier nations would help provide the poorer countries with such health care and services.[56]

What Sachs and his colleagues projected, in terms of dollars and cents, is that all of the wealthy nations of the world must devote one tenth of 1% of their gross national product (or $0.01 for every $10 of income) toward supporting health services for the world's poor. Economists estimate that the combined income of the world's wealthiest nations is about $25 trillion a year. Thus, a multinational contribution of $25 billion a year, along with similar monetary donations from philanthropic and corporate resources and cooperative efforts from poor nations, could markedly reduce the world's disease burden; 21 000 lives could be saved each day under such a plan.[57,58] If the humane imperative is not enough, recall that with enhanced worldwide health, vast improvements are made in the world economic situation because of more productive labor forces in nations decimated by disease. If this task were begun today, the United Nations Commission estimates that by 2020, more than $360 billion dollars a year would be generated in other economic benefits.[59] More recently, 8 internationally renowned economists, including 3 Nobel Prize winners, met in Copenhagen to determine how $50 billion could be most effectively spent on improving the world in any way, including education, the environment, and social services. According to cost-benefit analysis, they determined that the 3 best investments were $27 billion for combating AIDS, $12 billion for malnutrition, and $13 billion for malaria.[60]

These endeavors can work. The global effort to eradicate smallpox through immunization programs was a stunning success. Recent programs organized by a consortium of foundations, health agencies, and pharmaceutical companies to reduce or eliminate African river blindness, trachoma, AIDS, and leprosy in developing nations have been extremely successful.[1] Nevertheless, one of the greatest challenges of the 21st century is to construct a global health organization, or set of organizations, to expand and refine the activities initiated more than 150 years ago at the first international sanitary conferences. With an understanding of the close association between health and human rights, as articulated by the United Nations and WHO, and the best practices of infectious disease control, as demonstrated over time, there is hope as long as the world community accepts the fact that investing in infectious disease control is critical to global health, security, and prosperity. As the early 20th-century public health pioneer Dr Hermann Biggs proclaimed in 1911, "Public health is purchasable."[61] But it is an investment that works best when purchased in advance rather than paid out as each crisis arises.

References

1. Koop C. E., Pearson C. E., Schwarz M. R., eds. *Critical Issues in Global Health.* San Francisco, Calif: Jossey-Bass; 2002.
2. World Health Organization. Six diseases cause 90% of infection disease deaths. Available at: http://www.who.int/infectious-disease-report/pages/ch2text.html. Accessed August 8, 2004.
3. Barnett T., Whiteside A. *AIDS in the Twenty-First Century: Disease and Globalization.* New York, NY: Palgrave/MacMillan; 2004.
4. Garrett L. *Betrayal of Trust: The Collapse of Global Public Health.* New York, NY: Hyperion; 2000.
5. Kelly L. *Globalization and Health: An Introduction.* New York, NY: Palgrave/MacMillan; 2004.
6. Farmer P. *Infections and Inequalities: The Modern Plagues.* Berkeley: University of California Press; 1999.
7. McNeill W. H. *Plagues and Peoples.* Garden City, NY: Anchor Books; 1967.
8. Markel H. *Quarantine! East European Jewish Immigrants and the New York City Epidemics of 1892.* Baltimore, Md: Johns Hopkins University Press; 1997.
9. Crosby A. W. *The Columbian Exchange: Biological and Cultural Consequences of 1492.* Westport, Conn: Greenwood Publishing Co; 1972.
10. Fidler D. P. The globalization of public health: the first 100 years of international health diplomacy. *Bull World Health Organ.* 2001;79:842–849.
11. Roemer M. I. Internationalism in medicine and public health. In: Porter D., ed. *The History of Public Health and the Modern State.* Atlanta, Ga: Rodopi; 1994:403–423.
12. Winslow C.-E. A. *The Conquest of Epidemic Disease.* Princeton, NJ: Princeton University Press; 1944.
13. Bynum B. F. Policing hearts of darkness: aspects of the International Sanitary Conferences. *Hist Philos Life Sci.* 1993;15:421–434.
14. Howard-Jones N. The scientific background of the International Sanitary Conferences, 1851–1938. *WHO Chron.* 1974;28(pt 1):159–171; (pt 2):229–247; (pt 3):369–384; (pt 4):414–426; (pt 5):455–470; (pt 6):495–508.
15. Ackerknecht E. H. Anticontagionism between 1821 and 1867. *Bull Hist Med.* 1948;22:562–593.
16. Von Pettenkofer M. *Cholera: How to Prevent and Resist It.* London, England: Baillière Tindall Cox; 1875.
17. Rosen G. *A History of Public Health.* Baltimore, Md: Johns Hopkins University Press; 1993 [1958].
18. Fee E. Introduction. In: Rosen G., ed. *A History of Public Health.* Baltimore, Md: Johns Hopkins University Press; 1993 [1958]:ix–lxvii.
19. Farley J. *Bilharzia: A History of Imperial Tropical Medicine.* Cambridge, Mass: Cambridge University Press; 2003.
20. MacLeod R., Lewis M. *Disease, Medicine, and Empire: Perspectives on Western Medicine and the Experience of European Expansion.* New York, NY: Routledge; 1988.
21. Curtin P. D. *Disease and Empire: The Health of European Troops in the Conquest of Africa.* New York, NY: Cambridge University Press; 1998.
22. Truby A. E. *Memoir of Walter Reed: The Yellow Fever Episode.* New York, NY: Paul B Hoeber; 1943.

23. LePrince J. A., Orenstein A. J., eds. *Mosquito Control in Panama: The Eradication of Malaria and Yellow Fever in Cuba and Panama*. New York, NY: GP Putnam's Sons; 1916.

24. Gorgas W. C. *Sanitation in Panama*. New York, NY: D Appleton & Co; 1915.

25. Rosenberg C. E. *The Cholera Years: The United States in 1832, 1849, and 1866*. Chicago, Ill: University of Chicago Press; 1962.

26. Humphreys M. *Yellow Fever and the South*. Baltimore, Md: Johns Hopkins University Press; 1992.

27. Bloom K. J. *The Mississippi Valley's Great Yellow Fever Epidemic of 1878*. Baton Rouge: Louisiana State University Press; 1993.

28. The rise of international cooperation in health. *World Health Forum*. 1995;16:388–393.

29. De Kruif P. *Microbe Hunters*. New York, NY: Harcourt Brace & Co; 1926.

30. Marcus A. Disease prevention in America: from a local to a national outlook, 1880–1910. *Bull Hist Med*. 1979;53:184–203.

31. Williams R. C. *The United States Public Health Service, 1798–1950*. Washington, DC: Commissioned Officers Association of the United States Public Health Service; 1951.

32. Fee E., Brown T. M. 100 Years of the Pan American Health Organization. *Am J Public Health*. 2002;92:1888–1889.

33. Bustamante M. E. *The Pan-America Sanitary Bureau: Half a Century of Health Activities, 1902–1954*. Washington, DC: Pan-American Sanitary Bureau; 1955.

34. Alleyne G. A. O. The Pan American Health Organization's first 100 years: reflections of the director. *Am J Public Health*. 2002;92:1890–1894.

35. Acuña H. R. The Pan American Health Organization: 75 years of international cooperation in public health. *Public Health Rep*. 1977;92:537–544.

36. Birn A. E. Skirting the issue: women and international health in historical perspective. *Am J Public Health*. 1999;89:399–407.

37. Birn A. E. "No more surprising than a broken pitcher"? maternal and child health in the early years of the Pan American Sanitary Bureau. *Can Bull Hist Med*. 2002;19:17–46.

38. Cueto M., ed. *Missionaries of Science: The Rockefeller Foundation and Latin America*. Bloomington: Indiana University Press; 1994.

39. McCullough D. *The Path Between the Seas: The Creation of the Panama Canal, 1870–1914*. New York, NY: Simon & Schuster; 1977.

40. Markel H., Stern A. M. The foreignness of germs: the persistent association of immigrants and disease in American society. *Milbank Q*. 2002;80:57–88.

41. Markel H. *When Germs Travel: Six Major Epidemics That Have Invaded America Since 1900 and the Fears They Have Unleashed*. New York, NY: Pantheon Books; 2004.

42. Howard-Jones N. The World Health Organization in historical perspective. *Perspect Biol Med*. 1981;24:467–482.

43. Charles J. Origins, history, and achievements of the World Health Organization. *BMJ*. 1968;4:293–296.

44. Preamble to the Constitution of the World Health Organization as adopted by the International Health Conference, New York, June 19–22, 1946; signed on July 22, 1946, by the representatives of 61 states. Official Records of the World Health Organization (No. 2: 100) and entered into force on April 7, 1948.

45. World Health Organization. Constitution of the World Health Organization [reprinted]. *Bull World Health Organ*. 2000;80:983–984.

46. Annas G. J. Human rights and health: the Universal Declaration of Human Rights at 50. *N Engl J Med.* 1998;339:1778–1781.

47. Brand J. L. The United States Public Health Service and international health, 1945–1950. *Bull Hist Med.* 1989;63:579–598.

48. Gostin L. O. International infectious disease law: revision of the World Health Organization's international health regulations. *JAMA.* 2004;291:2623–2627.

49. Williams G. WHO: the days of the mass campaigns. *World Health Forum.* 1988;9:7–23.

50. Williams G. WHO: reaching out to all. *World Health Forum.* 1988;9:185–199.

51. Fox R. Medical humanitarianism and human rights: reflections on Doctors Without Borders and Doctors of the World. *Soc Sci Med.* 1995;41:1607–1616.

52. Mahler H. Blueprint for health for all. *WHO Chron.* 1977;31:491–498.

53. Cueto M. *The Return of Epidemics: Health and Society in Peru During the Twentieth Century.* Burlington, Vt: Ashgate Publishing Ltd; 2001.

54. Fox D. M., Kassalow J. S. Making health a priority of US foreign policy. *Am J Public Health.* 2001;91:1554–1556.

55. Millennium development goals. United Nations Development Programme Web site. Available at: http://www.undp.org/mdg/. Accessed January 10, 2004.

56. Sachs J. D. Investing in health for economic development. Project Syndicate Web site. Available at: http://www.project-syndicate.org. Accessed January 10, 2004.

57. Sachs J. D. Helping the world's poorest. *Economist.* 1999;352:17–20.

58. Bloom B. R., Bloom D. E., Cohen J. E., Sachs J. D. Investing in the World Health Organization. *Science.* 1999;284:911.

59. Sachs J. D., Mellinger A. D., Gallup J. L. The geography of poverty and wealth. *Sci Am.* 2001;284:70–75.

60. Poole G. A. $50 billion question: world, where to begin? *New York Times.* June 4, 2004:A1–2.

61. Biggs H. M. Public health is purchasable. *Monthly Bulletin of the Department of the City of New York.* October 1911;1:225–226.

54

DISEASE, DIPLOMACY AND INTERNATIONAL COMMERCE

The origins of international sanitary regulation in the nineteenth century

Mark Harrison

Source: *Journal of Global History*, 1:2 (2006), 197–217.

Abstract

During the early nineteenth century, European nations began to contemplate cooperation in sanitary matters, starting a diplomatic process that culminated in the International Sanitary Conferences and the first laws on the control of infectious disease. This article examines the origins of these conferences and highlights certain features that have been neglected in existing scholarship. It argues that while commercial pressures were the main stimuli to the reform of quarantine, these were insufficient in themselves to explain why most European nations came to see greater cooperation as desirable. It places special emphasis on the diplomatic context and shows that the peace of 1815 produced a climate in which many European nations envisaged a more systematic and liberal sanitary regime.

The first International Sanitary Conference, held in Paris, in 1851, is generally regarded as a milestone in international sanitary cooperation. Although there was little agreement among the twelve nations that sent delegates to the conference, it established the principle that quarantine and similar sanitary measures ought to be fixed by international agreement, so as to minimize the expense and inconvenience arising from a multiplicity of practices. The Paris conference applied only to the Mediterranean but all subsequent international forums and laws on the control of infectious diseases stemmed from these tentative steps towards international sanitary collaboration, more than 150 years ago. Yet historians have shown comparatively little interest in the origins of the Paris conference or in attempts to control the spread of diseases across borders prior to 1851. Above all, we have little idea of why the idea of international collaboration suddenly became attractive to many countries in the decades before 1851: it was by no means an easy or natural evolution, as quarantine had typically been regarded as an instrument of foreign policy, to be used aggressively in furtherance of national interests.

In so far as an explanation has been attempted, it has stressed the growth of international commerce and particularly the trading interests of Britain and France.[1] The fact that these countries took the initiative would appear to suggest that they saw international agreement as a means of diminishing impediments to their maritime trade. Other factors, such as the growth of political liberalism have also been suggested as reasons why certain states sought to reduce the burden of quarantine, although there is little agreement about how far ideology had a consistent bearing upon sanitary policies.[2] Yet neither explanation seems sufficient in itself to account for the radical shift that was needed for states to contemplate cooperation in sanitary matters. As Peter Baldwin has noted, mercantile interests were far from uniform and tended to be regarded as having a rather narrow view, sometimes incompatible with the national good. Two important questions therefore arise. First, how and with what degree of success did mercantile groups enlist the support of others in their campaign to reform quarantine regulations? Second, how did the reform of quarantine come to be identified, not only with national interests, but with the welfare of humanity in general?

It is not possible here to reconstruct the process whereby the critics of quarantine were able to forge coalitions in their respective countries, but it is possible to examine the international context from which the desire for sanitary cooperation developed. As is well known, the Congress of Vienna (1815) brought to an end an atomized system of international relations in which armed conflict had been common. The system of diplomacy inaugurated at Vienna recognized the existence of different national interests but sought agreements that transcended them. Although this system fell into disarray in 1823, congresses were replaced by smaller conferences on specific topics, and these often proved to be more effective than the rather grandiose gatherings they replaced. It was in this context that the concept of international sanitary cooperation was first articulated, marking a fundamental shift from the state of affairs prior to 1815. While the growth of international trade loomed large in these discussions, other considerations were also important, not least the balance of power and the avoidance of war. Both within individual countries and in the international arena, the proponents of quarantine reform grew in support and stature as their campaign became enmeshed with these broader political and humanitarian concerns.

Quarantine's *ancien régime*

By the middle of the fifteenth century, legislation banning commerce with infected places was common in many Mediterranean countries, particularly those closest to reservoirs of plague in Central Asia. Although the plague was still regarded as a 'blight of God', prayer and penitence – formerly 'the first and sovereign remedy' – were gradually supplemented by more secular interventions.[3] Some countries, especially the Italian states, also began to develop permanent bureaucracies to administer quarantine and lazarettos, in the belief that plague was a contagious disease that could be prevented by thwarting its transmission.[4] This belief rested on two related observations. First, of all the maladies afflicting Europe, plague alone originated outside the continent; second, it appeared to be a specific disease, with easily recognizable symptoms that could be differentiated from common fevers. Quarantine was invariably imposed whenever the disease was reported in the Levant, which had long been regarded as the conduit of plague into Europe. It was also sometimes imposed against ships from the West Indies, when epidemic disease (most likely yellow fever) was known to be prevalent.[5] In the seventeenth century, these measures were usually *ad hoc* in nature rather than the subject of specific statutes.[6] Even in the Mediterranean, more vulnerable to plague than northern Europe because of its proximity to the Levant, quarantine stations were isolated and their practices irregular. In France, for instance, there were only two quarantine stations along the Mediterranean Sea, at Toulon and Marseilles. Contemporaries were struck by the lack of coordination between these stations and also by the fact that quarantine often continued to be imposed at the ports when the plague was ravaging the interior. This situation led, in 1683, to the first statute relating to quarantine, which began to standardize practices across the country.[7]

In many Mediterranean countries, quarantines came to enjoy a good measure of popular support and were widely credited with the freedom of certain countries from plague. Liberal quarantine regimes like those at Marseilles, however, were generally the exception rather than the rule, and other Mediterranean stations, such as those along the Barbary Coast, became notorious for malpractice and exorbitant charges. But in some European countries, most notably France and Britain, the eighteenth century saw increasing divergence of opinion on quarantine. While such measures continued to command popular support, the medical profession began to divide sharply over the utility of quarantine and the theory of contagion that underpinned it. At the same time, merchants involved in the export trade with the Levant grew increasingly critical of quarantine restrictions, which cost them a great deal through delays, charges and the destruction or damage of goods by fumigation in quarantine houses. Arrangements in the Mediterranean were the main cause of complaint but the enactment of quarantine statutes in northern countries during the eighteenth century constituted an additional burden.[8]

Perhaps the clearest example of this polarization of opinion was the response to the plague in Marseilles in 1720. The outbreak was immediately traced to a merchant vessel that had arrived from Syria, and neighbouring countries lost no time in imposing quarantine against French shipping; a sanitary cordon was also imposed around Marseilles and other infected provinces. The cordons appeared to prevent plague from spreading beyond southern France but some medical practitioners questioned the contagious nature of the disease. If plague were contagious, why did it appear only at certain times of the year? Might not epidemics be related to other factors, such as seasonal climatic changes and states of the atmosphere? Such ideas had steadily gained ground since the revival of Hippocratic medicine in the Renaissance, and by the late seventeenth century they were being clearly articulated by the English physician Thomas Sydenham (1624–89), amongst others.[9] Many of the medical practitioners who commented on the epidemic in southern France employed such explanations as an alternative or supplement to contagion. The fact that the Levant was afflicted more often than Europe was explained by the fact that it was subject to great heat, the plague 'poison' arising from the rapid putrefaction of dead animals and plants; likewise, plague tended to occur in Europe during the summer, when conditions approximated to those in the East. Quarantine therefore seemed to be unnecessary, as well as injurious to trade.[10]

In Britain, the incorporation of quarantine into statute law provoked similar debates. The first act was passed in 1710, and further legislation followed the arrival of plague in Marseilles, creating a quarantine station in the Medway and elevating the maximum penalty for evasion to death.[11] However, the draconian powers of the 1721 Act were modified as the threat from the Mediterranean diminished.[12] As in France, the broad consensus over preventative measures that had existed in the 1600s was beginning to break down: medical opinion was diverging and exporters were growing increasingly impatient of restrictions on trade. Critics claimed that quarantine in Britain was unnecessary if men boarding ships in the Levant were healthy, as the voyage of seven or eight weeks was long enough to ensure that plague was not present.[13]

Some critics went further and suggested that quarantine in Europe could be relaxed in view of the fact that ships leaving the Levant with foul bills of health were required to perform quarantine at Malta, Leghorn and Venice. But quarantine was far from infallible. In Spain, for instance, the authorities experienced great problems in imposing an embargo against ships from Marseilles, despite posting guards along the Mediterranean coast. Ships also attempted to dock in Spanish ports with fraudulent bills of health, which falsely claimed that the ships had sailed from non-infected ports. Cordons imposed along land borders were even more porous,[14] and plague epidemics were often blamed on illicit traders who stealthily crossed borders to evade customs duties and quarantine.[15]

Even supporters of quarantine admitted that this was a problem and some concluded that the answer lay in more efficient systems of disease notification, which would mean that quarantine could be resorted to selectively. The British physician William Brownrigg, for example, conceded that less resort need be had to quarantine if the bills of health issued from plague-infected countries were more reliable.[16] By the 1770s, bills were issued routinely by some of the Italian states and by foreign consuls in the Ottoman dominions. Bills normally declared the time and place from which they were granted, the names and numbers of crew and passengers, and indicated the health status of the vessel. They also recorded whether or not quarantine had been performed and the nature of any merchandise carried.[17]

One of the problems with the system was that consuls had to depend on unreliable sources of information. All it took for a consul to issue a foul bill of health was a single reported case in a Levantine city or its environs, and some British merchants suspected that consuls were deliberately fed false reports by their commercial rivals. 'The Greeks carry on three-fourths of the Dutch as well as the Italian trade', protested a group of Smyrna merchants, 'it is therefore their interest (and unfortunately that of every other nation) to depress ours as much as possible.' For this reason, the merchants, championed by the prison-reformer John Howard, advocated the construction of a model lazaretto in Britain, thereby dispensing with the need to quarantine ships in the Mediterranean. In view of the distance from the Levant, Howard proposed that a quarantine of no longer than forty-eight hours need be performed, if no cases of sickness developed among crew or passengers. Although the British government had hitherto rejected the idea on grounds of cost, the Levantine merchants claimed that a boom in trade with Turkey would more than repay it.[18]

Despite its obvious flaws, quarantine remained firmly entrenched for the rest of the century, both in the Catholic Mediterranean and in the Protestant North.[19] Quarantine was imperfect but it was the art of the possible, and to abandon any form of protection was incompatible with contemporary theories of statecraft, which viewed population as a source of wealth and power. Johann Peter Frank's multi-volume treatise, *A system of complete medical police*, exemplified this line of thinking. An exponent of enlightened absolutism, Frank proposed a comprehensive system to protect and improve the health of all persons through generous state provisions and the regulation of social relations. In this system, quarantine played an important part in protecting enlightened states – like that of his emperor, Joseph II of Austria – against the ingress of disease from their less diligent neighbours. 'It is one of the foremost tasks of the state to prevent persons or animals, goods, and all objects to which or whom contagions cling, from entering the country', he proclaimed, 'and there is no doubt that governments are entitled to use all suitable means that do not contravene international law in order to achieve this.'[20] Indeed, some writers advocated quarantine explicitly on mercantilist grounds, contrasting the absence of such measures in the plague-ravaged Ottoman provinces with more 'enlightened' regimes that were free from the disease.[21] However, writers such as Paskal von Ferro and Martin Lange argued that quarantine measures ought to be brought into conformity with enlightened government, minimizing inconvenience and disruption of trade.[22]

Despite calls for moderation, quarantine was often employed as a form of commercial protection or was used to sever the economic arteries of rival countries;[23] sanitary cordons were also attractive to states because they could be used to strengthen national and imperial borders. It was partly for this reason that the Venetian republic maintained a sanitary cordon against the adjacent Ottoman provinces of Istria and Dalmatia, but the most striking example is the 1,600 km cordon established by Austria-Hungary along its borders with the Ottoman Empire. The cordon was policed by watchtowers and roving bands of soldiers, ordered to shoot on sight those who crossed the border without performing quarantine. The sanitary functions of the cordon developed gradually from 1710, having originated in the Military Border established to defend against Ottoman invasion. This military and sanitary cordon constituted an important additional source of manpower for the Hapsburg Empire and troops raised in the border provinces to form the cordon were sometimes deployed elsewhere for purely military purposes.[24] Indeed, sanitary cordons were sometimes used to cloak the aggressive intentions of predatory nations. During the plague epidemics in Eastern Europe in 1770, for example, Prussia established a sanitary cordon that encroached upon Polish territory, its ostensibly defensive nature concealing Prussia's predatory intentions.[25]

For these reasons, sanitary matters began to figure prominently in international diplomacy by the 1770s, providing an early indication that some form of dialogue was necessary if damaging disputes and even conflict were to be averted. As the system of diplomacy became more professional,[26] decisions over whether or not to impose quarantine became more difficult and those responsible rarely took action without carefully considering the likely reactions of other states. For instance, when plague appeared in western Russia in 1771, threatening the port of St Petersburg, quarantine was imposed upon all goods brought to the city for export, in the hope that this would deter other countries from imposing embargos or quarantines against Russian shipping. But despite active diplomacy, fear of plague and commercial ostracism led most northern European countries to impose quarantine against Russia, much to the disappointment of the British mercantile community in St Petersburg.[27]

Nevertheless, mercantile opposition to quarantine was growing and was becoming quite influential in some regions that depended heavily on international commerce, such as the eastern seaboard of North America. Here, among Republicans such as Dr Benjamin Rush, a signatory of the Declaration of Independence, quarantine had also come to be identified with tyranny.[28] Free trade had long been associated with political liberty,[29] and the growing influence of such doctrines in the Anglophone world led a number of writers to equate quarantine with authoritarian regimes. For Protestant writers such as Dale Ingram and Sir Richard Manningham, the doctrine of contagion was merely a Popish fabrication, originally calculated to exclude certain delegates from the Council of Trent.[30] Yet, opposition to quarantine was not confined to mercantile groups and the doctors with whom they associated: those who travelled regularly by sea also came to resent the costs and delays occasioned by quarantine. The French explorer Corneille le Brun was one of many who complained of the great inconvenience of being detained in Mediterranean lazarettos while returning from the Levant to Europe.[31]

One of the chief problems facing merchants and travellers was the great variety of regulations imposed at ports in the Mediterranean: some maintained forty-day quarantines against all vessels from the Levant, regardless of their bills of health, while others settled for a period of only eighteen days. Irregularities in ships' manifests could also result in the impounding of vessels when there was no disease on board, and for this reason travellers from the Levant often purchased bills of health separately from those of the crew.[32] It was not sufficient, however, to oppose quarantine solely on grounds of inconvenience or even for commercial reasons; its opponents had to attack the doctrine of contagion on which quarantine was based and, even if they did not deny the possibility of contagion, they stressed the vital role of climate and meteorological conditions in epidemic disease. Colonial experience was crucial here, for the seemingly distinctive disease environments of Asia, Africa, and the Americas made a profound impression upon medical practitioners. Colonial practitioners worked consciously in the tradition of Sydenham and were increasingly vocal in their opposition to simplistic notions of contagion.[33] The surgeon John Wade, employed by the East India Company, declared that he had not encountered a 'single instance of contagion' during his service and added that most epidemics in hot climates were the product of miasma.[34]

Yet opposition to contagion and quarantine was by no means universal among medical practitioners with overseas experience. Senior military and naval medical officers, for example, tended to reaffirm official views on the control of diseases like plague and yellow fever.[35] Support for quarantine was also to be found among those practitioners working for trading concerns such as the English Levant Company. The physician Patrick Russell, who had experienced plague epidemics while working at Aleppo, acknowledged that it was affected by seasonal factors, but he also believed that plague could be communicated through contact between persons and through certain kinds of merchandise, such as clothing. It was therefore wise to maintain the precautions that had served Britain well, cautioned Russell, as the inconvenience caused by quarantine was preferable to the massive disruption that would be caused by an epidemic at home.[36]

Nevertheless, the revolutionary and Napoleonic wars tilted the balance of medical opinion towards those who sought to abolish or, more commonly, to reform quarantine. This may seem counter-intuitive in view of the fact that European armies suffered gravely from both plague and yellow fever,[37] yet overseas campaigns provided practitioners with the opportunity of studying these diseases at first hand, to observe how they spread, under what conditions they seemed to occur, and what effects they had on the human body. Plague and yellow fever were thus demystified and some medical practitioners came to regard them, not as separate diseases, but merely as varieties of common or garden 'epidemic fever'.[38] A growing number of practitioners claimed that these diseases were not contagious in any sense other than they could be conveyed in the breath of the sick,[39] and they placed more emphasis on the climatic and sanitary conditions necessary to produce the diseases in epidemic form.[40] The opponents of quarantine looked back at its chequered history, the frequent abuses of sanitary regulations for political ends, and portrayed it as a vestige of a less enlightened era.

Towards an international sanitary system

An additional impetus to the reform of sanitary legislation was provided by the recovery of international trade following the disruption of the French wars. The dynamic force behind the recovery was Britain, now the predominant sea power, although non-European states such as Egypt also played a significant part,[41] ushering in what some historians have referred to as a new wave of globalization.[42]

It is questionable whether the concept of globalization accurately describes the fractured nature of international trade at this time,[43] but the expansion of international commerce undoubtedly became more prominent in discussions over sanitary regulation. On the one hand, certain mercantile interests – particularly those involved in the booming cotton trade with Egypt – increased their demands for the relaxation of quarantine.[44] On the other, there was a heightened sense of the danger posed by infectious diseases originating outside Europe. Although many medical practitioners declared that these diseases were not contagious, epidemics caused alarm among the lay public, dispelling the complacency that followed the retreat of plague. The outbreak of yellow fever in the West Indies during the 1790s, for instance, aroused fears that troops and prisoners sent back to Europe would carry the disease,[45] and vessels were sometimes impounded, much to the frustration of naval authorities.[46] Epidemics of yellow fever in some Mediterranean ports in the early 1800s showed that these fears were justified,[47] while the appearance of plague on Corfu in 1816 caused great alarm because of the enlargement of trade between the northern Atlantic countries and the eastern Mediterranean.[48] Alien epidemics now stood alongside a host of other seemingly new diseases – principally nervous and digestive disorders – that were attributed to the luxurious and frenetic lifestyles produced by commercial and colonial expansion.[49]

This sense of vulnerability meant that most nations – especially those closest to the presumed sources of epidemics – were reluctant to abandon quarantine, their traditional defence against epidemic disease.[50] This was clearly illustrated by the response to the appearance of cholera in European Russia, in 1830, which led most states to fall back on quarantine, despite the lack of consensus about its causation and spread. As with plague and yellow fever, there was little agreement among medical practitioners about whether the disease was contagious or whether quarantine was of any use. For some, the slow and uneven spread of the disease provided evidence that quarantine did not work,[51] while for others it was proof that it had not been sufficiently enforced.[52] Likewise, the spread of the disease from East to West was enough to persuade many that it was in some sense contagious, while the fact that it spread very unevenly – geographically and socially – suggested that other factors were involved.[53] In general, the severity of quarantine and similar measures imposed against cholera depended on the extent to which commercial and manufacturing interests held sway. As Richard Evans has shown, authorities in Hamburg took little action in the fight against cholera during the epidemics of 1832 and 1848, while the Prussian authorities, less dependent upon commerce, insisted on the contagiousness of cholera and the need for restrictions of trade and population movement.[54] However, commercial interests – like the medical profession – were still divided on the issue of quarantine, and some thought moderate measures indispensable in preventing more damaging restrictions.[55]

It is perhaps surprising that cholera did not figure prominently in debates over quarantine in the 1830s and 1840s. The most important reason for this was that almost all the quarantine establishments in the Mediterranean had been created to deal with plague and it was not yet clear that cholera would become a perpetual threat. Cholera remained marginal to international discussions of quarantine until the late 1840s, following its second epidemic visitation in Europe, after which time it grew in importance in debates over sanitary regulation. However, at the first international sanitary conference in 1851, it was still less important than plague, and some states, such as that of Austria, had even requested that it be excluded from discussions.

The first suggestion that quarantine might be regulated on an international basis came from France, which entered a more liberal phase of government under Louis Philippe. The Orleanist regime enjoyed a relatively harmonious relationship with the Academy of Medicine, which had become increasingly hostile to contagion and quarantine. The abuse of sanitary cordons by the Bourbon monarchy had led to widespread criticism and had turned many away from quarantine to consider more liberal alternatives. In 1823, for example, a sanitary cordon assembled along the border with Spain to protect against yellow fever was used to restore the Spanish Bourbon monarch to power following a liberal revolt.[56] French merchants and diplomats in the Eastern Mediterranean were also protesting against the disruption caused by quarantine during outbreaks of plague and the high cost of detaining goods and persons in lazarettos.[57] The main causes of complaint were the quarantines imposed against plague after Muhammed Ali became Pasha (Ottoman viceroy) of Egypt in 1805. As part of his programme of modernization, Muhammed Ali began to impose quarantine against shipping from infected ports and took strict measures within his own territories to deal with epidemics.[58] The situation became more serious in 1831, when his army invaded the Ottoman province of Syria, engendering nearly two years of war and political tension between Russia, and France and Britain. In 1833, however, Muhammed Ali established a sanitary board with a consular commission that represented the interests of several foreign powers, arousing cautious optimism about the prospect of more extensive international cooperation.

It was in these circumstances that M. de Ségur Dupeyron, Secretary to the Supreme Council of Health in France, was charged by the Minister of Commerce with investigating the different modes of quarantine operating in the Mediterranean. He examined a number of lazarettos personally and took note of their rules for fixing the length of quarantine. Eschewing the speculation which he felt had been characteristic of medical works, Dupeyron adopted an historical approach, seeing present arrangements in the light of epidemics and quarantine arrangements over several centuries. He concluded that there was a close link between commerce and plague, pointing to the fact that the disease never seemed to occur in those countries whose commerce had been disrupted by war. All epidemics of plague in Europe also appeared to have spread outwards from the Levant, suggesting that the disease was contagious. Although sanitary precautions had been effective in some cases, he felt they were unnecessarily oppressive because they were imposed in an unsystematic way. In view of this, he made a number of suggestions to establish what he termed a 'reasonable and uniform system'. This included quarantines of shorter duration; abolition of quarantines of observation against vessels coming from the West Indies and the USA with clean bills of health; and, most importantly, forbidding arbitrary increases in the duration of quarantine.[59]

When Dupeyron's report was published, the diplomatic climate was not especially conducive to international cooperation. Although Britain and France had been ideologically aligned, in principle, since 1830, the so-called 'liberal alliance' was experiencing difficulties and in 1834–5 France was moving away from Britain in an effort to heal the diplomatic breach that had arisen between the Eastern and Western powers; by 1836, France was far closer to Austria than its erstwhile partner.[60] In 1838, however, the French government, which accepted the thrust of Dupeyron's report, proposed a conference of delegates from various European countries with ports on the Mediterranean, the aim being to agree upon a system of uniform quarantine arrangements. Contemporaneously, in Britain, free-trade agitators in parliament, such as the Benthamite MP Dr John Bowring, kept up the pressure with speeches and publications designed to demonstrate the non-contagiousness of plague and the uselessness of quarantine.[61] In November that year, the British government, along with other nations, agreed in principle to the French proposal.[62]

The most significant of these other powers was Austria, which had numerous quarantine stations along its borders with the Ottoman Empire and along the Danube, as well as substantial commercial interests in the eastern Mediterranean. The Austrians had been protesting for some years about 'impediments thrown in the way of navigation' in the Ionian Sea. The British administration of the Ionian islands appears to have imposed quarantines against vessels from the Levant that sometimes exceeded the fourteen-day period prescribed.[63] For its part, Britain was anxious to secure a reduction in quarantine, not only for commercial reasons, but because its naval vessels and mail ships were often subjected to long delays at quarantine stations in the Mediterranean.[64]

These tentative steps towards an agreement on quarantine exemplified the system of international relations inaugurated by the Congress of Vienna and which prevailed until the Crimean War.[65] It was fundamentally different to that which existed before 1815, when colonial rivalry between the Atlantic nations intermingled with the continental struggles of the Great Powers. The defeat of France brought to an end any hopes of regaining lost territory in India and North America and, although it was to colonize Algeria between 1829 and 1848, France did not see itself as an imperial rival of Britain until the last quarter of the nineteenth century. Indeed, its interests in Algeria gave France a greater incentive to work with Britain in order to moderate quarantine in Mediterranean ports.[66]

In the forty years after the Vienna congress, the Great Powers sought to work out their differences at the conference table rather than on the battlefield and, in such a system, there was less need or scope for the use of quarantine as a political weapon. Although abuses of quarantine continued to occur, they were increasingly seen as potential causes of discord between nations. Although there was no mention of quarantine in the Vienna settlement, the congress did agree on some related matters, such as freedom of navigation on the Rhine. Like subsequent agreements on traffic on the Danube, this was concluded partly to satisfy economic interests but also because economic cooperation was seen as conducive to peaceful coexistence.[67]

The 'conference system' that evolved following the failure of congress diplomacy remained dedicated to the peaceful solution of political problems. It was also more pragmatic and, in many respects, more successful, involving smaller gatherings of states which aimed to reach agreement on specific matters.[68] Although predominantly driven by the commercial and colonial interests of Britain and France, agreement over such issues as quarantine must be seen in the light of other considerations, with which they became increasingly intertwined, not least the desire to remove potential sources of tension between nations. In this sense, the effort to reach agreement on quarantine closely resembled previous and parallel discussions over navigation. The fact that the focus of sanitary discussions was the eastern Mediterranean made such an agreement all the more desirable, in view of the fact that the Levant had become a potential flash-point in international relations.

It is perhaps significant that attempts to convene an international conference coincided with rising tension sparked by another war between the Ottoman sultan and the rebellious province of Egypt, which again raised the spectre of Russian influence in Istanbul. Tension also rose between Britain and France because of French support for Muhammed Ali, but the French were unwilling to risk war with the Austrians and British, who had sent an expeditionary force to the Levant. The situation was defused after Egyptian forces retreated and by the Treaty of London (1840), in which the four principal European powers (Austria, Britain, Prussia and Russia) jointly guaranteed the security of the Ottoman Empire. As the British foreign secretary Lord Palmerston put it, the aim of all governments concerned was to 'agree upon a common course of policy, which may be calculated to accomplish purposes [i.e. the preservation of peace in the Levant] so essential for the general interests of Europe'.[69] The Straits Convention of the following year also made the prohibition of foreign naval traffic through the Bosphorous and Dardanelles a matter of international agreement rather than simply an Ottoman policy, as it had been before.[70] At the same time, there was an improvement in relations between Britain and France, following the dismissal of Thiers in 1840, and the subsequent fall from power of Palmerston and the Whig government. The two countries once again sought to work together amicably to resolve conflicts of interest, and this gave added momentum to discussions over quarantine.[71] According to the quarantine reformer Dr Gavin Milroy, everyone who had studied the subject – statesmen, travellers, merchants and physicians – had come to the conclusion that an international agreement on quarantine was vital to their 'common welfare'.[72]

Metternich claimed that it was now possible to relax quarantine in the Mediterranean because Egyptian measures against plague made its spread westwards less likely. The prospect of similar regulations being introduced in the Ottoman Empire also gave grounds for optimism. In 1838 the sultan asked the Austrian government to send him several experienced quarantine officials to assist in establishing quarantine stations throughout the Ottoman provinces. Most parts of the Empire had been severely affected by plague during the late eighteenth and early nineteenth centuries: in 1812 an estimated 300,000 people died during an outbreak in the greater Istanbul area and, as late as 1836, the disease had claimed the lives of 30,000 people in the Ottoman capital. Although its virulence was decreasing, plague continued to visit Istanbul and the Balkan provinces almost annually through to the middle of the century; moreover, the Empire faced a new threat in the form of cholera, which arrived from Russia in 1821. In the next three decades, seven epidemics of cholera spread through the Ottoman world, having arrived with pilgrims to the Holy cities of Mecca and Medina.[73] This new threat from the

East presented a great challenge to successive administrations which were attempting to modernize the Empire; they stunted population growth and disrupted the flourishing international trade promoted by railways and steam navigation.[74]

In seeking European expertise, the administrations of Mahmut II (1808–39) and Abdlmecit I (1839–61) were following precedents set in other branches of state, not least in the army. Moreover, the attempt to construct a sanitary infrastructure across the empire was in line with the rapid growth of the Ottoman state during the nineteenth century, with regulations in all ports expected to conform to instructions issued in the Ottoman capital.[75] However, the European powers saw the creation of a 'Commission of Public Health' in Istanbul as another means of exercising influence over the sultan and of securing concessions beneficial to European navigation.[76] Although the influence of foreign representatives on the Constantinople Council of Health,[77] as it became known, was rather less than the European powers had hoped, their representation, like the Straits Settlement of the following year, was symbolic of the sultan's waning independence.[78]

The establishment of the Constantinople Council showed heightened awareness of the need for international cooperation in sanitary matters, which had the effect of bringing Austria into closer cooperation with Britain and France.[79] But despite his initial support for a conference to discuss quarantine, Metternich and other foreign ministers were unable to agree about where to hold the meeting. These wrangles were in no sense untypical, as both Metternich and Palmerston tended to favour conferences over which they could exert control.[80] Talks resumed in 1843, again as a result of French initiative and the British foreign secretary Lord Aberdeen, one of the architects of the new *entente cordiale*, responded enthusiastically, declaring that 'great benefits would result from it to Mediterranean commerce and communications'. However, he felt that prior to offering an invitation to Russia and the Italian states, it would be wise for Britain, France and Austria to first reach agreement between themselves on key issues. He then hoped that Austria would exert its influence on the Italian states to induce them to cooperate. Aberdeen was keen that Russia be involved in the conference because it was a major regional power and any agreement was unlikely to be workable without it. He proposed the neutral port of Genoa as a venue.[81] Other departments of the British government were equally enthusiastic, noting that the mood internationally seemed more conducive to progress than ever before. Mr J. MacGregor of the Office of the Privy Council for Trade declared that 'A very decided tendency has been manifested on the part of the principal Powers, to assimilate in some degree the periods of detention, and at all events to relax very considerably the severity of the restrictions on merchandise and vessels'. He noted that 'the general good understanding which now prevails between this country and foreign Powers . . . encourage[s] the hope that the deliberations of such a conference . . . would result in the adoption of that general system of Quarantine which is so desired'.[82] It is therefore clear that the system of international diplomacy that developed after 1815 – with its overriding objective of preventing war in Europe – was a vital precondition to any agreement on international sanitary regulation. By contrast, the atomized nature of international relations that had existed before the French wars had meant that all attempts to mitigate the effects of quarantine through diplomacy were doomed to failure.

All the signs were, indeed, encouraging, with Britain and France showing their willingness to participate in a conference if it were convened in one of a number of neutral cities. The Austrians, however, were slow to respond and when they did, they did so with less enthusiasm than expected. Metternich considered a conference premature and insisted that the three principal parties first reach an agreement over technical matters such as the minimum and maximum terms of quarantine necessary for humans, the terms for various types of merchandise, and the best methods of disinfecting objects thought susceptible of contagion. This was not unlike Aberdeen's proposal, but the Austrians stated that they required a period of six months in which to consider the matter by themselves; Metternich also stated his preference for any such conference to be held in Vienna.[83]

While France awaited a response from Vienna, the British government commissioned its own investigation of quarantine in the Mediterranean from a former naval officer, Sir William Pym, the Superintendent of Quarantine at the Privy Council. In 1845 he made a detailed report on the numbers of persons and vessels quarantined at different stations, procedures for the handling of goods, charges levied, and so forth. Pym reached a similar conclusion to that of Dupeyron: that quarantine was necessary in some form but that it operated unsystematically. It was this arbitrariness, rather than quarantine *per se*, that posed the chief obstacle to trade in the Mediterranean.[84] On the basis of his investigation, Pym drafted a response to the issues raised by Metternich,[85] but the latter continued to procrastinate, telling British and French officials that he would only consider the matter once he had received information from the Austrian departments of the Interior and of Finance.[86]

How is one to explain the apparently contradictory position of the Austrian government? It does seem that there was a genuine desire on the part of Metternich to conclude an international agreement that would be potentially of great benefit to Austrian commerce. The records kept by quarantine stations in the Eastern Mediterranean show that Austrian ships were among those most commonly inconvenienced by quarantine.[87] Steam navigation had led to an increasing volume of trade with the East and there was also increasing pressure from within Austria to relax quarantine regulations along the border of the Hapsburg Empire, for both commercial and humanitarian reasons. Some prominent medical men, such as Professor Sigmund of Vienna, recommended that Austria rely more on sanitary measures than quarantine.[88] The Austrian Ambassador to Britain also told Lord Aberdeen in 1845 that a commission had been established 'with the desire to diminish the expenses of the Cordon Sanitaire, which it is said has completely failed in preventing intercourse across the frontier, and which offers unnecessary interruption to traffic'.[89] Metternich was similarly inclined but Austria's long boundary with the formerly plague-ridden Ottoman Empire meant that others were reluctant to abandon 'tried and tested' sanitary measures. The extent to which other foreign policy objectives affected Metternich's thinking is unclear, except in so far as an agreement between the various powers with interests in the Mediterranean was consonant with his broader aim to reach an accord with Russia as well as the Western powers. His diplomatic correspondence with Britain and France similarly stressed the need to ensure that a conference on quarantine included Russia simply because of its status as a power in the region.[90]

For Britain and France, the chief motives in seeking international agreement were of course related to their commercial and imperial interests. Growing French involvement in Algeria and its trade with the Eastern Mediterranean provided an obvious incentive to reform quarantine and, in the 1840s it took measures unilaterally to reduce quarantine in its Mediterranean ports. Medical opinion, too, was moving increasingly in support of the relaxation or abolition of quarantine. In Britain commercial interests were also becoming more influential and the repeal of the protectionist Corn Laws in 1846 encouraged free traders to seek reductions in other restrictions on trade. Critics of quarantine estimated that its annual cost to Britain amounted to between two and three millions pounds, with similar losses incurred by merchants in the Mediterranean.[91] In the late 1830s, Britain and other nations had also concluded a series of commercial and navigation treaties with the Ottoman Empire, with the aim of opening up areas of trade formerly prohibited to foreign merchants and of agreeing a moderate tariff on imports into the Ottoman dominions.[92] The attempt to reach an agreement on quarantine that involved the sultan was thus part of a more general process, whereby foreign powers were attempting to exploit Ottoman weakness in order to secure concessions on trade and navigation.[93]

But commercial interests were not the only factors that induced Britain to seek international agreement over quarantine. Quarantine was becoming a great inconvenience to the growing number of Britons who travelled to and from India by way of the Levant and there were increasing complaints about the 'absurdities' and 'irregularities' of quarantine in Mediterranean stations, particularly Alexandria.[94] Since quarantines and sanitary cordons had been established in Egypt in the early 1830s, European merchants and diplomatic staff had complained that they had been enforced selectively and that the system was inefficient;[95] the severe plague epidemic that affected Egypt in 1835 was sometimes used in support of these arguments. The tense relationship that existed between the British and Egyptian governments since the early 1830s continued to arouse suspicions that quarantine was being used to damage British interests. Muhammed Ali was deeply suspicious of the East India Company's establishment of a base in Aden and resented the presence of a British garrison adjacent to his territories.[96] The combined European force sent to assist the Ottomans in 1839 had also thwarted his ambitions in Syria.

In view of this, it is hardly surprising that the Egyptian authorities made use of one of the best opportunities they had to monitor the intentions of what they regarded as a hostile power. The advent of steam navigation led to an increasing volume of mail being sent through Egypt, to and from Britain and India, and packet agents in Alexandria and Cairo frequently complained that sanitary fumigation was used as a pretext to intercept, delay or destroy diplomatic communiqués.[97] Dr John Bowring also told the House of Commons in 1842 that 'Official dispatches were opened, perforated with awls, incised by chisels, dipped in vinegar . . . and at length transmitted to their destination in a mutilated, and scarcely legible condition.' He continued that: 'There was no doubt that political objects were sought for in the maintenance of quarantine in the east; and it was equally certain that political interests were promoted by them, and that these, and not the health of nations, were the principal motives for the great severity with which the regulations were enforced abroad.' It was not only the Egyptians who used quarantine in this way, he insisted, but also – to his shame – British consular officials. Yet there was no country that used quarantine for political ends so routinely as Russia. Bowring claimed that its quarantine officials were merely 'political functionaries' that 'arrested and released travellers at will. They took possession of all correspondence . . . they checked or facilitated commerce according to the passing interests of the moment . . . and in the name of public health', he declared, 'they had introduced a system of universal police and espionage.' In view of this, he insisted, the government ought to do all in its power to ensure that an international agreement was reached. His motion was enthusiastically supported by members of the government, including the Prime Minister, Sir Robert Peel.[98]

The revolutions of 1848 distracted attention from efforts to bring about an international conference on sanitary regulation. However, the French reopened negotiations with renewed vigour and were successful in persuading eleven other states with interests in the Mediterranean (including the Ottoman Empire) to agree to a conference in Paris in 1851. Most countries sent two delegates, a diplomat and a physician, the former in order to ensure that political and commercial matters were given due consideration. As the French Minister of Foreign Affairs insisted, it was necessary to find a *modus operandi* befitting an age of technical and industrial progress, and to strike a mutually beneficial balance between the needs of commerce and of public health. Just as new modes of communication were erasing the tyranny of distance, he argued, it was now time to remove political and commercial impediments that stood in the way of international harmony.[99] The mood internationally was receptive, too. Tension between Britain and France over the Spanish succession evaporated following the removal of the Orleans monarchy in 1848,[100] while the triumph of reaction elsewhere brought stability and a desire to avoid conflict.[101]

The Paris conference is usually considered a failure because its proceedings were marked by disagreement over key issues such as the transmissibility of cholera and because the resulting convention was signed by only three states – France, Sardinia and Portugal – and ratified by Sardinia alone.[102] Although the divisions were primarily between the Mediterranean countries, which were more reluctant to abandon quarantine, and Britain and France, which were eager for commercial and colonial reasons to liberalize it, the fault lines were numerous and often cut across each other. Despite Metternich's earlier optimism, Austrian delegates opposed any attempt to modify maritime quarantine and disinfection regimes in times of plague, and were particularly hostile to British proposals to reclassify susceptible merchandise so as to downgrade the threat from cotton, long regarded as a carrier of plague. Together with Russian delegates, they also opposed British proposals to abandon land-based cordons, which, however imperfect, were regarded as the only means of defending their empires against plague from the Levant. Yet Austrian (but not Russian) delegates backed the French and British position that cholera was not contagious in the same way as plague, and opposed the use of quarantines and sanitary cordons to control it.[103] As Baldwin has noted, public opinion was also important in affecting positions at the conference, often to the detriment of liberalization as in the case of most Italian states.[104] Yet the conference agreed in principle upon the basic aim of achieving agreement internationally over sanitary regulations, as well as the desirability of some specific measures, including the strengthening of sanitary surveillance in Egypt and the Ottoman Empire.[105]

Even this limited degree of consensus would have been unthinkable before 1815 but the nature of international relations in the four decades following the Vienna congress was such that it became less acceptable to use quarantines and sanitary cordons for overtly political purposes. From 1815, matters such as navigation and quarantine were considered partly with conflict avoidance in mind, especially in potential trouble spots like the Levant. And, from 1851, the attempt to reach an international consensus gathered momentum, with ten further international sanitary conferences being convened over the next half century, most of which were widely ratified. Unlike 1851, the primary concern at most of these conferences (1881 and 1897 excepted) was to devise an effective but not too disruptive means of preventing incursions of cholera from Asia. Until 1881, the conferences were attended and hosted by European countries only, but, in that year, a conference was held in Washington DC. The USA continued to be involved in European conferences but it simultaneously attempted to develop and lead international sanitary discussions in its own sphere of influence. A conference of South American states had already been held at Rio de Janeiro in 1887, but this was followed in 1902 by a Pan-American Conference at Washington DC, which resulted in the establishment of the Pan-American Sanitary Bureau. A few years later, in 1907, the first European international health organization, the Office International d'Hygiène Publique, was established in Paris.[106]

These measures and those that developed subsequently were the fruit of an evolving international consciousness, of which we see the first signs in the 1830s and 1840s. It is ironic that the growth of such institutions came at a time of mounting international tension. Although the idea of international sanitary cooperation was a brainchild of conference diplomacy, this system broke down with the outbreak of the Crimean War. Indeed, the first conference at Paris, in 1851, was as much the end of an era as the beginning of a new one. In the years that followed, disputes over quarantine escalated in tandem with rivalry between the imperial powers. For instance, after Britain's unilateral ending of the system of Dual Control of the Egyptian debt in 1882, France, its former partner in Egypt, sought every opportunity at international sanitary conferences to oppose British interests, by insisting on strict quarantine for vessels at Suez. As the Suez Canal, which opened in 1869, was a vital conduit for British eastern trade and for communications with India, quarantine measures at Suez affected Britain disproportionately. However the emergence of a united Germany and the formation of the Triple Alliance with Italy and Austria served as a counterweight to French demands. From 1885, after it had become a colonial power in East Africa, Germany and its partners sided with Britain in seeking relaxation of quarantine at Suez.[107] Quarantine was also the subject of contention between Britain and Russia, where it was used by both powers in their attempt to gain territorial and commercial influence in Central Asia.[108] Nevertheless, the foundations of an international sanitary order had been established and the sanitary conferences of the late nineteenth century provided a context in which such disputes could be moderated and their political impact blunted by international consensus.

Notes

The author wishes to thank the editors and referees, together with those who commented on earlier versions of this paper at Johns Hopkins University, the London School of Tropical Medicine and Hygiene, the University of Geneva, and the University of Valencia. The author is especially grateful to Professors Harry Marks, Graham Mooney and Josep Barona.

1 N. M. Goodman, *International health organizations and their work*, London: J. & A. Churchill, 1952, pp. 34–6; Howard-Jones, *The scientific background of the international sanitary conferences*, Geneva: WHO, 1975, p. 11; David P. Fidler, *International law and infectious diseases*, Oxford: Clarendon Press, 1999, pp. 21–37.

2 The classic statement of the relationship between ideology and sanitary policy is Erwin Ackerknecht's essay, 'Anticontagionism between 1821 and 1867', *Bulletin of the History of Medicine*, 22, 1948, pp. 562–93. However, as Peter Baldwin

has recently pointed out, the connection between politics and policy is far more complex than Ackerknecht's formulation suggests. See Peter Baldwin, *Contagion and the state in Europe 1830–1930*, Cambridge: Cambridge University Press, 1999.

3 *L'ordre public pour la ville de Lyon, pendant la maladie contagieuse*, Lyon: A. Valancol, 1670.

4 Ann G. Carmichael, *Plague and the poor in Renaissance Florence*, Cambridge: Cambridge University Press, 1986, pp. 110–21.

5 Paul Slack, *The impact of plague in Tudor and Stuart England*, Oxford: Clarendon Press, 1985, p. 324. Those who believed that yellow fever was a contagious disease often likened it to plague, some claiming it was different from plague only in degree rather than in kind. For example, Henry Warren, *A treatise concerning the malignant fever in Barbados, and the neighbouring islands: with an account of the seasons there, from the year 1734 to 1738, in a letter to Dr. Mead*, London: Fletcher Gyles, 1740.

6 In England, for example, quarantine was imposed by orders in council, which were to be implemented by the corporations governing ports. See Wellcome Library for the History and Understanding of Medicine, London (henceforth WLHUM), Western MS.3109, Thursday meeting book, Kingston-upon-Hull Corporation, 8 September 1668.

7 'Quarantaines', *Dictionnaire encyclopédique des sciences médicales*, Paris: P. Asselin & G. Masson, 1874, p. 24.

8 *Ibid.*, pp. 26–30.

9 David Cantor, ed., *Reinventing Hippocrates*, Aldershot: Ashgate, 2002.

10 Jean Baptiste Senac, *Traité des causes des accidens, et de la cure de la peste*, Paris: P-J. Mariette, 1744.

11 Arnold Zuckerman, 'Plague and contagionism in eighteenth-century England: the role of Richard Mead', *Bulletin of the History of Medicine*, 78, 2004, pp. 273–308.

12 Slack, *Impact*, pp. 330–2.

13 'Extracts of several letters of Mordach Mackenzie, M.D. concerning the plague at Constantinople', trans. 93, *Philosophical Transactions of the Royal Society*, 47, 1752, pp. 384–95; 'A further account of the late plague at Constantinople, in a letter of Dr Mackenzie from thence', trans. 87, *ibid.*, pp. 514–16.

14 WLHUM, Western MS.963, Balthasar de Aperregui, 'Ordenes relativos a sanidad y lazarettos en el Puerto de Barcelona, con motivo de la peste, en el año de 1714, y siguientes', Barcelona, 1752.

15 William Brownrigg, *Considerations on the means of preventing the communication of pestilential contagion and of eradicating it in infected places*, London: Lockyer Davis, 1771, p. 4.

16 Brownrigg, *Considerations*.

17 *Ibid.*, pp. 5–6.

18 John Howard, *An account of the principal lazarettos in Europe*, Warrington: William Eyres, 1789, pp. 25–7.

19 E.g. *Della peste ossia della cura per preservarsene, e guarire da questo fatalismo morbo*, Venice: Leonardo & Giammaria, 1784.

20 Johann Peter Frank, *A system of complete medical police*, ed. E. Lesky, Baltimore: J. H. V. Press, 1976, trans. by E. Vlim from 3rd edn., Vienna, 1786, p. 446.

21 Paskal Joseph Ferro, *Untersuchung der Pestanstekung, nebst zwei Aufsätzen von der Glaubwürdigkeit der meisten Pestberichte aus der Moldau und Wallachey, und der Schädlichkeit der bisherigen Contumazen von D. Lange und Fronius*, Vienna: Joseph Edlen, 1787.

22 Martin Lange, *Rudimenta doctrinae de peste*, Vienna: Rudolph Graeffer, 1784.
23 Mark Harrison, *Disease and the modern world: 1500 to the present day*, Cambridge: Polity, 2004, pp. 58–68.
24 Gunther E. Rothenberg, 'The Austrian sanitary cordon and the control of bubonic plague: 1710–1871', *Journal of the History of Medicine and Allied Sciences*, 28, 1973, pp. 15–23.
25 Herbert H. Kaplan, *The first partition of Poland*, New York and London: Columbia University Press, 1969, pp. 129–30.
26 D. McKay and H. M. Scott, *The rise of the great powers 1645–1815*, London: Longman, 1983.
27 John T. Alexander, *Bubonic plague in early modern Russia: public health and urban disaster*, Oxford: Oxford University Press, 2003, pp. 249–51.
28 Benjamin Rush, *An account of the bilious remitting yellow fever*, Philadelphia: Thomas Dobson, 1794; J. H. Powell, *Bring out your dead: the great plague of yellow fever in Philadelphia in 1793*, Philadelphia: University of Pennsylvania Press, 1949; William Coleman, *Yellow fever in the north: the methods of early epidemiology*, Madison: University of Wisconsin Press, 1987; Martin S. Pernick, 'Politics, parties and pestilence: epidemic yellow fever in Philadelphia and the rise of the first party system', in J. Walzer Leavitt and R. L. Numbers, eds., *Sickness and health in America: readings in the history of medicine and public health*, Madison: University of Wisconsin Press, 1985, pp. 356–71.
29 Carla G. Pestana, *The English Atlantic in an age of revolution 1640–1661*, Cambridge, MA: Harvard University Press, 2004.
30 Dale Ingram, *An historical account of the several plagues that have appeared in the world since the year 1346*, London: R. Baldwin, 1755; Richard Manningham, *A discourse concerning the plague and pestilential fevers*, London: Robinson, 1758.
31 Corneille le Brun, *Voyages de Corneille le Brun au Levant, c'est-à-dire, dans les principaux endroits de l'Asie Mineure, dans les Isles de Chio, Rhodes, Chypres, etc.*, Paris: P. Gosse & J. Neautme, 1732, p. 554.
32 John Taylor, *Travels from England to India, in the year 1789*, London: S. Low, 1799, vol. 1, pp. 114–5.
33 Some of the best examples are: James Lind, *An essay on diseases incidental to Europeans in hot climates*, London: T. Beckett & P. A. De Hondt, 1768; John Clark, *Observations on the diseases in long voyages to hot countries, and particularly to those which prevail in the East Indies*, London: D. Wilson and G. Nicol, 1773; Charles Curtis, *An account of the diseases of India*, Edinburgh: W. Laing, 1807. For a discussion of this literature, see W. F. Bynum, 'Cullen and the study of fevers in Britain, 1760–1820', in W. F. Bynum and V. Nutton, eds., *Theories of fever from antiquity to the enlightenment, Medical History* supplement no. 1, London: Wellcome Institute for the History of Medicine, 1981; Richard B. Sheridan, *Doctors and slaves: a medical and demographic history of slavery in the British West Indies, 1680–1834*, New York: Cambridge University Press, 1985; Mark Harrison, *Climates and constitutions: health, race, environment and British imperialism in India 1600–1850*, Delhi: Oxford University Press, 1999.
34 John P. Wade, *A paper on the prevention and treatment of the disorders of seamen and soldiers in Bengal*, London: J. Murray, 1793, pp. 5, 9.
35 Gilbert Blane, *Observations on the diseases incident to seamen*, London: Joseph Cooper, 1785, p. 128.
36 Patrick Russssell, *A treatise of the plague*, London: G. G. J. & J. Robinson, 1791.
37 John R. McNeill, 'The ecological basis of warfare in the Caribbean, 1700–1804', in M. Utlee, ed., *Adapting to conditions: war and society in the eighteenth century*, Tuscaloosa: University of Alabama Press, 1982; David Geggus, *Slavery, war, and*

revolution: the British occupation of Saint Domingue, 1793–1798, Oxford: Claren-don Press, 1982; Roger N. Buckley, *The British army in the West Indies: society and the military in the revolutionary age*, Gainesville: University Press of Florida, 1998.

38 P. Assalini, *Observations on the disease called the plague, on the dysentery, the opthalmy of Egypt, and on the means of prevention, with some remarks on the yellow fever of Cadiz*, trans. A. Neale, New York: T. J. Swords, 1806.

39 Margaret Pelling, 'The meaning of contagion: reproduction, medicine and metaphor', in A. Bashford and C. Hooker, eds., *Contagion: historical and cultural studies*, London: Routledge, 2001, pp. 15–38.

40 E.g. Hector M'Lean, *An enquiry into the nature, and causes of the great mortality among the troops at St. Domingo*, London: T. Cadell, 1797; James Clark, *A treatise on the yellow fever, as it appeared in the island of Dominica, in the years 1793–4–5*, London: J. Murray and S. Highley, 1797; J. Mabit, *Essai sur les maladies de l'armée de St.-Domingue en l'an XI, et principalement sur la fièvre jaune*, Paris: École de Médicine, 1804; Victor Bally, *Du typhus d'Amérique ou fièvre jaune*, Paris: Smith, 1814.

41 See A. G. Hopkins, ed., *Globalization in world history*, London: Pimlico, 2002; C. A. Bayly, *The birth of the modern world 1780–1914*, Oxford: Blackwell, 2004.

42 Robbie Robertson, *The three waves of globalization*, London: Zed Books, 2003; Rondo Cameron and Larry Neal, *A concise economic history of the world*, New York and Oxford: Oxford University Press, 2003.

43 See 'Globalization', in Frederick Cooper, *Colonialism in question: theory, knowledge, history*, Berkeley: University of California Press, 2005.

44 *Second report of the select committee appointed to consider the means of improving and maintaining the foreign trade of the country*, PP 1824.

45 National Maritime Museum ADM/F/27, letter from Office of Sick and Wounded Seamen to Admiralty Board, 19 August 1797.

46 In 1794, for instance, the British navy was irked by the prolonged quarantine in Lisbon of a captured French vessel containing valuable merchandise from Saragossa. The seemingly arbitrary extension of the quarantine led to protracted negotiations with the Portuguese secretary of state and other officials. See WLHUM, Western MS.7313, Thomas Mayne, Lisbon, 8 November 1794, to Sir Charles Hamilton, commander, HMS *Rodney*, Portsmouth.

47 See for example, J. Tommasini, *Recherches pathologiques sur la fièvre de Livorne de 1804, sur la fièvre jaune d' Amérique*, Paris: Arthus-Bertrand, 1812.

48 WLHUM, Western MS.3883, Maj.-Gen. Sir Charles Phillips, 'Letters and instructions to the officers during the plague at Corfu, 1816'.

49 E.g. Hugh Smith, *An essay on the nerves . . . to which is added an essay on foreign teas*, London: P. Norman, 1799; Thomas Trotter, *Medicina nautica: an essay on the diseases of seamen*, London: T. Cadell and W. Davies, 1797, pp. 9–10; Thomas Trotter, *A view of the nervous temperament*, London: Longman et al., 1807; James Johnson, *An essay on the morbid sensibility of the stomach and bowels*, London: T. & G. Underwood, 1827.

50 James McGrigor, *Medical sketches of the expedition to Egypt, from India*, London: J. Murray, 1804.

51 E.g. James McCabe, *Observations on the epidemic cholera of Asia and Europe*, Cheltenham: G. A. Williams, 1832, pp. 1–4.

52 West Sussex Record Office, Goodwood Papers, MS.1451, Sir Gilbert Blane to the Duke of Richmond, 28 November 1831, 30 November 1831; Richmond to Blane, 17 October 1831, 18 October 1831, 18 January 1832.

53 McCabe, *Observations*, pp. 5–6; William White, *The evils of quarantine laws, and non-existence of pestilential contagion*, London: Effingham Wilson, 1837. See

also Pelling, Cholera, pp. 24–5; Michael Durey, *Return of the plague: British society and the cholera of 1831–2*, London: Macmillan, 1979; Harrison, *Climates*, chap. 4.

54 Richard Evans, 'Epidemics and revolutions: cholera in nineteenth-century Europe', in P. Slack and T. Ranger, eds., *Epidemics and ideas*, Cambridge: Cambridge University Press, 1992, pp. 167–8; Richard Evans, *Death in Hamburg: society and politics in the cholera years 1830–1910*, Oxford: Clarendon Press, 1987.

55 Baldwin, *Contagion*, pp. 97–8.

56 On the rise of anticontagionist sentiment in France see Ackerknecht, 'Anticontagionism'; Ann F. La Berge, *Mission and method: the early nineteenth-century French public health movement*, Cambridge: Cambridge University Press, 1992, pp. 90–4; E. A. Heaman, 'The rise and fall of anticontagionism in France', *Canadian Bulletin of the History of Medicine*, 12, 1995, pp. 3–25.

57 See WLHUM, Western MS.4911, A. D. Vasse St. Ouen, French consul at Larnaca, Cyprus, to A. R. Roussin, French ambassador at Constantinople, 27 November 1834 to 26 April 1836.

58 La Verne Kuhnke, *Lives at risk: public health in nineteenth-century*, Egypt, Berkeley: University of California Press, 1990; Sheldon Watts, *Epidemics and history: disease, power, and imperialism*, New Haven: Yale University Press, 1997, pp. 35–9.

59 De Ségur Dupeyron, *Rapport adressé a son exc. le ministre du commerce, chargé de procéder a une enquête sur les divers régimes sanitaires de la Méditerranée*, Paris: L'Imprimerie Royale, 1834.

60 C. K. Webster, *Palmerston, Metternich and the European system 1830–1841*, London: The British Academy, 1934, pp. 19–21.

61 John Bowring, *Observations on the oriental plague, and on quarantine as a means of arresting its progress*, Edinburgh: W. Tait, 1838.

62 Earl of Aberdeen, to Lord Cowley, British Ambassador to France, 27 June 1843, *Correspondence respecting the quarantine laws since the correspondence last presented to parliament*, London: T. R. Harrison, 1846, PP 1846 [718], 45.

63 Prince Esterhazy, Austrian ambassador to Britain, to Palmerston, 19 November 1936, *Correspondence relative to the contagion of plague and the quarantine regulations of foreign countries, 1836–1943*, London: T. R. Harrison, 1843, PP 1843 [475], 54.

64 Palmerston to Sir Frederick Lamb, British ambassador to Austria, 11 June 1838, *ibid*.

65 Harold Nicolson, *The congress of Vienna: a study in allied unity 1812–1822*, London: Constable and Co., 1946; Henry A. Kissinger, *A world restored: Metternich, Castlereagh and the problems of peace 1812–22*, London: Weidenfeld and Nicolson, 1957; Charles Webster, *The congress of Vienna 1814–1815*, London: Thames and Hudson, 1963; Tim Chapman, *The congress of Vienna: origins, processes and results*, London: Routledge, 1998.

66 These efforts were grounded on a report on quarantine in the Mediterranean by the French academy of medicine chaired by Dr R. C. Prus and published in 1846. See George Weisz, *The medical mandarins: the French academy of medicine in the nineteenth and early twentieth centuries*, New York: 1995, p. 77.

67 F. S. L. Lyons, *Internationalism in Europe 1815–1914*, Leyden: A. W. Sijthoff, 1963, pp. 56–64.

68 F. R. Bridge and Roger Bullen, *The great powers and the European states system 1815–1914*, London: Longman, 1980, pp. 41–2.

69 Palmerston to Marquess of Clanricarde, 9 July 1839, correspondence relative to the affairs of the Levant, PP 1841 [304], 8, Session 2.

70 Coleman Phillipson and Noel Buxton, *The question of the Bosphorous and Dardanelles*, London: Stevens and Hayes, 1917, pp. 74–80.

71 Roger Bullen, *Palmerston, Guizot and the collapse of the entente cordial*, London: The Athlone Press, 1974, p. 334.

72 Gavin Milroy, *Quarantine and the plague: being a summary of the report on these subjects recently addressed to the royal academy of medicine in France*, London: Samuel Highley, 1846, p. 5.

73 Donald Quataert, 'Population', in H. Inalcik and D. Quataert, eds., *An economic and social history of the Ottoman empire*, vol. 2, Cambridge: Cambridge University Press, 1994, pp. 787–9.

74 Donald Quataert, *The Ottoman empire: 1700–1922*, Cambridge: Cambridge University Press, 2005, pp. 127–8.

75 The regulations were approved in May 1841 and were accompanied by detailed guidelines for all doctors in the sanitary service of the Ottoman empire. See *Papers respecting quarantine in the Mediterranean*, London: Harrison & Sons, 1860, pp. 81–7.

76 Metternich to Baron Langsdorff, French chargé d'affaires at Vienna, 13 July 1838, PP 1843 [475], 54.

77 The council consisted of sixteen members, with an Ottoman official as president; around half were sent by foreign powers, principally Britain, France and Austria-Hungary. See *Papers respecting quarantine*, p. 94.

78 Convention between Great Britain, Austria, France, Prussia, Russia, and Turkey respecting the straits of the Dardanelles and of the Bosphorous, PP 1842 [350], 44.

79 Webster, *Palmerston*, p. 24.

80 *Ibid.*, pp. 6–7.

81 Aberdeen to Lord Cowley, 27 June 1843, PP 1846 [318], 45.

82 J. Macgregor to Viscount Canning, 2 March 1844, PP 1846 [718], 45.

83 Metternich to Sir Robert Gordon, British ambassador to Austria, 24 May 1844; Gordon to Aberdeen, 31 May 1844; Canning to M. Lefevre, 17 April 1845; Canning to Lefevre, 12 September 1845, PP 1846 [718], 45.

84 Pym to the Earl of Dalhousie, 5 June 1845; Pym to Lefevre, 6 June 1845, PP 1846 [718], 45.

85 Pym to Lefevre, 22 September 1845, PP 1846 [718], 45.

86 Mr Magenis, Austrian ambassador to Britain, to Aberdeen, 15 December 1845, PP 1846 [718], 45.

87 See tables of vessels subjected to quarantine at Rhodes, *Papers respecting quarantine*, pp. 66–70.

88 General Board of Health, *Report on quarantine*, London: W. Clowes & Sons, 1849, pp. 78–9.

89 Magenis to Aberdeen, 15 November 1845, PP 1846 [718], 45.

90 Metternich to Langsdorff, 13 July 1838, PP 1843 [475], 54.

91 Speech by Bowring, 15 March 1842, Hansard, *Parl. debates*, col. 610.

92 See 'Copy of the tariff agreed upon by the commissioners appointed under the seventh article of the convention of commerce and navigation between Turkey and England', PP 1839 [549], 47; *Convention of commerce and navigation between her majesty, and the sultan of the Ottoman empire*, London: J. Harrison, 1839, PP 1839 [157], 50; Correspondence respecting the operation of the commercial treaty with Turkey, of August 16, 1838, PP [341], session 2, 8.

93 Note of the representatives of Austria, France, Great Britain, Prussia, and Russia at Constantinople, to the Porte, 27 July 1839, PP 1839 [205], 50; Correspondence relative to the affairs of the Levant, Part 3, PP 1841 [337], session 2, 8.

94 E.g. Arthur T. Holroyd, *The quarantine laws, their abuses and inconsistencies*, London: Simpkin, Marshall & Co., 1839.

95 *Papers respecting quarantine*, p. 26.

96 Campbell to Lord Palmerston, 27 March 1838, G/17/10, OIOC, British Library.

97 Lt.-Col. P. Campbell, East India Company agent, Cairo, to Peter Amber, 14 July 1835; Campbell to James Melville, 14 July 1837; Alexander Waghorn, EIC agent, Alexandria, to French post office, Alexandria, 18 July 1837, G/17/10, OIOC.

98 Hansard, *Parl. debates*, 15 March 1842, cols. 608–18.

99 *Procés-verbaux de la conférence sanitaire internationale, ouverte à Paris le 27 Juillet 1851*, vol. 1, 5 August 1851, pp. 3–4.

100 Bullen, *Palmerston*, pp. 337–8.

101 A. J. P. Taylor, *The struggle for mastery in Europe 1848–1918*, Oxford: Clarendon, 1954, p. 46.

102 Howard-Jones, *Scientific background*, pp. 15–16.

103 *Conférence sanitaire internationale*, 24 October 1851, pp. 23–25; 4 October 1851, pp. 8–9; 18 September 1851, pp. 3–12.

104 Baldwin, *Contagion*, p. 198.

105 *Conférence sanitaire internationale*, vol. 2, Annex to Proc. 29, 11 November 1851.

106 Fidler, *International law*, chap. 2.

107 Mark Harrison, *Public health in British India: Anglo-Indian preventive medicine 1859–1914*, Cambridge: Cambridge University Press, 1994, chap. 5.

108 E.g. Amir A. Afkhami, 'Defending the guarded domain: epidemics and the emergence of an international sanitary policy in Iran', *Comparative Studies of South Asia, Africa and the Middle East*, 19, 1999, pp. 122–34.

55

GLOBAL HEALTH GOVERNANCE

A conceptual review

Richard Dodgson, Kelley Lee and Nick Drager

Source: Discussion Paper 1, Geneva: World Health Organization and London School of Hygiene and Tropical Medicine, 2002, 27 pp.

Acknowledgements

This paper was written as part of a project entitled "Key Issues in Global Health Governance" funded by the Department of Health and Development, World Health Organization. The authors wish to thank Robert Beaglehole, Kent Buse, Jeff Collin and David Fidler for their helpful comments on previous drafts of this paper.

Preface

WHO's work in the area of Globalization and Health focuses on assisting countries to assess and act on cross border risks to public health security. Recognising that domestic action alone is not sufficient to ensure health locally the work programme also supports necessary collective action to address cross border risks and improve health outcomes.

In carrying out this work there was an increasing recognition that the existing rules, institutional mechanisms and forms of organization need to evolve to better respond to the emerging challenges of globalization and ensure that globalization benefits those currently left behind in the development process.

Consequently, as part of WHO's research programme on Globalization and Health, global governance for health was identified as an issue that required more detailed analysis to better inform policy makers interested in shaping the future "architecture" for global health.

Working in partnership with the Centre on Global Change and Health at the London School of Hygiene and Tropical Medicine, WHO's Department of Health and Development commissioned a series of discussion papers as a starting point to explore the different dimensions of global governance for health. The papers have been written from varying disciplinary perspectives including international relations, international law, history and public health. We hope these papers will stimulate interest in the central importance of global health governance, and encourage reflection and debate among all those concerned with building a more inclusive and "healthier" form of globalization.

Dr. Nick Drager
Department of Health and Development
World Health Organization

Abbreviations

EBF	extrabudgetary funds
FCTC	Framework Convention on Tobacco Control
GATT	General Agreement on Tariffs and Trade
GHG	global health governance
GPPPs	global public-private partnerships
HSD	Department of Health and Sustainable Development (WHO)
ICPD	International Conference on Population and Development
IFPMA	International Federation of Pharmaceutical Manufacturers Associations
IGO	intergovernmental organization
IHG	international health governance
IHR	International Health Regulations
IMF	International Monetary Fund
IR	International Relations
MSF	Medicins Sans Frontieres
NGO	nongovernmental organization
OECD	Organization for Economic Cooperation and Development
OIHP	Organization International d'Hygiène Publique
PAHO	Pan American Health Organization
PASB	Pan American Sanitary Bureau
SAP	structural adjustment programme
SPS	Sanitary and Phytosanitary Measures
TBT	technical barriers to trade
TFI	Tobacco Free Initiative
TNC	transnational corporation
TRIPS	agreement on Trade-Related Intellectual Property Rights
UNDDSMS	United Nations Department for Development Support and Management Services
UNDP	United Nations Development Programme
UNFPA	United Nations Population Fund

UNHCR	United Nations High Commissioner for Refugees
UNICEF	United Nations International Children's Emergency Fund/ UN Children's Fund
UNRRA	United Nations Relief and Rehabilitation Administration
WHA	World Health Assembly
WHO	World Health Organization
WTO	World Trade Organization

The solution lies not in turning one's back on globalization, but in learning how to manage it. In other words, there is a crying need for better global governance . . .

UN Deputy Secretary-General Louise Frechette (1998)

. . . global governance cannot replace the need for good governance in national societies; in fact, in the absence of quality local governance, global and regional arrangements are bound to fail or will have only limited effectiveness. In a way, governance has to be built from the ground up and then linked back to the local conditions.

R. Vayrynen, *Globalization and Global Governance* (1999)

1.1 Introduction

In today's world of changing health risks and opportunities, the capacity to influence health determinants, status and outcomes cannot be assured through national actions alone because of the intensification of crossborder and transborder flows of people, goods and services, and ideas. The need for more effective collective action by governments, business and civil society to better manage these risks and opportunities is leading us to reassess the rules and institutions that govern health policy and practice at the subnational, national, regional and global levels. This is particularly so as a range of health determinants are increasingly affected by factors outside of the health sector – trade and investment flows, collective violence and conflict, illicit and criminal activity, environmental change and communication technologies. There is an acute need to broaden the public health agenda to take account of these globalizing forces, and to ensure that the protection and promotion of human health is placed higher on other policy agendas (McMichael and Beaglehole 2000). There is a widespread belief that the current system of international health governance (IHG) does not sufficiently meet these needs and, indeed, has a number of limitations and gaps. In light of these perceived shortcomings, the concept of global health governance (GHG) has become a subject of interest and debate in the field of international health.

This paper seeks to contribute to this emerging discussion by reviewing the conceptual meaning and defining features of GHG.[1] This paper begins with a brief discussion of why GHG has become such a subject of discussion and debate. The particular impacts that globalization may be having on individuals and societies, and the fundamental challenges that this poses for promoting and protecting health, are explained. This is followed by a review of the history of IHG and, in particular, the traditional role of the World Health Organization (WHO). The purpose of this brief section is to draw out the distinction between international and global health governance, and the degree to which there is presently, and should be, a shift to the latter.[2] This is achieved by defining, in turn, the terms global health and governance from which the essential elements of GHG can be identified. This leads to an identification of key challenges faced by the health community in bringing about such a system in future. The paper concludes with suggestions on how the key types of actors and their respective roles in GHG might be defined further.

1.2 Health governance: the challenge of globalization

In broad terms, **governance** can be defined as the actions and means adopted by a society to promote collective action and deliver collective solutions in pursuit of common goals. This a broad term that is encompassing of the many ways in which human beings, as individuals and groups, organize themselves to achieve agreed goals. Such organization requires agreement on a range of matters including membership within the co-operative relationship, obligations and responsibilities of members, the making of decisions, means of communication, resource mobilisation and distribution, dispute settlement, and formal or informal rules and procedures concerning all of these. Defined in this way, governance pertains to highly varied sorts of collective behaviour ranging from local community groups to transnational corporations, from labour unions to the UN Security Council. Governance thus relates to both the public and private sphere of human activity, and sometimes a combination of the two.

Importantly, governance is distinct from *government*. As Rosenau (1990) writes,

> Governance is not synonymous with government. Both refer to purposive behaviour, to goal oriented activities, to systems of rule; but government suggests activities that are backed by formal authority ... whereas governance refers to activities backed by shared goals that may or may not derive from legal and formally prescribed responsibilities and that do not necessarily rely on police powers to overcome defiance and attain compliance.

Government, in other words, is a particular and highly formalised form of governance. Where governance is institutionalised within an agreed set of rules and procedures, regular or irregular meeting of relevant parties, or a permanent organizational structure with appropriate decision making and implementing bodies, we can describe these as the means or mechanisms of governance

(Finkelstein 1995), of which government is one form. In other cases, however, governance may rely on informal mechanisms (e.g. custom, common law, cultural norms and values) that are not formalised into explicit rules.

Health governance concerns the actions and means adopted by a society to organize itself in the promotion and protection of the health of its population. The rules defining such organization, and its functioning, can again be formal (e.g. Public Health Act, International Health Regulations) or informal (e.g. Hippocratic oath) to prescribe and proscribe behaviour. The governance mechanism, in turn, can be situated at the local/subnational (e.g. district health authority), national (e.g. Ministry of Health), regional (e.g. Pan American Health Organization), international (e.g. World Health Organization) and, as argued in Section 5, the global level. Furthermore, health governance can be public (e.g. national health service), private (e.g. International Federation of Pharmaceutical Manufacturers Association), or a combination of the two (e.g. Malaria for Medicines Venture).

Historically, the locus of health governance has been at the national and subnational level as governments of individual countries have assumed primary responsibility for the health of their domestic populations. Their authority and responsibility, in turn, has been delegated/distributed to regional/district/ local levels. Where the determinants of health have spilled over national borders to become international (transborder) health issues (e.g. infectious diseases) two or more governments have sought to cooperate together on agreed collective actions. This is discussed in Section 3. Growing discussions of the need to strengthen health governance at national, regional, international and, more recently, the global level has, in part, been driven by a concern that a range of globalizing forces (e.g. technological change, increased capital flows, intensifying population mobility) are creating impacts on health that existing forms of governance cannot effectively address. This has led to debates about, for example, the appropriate balance among different levels of governance, what roles public and private actors should play, and what institutional rules and structures are needed to protect and promote human health.

This paper sees **globalization** as an historical process characterised by changes in the nature of human interaction across a range of social spheres including the economic, political, technological, cultural and environmental. These changes are globalizing in the sense that boundaries hitherto separating us from each other are being transformed. These boundaries – spatial, temporal and cognitive – can be described as the dimensions of globalization. Briefly, the spatial dimension concerns changes to how we perceive and experience physical space or geographical territory. The temporal dimension concerns changes to how we perceive and experience time. The cognitive dimension concerns changes to how we think about ourselves and the world around us (Lee 2000b).

Many argue that globalization is reducing the capacity of states to provide for the health of their domestic populations and, by extension, intergovernmental

52

health cooperation is also limited. The impact of globalization upon the capacity of states and other actors to co-operate internationally to protect human health is fourfold. First, globalization has introduced or intensified **transborder health risks** defined as risks to human health that transcend national borders in their origin or impact (Lee 2000a). Such risks may include emerging and reemerging infectious diseases, various noncommunicable diseases (e.g. lung cancer, obesity, hypertension) and environmental degradation (e.g. global climate change). The growth in the geographical scope and speed in which transborder health risks present themselves directly challenge the existing system of IHG that is defined by national borders. The mechanisms of IHG, in other words, may be constrained by its statecentric nature to tackle global health effectively (Zacher 1999b).

Second, as described above, globalization is characterised by a growth in the number, and degree of influence, of nonstate actors in health governance. Many argue that the relative authority and capacity of national governments to protect and promote the health of domestic populations has declined in the face of globalizing forces beyond national borders that affect the basic determinants of health as well as erode national resources for addressing their consequences (Deacon et al. 1997). Nonstate actors, including civil society groups, global social movements, private companies, consultancy firms, think tanks, religious movements and organized crime, in turn, have gained relatively greater power and influence both formally and informally.[3] The emerging picture is becoming more complex, with the distinct roles of state and nonstate actors in governance activities such as agenda setting, resource mobilisation and allocation, and dispute settlement becoming less clear. New combinations of both state and nonstate actors are rapidly forming, in a myriad of forms such as partnerships, alliances, coalitions, networks and joint ventures. This apparent "hybridisation" of governance mechanisms around certain health issues is a reflection of the search for more effective ways of cooperation to promote health in the face of new institutions. At the same time, however, it throws up new challenges for creating appropriate and recognised institutional mechanisms for, *inter alia*, ensuring appropriate representation, participation, accountability and transparency.

Third, current forms of globalization appear to be problematic for sustaining, and even worsening existing socioeconomic, political and environmental problems. UNDP (1999), for example, reports that neoliberal forms of globalization have been accompanied by widening inequalities between rich and poor within and across countries. In a special issue of *Development*[4], authors cite experiences of worsening poverty, marginalisation and health inequity as a consequence of globalization. In some respects, these problems can be seen as "externalities" or "global public bads" (Kaul et al. 1999) that are arising as a result of globalizing processes that are insufficiently managed by effective health governance. As Fidler (1998a) writes, these deeply rooted problems "feed off" the negative consequences of the globalization of health, creating a reciprocal relationship between health and the determinants of health. Although many of these problems are most acute in the developing world, they are of concern to all countries given their transborder nature (i.e. unconfined to national borders).

Fourth, globalization has contributed to a decline in both the political and practical capacity (see reading) of the national governments, acting alone or in cooperation with other states, to deal with global health challenges. While globalization is a set of changes occurring gradually over several centuries, its acceleration and intensification from the late twentieth century has brought attention to the fact that states alone cannot address many of the health challenges arising. Infectious diseases are perhaps the most prominent example of this diminishing capacity, but equally significant are the impacts on noncommunicable diseases (e.g. tobacco-related cancers), food and nutrition, lifestyles and environmental conditions (Lee 2000b). This decapitating of the state has been reinforced by initiatives to further liberalise the global trade of goods and services. The possible health consequences of more open global markets have only begun to be discussed within trade negotiations and remain unaddressed by proposed governance mechanisms for the emerging global economy.

The fourth of the above points is perhaps the most significant because it raises the possibility of the need for a change in the fundamental nature of health governance. As mentioned above, IHG is structured on the belief that governments have primary responsibility for the health of its people and able, in co-operation with other states, to protect its population from health risks. Globalization, however, means that the state may be increasingly undermined in its capacity to fulfil this role alone, that IHG is necessary but insufficient, and that additional or new forms of health governance may be needed. Some scholars and practitioners believe that this new system of health governance needs to be global in scope, so that it can deal effectively with problems caused by the globalization of health (Farmer 1998; Kickbusch 1999). Globalization, in short, is an important driving force behind the emergence of GHG.

1.3 The origins of international health governance

1.3.1 The growth of health governance in the nineteenth century

A fuller understanding of the distinction between international and global health governance requires an historical perspective, of which a brief overview is provided here.[5] Historically, we can trace health governance to the most ancient human societies where agreed rules and practices about hygiene and disease were adopted. Early forms of IHG, in the form of cooperation on health matters between two or more countries, span many centuries with the adoption of quarantine practices amidst flourishing trade relations and the creation

of regional health organizations. The process of building institutional structures, rules and mechanisms to systematically protect and promote human health
across national borders, however, began more concertedly during the nineteenth century. Following the conclusion of the Napoleonic Wars, European
states formed a number of international institutions to promote peace, industrial development and address collective concerns including the spread of
infectious disease. This process of institutionalisation of IHG, according to
Fidler (1997), was a consequence of the intensified globalization of health
during this period.[6] Notably, these initiatives enjoyed the support of political
and economic elites across European societies who believed that the cross-
border spread of disease would hamper industrialisation and the expansion
of international trade (Murphy 1995; Fidler 1998a).

The first institution to be created during this period was the International
Sanitary Conference, with the first conference held in 1851. The achievements
of this meeting, and the ten conferences subsequently held over the next four
decades, were limited. In total, four conventions on quarantine and hygiene
practices were concluded, along with an agreement to establish an institution
for maintaining and reporting epidemiological data, and coordinating responses to outbreaks of infectious diseases (Lee 1998). Importantly, however,
the conferences formalised a basic principle that has defined subsequent
efforts to build IHG, namely the recognition that acting in cooperation
through agreed rules and procedures enable governments to better protect
their domestic populations from health risks that cross national borders. As
such, the institutions adopted were envisioned as an extension of participating
governments' responsibilities in the health field to the international (intergovernmental) level.

Along with this emerging sense of an international health community,
constructed of cooperating states, was a growing body of scientific knowledge
that was beginning to be shared in a more organized fashion (1998a). Scientific
meetings on health-related themes reflected substantial advances during this
period in understanding the causes of a number of diseases, such as cholera
and tuberculosis. In addition, international meetings were held on social issues
that impacted on public health, notably trafficking of liquor and opium. Between
1851–1913, eighteen international conferences on health were held (Box 1),
and twelve health-related international institutions[7] had been established by
1914 (Murphy 1995). Among the most prominent were the International
Sanitary Bureau (later the Pan American Sanitary Bureau) in 1902 and *Office
International d'Hygiene Publique* (OIHP) created in Paris in 1907. The OIHP
was a milestone in IHG in that it provided a standing (rather than periodic)
forum for countries to exchange ideas and information on public health
(Roemer 1994). This was followed in 1920 with the formation of the Health
Organization of the League of Nations. While a lack of resources and political
support restricted its activities, and inter-organizational competition with
the OIHP hindered the scope of its work, the organization emerged from

---

Box 1. World and European conferences on health: 1851–1913

1851	First Sanitary Conference, Paris
1859	Second Sanitary Conference, Paris
1866	Third Sanitary Conference, Instanbul
1874	Fourth Sanitary Conference, Vienna
1881	Fifth Sanitary Conference, Washington
1885	Sixth Sanitary Conference, Rome
1887	Liquor on the North Sea, venue unrecorded
1892	Seventh Sanitary Conference, Venice
1893	Eighth Sanitary Conference, Dresden
1894	Ninth Sanitary Conference, Paris
1897	Tenth Sanitary Conference, Venice
1899	Liquor Traffic in Africa, Brussels
1903	Eleventh Sanitary Conference, Paris
1906	Liquor Traffic in Africa, Brussels
1909	Opium, Shanghai
1911	Twelfth Sanitary Conference, Paris
1911	Opium, The Hague
1913	Opium, The Hague

Source: Murphy, C. N. (1994), *International Organization and Industrial Change: Global Governance since 1850* (Cambridge: Polity Press), p.59.

the interwar period with a strong reputation for data collection and public health research.

From the mid nineteenth century, the nongovernmental sector also began to grow and contribute to IHG, essentially filling gaps or supplementing government action. For example, religious missions and The Rockefeller Foundation's International Health Division (established in 1913) led the way in supporting health services and disease control programmes in many parts of the developing world. The International Committee of the Red Cross (established in 1863) succeeded in establishing the Geneva Convention, a precursor of future international health regimes in setting out norms of behaviour and ethical standards for treating casualties of war. Other notable NGOs created during this period were the League of Red Cross Societies (1919) and Save the Children Fund (1919).

By the 1920s, governmental and nongovernmental health organizations were contributing to a vision of IHG that was increasingly defined by humanitarianism. Many medical practitioners and public health officials building national public health systems at the national level (e.g. Margaret Sanger) became closely involved in designing these early international health institutions. Many of attended international scientific conferences from the mid nineteenth century, bringing with them a strong belief that international health cooperation should seek to provide health to as many people as possible. To achieve this vision of 'social medicine' required a strong emphasis on universality as a guiding principal, achieved through the inclusion of as many countries as possible in any international system of health governance that was formed.

1.3.2 International health governance after the Second World War

The postwar period brought a significant expansion in IHG through the establishment of new institutions and official development assistance for health purposes. Within the UN system, the World Health Organization (WHO) was created in 1948 as the UN specialised agency for health. Other organizations contributing to health were the UN Relief and Rehabilitation Administration (UNRRA) in 1943, UN International Children's Emergency Fund (UNICEF) in 1946 and UN High Commissioner for Refugees (UNHCR) in 1949. WHO was similar in a number of ways to the Health Organization of the League of Nations that preceded it. Above all, the ideal of universality was, and remains, central to its mandate and activities. As stated by the Constitution of WHO (1946), the overall goal of the organization is "the attainment by all peoples of the highest possible level of health". Even in the face of scepticism at the attainability of such a mandate, and challenges to the appropriateness of social medicine (Goodman 1971), WHO was founded with a strong commitment to addressing the health needs of all people. The universalism of WHO has been reaffirmed on a number of occasions since 1948, most clearly during the 1970s with the Health for All strategy and Renewing Health for All Strategy in the 1990s (Antezana et al. 1998).

WHO's pledge to universality, however, has been strongly defined by the sovereignty of its member states. The working assumption of the organization has been that "health for all" can be achieved by working primarily, if not exclusively, through governmental institutions, notably ministries of health. Universality, in this sense, is measured by number of member states. Where a large number of countries participate, such as the World Health Assembly (WHA), it is assumed that the health needs of all peoples are represented. The role of WHO, in turn, is designed as supporting the efforts of governments to promote and protect the health of their populations.

Beyond national governments NGOs have been allowed to apply for permission to enter into official relations with WHO since 1950 if it is concerned with matters that fall within the competence of the organization and pursues (whose aims and purposes are in conformity with those of the Constitution of WHO). In 1998, there were 188 NGOs in official relations (WHO 1998) from such diverse fields as medicine, science, education, law, humanitarian aid and industry. In principle, therefore, NGOs are recognised as important contributors to achieving the goals of WHO. In practice, however, the actual role NGOs have played has been limited. Lucas et al. (1997), for example, found that WHO has engaged with NGOs in its support at country level in contrast with trends within agencies and other UN organizations such as UNDP and UNICEF. At the headquarters and regional levels, officially recognised NGOs have observed proceedings of the World Health Assembly or meetings of the regional committees, and have limited access to programme-related meetings dealing with more specific health issues. However NGOs have not been routinely consulted despite their importance as channels of health sector aid since the 1980s (Hulme and Edwards 1997) increased.

This traditional focus on member states and, in particular, ministries of health has been in a context of greater diversity of policy actors. By the mid 1990s, the map of IHG was one of considerable uncertainty, as Zacher (1999bc) describes, fractured into an "organizational patchwork quilt". Alongside WHO has emerged a multiplicity of players, each accountable to a different constituency and bringing with them different guiding principles, expertise, resources and governance structures. The World Bank maintains a prominent place because of its unrivalled financial resources and policy influence. Regional organizations, such as the European Union, and other UN organizations (e.g. UNICEF, UNDP, UNFPA) retain health as an important component of their work but are more limited in membership and/or scope. The Organization for Economic Cooperation and Development (OECD) and World Trade Organization (WTO) approach health from an economic and trade perspective. Varied civil society groups, such as consumer groups, social movements and research institutions, also make substantial contributions to health development. Finally, the growth of the private sector actors in health, within and across countries, is notable. New fault lines and allegiances had emerged to form an increasingly complex milieu for health cooperation, with interests divided within and across countries and organizations. Undertaking a wide-ranging process of reform, WHO has sought to change some of its traditional governance features, notably its strong focus on ministries of health, by engaging other public and private sector actors, and creating new consultation mechanisms. As discussed in 4 below, there have been clear efforts to increase the involvement of the NGO sector in areas of WHO activities, such as tobacco, tuberculosis and HIV/ AIDS, since the late 1990s. At the same time, it has reiterated its commitment to universality as the defining principle of its activities. How to define, let alone achieve health for all, remains an enduring challenge.

In summary, IHG has evolved alongside an intensification of human interaction across national borders over a number of centuries, gradually becoming more institutionalised from the mid nineteenth century. During the twentieth century, this institutional framework has grown and spread, encompassing both rich and poor countries, in all regions of the world. The defining feature of IHG has been the primacy given to the state although non-state actorsand interests were ever present. By the late twentieth century, however, what Held et al. (1999) calls a "thickening" of the globalization process was challenging this statecentric system of health governance. It is within this context that discussions and debates about global health governance have emerged.

1.4 An emerging system of global health governance?

The precise origins of the term GHG are unclear, although many scholars and practitioners who use the term draw upon a number of different fields. These mixed origins mean that GHG can be difficult to define. This problem of definition is compounded by the fact that the term GHG is used widely in a number of different contexts. We can begin to overcome this problem of definition by breaking GHG into its component parts – global health and governance.

1.4.1 International versus global health

Globalization brings into question how we define the determinants of health and how they can be addressed. In principle, the mandate of WHO is based on a broad understanding of health[8], although in practice its activities have traditionally been biomedical in focus. Since the 1970s, efforts have been made to incorporate a more multisectoral and multidisciplinary approach into the organization's activities. For example, *Health for all in the 21st Century* links the attainment of good health to human rights, equity, gender, sustainable development, education, agriculture, trade, energy, water and sanitation (Antezana et al. 1998). Similarly, the replacement of the Global Programme on AIDS by UNAIDS was in large part due to a desire to go beyond a narrow biomedical approaches to HIV/AIDS (Altman 1999).

Globalization from the late twentieth century has emphasised even more poignantly the need for greater attention to the basic determinants of health including so-called non-health issue areas. In arguing for a reinvigoration of public health, McMichael and Beaglehole (1999) point to the need to address underlying socioeconomic (notably inequalities), demographic and environmental changes that global change is creating. Similarly, Chen et al. (1999) argue that globalization is eroding the boundary between the determinants of public (collective) and private (individual) health. For example, susceptibility to tobacco-related diseases, once strongly linked to, and blamed on, the lifestyle choices of individuals, is increasingly seen as attributable to the worldwide marketing practices of tobacco companies. The distinction between *global* health and *international* health therefore is that the former entails a broadening of our understanding of, and policy responses to, the basic determinants of health to include forces that transcend the territorial boundaries of states. Global health requires a rethinking of how we prioritise and address the basic determinants of health, and engagement with the broad range of sectors that shape those underlying determinants.

The need to address the basic determinants of health leads to the practical question of how to do so. Since at least the early 1990s, there has been a growing confusion of mandates among UN organizations that have substantial involvement in the health sector – WHO, UNICEF, UNDP, UNFPA and the World Bank. In large part, this has been due to efforts to develop multisectoral approaches to both health and development, as well as key areas (e.g. reproductive health, environmental health) that bring together the activities of two or more organizations (Lee et al. 1996). Globalization invites a further widening of the net of relevant organizations, requiring engagement with actors that have little or no formal mandate in the health field. Notable have been efforts to establish greater dialogue between WHO and the WTO. While trade interests have historically defined, and in many ways confined, international health cooperation, officially the two spheres have been addressed by separate institutions. Nonetheless, the multiple links between trade and health policy are well recognised (WHO 2002, Brundtland 1998; Brundtland 1999), resulting in high-level meetings between the two organizations since the late 1990s. At present, WHO holds official observer status on the Council of the WTO, and committees relating to Sanitary and Phytosanitary Measures (SPS) and Technical Barriers to Trade (TBT) agreements. However, the capacity to articulate public health concerns regarding, for example, the agreement on trade-related intellectual property rights (TRIPS), has been hampered by the framing of health among trade officials as a "non-trade issue", and as such the reluctance of certain countries to discuss health within the context of a trade negotiations. Moreover, the ability of WHO to influence the WTO has been hampered by the fact that states (many of which are members of both organizations) have accorded a higher priority to trade issues, rather than those relating to human health. As such, there remain considerable barriers to incorporating health as a legitimate and worthy concern on the global trade agenda.

1.4.2 The different meanings of governance

As described above, the ability of a society to promote collective action and deliver solutions to agreed goals is a central aspect of governance. As shown in Table 1 the term governance has been used in a number of different ways, ranging from the relatively narrow scope of corporate and clinical governance, to the broader concept of global governance.

Recent interest in governance within the development community can be traced to the late 1980s as part of a desire among aid agencies to address the uneven performance of low and middle-income countries to macro economic reforms (Dia 1993). The term **good governance** was introduced by the World Bank (1994) as an explanation for problems being experienced in many countries, namely the weakness of public sector institutions and management, and as a basis for setting further lending conditionalities. In this context, governance is defined as "the manner in which power is exercised in the management of a country's economic and social resources of development."

Table 1 Various uses of the term governance.

Type of governance	Characteristics
governance	• the actions and means to promote collective action and deliver collective solutions • "an exercise in assessing the efficacy of alternative modes (means) of organization. The object is to effect good order through the mechanisms of governance" (Williamson 1996: 11) • "The manner in which power is exercised in the management of a country's economic and social resources for development" (World Bank 1994)
corporate governance	• clear systems of transparency and accountability to investors • mechanisms for meeting social responsibility by corporations • "the framework of laws, regulatory institutions, and reporting requirements that condition the way that the corporate sector is governed" (World Bank 1994)
good governance (World Bank 1994)	• public sector management • accountability of public sector institutions • legal framework for development • transparency and information
good governance (UNDP 1997)	• management of nations affairs • efficiency, effectiveness and economy • liberal democracy • greater use of non-governmental sector
clinical governance	• "a framework through which NHS organizations are accountable for continuously improving the quality of their services and safeguarding high standards of care by creating an environment in which excellence in clinical care will flourish" (UK 1998)
global governance	• "not only the formal institutions and organizations through which the rules and norms governing world order are (or are not) made and sustained – the institutions of the state, inter-governmental co-operation and so on – but also those organizations and pressure groups – from MNCs, transnational social movements to the plethora of non-governmental organizations – which pursue goals and objectives which have a bearing on transnational rule and authority systems" (Held et al. 1999)

For governance to be "good", social and economic resources must be managed by a small efficient state that is representative, accountable, transparent, respectful of the rule of law, and supportive of human rights through programmes of poverty reduction.

The conceptualisation and application of the term good governance by the World Bank is seen by Leftwich (1993) as problematic in a number of ways. First, he argues that it is an extension of neoliberal-based policies, (for example, structural adjustment programmes) that are arguably themselves contributing to the problems experienced by many countries since the 1980s. Second, the World Bank focuses narrowly on the performance of public sector administration and management, while ignoring the importance of good governance for the private sector or donor community itself, along with levels of foreign debt, in influencing how countries have fared. Third, the prescriptive element of good governance again focuses on governments, while at the same time adopting a technocratic view of how governments should work.

Other development agencies have since taken up the term good governance as important components of their policies[9]. The UN Development Programme (UNDP) is a notable example. In seeking to go beyond public sector management, UNDP (1997) has incorporated a range of principles into its conceptualisation of good governance including legitimacy (democracy), freedom of association, participation, and freedom of the media. As Deputy Director of the UN Department for Development Support and Management Services A.T.R. Rahman (1996) states, "good governance is an overall process that is essential to economic growth, to sustainable development and to fulfilling UN-identified objectives such as the advancement of women and elimination of poverty".[10]

Another increasingly used term is **corporate governance.** Williamson (1996) defines corporate governance, for example, in terms of recent developments on transaction-cost approaches in economic theory. He writes that governance concerns institutional structures and accompanying practices (e.g. rules) that facilitate economic production and exchange relations. "Good" governance structures are those that effectively "mitigate hazards and facilitate adaptation". These can be simple or complex depending on the degree of hazard faced. Other writers on corporate governance similarly focus on mechanisms that enhance economic transactions. The underlying assumption of such approaches is that good corporate governance, in the form of improved (more democratic) systems of accountability and transparency for investors, will enhance the process of wealth creation and prevent greater regulation by governments (McRitchie 1998).

A broader perspective on corporate governance is more closely related to the definition of good governance put forth within the development community. This approach focuses more directly on the nature of social responsibility by business, rather than the enhancement of profits. There has been a growing movement to encourage the corporate sector to be more responsible, not only to shareholders, but to the wider communities within which they operate. The notion of corporate responsibility and citizenship has thus arisen in relation to such practices as fair trade, ethical investment and activist shareholders, social and environmental impact assessments, improved working conditions for workers in low-income countries, and the social auditing of companies (Cantarella 1996).

The values of management-oriented approaches to corporate governance have entered the health lexicon in the guise of **clinical governance**. In the UK, where the term that has become especially popular, clinical governance refers to "a framework through which NHS [National Health Service] organizations are accountable for continuously improving the quality of their services and safeguarding high standards of care by creating an environment in which excellence in clinical care will flourish." (UK 1998). Initially emerging as part of health sector reform, it has been a response in particular to differences in quality of care in parts of the country, and to public concerns regarding well-publicised cases of poor clinical performance. The focus, therefore, has been improving the quality of patient care through evidence based practice, collecting information to measure performance against agreed standards, providing ongoing education for health care professionals, and managing and learning from complaints (Scally and Donaldson 1998). Institutional mechanisms (e.g. National Institute for Clinical Excellence) and practices have been introduced for these purposes (Paris and McKeown 1999; The King's Fund 1999). Criticisms of clinical governance focus on whether there is anything new about its aims. Some argue that clinical governance offers little more than a confirmation of "the common sense message that we [doctors and health professionals] must all strive after quality in practising medicine" (Goodman 1998).

A further use of the term governance, and the focus of this paper, is **global governance** which can be broadly defined as

> not only the formal institutions and organizations through which the rules and norms governing world order are (or are not) made and sustained – the institutions of the state, inter-governmental cooperation and so on – but also those organizations and pressure groups – from MNCs, transnational social movements to the plethora of non-governmental organizations – which pursue goals and objectives which have a bearing on transnational rule and authority systems.
> (Held et al. 1999)

The concept of global governance has come to the health field from the discipline of International Relations (IR) within which a diverse, and theoretically riven, debate has developed on the specific nature of globalization, the emerging global order, key actors, and ultimate goals of global governance (Table 2). **Liberal-internationalist** scholars view the purpose of global governance as

Table 2 Theoretical approaches to global governance.

Central issue of global governance	Liberal-internationalism	Critical/Radical	Cosmopolitan democracy
Globalization	Multi-causal process – generates interdependence and 'zones of peace'	Economically driven – subject to contradictions	Multi-causal process with transformative potential
Nature of the current global order	Emerging post-Westphalian order	Global neoliberalism	Post-Westphalian order
Actors in global governance	States, international organizations corporations and NGOs etc.	Transnational capitalist class, elites through states, International organization and civil society.	States, peoples, international organization, corporations and social movements
Key actors in collective problem solving	States and international organization	Transnational capitalist class, international organization, states and civil society.	States, international organization, corporations and social movements
Nature of global governance	Reformist and top-down	Revolutionary and bottom-up	Transformationalist and participatory
Change towards	Liberal democratic consensus politics	Humane governance	Cosmopolitan democracy

Source: Adapted from McGrew A. (1997), "Globalization and Territorial Democracy: an introduction" in McGrew A. ed., *The Transformation of Democracy?* (London: Polity Press), p.20.

ultimately moving towards a more liberal democratic global order in which states and IGOs have equal roles. Within such an order it is envisaged that power and influence will flow in a top-down manner, although states and IGOs may be held accountable via a global assembly composed of representatives from national and global civil society (Commission on Global Governance 1995). In contrast, **radical/critical** scholars believe that the direction of global governance should be guided from the bottom-up. Emphasis is placed on the potential of actors from within (global) civil society (in particular social movements) to bring about more 'humane governance' (Gill 1998). **Cosmopolitan democrats** pursue a vision of global governance that embraces the diversity of people across national and other forms of identity within a shared political community. This ideal may be achieved, for instance, through consensus on universal principles (e.g. human rights), increased public scrutiny of existing IGOs, global referendums and an expanded international legal system (Held 1995; McGrew 1997). This is a somewhat simplistic summary of a substantial and intellectually rich literature.[11]

To summarise, the concept of governance has generally been used in two broad ways in relation to health. The first defines governance as a problem-solving approach to address the shortfalls of public and private institutions to function efficiently. Strongly influenced by recent developments in management and economic theory, good or better governance is equated with strengthening efficiency and effectiveness within existing institutional structures. The second takes a more transformative approach by finding existing forms of governance falling short in its responsiveness to the needs of society as a whole. Faced with a range of intensifying and/or new risks and opportunities, more effective governance is believed to be needed to respond to social change. This volume is located within this second view in its efforts to encourage wider discussion of the challenges posed by globalization, and the clearer vision needed to address them through global governance.

1.4.3 The essential elements of global health governance

From the above discussion, we can identify some essential elements of GHG and the challenges for achieving them. The first is the "deterritorialisation" of how we think about and promote health, and thus *the need to address factors which cross, and even ignore, the geographical boundaries of the state.* The formation of the international system of states in the sixteenth century, the birth of public health during the nineteenth century, and the creation of national health systems in the twentieth century have contributed to a system of governance that is premised on protecting the integrity of the state. IHG has been historically focused on those health issues that cross national borders, with the aim of protecting domestic populations within certain defined geographical boundaries through such practices as quarantine, cordon sanitaire, and internationally agreed standards governing the reporting of infectious disease, trade and population mobility. All of these efforts have been focused on the point of contact, the national border of states.

However, forces of global change, in various forms, have intensified cross-border activity to such an extent as to undermine the capacity of states to control them. The increased levels of international trade and movement of people are examples. Moreover, a wide range of others forces render national borders irrelevant. The worldwide flows of information and communication across the Internet; the ecological impacts of global environmental change; the frenzied exchange of capital and finance via electronic media; the illicit trade in drugs, food products and even people; and the global mobility of other life forms (e.g. microbes) through natural (e.g. bird migration) and manmade (e.g. bulk shipping) means render border controls irrelevant. Many of these global changes impact on health and requires forms of cooperation that go beyond IHG.

A second essential element of GHG is *the need to define and address the determinants of health from a multi-sectoral perspective*. Biomedical approaches to health have dominated historically in the form of disease-focused research and policy, the skills mix of international health experts and officials, and the primacy given to working through ministries of health and health professionals. A global system of health governance begins with the recognition that a broad range of determinants impact on population health including social and natural environments. In recent decades, this has been recognised to some extent through the increased involvement of other forms of expertise in health policy making (e.g. economics, anthropology) and links with other social sectors (e.g. education, labour). More recently, ministries of health and international health organizations have sought to engage more directly with sectors traditionally seen as relatively separate from health (e.g. trade, environment, agriculture) in recognition of "cross sectoral" policy issues at play. Informal consultations between WHO and WTO, for example, have been prompted by the importance of multilateral trade agreements to health.

The main challenge to achieving greater cross sectoral collaboration lies in the danger of casting the health "net" so widely that everything becomes subsumed within the global health umbrella. Opening up GHG too indiscriminately can dilute policy focus and impact, and raise questions about feasibility. The linking of traditional health and non-health issues also demands a clear degree of understanding and empirical evidence about cause and effect. Defining the scope of GHG, therefore, remains a balance between recognising the interconnectedness of health with a varied range of globalizing forces, and the need to define clear boundaries of knowledge and action.

The third essential element of GHG is *the need to involve, both formally and informally, a broader range of actors and interests*. As described above, while nonstate actors have long been an important part of the scene, IHG has been firmly state-defined. Health-related regional organizations (e.g. PAHO, European Union), along with major international health organizations such as WHO and the World Bank are formally governed by member states. Their mandates, in turn, are defined by their role in supporting the national health systems of those member states. The universality of their activities is measured by the number of member states participating in them. Defining criteria and measures of progress to address the burden of disease, health determinants and health status are focused on the state or groups of states.

GHG, however, is distinguished by the starting point that globalization is creating health needs and interests that increasingly cut across and, in some cases, are oblivious to state boundaries. To effectively address these global health challenges, there is a need to strengthen, supplement and even replace existing forms of IHG. Importantly, this does not mean that the role of the state or IHG will disappear or become redundant, but that they will rather need to become part of a wider system of GHG. Many existing institutions will be expected to play a significant role in GHG, and states will continue to be key actors. However, states and state-defined governance alone is not enough. Forms of governance that bring together more concertedly state and nonstate actors will be central in a global era (Scholte 2000). As described by the Commission on Global Governance (1995), "[global governance] must . . . be understood as also involving NGOs, citizen's movements, multinational corporations, and the global capital market," as well as a "global mass media of dramatically enlarged influence."

As described above, state and nonstate actors have long interacted on health governance. The difference for GHG will lie in their degree of involvement and nature of their respective roles, varying with the health issue concerned. Three brief examples illustrate this. First, relations among the diverse NGO community are constantly changing depending on the issue. On certain issues, they may be willing to form strategic networks or alliances with other NGOs, thus representing an important governance mechanism within GHG. Such a mechanism was formed around the global campaign against the marketing of breastmilk substitutes that led to the formation of the International Baby Food Action Network. Cooperation among the International Baby Food Action Network, UNICEF, WHO and selected governments led to the International Code of Marketing on Breast-Milk Substitutes in 1981. Like-minded NGOs also came together to form more permanent, but still highly fluid, global social movements around the environment and women's health. These movements opposed each other at the UN Conference on the Environment and Development (1992), yet worked together to propose an alternative view of development at the World Summit for Social Development in 1995. Close relations among the women's health movement, national governments and UNFPA was also a defining feature of the International Conference on Population and Development (1994). Relations between the women's health movement and some states, in particular the US, were so close that members of the women's health movement served on some of the official government delegations. Parties involved in the conference believed that such close relations played a key role in shaping the resultant commitment to reproductive health (Dodgson 1998).

A second example is the closer relations among state and nonstate actors characterising the emerging global strategy on tobacco control. Under the auspices of WHO, negotiations for a Framework Convention on Tobacco Control (FCTC) have been attended by officially recognised NGOs, along with state delegations. The Tobacco Free Initiative (TFI), WHO maintains that NGO participation is central to the overall success of the FCTC, and has supported the creation of a global NGO network to support the FCTC (i.e. Framework Convention Alliance). Links were also formed with representatives of the women's movement to ensure that tobacco and women's health was discussed during the Beijing Plus 5 process. At the same time, TFI has developed links with the business community, in particular, the pharmaceutical industry, to explore how nicotine replacement treatments can be made more widely available. Other coordination efforts have been focused on bringing together different UN organizations through the formation of a UN Ad Hoc Inter-Agency Task Force on tobacco control, and the holding of public hearings to encourage the submission of a wide range of evidence from different interest groups.[12]

These efforts to build formal links with such a diverse range of stakeholders to support global tobacco control policy is unprecedented for WHO, and a good example of emerging forms of GHG. It represents an important challenge to traditional ways of working for WHO in its efforts to tackle health issues with global dimensions (Collin et al. 2002). Ensuring state and nonstate actors work collectively on different levels of governance (i.e. global, regional, national[13] and subnational), the FCTC is an example of how "behind-the-border" convergence could be promoted in the future. The goal of adopting a legally binding treaty and associated protocols is also a new development in institutionalising global governance in the health sector. The FCTC is based on international regimes that have emerged to promote collective action on global environmental problems. These international regimes can be defined as "sets of implicit or explicit principles, norms, rules and decision-making procedures around which actors expectations converge in a given area of international relations" (Krasner 1983). In addition to the FCTC, other examples of international regimes in the field of health are the International Health Regulations[14], the International Code for the Marketing of Breast Milk Substitutes and the Codex Alimentarius (Kickbusch 1999). These examples of international health regimes demonstrate that they have played a significant role in IHG. The remit and organizational structure of the FCTC and its implementation suggest that such regimes will be a core feature of GHG in future.

A third example of state-nonstate governance is so-called global public-private partnerships (GPPPs) defined as "a collaborative relationship which transcends national boundaries and brings together at least three parties, among them a corporation (and/or industry association) and inter-governmental organizations, so as to achieve a shared health creating goal on the basis of a mutually agreed division of labour" (Buse and Walt 2001). Among the most prominent GPPPs are the Albendazole Donation Programme, Medicines for Malaria Venture and International AIDS Vaccine Initiative. The idea of building partnerships with business is at the centre of UN-wide views on the governance of globalization (Global Compact). For this reason, and the fact that GPPPs bring much needed resources to major health issues, the number of GPPPs is likely to grow in future. At the same time, like the FCTC process, GPPPs require a period of reflection on a range of governance issues. Buse and Walt (2001), for example, raise questions about accountability, transparency and long-term sustainability of GPPPs. They also ask who benefits, people who seek treatment or the pharmaceutical companies that gain good public relations. Some governments of low-income countries, a number of NGOs and UN institutions have expressed concerns about the viability of building links among actors with fundamentally differing objectives and interests. For example, Carole Bellamy, UNICEF Executive Director comments, "it is dangerous to assume that the goals of the private sector are somehow synonymous with those of the United Nations, because they most emphatically are not."[15]

Thus, global health emphasises the need for governance that incorporates participation by a broadly defined "global" constituency, and engaging them in collective action through agreed institutions and rules. The challenges of achieving GHG, defined in this way, are considerable. At the heart lies the need to define the core concept of democracy in the context of globalization in terms of political identity and representation. If existing forms of health governance are seen to be undemocratic, alternatives that appropriately balance actors and interests are needed. Systems for ensuring accountability and transparency must be agreed. There requires greater clarity about what contributions different actors make to GHG, and what governance mechanisms can ensure that these roles are fulfilled. The issue of meaningful participation and responsibility remains problematic. For example, the WHA is attended by WHO member states but there are inequities in capacity to follow proceedings and contribute to decision making. This is a challenge for many international organizations including the WTO. Conflicts are also likely to emerge and need to be resolved. The familiar yet enduring problem of coordination of international health cooperation remains unresolved. Overall, the principle of closer state-nonstate cooperation is an increasingly accepted one, but the "nitty gritty" of what this should look like in practice is only beginning to be explored within the health sector. This theme is taken up by discussion papers on the potential role of civil society and the private sector in this series.

1.5 Conclusions: beginning to define and shape the architecture for GHG

The task of defining and shaping a system of GHG in further detail, both as it appears to be currently evolving and more prospectively, begins with a number of important challenges for research and policy. The first, and perhaps the most fundamental, is the need to agree the normative framework upon which GHG can be built. There is a need to reach some degree of consensus about the underlying moral and ethical principles that define global health cooperation. As discussed in this paper, universalism has been a strong ethos guiding the emergence of social medicine, the Health for All movement from the late 1970s and, more recently, calls for health as a human right. Alongside such communitarian ideas have been approaches informed by principles of entitlement (economic or otherwise) and utilitarianism. Despite recent high-profile initiatives on "global health", an informed discussion about their normative basis remains to be carried out.

A second challenge is the need to define leadership and authority in GHG. As discussed above, health cooperation has evolved into an arena populated by a complex array of actors operating at different levels of policy and constituencies, with varying mandates, resources and authority. Figure 1 is an attempt to identify the key actors potentially concerned with GHG and their possible positions at a given point in time. WHO and the World Bank are shown as central because they represent the main sources of health expertise and development financing respectively. At the same time, they are accompanied by a cluster of institutions, state and nonstate, that fan outwards including, but are not restricted to, the International Monetary Fund (IMF),

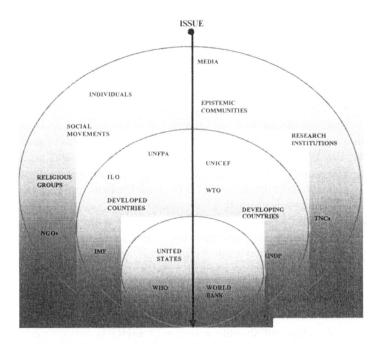

Figure 1 Global health governance mapped.

World Trade Organization (WTO), United Nations Children's Fund (UNICEF), International Labour Organization (ILO), United Nations Development Programme (UNDP), and United Nations Population Fund (UNFPA). Specific regional and bilateral institutions (e.g. USAID) are included as politically and economically influential.[16] GHG also includes the wide variety of actors within the private sector and civil society, the latter defined as "a sphere of social interaction between economy and state, composed above all of the intimate sphere (especially family), the sphere of associations (especially voluntary associations) and forms of public communication" (Jareg and Kaseje 1998). Some of these actors (e.g. Bill and Melinda Gates Foundation) have become highly prominent in recent years. Others, as described above, including NGOs, social movements, epistemic communities, professional associations and the mass media, can be influential on a more policy specific basis.

In this complex arena of actors, the issue of leadership and authority is a difficult one. As well as setting the normative framework for global health cooperation, leadership can provide the basis for generating public awareness, mobilising resources, using resources rationally through coordinated action, setting priorities, and bestowing or withdrawing legitimacy from groups and causes. The willingness of states to 'pool' their sovereignty and act collectively through mechanisms of GHG is one historically significant hurdle. The absence of a single institution, with the authority and capacity to act decisively, to address health issues of global concern is another. The panoply of vested interests that characterise global politics represents another clear difficulty. After the Second World War, the agreement to establish the World Health Organization was prompted by a strong collective recognition of the need to improve health worldwide. The global nature of many emerging health issues, including the threat of major threats to humankind (e.g. emerging diseases, antimicrobial resistance) may prompt similar consensus.

A third challenge for GHG is the need to generate sufficient resources for global health cooperation and distribute them appropriately according to agreed priorities. The present system is ad hoc in nature, reliant on the annual spending decisions of governments, and the goodwill of private citizens and companies. Efforts to provide debt relief and increase development assistance recognise the inherent inequities of current forms of globalization (UNDP 1999). Recent discussions about the creation of a Tobin Tax or equivalent surcharge, on global activities that rely on a secure and stable world (e.g. financial transactions, air travel), could generate substantial and much needed sums.

Fourth, the sovereignty of states is also a hurdle to giving "teeth" to global health initiatives because of the lack of effective enforcement mechanisms. With the exception of the International Health Regulations, which in itself is highly circumscribed in remit, WHO can recommend rather than command action by member states. The reporting of outbreaks of yellow fever, cholera and plague, for example, is traditionally reliant on governments who may not be willing to report such information for fear of causing adverse economic reactions. By definition, a global health issue is one where the actions of a party in one part of the world can have widespread consequences in other parts of the world. Reliance on voluntary compliance with agreed practices, such as the use of antibiotics and antimicrobials, without sufficient monitoring and enforcement, can lead to serious and even irreversible health impacts.

Finally, the enigma of how to achieve a more pluralist, yet cohesive, system of GHG stands before us. As the globalization of health continues, health governance will have to become broader in participation and scope. The proto forms of GHG that are presently emerging (e.g. FCTC, GPPPs) might be seen as examples of improving practice as they open up participation in health governance to a wider range of actors. Nonetheless, a critical evaluation of these forms of governance is yet to be undertaken, nor is it yet clear whether these emerging forms of GHG will achieve their objectives.

The task of moving forward this complex, yet much needed, debate can be facilitated by a number of further tasks that are the focus of future discussion papers in this series. The purpose of this paper has been to review the conceptual meaning of GHG and, in turn, to highlight the challenges faced in moving towards such a system. A second task is to better understand the historical context of IHG and GHG, and how this can inform the transition from one to the other. Many different types of governance mechanisms for health purposes have been tried and tested since the end of the Second World War, and it would be useful to explore these in relation to the criteria set in this paper. This is the subject of Discussion Paper No. 2.

The next task is to better understand the "nitty gritty" of global governance in terms of what, in concrete terms, it looks like in practice. This moves us into the legal realm where international lawyers have grappled with the formulation and implementation of governance at the global level. An examination of what currently exists within the health field, as well as other fields such as trade and environment, may shed light on future possibilities. While such a review can only be selective in nature, it can point to lessons for building mechanisms for GHG. This is the subject of Discussion Paper No. 3.

Lastly, there is the task of defining more clearly the potential role of nonstate actors within a system of GHG. Relationships, patterns of influence and agreed roles among state and nonstate actors within an emerging system of GHG are still emerging. This myriad of different actors, each with individual spheres of activity, types of expertise, resources, interests and aspirations, cannot yet be described as a "global society". As defined by Fidler (1998b), a global society is "made of individuals and non-state entities all over the world that conceive of themselves as part of a single community and work nationally and transnationally to advance their common interests and values." The ad hoc nature of GHG so far, however, suggests that a more concerted effort to define and describe existing and potential roles would contribute to policy debates on possible future directions. The potential role of civil society in GHG is the subject of Discussion Paper No. 4, and the potential role of the private sector is examined in Discussion Paper No. 5.

Notes

1 A more detailed analysis of the institutional forms and mechanisms of international and global health governance is provided in Fidler D. (2002), "Global Health Governance: Overview of the role of international law in protecting and promoting global public health," Discussion Paper No. 3.

2 A more detailed analysis of the historical dimensions of global health governance is provided in Loughlin K. and Berridge V. (2002), Historical Dimensions of Global Health Governance, Discussion Paper No. 2.

3 The emerging and potential role of civil society and private sector in global health governance are discussed in Discussion Paper Nos. 4 and 5.

4 *Development*, Special Issue on Responses to Globalization: Rethinking health and equity, December 1999, 42(4).

5 A more detailed analysis of the historical dimensions of global health governance is provided in Loughlin K. and Berridge V. (2002), Historical Dimensions of Global Health Governance, Discussion Paper No. 2.

6 Early regional health organizations include the Conseil Superieur de Sante de Constantinople (c. 1830), European Commission for the Danube (1856) and International Sanitary Bureau of the Americas (1902). For a history of health cooperation in the nineteenth century see Howard-Jones N. (1975), *The Scientific Background of the International Sanitary Conferences, 1851–1938* (Geneva: WHO History of International Public Health Series); and Weindling P. ed. (1995), *International Health Organizations and Movements, 1918–1939* (Cambridge: Cambridge University Press).

7 The twelve health-related international institutions established compares with five on human rights, three on humanitarian relief and welfare, and ten on education and research (Murphy 1995).

8 The Constitution of WHO defines health as "a state of complete physical, mental and social well being and not merely the absence of disease or infirmity."

9 For the UK government's view on good governance see Department for International Development (DfID), *Eliminating World Poverty: A Challenge for the 21st Century* (DfID, 1997). See also UN General Assembly, Resolution 50/225, 1996.

10 Since completion of this paper, the UNDP Poverty Report 2000, has expanded on the link between "good governance" and poverty relief.

11 For a more detailed discussion see Hewson and Sinclair (1999).

12 Interview with Douglas Bettcher, Framework Convention Team, Tobacco Free Initiative, Geneva, 9 December 1999.

13 Technical documents that have been written as part of the consultation process for the FCTC suggest that all signatory states should adopt an autonomous national tobacco control commission. See for example, A. Halvorssen, "The Role of National Institutions in Developing and Implementing the WHO Framework Convention on Tobacco Control", *Framework Convention on Tobacco Control: Technical Briefing Series*, No. 5 (1999).

14 Following a long process of review, the International Health Regulations (IHRs) are on the brink of being reformed to make them more effective and binding on states. Most significantly, the revised IHRs require the reporting of all "events of urgent international importance related to public health".

15 Interview with J. Ann Zammit, The South Centre, 9th December 1999. "UNICEF: Bellamy warns against partnership with private sector", *UN Wire*, 23rd April (1999).
16 This is not to suggest of course that these are the only bilateral actors to play a role in international health, United Kingdom's Department for International Development is one many other such institutions.

References

Altman D. (1999), "Globalization, political economy, and HIV/AIDS," *Theory and Society*, 28: 559–84.

Antezana F., Chollat-Traquet C. and Yach D. (1998), "Health for all in the 21st century", *World Health Statistics Quarterly*, 51(1): 3–4.

Ball C. and Dunn L. (1995), *Non-Governmental Organizations: Guidelines for Good Policy and Practice* (London: The Commonwealth Institute).

Brundtland G. (1998), "Speech of the WHO Director-General", *Ad hoc Working Group on Revised Drug Strategy*, Geneva, 13 October.

Brundtland G. (1999), "International Trade Agreements and Public Health: WHO's Role", *Conference on Increasing Access to Essential Drugs in a Globalized Economy*, Amsterdam, 25–26 November.

Buse K. and Walt G. (2000), "Global public-private health partnerships: Part I – a new development in health?" *Bulletin of the World Health Organization*, 78(4): 509–561.

Buse K. and Walt G. (2000), "Global public-private health partnerships: Part II – what are the health issues for global governance?" *Bulletin of the World Health Organization*, 78(5): 699–709.

Cantarella F. (1996), "Corporate social solutions," *The Corporate Board: Journal of Corporate Governance*, November 1996.

Chen L., Evans T. and Cash R. (1999), "Health as a Global Public Good" in Kaul I., Grunberg I. and Stern M. eds., *Global Public Goods: International Co-operation in the 21st Century* (Oxford University Press): 285–89. Collin J., Lee K. and Bissell K., (2002), "The Framework Convention on Tobacco Control: The politics of global health governance, Third World Quarterly, 23(2).

Commission on Global Governance, *Our Global Neighbourhood* (Oxford: Oxford University Press 1995).

Deacon B. (1997), Global Social Policy (London: Sage).

Dia M. (1993), *A Governance Approach to Civil Service Reform in Sub-Saharan Africa*, World Bank Technical Paper, No. 225, Washington D.C.

Dodgson R. (1998), "The Women's Health Movement and the International Conference on Population and Development", *PhD Dissertation*, University of Newcastle upon Tyne, UK.

Farmer P. (1996), "Social Inequalities and Emerging Infectious Diseases." *Emerging Infectious Diseases*, 2(4): 259–66.

Fidler D. (1997), "The Globalization of Public Health: Emerging Infectious Diseases and International Relations," *Indiana Journal of Global Legal Studies*, 5(1): 11–51.

Fidler D. (1998a), "International Law and Global Public Health," International Colloquium on Public Health Law, Durban, South Africa, 22–24 November.

Fidler D. (1998b), "Microbialpolitik: Infectious Diseases and International Relations," *American University International Law Review*, 14(1): 1–53.

Finkelstein L. (1995), "What is global governance?" *Global Governance*, 1(3): 367–72.

Frechette L. (1998), "What do we mean by global governance?" Address by the UN Deputy Secretary-General, Global Governance Autumn Meetings Series, Global Governance and the UN: Beyond Track 2, Overseas Development Institute, London, 8 December.

Gill S. ed. (1997), *Globalization, Democratization and Multilateralism* (London: Macmillan).

Goodman N. (1971), *International Health Organizations and Their Work* (London: Livingstone Churchill).

Goodman N. (1998), "Clinical Governance", *British Medical Journal*, 317 (19 December): 1725–27.

Held D. (1992), "Democracy: From City States to Cosmopolitan Order?" in Held D. ed. *Prospects for Democracy* (London: Blackwell Publishers).

Held D. (1995), *Democracy and the Global Order* (Stanford: Stanford University Press).

Held D., McGrew A., Goldblatt D. and Perraton J. (1999), *Global Transformations: Politics, Economics and Culture* (Stanford: Stanford University Press).

Hewson M. and Sinclair T. (1999), "The Emergence of Global Governance Theory" in Hewson M. and Sinclair T. eds. *Approaches to Global Governance Theory* (New York: SUNY): 3–22.

Hulme D. and Edwards M. (1997), *NGOs, States and Donors, Too Close for Comfort?* (London: Macmillan).

Jareg P. and Kaseje D. C. (1998), "Growth of Civil Society in Developing Countries: Implications for Health", *The Lancet*, 351 (14 March):

Kaul I., Grunberg I. and Stern M. (1999), *Global Public Goods, International Co-operation in the 21st Century* (Oxford: Oxford University Press).

Kickbusch I. (1997), "New players for a new era: responding to the global public health challenges." *Journal of Public Health Medicine*, 19(2): 171–78.

Kickbusch I. (1999), "Global + Local = Global Public Health," *Journal of Epidemiology and Community Health.* Kickbusch I. (1999), "Global Public Health: Revisiting health public policy at the global level," *Health Promotion International.*

Kickbusch I. (1999), "Shifting global environments for health and development," Keynote Address to 6th Canadian Conference on International Health, Canadian Society for International Health, Ottawa, 14 November.

Krasner (1983) ed., *International Regimes* (Ithaca, NY: Cornell University Press).

The King's Fund (1999), "What is clinical governance?" *Briefings*, London.

Lee K. (1998), *Historical Dictionary of the World Health Organization* (New Jersey: Scarecrow Press).

Lee K. (1998), "Shaping the future of global health co-operation: where can we go from here?" *The Lancet*, 351 (March 21): 899–902.

Lee K. (2000a), "An overview of global health and environmental risks" in Parsons L. and Lister G. eds. Global Health, A Local Issue (London: The Nuffield Trust), pp. 34–46. www.nuffieldtrust.org.uk

Lee K. (2000b), "The impact of globalization on public health: Implications for the UK Faculty of Public Health Medicine," *Journal of Public Health Medicine*, 22(3).

Lee K. (2001), "Globalization – A new agenda for health?" in McKee M., Garner P. and Stott R. eds. *International Co-operation and Health* (Oxford: Oxford University Press), Chapter 2.

Lee K., Collinson S., Walt G. and Gilson L. (1996), "Who should be doing what in international health: a confusion of mandates in the United Nations?" *British Medical Journal*, 312, 3 February: 302–307.

Leftwich A. (1993), "Governance, Democracy and Development in the Third World", *Third World Quarterly*, 14(3): 605–21.

Lucas A., Mogedal S., Walt G., Hodne Steen S., Kruse S. E., Lee K. and Hawken L. (1997), *Cooperation for Health Development, The World Health Organization's support to programmes at country level* (London: Governments of Australia, Canada, Italy, Norway, Sweden and the U.K.).

McGrew A. ed. (1997), *The Transformation of Democracy* (London: Polity Press).

McMichael A. J. and Beaglehole R. (2000), "The changing global context of public health", *The Lancet*, 356: 495–99.

McRitchie J. (1998), "Corporate governance, Enhancing the Return on Capital Through Increased Accountability." http://www.corpgov.net

Murphy C. (1994), *International Organization and Industrial Change, Global governance since 1850* (London: Polity Press).

Paris J. A. G. and McKeown K. M. (1999), "Clinical governance for public health professionals," *Journal of Public Health Medicine*, 21(4): 430–34.

Rahman A. T. R. (1996), *UN Development Update*.

Roemer M. (1994), "Internationalism in Medicine and Public Health" in Porter D. ed., *The History of Public Health and the Modern State* (London: Clio Medica/ Wellcome Institute).

Rosenau J. N. (1995), "Governance in the Twenty-first Century", *Global Governance*, 1(1).

Scally G. and Donaldson J. (1998), "Clinical governance and the drive for quality improvement in the new NHS in England", *British Medical Journal*, 317 (4 July): 61–65.

Scholte J. A. (1997), "The Globalization of World Politics", in: John Baylis and Steve Smith (Eds), *The Globalization of World Politics: An Introduction to International Relations* (Oxford University Press), Chapter 1.

Scholte J. A. (2000), Globalisation: A Critical Introduction (London: Palgrave].

Sikkink K. (1986), "Codes of conduct for transnational corporations: the case of the WHO/UNICEF code," International Organization, 40: 817–40.

UK Department of Health (1998), *The new NHS, a first class service* (London: HMSO).

UNDP (1997), *Reconceptualising Governance* (New York: Management Development and Governance Division). Vaughan J. P., Mogedal S., Walt G., Kruse S. E., Lee K. and de Wilde K. (1996), "WHO and the effects of extrabudgetary funds: is the Organization donor driven?" *Health Policy and Planning*, 11(3): 253–64.

Vayrynen R. ed. (1999), Globalization and Global Governance (New York: Rowman & Littlefields).

Williamson O. (1996), *The Mechanisms of Governance* (Oxford: Oxford University Press).

World Bank (1994), *Governance: The World Bank's Experience* (Washington D.C.: IBRD).

World Bank (1997), *World Development Report, The State in a Changing World* (Washington D.C.: IBRD).

WHO (1995), "The rise of international co-operation in health." *World Health Forum*, 16(2):

WHO (1998) www.who.int/ina-ngo/ (accessed 22 March 2001)

WHO (2002), Health and Trade: Towards Common Ground (Geneva:WHO/HDE).

Zacher M. (1999a), "Global Epidemiological Surveillance: International Cooperation to Monitor Infectious Diseases" in Kaul I., Grunberg I. and Stern M. (1999), *Global Public Goods, International Cooperation in the 21st Century* (Oxford: Oxford University Press).

Zacher M. (1999b), "Uniting Nations: Global Regimes and the United Nations System" in Vayrynen R. ed. *Globalization and Global Governance* (New York: Rowman and Littlefield Publishers).

56

NEW PLAYERS FOR A NEW ERA
Responding to the global public health challenges*

Ilona Kickbusch

Source: *Journal of Public Health Medicine*, 19:2 (1997), 171–8.

Introduction

Many of the institutions and approaches established after World War II are no longer functional for the challenges of the twenty-first century.

In relation to the Group of Seven (G7), a recent foreign affairs commentary in the *New York Times* took up this point. It proposed a very different composition of the group, which at present includes Canada, France, Germany, Great Britain, Italy, Japan, and the USA. The composition could be as follows: '(1) China. (2) Japan. (3) The US. (4) Germany. (5) Rupert Murdoch, because he is . . . putting together the first truly global telecommunications network and he scares everybody in every market. (6) Bill Gates of Microsoft, because through his software he is building the first truly global marketplace, . . . he is doing more to enlarge the global market for goods and services than any trade minister. (7) Mother Teresa, because she understands that promoting economic efficiency – a G7 speciality – is not the same as building a caring society.' Other lists in the article include countries such as India and Brazil, and the new global organization, the WTO (World Trade Organization), and most innovatively one list adds Michael Jordan, the US basketball player 'because his personal GNP is bigger than half the countries of the world, and because he is so cool and would definitely liven up that stupid group photo they take every year of seven white guys in suits'. This membership would definitely increase the interest of my 12-year-old son in the dealings of the G7.

This creative speculation about significant membership in world bodies highlights two questions:

- Who really matters – and who should participate in defining the problem?
- What really makes a difference in terms of solutions?

The vacuum

To me, the parallels to the public health debate are obvious. Too often, I get the impression that public health exists in a vacuum – the organizational infrastructure of many public health departments or the curricula of most schools of public health do little to counterbalance this impression. Even the so-called renaissance of public health and many of the contributions under the heading 'new public health' do not think 'outside the dots', as it has become fashionable to say in management theory.

This applies to the knowledge base, the conceptual base and the organizational and policy base of public health within our societies. The innovations that have occurred have frequently been introduced (often with much opposition) in the name of health promotion, but have not been able to move centre stage yet in the public health–health policy discourse, even though lip service is continuously paid to them.

I would venture that at this point most proposals for 'a new public health' are still inherently traditional, separating public health from what really matters and therefore marginalizing it rather than placing it in the centre of health development and health care reform where it should be. Most importantly, most proposals do not address the challenges public health must face in view of increasing globalization.

Looking at the bright side, we can argue that it already constitutes a renaissance to be talking again about public health to the extent that we do (new or old), in view of the fact that for quite some time it was a term that was considered outmoded – others took its place in a long succession: community medicine, social medicine, primary health care, health promotion, to name but a few. The demise or eclipse of public health was linked to many factors – the increasing power of clinical medicine, the upsurge of behavioural epidemiology (at one point Milton Terris was forced to exclaim: 'there can be no epidemiology without public health'), the rise of the environmental movement, the dominance of health research by an individualistic, bio-medical paradigm. Partly the very success of public health has led to a lack of visibility and/or demise of the discipline and system that has brought about many of the significant health gains of this century. And what remains is often threatened by the new climate of cost cutting and economic reform.

It would seem therefore that 'today more than ever public health institutions world-wide . . . need to redefine their mission in the light of the increasingly complex milieu in which they operate' (Julio Frenk, Mexico).

The mission of public health

Let me start from the mission of public health. I have come to most prefer the following definition by the US Institute of Medicine (IOM) in 1988: 'fulfilling societies' interest in assuring conditions in which people are healthy'.

This definition is short, precise and a large order: in present language it means acting on the determinants of health.

The Ottawa Charter for health promotion reiterates this: 'The fundamental conditions and resources for health are peace, shelter, education, food, income, a stable eco-system, sustainable resources, social justice and equity. Improvement in health requires a secure foundation in these basic prerequisites.'

As we go systematically through these points and analyse what is happening in most countries around the globe we can note:

- a growing inequity in health as measured in life expectancy and healthy life expectancy within countries and between countries, as outlined in the World Health Report 1995 by WHO[1] with its focus on poverty;
- a growing unwillingness to invest in public housing, infrastructure, education, basic preventive services, and basic public health;
- an unwillingness to look at the organization of work – its division during the life cycle, between generations, between men and women and globally; and
- a drawing back from international initiatives and foreign aid.

Anyone who has read the history of public health feels trapped in a time machine and transported back to the nineteenth century rather than forward in *Star Trek* to the twenty-first.

The key challenges

Health policies are not yet reacting to the fact that we are on to a new revolution – a total restructuring of our societies and the way they function: 'how people live, love, work and play' to paraphrase the Ottawa Charter. And as with the industrial revolution 100 years ago, it is a global revolution, based on new types of interdependences. There are several ways to look at the key challenges; to a certain extent they reflect a hierarchy of decision-making.

(a) The US Institute of Medicine recently put forward six factors that will most influence health over the next 20 years:

    (i)   human demographics and behaviour;
    (ii)   technology and industry;
    (iii)   economic development and land use;
    (iv)   international travel and commerce;
    (v)   microbiological adaptation and change;
    (vi)   breakdown of public health measures.

Do schools of public health include these issues in their curriculum? Do our own health policies refer to these factors? Do health professionals push for a public debate on matters that are as important to our future as sewer systems were to nineteenth-century cities?

(b) WHO has identified seven key areas for health promotion action that will be discussed at the upcoming WHO conference in Indonesia in 1997 on 'Moving health promotion into the 21st century':

(i)   habitat;
(ii)   families;
(iii)   work;
(iv)   ageing;
(v)   violence;
(vi)   markets;
(vii) communications.

In nearly all of these areas, WHO is launching or implementing major programmes and projects to develop global responses – but still many key donors remain focused on infectious diseases.

(c) The United Nations Research Institute for Social Development (UNRISD) has identified six consistent trends that are shaping institutional change:

(i)   the spread of liberal democracy;
(ii)   the dominance of market forces;
(iii)   the integration of the global economy;
(iv)   the transformation of production systems and labour markets;
(v)   the speed of technological change;
(vi)   the media revolution and consumerism.

The aim

To build the next step of the argument, let us look at what the same IOM report defines as the aim of public health: 'to generate organized community effort to address the public interest in health by applying scientific and technical knowledge to prevent disease and promote health'.

Now I would fully concur with the focus on organized community effort, but I put forward that a very changed environment calls for public health responsibility and action that goes beyond 'preventing disease and promoting health'. When public health was first established, the medical care sector (what we now call health services) was negligible, both in quantitative and qualitative terms. Also, the demographic composition of our societies was markedly different.

Today, the 'health sector' accounts for 10 per cent or more of the GNP in most developed countries with a range of other sectors (i.e. the building industry) dependent on its continuing growth. It is one of the largest single sectors, with significant employment effect, particularly for women. In such an environment, public health cannot be solely concerned with prevention and health promotion, while the minds of politicians, the media and the public are dominated by the curative sector in terms of distribution, financing, access, quality, etc.

We cannot continue to see public health as a 'separate subsystem of services provided by the state'; that would lead to increasing marginalization (i.e. the Clinton health plan hardly mentioned public health). At the same time, the health services agenda must not be allowed to overshadow the population health agenda. A difficult balancing act indeed. And even more crucial for developing countries which face serious investment decisions.

We must begin to understand public health as a much broader organized social response to both the production of health and the consumption of health services – particularly as a basis for development policies.

The IOM report says that the organized community effort that is public health is addressed: 'by private organizations, by individuals as well as by public agencies'. It indicates that the health of the public is not just a government concern, but a joint societal effort where, in particular, the contribution of the private sector needs to increase significantly, yet be held accountable in new ways.

The conceptual base

These two, at first instance paradoxical, directions – more public health action on the determinants of health and more public health concern with the health care system – come together in the concept of health gain. This, to my mind, is one of the key intellectual concepts on which to build a new public health. It moves the debate from the assumption that we create health by eliminating disease to a public health paradigm based on the creation/production of health.

Obviously, health gain must not be treated as a purely economic category – and this is crucial for the further debate on public health. In order to underline this I have proposed three basic questions that outline the intellectual and operational challenge implied in such a concept.

- What creates health? Where is it created?
- Which investment produces the largest health gain?
- Does this investment help reduce health inequities and does it ensure human rights?

Such an investment example was recently displayed in a full page advertisement in the *New York Times*, financed by a group of business representatives in response to proposals by the Republican Congress (see Figure 1).

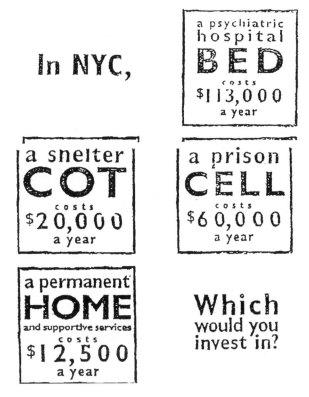

Figure 1 Part of an advertisement in the *New York Times*, financed by a group of business representatives.

The issues – the scope

If the above is accepted, then a new public health has its foundation in a knowledge base that builds on the truly interdisciplinary study of:

- the determinants of population health and its distribution;
- the organized social response to these determinants.

It is clear that public health at present is weak on both counts, and this is reinforced if we look at the changing issues public health needs to confront.

These issues can be defined and classified in very different ways depending what school of thought one adheres to. On the whole though, they present the elements of a Rubik cube that we need to tackle with a new public health paradigm.

(a) They can be seen as 'health issues' such as AIDS, smoking, drug abuse and/or as wider environmental and ecological issues, such as toxic waste, environmental degradation. Not only do these problems constitute an additional problem range of the public health agenda, they also contribute to its change of focus and style of operations – working with AIDS organizations or the environmental movement requires a different style than food safety regulation or they can also be seen as social issues that increasingly enter the health arena – such as violence, teenage pregnancy, social isolation – and that call for new types of interventions and a new epidemiological base.

(b) The next analytical level starts from actual cause of death, along the lines of the model outlined by McGinnis and Foege for the USA on the basis of 1990 data. It juxtaposes the diseases with the actual causes of death (Table 1). This approach allows a clear action agenda and is more easily outlined to the public.

(c) The World Health Report 1995 outlines the issues in terms of killers, disease incidence, and burden and disability:

- the biggest group of killers remains infectious diseases and parasitic diseases (16.4 million lives every year);
- disease incidence – diarrhoea in children under five years old (1.8 billion episodes a year, 3 million children die); sexually transmitted diseases (297 million new cases every year);
- disease burden – goitre (655 million sufferers); chronic lung disease (600 million sufferers);
- disability caused – biggest cause of disability: mood disorders (59 million); blindness (27 million); leprosy (2.5 million).

WHO, together with many partners, has shown that a difference can be made and has been made in global health. Table 2 highlights some improvements achieved in the last 15 years. But the new and pressing challenges call on us to move faster and be more determined: we need to prepare for the new challenges while the old are still with us.

Table 1 Number of deaths in the United States in 1990.

Actual causes of death	
Tobacco	400 000
Diet–inactivity patterns	300 000
Alcohol	100 000
Certain infections	90 000
Toxic agents	60 000
Firearms	35 000
Sexual behaviour	30 000
Motor vehicles	25 000
Drug use	20 000
Total	1 060 000

Table 2 Some selected global health targets by the year 2000.

Indicator (Global)	1980	1993–94	Targets by the Year 2000
Life expectancy at birth	61	66	Over 60 years in all countries (26 countries still to reach 60 years)
Infant mortality	82	68	50 per 1000 live births or under, in all countries
Under-5 mortality	117	92	70 per 1000 live births or under in all countries
Dracunculosis prevalence (Guinea-worm)	12 million	3 million	Eradication of dracunculosis
Leprosy prevalence	10.5 million	5.5 million	Elimination of Leprosy
Malnutrition (children under 5)	–	35.8%	Reduction by at least 50%
% of world population having access to:			
• Safe water	52%	71%	85%
• Sanitation	24%	56%	75%
Average rate of children immunized against six diseases. diphtheria, pertussis, tetanus, measles, poliomyelitis and tuberculosis	20%	80%	at least 90%

But, as outlined earlier, the public health agenda in the 1990s and beyond also includes the overall systems challenges of health policy, particularly in view of increasing privatization, a focus on guidance and planning of health care provision (often reinforced through the new purchaser–provider splits), assessment and control of medical technology, the ethical issues arising from the health care system and progress in biomedical research, the appropriateness and quality of care, and the issues of ageing, dying and death.

The scope of public health has therefore expanded considerably: this means a new public health cannot 'restrict' itself to functions as would have been outlined classically in disease control and sanitation, and the standard setting in terms of safety standards for hygiene, food safety, air pollution, as essential as all these measures are. It becomes part and parcel, if not the driving force, of a new type of development agenda.

The measures, the policies and the economics of health creation need to be driven by an organized community effort, from the local through to the global level.

New players

This leads me back to where I started. Now, as with the G7, it is obvious that these challenges cannot be met by public health or even the health care system alone. We must aim to create public health approaches and alliances that will respond to the new and global health challenges and that open up means for real solutions: we must start thinking of global health not just in terms of minimum health care, a moral obligation to save children from dying, or a possible market place for health care products. Instead, we must begin to understand global health in terms of health security that transcends national boundaries.

Population health is increasingly being influenced globally by developments in the private sector. Three major players stand out, and in many cases form a highly influential triad:

1   The health care industry, which will continue to grow dramatically, totally restructure itself and continue to be one of the key markets of the future, last but not least in terms of export to the middle income economies. Hospitals/health service institutions will increasingly compete, strengthen their accountability and health gain orientation through managed care, and will increasingly enter the arena of community health, as is already the case in the USA, where community based projects and assessments allow hospitals to keep a tax-free status. Areas that were seen to be the unique responsibility of the state will be seen to move into the private sector or into a public/private mix – both in the developed and the developing world.

2   The information industry, which is the mega growth market of the present and which increasingly helps create and structure how we live and what we think (just correlate the thought of 2 billion teenagers worldwide by the year 2001 and a global network of the MTV type). Not only will this industry structure global patterns of consumption, it will aim at satisfying the public's interest in health matters through massive expansion of its health programmes. In the USA, first pilots are being run on 24-hour health channels, health matters are ideal for interactive television programming, health information (on self-medication, self-care, prevention, etc.) will increasingly be offered through private information services, as will on-line information services for health professionals (telemedicine, health on-line). Epidemics today are 'made' by global media – plague, Ebola, BSE.

3   The 'lifestyles industry' of products (foods, drinks, cigarettes), as well as the sports and leisure and tourist industry, and the many health-related services, such as fitness institutes, weight watchers, etc., will continue its rapid expansion. Already, tourism is the world's largest industry: it has 10 per cent of the global workforce, 10 per cent of world GNP and

10 per cent of all consumer spending. The cigarette is the most widely distributed global consumer product on earth, the most profitable and the most deadly. The average profit margin on a cigarette has been about 35 per cent. Owing to diversification, about 10 per cent of everything on the shelf in American supermarkets is a product of one large tobacco company. A whole generation of kids is confronted with a development that has transformed sports into entertainment and it has been a shoe company that has pushed world-wide a new range of sports activities, body image and self-esteem (including women).

These three growth sectors are amplified by the lobbies of those dependent on these markets: advertising agencies, television and print media for advertising revenue.

Where to from here?

There is no choice but to break through the public health bubble and exercise the public health virtue of foresight.

I venture that what is at present happening in the media industry will happen increasingly in health, meaning the interlinkage of separate functions or 'industries' to a new type of service and product. As computer hardware firms buy up software producers, link with telephone and cable companies and go global as 'mega media' – so we will see a similar development in the health care industry.

For example, a major American communications company is now entering the arena of medical self-help videos to be sold for US$20 in drugstores, mass marketing chains and through Health Maintenance Organizations (HMOs). (Note: the company invested US$20 million in the project and will spend US$15 million on a national advertising campaign.)

The pharmaceutical industry, for example, will redefine its product to be 'health' rather than a pill which can be bought at a chemist or in a pharmacy – it will get involved in direct health care provision (hospital chains), home order systems (for self-medication), health advice on-line (interactive television, 24-hour health line, etc.), and health software development.

Is public health prepared? Is the answer control, standard setting, joint ventures or laissez-faire? What forms of co-operation must be sought?

The road map

We do have the first outlines of a road map to tackle these issues. The Ottawa Charter and health promotion have early on laid the ground for a thinking based on determinants of health and oriented towards health investment and health gain. The strategies that the Charter outlined have stood the test of time. In many cases, it is only now that countries show signs of serious political implementation. Let me remind you of those agendas:

- Healthy public policy – the refocusing of a public health community that had got sidetracked into individualistic behavioural epidemiology on a determinants of health debate. This debate has now seriously started.
- Supportive environments – highlighting the role of social factors in health and through that the importance of the social sciences to any future-oriented public-health thinking (political science, organizational sociology, social psychology and the like); the public health strategy called 'the settings approach' has emerged out of this.
- Community action – highlighting participation and involvement as a key factor in change for health and recognizing the need for community action and advocacy.
- Personal skills – highlighting the need for broader health skills and life skills rather than just health knowledge.
- Reorienting health services – highlighting the need to reorient the health sector towards a health gain perspective.

Let me highlight two strategic areas where a new public health needs to focus activities and sharpen its approaches – although they also seem juxtaposed at first:

- more action on the social health components, particularly through local strategies; and
- more action on global issues.

They come together as part of a sustainable development agenda. Naisbitt has called this the 'global paradox'.

With its 'settings' projects, WHO has shown foresight in aiming to find new approaches to strengthen commitment to health where it is created: projects such as 'Healthy Cities' have led to spin–offs such as 'Healthy Islands' and 'Healthy Villages' – each type of project in turn respecting and building on the specific regional context. This year's World Health Day has been designated to 'Healthy Cities' – and the amount of energy that has been generated at city level using local resources shows that creative public health strategies can get political and popular commitment throughout the world.

Similar experiences have been gained with settings projects that are organization-based, such as health-promoting schools, hospitals, workplaces, even prisons. They, in turn, look at the changing nature of institutions and the contribution of health as a way forward to better institutional performance. Health promotion has availed itself of organizational development strategies tested in the private sector, showing the value of crossover and experience exchange between public and private sectors.

These projects and approaches have an added value that is often neglected, but constitutes the core of WHO's definition of health as social wellbeing.

A key feature of modern societies is social disintegration and the helplessness of formal structures and institutions to respond. Settings projects act as mediating structures for civil society – and provide a counterbalance at the local, national and global level through integration, participation and open communication channels. We will learn over the years that frequently the process is as important as the targeted outcome, particularly in relation to larger social goals. An example is the statement from one of the Eastern European countries involved in the health-promoting schools project, stating: 'This project is important because it allows us to invest in our children and young people and provides them – together with their teachers – with a space to practice democratic behaviour.' Naisbitt calls this 'the spread of governance without government, globalization from below'.

Let me move then to the other component of the global paradox, the globalization of industry and trade, of communications and travel. WHO in revisiting the 'Health for All Strategy' is aiming to define the key components of what constitutes good global governance for health. Five principles are beginning to emerge:

1 Focus on health and its determinants, with the aim to reduce the enormous health gaps that persist and have been widening across the globe.
2 Understand health as a global commons and resource. No longer is 'my' health safe if I don't care about 'your' health; AIDS, Ebola, the BSE scare and many similar issues, particularly in the environmental arena, demonstrate this.
3 Ensure health security in view of increasing economic pressures – tobacco, primary health care provision.
4 Invest where it matters – women, schooling, country-based services.
5 Work in partnerships, create alliances.

We have seen the first positive signals of these messages being heard: health is becoming more important in the agendas of the development banks, it has moved up on the agendas of the global summits – but we are still far removed from a new global contract on health which strengthens the elements laid out in Alma Ata towards a concept of joint stewardship of a global commons. It cannot be acceptable that in the space of a day passengers flying from Japan to Uganda bridge 37 years difference in average life expectancy, and even the train ride from Vienna to Budapest bridges an average of seven years.

The harsh reality is that about $260 is spent per capita per year on marketing products, while some countries have an average of $4 per capita per year to spend on health. These imbalances need to be addressed through a global public health strategy that seeks a systematic dialogue with the three key industries that I have mentioned earlier. A number of 'responsible partnerships for global health' through a global health promotion alliance could be considered.

But we also need to make proposals for new rules of the game: already a number of countries are using the model of dedicated taxes to increase the resources for health promotion, usually focused on the tobacco tax. Another model that could be considered in order to address global imbalances is a dedicated tax on advertising and marketing, a portion of the proceeds of which could support public health and health promotion projects world-wide.

It is a great challenge indeed to work on new norms, rules of conduct, accountability and decision-making. How difficult this is is illustrated every day in the debate over regulating the World Wide Web, counteracting the onslaught of the tobacco industry, keeping up with the pace, size and diversity of the changes under way in nearly every sector of life.

The key problem is surely to stay on the political agenda in a period of time where 'the political economy of the post-modern age is centred on the production and distribution of public attention' (Greenpeace).

The challenge for the discipline

The challenge for public health can be summarized in seven categories of change:

- Change of context: global new social baseline.
- Change of scope: multisectoral, interrelated, social environments.
- Change of institutional focus: health system, other systems.
- Change of goal: health gain outside health system/health care.
- Change of partners: alliances, private, business, NGO (non-government organization), public/private mix.
- Change of site: from the individual to the setting and social environment; global?
- Change of style: participatory, multisectoral, communications oriented, policy.

The managing of this change process for the discipline and for the operational dimension requires a new type of public health leadership, a leadership that sees its skill in setting a health gain agenda, advocating for it and mediating between the major partners to achieve it. This means working with at least five key sectors:

- citizens, consumers, NGOs;
- health care industry, providers (public and private), professional organizations;
- public health/scientific community;
- policy-makers, parliamentarians;
- private sector: communications, lifestyle industries, leisure, tourism.

I would like to propose that we start thinking global public health 'outside the dots' with new players:

- Why not an alliance between the international civil aviation authorities (or some major airlines), the pharmaceutical industry and WHO to fight those 16 million deaths owing to infectious diseases and the 300 million odd cases of sexually transmitted diseases? Twenty cents on each international ticket, not as a tax but as a voluntary agreement.
- Why not a major campaign to increase women's literacy combined with skills for health and banking in an alliance between the WHO, the World Bank, UNICEF, and a group of telecommunications networks that are out to conquer the most populous countries? This would include making women more knowledgeable about health care provision, sexual health, and self-medication.
- Why not a global safe sex campaign for teenagers on those networks they are just dying to see linked to those products they are just dying to wear, promoted by those people they are just dying to be (that is where Michael Jordan comes in)? In the year 2001 there will be 2 billion teenagers world-wide.
- Why not an alliance of responsible politicians together with WHO, the World Bank, the health industry, the communications industry on 'the economies of health and well-being' following through on The World Health Report 1995 and the World Development Report 1993[2] – reported on with the same big bang as G7? Such a group would put forward a Club of Rome type of report outlining what ill health costs the world (all of us) and what health security threats it involves. It would cost a meagre US$500 million to eradicate polio. It takes about US$100 to 200 million in advertising and promotion to launch a new cigarette brand.
- A health alliance between the seven most populous countries in the world to tackle common problems and to learn from each other how to bring health promotion to scale, focusing on application of what we know (and would include much of the above).

The paradox

Let us face up to it: much of health research is not about the real world. It likes to focus on interventions; it loves controlled environments. But our environments are not controlled.

The health theme permeates advertising, soap operas and sitcoms to the extent that the most recent trend is to say that the product is not healthy. High profits are made in private health, while we face the extreme difficulty of generating a real interest in public health.

It is these kinds of factors we need to face up to when we look at public health in the twenty-first century. We must combine the art of the possible and the art of innovation. And we must set ourselves challenging goals.

Let me end with a quote by Oscar Wilde: 'A map of the world that does not have Utopia on it is not worth looking at.'

Note

* Lecture given on the occasion of the Queen Elizabeth The Queen Mother Lecture, Newcastle upon Tyne, UK, 28 March 1996.

References

1 *The World Health Report 1995*. Geneva: WHO, 1995.
2 *World Development Report 1993*. Washington, DC: The World Bank, 1993.

57

GLOBALIZATION AND CHOLERA

Implications for global governance

Kelley Lee and Richard Dodgson

Source: *Global Governance*, 6:2 (2000), 213–36.

Plague and pestilence have become an increasingly popular theme since the end of the Cold War among policymakers, journalists, fiction writers, and film directors searching for new threats to personal and national security. Ill health and, in particular, infectious diseases have generated a spate of popular, and often alarmist, literature.[1] This has been accompanied by growing high-level concern within governments and the medical community with global health issues that threaten national interests.[2] The emphasis in many of these discussions has been on emerging health threats that are perceived to pose potentially sudden and serious dangers to public health.

We begin this essay with the premise that the process of globalization has particular impacts on health and that there is a clear need to better understand and more effectively respond to these impacts. However, without underplaying the dangers posed by health emergencies caused, for example, by the genetic mutation of viral agents or epidemics of emerging infectious diseases, we seek to develop a broader understanding of the historical and structural factors behind the health challenges posed by globalization. As we discuss later, globalization can be defined as a process that is changing the nature of human interaction within a range of social spheres. Globalization's impact on health can be seen as part of a longer historical process firmly located in social change over decades, and perhaps centuries, rather than recent years.

From this perspective, an understanding of global health issues at the turn of the twenty-first century could benefit substantially from the voluminous literature on globalization from international relations, including the subfields of social and political theory and international political economy. This is a rich and highly relevant literature. It documents what structural changes are occurring toward a global political economy, how power relationships are embedded within this process of change, what varying impacts this may have on individuals and groups, and to what extent global governance could effectively mediate this process. These issues counterbalance the strong focus in the health literature on biomedical research, information systems, and other technical solutions. Although health is a classic transborder issue, it continues to receive limited attention in international relations.

We seek to bring together the international relations and health fields for two purposes. First, knowledge of the globalization process can be used to better understand the nature of health issues and the development of effective responses to them. To explore this link, we analyze cholera from the nineteenth century to the present, with particular attention to the seventh pandemic (1961–present). We argue that the particular form that globalization takes has created social conditions that have influenced the transmission, incidence, and vulnerability of different individuals and groups to the disease. Thus, we compare epidemiological patterns of the disease alongside changing patterns of human migration, transportation, and trade.

Second, knowledge of health and disease can be used to better understand the nature of globalization, because globalization is a highly contested concept, infused with embedded interests and having both positive and negative consequences.[3] Cholera has mirrored this process, highlighting the contradictions of globalization in its present form. A significant and often overlooked threat to human health, therefore, is the particular form globalization took in the late twentieth century. Thriving in the midst of increased poverty, widening inequalities within and across countries, pressures to shrink the public sector, and global environmental change, cholera can be seen as a reflection of the ills of globalization itself.

From analysis of this dual relationship between globalization and cholera, we conclude by considering the implications for existing mechanisms of international health cooperation. Following a brief review of measures for the transborder prevention, control, and treatment of infectious diseases, we explore the need for a system of global governance. We propose a definition of global governance for health and discuss key functions and characteristics that may be needed to protect human health on a global scale.

Globalization and health: a conceptual framework

An understanding of the linkages between globalization and health depends foremost on one's definition of globalization and precise dating of the process. In this essay, we define globalization as a process that is changing the nature of human interaction across a range of social spheres, including the economic, political, social, technological, and environmental. This process is globalizing in the sense that many boundaries hitherto separating human interaction are being increasingly eroded. These boundaries—spatial, temporal, and cognitive—can be described as the dimensions of globalization.[4]

The *spatial dimension* concerns change to how we experience and perceive physical space. Roland Robertson writes of "a sense of the world as a single place" because of increased travel, communication, and other shared experiences.[5] Conversely, this "death of distance"[6] has also led to more localized, nationalized, or regionalized feelings of spatial identity. As such, globalization can be seen as a reterritorializing rather than deterritorializing process. Second, the *temporal dimension* concerns change to the actual and perceived time in which human activity occurs, generally toward accelerated time frames. A good example is currency trading of U.S.$1.7 trillion worldwide each day, two-thirds of this amount retraded after less than seven days. The speed of communication (e.g., facsimile, email) and transportation (e.g., high-speed train, Concorde jet) has also accelerated social interaction. Third, globalization has a *cognitive dimension* that affects the creation and exchange of knowledge, ideas, beliefs, values, cultural identities, and other thought processes. Change has been facilitated by communication and transportation technologies that have enabled people to interact more intensely with others around the world. The production of knowledge has also become more globalized through research and development, mass media, education, and management practices. Contrasting forces are at play that, on the one hand, homogenize cognitive processes for better or worse (e.g., global teenager) and, on the other hand, encourage greater heterogeneity (e.g., religious fundamentalism).

In addition to the precise nature of globalization, the timing of the process has been subject to dispute. Some believe that it is a relatively recent phenomenon defined foremost by the activities of multinational corporations and their striving for global economies of scale.[7] While others agree that social relations have become more intense during the past ten to twenty years, they argue that such relations are not fundamentally new. Anthony Giddens and Robertson, for example, argue that globalization has historical roots from the fifteenth century.[8] Giddens asserts that, since the fifteenth century, globalization has developed with modernity. Robertson, however, disputes the view that globalization has followed a single *telos* or that its emergence can be linked to a single force such as modernity. Instead, he argues that there are a number of historical stages to globalization (Table 1), each characterized by what are currently regarded as features of a modern society and global system. These include, for instance, human migration, a system of global trade, urbanization, and the growth of international governance.

It is this conceptualization of globalization occurring across multiple spheres and dimensions and a time frame of centuries that we adopt in this essay as a useful framework for understanding its complex impacts on health. Briefly, the geographical spread of disease can be closely correlated with the migration of the human species across the globe. Robert Clark writes, "In becoming global, humans, plants, animals, and diseases have coevolved; i.e., evolved together as a package of interdependent life systems."[9] With the spread of human populations came changes to social organization into larger

Table 1 Robertson's historical stages of globalization.

Stage	Time Scale	Spatial Center	Characteristics
Germinal	Circa 1500–1850s	Europe	Growth of national community, accentuation of the concept of the individual, spread of Gregorian calendar
Incipient	Circa 1850–1870s	Mainly Europe	Shift toward homogeneous unity of the state, formalized international relations
Takeoff	Circa 1870–1920s	Increasingly global	Inclusion of non-European states into international society, World War I, League of Nations
Struggle for hegemony	Circa 1920–1965	Global	Wars or disputes about the shape of the globalization process, atomic bomb, UN
Uncertainty	Circa 1965–present	Global	Inclusion of Third World, moon landing, end of Cold War, environment, HIV/AIDS

Source: Roland Robertson, *Globalization: Social Theory and Global Culture* (London: Sage, 1992).

communities with different lifestyles, notably from hunting and gathering to agricultural and animal husbandry, to sustain such communities. Changes to disease patterns followed—increased zoonosis (e.g., tuberculosis, rabies, salmonella, helminths), nutritional ills, and dental decay. The establishment of permanent communities, accompanied by systems of irrigation and often ineffective sanitation and water supplies, led to increased diseases such as malaria and schistosomiasis.[10]

As J. N. Hays points out, human settlements on different continents remained relatively isolated until the late fifteenth century when the age of exploration brought Europe into contact with the Americas. Coinciding with a greater concentration of human populations into larger communities, the impact of the spatial dimension of globalization on health became increasingly evident. Periodically, epidemics could now become pandemics through intercontinental trade, migration, and imperialism. During this period, diseases such as plague and influenza traveled the silk route from Asia into Europe, or by ship to ports throughout the old and new worlds. Similarly, typhus from Asia and syphilis from the Americas were brought to Europe, while Europeans intro-duced measles, smallpox, typhus, plague, and other diseases to the new world, thus precipitating "the greatest demographic disaster in history."[11]

The greater frequency and intensity of human interaction across continents eventually made the temporal dimension of globalization more prominent. From the seventeenth century, industrialization, rapid urbanization, military conflict, and imperialism brought increased vulnerability to many populations. Coupled with inequalities in living standards and a lack of basic medical knowledge, many communicable diseases (e.g., syphilis, typhus, tuberculosis, and influenza) spread more rapidly than ever before. Another disease, the infamous "potato blight," was also able to travel quickly from the northeast of North America in 1840 to Europe by ship in 1845, eventually causing widespread starvation, notably in Ireland.[12]

By the late eighteenth century, these changes to the spatial and temporal dimensions of health risks and determinants led to greater efforts to develop public health knowledge and practice to respond to them. The nineteenth century brought the initiation of bilateral and regional health agreements, giving way from 1851 to periodic International Sanitary Conferences to promote inter-governmental cooperation on infectious disease control. This was accompanied by major advances in medical knowledge, including vaccination and microbiol-ogy, which were increasingly shared at international scientific meetings. This process of knowledge creation and application across countries signaled the cognitive dimension of globalization in health, which gained further momentum with the professionalization of the health field, creation of research and training institutions worldwide, and growth of scientific publications. Yet, as we show later, how health and ill health within and across societies were understood cannot be separated from prevailing beliefs and values characterizing these later stages of globalization. The creation of the World Health Organization (WHO) in 1948 was fueled by the postwar faith in scientific and technical solutions to defeat ill health, a belief that would be seriously shaken by the uncertainty of this phase of globalization in the late twentieth century.

Cholera in the time of globalization: the first six pandemics

We argue that an analysis of cholera from the nineteenth century can offer important insights into the nature of globalization and the specific challenges it poses for human health. Cholera is caused by the ingestion of an infectious dose of a particular serogroup of the *Vibrio cholerae* bacterium.[13] The bacterium is usually taken into the body through contaminated water or food, then attaches itself to the lining of the human bowel and produces a poison (enterotoxin). The infection is often mild or without symptoms, but approximately one in twenty cases is severe. In severe cases, cholera is an acute illness characterized by repeated vomiting and profuse watery diarrhea, resulting in rapid loss of body fluids and salts. During this stage, the disease is highly infectious through further contamination of local water, soil, and food. Without treatment, this can lead to severe dehydration, circulatory collapse, and death within hours.[14]

Medical historians have long recognized that the epidemiology of cholera has been intimately linked to social, economic, and political change. Cholera had been confined for centuries to the riverine areas of the Indian subcontinent with occasional appearances along China's coast introduced by trading ships and in the Middle East transported by pilgrims traveling to Mecca. The pattern of the disease changed dramatically, however, in the early nineteenth century with the first of six pandemics over the next hundred years (Table 2). The intensification of human interaction during this period through imperialism, trade, military conflict, and migration (e.g., slave trade) was a significant factor. The first pandemic occurred between 1817 and 1823, with cholera suddenly moving far beyond its historical boundaries. A number of changes contributed to its spread in that period: the movement of British troops and camp followers throughout the region, construction of irrigation canals without sufficient drainage ditches to raise cash crops, building of a national railway system, impoverishment of rural people by land reforms and taxation, and mass migration as a result of economic hardship. For the first time, cholera became endemic throughout South Asia, from which it was then transported to the Far and Middle East via burgeoning trade links (e.g., tea, opium), religious pilgrimage, and notably military expansionism.

The geographical pattern of cholera during the next five pandemics continued to mirror human activity, spreading from country to neighboring country. Corresponding with the intensification of links between Asia, Europe, and the Americas, cholera became a worldwide disease in 1826. From India, the disease moved beyond Asia to Europe, the Americas, and to a lesser extent Africa; it traveled via immigration, troop movements during times of war and peace (e.g., Crimean War), and the slave trade. A particularly important factor was immigration from Europe to North America. Cholera first arrived in New York in June 1832 via immigrants from Dublin who, in turn, traveled inland via wagon train. This extended the second pandemic across North America and then south to the Caribbean and South America. Immigrants then became a repeated source of reinfection, facilitated by the building of the intercontinental railway.[15]

This close link between epidemiology and mode of transport can be observed throughout the history of the first six cholera pandemics. As well as extending the geographical incidence of the disease, the speed at which it spread also corresponded with prevailing technology. Until the twentieth century, cholera was limited to travel by land and sea. Compared to the seventh pandemic, which we discuss later, the rate of spread was relatively slow. For example, it took the disease three months to cross the sea via trade routes from Hamburg (where it arrived in August 1831) to Sunderland in the northeast of England (where it arrived in October 1831). During later pandemics, the introduction of the steamship led to cholera spreading more quickly across major bodies of water. Hence,

Table 2 First six cholera pandemics, 1817–1923.

Date	Geographical Pattern of Spread
1817–1823 (6 years)	India (1817) Ceylon, Burma, Siam, Malacca, Singapore (1818–1820) Java, Batavia, China, Persia (1821) Egypt, Astrakhan, Caspian Sea, Syria (1823)
1826–1838 (12 years)	India (1826) Persia, Southern Russia (1829) Northern Russia, Bulgaria (1830) Poland, Germany, Austria, England, Mecca, Turkey, Egypt (1831) Sweden, France, Scotland, Ireland, Canada, United States (1832) Spain, Portugal, Mexico, Cuba, Caribbean, Latin America (1833) Italy (1835)
1839–1855 (16 years)	India, Afghanistan (1839) China (1840) Persia, Central Asia (1844–1845) Arabian Coast, Caspian and Black Seas, Turkey, Greece (1846–1847) Arabia, Poland, Sweden, Germany, Holland, England, Scotland, United States, Canada, Mexico, Caribbean, Latin America (1848) France, Spain, Portugal, Italy, North Africa (1850)
1863–1874 (11 years)	India (1863) Mecca, Turkey, Mediterranean (1865) Northern Europe, North America, South America (1866–1867) West Africa (1868)—limited
1881–1896 (15 years)	India (1881) Egypt (1883) North Africa, Southern Mediterranean, Russia China, Japan United States, Latin America (1887)—limited Germany (1892)
1899–1923 (24 years)	India (1899) Near and Far East Egypt, Russia, Balkan Peninsula Southern Europe, Hungary China, Japan, Korea, Philippines

Sources: Compiled from K. Kiple, ed., *The Cambridge World History of Human Disease* (Cambridge: Cambridge University Press, 1993), pp. 642–649; D. Barua, "The Global Epidemiology of Cholera in Recent Years," *Proceedings of the Royal Society of Medicine* 65 (1972): 423–432. *Note*: Accurate historical data on the epidemiology of specific infectious diseases is notoriously incomplete, given the absence of standard reporting systems (e.g., lists of notifiable diseases), incompleteness of demographic data, and differences in disease nomenclature. This table draws on the limited data available to illustrate the general geographic pattern of early cholera pandemics. The spread of the disease by year and country cannot always be provided comprehensively.

in 1848 cholera advanced from Poland to New Orleans in just over seven months. This more rapid move also coincided with the approximate doubling of railway lines and tonnage of steamships in operation,[16] correlating with the rapid spread of the disease throughout the Americas. By the time of the third and fourth pandemics, the spread of cholera into South America was hastened by the opening of the Panama Canal. A similar pattern can be observed in the Middle East with the opening of the Suez Canal.

Another feature during this period was cholera's close association with prevailing social conditions that enabled the disease to spread so widely and repeatedly, in the process becoming endemic in many parts of the world. In India, the cumulative effect of profound changes to local societies and ecology was, as Sheldon Watts writes, the transformation of a merely local disease, endemic in Bengal, into a chronic India-wide problem by 1817 and soon afterward an epidemic disease of worldwide proportions.[17] As cholera spread, it found fertile conditions for epidemic transmission in nineteenth-century industrialization. Poor sanitation, poverty, malnutrition, overcrowding, ignorance, and a lack of basic health services allowed cholera to flourish in the new urban centers of Europe and North America. Such was the link between cholera and social inequality during this period that the disease added impetus to fermenting unrest. In Russia, an uprising by revolutionaries known as the "cholerics" in the 1830s was because of the belief that the disease was actually a plot to kill off the poor. Although Czar Nicholas I quelled the movement, cholera continued to inflame class conflict across Europe.

By the middle of the nineteenth century, health policies to control epidemic diseases began to be adopted. But the link between disease and the squalid conditions of the poor had not yet been made officially. The experiences of Florence Nightingale with cholera during the Crimean War led the British Army to establish sanitary engineering as a new branch.[18] The first U.K. Public Health Act was adopted in 1848, followed by the creation of a General Board of Health, although cholera continued to be blamed on immorality and a lack of "proper habits."[19] Despite John Snow's historic gesture in 1854,[20] it was not until the discovery by Robert Koch in 1883 of the bacillus *Vibrio cholerae* as the causative agent of cholera that the relative inertia of government bodies toward the lack of safe drinking water and sanitation for poor people finally ended. This was gradually followed by the establishment of a public health infrastructure, eventually supported by a system of regulation and social welfare.

Internationally, governments complemented national efforts with meetings to promote cooperation and improve public sanitation. Between 1851 and 1911, twelve International Sanitary Conferences were held, which led to the formation of international public unions, such as the International Association of Public Baths and Cleanliness. In 1907, the Office International d'Hygiène Publique (OIHP) was created to standardize surveillance and reporting of selected communicable diseases, including cholera. Following establishment of the League of Nations, the work of these international public unions continued under the auspices of the League's Health Commission. In particular, the commission "established new procedures for combating epidemics and initiated studies in child welfare, public health training and many other subjects."[21] All of these efforts proved to be the forerunners of increasingly organized international health cooperation, leading to the eventual creation of the World Health Organization in 1948.

In summary, the first six pandemics of cholera can be understood in close relation to the prevailing socioeconomic and political structures of the period. From a local disease, cholera became one of the most widespread and deadly diseases of the nineteenth century, killing estimated tens of millions of people.[22] Not coincidentally, cholera traveled the same routes around the globe as European imperialism. The disease, in this sense, was an integral part of this stage of the globalization process, affected by changing spatial, temporal, and cognitive dimensions of human interaction but, in turn, also influencing the articulation or particular form that globalization has taken. It is within this historical context that the seventh pandemic can be understood.

Globalization and the seventh pandemic: mirror, mirror on the wall

The seventh cholera pandemic began in 1961 in Sulawesi, Indonesia, after a gap of thirty-eight years. The disease remained endemic in a number of regions, including South and Southeast Asia, and cases were reported regularly until the 1960s. Nonetheless, there was a declining incidence overall, and worldwide transmission did not occur. The primary reasons were improvements in basic sanitation and water supplies in many countries, backed by international health cooperation. Until 1961, it was thought that cholera was disappearing.

But in 1961, cholera presented a new and unexpected challenge (Table 3). Unlike previous pandemics, which are believed to have been the result of the classical biotype, the cause of this new pandemic was discovered to be a different biotype of *Vibrio cholerae*, known as El Tor.[23] Although less virulent, this new strain has proven more difficult to eradicate. El Tor cholera causes a higher proportion of asymptomatic infections, allowing carriers to spread the disease through contamination of food or water. It survives longer in the environment and shows greater resistance to antibiotics and chlorine. It can also live in association with certain aquatic plants and animals, making water an important reservoir for infection.[24]

From Indonesia, El Tor cholera moved west to reach India and the Middle East by 1966. In 1970, it reached southern Europe (Russia) and north, east, and west Africa. By 1971, outbreaks had been reported in thirty-one countries, one-third of them experiencing the disease for the first time. In that year, 150,000 cases were reported, including some 50,000 cases in West Bengal refugee camps. In most newly affected countries, the disease caused severe outbreaks with mortality rates of 40 percent or higher.[25] A year later,

Table 3 Seventh and eighth cholera pandemics, 1961–present.

Pandemic, Date, Type[a]	Countries
Seventh pandemic, 1961–present, El Tor biotype	Indonesia (1961)
	Indo-Pakistan Subcontinent (1963–1964)
	West Pakistan (Bangladesh), Afghanistan, Iran, Uzbekistan, Thailand (1965)
	Iraq (1966)
	Laos, South Korea, Hong Kong, Macao, Nepal, Malaysia, Burma, East Pakistan (1969)
	Russia (Astrakhan, Odessa/Kersh), Turkey, Czechoslovakia, France, U.K.,[b] Lebanon, Israel, Syria, Jordan, Libya, Tunisia, Dubai, Kuwait,[b] Saudi Arabia, Somalia, Ethiopia, Guinea, Sierra Leone, Liberia, Ghana, Côte d'Ivoire, Mali, Togo, Dahomey, Upper Volta, Nigeria, Niger, Japan[b] (1970)
	Muscat, Oman, Yemen, Morocco, Algeria, Cameroon, Chad, Mauritania, Senegal, Kenya, Uganda, Madagascar,[b] Spain, Portugal, France,[b] Sweden,[b] West Germany[b] (1971)
	United States (1973)
	Peru, Colombia, Chile, Bolivia, Brazil, Ecuador, Guatemala, Honduras, Mexico, Nicaragua, Panama, Venezuela (1991)
	Argentina, Belize, Costa Rica, El Salvador, French Guyana, Guyana, Surinam (1992)
	Paraguay (1993)
	Zaire, Ukraine (1994)
Eighth pandemic, 1993–present, 0139 Bengal serogroup	India, Bangladesh (1993)
	Pakistan, Thailand (1994)
	10 Southeast Asian countries, United States[b] (1995)

Sources: D. Barua, "The Global Epidemiology of Cholera in Recent Years," *Proceedings of the Royal Society of Medicine* 65 (1972): 423–432; Paul Epstein, "Emerging Diseases and Ecosystem Instability: New Threats to Public Health," *American Journal of Public Health* 85, no. 2 (February 1995): 168–172.

Notes: a. Many serogroups of *Vibrio cholerae* have been identified. During the first to seventh pandemics, only the 01 serogroup (of which two biotypes exist) caused cholera. Its classic biotype caused the first six pandemics and its El Tor biotype caused the seventh pandemic. A different serogroup—0139 Bengal—caused the eighth pandemic, and it is the first non 01 serogroup to have caused cholera.

b. Shows imported cases.

it reached the southeastern Mediterranean and eastern Europe. M. Narkevich and others describe the pandemic up to the 1990s as falling into three periods: 1961–1969, 1970–1977, and 1978–1989. The peak of the pandemic was during periods 1 and 2 (1967–1974), after which morbidity declined until 1985. Then, from 1985 to 1989, the pandemic seemed to accelerate once again, with 52,000 cases reported in thirty-six countries. In total, between 1961 and

Table 4 First three periods of the seventh cholera pandemic, 1961–1989.

Date	Reported Cases	Countries Reporting
1961–1969	419,968	24, mainly in Asia
1970–1977	706,261	73 (27 Asia, 32 Africa, 12 Europe, 2 Americas)
1978–1989	586,828	83

Source: Adapted from M. Narkevich et al., "The Seventh Pandemic of Cholera in the USSR, 1961–89," *Bulletin of the World Health Organization* 71, no. 2 (1993): 189–196.

1989, approximately 1.72 million cases of cholera were reported to WHO from 117 countries (see Table 4).[26]

Explanations for the origins of the pandemic were similar to previous ones, namely transmission around the world from an endemic country via travel. As Leonard Bruce-Chwatt observed, the impairment of sanitation on many Indonesian islands because of overpopulation of urban peripheries, military operations, and other disturbances, combined with certain cultural habits (e.g., use of night soil), allowed cholera to reach epidemic proportions.[27] However, the epidemiology of this pandemic has proven different in two fundamental ways: it has been more geographically widespread (spatial dimension) and has lasted longer (temporal dimension). First, the seventh pandemic has encompassed a large number of countries that have either never experienced cholera before, not done so for many decades, or never to such an intensity. In many parts of Africa, in particular, public health officials have experienced difficulty controlling the disease largely because of a lack of adequate surveillance, treatment, or prevention measures. As D. Barua wrote, "All the factors favoring endemicity of cholera exist in present-day Africa, particularly in the populous coastal and riverine areas, where there is little possibility of improving water supply, waste disposal and personal hygiene in the near future. In all probability, cholera is going to become, if it is not already, entrenched in this continent at least temporarily."[28] Barua's predictions have proven correct, and cholera has now become endemic throughout west, east, and southern Africa for the first time.[29]

This unprecedented geographical spread is also observable in the Americas, where the majority of cases have occurred in the 1990s. After disappearing from the Western Hemisphere for almost a century, El Tor cholera was simultaneously reported in two cities in Peru in January 1991. By mid-February, there were 12,000 confirmed cases. WHO described how the epidemic moved with "unexpected speed and intensity," traveling quickly 2,000 kilometers along the coast to Ecuador. By March–April, it had reached Colombia and Chile. By the end of the year, the epidemic had reached a new country every month, resulting in nearly 400,000 cases and more than 4,000 deaths. This was more than the total number of reported cases worldwide for the previous five years. The epidemic continued into 1992, with more than 300,000 cases and 2,000 deaths in twenty countries.[30]

The second difference of the seventh pandemic has been its duration so far—thirty-nine years. This has been by far the longest pandemic, and it shows few signs of having run its course. As we discussed earlier, cholera took several months to spread from country to neighboring country during the nineteenth century, transported by land or sea. El Tor cholera has also traveled readily by land and sea. It is believed, for example, that the disease was imported into Turkey and Lebanon in the early 1970s by workers coming from neighboring affected countries. Similarly, severe outbreaks in Mali, Ghana, Niger, Nigeria, and Chad were traced to the arrival of individuals from infected areas. In India, an outbreak in 1971 was primarily among refugees from the former East Pakistan.[31] Perhaps most dramatically, it is thought that the epidemic in Latin America began after a ship from China emptied its ballast tanks in Peruvian waters. The vibrio then infected local seafood eaten by local people. El Tor is also thought to have arrived on the U.S. Gulf Coast in the hulls of ships from Latin America.[32]

Since the 1960s, however, the reduced cost of transportation and the addition of faster technologies (e.g., high-speed rail, ocean liners, and air travel) have brought unprecedented movement of human populations to and from endemic areas. Since the 1960s, mass travel (growth of 7.5–10 percent per annum) has been growing at a rate faster than global population growth (growth of 1.5–2.5 percent per annum).[33] This intensification of human mobility has posed new problems for public health officials, including their capacity to contain serious outbreaks of infectious disease. K. F. Kaferstein, Y. Motarjemi, and Douglas Bettcher note that "over the last two hundred years, the average distance travelled and speed of travel have increased one thousand times, while incubation periods of disease have not."[34] As the average journey time of an airliner or a bulk carrier is much shorter than the incubation period of a disease, these different forms of transportation are believed responsible for the increased spread of disease from one location to another.[35] Air travel, for instance, brings large numbers of people into close contact with each other within an enclosed space. In relation to cholera, the disease has been spread via contaminated food served on airplanes[36] and through global trade in food products (e.g., shellfish, frozen coconut milk).

Furthermore, the epidemiology of the disease has been geographically unpredictable. Whereas in the past cholera could be monitored from country to neighboring country, more recently it has "jumped" continents. In 1973, for instance, forty passengers traveling from London to Australia were infected with cholera from contaminated food taken on board in Bahrain.[37] Similarly, thirty-one passengers were found to have cholera on a flight bound to Los Angeles from Buenos Aires, Argentina, in 1992.[38] At least seventy-five people contracted cholera by eating cold seafood salad loaded on a flight at Lima, Peru, bound for California.[39] It is estimated that, for air travelers from the United States to India, the reported rate of cholera cases is 3.7 cases per 100,000 travelers.[40] It is this "hypermobility" of the causative agent via worldwide transportation networks that has been a key factor in the continuation of the pandemic.

Technological change, however, does not tell the entire story of cholera in the late twentieth century. Indeed, like previous pandemics, socioeconomic and political structures have also been central. The 1920s to 1960s were perhaps a "boom" period for public health systems. Many countries created national health systems. And the aid to the health sector grew through bilateral aid agencies, multilateral organizations (e.g., WHO, UNICEF), charitable foundations (e.g., Rockefeller Foundation), and other nongovernmental organizations (e.g., Save the Children Fund, Oxfam). Although it was clear that not all benefited equally from this intense period of health development, facilitated by advances in medical knowledge, there was a feeling that progress against many traditional scourges of humankind was being achieved. Eradication campaigns against malaria and (more successfully) smallpox were reflections of this belief in the triumph of science over disease.

The seventh pandemic has been a reminder, however, of the persistent and, in many cases, growing inequalities that remain within and across countries. Life expectancy ranges from forty-three years in the poorest countries to an average of seventy-eight years in higher-income countries. Three-fifths of people in the developing world lack access to safe sanitation, one-third to clean water, and one-fifth to modern health services of any kind.[41] The initial outbreak of cholera in the early 1960s took advantage of these conditions to spread among the have-nots in many different societies. By the early 1970s, the pandemic seemed to peak, and cases gradually decreased over the next decade.

By the 1980s, however, cholera began to benefit from fundamental changes in many public health systems around the world. Despite the launch of the primary health care movement in 1978 by WHO and UNICEF, the 1980s saw a pulling back of the state from the financing and provision of health care. Detailed analysis of this period of health sector reform can be found elsewhere.[42] Briefly, as part of the World Bank's structural adjustment program, many lower-income countries were encouraged to reduce public expenditure on health throughout the 1980s and 1990s.[43] Globally, health sector reform in higher- and lower-income countries included policies to encourage market forces to play a greater role in health systems.[44] There was growing evidence in the late 1990s that these policies have impacted adversely on public health capacity in many countries,[45] and the growing awareness of globalizing forces has led to efforts to redefine public health functions in countries around the world.[46]

It was in this context that cholera opportunistically spread in the early 1990s. In Latin America, the adverse impacts of globalization on health systems have included increased national debt, rapid urbanization, environmental degradation, inequitable access to health services, and reduced public expenditure on public health infrastructure.[47] Cholera then arrived in 1991, spreading rapidly across the continent in an epidemic of 1.4 million cases and more than 10,000 deaths in nineteen countries.[48] This scenario has not, however, been confined to Latin America. In October 1994, El Tor cholera was reported in the former Soviet Union amid economic instability, deteriorating health services, drought, and poor hygiene. The most serious outbreak occurred in ten cities in the Ukraine and threatened a population of 50 million people.[49] As the head of the Ukrainian parliament stated at the time, "The spread of cholera and other infectious diseases is the calling card of an economy in trouble."[50]

Another contributory feature of the global political economy to the seventh pandemic has been the mass migration of people. In the early 1990s, it was estimated that 500 million people crossed international borders on commercial airlines annually. There are 100 million migrants in the world today, with an estimated 70 million people, mostly from low-income countries, working legally or illegally in other countries. In addition, a large proportion (30 million) of total migrants do so involuntarily, including 20 million refugees.[51] Enforced migration has become a particular feature of Africa, where 16 million people have been internally displaced.[52] In many cases, such migration has been a cause and effect of "complex emergencies," which have "a singular ability to erode or destroy the cultural, political, and economic integrity of established societies."[53] Given large numbers of displaced people, resulting in overcrowded living conditions, poor sanitation, unclean water supplies, and malnutrition, cholera has become a familiar feature. For example, the mass population movements as a result of the Pakistani-Indian war in 1971 led to thousands of deaths from cholera and further spread of the disease.[54] Between 1987 and 1991, cholera was diagnosed in Mozambican refugees as they migrated from their home villages to camps in Malawi.[55] In August 1994, El Tor cholera broke out in relief camps in Goma, Zaire, among Rwandan refugees. Within twenty-four hours, 800 people had died; the epidemic eventually caused 70,000 cases and 12,000 deaths.[56]

Finally, globalization in its present form is believed to be contributing to changes in the natural environment that enable infectious diseases such as cholera to thrive.[57] Like the British-built irrigation canals in India, which increased the incidence of malaria and cholera, rapid urbanization and industrialization without sufficient attention to sustainable economic development have led to contamination of drinking water. Historically, the Ganges River has symbolized purification for Hindus, who believe drinking and bathing in its waters will lead to salvation. Today twenty-nine cities, seventy towns, and countless villages deposit about 345 million gallons of raw sewage a day directly into the river. Factories add another 70 million gallons of industrial waste and farmers another 6 million tons of chemical fertilizers and 9,000 tons of pesticides.[58] Perhaps more worrisome still, it is believed that widespread changes in coastal ecology are generating "hot systems" in which mutations of the cholera organism are being selected and amplified under new environmental pressures and then transferred to human populations through the food chain. This is the explanation for the appearance of *Vibrio cholerae* 0139 Bengal

in 1992, a new strain of cholera and the first non 01 strain capable of causing epidemics, signaling the beginning of the eighth pandemic.[59]

In summary, the seventh pandemic is a reflection of the contradictions of
globalization in the late twentieth century. As in previous pandemics, cholera
and deprivation remain closely linked. Development of national health systems
worldwide led to the reduction and to what was hitherto believed to be the
eradication of cholera in many parts of the world. The global spread of cholera
since the early 1960s, however, has revealed persistence and growing inequalities within and across countries. Other features of globalization, notably
mass migration, social instability, and environmental degradation, present
the disease with the opportunity to establish itself in new areas of the world.
Cholera, in short, is a mirror for understanding the nature of globalization.

At the same time, an understanding of globalization is needed to explain
the distinct epidemiological profile of El Tor cholera. Through changes in
human interaction spatially, temporally, and cognitively, cholera has become
more geographically widespread and persistent over time. That the disease can
"jump" across continents within hours, for example, poses new challenges for
national health systems. Indeed, the globalization of cholera may require new
responses that more closely integrate different levels and types of governance.

Global governance for health: learning lessons
once again from cholera

The emergence of global governance as a central concept in international
relations responds to a perceived change in the nature of world politics. In
contrast to international governance, the defining feature of global governance
is its comprehensiveness. Global governance views the globe as a single place
within which the boundaries of the interstate system and nation-state have been
eroded. Although the nation-state remains an important actor, processes and
mechanisms of global governance are growing to encompass the structures
of international governance that manage the system of nation-states. The
emerging processes and mechanisms of global governance can be seen as
forms of supraterritorial authority.[60]

The processes and mechanisms of global governance are diverse, as are
the actors and structures that participate within them. In addition to nation-
states, these actors include international institutions, governmental organizations,
various nonstate actors, regimes, values, and rules.[61] These different actors compete with each other to shape the nature of global order, the establishment of
which is the main purpose of global governance. Global governance may be
used to stabilize and expand market capitalism on a global scale, as sought by
the International Monetary Fund (IMF) and World Bank, or to establish an
order based on greater social justice and redistribution of global resources.[62]

Although scholars, practitioners, and policymakers in the health field may
not explicitly recognize or widely use the term *global governance*, there is

growing recognition of the need to establish more effective mechanisms for addressing a range of global health issues. Such issues are wide-ranging and are reviewed elsewhere.[63] Developing responses to them lead to questions concerning scope of activity, distribution of authority, decisionmaking process, institutional structure, and resource mobilization and allocation.

The development of an effective system for the prevention, control, and treatment of infectious diseases is perhaps the classic transborder health issue. It has long been recognized that diseases do not recognize national borders and that states acting alone are unable to prevent their spread. In recent years, this message has been stated with renewed vigor in relation to emerging and reemerging diseases and globalization. As a U.S. report warns, "The modern world is a very small place, where any city in the world is only a plane ride away from any other. Infectious microbes can easily travel across borders with their human and animal hosts. . . . [And] diseases that arise in other parts of the world are repeatedly introduced into the United States, where they may threaten our national health and security."[64] Similarly, Paul Farmer writes that "EIDs [emerging infectious diseases] have often ignored political boundaries, even though their presence may cause a certain degree of turbulence at national borders. The dynamics of emerging infections will not be captured in national analyses, any more than the diseases are contained by national boundaries."[65]

A brief review of the existing institutional framework for international cooperation on infectious diseases shows a strong emphasis on biomedical understanding of human disease and state-based health systems. Since its founding in 1948, WHO has carried out surveillance and monitoring of various infectious diseases. Diseases deemed to pose a particular international threat, however, have been governed since 1951 under the International Health Regulations (IHR), a consolidation of various International Sanitary Conventions adopted from the nineteenth century onward. Over the years, the IHR have been periodically updated to take account of changing health needs (e.g., removal of smallpox from the list of notifiable diseases after eradication). In their present form, the IHR set out procedures for limiting the transmission of infectious disease via shipping, aircraft, and other modes of transport. The regulations do not control the movement of international traffic directly but concentrate on controlling the spread of disease where transborder conveyance may occur. The IHR also call on states to "report to WHO, within specific periods, cases of these three diseases [i.e., cholera, plague, and yellow fever] within their territories. Second, to facilitate reporting and deter unnecessary interference with international travel and trade, members must limit their responsive health measures (applied to international traffic for the protection of their territories against these diseases) to maximum measures permitted by these regulations."[66]

Responsibility for the IHR and other infectious disease–related activities falls on WHO's Cluster on Communicable Diseases (CDS), formerly the

Division of Emerging and Other Communicable Disease Surveillance and Control (EMC) (now referred to as Communicable Disease Surveillance and Response).

Other international agreements concerned with infectious diseases are the WHO and Food and Agriculture Organization's Codex Alimentarius, the World Trade Organization's Agreement on the Application of Sanitary and Phytosanitary Measures, and the International Civil Aviation Organization's Facilitation to the Convention on International Civil Aviation. Supporting international cooperation, in principle, is a network of national health systems led by ministries of health in each member state and extending to national health services, research institutions, public health laboratories, and monitoring and surveillance systems. Together, it is assumed that WHO coordinates top-down guidance and information, provided from the bottom up by national health systems.

In practice, there are gaps at both the international and national levels. Internationally, the IHR cover only three diseases, and WHO does not have the means to enforce compliance with even these limited stipulations. International surveillance and monitoring relies on the goodwill of governments, but fears of adverse effects on trade or tourism can lead to underreporting. India lost an estimated U.S.$1,700 million in exports, tourism, and transportation services because of the outbreak of plague in 1996.[67] Exports of shellfish by Latin American countries were similarly affected by reports of cholera in the region. Although efforts are in play to revise the IHR to stipulate reporting of "syndromes" rather than diseases, the question of authority remains.

Another difficulty lies in the limited resources available to mount rapid responses to major transborder outbreaks. Given the limits of WHO resources, the U.S. Centers for Disease Control (CDC) at times has stepped in more quickly in health emergencies (e.g., the outbreak of Ebola in northern Zaire in 1976 and the refugee camps in Goma, Zaire). At the national level, variation in health capacity is even more acute. Many lower-income countries have less than U.S.$4 per capita to spend on health care annually.[68] Structural adjustment programs place further pressure on public health expenditure, and the World Bank continues to attribute problems, such as the reemergence of cholera, on the failure to privatize rather than on a crisis in resources. As one World Bank study concludes,

> The return of cholera in 1991 to Latin America and [the] Caribbean region was only a symptom of the deep-seated problems and the fragility and inadequacy of publicly operated water supply and sanitation systems. Consequently, the agencies that operate these systems are entering a crucial phase of deciding whether they can greatly improve their operations while remaining in the public sector or whether they should seek increasing private sector financing and participation in both operations.[69]

109

To address these deficiencies, international efforts have focused on improving surveillance, monitoring, and reporting systems. WHO is now working to create a Global Surveillance Network using electronic links for rapid exchange of information.[70] In 1994, the Program for Monitoring Emerging Diseases (ProMED) was created with the impetus of sixty prominent experts in human, animal, and plant health. Accessed via the Internet, ProMED is intended to be a global system of early detection and timely response to disease outbreaks. Similarly, the Global Health Network was established to monitor the spread of emerging infectious diseases through links with public health organizations, multilateral organizations, NGOs, and independent research centers. Although such technology is clearly a vital feature of a global system of disease control, this emphasis on technical issues highlights two further flaws in the present system of international health governance.

First, underlying these initiatives is a rational model of policymaking, which assumes that lack of information is the key factor in the globalization of infectious disease. However, as we argue in this essay, the seventh cholera pandemic has been shaped by the structural features of the global political economy that have contributed to the vulnerability of certain populations and environments within and across countries. Second, globalization in its present course has created transborder externalities in the form of health risks that increasingly defy state-centric approaches of the past. Although national epidemiological data remain significant, there is also a need for disaggregated data that allow comparisons and analysis within and across countries and regions. Furthermore, focusing on control measures at the national level amid intensified human interaction has so far reinforced a fortress mentality among many governments.[71] Yet effective control of all infectious diseases at national borders is neither practicable nor ethical. Many diseases remain asymptomatic or have long periods of incubation.

It is here that the existing literature on global governance may offer ideas for creating new forms of authority and institutional linkages to address the challenges of global health. To begin with, the global governance literature highlights the need to be more comprehensive in our approach to global health. Needed, for instance, is a greater appreciation of the link between health and the environment. Douglas Bettcher and Derek Yach point out that public health issues are central components of sustainable development programs and should be incorporated into the system of global governance that has emerged from the United Nations Conference on the Environment and Development (1992) around sustainable development.[72] Piggybacking on strategies for global sustainable development may boost the chances of a system of global health governance being established. Similar linkages between health and changing governance of other sectors, such as agriculture, transportation, communications, and trade and finance, need far greater exploration.

Another central theme of the global governance literature is the need to ensure that the processes and mechanisms of global governance have the support of those governed. Various proponents of global governance agree that there is a need to reform the UN's core institutions so that they are more democratic and representative of the global population. WHO, for example, is an organization often described as governed by a "medical mafia" and influenced by the extrabudgetary funding of a small number of donor governments.[73] At the national and subnational levels, as well, there have long been calls for going beyond the traditional focus on ministries of health and government institutions. Civil society, in particular, is identified as requiring a greater role in policymaking at many levels. For example, the influence of certain global social movements, such as the women's health movement, has been recognized as positively contributing to the democratization of certain policy issues (i.e., population policy).

The nation-state and existing institutions of international health governance (e.g., the WHO and IHR) will remain central to any future system of global health governance. The challenge for scholars and policymakers is how to construct processes and mechanisms of global health governance that recognize the interests of nation-states and civil society. This is a massive challenge, yet recent developments in global health governance suggest some optimism about the ability to meet it. For example, plans for a Framework Convention on Tobacco Control bring together shared interests across nation-states, civil society, and the business community (e.g., the pharmaceutical sector) for a more comprehensive effort to control the production and consumption of tobacco. WHO's policy document "Health for All in the 21st Century" adopts a similar approach to deal with persistent inequalities in health within and across countries.[74] These initiatives are directly concerned with strengthening global health governance, proposed by an intergovernmental organization (i.e., WHO) and supported by an amalgam of member states, civil society groups, and individuals.

Finally, there is a need for critical analysis of health determinants that conceptualize social change in the context of long-term and fundamental socioeconomic structures, rather than shorter-term, technically specific change. Such an approach leads to a recognition of the structure-agent links that exist between globalization and health, including the possibility that present forms of globalization are, in fact, incompatible with human health. Importantly, critical theorists see globalization as a historical process constructed not by rationality but by embedded power relations and consequences. Locating cholera and other global health issues within this reflexive starting point therefore seeks to address, and ultimately redress, the underlying causal factors behind ill health.

Conclusion

In summary, we have analyzed cholera from the nineteenth century as a case study of the links between globalization and health. How human populations

have lived—population size and distribution, social structure, cultural practices, distribution of resources—has historically been linked to patterns of
health and disease. We have also sought to show how globalization is changing
the nature of human societies across the world and, consequently, the health
of populations. At the same time, cholera has been reflective of particular
features of globalization from its earlier stages to the present.

Globalization has shaped the pattern of the disease, the vulnerability of
certain populations, and the ability of public health systems to respond effectively. The contributing features of globalization to the epidemiologically
distinct seventh pandemic have included socioeconomic instability, intensified
human interaction and mobility, environmental degradation, and inequalities
within and across countries.

As public health systems have struggled to control the seventh pandemic,
reports of an eighth pandemic came in 1993. As we described earlier, the
new pandemic involves a new strain of *Vibrio cholerae*, believed hardier than
El Tor cholera in terms of environmental adaptation. Its emergence is thought
to have resulted from changes to coastal ecologies in South Asia. By 1995,
the pandemic spread to Calcutta, India, with 15,000 cases and 230 deaths,
and then moved rapidly to Dhaka, Bangladesh, where 600 cases were reported
daily. Severe flooding in Bangladesh in 1998 worsened conditions significantly.
Reaching 100,000 cases by 1996, the disease has since spread to Pakistan,
Thailand, and ten other Southeast Asian countries. Travel-associated cases
have been reported in the United States, Europe, and Japan.[75] Cholera is
poised, it seems, to offer yet another opportunity to learn hard lessons.

Notes

Kelley Lee is senior lecturer in International Health Policy at the London School of
Hygiene and Tropical Medicine. She is author of *Historical Dictionary of the World
Health Organization* (1998) and chairs the WHO External Advisory Group on
Globalization and Health. Richard Dodgson received his doctorate from the University
of Newcastle upon Tyne, England. He has taught at the University of Newcastle
upon Tyne, the University of Durham, and Sunderland University.

1 Richard Preston, *The Hot Zone* (New York: Corgi, 1994); Leslie Garrett, *The
   Coming Plague: Newly Emerging Diseases in a World Out of Balance* (New York:
   Farrar, Straus & Giroux, 1994); Frank Ryan, *Virus X: Understanding the Real
   Threat of the New Pandemic Plagues* (London: HarperCollins, 1996).
2 Institute of Medicine, *Emerging Infections: Microbial Threats to Health in the
   United States* (Washington, D.C.: National Academy Press, 1992); U.S. Committee
   on International Science, Engineering, and Technology Policy (CISET), *Global
   Microbial Threats in the 1990s* (Washington, D.C.: Working Group on Emerging
   and Re-emerging Infectious Diseases, 1995); Institute of Medicine, *America's Vital
   Interest in Global Health* (Washington, D.C.: National Academy Press, 1997).
3 Louise Amoore, Richard Dodgson, Barry Gills, Paul Langley, Don Marshall,
   and Iain Watson, "Overturning Globalisation: Resisting the Teleological, Reclaiming
   the Political," *New Political Economy* 2, no. 1 (1997): 179–195.

4 Kelley Lee, "Globalisation and Health Policy: A Review of the Literature and Proposed Research and Policy Agenda," in Pan American Health Organization, *Health and Human Development in the New Global Economy* (Washington, D.C.: Pan American Health Organization, 2000).

5 Roland Robertson, *Globalization: Social Theory and Global Culture* (London: Sage, 1992).

6 F. Cairncross, *The Death of Distance* (Cambridge: Harvard Business School Press, 1997).

7 Alan Rugman and Michael Gestrin, "New Rules for Multilateral Investment," *International Executive* 39, no. 1 (1997): 21–33.

8 Anthony Giddens, *The Consequences of Modernity* (London: Polity Press, 1990); Robertson, *Globalization*.

9 Robert Clark, "Global Life Systems: Biological Dimensions of Globalisation," *Global Society* 11, no. 3 (1997): 280.

10 Mark Nathan Cohen, "The History of Infectious Disease," in Mark Nathan Cohen, *Health and the Rise of Civilization* (New Haven: Yale University Press, 1989); Arno Karlen, *Man and Microbes, Disease and Plagues in History and Modern Times* (New York: Simon & Schuster, 1995).

11 J. N. Hays, "New Diseases and Transatlantic Exchanges," in J. N. Hays, *The Burdens of Disease, Epidemics and Human Response in Western History* (New Brunswick, N.J.: Rutgers University Press, 1998), pp. 62–77, quotation from p. 72.

12 Cohen, "The History of Infectious Disease."

13 There are more than sixty serogroups of *Vibrio cholerae*, but only serogroup 01 causes cholera. Serogroup 01 has two biotypes (classical and El Tor), and each biotype has two serotypes (Ogawa and Inaba).

14 World Health Organization, *Guidelines for Cholera Control* (Geneva: WHO, 1993).

15 R. S. Speck, "Cholera," in K. F. Kiple, ed., *The Cambridge World History of Human Diseases* (Cambridge: Cambridge University Press, 1993), p. 647.

16 Eric Hobsbawm, *The Age of Capital: 1848–1875* (London: Weidenfield & Nicolson, 1975), p. 310.

17 Sheldon Watts, "Cholera and Civilization: Great Britain and India, 1817 to 1920," in Sheldon Watts, *Epidemics and History, Disease, Power and Imperialism* (New Haven: Yale University Press, 1997), pp. 167–212.

18 R. S. Bray, *Armies of Pestilence: The Effects of Pandemics on History* (Cambridge: Lutterworth Press, 1996), pp. 180–183.

19 Watts, "Cholera and Civilization," p. 194.

20 Amid a severe cholera outbreak in London, John Snow found a concentration of cases around a pump in Broad Street. Hoping to prove his theory that cholera is a waterborne disease, he removed the pump handle in front of public officials; and the outbreak was contained.

21 David Armstrong, *The Rise of International Organisation: A Short History* (London: Macmillan, 1982), p. 43.

22 Bray, *Armies of Pestilence*.

23 The causative agent is named after the El Tor quarantine camp on the Sinai Peninsula, where it was first isolated in 1905 from the intestines of pilgrims returning from Mecca.

24 World Health Organization, *Guidelines for Cholera Control*.

25 Leonard Bruce-Chwatt, "Global Problems of Imported Disease," *Advances in Parasitology* 11 (1973): 86.

26 M. Narkevich et al., "The Seventh Pandemic of Cholera in the USSR, 1961–89," *Bulletin of the World Health Organization* 71, no. 2 (1993): 189–196.

27 Bruce-Chwatt, "Global Problems of Imported Disease."

28 D. Barua, "The Global Epidemiology of Cholera in Recent Years," *Proceedings of the Royal Society of Medicine* 65 (1972): 423–432.

29 J. van Bergen, "Epidemiology and Health Policy—A World of Difference? A Case-Study of a Cholera Outbreak in Kaputa Distict, Zambia," *Social Science and Medicine* 43, no. 1 (1996): 93–99.
30 Richard Guerrant, "Twelve Messages from Enteric Infections for Science and Society," *American Journal of Tropical Medicine and Hygiene* 51, no. 1 (1994): 27.
31 Barua, "The Global Epidemiology of Cholera in Recent Years," pp. 426–448.
32 S. McCarthy, R. McPhearson, A. Guarino, and J. Gaines, "Toxigenic Vibrio Cholerae 01 and Cargo Ships Entering Gulf of Mexico," *Lancet* 339 (1992): 624–625.
33 Andrew Cliff and Peter Haggett, "Disease Implications of Global Change," in R. J. Johnston, P. J. Taylor, and M. J. Watts, eds., *Geographies of Global Change: Remapping the World in the Late 20th Century* (Oxford, England: Blackwell, 1995), p. 209.
34 K. F. Kaferstein, Y. Motarjemi, and Douglas Bettcher, "Foodborne Disease Control: A Transnational Challenge," *Emerging Infectious Diseases* 3, no. 4 (1997): 8.
35 Bruce Jay Plotkin and Ann Marie Kimball, "Designing an International Policy and Legal Framework for the Control of Emerging Infectious Diseases: First Steps," *Emerging Infectious Diseases* 3, no. 1 (1997): 1–9.
36 David L. Heymann and Guenael R. Rodier, "Global Surveillance of Communicable Diseases," *Emerging Infectious Diseases* 4, no. 3 (1998): 1–5.
37 Bruce-Chwatt, "Global Problems of Imported Disease," p. 87.
38 William Booth, "Cholera's Mysterious Journey North," *Washington Post*, 26 August 1991.
39 Robert Tauxe, Eric Mintz, and Robert Quick, "Epidemic Cholera in the New World: Translating Field Epidemiology into New Prevention Strategies," *Emerging Infectious Diseases* 1, no. 4 (1995): 141–146.
40 J. Todd Weber, William C. Levine, David P. Hopkins, and Robert V. Tauxe, "Cholera in the United States, 1965–1991," *Archives of Internal Medicine* 154 (14 March 1994): 551–556.
41 Barbara Crossette, "Kofi Annan's Astonishing Facts," *New York Times*, 27 September 1998, p. WK16; United Nations Development Programme, *Human Development Report* (New York: UNDP, 1998).
42 Antonio Ugalde and J. Jackson, "The World Bank and International Health Policy: A Critical Review," *Journal of International Development* 7, no. 3 (1995): 525–542.
43 World Bank, *Financing Health Services in Developing Countries: An Agenda for Reform* (Washington, D.C.: IBRD, 1987); World Bank, *World Development Report: Investing in Health* (Washington, D.C.: IBRD, 1993).
44 Mary Ruggie, *Realignments in the Welfare State: Health Policy in the United States, Britain, and Canada* (New York: Columbia University Press, 1996).
45 Ankie Hoogvelt, *Globalisation and the Postcolonial World: The New Political Economy of Development* (London: Macmillan, 1997); Robert Beaglehole and Ruth Bonita, *Public Health at the Crossroads, Achievements and Prospects* (London: Cambridge University Press, 1997).
46 Douglas Bettcher, Steve Sapirie, and Eric Goon, "Essential Public Health Functions: Results of the International Delphi Study," *World Health Statistics Quarterly* 51 (1998): 44–54.
47 Alberto Cardelle, "Health Care in the Time of Reform: Emerging Policies for Private-Public Sector Collaboration in Health. *North-South Issues* 6, no. 1 (1997): 1–8.
48 Jose Sanchez and David Taylor, "Cholera," *Lancet* 349 (21 June 1997): 1825–1830.
49 World Health Organization, *The World Health Report 1996: Fighting Disease, Fostering Development* (Geneva: WHO, 1996).
50 Alexander Moroz, quoted in Ryan, *Virus X*, p. 108.
51 Mary Wilson, "Travel and the Emergence of Infectious Diseases," *Emerging Infectious Diseases* 1, no. 2 (1995): 39–46.

52 "Migration: The Facts," *New Internationalist*, no. 305 (1998): 18.
53 Mark Duffield, "Complex Emergencies and the Crisis of Developmentalism," *IDS Bulletin* 25, no. 4 (1994): 38. Duffield defines complex emergencies as "protracted political crises resulting from sectarian or predatory indigenous responses to socioeconomic stress and marginalisation."
54 A. Zwi, "Cholera in South Africa," *South African Outlook* 11 (1981): 172–177.
55 Susan Cookson et al., "Immigrant and Refugee Health," *Emerging Infectious Diseases* 4, no. 3 (1998): 1–2.
56 Sanchez and Taylor, "Cholera"; Heymann and Rodier, "Global Surveillance of Communicable Diseases," p. 2.
57 A. J. McMichael, B. Bolin, R. Costanza, G. Daily, C. Folke, K. Lindahl-Kiessling, E. Lindgren, and B. Niklasson, "Globalization and the Sustainability of Human Health: An Ecological Perspective," *BioScience* 49, no. 3 (1999): 205–210.
58 Crossette, "Kofi Annan's Astonishing Facts."
59 Paul Epstein, "Emerging Diseases and Ecosystem Instability: New Threats to Public Health," *American Journal of Public Health* 85, no. 2 (February 1995): 168–172.
60 Jan Aart Scholte, "The Globalization of World Politics," in John Baylis and Steve Smith, eds., *The Globalization of World Politics: An Introduction to International Relations* (Oxford: Oxford University Press, 1997), pp. 13–30.
61 James Rosenau, "Governance in the Twenty-first Century," *Global Governance* 1, no. 1 (January–April 1995): 13–43.
62 André C. Drainville, "The Fetishism of Global Civil Society," in M. P. Smith and L. E. Guarnizo, eds., *Transnationalism from Below* (London: Transaction Publishers, 1998), p. 37; Richard Falk, *On Humane Governance: Toward a New Global Politics* (Cambridge, England: Polity Press, 1995).
63 Lee, "Globalisation and Health Policy."
64 U.S. Committee on International Science, Engineering, and Technology Policy, *Global Microbial Threats in the 1990s.*
65 Paul Farmer, "Social Inequalities and Emerging Infectious Diseases," *Emerging Infectious Diseases* 2, no. 4 (1996): 259–266.
66 Quoted in Plotkin and Kimball, "Designing an International Policy and Legal Framework," p. 3.
67 Collette Kinnon, "Globalization, World Trade: Bringing Health into the Picture," *World Health Forum* 19 (1998): 397–406.
68 World Health Organization, *The World Health Report, 1995: Bridging the Gaps* (Geneva: WHO, 1995).
69 Emanuel Idelovitch and Klas Ringskog, *Private Sector Participation in Water Supply and Sanitation in Latin America* (Washington, D.C.: World Bank, Directions in Development Series, 1995).
70 World Health Organization, *Global Cholera Update* (Geneva: WHO, 1998).
71 Institute of Medicine, *America's Vital Interest in Global Health.*
72 Douglas Bettcher and Derek Yach, "The Globalisation of Public Health Ethics?" *Millennium: Journal of International Studies* 27, no. 3 (1998): 495.
73 D. Pitt, "Power in the UN Superbureaucracy: A New Byzantium?" in D. Pitt and T. Weiss, *The Nature of United Nations Bureaucracies* (London: Croom Helm, 1992), chap. 2; P. Vaughan, S. Mogedal, S. E. Kruse, K. Lee, G. Walt, and K. de Wilde, *Co-operation for Health Development: Extrabudgetary Funds and the World Health Organisation* (Oslo: Governments of Australia, Norway, and the United Kingdom, 1995).
74 World Health Organization, "Health for All: Policy for the 21st Century," WHO Doc. WHA51/5, May 1998.
75 Sanchez and Taylor, "Cholera."

58

GOVERNING THE
GLOBALIZATION OF
PUBLIC HEALTH

Allyn L. Taylor

Source: *Journal of Law, Medicine & Ethics*, 32:3 (2004), 500–8.

The number and the scale of transboundary public health concerns are increasing. Infectious and non-communicable diseases, international trade in tobacco, alcohol, and other dangerous products as well as the control of the safety of health services, pharmaceuticals, and food are merely a few examples of contemporary transnationalization of health concerns. The rapid development and diffusion of scientific and technological developments across national borders are creating new realms of international health concern, such as aspects of biomedical science, including human reproductive cloning, germ-line therapy, and xenotransplantation, as well as environmental health problems, including climate change, biodiversity loss, and depletion of the ozone layer. Growth in international trade and travel, in combination with population growth, has served to increase the frequency and intensity of health concerns bypassing or spilling over sovereign boundaries.

Although health has traditionally been seen an area of limited multilateral cooperation, there is growing awareness that contemporary globalization has led to the proliferation of cross border determinants of health status and is undermining the capacity of nation states to protect health through domestic action alone. Consequently, globalization is creating a heightened need for new global health governance structures to promote coordinated intergovernmental action.

This emerging need for new mechanisms and models for collective health action is a fundamental force behind the rapid expansion of international health law. Today, the growing field of international health law encompasses treaties and other legal instruments addressing diverse and complex concerns and is increasingly recognized as integrally linked to most other traditionally defined international legal realms.

Despite growing awareness of the capacity of conventional international law to serve as a dynamic tool for multilateral health cooperation in an increasingly interdependent world, little scholarly consideration has been paid to how twenty-first century global health lawmaking should be managed from an international institutional basis.[1] With multiple international organizations sharing lawmaking authority for global health and with other actors engaged in the international legislative process, international lawmaking shows potential for fragmented, uncoordinated, and inefficient sprawl.

This article seeks to contribute to the emerging discussion on global health governance by examining how globalization and the rising need for new global health governance structures is a driving force behind the expansion of conventional international health law. The article considers the complexities associated with using conventional vehicles to advance international cooperation and the inherent limitations of the international legislative process. It examines whether the present institutional framework is adequate and appropriate to meet the emerging global health law governance needs of the world community and whether leadership by the World Health Organization could strengthen global coordination and effective implementation of future developments in this rapidly evolving domain of international legal concern. Conventional international law is the primary international legal vehicle by which international organizations can advance international legal cooperation, so the article focuses on treaty law rather than other sources of international law.

The evolution of international law related to public health

Globalization and the expanding domain of international health law

It has been widely observed that globalization has critical implications for public health and global public health governance.[2] A dominant characteristic of contemporary globalization is that it has introduced or expanded risks to health that transcend national borders in their origin or impact.[3] Such risks may include emerging and re-emerging infectious diseases, global environmental degradation, food safety, and an array of non-communicable diseases as well as trade in harmful commodities such as tobacco.

For example, the magnitude of the global impact of catastrophic appearances of new infectious diseases and the violent worldwide reemergence of old contagions has vividly evidenced the globalization of public health. Over the last two decades nations worldwide have been confronted with outbreaks of virulent strains of many old diseases and over thirty newly recognized pathogens, including, most notably, HIV/AIDS. Most recently, the well-publicized global threats of severe acute respiratory syndrome (SARS) in late 2002 and 2003 and outbreaks of both human (H3N2) and avian (H5N1) influenza less than a year later captured public and media attention. The

SARS epidemic spread rapidly from its origins in southern China until it had reached more than 25 other countries within a matter of months. In addition to the number of patients infected with the SARS virus, totaling more than 8000 cases and 774 known deaths, the disease had profound economic and political repercussions in many of the affected regions. Reports in early 2004 of isolated new SARS cases and a fear that the disease could reemerge and spread put public health officials on high alert for any indications of possible new outbreaks. Concerns about rapid worldwide transmission of communicable diseases were confounded by epidemic outbreaks of both human (H3N2) and avian (H5N1) influenza in 2003–2004. Although these two recent epidemics have thus far had a limited relative impact on global health, the magnified public attention has promoted a mobilizing vision for coordinated health action and, in some cases, jolted global awareness and appreciation of the interconnectedness between domestic and international health.

The impact of increasing global integration for the globalization of public health is not, of course, an entirely new phenomenon. It has long been recognized that challenges to health are increasingly international[4] and have led to the obsolescence of the traditional distinction between national and international health policy.[5] However, contemporary globalization has had an unprecedented impact on global public health.

As Dodgson, Lee, and Drager have observed, the dramatic growth in geographical scope and speed with which contemporary transborder health risks have emerged has effectively challenged the established system of health governance defined by national boundaries.[6] Contemporary globalization has thus contributed to the rapid decline in the practical capacity of sovereign states to address contemporary health challenges through unilateral action alone and has amplified the need for health governance that transcends traditional and increasingly inadequate unilateral national approaches.

Conventional international law – treaty law – has received new prominence as a tool for multilateral cooperation in the public health field as states increasingly recognize the need to complement domestic action in the health sector with cross-sector and cross-border action to protect the health of their populations. The momentum of globalization is such that governments must turn increasingly to international cooperation to attain national public health objectives. Globalization has increased the need for new, formalized frameworks of international collaboration, including conventional international law, to address emerging global health threats and to improve the health status of poor states that have not benefited from globalization – the so-called "losers" of globalization.[7] Global health governance is, therefore, not about one world government, but about institutions and legal practices that facilitate multilateral cooperation among sovereign nation states.[8]

Globalization has also impacted the development of international health law, because increasing global integration has compounded the impact of other contemporary global developments that are strongly connected with health status and thereby magnified the need for frameworks for international cooperation. For example, the spread of communication and information technologies has dramatically accelerated the rate of scientific progress and its diffusion and application around the globe. This rapid worldwide dissemination of recent advances in scientific knowledge and technology has advanced international agreement and action by providing the evidence base and the technological tools needed for effective national action and international cooperation in a wide range of treaties – including those concerned with the safety of chemicals, pesticides, and food and the disposal of hazardous wastes. At the same time, however, the use of environmentally damaging technologies has also contributed to the codification of international law by propelling global health threats such as biodiversity loss, marine pollution, depletion of the ozone layer, and climate change. Further, continuing scientific progress and developments are generating ongoing global debate on codifying new international commitments, including global bans on certain novel technologies, such as reproductive human cloning.[9]

Issue linkage

Globalization has contributed to the expansion of international health by contributing to enhanced appreciation of the interconnectedness of contemporary global concerns and, concomitantly, the "linkage" of health to other international legal issues. International legal scholars have conventionally compartmentalized and treated substantive subject matters such as human rights, environmental protection, health and arms control, as discrete, self-contained areas with limited connections.[10] Students of international law have only recently begun to recognize the nexus among different realms of international law, such as trade and human rights, and human rights and environmental protection.[11]

The evolution of the concept of international security, a realm at the fore of the global community's political agenda, provides an interesting example of this phenomenon. The traditional understanding of international security has come under increasing scrutiny in recent years with growing support for a comprehensive and multisectoral conceptualization of security that addresses the wide-ranging factors that impact on the vulnerability of people. The linkage between health and security sits squarely at the center of this movement. For instance, in May 2003, the Commission on Human Security released a report proposing a new security framework that focuses directly on improving the human condition, including a key public health component.[12]

As a further example, the development agenda has evolved over the past few years from a view focused exclusively on unbridled and "trickle-down" economic growth, towards a more holistic perspective that economic growth should be cased by multidimensional concepts such as sustainable development and human development. The concepts of human development and sustainable development encompass the idea of expanded intersectoral action and coordination of economic, social, and environmental policy to improve the human condition. Health and the relationship between improved health and development are at the core of this development agenda.[13] At the same time as these developments public health policy-makers have expanded intersectoral global public health action to address the increasingly evident intersectoral determinants of health status, including poverty, education, technology, and the environment.

These global public policy developments have important implications for the conceptualization and advancement of international health law.[14] As a consequence of "issue linkage" international health law is increasingly understood to be a key component of other international legal regimes, including labor law, human rights, environmental law, trade, and arms control. For example, the extraordinary growth of international trade means the link between health and trade in a number of the World Trade Organization (WTO)'s treaties is becoming increasingly manifest in a wide range of areas including access to medicines, food security, nutrition, infectious disease control, and biotechnology.[15] In addition, as noted above, health has been linked to international peace and security issues in multiple contexts, including those of HIV/AIDS, and biological and other weapon systems. Overall, health is emerging as a central issue of multilateralism as a consequence of issue linkage in combination with the widespread impact of globalization.

"Issue linkage" is not limited to mere doctrinal debates, but also impacts contemporary codification efforts. Coordinated action on health and other traditionally distinct substantive concerns has become increasingly commonplace in international legislative projects. For example, as described above, sustainable development encompasses the idea of intersectoral coordination of environmental, economic, and social policy to improve the human condition.[16] The praxis of sustainable development informed the 1992 Rio Declaration on Environment and Development and has been elaborated in a number of international instruments, including the Conventions on Climate Change and Biological Diversity.

As a further example, the evolution of international health law has been very much tied to the protection and promotion of human rights related to physical and mental integrity.[17] The principal international legal basis for the right to health and other human rights relevant to health is found in the core instruments of human rights law: the International Bill of Rights which consists of the Universal Declaration of Human Rights (1948), the International Covenant on Economic, Social and Cultural Rights (1966), and the International Covenant on Civil and Political Rights (1966). However, there has been an emerging global understanding, arising primarily from public health approaches to HIV/AIDS, that human rights and public health are intertwined and interdependent.[18] Consequently, the domain of human rights in relation to health has expanded conspicuously in the last decade or so with bodies of the United Nations system paying increasing attention to the interrelation between health and human rights, and tailored human rights instruments now address the rights of particular populations, such as persons with HIV/AIDS and disabilities, women, children, migrant workers, and refugees[19] and, most recently, the interrelation between the human right to health and access to medicines.

The promise and limitations of international law for global health governance

Health has emerged as a key global policy issue as a consequence of the globalization of public health, including the recently enhanced appreciation of the centrality of health to most realms of international relations.

Contemporary international health law includes a wide and growing diversity of international concerns. The scope and depth of contemporary international health law and its nexus with other realms of international legal concern reflects growing multilateral concern with and international cooperation to address the impact of contemporary globalization on public health, including aspects of biomedical science, human reproduction and cloning, organ transplantation and xenotransplantation, infectious and non-communicable diseases, international trade and the control of safety of health services, food and pharmaceuticals, and the control of addictive substances such as tobacco and narcotics.[20] As described above, international health law is also increasingly linked with other realms of multilateral concern. Arms control and the banning of weapons of mass destruction, international human rights and disabilities, international labour law and occupational health and safety, environmental law and the control of toxic pollutants, nuclear safety and radiation protection, and fertility and population growth are all intimately related to the domain of international health law.[21] The current configuration of international health law and the contribution of intergovernmental organizations to its development have recently been examined.[22]

Globalization is creating new and increasingly difficult governance needs. In the realm of public health, enhanced cooperation among nation states is proving increasingly necessary to address the rising number and complexity of transboundary health problems. Global health governance in the twenty-first century, therefore, is likely to include expanded use of international law through the codification of new agreements and the adaptation of existing ones as nations at all levels of development increasingly recognize the need to provide a framework for coordinated action in an increasingly interdependent world. Global health development strategies, including the codification and implementation of treaty law, will be needed to address increasingly complex, intersectoral, and interrelated global health problems.

The burgeoning literature examining health and international health law as global public goods testifies to the increasing significance of conventional international law as a mechanism for future international collective action in this era of globalization.[23] The interdependence and integration associated with globalization means that providing global public goods such as public health increasingly requires action to be undertaken at the global level through effective international cooperation.

Notably, the ever-expanding sense of global health interdependence and global health vulnerability fostered by contemporary globalization may also, over time, become a powerful factor in overcoming the penchant for isolationism or unilateralism that, at times, has characterized the foreign policy of some powerful states, including, most notably, the United States, and thus contribute to the relevance of international health law by encouraging both the codification and implementation of effective international commitments.

Conventional international law is, of course, an inherently imperfect mechanism for international cooperation and the international legislative process is characterized by numerous and manifest limitations – including challenges to timely commitment and implementation – although considerable advances have been made in the last few decades.[24]

Globalization has also, in some respects, magnified the complexity of using conventional international law as an effective vehicle for intergovernmental cooperation. Increasing global interdependence may, as suggested above, enhance the codification and implementation of effective international health commitments by expanding awareness of global health vulnerability and the need for collective and concerted action. However, while contemporary health challenges are of concern to all countries because of their transborder character, many such problems are particularly acute in the poorest nations that are in the weakest position to negotiate effective and collective international obligations. Further, the deepening of poverty and accentuation of health inequalities among and within countries as well as the expanding numbers of increasingly complex and multifarious transnational health concerns and determinants of health status considerably compounds the challenge of using international legislation as a means to promote global public goods. In addition, as described further herein, the expansion in the number and power of non-state actors in the health domain is impacting on the capacity of traditional modes of state-to-state cooperation, including international law, to address global health concerns.

Despite the conspicuous limitations of the international lawmaking process and the inherent challenges associated with using treaties to promote international collective action in a globalizing world, treaties can be useful for raising public awareness and stimulating international commitment and national action. As an increasing number of health threats are global in scope or have the potential to become so, international treaties and other such legal mechanisms are of vital and ever-increasing importance and are an essential, albeit limited, component of future global health governance.

Global health governance and international law: the institutional framework

Contemporary global health governance

In recent years there has been considerable development in the field of international organization with the number of intergovernmental organizations active in the domain of health and other fields of international relations growing dramatically. A diversity of intergovernmental organizations now contribute to the elaboration of the increasingly complex and multivaried field of international health law.[25] These include the United Nations and its agencies, organs, and other bodies, and international and regional organizations outside of the United Nation's system. Within the comprehensive United Nations system, for example, organizations with significant involvement in the health sector include WHO, UNICEF, FAO, UNEP, UNDP, UNFPA and The World Bank. Globalization has also expanded the web of relevant international organizations in the field of global health, including, notably, the WTO. Overall, an increasing number of intergovernmental organizations with express lawmaking authority and relevant mandates have served as platforms for the codification of international law related to health; others have influenced contemporary international law in this field.

More than fifty years after the founding of the United Nations, the world has changed dramatically and there has been a multiplication of non-state actors in international health with the private sector becoming an increasingly important player in health governance. These non-state actors include a wide assortment of foundations, religious groups, nongovernmental agencies and for-profit organizations – such as the pharmaceutical industry – with a powerful influence on international health policy, including global lawmaking. Innovative "international health coalitions" that involve diverse global health actors,[26] such as health research networks and public-private partnerships are also increasingly commonplace and have an important influence on contemporary global health governance.[27]

The growing significance of non-state actors in global health governances combined with widespread criticism of the United Nations and its specialized agencies, including WHO, has led some commentators to suggest a declining and, perhaps, dwindling role for intergovernmental organizations in global health governance. Further, it is argued that globalization is not only reducing the capacity of national governments to address health challenges alone, but also, by extension, collectively through intergovernmental institutions.[28] The rise of innovative health coalitions, which often incorporate international organizations, is considered as a particular challenge to the continued authority of international organizations. Some commentators have emphasized a gradual reallocation of power from intergovernmental organizations to private-sector actors and the innovative health coalitions which have gained increasing power and influence in global health governance.[29] According to this view, the overall growth in the number and degree of influence in non-state actors in health governance has led to blurring of the distinct roles of state and non-state actors in governance activities such as resource mobilization[30] and contributed to a reallocation of authority and, perhaps, legitimacy in health governance.

Although globalization has facilitated the rise and influence of new non-state actors in health, increasing global health interdependence in fact requires that multilateral organizations play a larger role in international health co-operation[31] – at least in the emerging realm of international health lawmaking and implementation. As this article has illustrated, contemporary globalization has brought about profound changes in the international context creating a greater need for meaningful intergovernmental coordination than ever before. At the same time, it is widely recognized that globalization has tended to weaken, diminish, and even fragment the state, but it has not crushed, destroyed, or replaced it. Ultimately, states retain the final authority and responsibility to decide which issues are considered and negotiated at the international level and implemented into domestic law and policy. Hence, while the growing influence of new health actors may have led to the blurring of traditional roles in some aspects of international health, this is not the case for international health lawmaking.

The vast majority of international legislative projects are conducted under the auspices of international organizations. Public international organizations are institutional mechanisms for multilateral cooperation and collective action. Their organizational structures and formal administrative arrangements provide stable negotiating forums for member states in realms within their relevant legal authority, thereby anchoring and facilitating intergovernmental coopera-tion.[32] Private-sector actors cannot replace international organizations as institutional focal points for global debate and codification of binding norms by state actors. Consequently, as this article has illustrated, public international organizations with relevant lawmaking authority will provide increasingly important vehicles through which states can develop and implement public policy as global integration progresses.

Institutional overload

The proliferation and patchwork development of multilateral organizations with overlapping ambitions and legal authority creates the risk that interna-tional health law may develop in an inconsistent and suboptimal manner. The experience of international environmental law over the last twenty years provides a cautionary example that demonstrates that uncoordinated lawmaking activity by different intergovernmental organizations may have counterproductive and inconsistent results.[33] Scholars argue that, as a consequence of the absence of an umbrella environmental agency, global environmental governance has suffered from "institutional overload."[34] That is, the plethora of treaties and organizations relating to the environment has exceeded the capacity of states to effectively participate in and comply with them. The inefficient management of global environmental lawmaking has, in part, led some commentators to identify the need for the establishment of a new public international organization – the "World Environment Organization."[35]

There is significant risk that a similar condition of "institutional overload" and inconsistent standard-setting will emerge in international health, a development which will detract from efforts to address the important global risks to health and to manage the new technologies with great potential to advance global public health. For example, dramatic advances in the field of biomedical science – a realm with vast opportunities and risks to global public health – has recently triggered numerous, uncoordinated regional and global initiatives,[36] which have considerably complexified rather than rationalized the global legal framework.

At the global level, UNESCO, WHO, the United Nations Commission for Human Rights, UNEP and the WTO have all contributed to the elaboration of international instruments in this rapidly evolving field without any meaningful institutional consultation, coordination or planning. The first international instrument to address a broad range of human rights and public health implications of biotechnology, the Universal Declaration on the Human Genome and Human Rights was adopted by the UNESCO General Conference in 1997. More recently, in 2003, UNESCO adopted an International Declaration on Human Genetic Data and, at the time of this writing, is in the process of preparing to negotiate a new proposed Declaration on Universal Norms on Bioethics. During this same period of time, the United Nations Commission for Human Rights has adopted resolutions pertaining to human rights and bioethics with implications for public health,[37] while WHO has also adopted resolutions and recommended standards on the social, ethical, and scientific implications of biotechnology, including human reproductive cloning.

There is growing evidence of fragmentation, duplication, and inconsistency in this highly complex realm, particularly with respect to binding instruments that have been adopted under the auspices of the assorted international organizations involved in the field. For example, some of the aspects of the biotechnology revolution for biodiversity are addressed in the United Nations Environment Programme's Convention on Biological Diversity and Biosafety Protocol. At the same time, the WTO's Convention on Trade-related Aspects of Intellectual Property establishes standards for protection of intellectual property applicable to biotechnology and several other WTO agreements also apply to biotechnology-related trade disputes. Most recently, in December 2001, the United Nations General Assembly established an Ad Hoc Working Group of the Sixth Committee to consider a proposed new treaty to ban the reproductive cloning of human beings. This negotiation process has been stymied by a split between those states, led by the United States, that favor a broad-based cloning treaty that bans all human cloning, including thera-peutic cloning, and those states that favor a treaty with a narrow focus on human reproductive cloning. In the absence of consensus on the scope of the proposed instrument, in late 2003, the United Nations Member States agreed to postpone discussions of the proposed treaty until late 2004.[38] Notably, no consideration has been given to extending the scope of the treaty to compre-hensively address critical and timely issues in species altering technology, such as germ line therapy.[39]

These examples illustrate that international law in biotechnology is develop-ing in a splintered and disconnected manner as intergovernmental organizations with overlapping claims to legal jurisdiction are addressing isolated aspects of the genetics revolution in a piecemeal and incomplete manner.[40] Instead of fostering effective interagency coordination and strengthened multilateral cooperation to harness the genetics revolution to advance global public health, the splintered legal process is aggravating uncertainty about the legal regime that governs biotechnology. This is partly because standards adopted under the auspices of different international organizations are being developed in increasingly contradictory ways, including conflicting legal standards related to intellectual property.[41]

This suggests that, similar to the experience of international environmental law, the multiplicity of public international organizations engaged in standard-setting in biotechnology is also likely to lead to "treaty congestion" and over-whelm the capacity of states to participate in the lawmaking enterprise and to implement international commitments. In some respects "institutional overload" in biotechnology appears to be leading to a situation of normative overkill. At the same time, the emerging patchwork of international law in biotechnology may still fail to comprehensively address the most important implications of the genetics field for human health. Despite the extensive international legislative activity in this area, there is no legally binding global instrument even under consideration that addresses the considerable public health implications of the globalization of biotechnology.

Advancing global health law governance

An international health law mandate for WHO

Lessons from the experience of the last several decades of global environ-mental governance and recent codification efforts in biotechnology illustrate that the international health law enterprise necessitates more effective collective management. More effective institutional coordination than exists in the current decentralized organizational framework is also needed because the phenomenon of "issue linkage" in contemporary lawmaking confounds the conundrum of contradictory international health law rules developed under the auspices of different organizations with overlapping legal authority. In international law generally, the question of issue linkage is increasingly understood to concern the allocation of legal jurisdiction among international organizations.[42]

The World Health Organization has a unique directive to provide leadership and promote rational and effective development of the evolving field of international health law. As the largest international health organization, WHO has wide-ranging responsibilities to address global public health concerns based on responsibilities assigned by its constitution and its affiliation with the United Nations.[43]

The structure of the relationship between the United Nations and WHO is grounded in the United Nations Charter and, in particular, those sections that describe the objectives of the United Nations. Article 55 of the Charter describes the goals that the United Nations has pledged to promote among its members, including solutions of international, economic, social, health, and related problems. As the specialized agency with the primary constitutional directive to act as the "directing and co-ordinating authority" on international health work, WHO has the cardinal responsibility to implement the aims of the Charter with respect to health. Although the broad idea that WHO should promote coordination throughout the United Nations system is not new to global health governance literature, it deserves more serious consideration in this neglected realm of international health lawmaking because of the implications of the current leadership vacuum.

System-wide coordination does not mean full centralization of all international health lawmaking functions under WHO's auspices. For at least six reasons, consolidation of all international health law making functions under WHO is neither feasible nor desirable. First, as described the field of international health law is growing rapidly encompassing more diverse and complex concerns, in part, as a consequence of issue linkage. Although health is a component of an increasing number of such codification efforts, not all such treaty enterprises fall squarely within WHO's core mandate. Second, as described further herein, WHO currently has highly limited experience in international health lawmaking and management of global legal developments. Therefore, WHO lacks the requisite capacity to undertake full centralization of all lawmaking functions in this rapidly developing field. Third, expanding WHO's mandate to address all aspects of international health law codification could also deplete the organization's existing resources and potentially undermine the ability of the institution to fulfil its well-established and essential international health functions.

Fourth, member states are highly unlikely to limit their autonomy and freedom of action by granting WHO such broad jurisdiction or, given current economic conditions, to provide it with the vast new resources needed to implement such an expansive new mandate. Fifth, other international organizations with overlapping legal jurisdiction would undoubtedly defend against full centralization under the auspices of WHO.[44] WHO has no binding authority over the activities of other autonomous intergovernmental organizations and, regrettably, competition rather than coordination has been a traditional stamp of organizational relations throughout the United Nations system.

Fifth, it is important to recognize that there are some advantageous aspects of the decentralization of the international lawmaking enterprise. In particular, as Doyle and Massey have observed, decentralization generates opportunities for international organizations to specialize and promotes innovation.[45] For example, some existing international organizations, such as the Food and Agriculture Organization of the United Nations, have substantial specialized technical expertise and legal experience that will make an important contribution to future lawmaking efforts. The growing complexity and interconnectedness of global health problems suggest that certain situations will require moving beyond the "single instrument and single institution" approach.[46] Notably, in the realm of international environmental law, decentralization of the actual lawmaking enterprise among different institutions has been recognized as a critical factor in the regime's widely recognized dynamism.[47]

While all lawmaking functions should not be consolidated under WHO auspices, WHO leadership in coordinating codification and implementation efforts among the diverse global actors actively engaged in health lawmaking could, in theory, foster the development of a more effective, integrated and rational legal regime and, consequently, better collective management of global health concerns. Expectations of WHO's capacity to manage the international health law enterprise must be reasonable and pragmatic, however. It is important to recognize that effective coordination of international legal efforts cannot be guaranteed by WHO or by any other intergovernmental organization. Efficiency of international standards and consistency among different treaties may not always be a priority among states codifying international commitments or the wide array of global health actors, including other autonomous intergovernmental organizations, that influence the international legislative process. Although effective coordination of the increasingly complex international health law regime cannot be assured, an effort to rationalize the international health law enterprise should pursued with reasonable expectations and awareness of the limitations of organizational action.

Organizational and political capacity

A fundamental precept in global governance is that the "the mandate should fit the organization and vice versa."[48] While WHO clearly has the legal capacity to serve as a platform for international health law coordination efforts, a key question that remains is whether or not it has the necessary organizational and political capacity to meet the complex new challenges associated with the international health law leadership mandate proposed in this article.

WHO is unique among United Nations specialized agencies in that the Organization has traditionally neglected the use of international legislative strategies to promote its global public policies. Despite wide-ranging advancements in international lawmaking by numerous intergovernmental organizations since the founding of the United Nations over fifty years ago, until recently, WHO encouraged the formulation of binding international standards in very limited and traditional contexts and never promoted the use of its constitutional authority to serve as a platform for treaty negotiations in any area of public health. A decade ago, I attributed WHO's "traditional conservatism" about the use of legal institutions largely to its cultural predispositions – its organizational culture.[49]

Some observers continue to marginalize the role of WHO in international law, but it is unclear whether and to what extent the conceptualization of WHO's traditional culture is still relevant. Under the leadership of Dr Gro Harlem Brundtland, Director-General of WHO from 1998–2003, there were wide-ranging changes in WHO's traditional organizational behavior. During Brundtland's tenure international law became more widely integrated into WHO's work than at any other time in the Organization's history. Among other things, the Organization initiated efforts to explore practical linkages between health and other realms of international law and develop and influence relevant global public policy. For example, some concrete efforts were made to establish a broader dialogue between WHO and the WTO in order to promote health as a legitimate concern on the global trade agenda and currently WHO holds official observer status on the Council of the WTO and some of its key committees.[50] As a further example, notable strides were made to address the Organization's historical neglect of the linkage between health and human rights.[51] Among other things, the Organization established its first health and human rights adviser post and sought to strengthen is role in providing technical, intellectual and political leadership in the field.[52]

Two international legislative projects were also effectively launched in the last five years. First, the Organization rejuvenated the process of revising and updating the International Health Regulations, potentially a key international instrument in the area of communicable disease control. Second and, perhaps, most significantly, WHO revived and accelerated the process of negotiating and adopting its first convention – the Framework Convention on Tobacco Control – an idea that had been initiated in the early 1990s[53] and formally proposed in an independent feasibility study for WHO in 1995,[54] but had languished prior to the election of Brundtland. With a strong push from WHO in the late 1990s, the idea of a WHO tobacco convention became a viable international negotiation process involving over 160 countries. A final draft of the Convention was adopted by the World Health Assembly, the legislative organ of WHO, in May 2003, just prior to the end of Brundtland's term as Director-General.

As I have described elsewhere, these legal developments may herald a "turning-point": a new era in international health cooperation and, perhaps, an important step towards a new international health law leadership role for

WHO.[55] The Organization's unprecedented consideration of the role of international law and institutions in promoting public health policies in tobacco control and other realms of international health law concerns suggests a rethinking, reformulation and expansion of the organization's traditional scientific, technical approaches to public health.

The question that remains is whether or not the organizational changes initiated under Brundtland, a unique WHO head because of her unconventional background in international lawmaking and diplomacy as well as public health, reflect merely limited and inconsequential deviations from established procedures or key steps towards genuine adaptation or evolution WHO's conservative culture[56] that will be sustained and fostered under WHO's new Director-General, Dr. Jong-wook Lee, and beyond. The process of change in international organizations is stimulated by a variety of factors external and internal to the institution, including organizational leadership. The heads of international organizations typically have considerable agenda-setting power and leadership change and institutional change frequently go hand in hand in international organizations.[57]

At the time of this writing Dr. Lee, a distinguished international health practitioner who had been at WHO for a substantial number of years prior to his election as Director-General, has been in his new office for less than a year. It is, therefore, perhaps too soon to conclude whether or not his administration is committed to expanding WHO's leadership in international health law and whether or not new practices in this realm will be successfully institutionalized and integrated into the regular processes of the Organization. However, in a perhaps noteworthy early signal of Lee's support for international legal approaches for public health, on July 30, 2003 the Organization announced internal structural changes, including the creation of a new department incorporating ethics, trade, human rights and law. Prior to Lee's restructuring of the institution, WHO's work on these areas was conducted by discrete departments with limited connections to one another and substantial overlaps in mandates. The consolidation of these realms under a single department at WHO has the potential to significantly rationalize, coordinate, and advance WHO's work on international health law. More importantly, however, current conditions of increasing financial stringency at WHO, including increased reliance on the private-sector, may serve to limit or inhibit WHO's autonomy to promote the advancement of international health law.

Ultimately, WHO's capacity to fulfill the leadership mandate described depends on political support from its member states, particularly the major powers who provide the majority of the Organization's budget. The willingness of governments to support this mandate will depend on factors external and internal to WHO. For example, consistency of legal regimes may not always be a priority, or even a goal, for states facing competing interests (principally from private-sector actors). Furthermore, the broadened mandate has important implications for WHO's budget and resources, which must be supported by states who may also face conflicting financial priorities. As described, WHO has been operating under the conditions of a declining budget in real terms, limiting its autonomy to effect decisions independent of its Member States and compounding pressure on the Organization to institute reforms and implement programmes that are responsive to the demands of key donors.

Governmental support of an expanded international health law mandate, in the near future, may also depend partly on assessment of the institution's existing strengths and past successes in contributing to the codification and administration of global health law. To this end, the 2003 WHO Framework Convention on Tobacco Control, the first treaty to be adopted under the auspices of the WHO in its fifty plus year history, may serve as a critical test of WHO's organizational and political capacity to provide leadership in future international health law efforts. The treaty will enter into force for state parties if and when it is ratified by forty states.

Much has been written about the effectiveness of the FCTC negotiation process in promoting national and international tobacco control.[58] However, viewed as an international instrument, there are number of aspects of the FCTC that raise the concern that the treaty itself may have limited impact in promoting effective national and international action for tobacco control, including the elaboration of detailed protocol agreements, assuming it ultimately enters into force. The FCTC is modeled upon the framework convention-protocol approach, an approach to international lawmaking made popular in the realm of international environmental law.[59] Although there is no single definition of a framework convention, such treaties tend to establish broad obligations and concrete institutions of global governance that provide a platform to promote negotiation and codification of detailed obligations in future protocol agreements. While the FCTC tends to establish broad obligations, the text is lacking many of the core institutional arrangements found at times in framework conventions, such as a prescribed annual or biannual meeting of the contracting parties, which serve as the bedrock for an ongoing international legislative enterprise.

Despite some of the manifest limitations of the final text of the FCTC, governments' evaluations of WHO's role in the FCTC process are unlikely to depend on the substantive outcome of the FCTC – whether the Convention and its proposed protocols are relatively effective or ineffective at promoting multilateral coordination to counter the tobacco pandemic or even if the FCTC ever enters into force. Intergovernmental organizations have important catalytic functions in treaty development, including the preparation of draft texts of the treaty. Ultimately, however, international organizations have limited capacity to influence the factors that encourage states to adopt, ratify, and implement effective commitments.

Rather, the willingness of states to use WHO as a platform, catalyst, and coordinator for international health law negotiations in the near future may depend on governments' final evaluations of WHO's effectiveness as a co-ordinator and manager of the FCTC negotiations and, potentially, the treaty regime. That is, governments are likely to collectively assess whether or not WHO provided the administrative coordination and public health expertise necessary to advance complex, multilateral negotiations in international health. Most importantly, perhaps, governments may evaluate WHO's capacity to address global health law matters in the near future on the basis of their collective assessment of whether or not WHO was able to serve as an honest broker for all states participating in the negotiation exercise. Some degree of tension between international organizations and their member states is commonplace in contemporary treaty negotiations. However, the states' col-lective judgment about the ability of an international organization to function as a neutral platform for all participating states is a critical element of the organization's ongoing political capacity to serve effectively as a center for international debate and codification.

In any assessment of WHO's performance as platform for the negotiations of the FCTC there are bound to be differences in judgment. Even so, perhaps many would agree that the institution's performance presents a mixed picture with some important successes and some major weaknesses. To this end, it is perhaps notable that in 2001, at the height of the FCTC negotiations, two new international legislative projects with potentially significant public health implications were initiated, the proposed convention banning the reproductive cloning of human beings and, as will be discussed further herein, a proposed Comprehensive and Integral International Convention on Protection and Promotion of the Rights and Dignity of Persons with Disabilities. Although WHO has the legal authority to serve as a platform for the negotiation of these proposed treaties, in both cases states chose an alternative forum.[60] Perhaps notable as well, in the final text of the FCTC adopted in May 2003 Member States included a provision that granted WHO the status of interim treaty secretariat with the permanent secretariat to be designated after the treaty enters into force. For a variety of reasons WHO is ultimately likely to be awarded the permanent secretariat if the treaty enters into force. Nevertheless, the FCTC provision on WHO interim secretariat status is rather unusual since specialized agencies tend to be customarily granted permanent secretariat status without such an interim period in treaties negotiated solely under their auspices.

Taking the agenda forward: recommendations for WHO global health governance leadership

Global health problems pose important legal challenges for the international community. The increasingly globalized nature of public health problems calls for an unprecedented degree of international cooperation and leadership by the World Health Organization.

It is, of course, important that expectations for organizational action in this realm remain realistic. As described herein, WHO has highly limited experience and resources in international health lawmaking and coordination. In other realms of international concern, the capacity of international organizations in international lawmaking and mobilization has developed over a generation. Consequently, it may take years before WHO is able to build the requisite expertise to provide maximum leadership in international health law cooperation, mobilization, and codification. Further, as described above, effective coordination of international legal efforts cannot be guaranteed by WHO or by any other intergovernmental organization in a world of autonomous states. Recognizing these inherent limitations, an effort to rationalize the international health law enterprise is essential and should be advanced.

It should be recognized that concerns about the fragmented nature of the legal system and the absence of a coordinated approach to norm-creating process are not unique, of course, to international health or even international environmental law. Rather, concerns about conflicts among norms and conflicts of legal jurisdiction cut across a variety of international legal disciplines. A variety of commentators have urged that international organizations should forge more effective linkages to promote coherent norm development. To this end, increased attention is being paid to the various institutional and legal mechanisms that can be used to enhance inter-organizational collaboration, including, most notably, organizational leadership and oversight structures. This article cannot fully describe the strategies that WHO could use to promote rational management of international legal developments. However, scholarship in international environmental law suggests some important starting points.[61] In particular, WHO can provide leadership and promote more coherent and effective development of international health law by endeavoring to serve as coordinator, catalyst and, where appropriate, platform for important international health agreements.

Promoting global dialogue and agenda setting

WHO can catalyze more effective and coordinated international health cooperation by promoting global awareness of international health law concerns and contributing to the "agenda-setting"[62] that is acutely needed in this realm.

One of the major challenges in effective management of public health problems of international legal concern is mobilizing public awareness as well as national political commitment and action. Global health problems battle for political attention against other international issues. At the same time, public health remains low on the priority list for national action or international cooperation in many states.

WHO can establish a key role for itself in catalyzing international agreements and national action by, among other things, establishing a mechanism of educating and informing national policy-makers of critical public health issues ripe for international legal action. Among other things, WHO can institutionalize an open and inclusive process for identifying priority issues for international legal cooperation and promoting them among relevant constituencies. By identifying priorities for international legal action and coordinating relevant public health and legal information, WHO can serve a critical role and meet an essential need by building global dialogue and educating governments, other global health actors, including other inter-governmental organizations, and the public about global health issues of legal concern. Critical to the success of such a process is the establishment of a mechanism to extend the dialogue to national policy-makers beyond ministries of health that form the traditional core of WHO's constituency. Effective coordination of such a process with other relevant intergovernmental organizations may serve to expand the network of national actors involved in the global heath law dialogue, promote national awareness and commitment, and contribute to the rationale development of the international legal regime.

In addition, constructing a more effective dialogue between states and the web of other global health actors will be a critical component of better collective management of international health law in the future. The rise of new global health actors, including civil society, religious groups, foundations, the private sector and broad international health coalitions has considerably complexified health governance and highlighted the limitations of the traditional state-centered focus of international law. Indeed, the complex network of governance structures that are burgeoning around the legal structures being established by the state-centered system indicates the need for an inclusive approach to engagement with new global health actors.

As a highly prominent international organization, WHO has the opportunity to play a pivotal role in building a dialogue among states and other health actors and in setting and launching the international health law agenda. Through these and other measures, WHO may promote global dialogue, build effective partnerships and stimulate more coordinated and, perhaps, more effective governmental and intergovernmental action.

Monitoring international health law developments and promoting coordinated institutional action

WHO can also promote effective consideration, better collective management, and development of international legal matters by monitoring and actively participating, where appropriate, in the increasing array of treat efforts initiated in other forums that have important implications for global public health. For example, in December 2001, the General Assembly of the United Nations established an Ad Hoc Committee to consider proposals on a Comprehensive and Integral International Convention on Protection and

Promotion of the Rights and Dignity of Persons with Disabilities. As a specialized agency of the United Nations system, WHO could contribute to this codification effort as an official observer to the negotiation sessions. However, the Organization did not contribute to the early sessions of the Ad Hoc Committee. WHO could make a significant contribution to this codification effort, and the development of international health law generally, by monitoring the legislative process and by informing and educating state delegations participating in negotiations about relevant public health and legal information.

Among other things, WHO could provide details of the global incidence of disabilities, and public health considerations involved in human rights issues of accommodation and access for persons with disabilities. Moreover, WHO may be able to broaden the dialogue and promote a comprehensive public health approach to disability by bringing forth information and stimulating global public debate on aspects of prevention, treatment and rehabilitation that may be ripe for national practice and, potentially, for inclusion in the text of the proposed treaty.

Further, as described above, WHO should incorporate other intergovernmental organizations with relevant mandates in the global dialogue on global health law priorities to promote more coordinated and rational development of the legal regime.

Platform for treaty negotiations

WHO can also effectively steer intergovernmental health cooperation by serving, where appropriate, as a platform for the codification and implementation of international legal agreements. The recent experience of biotechnology indicates that unless WHO plays a legislative role critical global public health issues may not be addressed in a timely and effective manner and may be subject to excessive institutional fragmentation and critical gaps. WHO is the only public international organization that brings together the institutional mandate, legal authority, and public health expertise for the codification of treaties that principally address global public health concerns.

Given the problems of legal jurisdiction raised by issue linkage and overlapping legal authority among various international organizations, a thorny question is which types of issues will benefit from codification under WHO's auspices. This needs to be decided on a case-by-ease basis and there may always be differences in judgment. However, WHO is the appropriate institutional setting for the elaboration of legal standards encompassing issues, such as tobacco control, that overlap with other realms of international concern (such as human rights, trade, agriculture, customs, and the environment) but are at the heart of the public health mandate of WHO and are beyond the central mission of another public international organization.

Conclusion

International health law can make an important contribution to the framework for global cooperation and coordination on public health matters in an increasingly interdependent world. An essential component of global health governance in the twenty-first century is an effective and politically responsive institution to promote collective supervision as well as the coherent development of this rapidly evolving field. The extent to which WHO can and will be able to provide such leadership in international health law will have an important influence on the collective ability of intergovernmental organizations to promote effective global cooperation to advance global public health.

References

1. A. L. Taylor, "Global Governance, International Law and WHO: Looking Towards the Future," *Bulletin of the World Health Organization* 80 (2002): 975–80.
2. K. Lee, "Shaping the Future of Global Health Cooperation: Where Can We Go From Here?" *Lancet* 351 (1998): 899–902.
3. K. Lee, "An Overview of Global Health and Environmental Risks," in L. Parsons and G. Lister, eds., *Global Health: A Local Issue* (London: The Nuffield Trust, 2000): 34–46.
4. F. Grad, "Public Health Law: Its Forms, Function, Future and Ethical Parameters," *International Digest of Health Legislation* 49 (1998): 19–40. A. L. Taylor, "Making the World Health Organization Work: A Legal Framework for Universal Access to the Conditions for Health, *American Journal of Law and Medicine* 18 (1992):301–46.
5. G. A. Gellart, et. al., "The Obsolescence of Distinct Domestic and International Health Sectors," *Journal of Public Health Policy* 10 (1989): 421–25.
6. R. Dodgson, K. Lee, and N. Drager, *Global Health Governance: A Conceptual Review,* (London: Center on Global Change & Health, London School of Hygiene & Tropical Medicine, 2002).
7. N. Drager and R. Beaglehole, "Globalization: Changing the Public Health Landscape," *Bulletin of the World Health Organization* 79 (2001): 803–09; D. Woodward, et. al., "Globalization and Health: A Framework for Analysis and Action, "*Bulletin of the World Health Organization,* 79 (2001): 875–81; A. Woodward, et. al., "Protecting Human Health in a Changing World: the Role of Social and Economic Development," *Bulletin of the World Health Organization,* (2000):1148–55; Dodgson, Lee, and Drager, *supra* note 7.
8. D. Nynar, "Towards Global Governance," in *Governing Globalization* (Oxford: Oxford University Press, 2002): 3–18.
9. R. Adorno, "Biomedicine and International Human Rights Law: In Search of a Global Agenda," *Bulletin of the World Health Organization* 80 (2002): 959–63; G. J. Annas, L. B. Andrews, and R. M. Isasi, "Protecting the Endangered Human: Towards and International Treaty Prohibiting Cloning and Inheritable Alterations, *American Journal of Law and Medicine* 28 (2002):151–78; A. L. Taylor, "The Contribution of International Law to a Global Bioethic: The Proposed

United Nations Convention Against the Reproductive Cloning of Human Beings," in J. Andreson, ed., *Once in a Lifetime: Interdisciplinary Perspectives on Cloning and Genetic Technologies* (Cambridge: Cambridge University Press [in press]).

10. P. Sands, "Sustainable Development: Treaty, Custom and the Cross-fertilization of International Law," in A. Boyle, and D. Freestone, eds., *Sustainable Development and International Law* (Oxford: Oxford University Press, 1999):39–60.

11. J. E. Alvarez, ed., "Symposium: The Boundaries of the WTO," *American Journal of International Law* 96 (2002): 1 Taylor, infra, note 23. 158.

12. Commission on Human Security, *Human Security Now: Protecting and Empowering People* (2003), *at* <www.humansecurity-chs.org.>

13. A. Woodward, *supra* note 11; G. H. Brundtland, Address to the World Business Council for Sustainable Development: our Common Future and Rio 10 years after: How far Have We Come and Where Should we be Going? November 4, 1999, Berlin, *available at* <http://www.who.int/directorgeneral/speeches/1999/english/19991104_berlin.html.>

14. Taylor, *supra* note 1.

15. World Health Organization, *WTO Agreements and Public Health*, (Geneva: World Health Organization, 2002).

16. Sands, *supra* note 11.

17. H. D. C. Abbing, "Health, Human Rights, and Health Law: the Move Towards Internationalization, with a Special Emphasis on Europe," *International Digest of Health Legislation*, 49 (1998): 101–12; S. Gruskin and D. Tarantola, "Health and Human Rights," in Detels, *supra*. note 4, at 311–57; A. L. Taylor et. al., "International Health Law Instruments: An Overview," in R. Detels, et. al., eds., *Oxford Textbook of Public Health: The Scope of Public Health* (Oxford: Oxford University Press, 2002): 359–86.

18. Gruskin and Tarantola, *supra* note 18.

19. *Id.*

20. Grad, *supra* note 1.

21. *Id.*

22. Taylor, *supra* note 23.

23. L. C. Chen, T. G. Evans, and R. A. Cash, "Health as a Global Public Good," in I. Kaul, I. Grunberg, and M. Stern eds., *Global Public Goods: International Cooperation in the 21st Century* (London: United Nations Development Programme, 1999): 284–305; R. Smith, et. al. eds., *Global Public Goods for Health: Health Economic and Public Health Perspectives* (Oxford, Oxford University Press, 2002).

24. P. C. Szasz, "International Norm-Making," in E. B. Weiss, ed., *Environmental Change and International Law* (Tokyo: United Nations University Press, 1992): 340–84.

25. Taylor et. al., *supra* note 23.

26. Chen, *supra* note 24.

27. *Id.*; K. Buse and G. Walt, "Global Public-Private Partnerships: Part 1 – a New Development in Health?" *Bulletin of the World Health Organization* 78 (2000): 549–61. M. R. Reich, ed. *Public–Private Partnerships for Public Health* (Cambridge: Harvard University Press, 2002).

28. Dodgson, Lee, and Drager *supra* note 7.

29. Chen, *supra* note 24.

30. Dodgson, Lee, and Drager, *supra* note 7.
31. G. Walt, "Globalisation of International Health," *Lancet* 351 (1998): 434–37.
32. D. Kapur, "Processes of Change in International Organizations," in Nynar, *supra* note 9, at 334–55.
33. S. Charnovitz, "A World Environment Organization," *Columbia Journal of Environmental Law* 27 (2002): 323–62; M. W. Doyle and R. I. Massey, "Intergovernmental Organizations and the Environment: Looking Towards the Future," in P. R. Chasek, ed., *The Global Environment in the Twenty-First Century: Prospects for International Cooperation*, (Tokyo: United Nations University Press, 2000) 411–26; P. Birnie and A. Boyle, *International Law and the Environment*, (Oxford: Oxford University Press 2002).
34. P. M. Haas, R. O. Keohane, and M. A. Levy, *Institutions for the Earth: Sources of Effective International Environmental Protection*, (Cambridge: MIT Press, 1993).
35. Charnovitz, *supra* note 34.
36. A. L. Taylor. "Globalization and Biotechnology: UNESCO and an International Strategy to Advance Human Rights and Public Health," *American Journal of Law and Medicine* 25 (1999): 479–541.
37. See, e.g., United Nations Commission for Human Rights, Resolution 2001/71 on Human Rights and Bioethics, April 25, 2001.
38. U. N. Wire, *Discussion of U. N. Treaty on Human Cloning Delayed Two Years*, November 6, 2003.
39. Taylor, *supra* note 10.
40. S. D. Murphy, "Biotechnology and International Law," *Harvard Journal of International Law* 42 (2001): 47–139; S. Pridan-Frank, "Human Genomics: A Challenge to the Rules of the Game of International Law," *Columbia Journal of Transnational Law* 40 (2001): 619–76.
41. *Id.*
42. J. P. Trachtman, "Institutional Linkage: Transcending "trade and . . . ," *American Journal of International Law* 96 (2002): 77–93.
43. Taylor, *supra* note 23; G. L. Burci and C. H. Vignes, "World Health Organization," in *International Encyclopedia of Laws* (Dordrecht: Kluwer [in press]).
44. Doyle and Massey, *supra* note 34.
45. *Id.*
46. P. C. Szasz, "IAEA Safeguards: Sanctions," in P. C. Szasz, *Selected Essays on Understanding International Institutions and the Legislative Process* (New York: Transnational Publishers 2001): 201–20.
47. *Id.*
48. Doyle and Massey, *supra* note 34.
49. Taylor, *supra* note 5.
50. Dodgson, Lee, and Drager, *supra* note 7.
51. Taylor, *supra* note 5.
52. World Health Organization, "The-State-of-the-Art: A Human Rights Based Approach in WHO," Report to the Second Interagency Workshop on Implementing a Human Rights-based Approach in the Context of UN Reform, Stamford, USA, May 5–7, 2003.
53. R. Roemer, J. Larvivier, and A. Taylor, "The Origins of the WHO Framework Convention on Tobacco Control," forthcoming in *American Journal of Public Health*.

54. A. L. Taylor and R. Roemer, "An International Strategy for Tobacco Control," (Geneva: World Health Organization: 1996) (WHO document WHO/PSA/96.6).
55. Taylor, *supra* note 1.
56. *Id.*
57. Kapure, *supra* note 33.
58. Roemer, LaRiviere, and Taylor, *supra* note 54.
59. Taylor and Roemer, *supra* note 55.
60. G. L. Burci and C. H. Vignes, *The World Health Organization* (The Hague: Kluwer Law International, 2004).
61. Doyle and Massey, *supra* note 34.
62. *Id.*

59

THE GLOBALIZATION OF PUBLIC HEALTH, I

Threats and opportunities

Derek Yach and Douglas Bettcher

Source: *American Journal of Public Health*, 88:5 (1998), 735–44.

Abstract

The globalization of public health poses new threats to health but also holds important opportunities in the coming century. This commentary identifies the major threats and opportunities presented by the process of globalization and emphasizes the need for transnational public health approaches to take advantage of the positive aspects of global change and to minimize the negative ones. Transnational public health issues are areas of mutual concern for the foreign policies of all countries. These trends indicate a need for cross-national comparisons (e.g., in the areas of health financing and policy development) and for the development of a transnational research agenda in public health.

A web of trade, investment, diplomacy, grassroots action and telecommunications is forging a global village from which our sense of commitment to the other half is strengthened.[1]

Globalization and liberalisation are a fast, new express train and countries have been told that all they need to do was to get on aboard. . . . Those that fail to get aboard will find themselves marginalised in the world community and in the world economy.[2]

The double face of globalization, one promising and the other threatening, is a fact of life as humanity is being catapulted into a more interdependent future and a new millennium. Globalization not only refers to economic processes or the development of global institutions but also describes the interconnection between "individual life" and "global futures."[3] More specifically, globalization is defined as the process of increasing economic, political, and social interdependence and global integration that takes place as capital, traded goods, persons, concepts, images, ideas, and values diffuse across state boundaries.[4] The roots of globalization can be traced back to the industrial revolution and the laissez-faire economic policies of the 19th century. However, the globalization of the late 20th century is assuming a magnitude—and taking on patterns—unprecedented in world history.[5,6] It not only embraces the liberalization of financial markets and trade but encompasses transboundary problems such as destruction of the ozone layer.[7]

The link between the lives of individuals and the global context of development is evident in another face of globalization, an often forgotten one: global health futures are directly or indirectly associated with the transnational economic, social, and technological changes taking place in the world. As a result, the domestic and international spheres of public health policy are becoming more intertwined and inseparable.

Since the achievement and maintenance of the health of populations is an integral part of sustainable development, the health impacts of globalization, both positive and negative, are key policy issues. Health development in the 21st century must take advantage of the opportunities afforded by global change and, at the same time, minimize the risks and threats associated with globalization so that the dramatic improvements in the health of the world's population achieved in this century can be maintained and advanced in the next one. The main theme of this paper is that the challenges posed by globalization make collective action imperative and mutually beneficial.

The globalization of public health

The health benefits to developing countries of increased trade, diffusion of appropriate technologies, and acceptance of human rights throughout the world were emphasized by Roemer and Roemer in 1990.[8] According to the Roemers' analysis, cross-national exchanges have facilitated the diffusion of technological innovations such as effective methods of contraception, techniques for obtaining safe drinking water, low-cost refrigeration, efficient transport and communication technologies, and new therapeutic agents that can effectively treat leprosy, schistosomiasis, trachoma, onchocerciasis (river blindness), and many other diseases. Nevertheless, the Roemers also recognized some of the negative aspects of trade liberalization for health, such as the US threat of trade sanctions against 4 Asian countries in the 1980s if American cigarette companies were not given free access.[8]

The perception of the world has shifted a great deal in the few years since the Roemers' important commentary. The end of the Cold War and of a world characterized by 2 competing social/political systems has unleashed massive global changes. With these changes, our health development paradigm —in other words, our road map for seeing the world—must also shift. This transformed world is characterized by increased competition for market share, liberalization of trade and finance, and global communications. In the health sector, for example, the liberalization of health services under the provisions of the General Agreement on Trade in Services has the potential to blur the boundaries between national and "globalized" health sectors. (The General Agreement on Trade in Services is the first set of multilateral rules governing fair and nondiscriminatory trade in services. It was one of the major components of the Uruguay Round package.) Transformations such as these are generating "powerful transnational dynamics" and suggest that we are on the verge of a "global health village" in which some health problems primarily concern particular countries, while others are of common concern.[9] Moreover, national health systems are becoming transnationalized: the ease and rapidity of communications have facilitated the diffusion of ideas, ideologies, and policy concerns relating to health care (as well as diseases), thereby fostering a global culture of reform.[10]

The domain of globalization includes many interconnected phenomena and risks that affect the sustainability of health systems and the well-being of the populations of both developing and industrialized countries. Although not intended to be a complete list, the transnationalization of health risks and disease is depicted in Table 1. (Refer to a recent article by John Last[11] that evaluates the quality of evidence for various health-related features of global change.)

At the same time, it should not be assumed that the implications of globalization for public health are all negative. Seriously addressing the risks and negative aspects of increasing global interdependence could help to sustain the process of economic and political globalization. Many of the risks cited in Table 1 could be turned into opportunities for improving our global health future. For instance, if modern information technologies are accessible and affordable to developing countries, the potential benefits are extensive: the uses of modern information technology in health include telemedicine, interactive health networks, communication services between health workers, human resource development and continuing education, and distance learning.[12] However, making these technologies available in the poorest communities of the world may require special government incentives, including incentives that could be at odds with norms governing liberalization of trade and removal of special subsidies.[13]

Adoption of proactive policies that protect essential health system functions from downsizing and privatization would ensure that core components of national health systems are protected as a matter of public safety. Another positive intervention would involve the global media, which could play a major role in health promotion in terms of preventing a portion of the estimated 10 million deaths per year (70% in developing countries) that are expected

Table 1 Health and global change.

Global Transnational Factor	Consequences and Probable Impact on Health Status
Macroeconomic prescriptions	
Structural adjustment policies and downsizing[14]	Marginalization, poverty, inadequate decreased social safety nets[a]
Structural and chronic unemployment	Higher morbidity and mortality rates[b]
Trade	
Tobacco, alcohol, and psychoactive drugs	Increased marketing, availability, and use[b]
Dumping of unsafe or ineffective pharmaceuticals	Ineffective or harmful therapy[b]
Trade of contaminated foodstuffs/feed	Spread of infectious diseases across borders[b]
Travel	
More than 1 million persons crossing borders/day	Infectious disease transmission and export of harmful lifestyles (e.g., high-risk sexual behavior)[c]
Migration and demographic	
Increased refugee populations and rapid population growth	Ethnic and civil conflict and environmental degradation[c]
Food security	
Increased demand for food in rapidly growing economies, for example, countries in Asia	Structural food shortages as less food aid is available and the poorest countries of the world are unable to pay hard currency[b]
Increase in global food trade continuing to outstrip increases in food production, and food aid continuing to decline[15]	Food shortages in marginalized areas of the world; increased migration and civil unrest[a]

Table 1 *(cont'd)*

Global Transnational Factor	Consequences and Probable Impact on Health Status
Environmental degradation and unsustainable consumption patterns	
Resource depletion, especially access to fresh water	Global and local environmental health impact[b]
Water and air pollution	Epidemics and potential violence within and between countries (water wars)
Ozone depletion and increases in ultraviolet radiation	Introduction of toxins into human food chain and respiratory disorders
	Immunosuppression, skin cancers, and cataracts[16]
Accumulation of greenhouse gases and global warming	Major shifts in infectious disease patterns and vector distribution (e.g., malaria), death from heat waves, increased trauma due to floods and storms, and worsening food shortages and malnutrition in many regions of the world[16]
Technology	
Patent protection of new technologies under the trade-related aspects of intellectual property rights agreement	Benefits of new technologies developed in the global market are unaffordable to the poor[c]
Communications and media	
Global marketing of harmful commodities such as tobacco	Active promotion of health-damaging practices[b]
Foreign policies based on national self-interest, xenophobia, and protectionism	Threat to multilateralism and global cooperation required to address shared transnational health concerns[c]

[a]Possible short-term problem that could reverse in time.
[b]Long-term negative impact.
[c]Great uncertainty.

to occur from smoking-related diseases in year 2020.[17] The global media could also help to reverse the disastrous effects that smoking-related deaths will have on the health and economies of both developing and industrialized countries.

Policy implications

The policy implications of globalization and transnational trends were one of the major themes of last year's Denver Summit of the Eight (G-8). The leaders of the major industrialized countries observed the following:

> The process of globalization, a major factor underlying the growth of world prosperity in the last fifty years, is now advancing rapidly and broadly. More openness and integration across the global economy create opportunities for increased prosperity. . . . At the same time, globalization may create new challenges. The increasing openness and interdependence of our economies, with deep trade linkages and ever greater flows of private capital, means that problems in one country can spill over more easily to affect the rest.[18]

The G-8 summit stressed that countries must collaborate in confronting shared problems such as climate changes, environmental health issues, the spread of infectious diseases, trafficking in illicit drugs, and ethical issues surrounding technological developments such as cloning. Unilateral efforts will not be successful.

As the world becomes more interdependent, the objectives of national foreign policies will need to be reexamined; traditional concepts of national security based on the ability to resist armed aggression are being supplemented by notions of "shared human security."[19] For instance, the control and surveillance of communicable diseases has become a matter of preventive diplomacy.[20] In a similar vein, World Health Organization Director-General Hiroshi Nakajima notes that

> foreign policies based on narrow interests of isolationism and pro-tectionism will reduce the creative spirit of international scientific investigation. . . . The global [health] development strategies needed to address these complex and inter-related problems will require innovative, intersectoral interventions, involving a high degree of international cooperation and political will.[21]

As part of renewing the health-for-all policy for the 21st century, the World Health Organization proposes that governments will need to work together to develop a broader base for international relations and collaborative strategies that will place greater emphasis on international health security. A draft of a new policy being developed by the organization emphasizes that addressing the threats to health security should include the health consequences of trade in commodities harmful to health, violations of human rights, transnational disease threats, environmental degradation, migration and population growth, and inequities between and within countries.[22]

These shared areas of foreign policy concern must be translated into well-defined strategies. The following are needed to deal with the major transnational health issues[6,22]:

- Global intersectoral action through transnational cooperation and partnerships, for example, between the health sector and trade/finance sectors both within countries and at the international level.
- An enhanced role for international legal instruments, standard setting, and global norms.
- More comprehensive forms of global vigilance, research, monitoring, and assessment. Information on health status and the global determinants of health is vital for defining future actions in a rapidly changing policy environment.
- Global research programs that concentrate on developing cost-effective technologies to improve the status of the poor.
- Human resource development in certain underdeveloped areas (e.g., public health law).
- Ongoing comparative assessments and cross fertilization of experiences regarding health system reform.

In conclusion, national health systems are increasingly being influenced by global factors that transcend state borders. These trends call for cross-national comparisons of health systems; this will allow for the sharing of information and the development of a transnational research agenda. Moreover, the globalization of public health will act as a strong impetus for global actions to address these areas of shared concern.

Acknowledgments

We wish to thank Dr F. S. Antezana, Deputy Director-General AI, World Health Organization, for his intellectual input and support of this work; Milton I. Roemer and Ruth Roemer for their comments on an earlier version of this paper; the Rockefeller Foundation for hosting a meeting in Bellagio (March 1997) at which an earlier version was presented; and the Canadian donors (Canadian International Development Agency, Canadian Public Health Association, and Health Canada) for their support of the International Meeting on Intersectoral Action for Health (April 1997), which served as a forum for discussing the general conceptual framework of this paper.

References

1. Speth J. G. Europe provides a guide to shrinking the world's rich-poor gap. *International Herald Tribune*. February 3, 1997:6.

2. Corea G. Globalization—the opportunities and dangers for Sri Lanka. *Daily News* (Colombo, Sri Lanka). December 11, 1996:8

3. Giddens A. Anthony Giddens on globalization. *UNRISD News*. 1997;15:4–5.

4. Hurrell A., Woods N. Globalization and inequality. *Millennium J Int Stud*. 1995;24(3):447–470.

5. Ruggie R. At home abroad, abroad at home—international liberalization and domestic stability in the new world economy. *Millennium J Int Stud*. 1995;24(3):507–526.

6. Bettcher D. *Think and Act Globally and Intersectorally to Protect National Health*. Geneva, Switzerland: World Health Organization; 1997. WHO document PPE/PAC/97.2.

7. Bonvin J. Globalization and linkages: challenges for development policy. *Development*. 1997;20(2):39–42.

8. Roemer M., Roemer R. Global health, national development, and the role of government. *Am J Public Health*. 1990;80:1188–1192.

9. Chen L., Bell D., Bates L. World health and institutional change. In: *Pocantico Retreat, Enhancing the Performance of International Health Institutions*. New York, NY: Rockefeller Foundation; 1996:9–21.

10. Altenstetter C., Björkman J. W. Globalized concepts and localized practice: convergence and divergence in national health policy reforms. In: Altenstetter C., Björkman J. W., eds. *Health Policy Reform, National Variations and Globalization*. London, England: Macmillan; 1997:1–16.

11. Last J. M. Human health in a changing world. In: *Public Health and Human Ecology*. 2nd ed. Stamford, Conn: Appleton & Lange; 1998:395–425.

12. *Health Informatics and Telemedicine*. Geneva, Switzerland: World Health Organization; 1997. WHO document EB99/INF.DOC./9.

13. Adams O. *International Trade in Health Services: Some Key Issues*. Geneva, Switzerland: World Health Organization; 1997.

14. Martikainen P., Valkonen T. Excess mortality of unemployed men and women during a period of increasing unemployment. *Lancet*. 1996;348:909–912.

15. *Food Security Assessment*. Rome, Italy: Food and Agricultural Organization; 1996. FAO document WFS 96/TECH/7.

16. McMichael A. J., Haines A., Sloof R., Kovats S., eds. *Climate Change and Human Health—An Assessment Prepared by a Task Group on Behalf of the WHO, WMO, and UNEP*. Geneva, Switzerland: World Health Organization; 1996.

17. *Tobacco Alert: The Tobacco Epidemic, a Global Public Health Emergency*. Geneva, Switzerland: World Health Organization; 1996.

18. *Final Communique of the Denver Summit of the Eight*. Denver, Colo: Group of Eight Countries; 1997.

19. Alleyne G. Health and national security. *Bull Pan Am Health Organ*. 1996;30:158–163.

20. O'Brien E. The diplomatic implications of emerging diseases. In: Cahill K. M., ed. *Preventive Diplomacy*. New York, NY: Basic Books; 1996:244–268.

21. Nakajima H. Global health threats and foreign policy. *Brown J World Aff*. 1997;IV:319–332.

22. *Health for All in the 21st Century*. Geneva, Switzerland: World Health Organization; 1998. WHO document EB101/8.

60

THE POLITICS OF GLOBAL HEALTH GOVERNANCE

Whatever happened to "Health for all by the year 2000"?

Caroline Thomas and Martin Weber

Source: *Global Governance*, 10:2 (2004), 187–205.

The discourse on global health governance (GHG) has received a significant boost in the context of the renewed efforts to tackle the global acquired immunodeficiency syndrome (AIDS) pandemic. Although there is a large body of literature that deals with questions relevant to GHG from the perspectives of various issues and interest groups, the discipline of international relations (IR) has proved slower in providing systematic approaches to interpreting and analyzing GHG. There are various reasons for this, but among the most significant is probably the general paucity of the IR global governance literature to date.[1] A great amount of scholarly effort is still directed primarily at clarifying global governance conceptually, at amending existing theoretical approaches toward its inclusion, and at developing methodologies that reflect these theoretical concerns adequately. The case of GHG offers a number of interesting insights that ought to advance conceptual as well as political debates.

In this article, we approach the problems of GHG by considering the competing political projects that underpin respective GHG conceptions, the actors that represent, defend, and advance them, and the structures that frame debates and policy initiatives. We begin by briefly outlining the scope and nature of the current global health situation, arguing that the main challenge for contemporary GHG is to reestablish within the policy environment the linkage between specific disease-oriented health care interventions and the underlying socioeconomic context. In the next part, we analyze the changing nature and orientation of GHG over the past twenty-five years, using the declarations made at Alma Ata in 1978 and Okinawa in 2000 as signposts indicating two very different trends in GHG. Within this section, we explore the political

148

legacies of two phases of global governance, in broad-brush terms of social democracy and neoliberalism, as a backdrop against which to chart, analyze, and interpret shifts in the GHG discourses. In the final part of the article, we explore recent inputs into the GHG discourse from a wide spectrum of actors, ranging from the World Health Organization (WHO) through to activist nongovernmental organizations (NGOs). We suggest that in their varying hues, these actors have attempted to reintroduce the wider social concerns constitutive of a more integrated approach to health care, which would locate specific interventions within a broader project of socioeconomic transformation.

Setting the scene: the challenge for GHG

To an outsider looking in, advances made in responding to health challenges seem inadequate when considered against the exacerbated health risks and problems faced by large populations. As Gro Harlem Brundtland formulated the problem in her address to the World Health Assembly (WHA) in 1998, "Never have so many had such broad and advanced access to healthcare. But never have so many been denied access to health."[2] Crucially, "growing health disparities between the world's wealthy and the world's poor" offset the measurable advances in global health care, such as a general rise in life expectancy from forty-eight years in 1955 to sixty-six in 1998.[3]

Poverty and inequality continue to provide the key context of terminal health problems, with the immediate cause for most deaths among the poor being a disease for which there is a cure. The WHO suggests that 50–90 percent of drugs in the developing and transitional economies are paid for out of pocket, reaffirming that the burden falls heaviest on the poor.[4]

The inequality issue has been highlighted in the context of the recent debate over human immunodeficiency virus (HIV) and poverty—informed significantly by the controversial remarks on the causes of HIV-related deaths by Thabo Mbeki—and the ensuing campaign for broad-based access to antiretroviral (ARV) drugs. Perhaps more than any other disease, HIV/AIDS reflects entrenched and growing global disparities, inequality, and exclusion, together with a salient retrenchment of a North-South divide.[5]

The most challenging problem for GHG, and one that is certainly not composed of but rather exposed more starkly by the AIDS crisis, remains the reestablishment of the linkage in the policy environment between disease-oriented health care intervention and the broader socioeconomic environment. Inequality of access to health mirrors broader socioeconomic inequality. It is in this sense that the GHG agenda must engage with the implications of a health policy environment that has been shaped pervasively by inequalities reproduced through global economic governance.

How are these challenges reflected in current approaches to GHG and to what extent are they likely to be met? In the next section, we reconstruct briefly the different legacies of two phases in global governance, each of which respectively spawned distinctly different academic and policy approaches. We argue that the issues raised between these two clusters are constitutive of the current crisis in GHG.

GHG discourses: from Alma Ata to Okinawa

The aim of this section is to explore and analyze the changing nature and orientation of GHG from the Alma Ata conference of 1978 to the Okinawa G8 summit of 2000. Each of these occasions resulted in major statements of GHG. However, to do this, it is first necessary to sketch the shifting history of global governance from the 1970s to the present—from the relatively open, multilateral UN-forums to the formalized and narrowly defined policy environments of the neoliberal global governance institutions of the 1980s to the present. This broader historical trajectory of global governance provides the context and important insights for our analysis of GHG from Alma Ata to Okinawa.

Shifting history: two legacies of "global governance"

We consider two legacies of global governance, representing two phases in its historical trajectory. The first phase broadly covers the 1970s when the prospects for multilateralism were relatively strong and the UN system was the forum for the development of global governance. This phase was marked by the plausibility of global social democracy; it encompassed the call for a New International Economic Order (NIEO) and the Alma Ata declaration, a milestone in health care discourse. The second phase covers the late 1970s onward, when the institutional development of global governance occurred more noticeably through global economic institutions, such as the International Monetary Fund (IMF), the World Bank, and more recently the World Trade Organization (WTO).

During the earlier phase, global governance appeared most clearly focused and unfolding through the UN system. The reasons for this are varied. However, a few trajectories shaped the possibility of a window of opportunity for a social democratic project of global governance during the 1970s and, in its late stages, up until the early 1980s. With the period of détente in the bipolar world system and the relative decline of U.S. global hegemony, the UN provided a forum for the emergence of a coalition of postcolonial states that culminated in the formation of the G-77 and the proclamation of the need for an NIEO.[6] This coalition was initially very successful at turning the primary focus in the UN away from the concerns immediately associated with the remits of the Security Council and onto the UN's role in shaping the perceptions and policies on global socioeconomic problems.

The upshot for the shape and form of global governance anticipated in this context was clearly a conception based on international global governance, requiring an executive function by UN agencies—for instance, the UN Conference on Trade and Development (UNCTAD) and, complementarily, significant increases in funds to these bodies. The world economic background to these efforts to consolidate multilateral governance in the sense of an NIEO was the capacity crisis of the late 1960s and early 1970s in advanced capitalist economies[7] and the gradual transition from an international to a global world economy.[8]

The implications of the NIEO for GHG can be assessed only tentatively, as the NIEO did not include explicit policy framework recommendations on this issue. Yet its general thrust of integrating economic and social concerns means that the undeniable exacerbation of the global health crisis through economic inequality would have constituted a much smaller problem than what is currently experienced.[9]

The 1978 Alma Ata declaration, which enshrined health as a fundamental human right, and its subsequent adoption by the WHO's World Health Assembly (WHA) in 1981, belong in the context of the politics of the NIEO. The declaration itself was drafted in the spirit of UN multilateralism[10] as a declaration of intent in solidarity of the signatories. The adoption by the WHO/WHA of the goals of the declaration to provide egalitarian health care on a global scale in accordance with a needs-based approach offers an important insight. It highlights the way in which UN governance at that historical juncture moved closer than ever to bridging the gap between declarative/symbolic global politics, on the one hand, and substantive policy development, on the other. The UN system was responsive to and transmissive of what was at least a social-democratic, if not transformative, agenda for global governance. The combined political might of the tentative OPEC/G-77 coalition "democratized" the UN more substantially during a time of East-West stalemate and a lapse in hegemonic leadership in the North. Despite the more radical challenges continuously posed by the members of, for instance, the Third World Forum,[11] the expressive social-democratic compromises can be seen to have commanded both plausibility and practicability in at least a general sense.

The second phase of global governance discussed here is characterized by governance according to neoliberal principles, with the Okinawa summit providing a milestone for the health policy discourse during this period. The phase began during the late 1970s, as the challenges to the political thrust of the NIEO were stepped up. There was a shift in emphasis in the institutional focus of global governance. Whereas the G-77's agenda was advanced mainly through the more parliamentary structures of the UN system, the response to the challenge posed by the call for an NIEO was fashioned through the functionally delimited policy domains of global financial institutions (GFIs) and the evolving multilateral trading system under the General Agreement on Tariffs and Trade (GATT). If the third world challenge to a crisis-ridden and crisis-inducing Northern economic hegemony drew its political force partly from the generality of its reform and transformation demands, the reassertion of Northern dominance proceeded via the piecemeal framing and reconstructing of economic reform proposals and packages along "Reagonomics" lines. Thus, disciplinary neoliberalism[12] in global political economy became extended through institutions in which the political momentum created for the G-77 proved relatively powerless. The constitutive purposes and remits of these institutions circumscribed the modes of engagement. Contemporaneously, a governance agenda was advanced for the structuring of developing states' political institutions. This focused on the administrative and law enforcement–oriented functions of the state/bureaucracy complex that were to be legitimized via democratic minimalism.

GHG: Alma Ata to Okinawa

In this section, the broader changes charted above provide a map for analyzing the changing nature and orientation of GHG. This can be studied by examining in more detail developments from the Alma Ata–inspired "Health for All" strategy in 1981 to the current UN health goals, sanctioned at the G8 summit in Okinawa in July 2000.

The 1978 declaration of Alma Ata cemented the notion of health care as a universal human entitlement and thus as a good, access to which should not be determined by particular economic circumstances. This was to be secured by a participatory process of comprehensive primary health care (PHC) in the context of multisectoral development. The WHO commented that the shape of PHC "is determined by social goals, such as the improvement of the quality of life and maximum health benefits to the greatest number."[13] Thus the declaration was in the spirit of the UN General Assembly, which had already incorporated health as a fundamental human right in the Covenant on Economic, Social and Cultural Rights. The Alma Ata declaration affirmed the responsibility and the crucial role assumed by states and the international community in providing sustainable health care but complemented this affirmation with an explicit recognition of the significant contributions made by households and communities. At least in intent, this was to reflect the experiences of health care improvements induced in the developing world by the establishment of rural health care systems and extension services based on community level access. In 1981, the WHO's WHA endorsed the "health for all by the year 2000" strategy, which was to translate the Alma Ata declaration of 1978 into a reality.

When considering the current global health situation, it is not only obvious that health for all was not achieved by the year 2000, but also that the prospects for significant progress have not improved. At the international level, health goals have been revised and are defined much more narrowly now around specific diseases and specific goals of quantifiable scope,[14] precluding any comprehensive engagement with the issues of universal human rights and socioeconomic transformation, which had previously been identified as crucial to integrated approaches. In May 1998, the WHA, recognizing that the original health for all goals would not be achieved by 2000, passed the new World Health Declaration and endorsed the new policy "Health for All in the 21st Century."[15] While this renewed health for all policy endorses social-democratic principles in terms of a fundamental human right to health, the policy responses supported by the WHO to achieve this goal in the context of globalization, such as public-private partnerships, are the subject of critical evaluation.[16] (See below in relation to policy responses to the challenge of HIV/AIDS.)

These shifts in the scope and general nature of GHG indicate the relocation of the global political project from the more discursively sensitive UN bodies, whose anchoring in parliamentary structures ensure at least some form of a forum of "political will–formation" for global governance, to the functionally defined GFIs and the WTO, ostensibly presented as "nonpolitical" but exhibiting the legitimation problems diagnosed for "new constitutionalism."[17] This means that whereas the achievement of health as a human right as envisaged at Alma Ata required health to be seen as a public good,[18] the neoliberal development orthodoxy of the 1980s and early 1990s interpreted it instead in terms of its privatization potential. The overarching neoliberal development strategy—based on the promotion of economic growth through structural adjustment of national economies and the liberalization of trade, investment, and finance—was to provide the context for the development of global and national health care policies. The new economic orthodoxy that envisaged the comprehensive withdrawal of state influence in markets had the effect of crowding out any political momentum created for cooperative approaches that included redistributive provisions.

This development strategy affected health governance and the actual health of peoples and people both indirectly and directly. The relationship between the neoliberal development project and health inequality has been explored in a number of highly critical recent publications.[19] The role of the market in determining entitlement to health increased, while the role of the state decreased.[20] Importantly, the PHC strategy was modified/derailed almost before it got going. Selective primary health care (SPHC) became the mantra. In terms of policy response, this meant a focus on specific interventions, such as immunization and oral rehydration, rather than an integrated approach to social transformation and community empowerment. The latter had been regarded as crucial to the success of comprehensive health care regimes. Capturing the logic of the SPHC approach quite well, Banerji refers to such interventions as "prefabricated global initiatives" and notes a resemblance between them and the equally prefabricated structural adjustment solutions that pay little regard to local variations (see below).[21]

Expressed in terms of the conception of "society" or societies, underpinning the political shift toward such approaches, the responses to challenges to GHG became framed in terms of functional differentiation. The market-based logic of production and distribution of health "hardware" (drugs and the machinery for health-oriented infrastructure) is set apart operationally from concerns and problems that cannot be expressed in terms of the logic of an economic system.[22]

The piecemeal policy approach to health interventions took place in the direct context of another component of neoliberal global governance: structural adjustment programs (SAPs). The indirect effects of SAPs on health are well documented (for example, the UN Children's Fund, 1987)[23] and have generally lead to criticisms of the dilemmas they have posed for Southern states and societies. Equally, the direct effects have been studied, as seen, for instance, in reports on the exclusion of those who cannot pay through the imposition of user fees and other cost-recovery mechanisms.[24] Confronting the trends toward the comprehensive introduction of payments for what were previously understood to be "public goods," Stephen Browne, director of poverty programs at the UN Development Programme (UNDP), remarks that "user fees are a deterrent to universal education and universal health."[25] World Bank research shows that user fees in health and education result in a lower take-up rate and that the abolition of such fees generally has the desired converse effect. Moreover, user fees beyond the health sector often impact directly on health.[26]

During the 1990s, there was a gradual realization that the process of economic globalization was accompanied by an increasingly pertinent uneven distribution of economic benefits. This resulted in a modification of the overarching global development policy to ameliorate its worst effects. Thus, there was a greater emphasis on targeted poverty reduction through such mechanisms as safety nets and microcredit, public-private partnerships, and debt relief through the Heavily Indebted Poor Countries initiative (HIPC).[27] The notion of good governance became fashionable, and greater efforts were made by multilateral institutions to involve civil society in policy development and implementation. During this period, as already implied in our survey of the greater political trajectories, the WHO lost ground also as a policy provider to the World Bank. In addition to the poor leadership of the WHO's director-general, Hiroshi Nakajima, the enhanced role accorded to the World Bank by the major donors in the context of the restructuring of development policy meant that the World Bank became the main source of funding for the health sector. With its direct links into ministries of finance and ministries of planning, the World Bank became the main multilateral agenda setter in the health field.[28]

This modification in the overarching development strategy and the changing relations between key multilateral institutions were reflected in health policy. On the face of it, there appeared to be an increasing realization in official policy circles that a better balance had to be struck between the goals of economic growth and social and environmental goals, including health. In 1993, the World Bank published its report "Investing in Health," which announced the importance of growth with equity. Some analysts applaud the report for pressing all the right buttons, such as the importance of female education and greater access to health care, but others make a more critical assessment. David Werner and David Sanders, for example, suggest that while the report on first reading sounds "comprehensive, even modestly progressive," in reality this was not the case.[29] For them, the Bank's "new" approach represented 1980s wine in 1990s bottles. Growth, trickle down, and structural adjustment principles underlay the new terminology, which borrows the concepts of social democracy more or less out of political expediency.[30]

In the late 1990s, again reflecting the approach and terminology of global development policy, the emphasis in global health policy was on increasing the involvement of a wide range of stakeholders. Emphasis was placed on public-private partnerships and on the role of benefactors to tackle specific health problems, such as malaria (Rollback Malaria Campaign), vaccines (Global Alliance for Vaccines and Immunization, GAVI), and the problem of access to drugs for the treatment of HIV/AIDS (UNAIDS-pharmaceutical industry initiative). At Okinawa, the notion of an enhanced role for the private sector and for public-private partnerships was given further legitimacy.

Market-based entitlement thus increasingly meant that those who needed drugs did not have access to them because they could not afford to buy them. As for arguments stressing the failure of states, it is true that most had failed to implement PHC, partly due to a lack of political will and partly due to numerous other constraints, including those imposed by structural adjustment, fluctuating commodity prices, crippling debt repayments, arms purchases, and corruption.

However, where PHC had been seriously attempted (such as in Cuba, India [Kerala], and Costa Rica) there had been great successes.[31] In all these cases, policies toward enhancing socioeconomic equality had been actively pursued by the national or federal state government. Yet in the mid- to late 1990s, the emphasis was still on a narrowly circumscribed role for the state, so the concept of public provision (national or global) was not seen as an appropriate alternative. While rhetorically "stakeholder partnerships" were (and are) the order of the day, typically not all stakeholders are included, as we see below in relation to HIV/AIDS, and not all partnerships function in the spirit of the concept.

This exploration of changing ideas and practice of health governance from Alma Ata to Okinawa would be inadequate without reference to the WTO, the most recent global economic governance body with significant development implications. The WTO impacts on health across a variety of areas, from the general level of "trade creep" over public health concerns to the particular areas, such as the Agreement on the Application of Sanitary and Phytosanitary Measures (SPS).[32] The question of intellectual property rights under the trade-related intellectual property rights (TRIPS) agreement (see below) are important in terms of structuring access to medicines and issues of equity. Also potentially crucial in terms of equity over the next few years will be the General Agreement on Trade in Services (GATS). Although a

GATS may not inherently prejudice the development of more inclusive and comprehensive approaches to GHG, the current agenda remains firmly tied to the disembedding logic referred to above and reflects in particular the interests of beneficiaries from trade in financial capital rather than the "localized" goods and services.[33] Critics have warned of the consequences of further entrenchment of the disembedding logic with reference to the provision of health based on public goods.[34] Explored in the context of WTO/GATS implications for the adaptive pressure on domestic health care policies, they make a pertinent point. The neoliberal hegemony, spearheaded in particular by U.S. trade negotiators, produces restrictions on the prospects for public health services in conjunction with enhanced prospects for corporate profit but offers little or no prospect for addressing persistent inequalities.[35]

It is interesting to note that over this period, the emphasis in the presentation of the ill health–poverty relationship has changed. Ill health, of course, contributes to poverty, as it directly affects the often subsistence-oriented economic activities of poor people. Decreasing productivity leads to increasing poverty. The vicious cycle is completed when this in turn leads to further deterioration in health. However, over the last two decades, the presentation of the balance of this relationship has shifted from ill health as a result of poverty, prevailing socioeconomic structures, and the dominant model of development, to conceptions of health in terms of opportunity for poverty reduction and for development. Whereas poverty was portrayed as the primary cause of ill health, now the emphasis has shifted, and ill health is presented more as a key cause of poverty and loss of economic productivity and earnings. The latter is clear in the December 2001 report of the WHO's Commission on Macroeconomics and Health, chaired by Jeffrey Sachs.[36]

These developments may galvanize some dedicated funding for particular problems, and this is both very necessary and urgent.[37] However, ultimately they may not serve well the realization of health as a human right. The consumer-oriented rhetoric of health service provision contained in the new rhetoric places the emphasis on the potential of medicine to remedy health problems, and indirectly poverty, rather than focusing on issues of equity and social transformation as the route to health. To view HIV, malaria, tuberculosis (TB), and other diseases in terms of lost economic productivity conceals that there is a growing body of evidence that suggests that socioeconomic factors influence health and well-being more than medical intervention.[38] While this analysis does not dismiss the importance of such interventions—clearly they are vital—it does suggest that it would be a mistake to take our eyes off the comprehensive need for socioeconomic transformation.

HIV/AIDS and the legacies of Alma Ata and Okinawa

The HIV/AIDS crisis, having been neglected by key agents of global governance for twenty years, became the focus of attention at the turn of the new century.

On 10 January 2000, the UN Security Council met to discuss the challenge of HIV/AIDS, and in July 2001, a UN General Assembly Special Session (UNGASS) was convened to address the problem. The G8 has also considered the problem. Therefore, over the last two years in a relatively short space of time, this disease has been transformed from a health issue into a security issue and most recently into a development issue.

As the symptoms of HIV are treatable and the disease itself can today be controlled to enhance both the patient's life prospects and quality of life, the issue of access to medication assumes an obvious pertinence in this case.[39] When considered in the context of the immensity of the problem, plus the unequal global distribution of the burden of the disease, it is obvious that countries with the greatest constraints on their budgets would be the very ones having to spend the most on HIV-related care. How is this challenge reflected in current approaches of GHG?

The global response to date has focused on piecemeal investments based on loans, discounts, or donations. Policy has been framed in terms of the rights of corporations rather than the human right to health. Corporations are keen to uphold their patent rights, thus safeguarding profits (mostly accrued in the North) into the future. The efforts of a few developing countries to pursue legitimate strategies to secure drugs for their people at more affordable prices have been obstructed by pharmaceutical companies and by some Northern governments, notably the United States.[40] (In theory, the WTO's TRIPS allows for the use of compulsory licensing [Article 31] and parallel importing [Article 6] to increase access to affordable drugs for infected citizens).[41]

The piecemeal approach outlined above is often presented in the language of partnerships. A key problem with these "partnerships" is that they are not based on substantive conceptions of equality that underpin, for instance, the health for all ideal, and that those in whose interests they are avowedly developed are in general excluded from their negotiation. For serious partnerships to develop, developing countries must be fully involved in deliberations with companies and UN organizations.[42]

The global policies currently in vogue for tackling the HIV/AIDS pandemic are likely to bring only limited short-term gains while enhancing significantly risks and vulnerabilities in the future. A cursory glance at the conditions for establishing workable society wide health infrastructures for administering ARVs makes this clear. Unless GHG in conjunction with the national and localized extension agencies get it right, a focus on "providing drugs" is likely to lead to significant adverse effects—for instance, increases in patient risks and the accelerated emergence of drug-resistant strains.[43]

There is growing recognition in several quarters that GHG, in order to be relevant in the context of the massive and deepening global inequality, poverty, and exclusion that characterize the AIDS pandemic, must facilitate the socioeconomic conditions that make health for all realizable. Under current conditions, and given the magnitude of the problem, this seems conditional on comprehensive regulatory and sociopolitical intervention with great emphasis on redistribution. So far this is absent in the GHG response.

The reform of GHG

The "Okinawa" agenda for GHG has been dominated by a limited set of actors who, albeit to differing degrees, have either encouraged and/or legitimated the continued disembedding of GHG from these wider concerns for social justice from which it is inseparable. There have been a few expressions of concern (such as by UNICEF), directed toward bringing about a reintroduction of wider social concerns within the current formal global governance patchwork. Yet these arguments for a more integrated approach have been without significant effect. In the light of recent clashes over access to HIV-related medication, the WHO has been playing a more confident role under the leadership of Gro Harlem Brundtland and her successor. In particular—and echoing the concerns of the G-77 coalition in the context of the NIEO—the WHO has taken on explicitly the issue of the inequality of access. In May 1999, the fifty-second World Health Assembly gave the WHO the mandate to do more work on trade-related issues, including the impact of global trade governance on access to drugs. The WHO was asked to study the effects of international trade agreements on health. NGOs are working with the WHO to track prices and access to essential drugs.[44] This research is seen as directly linked with enhancing Southern governments' political clout with reference to negotiating and defending affordable access. In the course of the engagement of global economic governance over health concerns, this newly emboldened coalition of interests and outlooks has aided the developing country "victory" at the Doha Round of the WTO.[45] Doha included a formal commitment to the health emergency measures already contained under TRIPS article 31, which had been the subject of the pharma-industry's challenge to Southern governments (most notably Brazil and South Africa).[46] Since Doha, however, continued bilateral pressure by the United States has restricted and delayed the production of cheaper generic drugs, thus revealing the hollow nature of the Doha victory.[47]

Agents of change

If recent attempts to shape GHG into more egalitarian terms have echoed the agenda set by the Alma Ata declaration, it is important to acknowledge that today the circumstances and the form and thrust of such a political project differ significantly. This can be gauged with reference to the range of actors—and their efficacy—involved in contesting the current consensus and the institutional and organizational environment within which this contest occurs. We have outlined the latter above—a more formalized global arena of political institutions, rules, and modes of interaction that evolved out of the 1980s–1990s efforts to secure and institute international commerce. With regard to the former, the agents of "egalitarian" politics of GHG belong, in general, to a more pluralized context of complex alliances, cooperation, and multiple publics on which the force of the political challenge depends. We consider, in turn, states, organizations, and social movements.

States

Rather than reflecting, as in the case of the NIEO, a relatively coherent challenge to the dominant world order, backed up by a strong coalition, today's state actors involved in contesting the inegalitarian distribution of entitlements to health care involve a few, relatively well positioned representatives of Southern concerns. The relatively higher economic performance of, for instance, Brazil and South Africa renders their status as markets, rather than as recipients of health care aid, more plausible, at least in the midterm future. Hence, the focus of pharmaceutical companies on preventing such states from establishing norms of "good practice," which contravene the corporate agenda of securing profits projected on intellectual property agreements. The states mentioned above have acted individually. However, as documented by the Doha Round, we are beginning to see strength in numbers and more concerted action internationally. This was already clear, for example, at the Geneva World Summit for Social Development in June 2000, when G-77 countries pushed a proposal for the final conference text to protect essential medicines from patentability. Although they did not achieve this, they did succeed in getting an affirmation of countries' rights to freely exercise their legal options.[48]

Organizations

The organizational side can be approached by considering the top-down and bottom-up continuum of organizational actors. On the one hand, there are the institutions of global economic governance (World Bank, IMF, WTO) projecting claims to a new "post–Washington Consensus," with greater emphasis on social and political questions and less focus on the economic orthodoxies of the SAP period. Yet its current programs typically continue to stress market-based responses to the challenges posed by globalization. While this captures some degree of the imbalance that persists in the *international* system, where Northern countries continue to hold on to advantageous subsidies and tariff barriers, the focus on trade liberalization distorts again the way in which the benefits of trade-led growth get distributed. The *international* focus on terms of trade and balance of trade distracts from an analysis of the *global* reproduction of inequality and immiseration.[49]

The bottom-up perspective in the field of organizational actors has seen NGOs, government-related international nongovernmental organizations

(GRINGOs), and government-organized nongovernmental organizations (GONGOs) gain greater access to global governance bodies, a development that is often offset by a degree of decoupling from their social movement bases, where such a base existed or was important in propelling the respective organizations onto the international political scene. The move from protest to consultation entails, politically, a narrowing of the informal power base, which often enabled the accession of the NGOs in the first place. This highlights, on the one hand, the problematic representative status of NGOs and, on the other hand, the implications of conceptions of cooperation versus co-optation.[50] More generally, to assume that NGOs and their hybrid siblings are unequivocal agents of progressive change is, of course, hugely misleading. Many NGOs effectively function as lobbying groups, often with narrow agendas and sometimes in ways more conducive to the continuation of existing power relations (see, for example, the role of the International AIDS Economics Network [IAEN], which is, at best, politically ambivalent). The conflictual map of civil society, drawn already by Hegel, serves as a warning against shortcutting assessments of political efficacy and purpose of its agents.[51]

Social movements

Social movements are "by definition fluid phenomena."[52] They differ from organizations and individual "events" (protests), yet their political clout is crucial to both these aspects of "politics from civil society." Insofar as momentum is building for sustained challenges to currently dominant modes in the formation of global governance, social movements can be seen as the sites at which politicization occurs; thus events such as the reiterative protest assertions in the context of global summits begin to take on features of a social movement.

Health activists, scholars, and citizens concerned with the encompassing conception of health policy outlined above are part of this reassertion of "egalitarian" politics, realizing, for instance, the potential significance of the WTO, not only for general issues of inequality but for health issues in particular.[53] Awareness raising and campaigning on health trade issues are gathering momentum as activists see the importance of putting health at the center of trade debates rather than on the periphery. Responses occur both in targeted issue areas, where campaigns focus on expertise-driven intervention in the technical processes of policymaking, and in the broader context of fostering general public debate about the nature of emerging global health governance.

The twin roles of NGOs and (egalitarian) social movements in constructing a governance-relevant "complex multilateralism"[54] in the more general sense is discernible in their persistence to promote more comprehensive conceptions of social justice, which address not only the distribution of health care, but also the conditions of health in general. Ultimately, the challenge of health is viewed by these actors as basically the challenge of socioeconomic equity and development from the local to the national, regional, and global level.

As Robert Beaglehole and Ruth Bonita note, "The main variation in health status among countries result from environmental, socio-economic and cultural factors, and medical care is of secondary importance."[55]

Conclusion

Reform of health governance will have to occur at many levels, yet its constraints are now significantly constructed internationally and at the global level. The required changes will have to be profound to make a significant and sustainable difference. There are examples of great achievements on very limited resources where social equity is prioritized. (For instance, TB control programs are cited as successful in this respect.)[56] However in some regions, notably Africa, the challenge symbolized by AIDS, but laden with far-reaching ramifications, is so great that possibly little short of a Marshall Plan is needed to make a big difference.

Is this likely? There are few signs of it at the moment, but there are, at least, signs of limited reform. Poverty reduction is back on the World Bank agenda and equity has returned to the policy discourses of the WHO agenda. Gro Harlem Brundtland stated in 1999 that the problem of "access . . . amounts to a moral problem, a political problem and a problem of credibility for the global market system," an assertion that at least helps to focus the ongoing debates in more inclusive terms.[57] The market-driven agenda for health policy implementation relied crucially on the continued promises of the eventual trickle-down of economic benefits from a generally buoyant global economy. However, the current slowdown and impending recessions may refocus and reinvigorate the politics of "re-embedding," of redistribution, and of the protection of social and political achievements, rather than their erosion through their colonization with market rationalities. Perhaps the pendulum is just beginning to swing back in favor of social justice, and the next step will be a more vigorous promotion of health in terms of public goods at all levels, from the local to the global.

Notes

1 Craig Murphy, "Global Governance: Poorly Done and Poorly Understood" *International Affairs* 14, no. 1 (2000): 3–27.
2 Cited by Joyce Millen, Alec Irwin, and Jim Yong Kim, "Introduction: What Is Growing? Who Is Dying?" in Millen, Irwin, Kim, and John Gershman, eds., *Dying for Growth: Global Inequality and the Health of the Poor* (Monroe, Maine: Common Courage Press, 2000), p. 4.
3 Ibid.
4 WHO, "The Rationale of Essential Drugs," available online at www.who.int/medicines/edm-concept.html (accessed January 2001).
5 The disproportionate impact of major health challenges on Southern countries and the roles of poverty and inequality were noted at the fifty-third World Health Assembly, May 2000.

6 Robert Cox, "Ideologies and the New International Economic Order," in Robert Cox and Tim Sinclair, eds., *Approaches to World Order* (Cambridge: Cambridge University Press, 1996), p. 237.

7 Heloise Weber, "Reconstituting the 'Third World'? Poverty Reduction and Territoriality in the Global Politics of Development," *Third World Quarterly* 25, no. 1 (2004).

8 Cox and Sinclair, *Approaches to World Order*, p. 528.

9 Evidence for the positive effects of redistribution on general well-being is provided in UNICEF's annual State of the World's Children reports, which suggest a link between social equity and health. For particular country experiences, see David Werner and David Sanders, *The Politics of Primary Health Care and Child Survival* (Palo Alto: Health Wrights, 1997), and Aviva Chomsky, "The Threat of a Good Example: Health and Revolution in Cuba," in Millen et al., *Dying for Growth*, pp. 331–358. David Coburn's article "Income Inequality, Social Cohesion and the Health Status of Populations: The Role of Neoliberalism," *Social Science and Medicine* 51 (2000): 139–150, has stimulated a lively debate.

10 Cox and Sinclair, *Approaches to World Order*, pp. 494–519.

11 Ibid., pp. 380–381.

12 Stephen Gill, "Globalisation, Market Civilisation, and Disciplinary Neoliberalism," *Millennium* 24, no. 3 (1995): 399–424.

13 WHO/UNICEF, *Primary Health Care*, Report of the International Conference on Primary Health Care, Alma Ata, 6–12 September 1978 (Geneva: WHO, 1978), p. 38.

14 The G8 summit in Okinawa, July 2000, set numerical targets on major infectious diseases to be achieved by 2010. See http://www.g8kyushuokinawa.go.jp/ (accessed 1 March 2001).

15 See http://www.who.int/archives/hfa/default.htm (accessed July 2002).

16 Caroline Thomas, "Trade Policy and the Politics of Access to Drugs," *Third World Quarterly* 23, no. 2 (2002): 251–264.

17 Gill, "Globalisation, Market Civilisation, and Disciplinary Neoliberalism."

18 We are aware of the problems created for using "public goods" as a normative standard in the context of the adoption of the public goods discourse by the IFIs and the WTO. The issue requires an in-depth critical reconstruction of shifts in the conception of what is properly such a good. For the purpose of our argument, public goods are conceived ideally as provided equally on a not-for-profit and needs basis.

19 Debabar Banerji, "A Fundamental Shift in the Approach to International Health by WHO, UNICEF, and the World Bank: Instances in the Practice of 'Intellectual Fascism' and Totalitarianism in Some Asian Countries," *International Journal of Health Services* 29, no. 2 (1999): 227–259; Millen et al., *Dying for Growth*; Evelyne Hong, *Globalisation and the Impact on Health: A Third World View* (Penang, Malaysia: Third World Network, 2000), available online at www.twnside.org.sg (accessed 10 December 2000).

20 Werner and Sanders, *The Politics of Primary Health Care and Child Survival*; Daniel Drache and Terry Sullivan, eds., *Market Limits in Health Reform: Public Success, Private Failure* (London: Routledge, 1999).

21 Banerji, "A Fundamental Shift," p. 239.

22 Elmar Altvater and Brigit Mahnkopf, "The World Market Unbound," *Review of International Political Economy* 4, no. 3 (1997): 448–471.

23 Giovanni Cornia, Richard Jolly, and Frances Stewart, eds., *Adjustment with a Human Face*, vol. 1: *Protecting the Vulnerable and Promoting Growth*, A Study by UNICEF (Oxford: Clarendon Press, 1987).

24 Werner and Sanders, *The Politics of Primary Health Care and Child Survival*, pp. 102–104.

25 Lean Ka-Min, "User Fees Blamed for Cholera Outbreak in South Africa," 26 October 2000, available online at http://www.twnside.org.sg/title/cholera.htm (accessed 21 November 2000).

26 Ibid., p. 1.

27 Heloise Weber, "The Imposition of a Global Development Architecture: The Example of Microcredit," *Review of International Studies* 28, no. 3, (July 2002): 537–556.

28 Kent Buse and Catherine Gwin, "World Health: The World Bank and Global Cooperation in Health: 'The Case of Bangladesh,'" *Lancet*, no. 351 (1998), pp. 665–669; Kamran Abbasi, "The World Bank and World Health: Changing Sides," *British Medical Journal*, no. 318 (27 March 1999): 865–869.

29 Werner and Sanders, *The Politics of Primary Health Care and Child Survival*, p. 104.

30 Alex Callinocos, *Against the Third Way* (London: Routledge, 2000).

31 Chomsky, "The Threat of a Good Example."

32 Meri Koivusalo and Michael Rowson, "The WTO: Implications for Health Policy," *Medicine. Conflict and Survival* 16 (2000): 175–191; Meri Koivusalo, *The World Trade Organisation and Trade-Creep in Health and Social Policies*, GASPP Occasional Paper No. 4 (Helsinki: STAKES, 1999).

33 Altvater and Mahnkopf, "The World Market Unbound," p. 459.

34 David Price, Allyson Pollock, and Jean Shaoul, "How the WTO Is Shaping Domestic Policies in Health Care," *Lancet* 354, no. 9193 (27 November 1999).

35 Ibid., p. 1891.

36 Jeffrey Sachs, ed., *Macroeconomics and Health: Investing in Health for Economic Development* (Geneva: WHO, 2001).

37 WHO, *World Health Report* (Geneva: WHO, 2000).

38 Thomas McKeown, *The Origins of Human Disease* (Oxford: Blackwell, 1988); J. Fraser Mustard, "Health, Health Care and Social Cohesion," in Drache and Sullivan, *Market Limits in Health Reform*, pp. 329–350.

39 Panos Institute, *Beyond Our Means? The Cost of Treating HIV/AIDS in the Developing World* (London: Panos, 2000), p. 3; Paul Rogers, "War on Want," available online at www.opendemocracy.net (posted 13 February 2002).

40 Thomas, "Trade Policy and the Politics of Access to Drugs."

41 Ibid.

42 Manto Tshabalala-Msimang, "Cheaper AIDS Drugs for South Africa? Minister Tells of Progress," Health Systems Trust, available online at http://hst.off1:.za/view.oho3?id=20001004 (accessed 24 October 2000).

43 A. D. Harries et al., "Preventing Antiretroviral Anarchy in Sub-Saharan Africa," *Lancet* 358, no. 4 (2001): 410–414.

44 Margaret Duckett, "Compulsory Licensing and Parallel Importing," ICASO Background Paper, July 1999, p. 7, available online at www.icaso.org (accessed 10 October 2000).

45 Sanjoy Bagehi, "What Happened at Doha?" *Economic and Political Weekly*, India (29 December 2001).

46 Patrick Bond, "A Political Economy of South African AIDS," *ZNet Commentary*, 16 July 2000, available online at www.spiraldynamics.com/documents/hotspots/Africa/SA_AIDS_Bond.htm (accessed 22 November 2000); Thomas, "Trade Policy and the Politics of Access to Drugs"; sec also www.tac.org.za/archive.htm (accessed December 2000).

47 Oxfam, "US Bullying on Drug Patents: One Year After Doha," Oxfam Policy Paper No. 33, available online at www.oxfam.org.uk/policy/papers/33bullying/33bullying.html (accessed 22 November 2002).

48 Celia Oh, "TRIPS and Pharmaceuticals: A Case of Corporate Profits over Public Health," available online at http:twnslde.org.sg/title/twr120a.htm (accessed 14 November 2000).

49 Julian Saurin, "The Global Organisation of Disaster Triumphant," paper presented at the ISA biannual global convention in Chicago, February 2001.

50 Inge Kaul, Isabelle Grunberg, and Marc Stern, eds., *Global Public Goods: International Cooperation in the Twenty-first Century* (New York: Oxford University Press, 1999); Lincoln Chen, Tim Evans, and Richard Cash, "Health as a Global Public Good," in Kaul, Grunberg, and Stern, *Global Public Goods*, pp. 284–304; Inge Kaul and Michael Faust, "Global Public Goods and Health: Taking the Agenda Forward," *Bulletin of the World Health Organisation* 79, no. 9 (2001).

51 See, for an extensive discussion, Alejandro Colas, *International Civil Society* (Cambridge: Polity Press, 2002).

52 Donatella Della Porta and Mario Diani, *Social Movements: An Introduction* (London: Blackwell, 1999), p. 17.

53 Ronald Labonte, "Healthy Public Policy and the WTO: A Proposal for an International Health Presence in Future Trade/Investment Talks," *Health Promotion International* 13, no. 3 (1998): 245–256; Enis Baris and Kari McLeod, "Globalization and International Trade in the Twenty-first Century: Opportunities for and Threats to the Health Sector in the South," *International Journal of Health Services* 30, no. 1: 187–210.

54 Robert O'Brien, Anne-Marie Goetz, Jan Aart Scholte, and Marc Williams, *Contesting Global Governance* (Cambridge: Cambridge University Press, 2000), p. 206.

55 Robert Beaglehole and Ruth Bonita, "Public Health at the Crossroads: Which Way Forward?" *Lancet* 351, no. 21 (February 1998): 590–592.

56 Harries et al., "Preventing Antiretroviral Anarchy in Sub-Saharan Africa," pp. 410–411.

57 Gro Harlem Brundtland, "Towards a Strategic Agenda for the WHO Secretariat," Statement by the Director General to the Executive Board at Its 105th Session, WHO, EB105/2, 24 January 2000, p. 7.

61

ACHIEVING MILLENNIUM DEVELOPMENT GOALS FOR HEALTH

Building understanding, trust and capacity to respond

Timothy John Downs and Heidi Jane Larson

Source: *Health Policy*, 83 (2007), 144–61.

Abstract

Biomedical interventions promise achievement of health-related Millennium Development Goals provided social-, capacity- and knowledge-based constraints to scaling up and reaching marginalized people at risk, are addressed, and balance between prevention and treatment is struck. We argue for a new approach: multi-stakeholder capacity building and learning for empowerment: MuSCLE. MuSCLE is used as a way to frame three systemic weaknesses in traditional health science and policy approaches: (1) a lack of engagement with people at risk to build a collective understanding of the contexts of health problems, including social drivers; (2) a lack of multi-criteria evaluation of alternative interventions; (3) a lack of attention paid to integrated capacity building. The MuSCLE framework responds in three ways: (1) participatory assessment of the ecological, socio-cultural, economic and political contexts of health, identifying priorities using risk and vulnerability science, and modeling drivers; (2) selection among intervention alternatives that makes ecological, socio-cultural, economic and political tradeoffs transparent; (3) integrated capacity building for sustainable and adaptive interventions. Literature and field lessons support the argument, and guidelines are set down. A MuSCLE approach argues for a transformation in health science and policy in order to achieve Millennium Development Goals for health.

1. Introduction

In 2000, the Millennium Declaration set out ambitious targets – Millennium Development Goals (MDGs) – for substantial reductions in poverty and hunger, child mortality, and disease as well as significant improvements in maternal health, gender equality, primary education, and environmental sustainability. In 2005, in the 5-year progress report, the UN concluded that business-as-usual approaches will not get us there: "if current trends persist there is a risk that many of the poorest countries will not be able to meet many of [the MDGs]" [1]. Investment of political and intellectual capital and planned mobilizing of financial capital have never been stronger. By 2015, all 191 member states of the United Nations have pledged to meet the MDGs [2].

The UN Millennium Project (MP) is an independent advisory board commissioned by the Secretary General to advise on strategies to achieve the MDGs [3]. The MP views country-level changes as key to achieving the goals: improvements in governance; engaging and empowering civil society; promoting entrepreneurship; mobilizing domestic resources; increasing aid; reforming global trade policies that favor rich nations [3]. Their report calls for a "bold, needs-based, goal-oriented investment framework over 10 years" [3, p. 24], and recommends that "countries" (i.e. central governments) follow four-steps: (i) map dimensions and underlying determinants of extreme poverty; (ii) use poverty maps to undertake needs assessment for public investment; (iii) convert the assessment into a 10-year action plan; (iv) include a 3–5-year "quick win" poverty reduction strategy within the plan. For rapid scale-up of interventions to a national scale the MP further states governments must: (a) set out objectives and work plans with clear deliverables and timelines; (b) build national and local capacity for management, human resources and infrastructure; (c) adopt replicable, locally appropriate delivery mechanisms for interventions; (d) monitor progress and allow mid-course correction. The MP recognizes that involvement and ownership by communities, and long-term donor funding and technical assistance are conditions for success. It strategically targets countries with governance that is weak because of weak capacity, not because of corruption or a lack of will.

The MP task force reports for the health-related MDGs have laid out a comprehensive set of recommendations and priority actions. However, the recommendations tend to be prescriptive and descriptive, rather than being operational and empowering. An inclusive, transparent and evidence-based process for turning the MP recommendations into actions is still needed.

This paper focuses on how to achieve the MDGs for health on the ground in partnership with multiple stakeholders. We argue for a transformative multi-stakeholder process that fosters social learning and strengthens social capital with three main features:

166

(1) Part]icipatory, systems-based assessment of the ecological, socio-cultural, economic and political contexts of health challenges and responses, identifying priorities using risk and vulnerability science, and modeling drivers.
(2) Selection among intervention alternatives that makes ecological, socio-cultural, economic and political tradeoffs transparent.
(3) A support system of capacity building to sustain selected interventions, and adapt to changing conditions and priorities over time.

The objective of the paper is to make the case for a "MuSCLE"-type process – multi-stakeholder capacity building and learning for empowerment – by exploring its theoretical and practical foundations, drawing from literature traditionally outside the scope of biomedical and public health fields, and supported by lessons from the field.

2. Social learning framework

The organizing framework for MuSCLE is a multi-stakeholder process that fosters social learning and strengthens social capital. Social learning has been defined as "a framework for thinking about knowledge processes that underlie social adaptation and innovation" [4, p. 64]. Much useful knowledge of social learning has come from natural resource management experience in developing countries, but has yet to be applied to health. Guangxia and Lianmin [5] found that effective social learning for forest management in Chinese study sites occurred as a result of a productive cycle of conflict and consensus. Strong cultural values allowed villagers to share the goal of forest conservation, and stakeholder interaction was mediated by respected elders. Success resulted from social learning, effective leadership and effective communication. Effective leaders – innovators – are able to exploit culturally accepted networks to stimulate collective action for change, and also accommodate special interests of some stakeholders. Biomedical professionals are often skeptical of community-based health approaches, but this stems from a perception that any such methods will exclude biomedical science and knowledge of proven intervention technologies. We advocate health scientists, practitioners, policy makers and communities-at-risk work together as a knowledge collaborative.

Buck et al. [6] signal four aspects of effective social learning for forest management, equally relevant to health: (i) conflict mitigation based on understanding power relations; (ii) an innovation and problem solving climate; (iii) communication and relationship building; (iv) capacity building and organizational development. Daniels and Walker [7] claim mutual learning derived from the interaction of differing values, capacities, perspectives, methods and historical experiences can transform collective understanding. Potential barriers include insufficient trust and transparency among participants, and resistance from power and knowledge elites – including some donors and "experts" – who are invested in the status quo.

167

2.1. Communication for social change

A growing number of development communication specialists are calling for an approach, which stimulates debate and dialogue. Recognizing the limits of traditional communication in development which is more focused on changing individual behaviors, the emerging communication for social change approach champions public and private dialogue through which people define who they are, what they want and how they can achieve it. The approach aims to change emphasis: (a) away from people as the objects for change and toward communities as agents of their own change; (b) away from designing, testing and delivering messages and toward fostering dialogue and debate; (c) away from a focus on individual behaviors and toward better understanding of social norms, policies, culture and the need for an enabling environment; (d) away from persuading people to do something and toward negotiating the best way forward in a partnership; (e) away from technical experts in "outside" agencies dominating a process and toward the people most affected by the problem playing a central role [8]. The experience of the global polio eradication initiative, paralyzed by a boycott against vaccination by a poor, politically marginalized group in Northern Nigeria, is a compelling example of the need to take in account the broader socio-cultural and political contexts of health initiatives and actively engage those most affected early in the planning (Box 1).

Beyond the polio case, current global health challenges expose the serious limitations of traditional bio-medical approaches for both explaining health disparities and responding adequately to them. More evident than ever, the fields of biomedicine and public health must join forces with each other, and with key disciplinary allies – anthropology, environmental science, political ecology, political economy, management science to name but a few – to encompass socio-cultural, political, economic, and ecological vulnerability factors [9–12 among many]. Arguably, HIV/AIDS research has learned the most about the need to work with people at risk, and has also advanced the science of vulnerability assessment considerably [13–17 among many]. Lessons from the field of HIV/AIDS also provide empirical evidence that supports a MuSCLE-type approach (Box 2).

2.2. Participatory methods

While people's participation in policy and development decisions that impact them is a widely accepted, human rights-based principle, effective participation is often unrealized. Community-based water management experience in developing countries provides one sound literature footing [21–32]. Methods used for over 20 years by development practitioners include participatory rural appraisal (PRA), applied in Africa and Asia since the 1980s, and participatory action research (PAR), applied from 1994 to 1998 by IRC and partners in Nepal, Pakistan, Kenya, Cameroon, Guatemala and Colombia [21].

Box 1. Embattled polio vaccination shows perils of ignoring socio-political and cultural factors

In 2000, in the midst of the global polio eradication initiative, Nigeria had reduced the total number of cases of polio to 28. In mid-2003, following persuasion by religious leaders questioning the safety of the vaccine, the governor of Kano State in Northern Nigeria declared a boycott on polio vaccination across the state. The boycott lasted 11 months, while numbers of polio cases escalated to nearly 800 in Nigeria and polio cases – traced to Nigeria – emerged in 15 countries which had not seen a case of polio for over a year, some for over four years. Although the boycott ended in mid-2004, the cost of the refusal to vaccinate continued into 2005, when two more countries saw outbreaks, after not having seen polio in over six years.[1] The polio virus had jumped continents from Africa to Asia because of the refusal to vaccinate by one of the poorest, disenfranchised communities in the world. The polio eradication program was perceived as externally imposed both by a central government and the "West", which according to local Muslim religious leaders, was intent on sterilizing Muslim populations through the polio vaccine. There was also a general frustration among communities that they were not receiving health services they perceived as being high priority. Similar vaccination refusals had emerged in Northern India, for some of the same reasons. The strategy that successfully turned the resistance around in India included building alliances with local Muslim medical colleges and trusted local leaders. In Nigeria, the boycott ended due to a combination of a locally led investigation of the safety of the vaccine, a change in the vaccine source to dominantly Muslim Indonesia, local and global political pressures due to the growing polio outbreak in and outside of Nigeria, increased involved of local community members in the vaccination campaigns (vaccinators from the local area rather than from other parts of the country), and building alliances with trusted religious leaders in and outside of Nigeria, e.g. AlAzhar University in Cairo).

An increasing number of environment-development scholar-practitioners recognize the need for a new conceptual and operational framework for poverty eradication and health promotion: a "bottom-up meets top-down" approach that brings governments and communities together to better understand then solve problems. As Martin Luther King declared: "No great victories are won in a war for the transformation of a whole people without total participation" [33].

Participation by those at risk in health research projects has tended to be limited to the provision of solicited information about exposure to risk and

Box 2. Confronting HIV/AIDS collaboratively makes inroads

The response to HIV/AIDS has been a pathfinder in multi-stakeholder, trans-disciplinary approaches and vulnerability science. HIV/AIDS was the first health issue to be "owned" widely outside of the health sector and the first disease-specific issue to be tabled at the UN Security Council. While sectors outside of health have long recognized the importance of addressing AIDS, the challenge was in negotiating and understanding so many different partners' roles in the response. When asked why communities in the South Pacific were so able to quickly mobilize themselves to organize funerals and all the rituals which surround them, even getting the word out to relatives living on remote islands, while health programs rarely saw such mobilization efforts, the response was "Everyone knows their role. Everyone knows exactly what they need to do for a funeral." [18].

Insights such as "everyone knows what they need to do" have been important cues to guide the response to HIV/AIDS. Other lessons learned from HIV/AIDS, include the importance of sensitive issues being communicated by trusted community members, not technical "specialists" from a far-away place. In Argentina, having drug users design AIDS prevention messages was "valuable for their own recuperative process, as well as being effective for identifying appropriate language or jargon." [19]. In Rwanda, similar experience meant that prevention programs engaged "people who live in the same area, share the same ways of life, speak the same language and even have the same jokes and idioms" in order to ensure that important AIDS prevention information was more easily understood [20].

health effects [34–41]. However, the tide is turning towards more collaborative methods; a special issue of the U.S. National Institute of Environmental Health Science (NIEHS) journal Environmental Health Perspectives dedicated to the future of environmental health research featured three articles on active collaborations between scientists and communities at risk that resonate with elements of MuSCLE [42–44]. NIEHS has funded an ongoing project (Downs is co-PI) that tests MuSCLE on the ground (Box 3). This reflects a growing awareness of the need to encompass socio-cultural, political, economic, and ecological vulnerability factors in explaining and addressing health disparities [9,10,12 among many].

2.3. Proposed learning cycle

Appropriate, well-designed multi-stakeholder engagement with all four stages of an adaptive learning cycle (Figure 1) – assessment and modeling, planning, implementation, and monitoring – is central to attaining the MDGs through

---

Box 3. MuSCLE approach gains traction in old urban industrial city

We are gaining practical experience of a MuSCLE approach in inner city, marginalized communities of Worcester, Massachusetts, once heartland of the industrial revolution in the USA, now blighted by pollution burdens and socio-economic pressures. Action research funded by the National Institute of Environmental Health Science's "Environmental Justice: Partnerships for Communication" Program is being undertaken during 2004–2008 by a collaborative comprising five main stakeholders: Clark University; Family Health Center (primary care facility with 30 years experience); Regional Environmental Council (environmental health outreach NGO with 20 years experience); the Worcester Youth Center (community-based organization providing youth development services to at-risk youth); and representatives of the target population—vulnerable residents. Target neighborhoods are Main South and Piedmont, which represent conditions of high risk and vulnerability because of ecological, socio-political, economic and cultural vulnerability factors. Priority stressors include: (a) chronic pollution (e.g. lead in household paint, dust and soil, mold, particulate matter indoors and outdoors); (b) lack of green-space for recreation; (c) abundance of brownfields (vacant lots and abandoned factories suspected to be, or known to be contaminated); (d) pervasive trash, sidewalk and street disrepair; (e) a climate of insecurity, drug abuse and crime. The population is of highly ethnic diversity (25% immigrant or refugee, with over 40% Latino). Over 40% live below the poverty line, many in old rented, delapidated housing.

Working groups of stakeholders have become task forces mobilized to tackle specific priority issues: health impacts, health services, pollution, and trash. Their action planning and capacity building is informed by mixed-methods, trans-disciplinary research with three aspects: (i) household surveys of health problems, vulnerabilities and existing capacities to cope; (ii) focus groups and listening sessions to discuss issues, resources and needs openly and informally; (iii) environmental sampling. Teenagers from the Youth Center are trained as part of the research team, and are involved in action planning that targets asthma, greenspace and youth activity initiatives.

---

a MuSCLE-type approach. The main stakeholders encompass: communities at risk (including women, children and minorities); local, district and state government agencies; non-governmental health organizations; the private sector; donors; and academics. The cycle reflects Holling's [45] ecological concept of complex systems 'backlooping' to remain adaptive to ever-changing conditions.

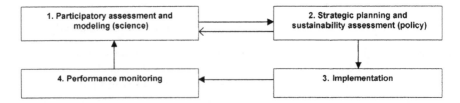

Figure 1 Multi-stakeholder learning cycle at the core of MuSCLE. We place stakeholders into a dynamic experiential learning cycle that includes all four stages
of a typical project: assessment, planning, implementation and monitoring.
Note the two-way interchange between assessment and planning, and
how monitoring re-informs our understanding. Thus, learning is adaptive
to changing conditions and priorities over time. In practice, stages of the
learning cycle overlap. Priority problems are addressed first and as tangible
benefits become visible, stakeholder buy-in is accrued and sustained.

In practice the stages of the learning cycle are quasi-sequential, to allow known
urgent problems to receive quick attention, and sustain buy-in from stakeholders.

Social learning and social capital building lie at the core of health and development progress. Three of the 10 core recommendations of the Millennium
Project [3, p. 1–3] acknowledge this. One states "developing country governments
should craft and implement the MDG-based poverty reduction strategies in
transparent and inclusive processes, working closely with civil society organizations, the domestic private sector, and international partners". The second
recommends that "civil society organizations should contribute actively to designing policies, delivering services, and monitoring progress". A third calls for
launching a "massive effort to build expertise at the community level . . . expertise in health, education, agriculture, nutrition, infrastructure, water supply
and sanitation, and environmental management . . . and training to promote
gender equality and participation". The reality remains that meaningful stakeholder participation remains largely ad hoc. Although participation in local
development projects is commonplace, participation by those most affected in
higher decision-making forums such as public health policy making is rare.

3. Systems understanding

3.1. Health as a dynamic system

Health is part of a much larger human–environment dynamic system, disease
a biological signal of stress. Therefore a participatory, trans-epistemological
approach to assessment is crucial, taking stock of the socio-cultural, political,
economic, and ecological contexts of health, and integrating different types
of knowledge, including anecdotal and indigenous types. With this fuller
contextual analysis, risks and vulnerabilities can be used to identify and
anticipate priority problems. A systems-based perspective also allows us to

model what is driving the risks and vulnerabilities in a given context, and act strategically to control drivers and prevent disease.

A strong argument can be made that only by employing such inclusive, collaborative approaches can we build an adequate understanding and a sustainable response to health needs. Expanding the World Health Organization's [46, p. 5] Pressure → State → Impact → Response (PSIR) model into seven levels – including drivers, pressures, state changes, exposures (contact over time with risk agents), vulnerabilities (amplifiers or attenuators of risk), effects (disease expression) and societal responses (interventions and policies) – will be instrumental for sustainable health gains (Figure 2). There are interdependencies among levels, and feedbacks, making the model non-linear.

We must also place the health systems model in its relevant, health-centered political, socio-cultural, economic and ecological contexts: a 'model within models'. For example, a model of the political context explains how power is distributed within the society, how health and development policy decisions are made, and the relationships among stakeholders, and is fundamental to effective intervention. A socio-cultural perspective is needed that describes gender dynamics, youth–adult relations, tribal and ethnic dynamics. Social drivers of health that result from these contexts and dynamics need special attention in a systems model. A model of the economic system tends to reflect power relations and help explain them, and places health in the

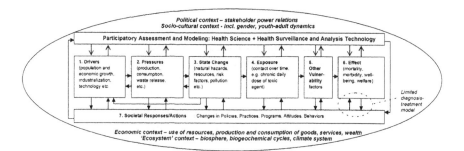

Figure 2 Societal–ecological health system levels. A health system is socially and ecologically dynamic and fuller understanding of these dynamics allows for a more comprehensive, multi-level and sustainable health response. Some drivers (e.g. clean technologies) lead to positive health outcomes while others (e.g. polluting technologies) lead to negative ones. Social drivers include those associated with power relations among and within stakeholder groups, e.g. ethnic group dynamics, gender dynamics and youth-adult dynamics. Cultural drivers include belief systems and behavioral norms. Traditional biomedical approaches tend to focus only on health effects (level 6) and specific treatments (e.g. vaccines, drugs). Interactions are shown among levels 1, 2 and 3, and between responses and each level, so the system is non-linear with multiple feedbacks. Participatory assessment and modeling is shown as an enabling part of the societal response. Four types of context are also shown.

context of the stock and flows of wealth, different types of capital, goods and services. Understanding the economic context of health challenges is especially important in a rapidly globalizing economy since economic forces operate at multiple geographical and political scales. A prime example of this is the role of large pharmaceutical companies and large donors in health system dynamics. At the societal response level of Figure 2, it is important for health innovators to understand the existing health care system's structure, organization and function, its strengths and weaknesses, and its capacity building needs and priorities. Lessons from the management sciences on process innovation need to be applied to strengthen technical and administrative capacity, especially human resources (see Section 5).

Data at each level of Figure 2 can be gathered, for example, in a GIS spatial database that allows data layers to be viewed separately or together. Today's GIS technology can be combined with statistical software so that multiple correlations and regressions and spatial cluster analyses on point-pattern data (like disease cases) can be carried out to improve scientific understanding of the relationships between key variables and parameters. Mapping health risk "hot spots" with GIS has great potential: triangulation can proceed as follows:

(1) Start with health effects data (level 6) and work back to explore known or suspected risk/vulnerability factors that may explain health outcomes (epidemiological "back-casting").
(2) Start with state variables such as pollution, exposures and vulnerabilities and work forward can help predict health outcomes (quantitative risk analysis "forward-casting").
(3) Examine local and anecdotal information on perceived causes and effects that can contribute to the overall assessment.

Acute respiratory infections (ARIs, e.g. child pneumonia) and enteric infections (diarrheas) are the number one and two killers of children under five [47]. Environmental state variables for ARIs and enterics include particulate matter levels in personal air, and pathogen levels in drinking water, respectively (level 3, Figure 2). Exposure indicators are dose rates of these contaminants (level 4). Candidate vulnerability indicators for many health problems (level 5) include nutritional status, literacy, education level, income, age, gender, and access to health care. Sharing data-gathering tasks among multiple stakeholders is a practical way to enrich the scope of the analysis. Few diseases illustrate the need for systems-based understanding and multi-level indicators and responses better than malaria (Figure 3 and Box 4).

3.2. Prioritizing health problems

How do we prioritize health problems and identify those most vulnerable? Risk and vulnerability theory (RVT) offers a sound, evidence-based approach

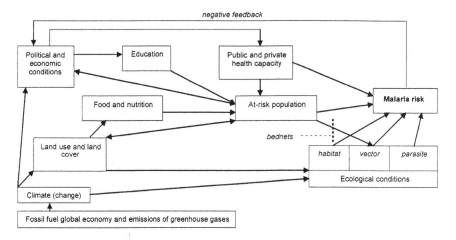

Figure 3 Malaria system. The model shows the need to understand the contextual richness of the disease, identify drivers. Interventions based on systems understanding emphasize prevention, are more strategic, sustainable and cost-effective; bednets should be one component of an integrated response (after Ref. [48]).

Box 4. the battle with malaria: a loud call for collaboration with vulnerable communities and systems-based understanding

We are also using the approach with local partners to design community-based malaria intervention in the Western Highlands of Kenya. Malaria has been described as a national tragedy for Kenya, killing over 90 children under five a day [49]. Insecticide-treated bednets (ITNs) are a mainstay of existing programs, like the global Roll-Back Malaria program launched by WHO and the World Bank in 1998. But ITNs are often unaffordable or otherwise inaccessible to the rural poor, especially those in remote rural areas. Even when a household can buy one, it is often the male head of household who sleeps under it, leaving vulnerable children exposed. The nets are often considered uncomfortable and may only last a year [50]. Millennium Project calls for free bednets [3], but this perpetuates dependency, and leaves structural drivers unaddressed (Figure 3).

As well as the limitations of existing ITN-based programs, drug therapies are another mainstay with serious constraints on the ground. In the Bunda District, Mara Region of Western Tanzania, for example, a community survey showed that while the District promotes the use of the sulfur drug SP (of which it has a large supply), people dislike its side effects and self-medicate with chloroquine. But local malaria resists both SP and chloroquine [50]. Meanwhile, WHO recommends artemisinin as a first line therapy [51]. Recently, the Government of Zambia and the Roll Back Malaria Program have formed a Malaria Control and Evaluation Partnership supported by a 9-year US$35 million grant from the Gates Foundation. The Zambian Health Ministry will coordinate efforts to purchase and distribute hundreds of thousands of ITNs, thousands of doses of artemisinin combination therapy, and enough insecticide to spray the walls of eligible homes in Zambia. This top-down approach, while larger in scale and more integrated, still lacks the features we advocate, and its impact could be greatly increased were they to be included in revised strategies.

Looking at the persistent human tragedy of malaria though the MuSCLE lens, it is possible to view the potential for much more sustainable, integrated solutions. These solutions may combine several or all of the following components for a contextualized response: (i) ITNs provided free from the outside; (ii) establishment of a local cottage industry to make affordable ITNs with local materials and skills (perhaps treated with a natural insecticide); (iii) an educational program to raise awareness of risks and simple ways to mitigate them; (iv) vulnerability reduction that tackles socio-economic and cultural factors that heighten risk (lifestyle and livelihood strategies); (v) drug therapy based on artemisinin made available at local clinics; (vi) improved nutrition and iron supplements (malaria contributes to iron-deficiency anemia); (vii) careful, targeted insecticide spraying; (viii) re-vegetation that cools the landscape to temperatures below the breeding range of mosquitoes; (ix) swamp reclamation (cool, shaded swamps are not a vector habitat); (x) swamp conversion to cropland that uses the fodder crop nappier grass to shade shallow irrigation channels that otherwise become habitat; (xi) changing other land-use practices that encourage the vector, for example stopping brush-clearing that people perceive to be effective but which perversely increases the vector habitat of warm stagnant puddles created by cattle hoofprints. To promote social learning, as well as local stakeholder working groups, we plan to employ health promoters from the affected communities (to be trained in malaria etiology, prevention and treatment methods, and risk communication). Networks are to be set-up to link communities, share knowledge, and build social capital and collective capacity.

to prioritization. "Risk" is the probability of an outcome multiplied by the severity of the consequence should it occur [52]: risk "hot spots" are where both probability and consequence are high. WHO [53, p. 52] defines risk as the "likelihood of identified hazards causing harm in exposed populations in a specific time frame, including the magnitude of that harm and/or consequences".

Quantitative risk assessment (QRA) involves identification of hazards (specific toxicities of chemical and biological agents), dose–response relationships that model the probability of a given health effect as a function of exposure, and exposure assessment that estimates contact between agents and human targets over time. QRA yields a risk estimate in terms of order-of-magnitude individual or population-level probabilities of a particular disease or endpoint.

An extension of risk theory, vulnerability is defined as: "differential capacity to deal with hazards, based on the position of groups and individuals within both the physical and social worlds" [54, p. 59]. Vulnerability may be analyzed in terms of potential exposures, susceptibility to harm, and ability to avoid exposure and cope with harm [55]. Vulnerability comprises: (1) differential exposure to risk agents or stressors, like toxics, floods, droughts, hurricanes; (2) differential susceptibility or sensitivity to adverse outcomes if exposed; (3) differential preparedness to respond to stressors; (4) differential 'coping', 'resilience' or 'adaptability' or ability to recover from adverse effects [55,56]. Coping or adaptability involves finding ways to reduce risks by either reducing the probability of an adverse outcome and/or the severity of the outcome should it occur.

Thus high vulnerability to disease can be explained by a combination of three determinants: (a) enhanced sensitivity/susceptibility to adverse outcomes from higher-than-background exposure to risk agents (biological, chemical, social, political, and economic) plus a higher probability of adverse response as a result; (b) reduced capacity to adapt autonomously; (c) severely reduced or zero planned adaptive capacity. Differential exposure to risks is a function of the quality of the environment(s) people come into contact with, and the type and amount of contact they have: time–activity–environment patterns. Differential sensitivity may be a function of gender, age, immune status, etc. (e.g. lead poisoning in infants and small children), while differential adaptability is a function of socio-economic variables. Vulnerability assessment owes much to epidemiology, especially in the case of HIV/AIDS [13–17].

For policy, a risk and vulnerability approach combined with systems understanding (Figure 2) expands the range of interventions available to reduce vulnerability. Vulnerability and sustainability can be considered two halves of the same environment-development coin: vulnerability is reduced, sustainability increased, when adaptive capacity is strengthened. The attention that should be paid to capacity building is also reinforced with this duality (see Section 5). A vulnerability approach to assessment also stimulates dialogue and social learning as it creates a space of convergence among different disciplines (e.g. health science, geography, economics and anthropology), types of knowledge (local, anecdotal, indigenous, scientific), and interests.

4. Selecting among interventions

Once priority health problems have been identified and placed in their societal and ecological contexts, stakeholders need to identify alternative solutions/

interventions and compare the ecological, socio-cultural, economic and political tradeoffs among them; i.e. undertake an assessment of their relative sustainability. We seek cost-effective, efficient and sustainable interventions. Cost effectiveness is best estimated in terms of expected changes in the risk of disease (prevalence and incidence) and/or changes in disability adjusted life years (DALYs) per unit resource cost, with resources measured in terms of money, personnel and information.

The call for a new type of multi-criteria analysis to guide decision making stems from a realization of the limitations of two closely linked conventional practices: environmental impact assessment (EIA) and cost–benefit analysis (CBA). EIA is applied to the screening of proposed development projects like roads, hospitals, dams, and factories. It suffers from bias in favor of proposed projects, discourages active participation by the public, and has become a regulatory end in itself, rather than a means to better development choices as originally intended [57]. CBA is widely used to screen and select among project or policy alternatives. Heinzerling and Ackerman [58] launched a strong critique of the method, listing major weaknesses: (i) more efficient decisions are not possible because reducing the value of life, health and nature to monetary units is flawed; (ii) use of monetary discounting systematically and improperly devalues long-term environmental risks and health effects, and any action that protects the interests of future generations; (iii) CBA also reinforces existing patterns of economic, ecological and socio-political inequities, since the method ignores how costs and benefits are distributed in society; (iv) the method as practiced is far from being transparent or objective, and the top-down nature of analysis precludes participation by people most affected by the decisions. They also highlight weakness in practical implementation: benefits are often not quantified (or cannot be), and costs are often skewed in favor of an option preferred by those undertaking or paying for the analysis.

Daly and Cobb [59] scrutinized CBA, arguing it only works as a rational model if one can compare investing in a given project with depositing money in a bank and accruing interest. Satisfaction of many social, political, cultural and ecological needs, either within a current generation or a future one, cannot be valued exclusively in this way [59]. While the use of CBA in policy and regulation is treated with growing skepticism by scholars [58–62] when incorporated as part of a wider multi-criteria assessment, the limitations of CBA can be overcome. Criteria for health intervention selection can include the following: (a) social/health criteria: projected positive and negative impacts ("benefits" and "costs", respectively); (b) economic criteria: projected positive and negative impacts in terms of resources (personnel, money, information, facilities); (c) ecological criteria: the projected positive and negative impacts in terms of ecology and the natural environment.

This type of transparent multi-criteria sustainability assessment of alternative interventions and scenarios, with stakeholder agreement on which alternatives to compare, criteria to employ and how impacts' tradeoffs are estimated, is basic to fostering both trust and ownership of interventions. It is particularly important to compare scenarios of the future for unstable infectious diseases like malaria and AIDS, assuming each of the different interventions considered. What does a business-as-usual future of AIDS, and malaria look like 10 years, 20 years from now (based on our Fig. 2 understanding), and how do alternatives compare? Integrated solutions that control system drivers, and meld prevention and treatment can be devised and compared against the baseline conventional approach. Notably, such sustainability assessment is both conducive of stakeholder dialogue and social learning, and a result of them. Revealing the possibility of an alternative, more positive future – especially for those who see none – is a transformative process.

5. Building capacity

The last feature of the MuSCLE framework is building societal capacity to sustain selected interventions, and adapt to changing conditions and priorities over time. According to UNDP [63], capacity building is the sum of efforts to develop, enhance and utilize the skills of people and institutions. Systematized capacity building is fundamental to sustainable poverty reduction and health promotion under the MDGs. Participatory integrated capacity building (PICB) is an approach synthesized from literature, international experiences and empirical evidence [64–66]. Case studies of many types of development projects were compared based on their relative sustainability and key characteristics. Relatively sustainable projects were those yielding a steady stream of net benefits over time after external donor support was withdrawn. Such projects were in the minority (10% of the sample) and distinguished themselves from the majority of case studies by having two distinct predictors of success: (a) a project process that built several complementary levels of capacity among stakeholders and the wider society they represented; (b) constructive stakeholder interaction that fostered trust, ownership of a problem and its solution, and empowerment. The approach was originally developed to build multi-stakeholder capacity to sustain urban water supply and sanitation in Mexico [64] and was later extended conceptually to sustaining health risk mitigation [65]. Evidence suggests that to sustain net benefits over time requires the co-strengthening of six interdependent levels of societal capacity:

(1) Political will and financial seed capital to initiate transitions and improve existing policies and practices.
(2) Human resource strengthening—education, training, communication, and raising awareness within formal and informal institutions and among stakeholder groups.
(3) Information resource strengthening—monitoring, data synthesis, analysis and modeling to characterize baseline conditions, identify priority problems and infer drivers.

(4) Policy making and planning—the design, enactment and enforcement of responsive policies, practices, laws, regulations, tariffs, and rights, with equity, accountability and incentive mechanisms.

(5) Basic infrastructure and appropriate technologies—health care facilities, prevention and treatment technologies, and sanitation infrastructure.

(6) Enterprise development and investment stimulation—provision of products and services, stimulation of entrepreneurial activities (especially local) that provide economic sustainability to the health program, substitute seed finance, and subsidize the costs of primary care for the poor.

These six 'hexagonal' levels interact with each other to support the program objectives and health solutions at the center (Figure 4). To make the approach practical, each of the six levels is further broken down into smaller operational elements. For example, if reducing under-five mortality by two thirds is the goal (MDG 4), and we have identified a preferred 'most sustainable' package of disease-specific interventions for ARI, enterics, malaria, etc., the capacity building system supports the interventions as follows:

• Level 2 capacity may include a community education program for children and parents about reducing risks and adopting the interventions; training for health practitioners.

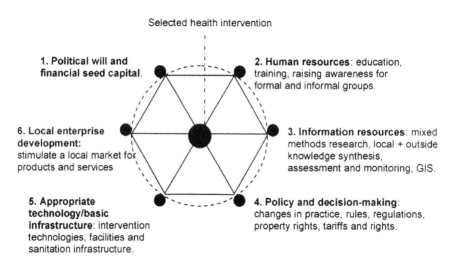

Figure 4 Capacity building system to sustain health interventions. (A) Based on the work of Downs [64–66], the health solution is sustained using a system of six different categories of capacities, shown here as a hexagon with the intervention/solution at the center. The intervention plan from the strategic planning stage (stage 2 of Figure 1) – answering what to do, how, where, when, why, with whom, at what cost – includes this hexagonal support system.

- Level 3 may include a GIS-based monitoring system to evaluate impacts of interventions.
- Level 4 may include responsive primary care policies and regulations with accountability.
- Level 5 may include health care facilities to deliver the intervention, and sanitation infrastructure.
- Level 6 may include ancillary health care and sanitation products and services.

For a full account of the application of this approach to health risk management, and urban water supply and sanitation in Mexican pilot cities, see Downs [65] and Downs [64], respectively. The hexagonal capacity building actually happens at two levels under MuSCLE: (a) micro-level: focused on the specific target priority problem and intervention, and built into the action plan; (b) macro-level: evolving from, and supportive of the social learning process as a whole.

6. Overall approach: implementation

We argue for multi-stakeholder capacity-building and learning for empowerment – MuSCLE – that fosters social learning and strengthens social capital. The MuSCLE process has three main features: (1) participatory, systems-based assessment of health challenges and responses; (2) selection among intervention alternatives that makes tradeoffs transparent; (3) a support system of capacity building to sustain adaptive interventions. In theory, the process is transferable across different, yet interrelated MDG sectors – health, energy, agriculture, industry, water – such that economies of scale can be exploited in severely resource-limited settings. It derives from and maintains a "living dialogue with genuine needs" that Havel (67, p. 119) advocates, favoring partnerships between formal and informal structures that encourage creative thought, communication and social learning. Table 1 describes generic guidelines for implementation, while Box 5 sets down 10 operating principles.

6.1. Risks and obstacles

Institutional inertia and resistance to new approaches must be overcome for the process to flourish. This is best done by making benefits explicit, proving the success of the approach in high-profile pilot projects, and demonstrating transferability. Three major risks are corruption, high transaction costs and destructive politics among stakeholders, but these risks can be minimized and/or mitigated by a carefully crafted MuSCLE approach that stimulates dialogue, builds collective understanding, and distributes the benefits of social learning and capacity building. The relationship between

Table 1 Practical guidelines for implementing a MuSCLE approach.

Step	Component of process	Description of activities	Milestone/Indicator of progress	Who?
1	Stakeholder and context preparation	Identify stakeholders and assemble existing general information about the geographical area where work is to be done: health, ecological, socio-political and economic conditions and characteristics. Include satellite imagery and GIS interpretation as appropriate.	Contextual information	Project initiators, facilitators.
2	Introduction to project and process	Hold preliminary scoping meeting to introduce project goals (could be MDGs) for the target population/area. Allow stakeholders to introduce themselves and their interests. Present the social learning cycle and revise the process. Receive feedback and revise the process as agreed. Agree upon project objectives.	Interest in project is garnered, stakeholders identified, political will sufficient.	Facilitators and stakeholder representatives.
3	Set-up working groups, and human resources	Organize four levels of working groups: i) steering group to oversee whole process, composed of representatives from the stakeholder groups (community*, public agency, private sector, academic, NGO, donor); ii) mixed methods research team to undertake field research activity and data gathering; iii) community-level working groups* to coordinate activity at the level of target communities, and provide local knowledge; and (as needed) iv) technical advisory group to provide technical support to other groups.* Include marginalized groups, women and children.	Working groups organized – human and social capital mobilized.	Facilitators and stakeholder representatives in respective working groups

4	Learning cycle Stage 1. Participatory assessment	Undertake detailed scoping sessions with local stakeholders, facilitated by community working groups. Assemble existing information and integrate into GIS database as appropriate. Identify key data gaps and design field sampling in a strategic way to maximize the information value per unit effort. Use mixed-methods research to gather new data, process and interpret. Identify priority problems and issues using risk/ vulnerability science, and drivers (build a model). Discuss results with the different working groups. Revise project objectives as needed.	Knowledge base and 'model'. Priority problems, needs, drivers identified. Process evaluation.	Working groups (with appropriate dynamics for the task)
5	Learning cycle Stage 2. Strategic planning	Identify all alternative responses and solutions to the priority problems and needs identified in 4 through open brains torming session. Screen the list using viability criteria (cultural, economic, technical) and keep a shortlist of viable alternatives. Submit the alternatives to selection using agreed-upon criteria (see 4.0) Select preferred option. Design action plan for this option that includes the integrated capacity building to sustain it over time (see 5.0).	Transparent planning leading to action plans. Process evaluation. Buy-in level.	Working groups
6	Learning cycle Stage 3. Implementation	Implement activities from the action plan on a timeline that prioritizes them based on their urgency and practicality at any given time. Some activities will require capacity to be built first.	Actions implemented. Process evaluated.	Working groups
7	Learning cycle Stage 4. Monitoring	Performance of actions undertaken with some key indicators used in step 4. Impacts of interventions are assessed, and compared to those expected by step 5 to refresh future selection.	Outcomes and impacts evaluated. Buy-in level.	Working groups
8	Learning cycle Back to Stage 1. Reassessment and remodeling	Results of monitoring are used to re-inform the assessment, the system model and to revise project objectives and plans accordingly. The cycle progresses as we learn more and build capacity.	Experience re-informs ongoing process. Sustained buy-in.	Working groups

The steps assume that funding has been obtained for a project in a target population and setting. If funding has not yet been obtained, initiators may undertake steps 1–2 and develop a funding proposal that competes for funds to complete the process. While the steps are generic, details of what happens and how is driven by specific project objectives and context. The working groups are informal and change as the project evolves and objectives change. Steps 4–8 reflect an iterative process, with knowledge and lessons learned being actively incorporated to improve understanding and progress.

Box 5. Guiding principles for a MuSCLE approach

(1) People-at-risk need to be full partners in understanding and solving their own health problems.

(2) Prevention and treatment options should be melded, with more emphasis on the former.

(3) Invest in social learning that builds trust, social capital and capacities to target priority health problems, stimulating ownership of problems and solutions.

(4) The partnership should comprise representatives from: (i) formal community-based organizations (CBOs); (ii) informal civil society groups (especially marginal groups, women and youth); (iii) academic researchers; (iv) donors; (v) governmental health agencies (local, district, state, including health practitioners); (vi) non-governmental agencies (NGOs); (vii) private sector businesses. Youth energy is a vital resource.

(5) Partners are involved in appropriate ways in all four stages of a learning cycle: assessment, planning, implementation and monitoring that re-informs assessment. Rules of engagement, and the roles and responsibilities of partners are explicit and agreed-upon by all those involved.

(6) Disruptive forces – corruption, destructive political interactions, and burdensome transaction costs – are to be monitored and mitigated. Understanding power relations and institutional frameworks is essential.

(7) The knowledge base about health conditions, characteristics, priorities and drivers is built collectively, inclusive of indigenous knowledge. Priorities are identified based on an evidence-based risk and vulnerability approach. The integrated systems-based understanding of health problems includes their socio-cultural, political and economic contexts. Any model should be as simple as possible, no simpler.

(8) Decision-making is transparent, with agreement about priority problems, viable alternative solutions, by what criteria they are to be compared, and how this is to be done.

(9) Capacity building benefits for partners are made explicit and equitable to ensure sustained buy-in and commitment, and action plans include the requisite capacity building needed to sustain solutions.

(10) Economies of scale across problems and sectors should be exploited for cost effectiveness, sustainability and maximum impact.

---

corruption and poverty has been explored by Downs [66] in the context of elites that regulate the flow of information within a society, and discourage community empowerment by placing high transaction costs on bureaucratic and legal procedures. The relationship among corruption, health, poverty and development is far from simple; scholar-practitioners need to undertake research to better understand it in a given setting [68–70]. Strong community ownership of a sanitation project on the Mexican side of the US–Mexico border, for example, successfully mitigated attempts by corrupt groups to gain control of the project [66].

High transaction costs are a major risk for multi-stakeholder projects, and have been partly responsible for skepticism with the public participation and partnership process. Falconer [71] flags the risks of high transaction costs for farmers and the state involved in inefficient participatory processes for agro-environmental schemes in the European Union. She recommends governments rationalize how farmers apply to different schemes, minimizing overhead costs, and promote longer-term capacity building for farmer networks. Successful NGOs build their own capacity to mitigate high trans-action costs, and can act as facilitators of a MuSCLE approach. Cameron [72] draws on 50 years of modern development economics, and the past 10 years of New Institutional Economics (NIE) to assert that NGOs working on micro-finance and income generation can be agents who redistribute transaction and transition costs, risks and uncertainties, in favor of the poor. Without due care, interactions among stakeholders may deteriorate into conflict that expends large amounts of social and financial capital, and leave project goals unmet. Businesses have significantly reduced transaction costs by internalizing them through diversified networks [73], and networks that cross-subsidize each others' capacities can attain formidable capacity in partnership.

Looking at the constraints and determinants of women's participation in local groups in Chad and Kashmir, Weinberger and Jutting [74] identified the risk that the middle classes appropriate the process, while the high opportunity costs and low bargaining power of the poor conspire to exclude them. This highlights the importance of any process being broadly repre-sentative of diverse interests in a community and horizontal in organization [18]. Working in China, Shenkar and Aimin [75] also remind us to pay attention to political dynamics and power relations among stakeholders (see Section 3.2). Trying to explain the failure of international cooperative ventures simply using limited theories of transaction costs, partner selection, or bargaining and learning may neglect an underlying destructive dynamic of political behavior. Svendsen and Svendsen [76] argue that prosperity dif-ferences between rich and poor countries can be explained by stocks and flows of social capital that promote informal human exchanges and the voluntary provision of collective goods like trust that mitigate destructive politics.

7. Conclusion

In his 1961 inaugural speech, President John F. Kennedy spoke provocatively of the need to "forge a grand and global alliance" against the "common enemies of Man: tyranny, poverty, disease and war itself" [77]. Arguably that need is greater now than ever. The case for using a MuSCLE-type approach to design health interventions – a trans-epistemological, multi-stakeholder process that fosters social learning and builds societal capacity for sustainable health improvement and poverty reduction – is compelling. Biomedical responses to global health concerns must evolve to become integral partners in this creative, organic and collaborative endeavor. Special attention needs to be paid to power relations among and within stakeholder groups, the social drivers of health, and the key role of youth in visioning, creating and owning healthier futures. The approach is necessarily transferable across development sectors and priorities, and can be scaled up or down to suit project objectives. A MuSCLE-bound process fostering ownership of health and poverty problems and their solutions promises significant progress; we should fully explore its potential between now and the 2015 horizon for significant poverty reduction progress. Without it, or something a lot like it, global health goals will remain unmet. With it those goals can not only be met, but likely surpassed.

Acknowledgements

Funding for the Worcester project is provided by the U.S. National Institutes of Health program *Environmental Justice – Partnerships for Communication*, grant# IR25ES013210-03. Funding for the malaria work is provided by the Global Environment Facility's *Assessment of Impacts and Adaptations to Climate Change/Advancing Capacity to support Climate Change/Adaptation* programs (AIACC/ACCCA). We thank the Harvard Center for Population and Development Studies for its ongoing support.

Note

1 Data table: www.polioeradication.org.

References

[1] UN. Millennium development goals report 2005; 2005. http://unstats.un.org/unsd/mi/pdf/MDG%20Book.pdf (consulted April 2006).

[2] UN. United Nations website; 2005. http://www.un.org/millenniumgoals/ (consulted January 2005).

[3] MP. Investing in development: a practical guide to achieve the millennium development goals. New York: Millennium Project, UN; 2005. http://www.unmillenniumproject.org/goals/goals02.htm (consulted 5 April 2005).

186

[4] Woodhill J., Röling N. G. The second wing of the eagle: the human dimension in learning our way to more sustainable futures. In: Röling N. G., Wagemakers M. A. E., editors. Facilitating sustainable agriculture. Cambridge: Cambridge University Press; 1998. p. 46–71.

[5] Guangxia C., Lianmin Z. In: Wollenberg E., Edmunds D., Buck L., Fox J., Brodt S., editors. Social learning in community forests. Jakarta, Indonesia: CIFOR and East-West Center; 2001. p. 109–26.

[6] Buck L. E., Wollenberg E., Edmunds D. Social learning in collaborative management of community forests: lessons from the field. In: Wollenberg E., Edmunds D., Buck L., Fox J., Brodt S., editors. Social learning in community forests. Jakarta, Indonesia: CIFOR and East-West Center. p. 1–20.

[7] Daniels S., Walker G. Rethinking public participation in natural resources management: concepts from pluralism and five emerging approaches. In: FAO. Pluralism and sustainable forestry and rural development. Proceedings of an international workshop. Rome: Food and Agriculture Organization; 1999. p. 29–48.

[8] Gray-Felder D., Deane J. Communication for social change: a position paper and conference report; 1999 (www.communicationforsocialchange.org).

[9] Kawachi I., O'Neill M. Exploration of health disparities. In: Goehl T. J., editor. Essays on the future of environmental health research: a tribute to Dr. Kenneth Olden. Research Triangle Park, NC: Environmental Health Perspectives and NIEHS; 2005. p. 100–7.

[10] Corburn J. Confronting the challenges in reconnecting urban planning and public health. American Journal of Public Health 2004;94(4):541–6.

[11] Larson H., Narain J. Beyond 2000: responding to HIV/AIDS in the new millennium. New Delhi: World Health Organization; 2001.

[12] Lebel J. Health: an ecosystem approach. Ottawa, Canada: International Development Research Center; 2003, 84 p.

[13] Galea S., Ahern J., Karpati A. A model of underlying socioeconomic vulnerability in human populations: evidence from variability in population health and implications for public health. Social Science Medicine 2005;60(11): 2417–30.

[14] Piwoz E. G., Bentley M. E. Women's voices, women's choices: the challenge of nutrition and HIV/AIDS. Journal of Nutrition 2005;135(4):933–7.

[15] Abel E., Chambers K. Factors that influence vulnerability to STDs and HIV/AIDS among Hispanic women. Health Care Women International 2004;25(8):761–80.

[16] Bates I., Fenton C., Gruber J., Lalloo D., Lara A. M., Squire S. B., Theobald S., Thomson R., Tolhurst R. Vulnerability to malaria, tuberculosis and HIV/AIDS infection and disease. Part 1. Determinants operating at individual and household levels. Lancet Infectious Disease 2004;4(5):267–77.

[17] De Moura S. L. The social distribution of reports of health-related concerns among adolescents in Sao Paulo, Brazil. Health Education Research 2004;19(2):175–84.

[18] Larson H. Light my fire: community mobilization and HIV/AIDS. Working paper prepared for UNAIDS, Geneva; 1998.

[19] Rossi D. Drug users involvement in AIDS prevention. In: Paper presented at the 10th international conference on AIDS. 1994.

[20] Murphy J. P. Pragmatism: from Pierce to Davidson. Boulder, CO: Westview Press; 1990.

[21] IRC. Community management: the way forward. Report of the workshop held 19–27 November 2001 in Rockanje, Netherlands; 2001a.

[22] IRC. From system to service—scaling-up community management. Report of the conference held 12–13 December 2001 in The Hague, Netherlands; 2001b.

[23] Bolt E., Khadka R. Water supply management by communities: a new challenge for support agencies. In: Sustainable development international. 3rd ed. London: ICG Publishing Ltd.; 2000. p. 65–70.

[24] Brikke F. Operation and maintenance of rural water supply and sanitation systems: a training package for managers and planners. Geneva, Switzerland: World Health Organization; 2000.

[25] CEFOC. Modèles de gestion privée oue déléguée de la maintenance de systèmes d'AEP. Training session on management of maintenance for drinking water in rural areas, EIER/ETSHER; 1999.

[26] Chambers R. Understanding professionals: small farmers and scientists. In: IADS occasional paper. New York: International Agriculture Development Service; 1980.

[27] Chambers R. Rural development: putting the last first. Longman; 1992.

[28] Estienne C. Making community management of piped water systems in the secondary towns of Senegal river valley more professional. In: Le Jalle C., et al., editors. Water supply and sanitation in peri-urban areas and small centers. GRET, Programme; 1999. p. 129–31.

[29] Livingstone A. J. Community management of small urban water supplies in Sudan and Ghana. In: WHO and WSSCC working group on operation and maintenance, operations and maintenance of water supply and sanitation systems: case studies. Geneva, Switzerland: World Health Organization; 1994. p. 44–56.

[30] Moriarty P. B. Broadening water supply to address rural livelihoods. In: Proceedings of the 27th WEDC conference, people and systems for water, sanitation and health. 2001.

[31] World Bank. World development report: infrastructure for development. Oxford, UK: Oxford University Press; 1994, 254 p.

[32] WSSCC. Vision 21: water for people—a shared vision for hygiene, sanitation and water supply. Geneva, Switzerland: Water Supply and Sanitation Collaborative Council; 2000.

[33] King M. L. Where do we go from here: chaos or community? New York: Harper & Row; 1967.

[34] Lynn F. M. Community-scientist collaboration in environmental research. American Behavioral Scientist 2000;44(4):649–63.

[35] Arcury T. A., Austin C. K., Quandt S. A., Saavedra R. Enhancing community participation in intervention research: farmworks and agricultural chemicals in North Carolina. Health Education and Behavior 1997;26(4):563–78.

[36] Ashford N. A., Rest K. M. Public participation in contaminated communities. Cambridge, MA: Center for Technology, Policy and Industrial Development, MIT; 1999.

[37] Couto R. Failing health and new prescriptions: community-based appro-aches to environmental risks. In: Hill C. E., editor. Contemporary health policy issues: an applied social perspective. Athens: University of Georgia Press; 1984.

[38] Israel B. A., Schultz A. J., Parker E. A., Becker A. B. Review of community-based research: assessing partnership approaches to improve public health. Annual Review of Public Health 1998;19:173–204.

[39] Lynn F. M., Busenburg G. Citizen advisory committee and environmental policy. Risk Analysis 1995;15:147–62.

[40] Scammell M. Environmental justice: partnerships for communication and com-munity-based prevention-intervention research, proceedings. Starkville: National Institute of Environmental Health Sciences and Mississippi State University; 1999.

[41] Schell L., Tarbell A. A partnership study of PCBs and the health of Mohawk youth: lessons from our past and guidelines for our future. Environmental Health Perspectives 1998;106(Suppl. 3):833–40.

[42] Northridge M. E., Shoemaker K., Jean-Louis B., Ortiz B., Swaner R., Vaughan R. D., Cushman L. F., Hutchinson V. E., Nicholas S. W. Using community-based participatory research to ask and answer questions regarding the environmental and health. In: Goehl T. J., editor. Essays on the future of environmental health research: a tribute to Dr. Kenneth Olden. Research Triangle Park, NC: Environ-mental Health Perspectives and NIEHS. p. 34–41.

[43] Wing S. Environmental justice, science and public health. In: Goehl T. J., editor. Essays on the future of environmental health research: a tribute to Dr. Kenneth Olden. Research Triangle Park, NC: Environmental Health Perspectives and NIEHS; 2005. p. 54–63.

[44] Cranmer J. M. The role of town meetings in environmental health research. In: Goehl T. J., editor. Essays on the future of environmental health research: a tribute to Dr. Kenneth Olden. Research Triangle Park, NC: Environmental Health Perspectives and NIEHS; 2005. p. 152–61.

[45] Holling C. S. Understanding the complexity of economic, ecological and social systems. Ecosystems 2001;4:390–405.

[46] WHO. Environmental health indicators: framework and methodologies. WHO, Geneva: Report WHO/SDE/OEH/99.10; 1999.

[47] WHO. Reducing mortality from major childhood killer diseases. Fact Sheet #180; 2005. http://www.who.int/child-adolescent-health/New_Publications/IMCI/fs_180.htm (consulted May 2005).

[48] Fischhoff B., Fischhoff I. R., Casman E. A., Dowlatabadi H. Integrated assess-ment of malaria risk. In: Casman E. A., Dowlatabadi H., editors. The contextual determinants of malaria, resources for the future. Washington, DC; 2002: 382 p (p. 331–48).

[49] Laakonnen H. Quoted in East African Standard April 20; 2005.

[50] Malaika Project. Malaika Project website; 2005. www. malaikaproject.org (consulted May 2005).

[51] WHO. The use of artemisinin and its derivatives as anti-malarial drugs; 1998. At: http://www.who.int/malaria/docs/artrep.htm#p7 (consulted May 2005).

[52] Wilson R., Crouch E. A. C. Risk–benefit analysis. Cambridge: Harvard University Press; 2001, 370 p.

[53] WHO. Guidelines for drinking water quality. 3rd ed. Geneva: World Health Organization; 2005.

[54] Clark, et al. Assessing the vulnerability of coastal communities to extreme storms: the case of Revere, MA, USA. In: Goehl T. J., editor. Mitigation, adaptation strategies for global, change; 1998. p. 59–82.

[55] Ahmad Q. K., et al. Summary for policy makers. In: McCarthy J. J., Canziani O. F., Leary N. A., Dokken D. J., White K. S., editors. Climate change 2001: impacts, adaptation and vulnerability. Contribution of the working group II to the third assessment report of the Intergovernmental Panel on Climate Change. Cambridge; 2001.

[56] NEJAC/EPA. Ensuring risk reduction in communities with multiple stressors: environmental justice and cumulative risks/impacts. Report developed from the national environmental justice advisory council meeting of 13–16 April 2004. Washington, DC: USEPA; 2004.

[57] Brown A. L. Decision scoping. In: Porter A. L., Fittipaldi J. J., editors. Environmental methods review: re-tooling impact assessment for the new century. The Press Club, Fargo, ND: Army Environmental Policy Institute (AEPI) and International Association for Impact Assessment (IAIA); 1998. p. 135–43.

[58] Heinzerling L., Ackerman F. Pricing the priceless: cost–benefit analysis of environmental protection. Washington, DC: Georgetown Environmental Law and Policy Institute, Georgetown University Law Center; 2002.

[59] Daly H. E., Cobb Jr J. B. For the common good: redirecting the economy toward community, the environment, and a sustainable future. 2nd ed. Boston: Beacon Press; 1994, 531 p.

[60] Goodstein E. Polluted data. American Prospect 8; 1997. At www.prospect.org.

[61] Richardson H. S. The stupidity of the cost–benefit standard. Journal of Legal Studies 2000;29:971–1003.

[62] Harrington W., Morgenstern R. D., Nelson P. On the accuracy of regulatory cost estimates. Journal of Policy Analysis and Management 2000;19: 297–322.

[63] UNDP. About Capacity 21; 2001. UNDP website: http://www.unescap.org/drpad/vc/orientation/M3anx_pic_c21.htm (consulted January 2005).

[64] Downs T. J. Making sustainable development operational: integrated capacity building for the water supply and sanitation sector in Mexico. Journal of Environmental Planning and Management 2001;44(4):525–44.

[65] Downs T. J. Sustainable health risk management and the role of cross-disciplinary professionals in developing countries: Mexican experience. Environment, Development & Sustainability 2001;3(1):60–81.

[66] Downs T. J. Changing the culture of underdevelopment and unsustainability. Journal of Environmental Planning and Management 2000;43(5):601–21.

[67] Havel V. Living in truth. London: Faber and Faber; 1986, 315 p.

[68] Qizilbash M. Corruption and human development: a conceptual discussion. Oxford Development Studies 2001;29(3):265–78.

[69] Caiden G. Corruption, development and underdevelopment. Journal of Public Administration Research and Theory; 1(4):484–8.

[70] Palmier L. Corruption, development and inequality. Journal of Public Administration Research and Theory 1990;10(4):475–6.

[71] Falconer K. Farm-level constraints on agri-environmental scheme participation: a transaction perspective. Journal of Rural Studies 2000;16(3):379–94.

[72] Cameron J. Development economics: the new institutional economics and NGOs. Third World Quarterly 2000;21(4):627–35.

[73] Lee J. W. The nature of Chaebol restructuring: two lessons from Professor Coase. Journal of International and Area Studies 2002;9(2):23–41.

[74] Weinberger K., Jutting J. P. Women's participation in local organizations: conditions and constraints. World Development 2001;29(8):1391–404.

[75] Shenkar O., Aimin Y. Failure as a consequence of partner politics: learning from the life and death of an international corporate venture. Human Relations 2002;55(5):565–601.

[76] Svendsen G. L. H., Svendsen G. T. On the wealth of nations: bourdieuconomics and social capital. Theory and Society 2003;32:607–31.

[77] Kennedy J. F. Presidential inaugural address. http://www.jfklibrary.org/j012061. htm.

62

BETWEEN ISOLATIONISM AND MUTUAL VULNERABILITY

A South-North perspective on global governance of epidemics in an age of globalization

*Obijiofor Aginam**

Source: *Temple Law Review*, 77 (2004), 297–312.

> We meet as we fight to defeat SARS, the first new epidemic of the twenty-first century. . . . Globalization of disease and threats to health mean globalization of the fight against them. SARS has been a wake-up call. But the lessons we have learned have implications that go way beyond the fight against this public health threat. . . . The events of the last few weeks also prompt us to look closely at the instruments of national and international law. Are they keeping up with our rapidly changing world?[1]

I. The crux of the argument

The transnational spread of infectious and non-communicable diseases in an era of globalization constitutes one of the most formidable challenges facing the normative orthodoxy of the Westphalian governance architecture. Exponents of "globalization of public health"[2] have explored the globalized nature of emerging and reemerging public health threats in an interdependent world. The recent transnational spread of severe acute respiratory syndrome ("SARS") from Asia to North America, as Brundtland observed in the quote above, is not only a wake-up call; it has once again challenged the legal and regulatory approaches to global health governance. This paper juxtaposes two contending approaches to public health governance: *isolationism* and *mutual vulnerability*, and argues for a reconfiguration of transnational health governance structures based on an inclusive humane globalism. Despite the powerful arguments canvassed by the exponents of globalization of public health, the stark realities of the contemporary South-North health divide has regrettably popularized isolationism, thereby impeding the emergence and sustenance of humane governance of global public health threats.

Isolationism is premised on the impression that the developing world is a reservoir of disease. In the discourse of hard-nosed realism, isolationism is a conscious effort to create a health sanctuary in the developed world that maximizes the health security of populations in Europe and North America. As SARS and other historical epidemics have infallibly proven, the argument canvassed by scholars of globalization of public health on the obsolescence or anachronism of the distinction between national and international health threats has become less recondite and unassailable in an interdependent world. Using SARS as the subject of analysis, this article explores the challenges of global governance of transnational epidemics in an interdependent world. I argue that global health governance orthodoxy has failed to respond adequately to public health challenges in a world characterized by South-North disparities.[3] I offer a reconstructive perspective that goes beyond the normative parameters of state-centric Westphalianism. The reconstruction draws from Richard Falk's "law of humanity," and David Held's "cosmopolitan social democracy:" a cosmopolitan or quasi-cosmopolitan framework that captures the South-North health divide based on the mutual vulnerability of all of humanity to the menace of disease in an interdependent world.

II. Isolationism and the evolution of public health diplomacy

Thus, the eleventh International Sanitary Conference in 53 years had as its essential purpose the protection of Europe against the importation of exotic diseases.[4]

Isolationism, a conscious effort to insulate populations within the geopolitical boundaries of a nation-state from exotic diseases, is as old as the history of public health diplomacy. Before the European-led international sanitary conferences in the nineteenth century that were driven by the European cholera epidemics in 1830 and 1847, Neville Goodman identified three dominant reactions by nation-states to the trans-boundary spread of disease.[5] The first was the predominant view that disease was a punishment from the gods that could only be cured by prayers and sacrifices.[6] The second reaction was the isolation of a healthy society from an unhealthy one through the practice of *cordon sanitaire* to prevent either importation or exportation of disease.[7] The third reaction was the practice of quarantine that enabled governments to isolate goods or persons coming from places suspected of suffering an outbreak of disease to protect the community from importation of exotic diseases.[8] Between the fourteenth and nineteenth centuries, almost the entire *civilized* world practiced some form of quarantine. This consisted mainly of imposing an arbitrary period of isolation on the ships, crews, passengers, and goods arriving from foreign sea ports and destinations believed to be reservoirs of major epidemic diseases, especially plague, cholera, and yellow fever.[9]

The nineteenth century, within which public health diplomacy evolved in Europe through the International Sanitary Conferences, raises intriguing questions on the transnational governance of infectious diseases. This is because the civilized-uncivilized construct invented in the Age of Columbus had become firmly entrenched in the vocabulary of nineteenth century international law and relations. Peter Malanczuk observed that the international community in the nineteenth century was virtually *Europeanized* on the basis of conquest and domination; the international legal system became an exclusive European club to which non-Europeans would only be admitted if they proved that they were civilized.[10] The *realpolitik* of nineteenth century public health diplomacy driven by the international sanitary conferences was the desire to protect civilized Europe from exotic diseases and pathogens that emanated from the uncivilized non-European societies. As Norman Howard-Jones observed, the international sanitary conferences were not motivated by a wish for the general betterment of the health of the world, but by the desire to protect certain favored (especially European) nations from contamination by their less-favoured (especially Eastern fellows).[11] Cholera presents an apt illustration of the European desire to keep exotic diseases far from reaching European territorial boundaries. Goodman observed that for centuries cholera, although terrible in rapidity and high morbidity, was considered a disease largely confined to Central Asia, particularly Bengal. But between 1828 and 1831, it was reported to have passed out of India and spread rapidly to the whole of Europe and to the United States.[12] From Punjab, Afghanistan, and Persia:

> [I]t reached Moscow in 1830 and infected the whole of Europe, including England, by the end of 1831. It reached Canada and the United States of America in the summer of 1832. . . . Another pandemic followed in 1847 and five others in the next fifty years. This was a new and terrifying disease to the Western world. . . .[13]

The entire gamut of the international sanitary conventions and regulations negotiated at each of the European-led international sanitary conference is replete with conscious efforts to insulate Europeans from exotic diseases. Both the sanitary convention and regulations negotiated at the first International Sanitary Conference in 1851 by eleven European states and Turkey on plague, cholera, and yellow fever were focused on ships "having on board a disease reputed to be importable."[14] According to David Fidler, the objective of protecting Europe from "Asiatic cholera" dominated the European-led international sanitary conferences of 1866, 1874, 1885, 1892, 1893, and 1894 because each of these conferences were convened after another cholera scare in Europe.[15] The four international treaties concluded between 1892 and 1897 followed the trend of European insulation from diseases of the *uncivilized*. While the 1892 International Sanitary Convention focused on the importation of cholera from the Suez Canal by Mecca Muslim pilgrims, the 1893 International Sanitary Convention focused broadly on policing European geopolitical boundaries against the importation of cholera. While the 1894 International Sanitary Convention focused on Mecca pilgrimages and maritime traffic in the Persian Gulf, the 1897 International Sanitary Convention focused on keeping plague out of Europe.[16] At the 1897 international sanitary conference convened specifically on plague, Great Britain, then the colonial overseer of India, was severely criticized by other European states because of a serious and persistent epidemic of plague from Bombay to the north-west littoral of India. Austria-Hungary proposed the 1897 international sanitary conference because it feared that its Muslim subjects from Mecca pilgrimage might bring plague with them after being in contact with pilgrims from India.[17]

Transiting to the twentieth century, public health diplomacy continued to evolve in the complex multilateral terrain of the civilized-uncivilized disease construct. Commenting on the 1903 consolidation of the 1892, 1893, 1894, and 1897 conventions, Howard-Jones observed that the 1903 international sanitary conference "had as its essential purpose the protection of Europe against the importation of the exotic diseases from the East."[18] Today, even in the age of globalization, the isolationist legacy of the nineteenth century public health diplomacy remains one of the dominant characteristics of global health governance. Notwithstanding the expansion of the international society through the establishment of the United Nations in 1945, and the decolonization and political self-determination of most African, Asian, and South Pacific entities in the 1960s and 1970s, contemporary public health Westphalianism is still embedded in a colonial-type relationship. The present South-North health divide conjures images of systematic exclusion of the *uncivilized* from the dividends of global public goods for health in the "emerging global village." Global governance, including global health, oscillates between the paradoxical challenges of what Upendra Baxi has explored as "Global Neighborhood and Universal Otherhood," a disguised or conscious entrenchment of age-old inequalities and structures which banish a sizable part of the developing world to the margins of global governance.[19]

The dominant perception in the developed world that the developing world is a reservoir of disease as a result of collapsed or even nonexistent public health infrastructure has led to isolationist national health policies in most of the global North. In nearly all the industrialized countries of the global North, immigrants from Africa are prohibited from donating blood to national blood banks because of the perception that every African blood is naturally tainted with malaria and other "*African*" diseases. Although the phenomenon of globalization has continued to erode geopolitical boundaries, globalization of public health has paradoxically reinforced the powers of nation-states in the global North to isolate potential immigrants who are perceived to be carriers of leading communicable diseases.[20] Immigration policies are now constructed around mandatory medical screening and testing of potential immigrants. Disease has emerged as a ground to shut the borders of Europe and North America against immigrants from Africa, Asia, South America, and the Caribbean. As Robert Kaplan observed in his widely cited essay *The Coming Anarchy*:

> As many internal African borders begin to crumble, a more impenetrable boundary is being erected that threatens to isolate the continent as a whole: the wall of disease. . . . Africa may today be more dangerous in this regard than it was in 1862. . . . As African birth rates soar and slums proliferate, some experts worry that viral mutations and hybridizations might, just conceivably, result in a form of the [acquired immunodeficiency syndrome ("AIDS")] virus that is easier to catch than the present strain.
>
> It is malaria that is most responsible for the disease wall that threatens to separate. Africa and other parts of the Third World from more-developed regions of the planet in the twenty-first century. Carried by mosquitoes, malaria, unlike AIDS, is easy to catch.[21]

Although countries often overreact to outbreaks of epidemics in other countries with trade, travel, and economic embargoes ostensibly to protect their populations, these embargoes are always more severe and isolationist when the disease or health threat emanates from a developing country. While science and risk assessment played some role in the ban of British beef by most European Union countries following the United Kingdom mad cow disease/bovine spongiform encephalopathy ("BSE") crisis and the recent United States' ban of Canadian beef as a result of the single BSE case in Alberta, the embargoes that followed the Indian plague outbreak in 1994, and the East African cholera outbreak in 1997, and the Ebola outbreak in Zaire (now Democratic Republic of the Congo) were pure isolationist policies by the developed world. Commenting on the economic embargoes that followed the Indian plague outbreak, David Heymann stated that such excessive measures included closing of airports to aircraft arriving from India, unnecessary barriers to importation of foodstuffs from India, and in many cases the repatriation of Indian guest workers even though many of them had not lived in India for many years.[22] In 1997, the European Community ("EC") imposed a ban on the importation of fresh fish from East Africa following an outbreak of cholera in remote areas in certain East African countries.[23] At the time of the ban, fish exports from the affected countries, Kenya, Mozambique, Tanzania, and Uganda, to the European countries stood at $230 million.[24] Is isolationism an effective public health strategy in an era of globalized epidemics? Does isolationism offer effective defenses against microbial forces that routinely disrespect geopolitical boundaries? History is in fact repeating itself. If *cordon sanitaire*, the dominant isolationist policy of European states in the nineteenth century was ineffective against the cross-border cholera epidemics of 1830 and 1847, then modern day isolationism would also be futile as globalization erodes national boundaries and renders populations within those boundaries vulnerable to the menace of disease. To gain deeper insights into the tension between isolationism and globalization of public health in the Westphalian system, we must explore the concept of mutual vulnerability in the dynamic of global health governance in an interdependent world.

III. Mutual vulnerability to disease in a globalizing world

Today, in an interconnected world, bacteria and viruses travel almost as fast as e-mail and financial flows. Globalization has connected Bujumbura to Bombay and Bangkok to Boston. There are no health sanctuaries. No impregnable walls exist between a world that is healthy, well-fed, and well-off and another that is sick, malnourished, and impoverished. Globalization has shrunk distances, broken down old barriers, and linked people. Problems halfway around the world become everyone's problem.[25]

Because globalization of public health postulates the anachronism of the erstwhile distinction between national and international health threats, it is now infallible that disease pathogens neither carry national passports nor respect the geopolitical boundaries of sovereign states. State sovereignty is an alien concept in the microbial world. With the contemporary globalization of the world's political economy, which is amply evidenced by the huge volumes of goods, services, and people that cross national boundaries, all of humanity is now mutually vulnerable to the emerging and reemerging threats of disease in an interdependent world. Mutual vulnerability, as employed in the global health context, is the accumulation of the vicious threats posed to humans by disease and pathogenic microbes in an interdependent world, the fragility of humans to succumb to these threats, and the obsolescence of the distinction between national and international health threats.[26] International trade, travel, intentional and forced migrations fueled by wars, conflicts, and environmental disasters propel the efficacy of mutual vulnerability as a phenomenon of "South-North dangers"[27] and one of the fundamental determinants of the contemporary Westphalian system.

The multiple dimensions of mutual vulnerability, although complex, are not at all new in humanity's encounter with disease. Historical accounts of the Plague of Athens in 430 BC,[28] the fourteenth century European bubonic plague (Black Death),[29] and the microbial consequences of the Columbian exchange between the Old and New Worlds,[30] suggest that one dimension of mutual vulnerability – the permeation of national boundaries by disease – is an entrenched feature of humanity's interaction with the microbial world. In contemporary public health diplomacy, the crisis of emerging and reemerging infectious diseases ("EIDs") reinforces our mutual vulnerability to disease in a globalizing world. The United States' Centers for Disease Control and Prevention ("CDC") defines EIDs as "diseases of infectious origin whose incidence in humans has increased within the past two decades or threatens to increase in the near future."[31] In 1995, the United States' government interagency Working Group on Emerging and Reemerging Infectious Diseases ("CISET") listed twenty-nine examples of new infectious diseases identified since 1973.[32] Some of the diseases in the list published by CISET include Ebola hemorrhagic fever (1977), Legionnaire's disease (1977), toxic shock syndrome (1981), Lyme disease (1982), acquired immunodeficiency syndrome ("AIDS") (1983), and Brazilian hemorrhagic fever (1984). The CISET Working Group categorized reemerging infectious diseases into three groups: (i) infectious diseases that have flared up in regions in which they historically appeared; (ii) infectious diseases that have expanded into new regions; and (iii) infectious diseases that have developed resistance to anti-microbial treatments and have spread through traditional and/or new regions because of such resistance.[33] Tuberculosis falls into each of the three categories of emerging and reemerging infectious diseases. It is an old disease that has reemerged in regions where it historically occurred, it has returned as a public health threat in the South and the North, and certain strains of tuberculosis have developed strong resistance to anti-microbial treatments.[34] Arno Karlen, in *Man and Microbes*, published a "partial list of new diseases" that first appeared between 1951 and 1993.[35] In Karlen's analysis, not even the most powerful country in the world, the United States, could insulate its populations from the outbreaks of Lassa fever and Legionnaires' disease suspected to have arrived in the United States from the developing world because "[h]igh-speed travel had created a global village for pathogens."[36] Even with an isolated disease like malaria, widely thought to be confined to Africa, high-speed travel, tourism, migration, and international airline networks have combined to entrench the disease firmly in the discourse of mutual vulnerability. Cases of "imported malaria" and "airport malaria" have reemerged in Europe, North America, and other regions of the world where the mortality and morbidity burdens of malaria constitute little or no threats to public health.[37] The disparities between the South and the North on the burdens of malaria are stark, with overwhelming malaria cases occurring in Africa. Nonetheless, airport and imported malaria can no longer be neglected, especially in Europe, because there have been reports of a surprising number of malaria deaths in countries of the North following unrecognized infection through a blood transfusion or a one-off mosquito bite near an international airport. Cases in Europe of airport malaria, which mostly occur in the absence of anamnestic signs of any exposure to malaria risk, are often difficult to diagnose.[38] From 1969 to 1999, confirmed cases of airport malaria have been reported in France, Belgium, Switzerland, the United Kingdom, Italy, the United States, Luxembourg, Germany, the Netherlands, Spain, Israel, and Australia.[39] Epidemiological data in Europe suggest that 1,010 cases were imported into the countries of the European Union in 1971; 2,882 in 1981; about 9,200 cases in 1991; and 12,328 cases in 1997.[40] In 1993, some thirty years after the eradication of malaria in the former Soviet Union, some 1,000 cases of malaria were registered in the Russian Federation and in the newly independent states: Belarus, Kazakhstan, Ukraine, Azerbaijan, Tajikistan, Turkmenistan, and Uzbekistan.[41] In the United Kingdom, 8,353 cases of imported malaria were reported between 1987 and 1992. A breakdown of this figure shows that United Kingdom nationals who visited their friends and relations in malaria endemic regions accounted for forty-nine percent of the cases, visitors to the United Kingdom accounted for nineteen percent, tourists accounted for sixteen percent, while immigrants and expatriates accounted for eleven and five percent respectively.[42]

The World Health Organization ("WHO") blames the global crisis of emerging and reemerging infectious diseases on "fatal complacency" as a result of antibiotic discovery, global eradication of smallpox, the progress made in rolling back the mortality burdens of measles, guinea worm, leprosy, poliomyelitis, and neo-natal tetanus.[43] This cautious optimism has turned into a fatal complacency that is costing millions of lives annually.[44] The emergence in the North of West Nile virus, airport and imported malaria, drug-resistant tuberculosis, and SARS through global travel, tourism, trade, and human migrations, provide the premise for an irrefutable conclusion: the distinction between national and international has become obsolete in an interdependent world. Populations within the geopolitical boundaries of Westphalian nation-states have now, more than ever before in recorded history, become mutually vulnerable to pathogenic microbes. Humanity is "on a hinge of history," and the Westphalian governance architecture must devise effective ways to protect humanity from advancing microbial forces.

IV. SARS and the tension between isolationism and mutual vulnerability

SARS, the first severe infectious disease to emerge in the twenty-first century, has taken advantage of opportunities for rapid international spread made possible by the unprecedented volume and speed of air travel. SARS has also shown how, in a closely interconnected and interdependent world, a new and poorly understood infectious disease can adversely affect economic growth, trade, tourism, business and industrial performance, and social stability as well as public health.[45]

In February 2003, an infectious disease in the form of an atypical pneumonia of unknown cause, SARS, was first recognized in Hanoi, Vietnam. In a few weeks, WHO was informed of similar outbreaks in various hospitals in Hong Kong (China), Singapore, and Toronto (Canada). Subsequent investigations by WHO traced the source of the outbreaks to a hotel in Hong Kong with a visiting physician from the Guangdong Province in China. The physician had treated patients with atypical pneumonia before traveling to Hong Kong and was symptomatic on arrival. The Chinese Ministry of Health, on February 11, 2003, informed WHO of an outbreak of acute respiratory syndrome involving over 300 cases with five deaths in the Guangdong province. On February

14, WHO was informed that the disease had been detected as far back as November 16, 2002, and that the outbreak was coming under control.[46] According to WHO, SARS has several features that constitutes a serious threat to global public health.[47] First, "there is no vaccine or treatment, forcing health authorities to resort to control tools dating back to the earliest days of empirical microbiology: isolation, infection control and contact tracing."[48] Second, the virus has been identified as a previously unknown member of the coronavirus family, and some coronaviruses undergo frequent mutation thereby frustrating the development of effective vaccines.[49] Both the epidemiology and pathogenesis of SARS are poorly understood. Third, SARS had a high case fatality ratio in the range of fourteen to fifteen percent.[50] Between November 2002 and April 2003, over 3,200 SARS cases were reported in twenty-four countries.[51]

SARS implicated the tension between isolationist national responses to goods and people from SARS-afflicted countries, and mutual vulnerability to the disease as a result of globalization and the speed of travel and trade. In part, this tension is epitomized by the heavy economic damage as a result of the embargoes and boycott of the SARS-afflicted countries, and the WHO's Global Outbreak Alert and Response Network that collaborated well with the United States' CDC and eleven laboratories around the world put together to identify the cause of SARS. In Canada, the economic cost of SARS was estimated at $30 million daily. It is projected that China and South Korea suffered some $2 billion in SARS-related tourism and economic losses. Visitor arrivals in China, South Korea, Singapore, and Canada dropped drastically as a result of the WHO travel advisories, isolationist responses, and over-reaction from other countries.[52] In Hong Kong, it was estimated that lost revenue from hotels, restaurants, and shops could amount to 0.5% of its total gross domestic product in 2003. Thailand, whose economy relied on tourism, barred visitors suspected of carrying the virus from entering the country.[53] This modern-day *cordon sanitaire*, when compared with the mutual vulnerability to SARS as a result of its rapid spread across national boundaries – from Asia to North America – underscores why global collaboration is the best way to fight epidemics in an age of globalization. Echoing the central theme of globalization of public health, Ilona Kickbusch observed with respect to the transnational spread of SARS that:

> Countries – small and large – will need to pool both sovereignty and resources based on a new mindset; they will need to acknowledge that while health is a national responsibility, it is also a global public good. . . . As a global community, we need to stop focusing on the reactive mode that fights disease by disease and outbreak by outbreak. We need to ensure the international legal framework for such a fight and develop sustainable financing of global surveillance, rapid global response and local capacity.[54]

The continued oscillation of public health diplomacy between *isolationism* and *mutual vulnerability* indicts the governance architecture of the Westphalian system and opens new vistas in global efforts to fight transnational epidemics.

V. Fidelity to humanity's health: a post-Westphalian exploration between "law of humanity" and "cosmopolitan social democracy"

Globalization of public health de-emphasizes the "territorialization" of public health risks simply because the concept of state sovereignty is alien to the microbial world.[55] Globalized public health requires a global policy universe and humane global health governance framework involving a multiplicity of actors – international organizations, private and corporate actors, and civil society. Exploring the politics of the "domestic-foreign Frontier," James Rosenau identified a policy response that treats the emergent "Frontier" "as becoming more rugged and, thus, as the arena in which domestic and foreign issues converge, intermesh, or otherwise become indistinguishable within a seamless web."[56] Thus:

> While foreign policy still designates the efforts of societies to main-
> tain a modicum of control over their external environments, new global
> interdependence issues such as pollution, currency crises, AIDS, and
> the drug trade have so profoundly changed the tasks and goals of
> foreign policy officials. . . .[57]

Global governance of transnational epidemics like SARS comes within the list of complex global issues that shape Rosenau's "domestic-foreign Frontier." Fashioning effective and humane global health governance accords will be difficult, but as Rosenau put it, "global governance is not so much a label for high degree of integration and order."[58] Governance of globalized public health threats in the 'Frontier' involves critical choices. What is most important is for evolving multilateral governance structures to focus on the "world" as its primary constituency, and humanity (human life) as the endangered species that it seeks to conserve. In an era of globalized epidemics, therefore, an indispensable part of post-Westphalian global governance architecture lies within the normative boundaries of Falk's "law of humanity"[59] and Held's "cosmopolitan social democracy."[60] According to Falk, "[t]he character of the law of humanity is not self-evident. It could mean law that is enacted by and for the peoples of the world, as distinct from the elites who act in law-making settings on behalf of states."[61]

The promise of civil society participation in humane governance is founded on the perceived or actual exclusion, by the state, of a sizable part of humanity from its protective structures from the Treaty of Westphalia 1648 to the present day.[62] This has led to vicious tensions between global policies, incubated in multilateral forums exclusively by nation-states acting as repositories of political power within geopolitical boundaries often perceived as not fully protective of human well-being, and an animation of transnational civic society agenda involving human rights, public health, the environment, and other substantive areas where states and market forces are perceived to be endangering public goods.[63] Falk uses "globalization-from-above" and "globalization-from-below" to explore the tension at the two extremes of law of humanity. In his metaphor of "predatory globalization," Falk argues that the governance frameworks of international institutions are now manipulated by market forces.[64] In a capital-driven, non-territorial world order, most states, especially developing countries, are unable to protect their citizens against decisions and policies of the World Bank, the International Monetary Fund, and the World Trade Organization within the colossal edifice of economic globalization.[65] Similar to this, Held's cosmopolitan social democracy postulates that:

> Political communities can no longer be considered . . . as simply 'discrete worlds' or as self-enclosed political spaces; they are enmeshed in complex structures of overlapping forces, relations and networks. . . . The locus of effective political power can no longer be assumed to be simply national governments – effective power is shared and bartered by diverse forces and agencies at national, regional and international levels.[66]

Reconstructing world order based on cosmopolitan social democracy, according to Held and Anthony McGrew, revolves around respect for international law, greater transparency, accountability, and democracy in global governance, a more equitable distribution of the world's resources and human security, the protection and reinvention of community at diverse levels, the regulation of the global economy through the public management of global financial and trade flows, the provision of global public goods, and the engagement of leading stakeholders in corporate governance.[67] Applied to the global health context, other cosmopolitan scholars like Thomas Pogge argue that the current distribution in national rates of infant mortality, life expectancy, and disease can be accounted for largely by reference to the existing world market system.[68] In contemporary global discourses, it has now been recognized, at least at the doctrinaire level, that health is a global public good.[69] As well, there now exists some persuasive evidence anchored on solid facts that significant financial and technical resources are urgently needed to address the mortality and morbidity burdens of killer infectious and non-communicable diseases, and the deadly partnership of poverty and ill health, in order to boost disease surveillance capacity in most of the Third World.[70] The pertinent question is whether emerging global health accords like the *Global Fund to Fight AIDS, Tuberculosis and Malaria*, and the *International Health Regulations* are cosmopolitan enough to catalyze a change in the sovereign mindset of poor and wealthy nation-states in the Westphalian system. Do they attract enough attention and resources to address the stark realities of contemporary South-North health divide? Do these accords place humanity as the epicenter of their core framework? Although this article does not provide all, or indeed any of the answers, the fact remains that the promise of global governance as a weapon against advancing microbial forces is uncertain. National, international, and global health regulatory institutions, as presently constructed, look like Michel Foucault's "panopticons," a strict spatial partitioning through which the North can catch every exotic disease from the South before it reaches their borders.[71] Regrettably, this isolationist global health governance policy has betrayed the public health trust that should drive interstate relations in an interdependent world. Deploring the betrayal of trust on which humane global public health architecture is presently constructed, Laurie Garrett observed that:

> The new globalization pushed communities against one another, opening old wounds and historic hatreds, often with genocidal results. It would be up to public health to find ways to bridge the hatreds, bringing the world toward a sense of singular community in which the health of each one member rises or falls with the health of all others.[72]

Leading epidemiologist, John Last reminds us that:

> Dangers to health anywhere on earth are dangers to health everywhere. International health, therefore, means more than just the health problems peculiar to developing countries. . . . There are several good reasons why we should be concerned about world health. The most obvious is self-interest: Some of the world's health problems endanger us all.[73]

While globalization has immersed all of humanity in a single microbial sea, global health governance constructed on South-North dichotomy and isolationist paradigms have left a sizable percentage of humanity, especially in the developing world, multilaterally defenseless in the face of advancing microbial forces. It is up to the future of global governance to humanize emerging and future global health accords to tackle global epidemics like SARS.

Notes

* An earlier version of this article was presented at the "SARS, Public Health and Global Governance" conference hosted by the Institute for International Law and Public Policy, Temple University James E. Beasley School of Law, Philadelphia, PA, March 24–25, 2004. I would like to thank Professors Jeffrey Dunoff and Scott Burris (Temple

University School of Law) for inviting me to present aspects of this article at the conference. I would also like to thank Professor Ronald Bayer (Columbia University School of Public Health), Ambassador Hans Corell (formerly of the United Nations), Dr. Mandeep Dhaliwal (International HIV/AIDS Alliance), Charles Weiss (Distinguished Professor, Georgetown University), Dr. Joanne Csete (Human Rights Watch), Professor Susan K. Sell (George Washington University), Professor David P. Fidler (Indiana University), and Sophia Gruskin (Harvard University) for their comments when I presented this paper at Temple University. This article was partly researched and written during my tenure as Global Security and Cooperation Fellow of the Social Science Research Council (SSRC) of New York. I would like to thank the SSRC for generously funding my GSC fellowship.

1 Gro-Harlem Brundtland, Past Director-General, WHO, Address at the 56th World Health Assembly, Geneva, Switzerland (May 18, 2003).

2 For a discussion of "globalization of public health," see generally David P. Fidler, *The Globalization of Public Health: Emerging Infectious Diseases and International Relations*, 5 IND. J. GLOBAL LEGAL Stud. 11 (1997); David Woodward et al., *Globalization and Health: A Framework for Analysis and Action, in* 79 BULL. WORLD HEALTH ORGAN. 875 (2001), *available at* http://www.scielosp.org/pdf/bwho/v79n9/v79n9a14.pdf; Kelley Lee & Richard Dodgson, *Globalization and Cholera: Implications for Global Governance*, 6 GLOBAL GOVERNANCE 214 (2000); Derek Yach & Douglas Bettcher, *The Globalization of Public Health, 1: Threats and Opportunities*, 88 AM. J. PUB. HEALTH 735 (1998); Derek Yach & Douglas Bettcher, *The Globalization of Public Health, II: The Convergence of Self-Interest and Altruism*, 88 AM. J. PUB. HEALTH 738 (1998).

3 I use the term "South-North" throughout this paper as suggested by IVAN L. HEAD in ON A HINGE OF HISTORY: THE MUTUAL VULNERABILITY of SOUTH AND NORTH 14 (1991). Professor Head expressed a preference for "South-North" as a more accurate reflection of the current international system. *Id.* He argued that "North-South" is misleading because "it lends weight to the impression that the South is the diminutive." *Id.*

4 NORMAN HOWARD-JONES, THE SCIENTIFIC BACKGROUND OF THE INTERNATIONAL SANITARY CONFERENCES 1851–1938, at 85 (1975).

5 NEVILLE M. GOODMAN, INTERNATIONAL HEALTH ORGANIZATIONS AND THEIR WORK 27–29 (2d ed. 1971).

6 *Id.* at 27.

7 *Id.* at 28.

8 For a history and discussion of the concept of quarantine, see *id.* at 29 (stating that quarantine derived from "forty-day (*quaranta*) isolation period imposed at Venice in 1403 and said to be based on the period during which Jesus and Moses had remained in isolation in the desert"); Paul Slack, *Introduction* to EPIDEMICS AND IDEAS: ESSAYS ON THE HISTORICAL PERCEPTION OF PESTILENCE 15 (Terence Ranger & Paul Slack eds., 1992); B. Mafart & J. L. Perret, *History of the Concept of Quarantine*, 58 MED. TROPICALE 14, 14–20 (1998) (French) (defining quarantine as "a concept developed by society to protect against outbreak of contagious diseases") (on file with author).

9 DAVID P. FIDLER, INTERNATIONAL LAW AND INFECTIOUS DISEASES 26 (1999); GOODMAN, *supra* note 5, at 31.

10 PETER MALANCZUK, AKEHURST'S MODERN INTRODUCTION TO INTERNATIONAL LAW 13 (7th ed. 1997). *See also* MOHAMMED BEDJAOUI, TOWARD A NEW INTERNATIONAL ECONOMIC ORDER 51–53 (1979) (discussing idea that international law in nineteenth century was synonymous with European imperialism); Antony Anghie, *Finding the Peripheries: Sovereignty and Colonialism in Nineteenth-Century International*

Law, 40 HARV. INT'L L.J. 1, 2 (1999) (stating that virtually all territories in Asia, Africa, and Pacific were governed by European law by end of nineteenth century).

11 Norman Howard-Jones, *Origins of International Health Work*, 6 BRIT. MED. J. 1032, 1035 (1950).

12 GOODMAN, *supra* note 5, at 38.

13 *Id.* (footnote omitted).

14 *Id.* at 46.

15 FIDLER, *supra* note 9, at 28–30.

16 *Id.* at 30.

17 HOWARD-JONES, *supra* note 4, at 78.

18 *Id.* at 78. *See also* FIDLER, *supra* note 9, at 31 (observing that "of the 184 articles in the 1903 International Sanitary Convention, 131, or approximately seventy-one percent of the treaty, deal with places (for example, Egypt, and Constantinople) and events (for example, Mecca pilgrimages) located outside Europe").

19 Upendra Baxi, *"Global Neighborhood" and the "Universal Otherhood": Notes on the Report of the Commission on Global Governance, in* 21 ALTERNATIVES 525, 544–45 (1996). I have applied Baxi's paradoxical matrix in the global health context. *See also* Obijiofor Aginam, *The Nineteenth Century Colonial Fingerprints on Public Health Diplomacy: A Postcolonial View*, 1 LAW SOC. JUST. & GLOBAL DEV. J. 1, 7–8 (2003) (discussing paradox between "global neighbourhood" and "universal otherhood"), *available at* http://elj.warwick.ac.uk/global/issue/2003-l/aginam.htm (last visited Sept. 7, 2004).

20 For an argument that globalization presents a paradox by opening the borders of developing countries to multinational corporations, from the North while shutting the borders of developed countries to immigrants, see Obijiofor Aginam, *Global Village, Divided World: South-North Gap and Global Health Challenges at Century's Dawn*, 7 IND. J. GLOBAL LEGAL STUD. 603, 610 (2000).

21 Robert D. Kaplan, *The Coming Anarchy, in* GLOBALIZATION AND THE CHALLENGE OF A NEW CENTURY: A READER 34, 40 (Patrick O'Meara et al. eds., 2000).

22 David Heymann, The International Health Regulations: Ensuring Maximum Protection with Minimal Restriction, Annual Meeting of the ABA, Program Materials on Law & Emerging & Re-Emerging Infectious Diseases (1996) (unpublished manuscript, on file with author). *See also* Laurie Garret, *The Return of Infectious Diseases*, FOREIGN AFF., Jan.–Feb. 1996, at 66, 74 (stating that India lost almost two billion dollars as a result of excessive measures following outbreak of plague).

23 *See* Commission Decision of 23 December 1997 concerning certain protective measures with regard to certain fishery products originating in Uganda, Kenya, Tanzania and Mozambique, 1997 O.J. (L356) 64 (banning importation of "fresh fishery products from, or originating in Kenya, Uganda, Tanzania and Mozambique" because of cholera epidemic); Commission Decision of 16 January 1998 on protective measures with regard to fishery products from, or originating in Uganda, Kenya, Tanzania and Mozambique and repealing Decision 97/878/EC, 1998 O.J. (L15) 43 (mandating testing of all frozen or fresh fishery products from or originating in Uganda, Kenya, Tanzania and Mozambique "to verify that they present no threat to public health").

24 FIDLER, *supra* note 9, at 80 n.158.

25 Gro-Harlem Brundtland, *Global Health and International Security*, 9 GLOBAL GOVERNANCE 417, 417 (2003).

26 I do not claim originality of the use of the concept of mutual vulnerability. For earlier uses of the concept to explore the political economy of South-North relations, development, and underdevelopment, see HEAD, *supra* note 3, at 185–87 (discussing global vulnerability to diseases such as AIDS and malaria); JORGE NEF, HUMAN

SECURITY AND MUTUAL VULNERABILITY: THE GLOBAL POLITICAL ECONOMY OF DEVELOPMENT AND UNDERDEVELOPMENT 13–26 (2d ed. 1999) (analyzing global vulnerability).

27 Ivan L. Head, *South-North Dangers*, FOREIGN AFF., Summer 1989, at 71, 84–86.

28 *Thucydides: History Of The Peloponnesian War, in* 6 GREAT BOOKS OF THE WESTERN WORLD 345, 399 (Robert Maynard Hutchins et al. eds., Richard Crawley trans., 1952) (suggesting that the plague, which devastated Athens, originated from Ethiopia and spread through Egypt and Libya before it reached Athens following movement of troops during war).

29 J. N. HAYS, THE BURDENS OF DISEASE: EPIDEMICS AND HUMAN RESPONSE IN WESTERN HISTORY 39–40 (1998) (arguing that path of Bubonic Plague originated in Central Asia, spread across Asian steppes in the 1330s, was carried by ship from Crimea to Sicily in 1347, and followed international travel and trading routes before arriving in major European sea ports before the end of 1348).

30 *See generally* ALFRED W. CROSBY JR., ECOLOGICAL IMPERIALISM: THE BIOLOGICAL EXPANSION OF EUROPE, 900–1900 (1986) (arguing that Europeans' successful displacement and replacement of native peoples in world's temperate zones has a biological, ecological origin); ALFRED W. CROSBY JR., THE COLUMBIAN EXCHANGE: BIOLOGICAL AND CULTURAL CONSEQUENCES OF 1492 (1972) (discussing exchange of disease and food supply following Columbus' finding new world); DOROTHY PORTER, HEALTH, CIVILIZATION AND THE STATE: A HISTORY OF PUBLIC HEALTH FROM ANCIENT TO MODERN TIMES (1999) (describing mutual interchange of biological and epidemiological trends of Old and New Worlds).

31 CDC, ADDRESSING EMERGING INFECTIOUS DISEASE THREATS: A PREVENTION STRATEGY FOR THE UNITED STATES 7 (1994). *See also* WHO, WORLD HEALTH REPORT 1996: FIGHTING DISEASE, FOSTERING DEVELOPMENT 15 (1996) [hereinafter WHO, WORLD HEALTH REPORT] (describing emerging infectious diseases).

32 NATIONAL SCIENCE & TECHNOLOGY COUNCIL COMMITTEE ON INTERNATIONAL SCIENCE, ENGINEERING, & TECHNOLOGY ("CISET"), INTERAGENCY WORKING GROUP ON EMERGING INFECTIOUS DISEASES, INFECTIOUS DISEASES: A GLOBAL THREAT 14 (Sept. 1995).

33 *See id.* (listing factors contributing to re-emergence of infectious diseases).

34 *See generally* JOHN CROFTON, GUIDELINES FOR THE MANAGEMENT OF DRUG-RESISTANT TUBERCULOSIS (1997) (discussing strategies for tuberculosis management); David P. Fidler, *Return of the Fourth Horseman: Emerging Infectious Diseases and International Law*, 81 MINN. L. REV. 771 (1997) (analyzing emerging and re-emerging infectious diseases).

35 ARNO KARLEN, MAN AND MICROBES 6 (1995).

36 *Id.* at 7.

37 For a distinction between "imported malaria" and "airport malaria," see Norman G. Gratz et al., *Why Aircraft Disinsection?, in* 78 BULL. WHO 995, 996–97 (2000) (stating that the "most direct evidence of transmission of disease by mosquitoes imported on aircraft is the occurrence of airport malaria, i.e. cases of malaria in and near international airports, among persons who have not recently traveled to areas where the disease is endemic or who have not recently received blood transfusions. Airport malaria should be distinguished from imported malaria among persons who contract the infection during a stay in an area of endemicity and subsequently fall ill.").

38 WHO REGIONAL OFFICE FOR EUROPE, STRATEGY TO ROLL BACK MALARIA IN THE WHO European Region 6 (1999), *available at* http://www.euro.who.int/document/e67133.pdf (last visited Sept. 7, 2004). *See also* Gratz et al., *supra* note 37, at 998 (stating that "[a]irport malaria is particularly dangerous in that physicians generally

have little reason to suspect it. This is especially true if there has been no recent travel to areas where malaria is endemic").

39 Gratz, *supra* note 37, at 998.

40 WHO REGIONAL OFFICE FOR EUROPE, *supra* note 38, at 6.

41 *Id.* at 3.

42 WHO, REPORT ON INFECTIOUS DISEASES: REMOVING OBSTACLES TO HEALTHY DEVELOPMENT 52 (1999).

43 WHO, WORLD HEALTH REPORT, *supra* note 31, at 1.

44 *Id.*

45 WHO Secretariat, *Revision of the International Health Regulations: Severe acute respiratory syndrome (SARS)*. 56th World Health Assembly, at 2, WHO Doc. A56/48 (May 17, 2003), *available at* http://www.who.int/gb/ebwha/pdf_files/WHA56/ea5648.pdf.

46 *Id.* at 1.

47 *Id.* at 2.

48 *Id.*

49 *Id.* at 2–3.

50 *Id.*

51 WHO, Cumulative Number of Reported Probable Cases of Severe Acute Respiratory Syndrome (SARS), *at* http://www.who.int/csr/sars/country/2003_04_15/en/print.html (Apr. 15, 2003).

52 Michael D. Lemonick & Alice Park, *The Truth about SARS*, TIME, May 5, 2003, at 50–51.

53 CENTER FOR STRATEGIC & INTERNATIONAL STUDIES, SARS's GLOBAL SPREAD DEMANDS INTERNATIONAL COLLABORATIVE CONTAINMENT EFFORTS, *at* http://www.globalization101.org/news.asp?NEWS_ID=49 (Apr. 14, 2003). For a detailed study on the economic cost of SARS, see Jong-Wha Lee & Warwick J. McKibbin, *Globalization and Disease: The Case of SARS*, AUSTRALIAN NAT'L UNIV. WORKING PAPERS IN TRADE & DEV., Working Paper No. 2003/16 (2003) (revised version of paper presented at the Asian Economic Panel, Tokyo, Japan, May 11–12, 2003), *available at* http://rspas.anu.edu.au/economics/publish/papers/wp2003/wp-econ-2003-16.pdf.

54 Ilona Kickbusch, *SARS: Wake-Up Call for a Strong Global Health Policy*, YALE GLOBAL ONLINE (Apr. 25, 2003), *at* http://yaleglobal.yale.edu/article.print?id=1476.

55 In adopting this view of globalization, I am a student of David Held and Anthony McGrew who defined globalization as "a process (or set of processes) which embodies a transformation in the spatial organization of social relations and transactions." DAVID HELD, et al., GLOBAL TRANSFORMATIONS: POLITICS, ECONOMICS AND CULTURE 16 (1999). *See also* JAN AART SCHOLTE, GLOBALIZATION: A CRITICAL INTRODUCTION 16 (2000) (characterizing globalization as "a spread of supraterritoriality").

56 JAMES N. ROSENAU, ALONG THE DOMESTIC-FOREIGN FRONTIER: EXPLORING GOVERNANCE IN A TURBULENT WORLD 5 (1997).

57 *Id.* at 20.

58 *Id.* at 10–11.

59 RICHARD FALK, LAW IN AN EMERGING GLOBAL VILLAGE: A POST-WESTPHALIAN PERSPECTIVE 33 (1998).

60 For a concise version of Held's perspective on cosmopolitan social democracy, see DAVID HELD & ANTHONY MCGREW, GLOBALIZATION/ANTI-GLOBALIZATION 118–36 (2002) (discussing reconstruction of world order). In exploring the discourses of Falk and Held, I do not suggest that "law of humanity" and "cosmopolitan social democracy" neatly overlap.

61 FALK, *supra* note 59, at 34.

62 *Id.* at 35.

63 *Id.* In using Falk's argument, I do not suggest that nation-states will become completely irrelevant in global governance or that they will automatically cede a significant part of their powers to civil society. Rather, I suggest that nation-states are no longer the only actors in global governance. A genuine dialogue between state and non-state actors is critically needed to review and fill the gap in the Westphalian system.

64 RICHARD FALK, PREDATORY GLOBALIZATION: A CRITIQUE 56 (1999).

65 *Id.*

66 HELD & MCGREW, *supra* note 60, at 123.

67 *Id.* at 131.

68 THOMAS W. POGGE, REALIZING RAWLS 237 (1989).

69 *See* David Woodward & Richard D. Smith, *Global Public Goods and Health: Concepts and Issues, in* GLOBAL PUBLIC GOODS FOR HEALTH: HEALTH, ECONOMIC, AND PUBLIC HEALTH PERSPECTIVES 3–8 (Richard Smith et. al. eds., 2003) (analyzing how global public good for health concept can best be utilized); Inge Kaul, Isabelle Grunberg, & Marc A. Stern, *Defining Global Public Goods, in* GLOBAL PUBLIC GOODS: INTERNATIONAL COOPERATION IN THE 21ST CENTURY 2–20 (Inge Kaul et al. eds., 1999) (introducing idea of global public goods).

70 *See* REPORT OF THE COMMISSION ON MACROECONOMICS & HEALTH (chaired by Jeffrey D. Sachs), MACROECONOMICS AND HEALTH: INVESTING IN HEALTH FOR ECONOMIC DEVELOPMENT 4 (2001) (recommending "that the world's low-and middle-income countries, in partnership with high-income countries, should scale up the access of the world's poor to essential health services."), *available at* http://www.un.org/esa/coordination/ecosoc/docs/RT.K.MacroeconomicsHealth.pdf (last visited Oct. 21, 2004).

71 For a discussion of Foucault's panopticism, see MICHEL FOUCAULT, DISCIPLINE AND PUNISH: THE BIRTH OF THE PRISON 195 (Alan Sheridan trans., 2d ed. 1995).

72 LAURIE GARRETT, BETRAYAL OF TRUST: THE COLLAPSE OF GLOBAL PUBLIC HEALTH 585 (2000).

73 JOHN M. LAST, PUBLIC HEALTH AND HUMAN ECOLOGY 337 (2d ed. 1998).

Part 11

ACTORS AND GOVERNANCE

63

WHO RUNS GLOBAL HEALTH?

[Lancet Editorial]

Source: *Lancet*, 373:9681 (2009), 2083.

The past two decades have seen dramatic shifts in power among those who share responsibility for leading global health. In 1990, development assistance for health—a crude, but still valid measure of influence—was dominated by the UN system (WHO, UNICEF, and UNFPA) and bilateral development agencies in donor countries. Today, while donor nations have maintained their relative importance, the UN system has been severely diluted. This marginalisation, combined with serious anxieties about the unanticipated adverse effects of new entrants into global health, should signal concern about the current and future stewardship of health policies and services for the least advantaged peoples of the world.

In this issue, Nirmala Ravishankar and her colleagues show quantitatively what many observers have seen qualitatively—the rising importance in global health of non-state and non-UN actors: the Global Fund, GAVI, World Bank, Gates Foundation, and non-governmental organisations. While those concerned with the world's health will be glad that development assistance for health has risen from US$5.6 billion in 1990 to $21.8 billion in 2007, they will also be concerned that the influence of intergovernmental agencies is being crowded out by donor-driven funding patterns that may not be fully responding to country needs.

These concerns are not merely theoretical. In WHO's first assessment of the effects of global health initiatives (GHIs, including the Global Fund, GAVI, PEPFAR, and the World Bank's Multicountry AIDS Programme) on health systems, the report card is mixed. It is certainly correct to say that GHIs illustrate a remarkable international commitment to diseases affecting millions of people already living in poverty. Access to medicines, such as antiretrovirals, has improved. Case detection of tuberculosis has increased. Coverage of insecticide-treated bed-nets has risen. There are emerging signs of some positive benefits in health equity, quality of services, innovative financing for health, task shifting, training, community participation, monitoring and evaluation, and the price of medical products.

But those "positive synergies" have also been accompanied by negative effects. We already know, for example, that GAVI's immunisation services support has encouraged over-reporting of vaccination success by recipient countries. The true situation in countries seems to be compounded by further problems. A team of scientists across 30 nations, and including WHO, UNICEF, UNAIDS, GAVI, the Global Fund, and the World Bank, now reveal several adverse effects of GHIs on health systems. Some of the most troubling harms include steepening inequalities in health services, reduced quality of services because of pressures to meet targets, decreases in domestic spending on health, misalignment between GHIs and country health needs, distraction of government officials from their overall responsibilities for health, the creation of expensive parallel bureaucracies to manage GHIs in countries, the weak accountability of a rapidly expanding GHI-funded non-governmental sector, and increased burdens on already fragile health workforces.

A further important finding by the WHO team is that GHIs have not taken the independent evaluation of their programmes sufficiently seriously. For initiatives that have many well-known researchers on their boards and advisory committees, this is an extraordinary failure. GHIs have been flying blind, apparently indifferent to knowledge about the effects of their investments in countries.

The WHO's Maximising Positive Synergies Collaborative Group makes five important recommendations: health systems strengthening needs to be a higher priority for GHIs; targets for GHIs need to include indicators for health systems; GHIs need to work harder to collect more reliable information about their effects; and donors need to increase their financial support of not only GHIs, but also health systems. A meeting in Venice next week, drawing together ministers from over 50 countries and leaders from several major GHIs, will discuss how to implement these proposals as a matter of urgency.

So who does run global health in 2009? The answer is a multiplicity of actors, old and new. But newer entrants should be careful what they wish for. WHO remains compellingly important to global health, for all its problems and relatively declining financial power. The health agency's influence might have been eroded during the past two decades. But thanks to WHO's technical leadership (forcing evaluation back onto the global agenda) as well as mistakes by GHIs (ignoring their own performance), the need for a strong, well-funded, and politically supported WHO has become a much sharper and convincing argument today than for many years.

64

THE NEW WORLD OF
GLOBAL HEALTH

Jon Cohen

Source: *Science*, 311:5758 (2006), 162–7.

An array of well-heeled new players has dramatically reshaped how wealthy countries tackle infectious diseases of the poor. But increasingly, these ambitious efforts are confronting their own limitations.

A revolution is under way that is fundamentally altering the way the haves of the world assist the have-nots. Over the past 7 years, a cadre of deep-pocketed, impassioned players has committed more than $35 billion to fight the diseases of the world's poor. At the forefront of these efforts is the Bill and Melinda Gates Foundation, which since 1999 has pledged $6 billion—roughly the budget of the World Health Organization (WHO) during the same time—to battling HIV/AIDS, malaria, tuberculosis, and other long-underfunded diseases.

Close on the foundation's heels are a half-dozen other massive new efforts, including the Global Fund to Fight AIDS, Tuberculosis, and Malaria, which has promised $4.8 billion to 128 countries, and the President's Emergency Plan for HIV/AIDS Relief (PEPFAR) from the Bush Administration that has pledged $15 billion to help selected countries. The Global Alliance for Vaccines and Immunization (GAVI), with half of the $3 billion in its coffers supplied by the Gates Foundation, is helping 72 countries fortify the immune systems of their children. And thanks in part to a star-studded cast that is championing the cause—including the rocker Bono, matinee idols Angelina Jolie and Richard Gere, former U.S. presidents Jimmy Carter and Bill Clinton, U.K. Prime Minister Tony Blair, U.N. Secretary-General Kofi Annan, and economist-cum-firebrand Jeffrey Sachs—stories on global health now routinely grace the covers of news magazines.

But amid all the heartfelt praise, the organizations at the forefront of the global health movement are now undergoing both increasing outside scrutiny and internal soul-searching about what they are actually accomplishing. Their goals are hugely, some would say impossibly, ambitious—for instance, upping childhood immunization rates to 90%, or providing "universal access" to anti-HIV drugs. And achieving these grand objectives is proving tougher than many anticipated. Many countries, for instance, face cumbersome procurement policies that make it difficult to translate dollars into drugs. Shortages of trained health-care workers mean that those drugs that are available may not be used properly. Corruption has bedeviled a few large grants, whereas many other aid recipients have found themselves drowning in the required paperwork.

The organizations leading the charge are also beset with growing pains, struggling with issues of accountability, credit, and even fundamental direction. There is also considerable confusion about how all these new entities fit together, as well as how they mesh with old-timers such as WHO, the United Nations Children's Fund (UNICEF), and the World Bank. "There've been lots of creative ideas and lots of new people," says Barry Bloom, dean of Harvard University's School of Public Health. "But there's one missing piece. There's no architecture of global health."

Seeds of change

No single event triggered the outpouring of funds for global health, says Columbia University's Sachs, who cites everything from an obscure 1978 health conference in the USSR to a 1993 report by the World Bank. Bill Gates has called the report, *Investing in Health*, a profound influence. In it the authors made the case that increasing funding for battling diseases in poor countries (then estimated at a mere $41 per person each year—1/30th what was spent in rich countries) would not only reduce the burden of disease but also dramatically improve the economies of poor nations.

Critical care. A counselor in South Africa explains the HIV test to children of an infected mother.

Until then, says Seth Berkley, who helped write the report and now heads the International AIDS Vaccine Initiative, health problems were seen "as a drain on the system"—not as a fundamental cause of poverty.

The exploding AIDS epidemic helped underscore the report's dire message about the link between poor health and poverty. AIDS also spawned a powerful activist community that highlighted the slow pace of drug development—and the vast inequities between rich countries and those too poor to afford powerful anti-HIV drug cocktails.

Even before the Gateses jumped in, Cable News Network mogul Ted Turner in 1997 pledged $1 billion, much of it for fighting disease, to the

United Nations to help the world's poor. Two years later, Bill and Melinda Gates began donating billions of dollars' worth of Microsoft stock to their foundation, which by 2001 had $21 billion in assets and a strong focus on global health. The size and boldness of their initial grants—including $750 million to kickstart GAVI—jolted public health veterans. "Everyone started dreaming," says Jim Yong Kim, who recently left the head job at WHO's HIV/AIDS program to return to Harvard University. "It was the first time we thought that way. Before, it was scraping for the pennies that would fall off the table."

Boosting vaccination

Because few interventions provide as much bang for the buck as vaccinating children, immunization programs have long been a cornerstone of public health efforts. Since the 1970s, WHO, UNICEF, and Rotary International together have staged massive campaigns that have substantially raised vaccination rates against many childhood diseases. In 1990, for instance, an estimated 75% of the world's children received the combined diphtheria-pertussis-tetanus (DPT) vaccine—a jump from 20% a decade earlier. But soon those efforts began to falter. DPT vaccination rates never climbed again throughout the 1990s. In addition, several years typically passed before developing countries received the benefits of new vaccines introduced into wealthy countries, and even then, vaccines often didn't reach the poorest of the poor.

Launched in 2000 as a public-private partnership outside the U.N. umbrella, GAVI set out to do things differently. Rather than stage pilot projects and then attempt to expand them from the "top down," it took a "bottom-up" approach, asking countries how they would use the money to increase coverage with existing and new vaccines. By hiring UNICEF to do bulk purchasing and distribution, GAVI hoped to drive down vaccine prices and prevent corruption simultaneously. Grants would be canceled if countries did not properly audit their own efforts. Leaders in the global health movement repeatedly refer to the "catalytic" and "galvanizing" impact that GAVI has had on how other organizations operate.

As of September 2005, GAVI had made 5-year commitments to 72 countries for $1.6 billion worth of support. This has led to the vaccination of some 100 million children, sparing more than 1 million from premature death due to *Haemophilus influenzae* B, pertussis, hepatitis B, measles, and other diseases, GAVI claims.

In many ways, GAVI's task is easier than those facing programs designed to treat HIV-infected people or to prevent the spread of malaria. Vaccines are, relatively speaking, a simple tool to use. "GAVI is pushing more money through systems that generally were working pretty well," says Roy Widdus, who led a now-defunct GAVI predecessor called the Children's Vaccine Initiative.

New global health efforts.

Organization	Focus	Year Launched	Donors	Pledged, Committed, Or Spent Funds*
Bill and Melinda Gates Foundation	Global health	2000	Bill and Melinda Gates	$6.2B
The Global Fund to Fight AIDS, Tuberculosis and Malaria	Financing treatment and prevention	2002	Governments, foundations, corporations	$8.6B
President's Emergency Plan for AIDS Relief (PEPFAR)	Financing and delivery of HIV/AIDS prevention and treatment	2004	U.S. government	$15B
International Finance Facility for Immunization	Financing vaccine delivery/GAVI	2005	U.K., France, Italy, Spain, Sweden	$4B
Multi-Country HIV/AIDS Program	Financing scale-up of existing government and community prevention and treatment efforts	2000	World Bank	$1.1B
Global Alliance for Vaccines and Immunization (GAVI)	Financing and delivery of childhood vaccines	1999	Gates Foundation, governments	$3B
Public-Private Partnerships	Drugs, vaccines, microbicides, diagnostics	n/a	Philanthropists, governments, industry	$1.2B
Anti-Malaria Initiative in Africa	Cut malaria incidence in half by 2010 in 15 countries	2005 (proposed)	U.S. government	$1.2B
United Nations Foundation	Children's and women's Health	1998	Ted Turner	$360M

* Overlap exists between organizations (e.g., PEPFAR money supports the Global Fund).

Even so, underimmunization of children remains a major concern. As UNICEF recently pointed out, more than 2 million children a year still die from vaccine-preventable diseases. GAVI has also had to reassess its own overly optimistic projections. GAVI initially envisioned that after 5 years of "bridge" funding, countries would have figured out how to finance and provide the increased immunizations themselves. But that's not happening, says Tore Godal, who headed GAVI from its inception until last January and now works as an independent health adviser in Geneva. Poor countries simply did not get the increase in health budgets that GAVI had anticipated, says Godal. As a result, GAVI recently decided to offer bridge funding for 10 years. Even so, it remains unclear whether countries can take over as initially envisioned.

William Muraskin, a history professor at The City University of New York, Queens College, criticizes GAVI for several "fundamental flaws." In an article published in the November 2004 *American Journal of Public Health*, he asserts that GAVI's bottom-up philosophy is illusory. He also contends that countries "had to be wooed" and "financially enticed" to accept GAVI's goals as their own. In particular, he questions the group's emphasis on hepatitis B vaccine. He points out that GAVI has immunized more children with it than all the other vaccines combined. "I'm not opposed to hepatitis B vaccination, but I do know that for many countries that adopted it, it was low man on the totem pole" compared to devoting resources to malaria, respiratory diseases, and malnutrition, he says.

Godal counters that no one forces countries to submit proposals. "It is up to the countries to decide what they want to apply for within the remit of GAVI," he says, adding that the hepatitis B vaccine indeed was a priority for many. GAVI Executive Secretary Julian Lob-Levyt says its most sobering challenge will be finding the money to purchase expensive new vaccines now on the horizon, such as those in the pipeline for pneumococcal disease, rotavirus, and human papillomavirus.

Gates fate?

In December 2004, officials at the Bill and Melinda Gates Foundation invited a power-packed group of outsiders to the Carter Center in Atlanta, Georgia, to discuss the direction of what had recently become the world's largest philanthropy. Former U.S. President Jimmy Carter attended the small gathering, as did a select group of leaders from academia and non-profits, the prime minister of Mozambique, WHO's Jim Kim, the director of the Wellcome Trust, and the president of the U.S. National Academy of Sciences. The group lavished praise on the Gateses, but a few participants voiced misgivings that the young foundation's global health program was starting to head off course. Carter in particular gave a blunt speech criticizing the program for having become too enamored with basic research at the expense

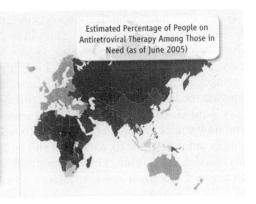

Pressing Needs Remain

Disease Burden and Funding Comparison

Estimated Percentage of People on Antiretroviral Therapy Among Those in Need (as of June 2005)

CONDITION	GLOBAL DISEASE BURDEN (million) DALYs*	R&D FUNDING ($Millions)	R&D FUNDING per DALY*
Cardiovascular	148.190	9402	$63.45
HIV/AIDS	84.458	2049	$24.26
Malaria	46.486	288	$6.20
Tuberculosis	34.736	378	$10.88
Diabetes	16.194	1653	$102.07
Dengue	0.616	58	$94.16

*Disability-Adjusted Life Year, a measure of healthy life lost.

SOURCE: MALARIA R&D ALLIANCE

of delivering drugs and preventives today. Patty Stonesifer, who co-runs the foundation with Bill Gates Sr., recalls the essence of Carter's message this way: "I'm an impatient man—I want to save some people now."

By and large, the global health community has appreciation that borders on reverence for the way the Gates Foundation has reinvigorated their efforts. And from the outset of its global health program, the foundation has attempted to fund projects like GAVI that deliver existing medicines as well as riskier basic research endeavors. Yet several people *Science* interviewed, who requested anonymity, complained that the foundation over the past 3 years has tilted too far toward duplicative, fundamental research that often fails and has also lost its nimble derring-do, becoming more like the U.S. National Institutes of Health (NIH). "How can Bill Gates have his name attached to an organization that's slower than the U.S. government?" asks one. "They've gone from being an easy foundation with which to deal to one that's very complicated and bureaucratic," says another.

Several critics attribute the shift to Richard Klausner, the former director of the U.S. National Cancer Institute (NCI), who ran the foundation's global health program from 2002 until announcing his resignation last September (*Science*, 16 September 2005, p. 1801). In particular, they point to two programs that started under Klausner's tenure.

One is Grand Challenges in Global Health, a bold effort to fund research that could lead to breakthroughs deemed most likely to improve health in poor countries. The foundation has won plaudits from both inside and outside the research community for aggressively seeking ideas from more than 1000 scientists around the world. But the process took too long, say critics—more than 2 years. And some are unhappy with the 43 final selections, most of which focus on fundamental, long-term, high-risk research. Critics say the Grand Challenges are diverting $436 million of foundation money to support the kinds of research that NIH should fund. Although several of the winning proposals are unusually inventive and provocative,

218

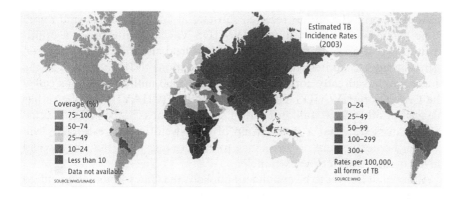

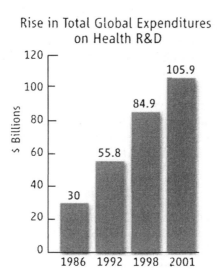

Raising the bar. The rise in funds has triggered a rise in expectations.

there is also a distinctly developed-world flavor to these labs: All but three projects are headed by researchers from the United States, Europe, or Australia. "The Grand Challenges are very, very much NIH stuff," says Peter Piot, head of the United Nations Joint Programme on HIV/AIDS (UNAIDS). "I always felt the strength of the Gates Foundation was that it was very serious money backed by a big name catalyzing work in developing countries."

Klausner says the foundation can't be all things to all people, explaining that the increased emphasis on research and development reflects the wishes of Bill and Melinda Gates. "It's a complicated set of tradeoffs," says Klausner, who also had strong outside support during his tenure.

Another project that has received substantial Gates funding—and raised some eyebrows—is the Global HIV/AIDS Vaccine Enterprise, a multi-institutional effort to draw a blueprint for the field and then create consortia of researchers to address the most critical questions. NIH, a partner in the enterprise, has already committed more than $300 million to what's called the Center for HIV/AIDS Vaccine Immunology (CHAVI), and Gates has pledged another $360 million to form similar groups. Some AIDS vaccine investigators fear that a small group of elite, well-funded researchers will receive the lion's share of the money to explore questions that they would have pursued without the extra help.

Although it has yet to be announced publicly, the Gates Foundation indeed plans to award part of its $360 million Enterprise money to at least two members of the CHAVI team. And another CHAVI team member won a $16.3 million Grand Challenges award from Gates to do related work.

Foundation officials defend their choices. Helene Gayle, who heads the HIV/AIDS program for the foundation, says, "There's a logic to going with success" and that they didn't want to exclude "the usual suspects" just because they were already well funded. Gayle adds that Gates is specifically working with NIH to make sure that they do not fund researchers for the same work twice. And she says the foundation made an effort to select lesser known people, too, in an attempt to create a network of researchers who might not otherwise collaborate. "So maybe some of the same players," says Gayle, "but we hope a different game."

AIDS aid

Funding on HIV/AIDS dwarfs that of any other infectious disease. Between 1996 and 2005, annual spending on AIDS programs in developing countries shot from $300 million to more than $8 billion, according to UNAIDS estimates, with most of this astonishing jump coming from the Global Fund, the World Bank's Multi-Country AIDS Program (MAP), and PEPFAR. In contrast, WHO says the next largest killers, malaria and tuberculosis, together receive less than $2 billion each year.

But people are questioning how much improvement this investment in HIV/AIDS is buying on the ground. A related concern is the amount of time grant recipients are spending simply sorting out the massive amounts of red tape created by the various programs and their overlapping agendas.

The biggest AIDS donor is the Global Fund. Like GAVI, the fund has rigorously avoided the top-down approach; it prides itself on being "country owned" and inclusive. Transparency and accountability are the buzzwords. The fund, which supports everything from providing antimalarial bed nets to anti-HIV drugs, has no staff permanently in countries and channels money through local financial institutions, as opposed to the World Bank. Rather than offering central drug procurement, the fund encourages countries to strengthen their own supply-and-distribution systems.

But critics say the goal of giving countries complete autonomy has come at too steep a price. The fund disburses money to countries only when they hit specific milestones, and since January 2004, they have been falling behind, according to Aidspan, a New York City–based watchdog of the Global Fund. The gaps in disbursement suggest that "deliverables" such as drugs and bed nets aren't reaching populations as quickly as hoped. "The thing I really want to know about is not dollars disbursed but pills in mouths," says Bernard Rivers, who heads Aidspan.

The fund is "a very good thing, but there are huge problems in terms of operating it," agrees Winstone Zulu, an AIDS and TB activist in Zambia. Zulu says other longtime donors closed their pocketbooks when the fund arrived, but that the new money has become ensnarled in bureaucratic tangles, and some critical programs in Zambia had to shut down.

Global Fund Director Richard Feachem agrees that it's a "mixed portfolio" when it comes to countries "turning the money into products." Procurement is a "key bottleneck," he says, as some countries have "sclerotic" procedures. "They were designed to prevent corruption, and they actually prevent procurement," says Feachem. "We're doing a lot of changing in thinking."

In two countries, Ukraine and Uganda, the fund suspended grants because of serious country mismanagement and outright corruption. A handful of

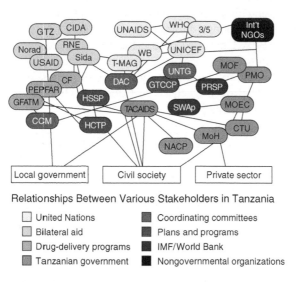

Relationships Between Various Stakeholders in Tanzania

☐ United Nations   ■ Coordinating committees
☐ Bilateral aid   ■ Plans and programs
▨ Drug-delivery programs ■ IMF/World Bank
▨ Tanzanian government   ■ Nongovernmental organizations

Thirty's a crowd. A confusing cluster of efforts aims to help Tanzania with its HIV/AIDS epidemic.

other countries have almost had their grants canceled for failing to reach milestones.

On top of these problems, the fund has never had as much money as its creators envisioned. "The Global Fund is chronically begging for money from the rich countries," says Sachs, one of its key proponents. "And this has meant that the Global Fund has not been as clear or inviting as it should have been to poor countries to put up very bold strategies." In the latest financing round this September, donors committed $3.7 billion for 2006–'07— far short of the projected $7 billion the fund says it needs.

The World Bank's much smaller MAP, which provides more flexible aid both to deliver medicines and to build health systems, faces similar concerns. A review of six MAP projects in 2004 found that the bank did not offer enough technical guidance, nongovernmental organizations (NGOs) were often included more in name than in practice, and none conducted adequate monitoring and evaluation.

The Bush initiative PEPFAR is the most recent entry into AIDS aid. It got off to a fast start in delivering drugs to people largely because of its top-down strategy that includes staff on the ground and central procurement. Salim Abdool Karim of the University of KwaZulu-Natal in South Africa says PEPFAR has been "amazingly successful" in his country and has had "much better politically sensitive management on the ground" than the Global Fund.

Yet Karim and many others take exception to some of PEPFAR's require-ments, which are tightly tied to the Bush Administration's conservative agenda. For instance, those who receive PEPFAR grants must have a policy "explicitly opposing prostitution," which Karim and others say has threatened their research and prevention efforts with sex workers. "This is reprehensible," says Karim. PEPFAR has also been criticized for devoting one-third of its prevention budget to abstinence programs, downplaying the value of condoms in the general population, and limiting the use of generic drugs by insisting that they first be approved by the U.S. Food and Drug Administration. (A U.S. Institute of Medicine panel is reviewing PEPFAR and plans to release its findings by this spring.)

A report issued in November 2005 by 600 treatment activists, *Missing the Target*, sharply rebuked the Global Fund, PEPFAR, the World Bank, and others for failing to work together as effectively as possible in delivering anti-HIV drugs. "A much more systematic approach to setting goals, meas-uring progress, and assessing and addressing barriers is needed."

Architectural indigestion

UNAIDS issued a report in May 2005 that had telling cartoons about the tangle of various stakeholders working on HIV/AIDS in Tanzania and Mozambique (see graphic). The illustrations could have spotlighted just as

Public-Private Partnerships Proliferate

The label "neglected diseases" packs a rhetorical wallop, as it conjures up needy causes that the world callously has ignored. But the phrase is losing some of its punch when it comes to malaria, tuberculosis, Chagas, dengue, visceral leishmaniasis, and African trypanosomiasis. Although profit-minded pharmaceutical companies have long shied away from research and development on drugs against maladies that mainly afflict the poor, 63 drug projects now under way are targeting these very diseases. As Mary Moran wrote in the September 2005 issue of *PLoS Medicine*, "The landscape of neglected-disease drug development has changed dramatically during the past five years."

Moran heads the Pharmaceutical R&D Project at the London School of Economics and Political Science. In its recent analysis of drug-development projects for neglected diseases (it did not analyze vaccines or diagnostics), Moran's team credited a raft of new "public-private partnerships" (PPPs)—80% of which are funded through philanthropies—for the surge in new efforts.

Pioneered by the Rockefeller Foudation and later by the Bill and Melinda Gates Foundation, PPPs link big pharmaceutical companies or smaller biotechs with academics, nongovernmental organizations,

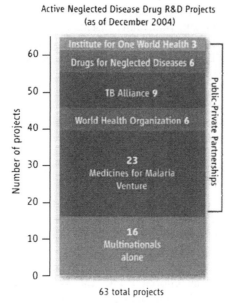

Active Neglected Disease Drug R&D Projects
(as of December 2004)

63 total projects

Business as unusual. PPPs account for nearly 75% of R&D projects under way to develop drugs to treat neglected diseases.

and multilateral groups such as the World Health Organization. Ten years ago, not a single PPP for global health existed. Today, there are nearly 100 of them, in the most liberal definition, with a combined war chest of more than $1 billion. "It's a seismic change," says Seth Berkley, head of the International AIDS Vaccine Initiative, which, at 10 years of age, is the granddaddy of PPPs for global health.

Moran and her co-workers predict that as many as nine products now in development will come to market in the next 5 years. In each case, the companies have agreed to sell any resultant drugs to poor governments at deep discounts or no profit. Moran's group further notes that between 1975 and 2000, the pharmaceutical industry developed a meager 13 new drugs for neglected diseases—and because of their high prices, only one was widely used.

Companies that enter into PPPs have little prospect of making money on the drugs they develop, but Moran notes that they face relatively limited financial risk because their partners typically pay for the most expensive part of the process: staging large, clinical trials. This "no profit-no loss" business model does offer big pharma benefits: a good public image and an introduction to developing-country markets and researchers who might help them elsewhere.

Although the entry of big pharma into this field is welcome—and, some say, long overdue—the problem is by no means solved, cautions Peter Hotez of George Washington University in Washington, D.C. In an article in the November 2005 issue of *PLoS Medicine*, he and his co-authors point out that many diseases remain neglected."When people speak of global health, the first thing you hear about is HIV/AIDS, malaria, TB, and you're liable to think that's all there is," says Hotez, who works on hookworm vaccines. Hookworm, schistosomiasis, leprosy, and 10 other neglected tropical diseases "affect at least as many poor people as the big three," they write. And they contend that for a mere 40 cents per person a year, four existing drugs could be used to quickly reduce the harm caused by seven of these scourges.

aptly the architecture of aid for tuberculosis, malaria, and other diseases that all have a plethora of eager new players trying to help.

The cartoons depict a spaghettilike squiggle of lines connecting dozens of bubbles that represent UNAIDS, WHO's 3 by 5 program (which failed to reach its goal of having 3 million people on treatment by the end of 2005), UNICEF, PEPFAR, the Global Fund, the World Bank's MAP, and a variety of other donors, local ministries, and NGOs. The overall effect is a comical mess, but the problem is anything but. "We were stepping on each other's toes, and in some countries it was destructive," says Debrework

Zewdie, who heads MAP and also sits on the board of the Global Fund. "Imagine the amount of time that countries spend catering to the different donors rather than fighting epidemics."

The UNAIDS report described a potential solution. In April 2004, the various stakeholders met in Washington, D.C., for a Consultation on Harmonization of International AIDS Funding and agreed to try to quell confusion by instituting a principle called "the three ones." It calls on each country to have one HIV/AIDS budget, one national AIDS coordinating committee, and one national monitoring and evaluation system that can report the same data to each donor.

As a follow-up to the D.C. consultation, UNAIDS formed a Global Task Team to analyze the "institutional architecture" that connects the various stakeholders in HIV/AIDS. Among the team's sweeping recommendations: establish a joint U.N.–Global Fund problem-solving team to address bottlenecks and develop a scorecard to rate performances of donors and recipients alike. "We're trying to bring some order into the universe," explains UNAIDS Director Piot.

Others are beginning to ask similar "architectural" questions about the broader universe of global health. In the November issue of *Nature Reviews Microbiology*, former GAVI head Godal argues for a more "holistic" approach that embraces the differences between bilateral, multilateral, and targeted approaches such as GAVI—rather than fighting about which one works best. "We need a summit of key players and a continuous kind of work plan to address issues in a systematic way and not on an ad hoc basis," says Godal.

If there's one universal, time-tested truth in the global battle against infectious diseases, it is this: easier said than done. For decades, rich countries have attempted to help poor ones, and poor ones have struggled to help themselves. Yet preventable, treatable, and even curable illnesses have continued to gain ground and cause massive suffering. The revolution that is sweeping through the global health effort has clearly brought more money, tools, creative ideas, and momentum than ever before. But the goal—narrowing the gap between aspirations and actions—remains a staggering challenge, and what already has become evident to many of the new and old players alike is that they have to monitor progress more vigorously, make midcourse corrections more quickly, and work together more effectively. Because at the end of the day, the question is not simply whether this revolution has done some good, but whether, as Jimmy Carter asked of the Gates Foundation, it has fully exploited all the remarkable possibilities.

65

ROLE CONFLICT?

The World Bank and the world's health

Kent Buse and Gill Walt

Source: *Social Science Medicine*, 50:2 (2000), 177–9.

Undoubtedly, the world's "preeminent development institution" has emerged as the world's foremost international health agency, thereby eclipsing, in certain domains, the positions of WHO and UNICEF (Buse, 1994). Most observers cannot fail to be impressed with the spectacular entrance of the World Bank on the international health scene: from the exponential increase in volume of lending to its position at the nexus of much policy debate. Many will have welcomed this development. It has raised the profile of health on international and national development agendas, has resulted in greater flows of resources to the sector, and has focused attention on critical issues such as financing, priority setting, and systemic reforms, inter alia.

While the transformation of the international health landscape, and the role of the Bank therein, as described in "The role of the World Bank in international health: renewed commitment and partnership" (De Beyer et al., 1997), raises a number of compelling issues, this response will limit itself to addressing five challenges confronting the Bank. These relate to how the Bank, as a large, complex lending institution, will manage key internal tensions while acting to safeguard the world's health.

First principles: the economists vs the rest

One of the strengths brought to the health sector by the Bank has been its economic analysis. Perhaps unsurprisingly, the battles within the Bank between economists and public health and other specialists have to date been won by the former. Consequently, health is viewed within the Bank, not as a right, an inherent good or a humanitarian product, but instead as an economic commodity (De Beyer et al., 1997). This philosophical starting point has clear implications for policy prescriptions, and ultimately health outcomes. Nevertheless, this philosophical position is not axiomatic. Economics is useful in that, like other disciplines, it can expose the value judgements in decisionmaking, yet economics cannot make value judgements any more scientifically than complementary disciplines. Ethical, cultural and political considerations have an equally legitimate claim to health policy (Green, 1992). Thus the first challenge facing the Bank is to acknowledge more explicitly the limitations of economic analyses and to embrace more fully other disciplinary approaches in its health policy discourse.

Banking on health: disbursement vs stakeholder ownership and capacity building

It is no secret that the Bank's management culture, staff policies and incentives, and business practices place salience on loan disbursement and quick, process-oriented results (Wapenhans, 1992). Where local capacity to conceive, design and implement projects is weak, there is a powerful incentive for Bank staff to assume responsibility to get things done and to do so as quickly as possible. Such pressure may run against good practice on the ground. For example, in the difficult social sectors, and particularly in the realm of systemic reform, development effectiveness requires ongoing and intensive policy dialogue, the full commitment of national and international stakeholders in programme formulation, and the strengthening of domestic capabilities. These processes will demand more time for listening and debate, perhaps initially the acceptance of lower standards, and call on the Bank for more substantive field presence. Yet, it is clear that staffing has not kept pace with the growing volume of lending and that the existing skill-mix does not meet demand (World Bank, 1997).

Thinking globally: thinking locally?

The emerging Bank agenda has at its core, support for health system reform in client countries, but the tension between global prescriptions and local diagnosis and solutions remains a challenge. The uncritical incorporation of cost recovery in lending programmes following publication of the Bank's "Agenda for Reform" (World Bank, 1987) is a case in point. Without proper regard for ensuring local, facility-level, retention of fees (to improve quality) and developing adequate capacity and systems for protecting the poor, service utilization for various population groups and illness categories were adversely affected, placing public health at risk (Gilson et al., 1995). Similarly, the concept of priority setting based on the analysis of burden of disease and cost-effectiveness runs the risk of being taken to absurd lengths as millions of dollars are spent in countries such as Bangladesh (and others) to generate the requisite data, for a methodology which remains highly problematic (Anand and Hanson, 1997). The challenge lies in adapting conceptual work to the specificities of local actors, contexts and processes.

Commitment and aid triage

A renewed commitment to the sector, backed up with increased lending and an enlarged knowledge brokering role, is heralded by the Bank in its recent sector strategy document (World Bank, 1997). However, this strategy obligates the Bank to practise greater country selectivity. Accordingly, those countries which do not meet some minimum threshold of "commitment", or embark upon an agreeable package of reforms, may not have access to Bank credits for further sector development. Selectivity may, in the short term, be at the expense of the health needs of the poor.

Leading vs learning

The Bank acts as a lightning rod, attracting fair and unfair criticism alike. However, in spite of its reputation for analytical competence, it may not be sufficiently open to debate, critical self-analysis or external review. One result is that Bank statements in the sector have tended to de-emphasize complexity and uncertainty, and to present policy prescription as received wisdom, with the attendant operational consequences noted above. The problem is compounded by institutional pressures which militate against learning. For example, excessive emphasis on lending expansion may thwart project evaluation. A recent review by the Bank's Operations Evaluation Department (Stout et al., 1997) found that a third of health projects had been rated "unsatisfactory" at completion. More damning was the finding that a "substantial majority" of projects had problems in common, suggesting that either task managers did not learn from past experience or that structures within the Bank impede change. The Bank has only performed one internal review based on detailed analysis of country-level experience (World Bank, 1992).

Of equal concern is the very limited extent to which the Bank is open to outside scrutiny. In the health sector, there have been only two "external" reviews "commissioned" by the Bank of its operations, although there are moves to remedy this situation (Stout et al., 1998). To its credit, the Bank has recently adopted a "disclosure" policy (World Bank, 1994). However, the policy is severely restrictive in terms of what enters the public domain, while investing considerable discretion with senior Bank officials to share material. The policy effectively ensures that only those in the trusted, inner circle can assess the work of the institution. How can the Bank balance the need to retain its "professional image" and facilitate learning in this complex environment?

Conclusions

There are encouraging signals that the Bank recognizes these tensions and is endeavouring to address some of them (World Bank, 1997; Stout et al., 1998). For example, the production of the *World Development Report* in 1993 (World Bank, 1993) was far more consultative and inclusive than previous policy statements of the Bank in the sector (World Bank, 1975, 1980, 1987, 1993). An effort is underway to develop indicators and measure the impact of Bank health operations (Stout et al., 1998). Yet if the Bank's involvement represents nothing more than the passing interest of economists, excited by the fiscal importance of the sector, perhaps our concern should be with the fate of other agencies which risk attrition in the face of the popularity currently enjoyed by the Bank. The Bank has some way to go to reconcile its role as a development bank and leading institution in the realm of health systems development.

References

Anand, S., Hanson, K., 1997. Disability-adjusted life years: a critical review, Journal of Health Economics 16, 685–702.

Buse, K., 1994. Spotlight on international organizations: The World Bank. Health Policy and Planning 9 (1), 95–99.

De Beyer, J. A., Preker, A. S., Feachem, R. G. A., 2000. The role of the World Bank in international health: renewed commitment and partnership, Social Science & Medicine 50 (2), 169–176.

Gilson, L., Russell, S., Buse, K., 1995. The political economy of user fees with targeting: Developing equitable health financing policy. Journal of International Development 7 (3), 369–401.

Green, A., 1992. An Introduction to Health Planning in Developing Countries. Oxford University Press, Oxford.

Stout, S., Evans, A., Nassim, J., Raney, L., 1998. Evaluating health projects: lessons from the literature. World Bank, Washington, DC, Discussion Paper.

Wapenhans, A., 1992. Effective Implementation: Key to Development Impact, Task Force Report. World Bank, Washington, DC.

World, Bank, 1975. Health Sector Policy Paper. World Bank, Washington, DC.

World, Bank, 1980. Health: Sector Policy Paper. World Bank, Washington, DC.

World, Bank, 1987. Financing Health Services in Developing Countries: An Agenda for Reform. World Bank, Washington, DC, Policy Study.

World, Bank, 1992. Population and the World Bank: Implications from Eight Case Studies. World Bank, Washington, DC, Operations Evaluation Department.

World, Bank, 1993. World Development Report 1993: Investing in Health. World Bank, Washington, DC.

World, Bank, 1994. Statement of Disclosure Policy as set out on 4 April, 1994. World Bank, Washington, DC.

World, Bank, 1997. Health, Nutrition and Population Sector Strategy. World Bank, Washington, DC.

66

THE CHANGING ROLE OF
THE WORLD BANK IN
GLOBAL HEALTH

Jennifer Prah Ruger

Source: *American Journal of Public Health*, 95:1 (2005), 60–70.

The World Bank began operations on June 25, 1946. Although it was established to finance European reconstruction after World War II, the bank today is a considerable force in the health, nutrition, and population (HNP) sector in developing countries. Indeed, it has evolved from having virtually no presence in global health to being the world's largest financial contributor to health-related projects, now committing more than $1 billion annually for new HNP projects. It is also one of the world's largest supporters in the fight against HIV/AIDS, with commitments of more than $1.6 billion over the past several years.

I have mapped this transformation in the World Bank's role in global health, illustrating shifts in the bank's mission and financial orientation, as well as the broader changes in development theory and practice. Through a deepened understanding of the complexities of development, the World Bank now regards investments in HNP programs as fundamental to its role in the global economy. (*Am J Public Health.* 2005; 95:60–70. doi: 10.2105/AJPH.2004.042002)

June 25, 2004, marked the 58th anniversary of the World Bank, which opened its doors in Washington, DC, in 1946. The International Bank for Reconstruction and Development, as it was initially called, was created at the Bretton Woods Conference in July 1944, along with its sister institution, the International Monetary Fund. At the outset, the bank's dual roles were reconstruction and development, as implied by its original name. Its primary function was to reconstruct Europe after World War II. However, unlike other specialized United Nations (UN) agencies the bank raised funds through private financial markets and received donations on a regular basis from the world's wealthiest countries.[1] With these funds, it provided interest-bearing and interest-free loans, credits, grants, and technical assistance to war-damaged and economically developing countries that could not afford to borrow money in international markets. These activities are ongoing, making the bank the "world's premier economic multilateral"[2] institution.

Over the course of more than 50 years, the bank's priorities and development philosophy—along with its role in the world—have changed from reconstructing Europe to alleviating poverty in developing countries. Perspectives on development also have changed dramatically during that time. New theories and evidence have deepened and transformed the international development debate and have influenced the bank's development practices and policy decisions. In particular, the bank now has a more sophisticated view of well-being, living standards, and poverty. In addition, evidence on the primary means of poverty reduction and development has accumulated throughout the bank's history, and the bank now has an improved, though still evolving, understanding of how to achieve development objectives. In the 1950s and 1960s, for example, when the prevailing wisdom was that economic growth was the key to development, the bank focused primarily on large investments in physical capital and infrastructure, because such investments were viewed as the most likely to increase national income.

However, in the 1960s through 1980s development theory shifted to encompass more than economic growth; it aimed at meeting individuals' "basic needs," because the objective was to provide all human beings with the opportunity for a "full life." This approach appealed to bank staff and especially to Robert McNamara, then president of the bank. Consequentially, the World Bank's focus began to slowly shift to investments in family planning, nutrition, health, and education. In the 1990s, the "Washington Consensus," which emphasized macroeconomic stability, privatization, trade liberalization, and public sector contraction, dominated development thinking, and the bank focused on open markets and economic management. However, lessons learned from this period of market-oriented reforms demonstrated that good governance, strong institutions, and human capital are critical for eradicating global poverty. Today, the bank views development as a holistic and multidimensional process that focuses on people in the societies in which it operates. This "comprehensive development framework" now gives health, nutrition, and population (HNP) programs a central place in the bank's work and mission.

The World Bank has gone from having virtually no presence in global health to being one of the leading global health institutions. Over time, its loans, credits, and grants to fund HNP programs have become substantial. The largest shift occurred over the past 20 years: World Bank support for social services such as health, nutrition, education, and social security grew from 5% of its portfolio in 1980 to 22% in 2003.[3]

The World Bank is now the world's largest external funder of health,[4] committing more than $1 billion annually in new lending to improve health, nutrition, and population in developing countries. Moreover, it is one of the worlds' largest external funders of the fight against HIV/AIDS, with current commitments of more than $1.3 billion, 50% of that to sub-Saharan Africa.[5] Because it allows long repayment periods (up to 35–40 years and a 10-year grace period), it provides the time and resources to address special problems, such as widespread disease epidemics.

The early years: Bretton Woods

In July 1944, delegates from 45 national governments convened in Bretton Woods, NH, to adopt the Articles of Agreement for the World Bank and the International Monetary Fund, establishing the 2 entities in international law.[6] The nascent bank was the first "multilateral development bank," a uniquely public sector institution created in a post–World War II era of intergovernmental cooperation. The International Monetary Fund, by contrast, was created to stabilize the international monetary system and monitor world currencies. A year later, the UN General Assembly convened in San Francisco, Calif, to draft the UN charter. A new era of multilateralism and intergovernmental cooperation had emerged.

By December 31, 1945, 29 governments had ratified the bank's Articles of Agreement. In March 1946, the board of governors of the World Bank and the International Monetary Fund were inaugurated in Savannah, Ga, where they adopted the institutions' bylaws and elected the bank's executive directors.[7] The board first met on May 7, 1946. The bank's first president, Eugene Meyer, took office on June 18, and the bank opened its world headquarters at 1818 H Street NW, Washington, DC, on June 25.[8]

The job of being the first bank president was challenging. In the 10th anniversary issue of *International Bank Notes*, Mr. Meyer noted that, "Finding the proper path for this new experiment in international cooperation was not easy. We had only the Articles of Agreement to guide us, and they provided only the sketchiest of outlines."[9]

Meyer resigned after 6 months and was succeeded by John McCloy, who held the position for 2 years, a period that initiated a rapid change in the World Bank's work and geographic orientation.

From reconstruction to development

McCloy helped shift the bank's focus from postwar reconstruction to economic development. On May 9, 1947, the bank authorized its first loan: $250 million to France for postwar reconstruction. By August 1947, it had authorized reconstruction loans to The Netherlands ($195 million), Denmark ($40 million), and Luxembourg ($12 million).[10] These first loans were for "reconstruction" (compared with project-specific loans), and they launched the nascent bank into international capital markets. However, the international community soon realized that, instead of piecemeal loans, European and Japanese reconstruction would require a full-fledged effort by international leaders. Hence, the Marshall Plan was established in June 1947.[11] Relieved of the reconstruction burden, the bank's directors turned their full attention to development.

In the postwar era, the prevailing wisdom in development theory was that economic growth (increasing gross national product or growth rates) was the key to development. Therefore, during this era the bank focused primarily on large investments in physical capital and heavy infrastructure. From 1948 to 1961, for example, 87% of its loans to less developed countries were for power and transportation. The remaining commitments provided for other forms of economic overhead, such as industry and telecommunications, and a small fraction (4%) was invested in agriculture and irrigation.[12] Moreover, from January 1949 through April 1961, the bank provided $5.1 billion to 56 countries for 280 different loans, primarily for economic development.[13] The first development loan ($13.5 million), effective on April 7, 1949, was to Chile's Corporacion de Fomento de la Produccion for 4 electric power projects and incidental irrigation.[14] The second development loan ($2.5 million), effective the same day, focused on machinery for Chilean agriculture. Education, health, and other social sectors were not provided for in the loans.[15]

This development theory and investment philosophy remained constant for most of the bank's first 2 decades, espousing the idea that public utility and transportation projects, financial stability, and a strong private sector were the primary means to development.[16] These types of projects were also easier to finance and were considered more appropriate for bank financing.[17] During this time, the World Bank shunned public investments in sanitation, education, and health.[18] One reason for this neglect, as previously mentioned, was the prevailing development paradigm that public utility investments and other economic infrastructure were the key to economic growth. Another reason related to the bank's culture as a "financial institution," because "by the early 1950s the bank's operations and development thinking had been set into a banker's mold."[19] This financial "mold" valued investments that showed a measurable and direct monetary return. As Edward Mason and Robert Asher explain in their book, *The World Bank Since Bretton Woods*,

> The contribution of social overhead projects to increased production . . . is less measurable and direct than that of power plants. . . . Financing them, moreover, might open the door to vastly increased

demands for loans and raise hackles anew in Wall Street about the "soundness" of the bank's management. It therefore seemed prudent to the management . . . to consider as unsuitable in normal circumstances World Bank financing of projects for eliminating malaria, reducing illiteracy, building vocational schools, or establishing clinics. . . .[20]

Some bank staff and advisors disagreed with this view. E. Harrison Clark, chief of the 1952 Survey Mission to Nicaragua, returned from that country with strong recommendations. The mission reported that

expenditures to improve sanitation, education and public health should, without question, be given first priority in any program to increase the long-range growth and development of the Nicaraguan economy . . . high disease rates, low standards of nutrition, and low education and training standards are the major factors inhibiting growth of productivity. . . .[21]

Despite these recommendations, none of the 11 loans Nicaragua received from the World Bank between 1951 and 1960 covered water, sanitation, health, or education.[22]

By virtually ignoring the social sectors, the World Bank charted a different course from the US government and other development institutions. From 1951 to 1954, more than 30% of US foreign aid to South Asia was for health, agriculture, and education.[23] In particular, US bilateral aid to Thailand for public health was a significant priority.[24] Although the primary motivation for US bilateral human resource lending in South Asia appeared to stem from the fear that poverty and ill health bred communist ideology,[25] such investments were consistent with the US postwar emphasis on individualism and human capacity and its confidence in science and medicine.[26] Other development institutions, such as the US Agency for International Development; Food and Agriculture Organization, UN Educational, Science, and Cultural Organization; United Nations Children's Fund (UNICEF); and especially the World Health Organization (WHO), also focused on improving public health.

The rationale for the bank's independent course was both academic and financial. Academic development dialogue at the time emphasized that economic growth was the principal tool for reducing poverty in developing countries and that social services investments would be counterproductive. Davesh Kapur et al. wrote, "Such measures would be temporary palliatives, at the expense of savings and productive investment; direct and immediate attacks on mass poverty would only squander limited national resources."[27]

This "trickle down" economic approach was reinforced by the idea that industrialization and urbanization were necessary for economic growth,[28] a view dominating bank thinking during most of the 1950s and 1960s.[29] Sociologists and economists agreed that urbanization was an inevitable component of development,[30] that income inequality was inevitably linked to economic growth,[31] and that growth, not distribution, should be the focus of development.[32]

The World Bank's financial interests were equally at odds with lending policies that favored social and human resources. Robert Cavanaugh, the bank's chief fundraiser and a bridge between the New York stock market— the bank's primary funding source—and the bank's lending instruments during this period, stated in 1961,

> If we got into the social field . . . then the bond market would definitely feel that we were not acting prudently from a financial standpoint . . . If you start financing schools and hospitals and water works, and so forth, these things don't normally and directly increase the ability of a country to repay a borrowing.[33]

Cavanaugh's statement reflected how the World Bank was influenced by potential financial market reactions, especially when it was trying to build a strong reputation within financial markets and development circles. Even if some bank officials thought health and education were important to development, academic and financial influences swayed the bank to put aside welfare matters for the first 25 years of its existence.

Investments in health, nutrition, and population programs

On April 1, 1968, Robert S. McNamara became president of the World Bank. During his long tenure (ending June 1981), he transformed the bank by moving poverty reduction to center stage. He sought to redefine the bank as a bona fide "development agency" and not just a financial institution[34] and was a forceful agent of change.

McNamara's arrival coincided with a shift in academic thinking and research about development. This shift began in the 1950s, when orthodox views of development[35]—focusing on economic growth—were questioned, and studies found that physical capital played a smaller-than-expected role in economic growth. Moreover, it appeared that a "residual factor" existed in macroeconomic statistical models.[36] This residual factor was believed to be investment in education, innovation, entrepreneurship, and, later, health.[37] The concepts of "human capital" and "human development"—investments in people—also gained acceptance.[38] The basic needs approach to development influenced the way academics and policymakers viewed development,[39] later forming the cornerstone of the US Agency for International Development program.[40]

These development ideas made sense to McNamara. They both appealed to him personally and were consistent with his own personal history, prior loyalties, and experience with the US government and the private sector. Moreover, internal bank studies and country mission reports revealed that hundreds of millions of people in developing countries were living in extreme poverty and lacking health clinics, primary and secondary schools, and safe drinking water.[41] Such conditions of "underdevelopment" were key barriers to productivity, economic growth, and poverty reduction, and poverty was a direct result of insufficient investments in health and education. Dragoslav Avramovic, acting head of the bank's economics department just before McNamara's arrival, was a strong critic of prevailing orthodox views. His critique of trickle-down economics later provided key aspects of McNamara's attack on poverty.[42] Although shifts in academic thinking about development influenced some bank staff in the 1960s, they did not take root in the bank's policies and institutional ethos until after McNamara arrived in 1968.

The bank's gradual shift toward more social sector lending began with an emphasis on population control, which McNamara regarded as the first step to alleviating poverty. In a landmark speech at the University of Notre Dame in 1969, he urged the international community to address population growth, the "most delicate and difficult issue of our era, perhaps of any era in history."[43] Population control was a major focus for other development agencies at the time, particularly the Ford Foundation and US Agency for International Development By 1970, McNamara had established the Population Projects Department in the World Bank and continued to advocate population control in speeches and dialogue with governments. In June 1970, the bank approved its first family planning loan ($2 million)—to Jamaica.[44] By the end of fiscal year (FY) 1973, the bank's lending in family planning totaled $22 million, less than 10% of that given for electric power ($322 million) and telecommunications ($248 million). It was an even lower fraction of that given for agriculture ($938 million) and transportation ($682 million).[45] On August 26, 1974, the report *Population Policies and Economic Development*, which analyzed the effect of rising populations on poverty, was published.[46] However, population control failed to develop into a strong lending program, perhaps because it could not meet the bank's interest in projects that were both acceptable to borrowers and attractive to bank shareholders.[47]

McNamara's attention then turned to nutrition, motivated in part by the International Conference on Nutrition, National Development, and Planning at Massachusetts Institute of Technology in 1971 and the International Nutrition Planning Program established in 1972 at the university and funded by the Rockefeller Foundation and US Agency for International Development.[48] In November 1970, biochemist James Lee became the bank's scientific advisor and was responsible for nutrition policy along with other areas of science.[49] In his speech at the bank's 1971 annual meeting, McNamara emphasized that "malnutrition is widespread and it limits the physical, and often the mental growth of hundreds of millions and it is a major barrier to human development."[50] By January 1972, the World Bank report *Possible Bank Actions on Malnutrition Problems* led to the establishment of a bank nutrition unit. In 1973, Alan Berg's book *The Nutrition Factor* and a 1973 nutrition policy paper, which called for a more active role in nutrition, reinforced McNamara's support for eventual bank lending in that area.[51] However, the bank did not approve its first loan for nutrition (to Brazil for $19 million) until 1976.[52]

Since 1970, McNamara had been advocating bank support of health and nutrition programs, as in speeches at Columbia University (1970) and the bank's annual general meetings (1972). In June 1973, he requested a health policy paper from bank staff.[53] The resulting 1975 *Health Sector Policy Paper* was 1 of the bank's first efforts to generate and disseminate knowledge on health policy issues. In 1974, 1 of the bank's most successful programs, the Onchocerciasis Control Program (OCP), was created to eliminate onchocerciasis (river blindness) and enhance country and regional control of the disease. This health initiative involved 11 countries in West Africa and was sponsored, along with the World Bank, by United Nations Development Program (UNDP), Food and Agriculture Organization, and WHO. It also involved the private sector and nongovernmental organizations. Onchocerciasis is caused by a parasitic worm and is spread by black flies that breed in fast-flowing water. The group determined they could stop flies from transmitting the disease by treating the water flow. The OCP also established a program of insecticide application to prevent the growth of black flies.[54]

Because the bank was not notably engaged in health issues at the time, its decision to tackle river blindness was a turning point. The program, which continued for some 30 years, protected an estimated 34 million people from river blindness and cleared nearly 25 million hectares of land for agricultural use.[55] The OCP gave the bank a boost in the health sector. In 1979, the bank established a health department and a policy to consider funding stand-alone health projects, as well as health components in other projects.[56]

These efforts in the health arena were influenced by the growing recognition in academic and policymaking development discourse that the basic needs approach was essential to poverty reduction.[57] McNamara, in particular, engaged with this dialogue. In his 1976 address to the annual general meeting of the board of governors in Manila, the Philippine Islands, he underscored the need to reexamine trickle-down economics and to focus on the unmet basic human needs of hundreds of millions of people in developing countries.[58] Over the ensuing years, he called for further research within the bank before endorsing a full-scale lending program for basic needs.

Despite its failure to become fully institutionalized in World Bank culture and policy, the basic-needs approach laid the foundation for further expansion in the bank's HNP sector. Official recognition of this shift came most publicly in the *World Development Report, 1980* which demonstrated that malnutrition and ill health were 2 of the worst symptoms of poverty and that both could be addressed by direct government action, with bank assistance. The report also suggested that improving health and nutrition would likely accelerate economic growth. After a series of research papers suggested that health and education were directly productive, these findings were incorporated in the *World Development Report, 1980* to argue for greater emphases on social sector lending.[59]

The bank translated development theory and research into action by creating the Population, Health, and Nutrition Department in October 1979 and allowing stand-alone health loans. A 1980 *Health Sector Policy Paper* was 1 of the first attempts to provide a rationale for stand-alone investments in the health sector.[60]

In 1980, the bank approved another nutrition loan—to the India Tamil Nadu Nutrition project. In 1984, it provided a $2 million grant for social emergency programs, and, in 1985, it gave a $3 million grant to the World Food Program for emergency food supplies to sub-Saharan Africa.[61] The creation of the Population, Health, and Nutrition Department became a landmark in the World Bank's involvement in health.

On February 10, 1987, the bank cosponsored—with WHO and United Nations Population Fund—a conference in Nairobi, Kenya, on safe motherhood.[62] This conference launched the bank's Safe Motherhood initiative, which was its first global commitment to health issues of this nature; the program is now in its 17th year. This initiative solidified the bank's commitment to family planning and maternal and child health. The public and financial commitments resonating from this initiative became important pillars of the bank's health sector work. Safe motherhood projects increased from 10 in 1987 to 150 in 1999, with an annual commitment of $385 million between 1992 and 1999–30% of total bank HNP lending.[63] Between 1987 and 1998, the bank supported safe delivery activities in 29 countries.[64] In 1987, it loaned $10 million for Zimbabwe's Family Health Project and $11 million to Malawi for its Second Family Health Project. In 1990, it supported a $267 million loan to Brazil's Second Northeast Basic Health Services Project.[65]

A second global health conference on safe motherhood, sponsored by the World Bank, WHO, UNICEF, and United Nations Population Fund, took place on January 30, 1989, in Niamey, Nigeria. A November 1989 bank report, *Sub-Saharan Africa: From Crisis to Sustainable Growth*, followed and called for doubling expenditures on human resource development.[66] Together, these events provided further momentum for investments in family planning and child and maternal health. In 1998, the bank loaned $300 million for India's Women and Child Development Project and $250 million for Bangladesh's Health and Population Program Project.[67] The bank's family planning work was not without controversy, however. Its *World Development Report, 1984: Population and Development* which emphasized governments' role in reducing fertility and mortality,[68] was criticized, as were its family-planning projects (drawn into abortion politics) in Latin America and elsewhere.[69]

Other noteworthy early HNP activities included the first loan in 1981 to Tunisia to expand basic health services, the 1987 study *Financing Health Services in Developing Countries: An Agenda for Reform*, and the bank's seminal *World Development Report, 1993: Investing in Health*.[70] The 1987 document, in particular, underscored the need for improved health sector financing and included user fees/charges, which are highly controversial, as 1 instrument for mobilizing resources. The *World Development Report, 1993* was a watershed in international health, giving the World Bank greater exposure and legitimacy in the health sector. The first *World Development Report* devoted entirely to health (signaling the bank's commitment), its overall aim was to make the case to the broader development community for investing in health. The *World Development Report, 1993* identified several major problems in international health systems, in particular, inefficient use of funds and human resources, inequitable access to basic heath care, and rising health care costs. As a result, the bank advocated several key recommendations for improving health: educating girls and empowering women, reallocating government resources from tertiary facilities to primary care, investing in public health and essential clinical services, and promoting private and social insurance and competition in health services delivery. Although generally well received, the report was criticized for introducing disability-adjusted life years (DALYs), for lacking a strong evidence base, and for promoting privatization.[71]

The World Bank's increasing involvement in global health

The *World Development Report, 1993* has been supplemented over the past decade with bank operational research and analysis, including the bank's Special Program of Research, Development and Training in Human Reproduction, the WHO/United Nations Development Program/World Bank Tropical Diseases Research Program, and the Global Micronutrient Initiative.[72] Since 1993, the bank has also increased its support of country-specific research and analysis of HNP issues, primarily through bank loans and credits, which has resulted in significant external HNP research funding in developing countries.[73] The World Bank's own Policy Research Department has also grown its interest in HNP issues and now spends $1 million annually (8% of the department's total research budget) on HNP studies.[74] Such policy research builds on the bank's comparative advantage in economic and intersectoral analysis related to health issues. Other areas of bank involvement in global health knowledge include training and seminars on HNP topics for policymakers in developing countries. Over the past several years, the bank has produced 210 country-specific HNP sector studies and staff appraisal reports and hundreds of country strategy documents on HNP topics,[75] including, for example, a study in Morocco on health financing and insurance.[76]

239

Although the bank's role in generating and disseminating global health knowledge is important, its main advantage compared with other international institutions is its ability to mobilize financial resources. By far the most dramatic change in its role in global health has been its increased financial support for HNP through loans, credits, and grants. Indeed, it is now the "single largest external source of HNP financing in low- and middle-income countries."[77] In contrast to approving only 1 HNP loan in 1970, it had financed 154 active and 94 completed projects in 1997 with a total of \$13.5 billion.[78] From 1987 to 1992 alone, it tripled its HNP lending, and the average number of new projects per year increased from 8 in FY 1987–1989 (\$317 million annually) to 21 in FY 1990–1992 (\$1.2 billion annually).[79] HNP projects grew from less than 1% of total World Bank lending in 1987 to nearly 7% in 1991.[80] By the end of FY 1996, the World Bank's new annual lending was \$21 billion, and 24% of that was directed to HNP (11% or \$2.4 million), education (8%), and social protection (5%).[81]

The types of HNP activities pursued by the bank also have changed over the past several years. Early projects focused primarily on strengthening countries' basic HNP infrastructure and services, specific diseases (e.g., OCP), and certain populations (e.g., rural development). However, a late-1990s review by the bank's Operations Evaluation Development Department of 120 projects conducted between FY 1970–1995 found that the narrow focus on capital investment failed to achieve the significant institutional and systematic changes necessary for project effectiveness. It also found that the bank's HNP portfolio was fragmented and of uneven quality.[82] This assessment has led the bank to shift its HNP activities away from basic health services toward broader policy reforms.[83] The Operations Evaluation Development Department review also called for a strategic policy direction and for lending supported by rigorous analysis and research. The bank responded with its 1997 *HNP Sector Strategy Paper*.[84] The review also recommended enhanced selectivity, involving a focus on country needs and an analysis of the costs, benefits, and risks (including political, institutional, and economic) of all planned HNP activities.

The World Bank also tried to tune into the international dialogue on the need to improve the effectiveness of development assistance through cooperation among agencies. A key lesson learned over the past decades is that institutions acting alone cannot meet complex HNP challenges. Thus, the bank has been working to strengthen its collaboration with other international organizations. In Brazil, Uganda, and Ghana, it collaborated with other donors through its sector-wide approach programs, which aim to bring multiple donors together to fund an entire sector, develop comprehensive sector-wide policies, and pursue similar policy objectives. Sector-wide approach programs are an improvement on the previously fragmented approach of multiple donors funding ad hoc projects without coordination, but they have not been without controversy.[85]

However, the World Bank recognizes that it must do more to strengthen its partnerships with client countries, civil society, stakeholders, and other agencies. Recently, it entered into collaborative agreements with WHO that will provide technical assistance for improving the design, supervision, and evaluation of bank-supported projects. The WHO and the World Bank are collaborating to advance international understanding of HNP issues, as was done, for example, through the recent Framework Convention for Tobacco Control, through which the bank worked with WHO to establish the evidence base on effective methods of curbing the prevalence and consumption of tobacco products.

Criticisms of the World Bank

The World Bank and its policies are among the most hotly debated and highly criticized in the global development community. With regard to health sector policies, key concerns involve user fees, structural adjustment, use of DALYs, and privatization.

In its 1987 report on financing, the bank highlighted user fees as an instrument for mobilizing resources. However, empirical evidence demonstrates that user fees reduce the demand for both necessary and unnecessary care and that they disproportionately affect poor and sick people. Evidence also suggests that such fees have not been overwhelmingly successful in raising revenue or enhancing efficiency. In its 1997 sector strategy, the bank claimed that it does not support user fees; however, it maintained that such fees are 1 tool for mobilizing resources. By contrast, critics prefer the bank to reject user fees entirely, a policy the World Bank has yet to pursue.

In the 1980s and 1990s, the bank pressured countries to adopt "structural adjustment" programs for their economies and to follow many prescriptions of the "Washington Consensus" by emphasizing economic management, macroeconomic stability, privatization, trade liberalization, and public sector contraction. This involved opening markets (trade liberalization), reducing government expenditures (in some cases for health), and privatizing state-owned enterprises. Critics argue that such programs reduce health care spending and have deleterious health effects.[86] UNICEF estimated that structural adjustment programs may have been associated with 500 000 deaths of young children in a 12-month period,[87] even though a 1998 study of the effect of structural adjustment operations on health expenditures and outcomes and the World Bank's own research[88] found no negative impact.[89] Still, much concern remains both within and outside the bank on the efficacy and negative effect of such programs, and the bank has moved away from endorsing them.

The bank also was criticized for introducing DALYs to global health assessments. It described DALYs in the *World Development Report, 1993* as a way to conceptualize and measure the global disease burden and to associate this burden with health and other social policies. Critics argue that DALYs lack a sound theoretical framework and are inequitable because they value years saved for the able-bodied more than for the disabled, the middle-aged more than the young or old, and the currently ill more than those who will be ill tomorrow.[90] By introducing DALYs, the bank contends it improved analysis of international health systems. Critics remain concerned with its use in global health, and the debate continues.

Critics also have been concerned about the negative effects of the World Bank's support for privatization in general and the health sector specifically.[91] Research focused on private markets in the health sector has demonstrated that a strong government is necessary to address market failures that occur in financing, consuming, and providing both personal and public health services. Insurance market failures, credit shortages, information asymmetries, and insufficiencies, in particular, can inhibit people from realizing economic benefits that accrue from collective risk reduction through risk pooling.[92] However, although the bank now admits that open markets and economic management are insufficient and that good governance and strong institutions are critical for eradicating poverty, in the health sector, more specifically, critics argue the bank needs to present a clearer position on the trade-offs between public and private financing and delivery of health services.[93]

Conclusion

The World Bank today is very different from the organization conceived at Bretton Woods in 1944. Its mission has changed from post–World War II reconstruction and development to worldwide poverty alleviation. Although the bank invested almost exclusively in physical infrastructure in its early days, its focus has broadened to include significantly more social sector lending. A major expansion of the bank's work in HNP took place between the late 1980s and late 1990s, and the bank is now the world's largest external funder of health and one of the largest supporters in the fight against HIV/AIDS.

The World Bank's role in global health has evolved through a better understanding of development, which the bank now sees as a holistic, integrated, and multidimensional task that should balance the strengths of the market and other institutions and focus on people in client countries.[94] This approach reflects, in part, a new paradigm of academic thought that development is the process of expanding the real freedoms people enjoy,[95] a concept set forth by Amartya Sen. Lessons learned from 50 years of development experience and theory suggest that economic growth, investments in infrastructure and physical capital, macroeconomic stability, liberalization, and privatization still matter, but that development is multifaceted and our understanding of it must be broad and inclusive. A number of key elements, including economic growth and stability, a thriving private sector, investment in people and physical assets, a sustainable environment, and sound institutions and policies are necessary to promote prosperity, reduce poverty, and improve the human condition.

In the late 1990s, the bank's *Voices of the Poor* study, which provided detailed interviews of impoverished people in developing countries,[96] showed that the experience and determinants of poverty are multidimensional. Poor people require not only higher incomes but also security and empowerment, opportunities for education, jobs, health and nutrition, a clean and sustainable environment, a well-functioning judicial and legal system, civil and political liberties, and a rich cultural life. Reflecting these views, the Bank's *World Development Report, 2000–2001* on Poverty[97] identified good health and nutrition and effective reproductive policies and health services as critical for allowing countries to break the vicious circle of poverty, high fertility, poor health, and low economic growth.

All of these changes in the bank's mission, leadership, research, and philosophy have made health, nutrition, and population programs priorities for its work and for the wider development community. The World Bank's evolution, like development research and thinking, has been slow and steady, suggesting that health's importance to development[98] is a concept with long-lasting implications.

Acknowledgments

The author is supported in part by a Career Development Award from the US National Institutes of Health (grant 1K01DA01635810).

The author thanks Kimberly Hannon and Susan Gatchel for administrative assistance, Linda Sage for editing assistance, and Washington University Center for Health Policy and School of Medicine for support.

Note

The author worked previously as a health economist in the health, nutrition, and population sector and as speechwriter to James D. Wolfensohn, president of the World Bank.

Human participant protection

No human participants were involved with this study

Endnotes

1 World Bank, "What is the World Bank," http://web.worldbank.org/WBSITE/EXTERNAL/EXTABOUTUS/0,,contentMDK:20040558~menuPK:34559~pagePK:34542~piPK:36600~theSitePK:29708,00.html (accessed February 27, 2004).

2 D. Kapur, J. P. Lewis, and R. Webb, *The World Bank. Its First Half Century, Volume 1: History* (Washington, DC: Brookings Institution, 1997), 2.

3 World Bank, "Ten Things You Never Knew About the World Bank," http://www.worldbank.org/tenthings/index.html (accessed March 5, 2004).

4 The Human Development Network, *Health, Nutrition, & Population*, World Bank Sector Strategy Paper (Washington, DC: World Bank, 1997).

5 World Bank, "What is the World Bank."

6 World Bank, "World Bank Group Historical Chronology 1944–1949," http://web.worldbank.org/WBSITE/EXTERNAL/EXTABOUTUS/EXTARCHIVES/0„contentMDK:20035657~menuPK:56307~pagePK:36726~piPK:36092~theSitePK:29506,00.html (accessed February 27, 2004).

7 Ibid.

8 World Bank, "Pages from World Bank History—Bank's 57th Birthday Retrospective," http://web.worldbank.org/WBSITE/EXTERNAL/EXTABOUTUS/EXTARCHIVES/0„contentMDK:20116771~pagePK:36726~piPK:36092~theSitePK:29506,00.html (accessed February 25, 2004).

9 World Bank, *International Bank Notes*, June 1956, quoted in World Bank, "Pages for World Bank History—Bank's 57th Birthday Retrospective."

10 World Bank, "Pages from World Bank History: Bank's First Development Loans," May 30, 2003, http://web.worldbank.org/WBSITE/EXTERNAL/EXTABOUTUS/EXTARCHIVES/0„contentMDK:20113929~pagePK:36726~piPK:36092~theSitePK:29506,00.html (accessed February 25, 2004); World Bank, "World Bank Group Historical Chronology 1944–1949."

11 Kapur, Lewis, and Webb, *The World Bank. Its First Half Century.*

12 Ibid, 85–86, 109–110.

13 Ibid, 85–86, 109–110.

14 World Bank, "Pages from World Bank History: Bank's First Development Loans."

15 Kapur, Lewis, and Webb, *The World Bank. Its First Half Century*, 82; World Bank, "Pages from World Bank History: Bank's First Development Loans."

16 E. S. Mason and R. E. Asher, *The World Bank Since Bretton Woods* (Washington, DC: Brookings Institution, 1973.)

17 L. Currie, *The Role of Economic Advisors in Developing Countries* (Seattle, WA: Greenwood Press, 1981).

18 Kapur, Lewis, and Webb, *The World Bank. Its First Half Century.*

19 Ibid, 85.

20 Mason and Asher, *The World Bank Since Bretton Woods*, 151–152.

21 World Bank, *The Economic Development of Nicaragua.* (Baltimore, MD: Johns Hopkins University Press, 1953), 22–23, quoted in Kapur, Lewis, and Webb, *The World Bank. Its First Half Century*, 111.

22 Kapur, Lewis, and Webb, *The World Bank: Its First Half Century.*

23 C. Wolf, *Foreign Aid: Theory and Practice in Southern Asia* (Princeton, NJ: Princeton University Press, 1960).

24 R. J. Muscat, *Thailand and the United States: Development, Security, and Foreign Aid* (New York: Columbia University Press, 1990).

25 Kapur, Lewis, and Webb, *The World Bank. Its First Half Century.*

26 R. A. Pastor, *Congress and the Politics of U.S. Foreign Economic Policy, 1929–1976* (Berkeley: University of California Press, 1980).

27 Kapur, Lewis, and Webb, *The World Bank. Its First Half Century*, 115.

28 J. Morris, *The Road to Huddersfield* (New York: Pantheon, 1963).

29 H. B. Chenery, "The Role of Industrialization in Development Programs," *American Economic Review* 45 (1955): 40; W. A. Lewis, "Economic Development with Unlimited Supplies of Labour," *Manchester School of Economic and Social Studies*

22 (1954): 131–191; W. A. Lewis, *Theory of Economic Growth* (London: George Allen and Unwin, 1955); B. F. Johnston and J. W. Mellor, "The Role of Agriculture in Economic Development," *American Economic Review* 51 (1961): 566–93; Kapur, Lewis, and Webb, *The World Bank. Its First Half Century.*

30 G. D. H. Cole, *Introduction to Economic History, 1750–1950* (London: Macmillan, 1952).

31 S. Kuznets, "Economic Growth and Income Equality," *American Economic Review* 45 (1955): 1–28.

32 Lewis, *Theory of Economic Growth.*

33 R. W. Cavanaugh, interview, World Bank Oral History Program, July 25, 1961, 63–64, quoted in Kapur et al., *The World Bank. Its First Half Century*, 119–120.

34 Kapur, Lewis, and Webb, *The World Bank. Its First Half Century.*

35 Lewis, *Theory of Economic Growth.*

36 M. Abramovitz, *Resource and Output Trends in the United States Since 1870,* Occasional Paper 52 (New York: National Bureau of Economic Research, 1956).

37 S. Enke, *Economics for Development* (London: Dennis Dobson, 1963).

38 T. W. Shultz, "Investment in Human Capital," *American Economic Review* 51 (1961): 11.

39 P. Streeten, *The Distinctive Features of a Basic Needs Approach to Development,* Basic Needs Paper 2, World Bank Policy Planning and Program Review Department, Washington, DC, August 10, 1977.

40 R. H. Sartorius and V. W. Ruttan, "The Sources of the Basic Needs Mandate," *Journal of Developing Areas* 23 (1989): 331–62.

41 Kapur, Lewis, and Webb, *The World Bank: Its First Half Century.*

42 Memorandum, Dragoslav Avramovic to George D. Woods, February 13, 1964, cited in Kapur, Lewis, and Webb, *The World Bank. Its First Half Century*, 208.

43 World Bank, "Pages from World Bank History—Bank Pays Tribute to Robert McNamara," March 21, 2003, http://web.worldbank.org/WBSITE/EXTERNAL/EXTABOUTUS/EXTARCHIVES/0,,contentMDK:20100171~pagePK:36726~piPK:36092~theSitePK:29506,00.html (accessed February 25, 2004).

44 World Bank, "World Bank Group Historical Chronology 1970–1979," http://web.worldbank.org/WBSITE/EXTERNAL/EXTABOUTUS/EXTARCHIVES/0„contentMDK:20035661~menuPK:56317~pagePK:36726~piPK:36092~theSitePK:29506,00.html (accessed February 27, 2004).

45 World Bank, "Pages from World Bank History: Excerpts from the 1973 Annual Report," http://web.worldbank.org/WBSITE/EXTERNAL/EXTABOUTUS/EXTARCHIVES/0,,contentMDK:20108747~pagePK:36726~piPK:36092~theSitePK:29506,00.html (accessed November 10, 2004).

46 World Bank, "World Bank Group Historical Chronology 1970–1979."

47 Kapur, Lewis, and Webb, *The World Bank. Its First Half Century.*

48 Ibid, 253.

49 Ibid.

50 World Bank, "Pages from World Bank History—Bank Pays Tribute to Bob McNamara."

51 Kapur, Lewis, and Webb, *The World Bank. Its First Half Century*, 253–254.

52 World Bank, "World Bank Group Historical Chronology 1970–1979,"

53 Kapur, Lewis, and Webb, *The World Bank. Its First Half Century.*

54 World Bank, "Pages from World Bank History: The Fight Against Riverblindness," March 14, 2003, http://web.worldbank.org/WBSITE/EXTERNAL/EXTABOUTUS/EXTARCHIVES/0,,contentMDK:20098846~pagePK:36726~piPK:36092~theSitePK:29506,00.html (accessed February 25, 2004).

55 Ibid.

56 Kapur, Lewis, and Webb, *The World Bank. Its First Half Century*, 345.
57 P. Streeten with Shahid Javed Burki, et al., *First Things First: Meeting Basic Human Needs in Developing Countries*, (Oxford: Oxford University Press, 1981).
58 R. S. McNamara, "To the Board of Governors, 1976, Manila, Philippines, October 4, 1976," in McNamara, *The McNamara Years at the World Bank* 337, quoted in Kapur, Lewis, and Webb, *The World Bank. Its First Half Century*, 266.
59 World Bank, *World Development Report, 1980* (New York: Oxford University Press, 1980).
60 The Human Development Network, *Health, Nutrition, and Population*.
61 World Bank, "World Bank Group Historical Chronology 1980–1989," http://web.worldbank.org/WBSITE/EXTERNAL/EXTABOUTUS/EXTARCHIVES/0,,contentMDK:20035663~menuPK:56318~pagePK:36726~piPK:36092~theSitePK:29506,00.html (accessed February 27, 2004).
62 Ibid.
63 The Human Development Network, *Safe Motherhood and the World Bank: Lessons From 10 Years of Experience*, (Washington, DC: The World Bank, 1999), 5.
64 Ibid, 33.
65 Ibid, 25.
66 World Bank, "World Bank Group Historical Chronology 1980–1989."
67 The Human Development Network, *Safe Motherhood and the World Bank*, 30.
68 World Bank, *World Development Report, 1984: Population and Development* (New York: Oxford University Press, 1984).
69 World Bank, "World Bank Group Historical Chronology 1990–1999."
70 World Bank, *World Development Report, 1993: Investing in Health* (New York: Oxford University Press, 1993).
71 K. Abbasi, "The World Bank and World Health: Under Fire," *British Medical Journal* 318 (1999), 1003–6.
72 The Human Development Network, *Health, Nutrition, & Population*.
73 Ibid, 11.
74 Ibid, 11.
75 Ibid, 13.
76 G. J. Schieber, J. P. Ruger, N. Klingen, A. M. Pierre-Louis, and Z. E. Driss, *Morocco Health Financing Brief*, World Bank Document (Washington, DC: World Bank, 1999); J. P. Ruger. "Health Financing and Insurance in Morocco" (paper presented at the Symposium on Health Sector Financing in Morocco, jointly sponsored by the Government of Morocco and the World Bank, Rabat, Morocco, June 1999).
77 The Human Development Network, *Health, Nutrition, & Population*, ix.
78 Ibid, ix.
79 World Bank, *World Development Report, 1993*, 169.
80 Ibid, 169.
81 The Human Development Network, *Health, Nutrition, & Population*, 69.
82 Ibid, 15.
83 Ibid.
84 The Human Development Network, *Health, Nutrition, & Population*.
85 Abbasi, "The World Bank and World Health: Under Fire."
86 M. Rao (ed.), *Disinvesting in Health: The World Bank's Prescriptions for Health* (Thousand Oaks, CA: Sage Publications, 1999).
87 UNICEF. *The State of the Worlds Children* (New York: Oxford University Press, 1989), 16–7.
88 World Bank, *Adjustment Lending: Policies for Sustainable Growth* (Washington DC: World Bank, 1990), 11; Abbasi, "The World Bank and World Health: Under Fire."

89 J. Van der Gaag and T. Barham, "Health and Health Expenditures in Adjusting and Non-Adjusting Countries," *Social Science and Medicine* 46 (1998): 995–1009.

90 Abbasi, "The World Bank and World Health: Under Fire"; S. Anand and K. Hanson, "DALYs: Efficiency Versus Equity," *World Development* 26 (1998): 307–10.

91 M. Turshen, *Privatizing Health Services in Africa* (New Brunswick, NJ: Rutgers University Press, 1999).

92 J. P. Ruger, D. Jamison, D. Bloom, "Health and the Economy," in *International Public Health: Disease, Programs, Systems, and Policies*, ed. M. Merson, R. Black, A. Mills, 617–66 (New York: Aspen Publishers, 2001); J. P. Ruger, "Catastrophic health expenditure" *Lancet* 2003 Sep 20; 362: 996–7.

93 K. Abbasi, "The World Bank and World Health: Interview with Richard Feachem," *British Medical Journal* 318 (1999): 1206–8; A. Wagstaff, "Economics, Health and Development: Some Ethical Dilemmas Facing the World Bank and the International Community," *Journal of Medical Ethics* 27(2000): 262–7.

94 World Bank, Comprehensive Development Framework, http://web.worldbank. org/WBSITE/EXTERNAL/PROJECTS/STRATEGIES/CDF/0,,pagePK:60447~ theSitePK:140576,00.html (accessed March 5, 2004).

95 A. K. Sen. *Development as Freedom* (New York: Knopf. 1999); J. P. Ruger, "Health and Development," *Lancet* 362 (2003): 678; J. P. Ruger, "Combating HIV/AIDS in Developing Countries," *British Medical Journal* 329 (2004): 121–2; J. P. Ruger, "Health and Social Justice," *Lancet* 2004; 364:1075–80; J. P. Ruger, "Ethics of the Social Determinants of Health," *Lancet* 2004; 364: 1092–97; J. P. Ruger, "Aristotelian Justice and Health Policy: Capability and Incompletely Theorized Agreements" (Ph.D. thesis, Harvard University, 1998).

96 D. Narayan, R. Patel, K. Schafft, A. Rademacher, and S. Koch-Schulte. *Voices of the Poor: Can Anyone Hear Us?* (New York: Oxford University Press, 2000); D. Narayan, R. Chambers, M. K. Shah, P. Petesch. *Voices of the Poor: Crying Out for Change* (New York: Oxford University Press, 2000).

97 World Bank, *World Development Report, 2000–2001: Attacking Poverty* (New York: Oxford University Press, 2001).

98 Ruger J. P. Millennium development goals for health: building human capabilities. *Bulletin of the World Health Organization.* 2004; 82(12):951–952.

67

THE GLOBAL GOVERNANCE OF COMMUNICABLE DISEASES

The case for vaccine R&D

Daniele Archibugi and Kim Bizzarri

Source: *Law & Policy*, 27:1 (2005), 33–51.

Fighting communicable diseases such HIV/AIDS, tuberculosis (TB), and malaria has become a global endeavor, with international health authorities urging the development of effective vaccines for the eradication of these global pandemics. Yet, despite the acknowledged urgency, and given the feasibility of effective vaccine development, public and private research efforts have failed to address a response adequate to the magnitude of the crisis. Members of the academic community suggest bridging this gap by devising research pull mechanisms capable of stimulating private investments, confident that competition-based market devices are more effective than public intervention in shaping scientific breakthroughs. With reference to the economics of innovation, the paper argues that, whilst such an approach would lead to a socially suboptimal production of knowledge, direct public intervention in vaccine R&D activities would represent a far more socially desirable policy option. In recognition of the current financial and political fatigue affecting the international community towards communicable disease control, the paper resorts to the theories of global public goods (GPGs) to provide governments, both in the North and in the South, with a powerful rationale for committing to a cooperative approach for vaccine R&D. The paper encourages the creation of a Global Health Research Fund to manage such exercise and proposes enshrining countries' commitments into an International Health Treaty. The paper ends by providing a number of policy recommendations.

I. Introduction: the current mismatch between global health needs and global health research

A. Current distribution of communicable diseases

At the dawn of the twenty-first century, despite 150 years of international health cooperation and numerous high-profile health summits, communicable disease control is still lacking adequate international political action: forty-two million people are currently living with HIV/AIDS around the world, thirty-nine million in developing countries (the South) alone. Infection rates are also on the increase: five million new HIV/AIDS infections were reported in 2002, with over 70 percent of these occurring just in sub-Saharan Africa (WHO 2003). Similarly, tuberculosis (TB) is responsible for the death of over two million individuals, and the infection of another seventeen million every year (WHO & UNICEF 2002), with an incidence of infection that is thirteen times higher in developing countries than in the industrialized world (the North). Malaria also, despite having been eradicated in the North[1] through an overall improvement in environmental conditions, still claims over one million lives and 400 million new infections each year in the South (Harvard Malaria Initiative 2000). The economic and social repercussions that entire regions experience as a result of these pandemics are tremendous. The United Nations (2001) estimates that AIDS alone will cause South Africa's GDP to fall by 17 percent by 2010, without taking into account falling workers' productivity, declining savings and investment, rising business costs, and decreasing life expectancy. Many other countries are also facing similar prospects, and comparable patterns are envisaged for malaria and TB (WHO & UNICEF 2002). As well as contributing to the economic decay, social fragmentation, and political destabilization of already volatile and strained societies, these global pandemics are also jeopardizing past and present development efforts aimed at bridging the increasing widening socio-economic divide between the North and the South.[2]

B. The need for vaccine R&D

Leading health organizations (International Aids Vaccine Initiative 2001; Médicins sans Frontières 2001a; WHO & UNICEF 2002) have argued with much vigor in favor of preventative immunization as representing the most effective tool in the fight against communicable diseases – the eradication of smallpox in 1977 as a result of WHO's Smallpox Eradication Programme representing the most remarkable example (see Fenner 1988 for a detailed analysis of the program's achievements). Yet, despite the success of preventative immunization and the authoritative opinion of experts, resources devoted to vaccine R&D continue to be minimal. The case of AIDS is exemplary.

The annual HIV/AIDS vaccine R&D expenditure still represents just 10 percent – about US$400 million – of the annual global HIV/AIDS anti-retroviral R&D spending (Esparza 2000; International Aids Vaccine Initiative 2002). For malaria and TB, vaccine R&D figures are even more disconcerting. The Malaria Vaccine Initiative[3] estimates that the total R&D for a malaria vaccine has not exceeded US$55 million, whilst for TB, the World Health Organization and United Nations' Children Fund (WHO & UNICEF 2002: 61) estimate that, since the early 1990s, vaccine R&D has not exceeded US$150 million.

C. Structure and objectives of this study

The paper will explore the possible explanations as to why vaccine R&D for major communicable diseases has been so inadequate in addressing the current health crisis. The following sections will provide an overview of current private and public research efforts in vaccine R&D, and will highlight the importance of incentives in determining R&D investments, arguing that geo-economic factors are responsible for the current lack of incentives. Through a global public goods approach, Section IV provides a rationale for convincing the international community to cooperate in the fight against communicable disease control by focussing on vaccine research and development. Sections V and VI advance estimates concerning the ideal R&D resources required, and propose the creation of an Global Health Research Fund for a coordinated approach to the management of these resources. Section VII supports the creation of an International Health Treaty in an attempt to insure member states' respect of their financial obligations to the proposed fund. The paper concludes by providing a number of policy recommendations.

II. The current state of scientific knowledge

A. How far are we from hitting the target?

The economics of innovation teach that, given the de facto uncertainty of all scientific investigation, no clear linear relationship between input and output can be assumed – the case for a cure for cancer being exemplary. Particularly with reference to the delivery of a vaccine for AIDS, malaria, and TB, experts believe science is still ten to fifteen years away from yielding the desired results (Kaufmann 2000; Malaria Vaccine Initiative 2003; WHO & UNICEF 2002). Despite this technical hurdle, it is the opinion of the very same experts that a knowledge gap alone does not explain the minimal investment geared towards vaccine R&D. To quote the authoritative opinion of the Rockefeller Foundation's deputy director, Scott Halstead, "the major impediment to basic vaccine science is not a gap in knowledge, rather a lack of serious financial commitments that precludes the yielding of tangible results" (Rabinovich, 1994). An opinion that is also shared by many other experts in the field, including Médecins sans Frontières (2001), the International AIDS Vaccine Initiative (2001, 2002), and the WHO and UNICEF (2002).

Though, if indeed a lack of incentives, as opposed to a knowledge gap, were to explain the current undermining of global efforts to fight communicable diseases, two aspects would need to be considered: (a) the type, and amount, of R&D expenditure of both profit-seeking and public non-profit agents; and (b) the influence that the distribution of the disease burden across countries exerts on global research agendas.

B. The private funding of health-related R&D

The UNDP (2001) reports that of the 1393 new drugs developed between 1975 and 1999, only sixteen (less than 1 percent) of these were relevant to tropical illnesses – including communicable diseases. The World Health Organization Commission on Macroeconomics and Health (2001: 90–91) explains that industry involvement in R&D activities concerning all major disease killers is very limited, and in the majority of cases it is simply non-existent. Similarly, the Harvard School of Public Health revealed in a recent study that, of the world's twenty-four largest drug companies, none maintain an in-house malaria research program (Médicins Sans Frontières 2001b).

This can be interpreted as a reflection of the profit-driven nature of private R&D. As Figure 1 illustrates, the bulk of the disease burden is confined to the

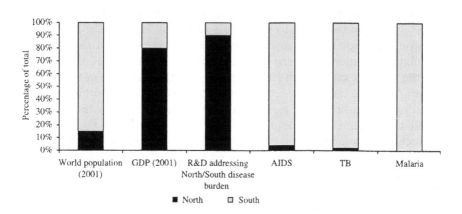

Figure 1 North/South Health and Resource Inequalities.
Sources: For World Population, see World Bank (2003: 235, Table 1, col. 1); for GDP, see World Bank (2003: 239, Table 3, col. 1); for R&D addressing North/South disease burden, see Médicins Sans Frontières (2001a); for AIDS, see UNAIDS & WHO (2002: 6); for TB, see UNDP (2002: 173, Table 7, col. 9); for Malaria, see UNDP (2002: 173, Table 7, col. 8).
North: high income countries. South: all others. (See UNDP 2002).

South, also home to the highest concentration of the world's poor, where 80 percent of the world's population concentrates just 20 percent of the world's GDP. As a consequence, this low purchasing power of the South has impeded the high "social" demand for vaccine R&D to be matched by an equally high "market" demand necessary to stimulate private investment. This would explain why, of the eleven different HIV clades currently identified, private vaccine research is focussing on clade B, the clade prevalent in Europe and North America – responsible for just 4 percent of the disease burden – whilst clades A and C, prevalent in Africa and responsible for 70 percent of all HIV/AIDS infections, receive minimal research effort (Barnet & Whiteside 2002; Kremer 2001). Moreover, the social pressure exerted over investors to treat their inventions as indivisibilities – as exemplified by the celebrated case between the South African government and the pharmaceutical industry over the AIDS anti-retroviral cocktail drug (May 2002; Seckinelgin 2002) – could cause private investors to be discouraged further from investing in a field already surrounded by much scientific uncertainty, and lacking adequate market demand.

C. Stimulating private R&D: the role of "purchasing commitments"

Many economists have attempted to devise a variety of mechanisms to stimulate privates' investment in neglected areas of medical research. One of the most celebrated proposals, indeed welcome by many IGOs (see the World Health Organization. Commission on Macroeconomics and Health 2001; Kaul et al. 2003: UNDP 2001) has been that of "purchasing commitments" (Kremer 2001). As described by Kremer, purchasing commitments entail a clear financial pledge by international organizations, such as UNICEF or WHO, to purchase a successful vaccine when and if developed. Kremer argues that, by committing to purchase a successful vaccine, the public sector would provide private investors with the market demand necessary to stimulate their interests, whilst it would leave the entire burden of the costs, and the risks associated with R&D activities, on the shoulders of the private sector. Although the private sector clearly necessitates of encouragement for investing in non-profitable markets, this approach presents a fundamental hurdle that deserves mentioning.

Purchasing commitments entail an entirely competitive spirit among research entities. As the economics of scientific and technological innovation teach, optimal knowledge production is reached by maximizing diffusion of all intermediate results, or rather through a highly cooperative approach to scientific inquiry (Nelson 1962). By contrast, the exclusivity of a prize, as suggested by Kremer, would force the various competing agents to maintain secret all intermediate results of their research, with an ultimate detrimental effect to vaccine knowledge production. Thus, despite the utility of encouraging private research in neglected areas of medical research, "purchasing commitments" are far from providing an ideal policy solution.

D. The role of the public sector

Back in 1962, Arrow had warned against the dangers of leaving to market forces alone the responsibility for providing the financial incentives necessary to stimulate scientific R&D since, the lack of profitable markets, indivisibilities, and scientific uncertainty, would cause private resources to be suboptimally allocated (Arrow 1962). With reference to activities with strong social implications, many classical economists, including Smith, Malthus, Ricardo, and indeed Arrow, suggested moreover that – in the event of a market failure – the state should bare the costs of their provision (Desai 2003). Within modern capitalist societies, the state and the market share the provision of a number of activities. With reference to scientific R&D, the public sector performs a variety of research activities through (a) a number of publicly owned infrastructures – such as academic research laboratories – and (b) by outsourcing research projects to private operators – as has been the experience of both space and military R&D programs. Especially within medical science, publicly funded R&D has played a fundamental role in major drug-lead discoveries. Publicly funded R&D has developed a number of antibiotics for many communicable diseases, drugs for treating tuberculosis, various types of chemotherapy to treat cancer, and more recently the development of anti-retrovirals for the treatment of HIV/AIDS (UNDP 2001). It is estimated that 70 percent of all drugs with therapeutic gains have been the direct result of the public sector's involvement (ibid.).

III. The geo-politics of vaccine R&D

A. The North-South paradox

If a lack of profitable markets explains the privates' disinterests towards communicable disease control, what could explain the public sector's disengagement? Figure 1 suggests that geo-political factors may be involved.

On one side of the hemisphere, the South concentrates 20 percent of the world's GDP, 90 percent of the total disease burden, and just 10 percent of the total R&D budget. In contrast, on the other side of the hemisphere, the North concentrates 80 percent of the world's GDP, 90 percent of the World's R&D budget, and less than 10 percent of the world's disease burden. These conditions have conferred the North, not only the resources and the competencies necessary to address these diseases, but also the power to set the global health research agenda. Regrettably though, many governments in the North, especially European, have favored financially the R&D of non-targeted academic activities and commercial areas that would increase the international competitiveness of national firms, rather than R&D activities that would benefit humanity as a whole (European Council 2002). The result has been a paradoxical situation, in which countries affected by the diseases lack the resources and expertise necessary to combat them, whilst countries holding both the resources and the expertise to fight them, lack a direct incentive for doing so.

B. The North/South health divide: a matter of political will

The case of the Global Fund To Fight AIDS, Tuberculosis and Malaria (GFATM) is exemplary to this political and financial *fatigue* of Northern government towards fighting communicable diseases globally. Established in 2002, under the auspices of the UN Secretary General, the fund has aimed at raising a total of US$8 billion a year through country's voluntary donations to fight major communicable diseases – although the Fund focuses on disease prevention and cure, as opposed to vaccine research and development (Tan, Upshur & Ford 2003). Despite the apparent initial political support from the international community, the fund has suffered severe financial constraints ever since its foundation. Most countries have in fact met only partially their financial obligations to the fund, with the USA in particular having contributed just 10 percent of the US$10 billion it agreed to donate by 2008 (Cunningham 2003). Far from being the exception, the Fund's lack of support follows the general trend that has distinguished Official Development Assistance (ODA) since the fall of the Berlin Wall, or rather a decreasing political and financial support to building bridges between the North/South socio-economic inequalities (World Bank 2003: 13).

Faced with this political indifference, many attempts have been made over the past thirty years to provide convincing arguments for inciting the North to play a proactive role in international cooperation, including global communicable disease control.

A most powerful rationale that has recently emerged, and has captured the interest of governments, and international governmental and non-governmental organizations, is that of global public goods (GPGs). Indeed, by looking at communicable disease control through a global public goods' lens, a persuasive justification can be developed for the North's cooperation in the fight against communicable diseases. The following section explores this rationale.

IV. Vaccine knowledge and communicable disease control as global public goods

A. Global public goods (GPGs): a definition

In her pioneering work, *Providing Global Public Goods: Managing Globalisation*, Kaul (2003) defines GPGs as goods exhibiting the following characteristics:

- non-excludable benefits – entailing the technical impossibility of excluding any one individual from consuming the good (i.e., the atmosphere, judicial systems, national defense);
- and/or non-rival benefits – by which the consumption of the good by one individual does not deprive others from consuming the same good (i.e., knowledge, see below);
- and whose benefits extend to all countries, people, and generations.

To these technical properties, Kaul adds a fourth and normative aspect, namely the dependency on international cooperation for an effective provision of GPGs.

Additionally, Kaul also distinguishes between what she defines *intermediate* global public goods, and *final* global public goods, or rather, global public goods whose provision is dependent upon the production of associate goods (Kaul, 2003). For the purpose of our argument, Kaul's definition will set the frame within which it shall be argued that both the control of communicable diseases, and the knowledge necessary to develop a vaccine for their eradication, can be considered global public goods – the former, final; and the latter, intermediate.

B. Vaccine knowledge as a GPG

In 1962, Arrow postulated that knowledge could be duplicated and diffused at zero or very low costs (Arrow 1962). Although this assumption has proven wrong for the majority of technological applications (see Pavitt 1999), in the case of the chemical and pharmaceutical industries the costs of knowledge duplication and diffusion can be minimal – given adequate supporting infrastructure (Mansfield, Schwartz & Wagner 1981). Moreover, knowledge is unique in its ability to diffuse from one individual to another without depriving the original withholder from continuing to enjoy its consumption and associated benefits. As noted by Thomas Jefferson, "he who receives an idea from me, receives instructions himself without lessing me" (Stiglitz 1999).

These de facto non-excludable and non-rival characteristics have distinguished knowledge as a public good (Correa 2003). However, in order to qualify as a *global* public good, vaccine knowledge would have to benefit more than one group of countries, populations, and generations. At present, the scientific community is concerned that, due to the geographic variation of the HIV virus genetic make-up, country-specific vaccines may fail to prove effective globally (Kremer 2001). International cooperation for the development of a universally effective vaccine might therefore be jeopardized by the self-interest of certain countries to develop a vaccine specific to their own needs only. Also looking at communicable disease control from a global public good perspective provides a convincing argument for pursuing cooperatively the development of a universal vaccine for communicable diseases.

C. Communicable disease control as a GPG

The GPG character of communicable disease control is best understood by juxtaposing it against the direct and indirect threats that the underprovision of communicable disease control poses globally. The following examples will highlight how, despite the unequal repartition of the disease burden across countries, communicable diseases bring states into a shared fate, consequently calling upon governments to act cooperatively in fighting against communicable diseases:

- *Cross border transmission* – international travel and trade are causing an increase in prevalence within industrial countries of diseases previously endemic to the South. In Switzerland, for example, new HIV infections are exhibiting similar characteristics to those fuelling the AIDS epidemic in Africa (Tenkorang & Conceiçao 2003). Similarly, the recent West Nile virus infections reported in the U.S., illustrate the physical boundless nature of communicable diseases (Kaul & Faust 2001);
- *Costly provision of national public goods* – the cross-border transmission of communicable diseases represents a direct negative externality for the country into which the disease enters – since the disease-importing country will have to bear the costs associated with the imported disease (i.e., prevention, treatment, vaccination, mortality, etc). This was recognized by the United States Congress in 2000, when it acknowledged in its Global AIDS and Tuberculosis Relief Act (2000), that "because of the ease of transmission of tuberculosis, its international persistence and growth pose a direct public health threat to those nations that had previously largely controlled the disease." Indeed, by failing to achieve global eradication, even disease-free countries will still have to incur the costs associated with immunization and treatment. The case of polio is exemplary. The incomplete eradication of polio is estimated to be costing the world US$1.5 billion a year (Aylward 2000). By contrast, it has been estimated that by achieving the eradication of smallpox, the United States recoups its contributions to the smallpox eradication programs once every twenty-six days. That is, every twenty-six days, the benefits accruing from *not* having to deal with smallpox, equal the U.S.'s total eradication costs (Tenkorang & Conceiçao, 2003);
- *Socio-economic repercussions* – as discussed in the introduction, HIV/AIDS is responsible for massive economic and social devastation in sub-Saharan Africa (Bell, Devarjan & Gersbach 2003). The United States assert that HIV/AIDS in Africa constitutes a national security threat not only because of cross-border HIV transmission, but because

it has the potential to destabilize the region and harm the economic, political, humanitarian, and strategic interests of other countries (Fidler 2001).

D. The necessity of international cooperation for communicable disease control

The examples reported above illustrate the non-excludable and non-rival characteristics associated with communicable diseases, highlighting the strong intergenerational and social and economic implications for all countries, including those currently disease-free. In particular, they highlight the GPG character of communicable disease control, given the inherent impossibility to exclude any one country from benefiting from the direct and indirect advantages accruing from the eradication of the diseases. Three main conclusions can therefore be drawn with reference to the GPG argument:

1. Vaccine R&D can be considered the *intermediate* GPG necessary for reaching the *final* GPG of communicable disease control.
2. The GPG character of both vaccine R&D and communicable disease control provides a strong case for public intervention in their provision.
3. The effectiveness of their provision will dependent on the international community's capacity to act cooperatively, since individual efforts will not be effective unless supported by a global structure.

Thus, despite the different degrees of threat posed to countries by communicable diseases, the global public good character of communicable disease control brings countries into shared fate. Consequently, countries should also be brought together as partners in reforming appropriately their public policy choices. The following section proposes an ideal framework on which countries should build a cooperative approach to the financing of vaccine R&D.

V. Creating a global health research fund

A. A central funding organization

In its 2001 report, the WHO Commission on Macroeconomics and Health proposed the creation of a Global Health Research Fund (GHRF) to support basic, biomedical, and applied sciences research on health problems of the poor. Although the report provides no details as to how this fund should be structured nor managed, we support amply its creation and we suggest a number of features that should characterise the fund:

- The GHRF should act as a complementary financing mechanisms to the Global Fund to Fight HIV/AIDS, Malaria and TB (GFAMT) by concentrating its mandate exclusively on vaccine research and development (hence knowledge production) – whilst the GFAMT would continue to provide financial support to outreach activities. The complementarity of the two funds would guarantee the global public good character of the vaccines developed;
- The fund would fall under the UN umbrella and, ideally, it would be coordinated by WHO in collaboration with all other UN agencies that might have a direct interest in the activities of the Fund, such as the United Nations Development Programme (UNDP), the United Nations Peoples Fund (UNFPA), and the United Nations Children Fund (UNICEF);
- WHO would be appointed as the primary coordinator of the fund, since WHO is the only global institution to benefit from the mandate to oversee international health cooperation and to guarantee the protection and promotion of global health commons. Moreover, WHO holds the ability to convene a broad array of actors, develop consensus, and mobilize resources. With respect to legitimacy, the World Health Assembly is currently attended by 191 member states, all of which have equal voting rights irrespective of size of financial contribution (Buse & Walt 2000). No other health-related organization can claim near universal membership of nation states, nor does it benefit from a technical network-support as extensive as that of WHO;
- The fund would be subject to the supervision of a Health Research Council – directly accountable to the World Health Assembly – and would be composed by members representing all stakeholders with an interest in vaccine R&D. Namely, these should include WHO and other UN representatives, scientists, members of academia, NGOs, industry, and southern peoples' groups, in order to account for both scientific and non-scientific matters, keep research activity within its scope, and avoid targeted research being transformed into disciplinary research;
- The fund should also function as a catalyst and cooperate with all international research initiatives geared towards the development of a vaccine for communicable diseases, such as WHO's own vaccine research programs, the WHO/UNAIDS Initiative for Vaccine Research, the Tropical Disease Research program – co-sponsored by WHO, UNDP, and World Bank – the International Aids Vaccine Initiative (IAVI), and the Global Alliance for Vaccine and Immunisation (GAVI);
- The fund should also aim at increasing funding to those groups obtaining more encouraging results. This evaluation would be performed by scientific peer review – a practice now common to many research-funding bodies, such as the U.S. National Institute of Health and the UK Medical Research Council. Members of the scientific community

258

should also be encouraged to exchange information with other research groups on a constant basis. This could be effectively managed by the Global Forum for Health Research established by WHO in 1996, and through customary academic channels – such as scientific journals, conferences, academic courses, Internet, and electronic fora.

B. Effectively managing the private outsourcing of R&D

There is no requirement that public financial commitment must also be performed by public institutions. As discussed earlier, in the case of space and defense, outsourcing R&D activity to private research centres has become a common practice – especially in the United States. Though, as argued also earlier, private contractors tend to disclose the minimum information, especially if they can trade any additional or unexpected result achieved via separate contracts. This can represent a major obstacle for the achievement of optimal knowledge production. The public contracting party would therefore need to master a high degree of competence in contract dealing and a strong leadership in directing research.

C. Privately funded research

Although this paper advocates a greater public commitment towards vaccine research, one cannot, and should not, aim at preventing private and profit-seeking agents from carrying out R&D activities in the field of immunization. Even in a residual position, the outcome of business-funded R&D could prove crucial to medical research. In the instance that the development of a successful vaccine for combating communicable diseases were the result of privately funded R&D, it would be necessary to negotiate the terms and conditions for licensing agreements – such as the type of remuneration (or compensation), and the exclusivity of the patent. Nothing should prevent the GHRF to purchase any successful vaccines through its annual budget. Alternatively, the GFATM could negotiate with patent holders the licensing right to reproduce and diffuse the vaccine via the payment of a royalty fee – issues associated with the duplication and diffusion of knowledge fall however outside the scope of argument (see Pogge (2002) for a radical proposition concerning the diffusion of essential knowledge to the developing world).

VI. Financing vaccine R&D for communicable diseases

A. The costs of developing a vaccine for AIDS, malaria, and TB

Estimates concerning the costs of drug development are very heterogeneous. Figures vary from US$50 million (WHO & UNICEF 1996) to almost US$900 million (Frank 2003; Tufts Center for the Study of Drug Development 2003) – though this appears to depend on whether the costs of clinical, pre-clinical, and post-approval tests are all accounted for (for a complete overview see DiMasi 1991; Frank 2003; WHO & UNICEF 1996; Miller 1998; TB Alliance 2001; Tufts Center for the Study of Drug Development 2003). The authoritative WHO Commission on Macroeconomics and Health (2001: 81) estimates that the cost of developing a vaccine for HIV/AIDS, malaria, and TB would require an ideal yearly R&D budget of US$1.5 billion. The Commission fails though to indicate how long this commitment would be required for – ideally until successful vaccines are developed. As mentioned earlier on, experts are of the opinion that HIV/AIDS, malaria, and TB vaccines are still ten to fifteen years out of reach (Kaufmann 2000; Malaria Vaccine Initiative 2003; WHO & UNICEF 2002), an opinion that is also supported by the economics of science. Grabowski and Vernon (1994) have shown that research projects in the medical/pharmaceutical field last on average ten years.

According to these estimates therefore, the cost of developing a vaccine for AIDS, malaria, and TB would require US$1.5 billion a year, for a potential fifteen-year period. This would total a comprehensive R&D budget of US$22.5 billion, a substantial sum, compared to the current patterns of vaccine R&D expenditure – which according to estimates here provided do not exceed US$600 million a year. Nevertheless, US$22.5 billion is an affordable sum for most countries in the North. The fight against communicable diseases would therefore be comparable in size to the Manhattan project, though it would have a far more socially constructive objective.

B. A proposed distribution of the financial burden

Table 1 illustrates a proposed distribution of the financial burden across countries according to the "Ability to Pay Principle" – or rather based on countries' GDP.[4] The largest overall contribution would come from the North, with the United States responsible for providing the single largest contribution, followed by that of the European Union and Japan. Developing countries would also provide a substantial financial contribution.

A considerable share of the funding should also be geared towards building local knowledge in, and transferring technology to, the South through the strengthening of programmes such as those initiated by IAVI and GAVI (see http://www.iavi.org and http://www.gavi.org), which aim at training local scientists by working in close collaborations with research laboratories in the North. Empowering the South with technical competencies necessary to perform medical R&D will contribute to bridging the current North/South health gap. However, the acquisition of knowledge is a long process that requires learning capacity, absorption of competencies,

Table 1 A Tentative Distribution of Requirements for Vaccine R&D.

	2001 GDP US$ billions	Vaccine R&D Requirements (total 15 years)* US$ billions	Vaccine R&D Requirements (per year)* US$ billions
World Total	31400.0	22.5	1.50
High Income Countries of *which*	25372.0	18.2	1.12
USA	9780.8	7.0	0.47
European Union 15	7181.7	5.1	0.34
Japan	4523.3	3.2	0.22
Low and Medium Income Countries	6025.0	4.3	0.29

*Proposals for pledges to an International Vaccine Fund Proportional to GDP.
Source: World Bank and elaborations.

and the building of local know-how (e.g., Lundvall & Johnson 1994; Pavitt 1999; Polanyi 1962).

VII. Implementation and implications: the case for an "international health treaty"

A. A proposed international health treaty

How could the idea here advocated of a GHRF be implemented? Vaccine R&D is certainly not the only area where a greater international cooperation, and internationally binding legal commitments have been advocated. For many years, it has been suggested to reinforce international health law in order to overcome some of the basic hurdles that constrain the WHO mandate, namely that of voluntary compliance mechanisms (see Fidler 2001). As has been well documented, WHO has historically preferred to use recommendations and persuasion to guide member states through the adoption of appropriate public health policies. Consequently, member states' compliance with WHO recommendations have remained voluntary, leaving public-health sovereignty of states legally unfettered by WHO's actions.

Among many critics, James Love (2003; Love & Hubbard 2004) has suggested creating an international health treaty as a mechanism for inciting governments' interest in communicable disease control. In particular, Love identified in an international health treaty the most appropriate legal mechanisms for ensuring countries' commitments towards funding R&D activities, including vaccine R&D for communicable diseases. Although this paper's primary objective is to provide a science policy approach to communicable

261

disease control, we believe that the general normative framework advocated by Love would benefit greatly the proposal of establishing a global health research fund. In particular, an international health treaty would need to focus on three main points:

Point 1. The Treaty would clearly stipulate that WHO member states have a legal and moral obligation not only to control communicable diseases, but also to promote the right to health both domestically and internationally, given the global public good character of communicable disease control. Member states would carry out this obligation through specific actions defined in Points 2 and 3;

Point 2. Member States would be required to meet the financial obligations to the GHRF – as proposed in Table 1 – and to the GFAMT in order to ensure the GPG character of communicable disease control;

Point 3. Member States would need to develop a coherent approach to health policy implementation by ensuring that domestic policies reflected international commitments (i.e., shift financial priorities from military to health programmes, devise tax incentives for the creation of philanthropic medical research foundations, promote international technology transfer programs, increase number of doctoral positions in the field of immunology).

An international health treaty would have the advantage to enshrine within international law the global public good character of communicable disease control and vaccine R&D, including the necessity for a cooperative approach to their provision. It would moreover provide governments with the necessary legal stimuli to meet their obligations to the GHRF.

VIII. Conclusions

In this paper we have applied the concept of global public goods as a powerful tool for a robust and rational approach to the cause of communicable disease control and vaccine R&D. More specifically, a GPGs-based approach has supported three main arguments:

1. The fact that both communicable disease control and vaccine knowledge require a form of global governance based on direct public intervention. This is also supported by the view that market forces alone are not the most appropriate device to provide financial investment for R&D devoted to basic human necessities;
2. The North has both direct and indirect incentives to commit its financial and technical resources to communicable disease control, even when affected just marginally by the diseases. Yet, an active involvement of

developing countries will also needed to generate appropriate capabilities in the long term and to achieve effective results on the field;

3. The distinction between *final* and *intermediate* GPGs has also allowed to make a strong case for focussing on vaccine R&D as an affective means of reaching the goal of eradicating communicable diseases – a proposition supported by ample evidence within the literature (i.e., WHO & UNAIDS 1999; WHO & UNICEF 1996, 2002).

The paper has also supported the argument in favor of the creation of a Global Health Research Fund to manage and coordinate R&D activity aimed at vaccine development, and has moreover proposed an ideal structure of the fund's mandate and operations. By reference to the economics of innovation and theories of GPGs, we have argued that the fund should be complementary to the GFATM in order to ensure the public good character of a vaccine by having the GHRF charged with the production side of knowledge, whilst the GFATM would insure its reproduction and global diffusion. The complementary role of the two funds could contribute substantially to the bridging of the North/South health divide. Although the development of a vaccine for AIDS, malaria, and TB would require US$22.5 billion – over a third of the current total health R&D spending – this sum is realistic by all means. The financial burden could be split across countries on the basis of the ability-to-pay principle. This would be consistent with the GPG character of fighting communicable diseases, since it would require countries to contribute proportionally to their financial and technical capabilities to produce the good of communicable disease control, as opposed to their share of the global disease burden. In recognition of the historical limitations of international law, we suggested ensuring a strong and continuous political/ financial commitment by the international community by including a binding obligation to fund vaccine R&D in the proposal of an international health treaty.

Given the advocacy aspect of our argument, it might be useful to make it explicit which communities are we addressing. First, we address global civil movements, an increasingly important player in international politics. Global civil movements have already played a crucial role in steering government priorities in key areas such as environment, disarmament, and human rights (see, e.g., Glasius, Kaldor & Anheier 2001, 2002, 2003). Concerning the health agenda, global movements have been particularly active in matters of knowledge diffusion, or rather access to drugs (see Shiva 2001). However, despite the present need to challenge the rules governing IPR regimes and realigning social needs with international trade law (see Coriat & Orsi 2002; Heller & Eisenberg 1998; Thurow 1997), we would urge these movements to also include in their priorities the need to increase publicly funded R&D for neglected diseases, since knowledge production is a precondition for its diffusion. As argued extensively in the paper, the current underprovision of communicable disease control is a reflection of lacking research environments, and not of diffusion mechanisms.

Second, we are addressing the academic community. In many cases, scientists hold the ability to direct strategically the priorities of their research. Governments do not have the information to direct scientific investigation unless there are scientists providing them with the technical expertise. Scientists could therefore devote increasing attention to the welfare implications and consequences of their work, and induce governments to devote more resources to global health priorities.

Last but not least, we address science policy analysts and advisors. In the last two decades there has been an increasing focus on science and technology as shapers of economic performance, rather than enhancers of social well-being. The circle of scholars of science and technology policy has been a close advisor to policymakers. If today, so much attention has been placed upon technologies for industrial innovation, and so little towards medical research for developing countries, it is due, in part, to the choices and priority setting of this community.

Whether governments will listen to a request for a change in priority setting will depend on the ability of global movements, scientific communities, and science and technology policy advisors to pursue common objectives.

Notes

1 The only high-income country with reported malaria cases is Korea (UNDP 2003: 258, Table 7, column 8).
2 North: OECD countries; South: all other countries.
3 Personal communication with Dr Walter Brandt, Senior Programme Officer, Malaria Vaccine Initiative, 17 June 2003.
4 According to the principle, the financial contribution capacity of countries is proportional to the country's GDP – membership fees to the United Nations for instance are calculated on the basis of the ability-to-pay principle.

References

Arrow, Kenneth (1962) "Economic Welfare and the Allocation of Resources For Invention." In *The Rate and Direction of Inventive Activity*, edited by R. Nelson. National Bureau of Economic Research. Princeton, N.J.: Princeton Univ. Press.

Aylward, Bruce (2000) "When is a Disease Eradicable? 100 Years of Lessons Learned," *American Journal of Public Health* 90: 1515–20.

Barnett, Tony, and Alan Whiteside (2002) *AIDS in the 21st Century: Disease and Globalisation*. New York: Palgrave MacMillan.

Bell, Clive, Shantayanan Devarajan, and Hans Gersbach (2003) *The Long-run Economic Costs of AIDS: Theory and Application to South Africa*. Washington, D.C.: World Bank.

Buse, Kent, and Gill Walt (2000) "The United Nations and Global Public-Private Health Partnerships." Paper presented at the Workshop: Public-Private Partnerships in Public Health, Harvard School Of Public Health, Boston, 7–8 April.

Correa, Carlos (2003) *Managing the Provision of Knowledge: The Design of Intellectual Property Laws.* In *Providing Global Public Goods: Managing Globalisation*, edited by I. Kaul, P. Conceição, K. Le Goulven & R. Mendoza. New York: Oxford Univ. Press.

Cunningham, Anne Marie (2003) "The Global Fund – All You Ever Wanted To Know." Available at http://www.geocities.com/jvidalalaball/TheglobalFund.doc.

Coriat, Benjamin, and Fabienne Orsi (2002) "Establishing a New Intellectual Property Rights Regime in the United States: Origins, Content and Problems," *Research Policy* 31: 1491–1507.

Desai, Meghnad (2003) *Public Goods: A Historical Perspective.* In *Providing Global Public Goods: Managing Globalisation*, edited by I. Kaul, P. Conceição, K. Le Goulven & R. Mendoza. New York: Oxford Univ. Press.

DiMasi, Joseph (1991) "Cost Of Innovation In The Pharmaceutical Industry," *Journal of Health Economics* 10(2): 107–42.

Esparza, Jose (2000) "Is an AIDS Vaccine Possible?," *UN Chronicle* 37(3): 22–23.

European Council (2002) *Presidency Conclusions.* Barcelona European Council. Brussels: EC.

Fenner, Frank (1988) *Smallpox and Its Eradication.* Geneva: WHO.

Fidler, David (2001) *International Law and Global Communicable Disease Control.* Geneva: WHO Commission on Macroeconomics and Health.

Frank, Richard (2003) "New Estimates of Drug Development Costs," *Journal of Health Economics* 22: 325–30.

Glasius, Marlies, Mary Kaldor, and Helmut Anheier (eds.) (2001) *Global Civil Society Yearbook.* Oxford: Oxford Univ. Press.

Glasius, Marlies, Mary Kaldor, and Helmut Anheier (Eds) (2002) *Global Civil Society Yearbook.* Oxford: Oxford Univ. Press.

Glasius, Marlies, Mary Kaldor, and Helmut Anheier (Eds) (2003) *Global Civil Society Yearbook.* Oxford: Oxford Univ. Press.

Grabowski, Henry George, and James Vernon (1994) "Returns to R&D on New Drugs Introductions in the 1980s," *Journal of Health Economics* 13: 383–406.

Harvard Malaria Initiative (2000) "The Ancient Scourge of Malaria." Available at http://www.hsph.harvard.edu/Malaria.

Heller, Michael, and Rebecca Eisenberg (1998) "Can Patents Deter Innovation? The Anticommons in Biomedical Research," *Science* 280: 698–701.

International AIDS Vaccine Initiative (2001) *A New Access Paradigm: Public Sector Actions to Assure Swift, Global Access to AIDS Vaccine.* New York: IAVI.

International AIDS Vaccine Initiative (2002) *When Will an AIDS Vaccine be Found? The State of Global Research.* New York: IAVI.

Kaufmann, Stephan. (2000) "Is the Development of a New Tuberculosis Vaccine Possible?," *Nature America* 6: 955–59.

Kaul, Inge, Pedro Conceição, Katell Le Goulven, and Ronald Mendoza (eds.) (2003) *Providing Global Public Goods: Managing Globalisation.* New York: Oxford Univ. Press.

Kaul, Inge, and Michael Faust (2001) "Global public goods and health: taking the agenda forward," *Bulletin of the World Health Organization* 79: 869–74.

Kremer, Michael (2001) *Public Policies to Stimulate Development of Vaccines and Drugs for Neglected Diseases*. Working Paper No. WG2. Geneva: Commission on Macroeconomics and Health.

Love, James (2003) "From TRIPS to RIPS: A Better Trade Framework to Support Innovation in Medical Technologies." Workshop on Economic issues related to access to HIV/AIDS care in developing countries held on 27 May 2003. Marseille: Agence nationale de recherches sur le sida/Institute d' économie publique.

Love, James, and Tim Hubbard (2004) "A New Trade Framework for Global Healthcare R&D," *PLoS Biology* 2(2): 147–50.

Lundvall, Bengt Ake, and Björn Johnson, (1994) "The Learning Economy," *Journal of Industry Studies* 1(2): 23–42.

Mansfield, Edwin, Mark Schwartz, and Samuel Wagner (1981) "Imitation Costs and Patents: An Empirical Study", *Economic Journal* 91: 907–918.

Mazzoleni, Robert, and Nelson, Richard (1998) "The Benefits and Costs of Strong Patent Protection: A Contribution to the Current Debate," *Research Policy* 27: 273–84.

May, Christopher (2002) "Unacceptable Costs: The Consequences of Making Knowledge Property in a Global Society," *Global Society* 16(2): 123–44.

Médicins Sans Frontières (2001a) *Fatal Imbalance: The Crisis in Research and Development for Drugs for Neglected Diseases*. Geneva: MSF.

Médicins Sans Frontières (2001b) *A Survey of Private Sector Drug Research and Development*. Switzerland: the Drugs for Neglected Diseases Working Group.

Miller, Henry (1998) "Rising Costs hold up Drug Discovery," *Nature*: 395: 835.

Nelson, Richard (1962) *The Rate and Direction of Inventive Activity*: National Bureau of Economic Research. Princeton, N.J.: Princeton Univ. Press.

Pavitt, Keath (1999) "On the Nature of Technology." In *Technology, Management, and Systems of Innovation*, edited by K. Pavitt. Cheltenham, UK: Edward Elgar.

Pogge, Thomas (2002) *World Poverty and Human Rights*. Cambridge: Polity Press.

Poku, Nana (2002) "Global Pandemics: AIDS." In *Governing the Global Polity*, edited by D. Held & A. McGrew. Cambridge: Polity Press.

Polanyi, Michael (1962) *Personal Knowledge. Towards a Post-Critical Philosophy*. London: Routledge & Kegan Paul.

Rabinovich, Regina (1994) "Vaccine Technologies: View to the Future," *Science* 265: 1401–4.

Seckinelgin, Hakan (2002) "Time to Stop and Think: HIV/AIDS, Global Civil Society, and People's Politics." In *Global Civil Society*, edited by M. Glasius, M. Kaldor & H. Anheier. Oxford: Oxford Univ. Press.

Shiva, Vandana (2001) *Protect or Plunder?: Understanding Intellectual Property Rights*. London: Zed Books.

Stiglitz, Joseph (1999) "Knowledge as a Global Public Good." In *Global Public Goods: International Cooperation in the 21st Century*, edited by I. Kaul et al. New York: Oxford Univ. Press.

Tan, Darrel (2003) "Global Plagues And The Global Fund: Challenges," *BMC International Health and Human Rights* 3(2): 1–9.

TB Alliance (2001) *The Economics of TB Drug Development*. New York: TB Alliance.

Tenkorang Dyna Arhin, and Pedro Conceiçao (2003) "Beyond Communicable Disease Control: Health in the Age of Globalisation." In *Providing Global Public*

Goods: Managing Globalisation, edited by I. Kaul et al. New York: Oxford Univ. Press.

Thurow, Lester (1997) "Needed: A New System of Intellectual Property Rights," *Harvard Business Review* (Fall): 95–103.

Tufts Center for the Study Of Drug Development (2003) *Outlook 2003 Report.* Boston: Tufts CSDD.

United Nations (UN) (2001) *HIV/AIDS: a Call To Action.* Paper presented at the African Summit On HIV/AIDS, Tuberculosis and Other Related Communicable Diseases, 24–27 April, Abuja, Nigeria.

United Nations Development Programme (UNDP) (2001) *Human Development Report 2001. Making New Technologies Work for Human Development.* New York: Oxford Univ. Press.

United Nations Development Programme (UNDP) (2003) *Human Development Report 2003. Millennium Development Goals: A Compact Among Nations to end Human Poverty.* New York: Oxford Univ. Press.

World Bank (2003) *World Development Report, Sustainable Development in a Dynamic World: Transforming Institutions, Growth, and Quality of Life.* New York: Oxford Univ. Press.

World Health Organization (WHO) (2003) *The World Health Report 2003.* Geneva: WHO.

World Health Organization (WHO) and UNAIDS (1999) *Report of the Overview of Vaccine Research in WHO and UNAIDS.* Geneva: WHO.

World Health Organization (WHO). Commission On Macroeconomics and Health (2001) *Investing for Economics Development.* Geneva: WHO.

World Health Organization (WHO) and United Nations Children's Fund (UNICEF) (1996) *The State of the World's Vaccines and Immunization.* Geneva: WHO.

World Health Organization (WHO) and United Nations Children's Fund (UNICEF) (2002) *State Of The World's Vaccine and Immunisation.* Geneva: WHO.

Laws cited

United States
Global AIDS and Tuberculosis Relief Act, Pub L No 106–264, HR 3519 (2000)

267

68

PUBLIC–PRIVATE PARTNERSHIPS FOR HEALTH

Their main targets, their diversity, and their future directions

Roy Widdus

Source: *Bulletin of the World Health Organization*, 79:8 (2001), 713–20.

Abstract

The global burden of disease, especially the part attributable to infectious diseases, disproportionately affects populations in developing countries. Inadequate access to pharmaceuticals plays a role in perpetuating this disparity. Drugs and vaccines may not be accessible because of weak distribution infrastructures or because development of the desired products has been neglected. This situation can be tackled with push interventions to lower the costs and risks of product development for industry, with pull interventions providing economic and market incentives, and with the creation of infrastructures allowing products to be put into use. If appropriately motivated, pharmaceutical companies can bring to partnerships expertise in product development, production process development, manufacturing, marketing, and distribution — all of which are lacking in the public sector. A large variety of public–private partnerships, combining the skills and resources of a wide range of collaborators, have arisen for product development, disease control through product donation and distribution, or the general strengthening or coordination of health services. Administratively, such partnerships may either involve affiliation with international organizations, i.e. they are essentially public-sector programmes with private-sector participation, or they may be legally independent not-for-profit bodies. These partnerships should be regarded as social experiments; they show promise but are not a panacea. New ventures should be built on need, appropriateness, and lessons on good practice learnt from experience. Suggestions are made for public, private, and joint activities that could help to improve the access of poor populations to the pharmaceuticals and health services they need.

Introduction

The disparities in health between rich and poor populations are, in a significant measure, attributable to a lack of access to drugs and vaccines as well as to differences in the geographical distributions of certain disease agents and sanitation. Historically, drugs and vaccines have become available through an informal division of responsibilities between public entities and private companies, all undertaking activities in accordance with their mandates or motivations. This division of labour constitutes a poorly defined partnership in which the outcomes desired by different parties have never been explicitly negotiated. In the more economically advanced countries it is generally regarded as reasonably successful, having led to the availability of a broad range of effective drugs and vaccines. However, this kind of system is not particularly responsive to the specific health needs of the world's poorest populations.

Substantial differences in health status have probably always existed between rich and poor populations and have certainly been documented for decades. Improved comparative data are now reinforcing the long-standing humanitarian and ethical concerns about inequalities in access to health products, health services, and resource allocation. Trends in increased travel, global awareness, information flow, and commerce — collectively termed globalization — have raised the level of interest about the possible causes and consequences of the uneven distribution of disease, particularly of emerging infections. As a result, increasing attention is being directed at the need to reduce global disparities in health.

Globalization has been accompanied by a reassessment of the strengths and limitations of public/governmental, private/commercial, and civil society institutions in grappling with world problems. Particularly in the health arena it seems to be recognized that intractable problems require not just better coordination of traditional roles but also new ways of working together in order to achieve a synergistic combination of the strengths, resources, and expertise of the different sectors.

With the aim of stimulating discussion on the most effective types of future action this paper presents a preliminary examination of experience in public –private partnerships. The focus is on partnerships between international or governmental agencies on the one hand and commercial pharmaceutical companies on the other. Most of these partnerships also include civil society bodies, e.g. nongovernmental organizations. Simple donations of funds or products by pharmaceutical companies, while potentially useful, are not considered here, nor is general corporate philanthropy.

Disparity in health between rich and poor

The health disparity between rich and poor countries results in average life spans of 77 and 52 years respectively (*1*). Deaths attributable to infectious diseases (Table 1) contribute most to the disparity. Deaths associated with diarrhoea and respiratory infection are rare in industrialized countries but are the major killers of children in developing countries. Diseases that do not occur in industrialized countries, e.g. malaria and schistosomiasis, or ones that are comparatively rare in these countries, e.g. tuberculosis and HIV/AIDS, impose a heavy burden on both adults and children in developing countries. The burden of morbidity from a number of untreated, debilitating but rarely fatal diseases in developing countries, including sexually transmitted infections, has a substantial impact on productivity.

Table 1 Deaths from infectious diseases worldwide, 1998[a]

Causes[b]	Deaths
No satisfactory vaccine available when data compiled	
AIDS	2 285 000 (27.47)[c]
Tuberculosis	1 498 000 (18.01)
Malaria	1 110 000 (13.34)
Pneumococcus	1 110 000 (13.22)
Rotavirus	800 000 (9.62)
Shigella	600 000 (7.21)
Enterotoxigenic *E. coli*	500 000 (6.02)
Respiratory syncytial virus	160 000 (1.92)
Schistosomiasis[d]	150 000 (1.80)
Leishmaniasis	42 000 (0.50)
Trypanosmiasis	40 000 (0.48)
Chagas disease	17 000 (0.20)
Dengue	15 000 (0.18)
Leprosy	2000 (0.03)
Subtotal	**8 319 000 (100)**
Satisfactory vaccine available	
Hepatitis B	1 000 000 (30.55)
Measles	888 000 (27.12)
Haemophilus influenzae type B	500 000 (15.27)
Tetanus	410 000 (12.52)
Pertussis	346 000 (10.57)
Cholera	120 000 (3.67)
Diphtheria	5000 (0.15)
Japanese encephalitis	3000 (0.09)
Poliomyelitis	2000 (0.06)
Subtotal	**3 274 000 (100)**
Grand total	**11 593 000**

[a] Source: unless otherwise indicated, ref. 2.
[b] Some pathogens are not included because etiology-specific estimates were not available.
[c] Figures in parentheses are percentages.
[d] Source: ref. 3.

An analysis of the differences in the disease burden between the poorest and the richest 20% of the world's population suggested that, in 1990, nearly 80% of the difference between the poor and rich in terms of death and disability-adjusted life years was attributable to communicable diseases (4). This is still likely to be true, as the incidences of HIV, malaria, and tuberculosis are increasing. Furthermore, the ageing of the population in the developing world can be expected to bring increases in the absolute burden of noncommunicable diseases (5).

Gwatkin & Guillot have also analysed the poor–rich health disparity in terms of the fraction of total burden attributable to various diseases (4). Pharmaceuticals exist that can treat most and prevent many of the diseases causing the bulk of morbidity and mortality in the pwoorer countries, with the caveat that for some diseases the available therapies require improvement in respect of ease of administration or length of treatment. Moreover, vaccines need to be improved for tuberculosis and developed for HIV/AIDS, malaria, and some other diseases. The disparity in health status probably results largely from differential access to drugs that are already available as well as to sanitation and safe water, which influence the transmission of some diseases.

Determinants of access to pharmaceuticals

The determinants of appropriate access to pharmaceuticals of acceptable quality can be categorized as in Box 1. In debates on how to improve access, drug affordability — interpreted as manufacturers' selling prices — is often simplistically singled out because it appears to be especially amenable to control. However, access presents a multifaceted problem and action is required on many fronts.

Each year, WHO compiles estimates from national experts on the percentages of countries' populations thought to have access to the essential drugs on the basic minimum list, most of which are off-patent. Figure 1 shows that in many countries, large numbers of people still have unacceptably low levels of access to basic drugs.

It is difficult to identify which of the determinants of access should be dealt with in order to achieve the greatest possible benefit. A lack of availability of any useful product is the dominant determinant of access for only a few diseases. In some instances, a better preventive product, such as a vaccine, would lead to improved disease control; in these cases, the product development step is essential. For many diseases, however, access is determined by the systems of pharmaceutical distribution and by economic factors.

An analysis of access to pharmaceuticals in sub-Saharan Africa during the 1980s and early 1990s indicated that there were major losses in therapeutic benefit because of inefficiencies in distribution systems (7). Given the economic problems in sub-Saharan Africa it is hardly surprising that the

---

Box 1. Determinants of access to pharmaceuticals

- **Availability** (i.e. whether a satisfactory product has been developed)
  - basic research
  - discovery
  - development
  - marketing

- **Accessibility**

  Quality, selection, prescribing, and use
  - Assurance of quality
  - Rational selection
  - Appropriate prescribing
  - Appropriate use, including patient compliance

  Effectiveness and efficiency of distribution system
  - reliable sources of supply
  - availability where needed

  Economic factors
  - resources for financing
  - costs
  - pricing policies and controls
  - price at point of use, including distributor mark-ups

  Knowledge and health-seeking behaviour of consumers
  - social norms
  - educational interventions
  - variations with socioeconomic status of potential consumers

---

situation is similar today, as confirmed by WHO's estimates of the scale of unsatisfactory access to essential drugs (Figure 1).

It is clear in sub-Saharan Africa, and it is probably also true in other parts of the world, that one of the major areas requiring attention is the inefficiency of pharmaceutical distribution systems. This is principally a responsibility of national governments. Additional analysis is needed so that global efforts can be guided. In this connection it would probably also be useful to assess the fraction of the burden attributable to each disease that might be reduced by access to off-patent drugs and vaccines (comprising 95% of the WHO model list of essential drugs); access to recently licensed/patented drugs and vaccines; and new products, yet to be developed. Different actions are already possible and are needed for each of these categories, but the required analysis has not yet been conducted.

It is important to recognize that the term "developing countries" now covers a wide range of economic well-being, ranging from poverty to relative

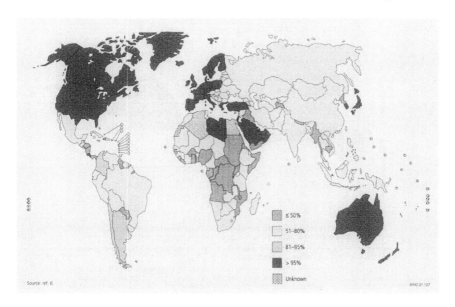

Figure 1 Percentage of population with regular access to essential drugs, 1997.

affluence. In Brazil, China, India, Indonesia, and Mexico, for example, there are moderate to large populations that are comparatively rich. Thus in the developing world there are countries and populations that can afford, much more easily than the poorest, to pay for health products and services either directly or, preferably, through schemes based on the principle of collective health insurance.

Interventions to improve access

The prospective market for products needed largely or exclusively in poorer developing countries is commercially unattractive in comparison with, for example, that linked to chronic health problems in affluent populations. In other words there is an unfavourable outlook for return on investment (Figure 2, segment B relative to segment A). The balance can be moved positively by the reduction of commercial expenditure (segment A) or by increased prospects of revenue (segment B).

Although there is considerable diversity in size, orientation, country location, and motivation among pharmaceutical companies, they consistently pay less attention to poor populations than those that are rich because of the need to provide a return to investors from the worldwide market (Figure 3).

Various interventions have been considered for stimulating product development and/or reducing infrastructural and economic barriers to access. These are generally grouped into pull and push interventions, as described below.

273

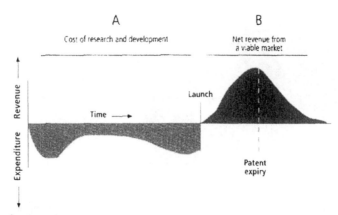

a For commercially attractive products, potential revenue (B) substantially exceeds the average costs to industry of research and development, including failures (A).

Expenditure on clinical studies, manufacturing, marketing, etc. continues after the launch but in the diagram are deducted from revenue in the interest of simplicity.

Costs to industry for vaccine development are reported to be approximately the same as those for drugs but with lower amounts spent in early development of vaccine concepts (that typically come from publicly funded basic research) and higher costs for production process development and efficacy trials. Many (but not all) vaccines have a relatively long life-cycle but revenue falls as competition increases.

Source: ref. 6.   WHO 01.137

Figure 2 Industry costs and revenue associated with product development[a].

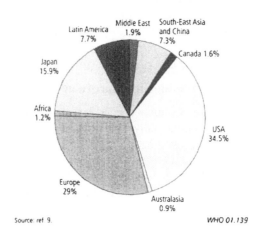

Source: ref. 9.   WHO 01.139

Figure 3 World pharmaceutical market, 1997.

Pull interventions

An economic incentive is required for industry to address the needs of developing countries in a sustained manner. Pull mechanisms should ideally include more attractive markets in the larger middle-income countries, where individuals themselves or their governments can afford to purchase products and, in the most impoverished countries, some sort of market-guarantee funding from external aid. Other possible pull interventions include tax credits on sales for priority products and early recommendations for product introduction from international organizations. The creation of health service infrastructures, allowing products and services to reach people in need, is essentially a pull mechanism since it is necessary to achieve a return on investment.

Push interventions

For industry to be attracted to the development of products for neglected diseases there must also be push interventions. These reduce the costs and risks to industry of developing the products. Push mechanisms can take many forms, such as public investment in basic research, sharing the costs of efficacy trials or other aspects of development, sharing the costs of production facilities, harmonizing international regulatory requirements, and introducing tax credits for investment in research and development.

Push and pull interventions typically require legislation or funding appropriations. They are generally created for a category of products, as in the orphan drug legislation in the United States of America. It was concluded at a recent conference that the most effective solution would probably be to create a mix of the two kinds of intervention (*10*).

However, a unique combination of challenges is faced in the progression of each product from research concept to wide utilization. In order to facilitate this progression there has frequently been a joining of forces by public and private sector organizations in new collaborative mechanisms. These public–private partnerships allow the different skills of the two sectors to be focused on the challenges specific to the products and diseases in question.

Although pharmaceutical markets in developing countries may expand, it appears that special arrangements will be necessary to meet the drug and vaccine requirements of some countries for the foreseeable future, including external financial assistance and, perhaps, concessionary or tiered pricing. Concessionary supply to the poorest countries is one of the most promising, although difficult, areas for public–private sector dialogue.

What forms have public–private partnerships taken?

The term "partnership" has recently been used to cover collaboration in general and the emerging forms of collaboration. However, it poorly represents the diversity of new relationships, a wide variety of which have been placed under the umbrella term of "public–private partnerships" (*11*).

Commercial pharmaceutical and other health-related companies have entered into a remarkable number of collaborations with public sector and civil society organizations in order to improve access to health products for poor populations. An initial inventory of over 70 collaborative relationships, mostly at the international level, has been established under the Geneva-based Initiative on Public–Private Partnerships for Health. These ventures involve a diversity of arrangements, varying with regard to participants, legal status, governance, management, policy-setting prerogatives, participants, contributions, and operational roles (*11*). Public–private partnerships for health should be distinguished from the trend to privatization, i.e. the private sector for-profit provision of health services. In the latter case, the public health policy goal and the rules under which for-profit entities operate are set and enforced solely by government agencies. The objectives of health partnerships are outlined in Box 2.

Among the legally independent, not-for-profit, public–private partnerships that have been established to deal with requirements for product development are the Medicines for Malaria Venture (for malaria drug replacements) (*12*), and the International AIDS Vaccine Initiative (for HIV/AIDS vaccines) (*13*). The Global Alliance for TB Drug Development is one of a number of partnerships that have just been launched (*14*).

The best known of the partnerships for disease control are the donation/distribution partnerships involving donations of albendazole (*15*), eflornithine (*16, 17*), leprosy multidrug therapy (MDT) (*18*), Malarone® (*19*), Mectizan® (*20, 21*), and Zithromax® (*22*). The contributions from the companies concerned have gone beyond the provision of products and have included involvement in supporting activities to ensure efficient distribution and effective use. Most of these donation/distribution programmes use products that are curative and relatively easy to administer in that few doses are required. Notwithstanding the health benefits, concerns have been expressed about these partnerships (*23*). When other services

---

Box 2. Objectives of a health partnership

- developing a product
- distributing a donated or subsidized product, to control a specific disease
- disease control through product donation and distribution
- strengthening health services
- educating the public
- improving product quality or regulation
- coordinating multifaceted efforts

---

are absent, partnerships directed to the distribution and utilization of donated products may not tackle the health problems of highest priority, as perceived locally. However, they are likely to be welcomed if they meet a need.

Particularly in relation to HIV/AIDS, partnerships are emerging which aim to strengthen health services. They include the Gates Foundation/Merck Botswana Comprehensive HIV/AIDS Partnership (24). Other partnerships, mostly aiming to improve coordination, are managed from within international organizations. The lodging of a partnership within a host organization significantly influences the rules governing its operations. Some so-called public–private partnerships could be more accurately described as public sector programmes with private sector participation. Collaborations in this category include the former Children's Vaccine Initiative, which had a secretariat in WHO, and the current Roll Back Malaria (25), Safe Injection Global Network (26), and Stop TB initiatives (27), all of which have secretariats in WHO. The successor to the Children's Vaccine Initiative, the Global Alliance for Vaccines and Immunization (28) has its secretariat in UNICEF, but the major funding vehicle associated with its work, the Global Fund for Children's Vaccines (29), is a legally independent, not-for-profit, private sector body.

Most partnerships have relied on the altruism of pharmaceutical companies and the prospect of good public relations. Few of the identified partnership have explicitly attempted to expand the sale of health products, for example by tapping new market segments. The exceptions include the social marketing of contraceptives and oral rehydration salts, and the creation of an otherwise unserviced market of the poorest countries for new vaccines, proposed by the Children's Vaccine Initiative in conjunction with UNICEF and WHO and subsequently implemented under the Global Fund for Children's Vaccines.

Apparent good practices for public–private partnerships are being analysed by various groups, including the Initiative on Public–Private Partnerships for Health.

Where should individual sector and partnership efforts focus in the future?

Partnerships between public/governmental entities, private/commercial entities, and civil society have a contribution to make in improving the health of the poor by combining the different skills and resources of various organizations in innovative ways. Public agencies clearly benefit from working in collaboration with the private sector in areas where the public sector lacks expertise and experience, e.g. in product development, production process development, manufacturing, marketing, and distribution.

However, there are areas, such as public health policy-making and regulatory approval, where the concept of partnership with for-profit enterprise is not appropriate. The purposes of partnerships should therefore be carefully considered and well articulated.

Partnerships appear to be most justified where: traditional ways of working independently have a limited impact on a problem; the specific desired goals can be agreed by potential collaborators; there is relevant complementary expertise in both sectors; the long-term interests of each sector are fulfilled (i.e. there are benefits to all parties); and the contributions of expertise and resources are reasonably balanced.

Public–private partnerships should not be expected to substitute for action on responsibilities that properly rest elsewhere. In particular, public sector agencies should continue to: fund fundamental research; set standards for product safety, efficacy, and quality; establish systems whereby citizens have adequate access to health products and services; use public resources in an efficient manner; and create environments in which commercial enterprise is appropriately motivated to meet the needs of whole populations.

Constructive analysis of the appropriateness, governance, accountability, operations, and benefits of partnerships is only possible when the subjects of analysis are properly defined. Such analysis requires the variation in arrangements for partnerships, particularly as regards legal status, to be taken into account.

Public–private partnerships should generally be viewed as social experiments that are attempting to learn how to tackle intractable health problems in better ways. There is no formula for constructing them and it is unlikely that a universally applicable one will be found. Criticisms of partnerships have been made (30) but it should be borne in mind that, without them, little new would be happening to tackle certain problems.

Public–private partnerships can be helpful but they are not a panacea. In the poorer countries, action is needed to overcome market failure and weak delivery systems that limit the availability and accessibility of pharmaceuticals and result in health disparities.

Certain actions by the public sector alone would mobilize new resources, strengthen demand, and allow market mechanisms to meet health needs in a broader range of countries, and more broadly within countries. Similarly, the for-profit private sector could also take some actions unilaterally to build a better base on which to construct partnerships. Building on these actions, collaborative efforts between the public and private sectors would yield added value. Examples of the contributions each sector could make individually and jointly are given in Box 3. Identifying the components of an appropriate strategy is relatively easy in comparison with the difficulties of implementation. It is necessary for all players, including many who are distrustful of those with whom they need to collaborate, to adopt a long-term view. Implementation requires long-term commitment. The onus of seeking new and more effective ways of working on intractable health problems rests as much — if not

Box 3. Action that could be taken by the public and private sectors

The **public sector** could:

- mobilize new resources for financing health, both within countries and from external sources, to help the poorest people;
- establish public health priorities for drugs, vaccines, diagnostics, and other health products;
- create fair health care financing systems to cover all people;
- assess the disease burden for major pathogens, country by country;
- assess the economic impact of diseases, country by country;
- conduct cost-effectiveness assessments for existing and anticipated products;
- strengthen research capability, including that associated with clinical trial sites in areas where certain diseases are endemic, through increased funding and training;
- support legislation that provides incentives or lowers the costs and risks of developing new or improved products for neglected diseases;
- support market segmentation for the poorest countries and price-tiering policies by industry;
- support market assurance mechanisms not only politically but also with solid financial appropriations.[a]

The **for-profit private sector** could:

- increase the use of devices such as licensing, tiered royalties, market segmentation, and tiered pricing to make products more accessible to all in need;
- allow wider access, under appropriate legal conditions, to chemical compound libraries in order to facilitate the search for new indications for old drugs;
- broaden personnel exchanges in order to allow public sector programmes to benefit from private sector skills, e.g. market/demand forecasting;
- create information policies in order to permit easier identification of partners for potential collaboration by interested parties.

The **collaborative efforts between the public and private sectors** could:

- agree on a working definition of the neediest countries and on how to target resources and special attention to them;
- estimate the need, demand, and uptake for existing and new products in developing countries collaboratively, since the public sector has the data and the private sector has the expertise;
- manage the challenges of concessionary supply to the poorer countries, including preventing the diversion of products from intended

beneficiaries to markets where prices are higher and the potential erosion of revenue from the richer markets necessary to support continued research and development;

- test and pilot new products earlier in developing countries to establish their potential benefits and reduce the delays that occur before the products become widely available;
- review partnerships engaged in donation/distribution and strengthening of health services, for lessons on distribution systems in poorer countries, and devise ways in which future efforts can apply the lessons within the framework of national plans and priorities;
- create additional partnerships, where necessary, in order to develop the products most needed to meet the health needs of the poor. This work should aim for products suitable for use under the conditions prevailing in poorer countries: simple administration and short-course treatment are desirable characteristics. Given the anticipated increase in the burden of noncommunicable diseases, it is advisable to look now at partnerships that would tackle the requirements of developing countries in this area.

[a] In the absence of efforts to make markets function effectively to meet health needs in as many countries as possible, the bilateral development assistance community will be faced with the unmanageable prospect of subsidizing health in many countries for the foreseeable future. In the absence of a prospect of some revenue and effective delivery systems, there is little reason to think that the interest of the pharmaceutical industry in the needs of poorer populations can be markedly increased solely by push interventions for product development.

more — on the public-sector, governmental and intergovernmental agencies as on the private sector institutions, as the former carry the responsibility for the public's health.

Acknowledgements

Funding for this work was provided to the Initiative on Public–Private Partnerships for Health of the Global Forum for Health Research by the Bill and Melinda Gates Foundation, the Rockefeller Foundation, and the World Bank.

Conflicts of interest

None declared.

References

1. **Sachs J.** Helping the world's poorest. *The Economist*, 14 August 1999: 16–22.
2. Children's Vaccine Initiative, 1999. *CVI Forum*. 1999, **18**: 6.

3. R. Bergquist, personal communication, 1999.
4. **Gwatkin D. R., Guillot M.** *The burden of disease among the global poor.* Washington, DC, World Bank, 1999.
5. **Murray J. L. C., Lopez A. D.** *Global burden of disease: a comprehensive assessment of mortality and disability from diseases, injuries and risk factors in 1990 and projected to 2020.* Boston, MA, Harvard School of Public Health, 1996.
6. M. Everard, personal communication, 1999.
7. *Better health in Africa.* Washington, DC, World Bank, 1994.
8. R. Ridley, personal communication, 2000.
9. Market report: 5 year forecast of the global pharmaceutical markets. IMS Health (Internet communication, 13 July 2001 at http://www.ims-global.com/insight/report/global/report.htm).
10. *Creating global markets for neglected drugs and vaccines: a challenge for public-private partnerships.* Report of a meeting held at Quail Lodge, Carmel Valley, C. A., 18–21 February 2000. San Francisco, C.A., Institute for Global Health, University of California, Berkley, CA.
11. **Widdus R. et al.** Towards better defining public-private partnerships for health. Geneva, Global Forum for Health Research, 2001 (in press).
12. *Medicines for Malaria Venture.* Geneva (Internet communication, 4 June 2001 at http://www.mmv.org/).
13. *International AIDS Vaccine Initiative.* New York (Internet communication, 4 June 2001 at http://www.iavi.org/) (4 June 2001).
14. *Global Alliance for TB Drug Development.* Geneva (Internet communication, 4 June 2001 at http://www.tballiance.org).
15. *Lymphatic filariasis.* Geneva, World Health Organization (Internet communication, 4 June 2001 at http://www.filariasis.org/).
16. *Sleeping sickness eflornithine.* Strasbourg, Aventis (Internet communication, 4 June 2001 at http://www.aventis.com/main/0,1003,EN-XX-10590-42250–,FF.html).
17. *Sleeping sickness eflornithine.* Geneva, International Federation of Pharmaceutical Associations (Internet communication, 4 June 2001 at http://www.ifpma.org/African.htm#WHO).
18. *Leprosy.* Geneva, World Health Organization (Internet communication, 4 June 2001 at http://www.who.int/lep/).
19. *Malarone.* GlaxoSmithKline (Internet communication, 4 June 2001 at http://www.malaronedonation.org/).
20. *Mectizan.* Atalanta, GA, Task Force for Child Survival and Development (Internet communication, 4 June 2001 at http://www.taskforce.org/MDP/).
21. *Mectizan.* Geneva, World Health Organization (Internet communication, 4 June 2001 at http://www.who.int/ocp/apoc/).
22. *International Trachoma Initiative/Zithromax.* New York, International Trachoma Initiative (Internet communication, 4 June 2001 at http://www.trachoma.org/).
23. **Kale O. O.** *Review of disease-specific corporate drug donation programmes for the control of communicable diseases.* Paper presented at conference on Drugs for Communicable Diseases: Stimulating Development and Securing Availability. Paris, Médecins Sans Frontières Foundation, 14–15 October 1999.
24. *Botswana Comprehensive HIV/AIDS Partnership.* Bill and Melinda Gates Foundation, Seattle, WA, (Internet communication, 4 June 2001 at http://www.gatesfoundation.org/pressroom/release.asp?PRindex=243).

25. *Roll Back Malaria*. Geneva, World Health Organization (Internet communication, 4 June 2001 at http://mosquito.who.int/).
26. *Safe Injection Global Network*. Geneva, World Health Organization (Internet communication, 4 June 2001 at http://www.injectionsafety.org/).
27. *Stop TB initiatives*. Geneva, World Health Organization (Internet communication, 4 June 2001 at http://www.stoptb.org/).
28. *Global Alliance for Vaccines and Immunization*. Geneva, UNICEF (Internet communication, 4 June 2001 at http://www.vaccinealliance.org/).
29. *Global Fund for Children's Vaccines*. Lyon, c/o Parteurop (Internet communication, 4 June 2001 at http://www.vaccinealliance.org/reference/globalfund.html).
30. *HAI*. Amsterdam, Health Action International (Internet communication, 4 June 2001 at http://www.haiweb.org/pubs/hailights/mar2001/mar01_lead.html).

69

GLOBAL PUBLIC–PRIVATE PARTNERSHIPS

Part II – what are the health issues for global governance?

K. Buse and G. Walt

Source: *Bulletin of the World Health Organization*, 78:5 (2000), 699–709.

This is the second of a two-part review of global public–private partnerships (GPPPs) for health development. Part I was published in the April issue of the *Bulletin* (vol. 78, No.4). The recent emergence of GPPPs is rapidly reconfiguring the international health landscape. While most multilateral and bilateral agencies are currently grappling with how to proceed, there is little information in the public domain concerning how individual partnerships work and to date very little consideration of the many implications of this trend. This paper differentiates between product-based, product development-based and issues/systems-based GPPPs and describes a number of examples of each type in the health sector. The benefits of these initiatives, not least the major resources which they harness for specific health problems, are identified. The final section of the paper explores the implications and dilemmas posed by GPPPs. It discusses whether or not shared goals can transcend conflicting values and mandates and how governance of partnership arrangements may transform and undermine certain attributes of multilateral organizations. The paper concludes that the current climate of goodwill between public and private sectors offers an opportunity that should not be missed: it can be used not only to foster new partnership but to ensure that partnership is truly in the interests of international public health.

Introduction

In Part I of this article, which appeared in the last issue of the *Bulletin*, we suggested that there have been a number of initiatives in which the corporate and public sectors sought collaboration in international public health through partnerships. That paper reviewed the concept of partnership and defined global public–private partnerships (GPPPs) as collaborative relationships which transcend national boundaries. Each partnership brings together at least three parties, among them a corporation (and/or industry association) and an intergovernmental organization, to achieve a shared health-creating goal on the basis of a mutually agreed division of labour. The paper described the context within which these partnerships are emerging, focusing particularly on changes confronting the United Nations and the corporate community during the 1990s.

While these partnerships are bringing major resources into international public health and have the potential to benefit large populations, they are also blurring traditional distinctions between public and private sector responsibilities and aims. The use of GPPPs in public health also raises a number of important questions of conflicts of interest, and implications for governance. This paper opens the debate on these issues, starting with a conceptual framework for understanding the different forms of global public–private partnership in the health sector, illustrated by a number of examples. It ends by exploring the implications of GPPPs for the 21st century, looking at issues of governance and equity.

What forms have GPPPs for health development taken?

GPPP categories

There are several ways to conceptualize and categorize partnerships. One is in terms of *constituent membership*, for example, donor–recipient or public–private. However, this is too broad to be very helpful for understanding GPPPs. Another categorization has been proposed by Mitchell-Weaver and Manning (*1*), who reason that as partnerships are primarily a set of institutional relations, they should be categorized by their *organizational form*. They differentiate between three institutional models on the basis of the degree to which private interests "participate in the strategic-level decision-making in the public interest". The *elite committee model* (sometimes called a board or conference) is characterized by negotiation among relatively equal partners so as to arrive at decisions by consensus. The committee does not implement decisions, rather the individual members influence the behaviour of their respective organizations to achieve partnership goals and/or influence public policy through network associations. In the health sector, the 'Global Business Council on HIV/AIDS', which involves the leaders of 15 major companies, is one example of such a model (*2*).

The second institutional form is the *NGO model*, involving nongovernmental organizations. Mitchell-Weaver and Manning suggest that the relationship between parties is essentially one of delegation. The public side provides organizational, material or financial resources to enable a private partner to carry out the public programme. The NGO model links the public with the private sector through resource transfers and is exemplified by the Sexually Transmitted Diseases Diagnostics Initiative (3).

The third is the *quasi-public authority model* in which a hybrid organization with both public and private characteristics is created by public sector institutions. Acting in the public interest, this type of organization provides goods and services or enables the private sector to enter a market. In effect, the quasi-public authority model creates favourable conditions for private enterprise to provide public services or goods. The Medicines for Malaria Venture (MMV) (4) and the International AIDS Vaccine Initiative (IAVI) (5) could both be said to be examples of this organizational form at the global level. Although this characterization is promising, it fails to provide a model in which the private sector is a dominant partner. Consequently, it would be difficult to situate a number of GPPPs, including most of the drug donation programmes, within this framework.

Another approach to categorization would be to base it on the nature of activity undertaken by the partnerships. One might, for example, differentiate among those partnerships which focus on *consultation* between public and private actors (e.g., the WHO Working Group with Pharmaceutical Industry), and those which involve *concertation* of policy between public and private actors (e.g., collaboration on standard setting), and those with a mainly *operational* function (e.g., engaged together in research and development or a drug donation programme). These categories are, however, far too broad and reveal little about how partnerships are governed or function.

Kickbusch & Quick (6) have categorized global health partnerships as based on the following: (1) existing products (e.g., deworming drugs for children); (2) product development (e.g., designing a refrigerator for use in developing countries); (3) services; (4) systems and settings (e.g., healthy cities); (5) issues (e.g., polio eradication); (6) health messages (WHO/UNESCO global malaria strategy); and (7) knowledge exchange (workplace health promotion). While the first two categories are distinct, the lack of specificity of the remaining categories results in some ambiguity. Although we feel that the approach to categorization based on institutional form (1) is worth further development, in this paper we use a goal-oriented, three-category classification of GPPPs: product-based, product development-based and issues/systems-based.

Examples of GPPPs

Some examples of these three types of partnership are provided in Tables 1, 2 and 3. The examples, mainly in the area of drugs and vaccines for communicable diseases, were chosen primarily on the basis of the availability of information, and include only a proportion of the better-known GPPPs currently operational. A number of GPPPs which deal with noncommunicable diseases, such as the WHO Partnership on Tobacco Dependence (7), and those which deal with the broader socioeconomic determinants of health (e.g. UNDP's Public–Private Partnership for Urban Environment) (8) are also emerging.

Product-based partnerships (Table 1) consist primarily of drug donation programmes, although partnerships also exist for the bulk purchase of products for public sector programmes in low-income countries, for example, female condoms (9) or AIDS medication (10). Drug donation programmes are generally established after the discovery that an existing drug (for animals or humans) is found to be effective in the treatment of some condition for which there is limited *effective demand*, due to lack of willingness and ability to pay, as was seen with AmBisome for the treatment of leishmaniasis. These types of partnership are usually initiated by the private sector. Pharmaceutical companies seek partnership with the multilateral sector to lower the cost and increase the chance of ensuring the drug reaches those who need it but cannot afford it. While private sector companies may seek short-term objectives through GPPPs such as the establishment of political contacts at global and country levels, it would appear that the longer-term objective is to establish their reputations as ethically oriented concerns. This end objective is not guaranteed, as product donation partnerships have been subject to controversy over dumping, dependency-creation and sustainability (11).

Product-development partnerships (Table 2) differ from product-donation partnerships in a number of respects. First, they are not targeted at specific countries. Second, these partnerships are generally initiated by the public sector (12). Third, the product-development partnerships are not based on ineffective demand so much as on *market failure*. Most of these products are perceived by the public sector as worthy of societal investment, but the market fails to allocate resources to their discovery and development because industry perceives that the potential returns do not justify the opportunity cost of investment. For example, although research on an AIDS vaccine is considered an important public good, industry is uncertain whether expenditure on research on it will yield a successful vaccine. Moreover, even if a vaccine is discovered, the private sector cannot be sure that a large enough market will exist to justify its development and commercialization. The potential cost of liability and regulation is another grey area (13).

Product-development GPPPs usually require the public sector to assume a number of risks associated with product discovery, development and/or commercialization (i.e., providing a public subsidy), thereby offsetting the opportunity cost of industrial involvement. A notable feature of a number of the product-development GPPPs is retention of the intellectual property rights by the partnership organization so as to retain leverage over

Table 1 Selected examples of product-based health GPPPs.

Name/Date	Partners	Goal	Scope
Mectizan® **Donation** **Programme/1987**	Merck & Co. WHO World Bank Task Force on Child Survival and Development National authorities and NGOs.	To eliminate river blindness by treating everyone who needs it with Mectizan®	• Drug donated until no longer required • All 34 endemic countries have at some time been provided with free Mectizan® • Cumulative value of donation is estimated at US$ 500 million. An additional US$ 200000 per year is spent on shipping plus the costs of the Mectizan® Expert Committee and its Secretariat
Malarone® **Donation** **Programme/1996**	Glaxo Wellcome Task Force on Child Survival and Development Medical Research Council, England National Institutes of Health, USA Centers for Diseases Control, Atlanta WHO World Bank Wellcome Trust National authorities	To help combat drug-resistant malaria in endemic countries where cost often limits access to new drugs	• Up to 1 million free doses per year globally through a targeted donation programme • Pilot donations in Kenya and Uganda
Albendazole **Donation** **Programme/199**	WHO/Division of Control of Tropical Diseases SmithKline Beecham Global Programme to Eliminate Filariasis National authorities and NGOs	To accelerate the effort to eliminate lymphatic filariasis	• Donation of albendazole to governments and other service providers until elephantiasis is eliminated • The value of the donation of up to 6 billion doses over 20 years is over US$ 1 billion
Zithromax® **Donation** **Programme/1998**	Pfizer Inc. E M Clark Foundation Conrad H Hilton Foundation Bill and Melinda Gates Foundation Helen Keller International International Trachoma Initiative GET 2020 (WHO Alliance for Global Elimination of Trachoma by 2020) National authorities and NGOs	To advance the global effort to eliminate blinding trachoma	• Two year partnership (in the first instance) • Donation of Zithromax® by Pfizer valued at US$ 60 million • Pfizer and Edna McConnell Clark Foundation each providing US$ 3.2 million to International Trachoma Initiative • Five of 16 WHO priority countries included (Ghana, Mali, Morocco, the United Republic of Tanzania and Viet Nam)

Table 2 Selected examples of product-development-based health GPPPs.

Name/date	Partners	Goal	Scope
Sexually Transmitted Infections Diagnostics Group (SDI)/1990	Academia WHO UNAIDS Rockefeller Foundation Program for Appropriate Technology in Health (PATH) Private sector on specific development projects	To identify, develop and introduce affordable sexually transmitted infections diagnostics	• Through the SDI, the public sector can identify and classify demand side of market and overcome product development and market penetration constraints
International AIDS Vaccine Initiative (IAVI)/1996	Fondation Marcel Mérieux Francois-Xavier Bagnould Foundation National AIDS Trust AIDS Vaccine Advocacy Coalition Albert B Sabin Vaccine Institute *Donors* World Bank UNAIDS Rockefeller Foundation AP Sloan Foundation Bill and Melinda Gates Foundation Department for International Development (DFID) Glaxo Wellcome Levi Strauss International and many others	To ensure the development of safe, effective, accessible, preventive HIV vaccines for use throughout the world	• Two vaccine development partnerships established between biotech companies and academia worth US$ 9 million in 1999 using 'social venture capital' • Unique intellectual property agreements – public sector holds rights • Bill and Melinda Gates Foundation contribution of US$ 25 million in 1999

Initiative	Partners	Objective	Notes
Medicines for Malaria Venture (MMV)/1998	Association of British Pharmaceutical Industries International Federation of Pharmaceutical Manufacturers Associations Wellcome Trust Rockefeller Foundation WHO/RBM/TDR World Bank Global Forum for Health Research DFID Swiss Development Cooperation (SDC) Glaxo Wellcome, Hoffman-La Roche	To support the discovery, development and commercialization of affordable drugs for malaria at the rate of one every five years through a public sector venture fund	• Public contribution of up to US$ 30 million/year • Private sector to provide gifts in kind worth up to US$ 2 million/ year • MMV retains patents for discoveries and will license out projects for commercialization to private companies. Royalties retained for financial sustainability
LAPDAP/1998	SmithKline Beecham WHO/Tropical Disease Research Programme DFID	To make available an affordable combination antimalarial tablet	• DFID, WHO and SmithKline Beecham to contribute one third of the development budget each
Malaria Vaccine Initiative (MVI)/1999	Bill and Melinda Gates Foundation PATH Private sector involvement through discovery and development partnership agreements	To accelerate the development of promising malaria vaccine candidates through identification and process development funding	• Bill and Melinda Gates Foundation contributed founding grant of US$ 50 million

eventual product pricing. Corporations may engage in product-development partnerships to mobilize a subsidy for research, to obtain assistance in carrying out clinical trials, or to pursue their own longer-term interests. Fundamentally, there is the certainty of some financial return (even if modest). Companies may also seek proximity or involvement in standard-setting and regulatory processes. Finally, companies may be seeking to portray themselves in a favourable light to help secure entry into emerging drug markets.

The *systems/issues-based partnerships* (Table 3) are a more eclectic group. Some have arisen to overcome market failures, such as the Malaria Vaccine Initiative (*14*). Some systems GPPPs have been established to complement the efforts of governments, such as the Secure the Future partnership (*15*), and others to tap non-medical private resources for disease control, such as the World Alliance for Research and Control of Communicable Diseases (*16*). A number of high profile issues-based GPPPs have recently been launched which seek to harmonize or bring strategic consistency to the approaches of various actors to single diseases, as well as to raise their profile on the health policy agenda. The Roll Back Malaria Global Partnership (*17*) and the Stop TB Initiative (*18*) are examples.

Are global public–private partnerships essential for health?

Shared goals and principles: can public and private be reconciled?

Definitions of partnership suggest a foundation of shared goals underpinned by agreement on key principles. The partnerships described in this paper have clear and uncontroversial goals. Of central importance to the global health agenda are the questions of who determines these goals, the processes by which they are determined, and to what extent the goals of GPPPs come to dominate the global health agenda. One might consider a continuum of partners' interests. At one end of the continuum are the interests of the UN: "our main stock in trade . . . is to promote values: the universal values of equality, tolerance, freedom and justice that are found in the UN Charter" (*19*). At this end of the continuum one also finds WHO's public health values and concern about inequities in health (*20*). The principles reflected in company policies may be at the other end of the spectrum with a concern to maximize profits so as to increase shareholder value. (This is not to suggest that these institutions and sectors are monolithic – but instead to make a broad generalization concerning different interests and values. Naturally there are exceptions and employees with widely varying values within both private and public sectors). At the centre of this continuum are the GPPPs where, it is hoped, the interests of both can be met.

Table 3 Selected examples of systems/issues-based health GPPPs.

Name/date	Partners	Goal	Scope
Children's Vaccine Initiative (CVI)/1991	UNICEF UNDP WHO World Bank Rockefeller Foundation Industry involved at the Task Force level and through Product Development Teams	To promote, coordinate and accelerate the development and introduction of new and improved vaccines	• CVI secretariat activities cost US$5–6 million per year
Global Programme to Eliminate Filiariasis (GPEF)/1998	CDC UNICEF World Bank WHO/CTD DFID SmithKline Beecham Merck & Co. Arab Fund Academia Placer Dome Centre for International Health International NGOs National authorities	To eliminate lymphatic filariasis as a public health problem by the year 2020	• Albendazole donated by SmithKline Beecham to governments and other service providers until elephantiasis is eliminated (several billion doses over 20 years) • Mectizan® donated by Merck to African countries co-endemic with onchocerciasis until it is eliminated • All 73 endemic countries to be successively covered by programme
Bill and Melinda Gates Children's Vaccine Program (CVP)/1998	Bill and Melinda Gates Foundation PATH Other partners have implementing role: UNICEF, WHO, World Bank, CVI, Ministries of Health, NGOs, academia, International Vaccine Institute, vaccine manufactures	To reduce or eliminate existing time lag between developing and developed world in the introduction of new vaccines for children	• Bill and Melinda Gates Foundation donated US$ 100 million as founding grant • Industry to contribute through donation of vaccines for model programmes, data for regulatory submissions, marketing information, financial and market surveys • Initial focus on 3 new vaccines in 18 countries • Programme to last 10 years
Secure the Future/1999	Bristol-Myers Squibb UNAIDS Harvard AIDS Institute Medical schools National authorities	To improve the state of HIV/AIDS research and community outreach in southern Africa	• Bristol-Myers Squibb donated US$ 100 million for five year partnership • Largest corporate donation for HIV/AIDS • Covers Botswana, Lesotho, Namibia, South Africa, and Swaziland

One critic of public–private partnerships argues, however, that the private sector has several mechanisms for maximizing profits which may conflict with the goal of better health (*21*). Among these is the reduction of costs by paying low wages and reducing the size of the workforce, thereby making people poorer. Is it possible that these private sector goals will ultimately dominate as the UN and industry move closer towards jointly defining their goals through GPPPs?

Alternatively, is it possible to ensure that core public and private identities and values are preserved in partnerships which limit themselves to specific win-win situations? Lenton of the international AIDS Vaccine Initiative (IAVI) has argued that shared goals are more important than shared values (*22*). In the short term, and with specific goals, it seems likely that goals can transcend disparate values and bind unlikely bedfellows together in a marriage of convenience. Literature is beginning to emerge on lessons learned on the "effectiveness" of health GPPPs (*4, 23, 24*). These emphasize the importance of: (1) clearly specified, realistic and shared goals; (2) clearly delineated and agreed roles and responsibilities; (3) distinct benefits for all parties; (4) the perception of transparency; (5) active maintenance of the partnership; (6) equality of participation; (7) meeting agreed obligations, inter alia. However, over the longer term the question arises of whether the values of the weaker partner are co-opted by the more powerful one. The answer to this question depends on the choice of private partners, as well as on the nature of GPPP governance.

Because of the potential clash between partners over principles and values, WHO, the World Bank and UNICEF all note the need to exercise caution over the selection of their private sector partners (*6, 25, 26*). In practice, given the short-term financial incentives that sometimes motivate UN organizations to enter into partnerships with the private sector, it may be difficult to refuse corporate offers which do not comply with all internal guidelines. For example, UNDP is alleged to be flouting its fundraising guidelines in pursuance of its Global Sustainable Development Facility initiative (*27*). In relation to health partnerships, Hancock urges "sober second thoughts" regarding the suitability of the pharmaceutical industry as a partner for WHO, at least in terms of health promotion, because of perceived or actual conflict of interests (*21*). He suggests instead that WHO's partners should be selected from industries which stand to profit economically from better health (e.g., life and health insurance, leisure and recreation, tourism and travel) and those that produce health (e.g., agri-food, housing). Hancock argues that at the global level, partnerships should be developed not with individual companies, who may wish to use the partnership for competitive gain, but with industry associations. He calls for a set of ethical criteria to guide the selection of partners.

Many multilateral and bilateral organizations are now aware of the need to give greater attention to this issue. WHO's proposed guidelines on partnership with the commercial sector single out tobacco producers and arms manufactures as incompatible partners (*28*), whereas other sections of the UN call for "creative partnership" with the arms industry (*29*).

Governance: representation, accountability and competence

Governance can be defined as "the process whereby an organization or society steers itself" (*30*). Broadly speaking, governance consists of the systems of rules, norms, processes and institutions through which power and decision-making are exercised. Good governance is thought to have four components: (1) representative legitimacy; (2) accountability; (3) competence and appropriateness; and (4) respect for due process (*31*). How is governance exercised in the global public–private health partnerships?

Representation

The area of *legitimate representation* in public–private partnerships raises both normative and operational issues. Normative issues determine whose interests should be represented in the partnership and whose should not. Most UN organizations derive some of their legitimacy from near-universal membership in their governing bodies. For example, the World Health Assembly is attended by representatives of 191 member states (although its state-centric bias raises its own problems of legitimacy), all of which have equal voting rights irrespective of size of financial contribution. In contrast, representation in GPPPs is both narrower and more eclectic. For example, no health GPPP can claim near universal membership of nation states (which would in any case make them unwieldy), but, more importantly, few partnerships include representation by low-income countries. Furthermore, not all GPPPs include WHO on their governing boards and technical committees, and in some cases it appears that the private sector representation is ad hoc and based on personal contacts.

The legitimacy of GPPPs will depend to a great extent on the expert committees that are established to advise them. Whereas the specialized agencies of the UN, such as WHO, rely on extensive networks of technical experts and have established means for selecting and operating expert groups[a], there are concerns that GPPP expert groups may be chosen from exclusive communities of expertise. They may also suffer from a lack of independence due to the sources of funding (*23*) and may have circumscribed powers (for example the Technical Advisory Group of the International Trachoma Initiative did not have the opportunity to advise on the choice of recipient countries (*32*). Although many analysts have drawn attention to the extent to which international agenda-setting and the formulation of policy are controlled by transnational policy elites (*33*), the implications of the increasing role of the private sector in such policy networks have barely been explored.

Accountability

Accountability is broadly concerned with being held responsible for one's actions. Both the public and private sectors have well-established mechanisms of accountability. In the private sector, management is accountable to the company's shareholders. In the public sector, administrative structures report to political structures that are ultimately accountable to the ruled through the contestability of political power. However, accountability within public–private partnerships may be less straightforward, partly because of the distance between the global partners and the beneficiaries, and the length of time needed for any impact to be felt. Bain (*34*) quotes Fox & Brown's study of transnational NGO networks which suggests that 'downward accountability' is often weak, and is particularly limited when geographical distances are great or international as well as local organizations are involved in a project. Given that accountability is dependent upon the clear specification of objectives, activities, roles and responsibilities, it will be more easily achieved in formal partnerships where these are spelled out. In contrast, partnerships whose goals and division of labour are vaguely defined will lack accountability. Moreover, actually holding a partner accountable presents difficult challenges. At the moment, systems of sanctions that can be applied to negligent partners do not appear to have been developed.

Two mechanisms of accountability are emerging among health GPPPs. In one model, the management and scientific groups report to the corporate sponsor directly. For example, in the Mectizan® Donation Programme, the Mectizan® Expert Committee reports to Merck & Co., its corporate sponsor, through bi-annual meetings, while the Secretariat reports monthly on financial expenditure (*23*). Similarly the Program for Appropriate Technology in Health (PATH), which provides the secretariat for the Bill and Melinda Gates Children's Vaccine Program, reports directly to Bill and Melinda Gates, its sponsors (*35*). Hence, in this model, the GPPPs are accountable first to their donors, and only indirectly to the public sector organizations and beneficiaries.

In another model, the management group reports to a governing body, whose members report back to their respective organizations. Hence, the secretariat of the International Trachoma Initiative will report on a six-monthly basis to its sponsors through the Governing Council. These reports will be shared with the wider trachoma network, notably the WHO Alliance for Global Elimination of Trachoma (*36*).

Competence

Partnerships raise difficult questions about *competence and appropriateness*. As global responsibility for specific health issues is transferred from WHO programmes to special GPPPs, there is some danger that WHO will fail to maintain expert groups on these issues as it tries to avoid duplicating the technical committees maintained under the aegis of the partnerships (whose membership is vetted by the corporate sponsors). Does this raise the spectre of the erosion of WHO's normative function? Where the private sector assumes a greater voice through partnership in WHO technical discussions, will global standards and norms increasingly reflect private interests, thereby jeopardizing their credibility? As an example, Muraskin (37) notes that the WHO Expert Committee on Biologicals (which established standards for vaccines) was criticized in the late 1980s on the level of standards set by the Organization. Many considered them unreasonably rigorous (thereby disadvantaging developing country industries) and too responsive to industry demands. Furthermore, will the proliferation of GPPPs exacerbate the fragmentation of international health organizations making it even more difficult to establish a coherent global health policy agenda?

The questioning of the component of governance concerned with *due process* is at a very early stage. Will due processes elaborated within the public sector be diluted to allow partnerships to proceed? There are some signs that this might be the case. For example, UNDP is alleged to have breached its own funding guidelines to accommodate specific corporate donations (27), and drug trials proposed under the Secure the Future partnership may erode global ethical norms governing clinical trials (38, 39). This points to the need for greater transparency and public disclosure of GPPP agreements and implementation.

Resources: who pays for partnership?

One of the notable features of a number of the partnerships is the volume of the resources at stake. For example, Pfizer's contribution to the International Trachoma Initiative is valued at an estimated US$ 63 million over a two-year period. During the first half of 1999, the Bill and Melinda Gates Foundation (with assets of over US$ 18 billion) made major grant commitments to a number of health GPPPs. These included US$ 100 million to the Bill and Melinda Gates Children's Vaccine Program, US$ 50 million to the Malaria Vaccine Initiative, US$ 25 million to the International AIDS Vaccine Initiative, and US$ 1 million to the International Trachoma Initiative. Meanwhile, Bristol-Myers Squibb donated US$ 100 million over five years to the Secure the Future partnership.

The total value of private funding to health GPPPs is difficult to estimate, but they clearly provide significant resources for specific health issues. Multilateral resources for disease control are paltry in comparison to the size of private funds for GPPPs. For example, the WHO 1998–99 total biennium budget for its Control of Tropical Diseases programme was US$ 29 million, while the TB programme received only US$ 7 million over the two-year period (40). In aggregate, private contributors to GPPPs are also significant in comparison to WHO's annual global budget, which is less than US$ 1 billion.

Notwithstanding the invaluable contribution of the private sector to health GPPPs, it appears that the costs (and risks) to the corporate sector may be relatively modest compared to the substantial gains in terms of public relations. First, many contributions are tax-deductible (hence the cost to the company is only approximately half the stated cost). Second, contributions may account for only a small fraction of the profits gained from a particular product. Regarding the Mectizan® Donation Program, for example, ivermectin is Merck & Co.'s second largest selling drug (for veterinary purposes), and between 1984 and 1989, sales were greater than those of any other animal health product in the world (41). Bristol-Myers Squibb's annual contribution of US$ 20 million to Secure the Future is just over 0.1% of the company's US$ 18.3 billion in annual sales – equivalent to less than one cent a share in each of the five years (42), although it would be more accurate to compare these figures against net profits rather than sales.

Third, the public sector contribution may account for the lion's share of the cost of the partnership's activities. For example, the Medicines for Malaria Venture (MMV) aims to raise up to US$ 30 million per year, most of which will come from public sources. Although the private sector partners have agreed to making gifts-in-kind, they have not made more than a vague commitment worth 'millions per year' (4). In other words, over a 10-year period the governing structure of MMV (including corporate representatives) will potentially control US$ 300 million of public funds, while the companies will contribute as they see fit. Even if it is argued that responsibility for the provision of health-promoting goods and services lies with the public sector, it is difficult to justify an equal involvement of the private sector in using these resources.

While GPPPs are clearly bringing new resources to international health, and currently play an essential role in drug and vaccine development, it is not axiomatic that all GPPPs are necessarily good for health. Where GPPPs are successful they can be spectacularly beneficial to health. However, it remains difficult to estimate the actual or potential health consequences of GPPPs (this is especially true for product-development partnerships) which are determined by the effectiveness of the initiative. For example, blinding onchocerciasis will soon cease to be a public health problem as a result of the Mectizan® Donation Program (43). Furthermore, product-development GPPPs represent only one form of GPPPs. In other types of partnership industry does not necessarily enjoy a 'natural' comparative advantage. In these cases the public sector may be able to deal with the health issue at stake without involving industry (Table 1, Table 3). Furthermore, the chequered history of the pharmaceutical industry's marketing of its products in developing countries (44) indicates the need to proceed with caution and to examine each proposed partnership according to appropriate guidelines and criteria. Guidelines may help ensure that the public institutions retain their core characteristics such as integrity, legitimacy, authority and neutrality. Such guidelines are still under development, for example within WHO (28), and have yet to receive adequate scrutiny and public debate.

Conclusions

In this article we have charted the growth of global public–private partnerships in health, suggesting that they fall roughly into three categories: product, product development and systems/issues. We have demonstrated that for both the private and the public sector partnership offers major benefits, given the perception that existing and emerging health problems cannot be successfully tackled by one sector alone. For the UN multilateral organizations, partnership with the private sector is seen to have (1) bestowed more business credibility and authority; (2) extended the UN's ability to fulfil its mandates though increased resources; and (3) provided access to private sector skills and management talents.

For the private sector, partnerships have (1) increased corporate influence in global policy-making and at the national level; (2) brought direct financial returns, such as tax breaks and market penetration, as well as indirect financial benefits through brand and image promotion; and (3) enhanced corporate authority and legitimacy through association with UN and other bodies. Many of these benefits of public–private partnerships are also true for bilateral donor agencies, with the added advantage of increased authority at the national level. For communities suffering from high rates of HIV infection, trachoma or onchocerciasis, or which will eventually be the beneficiaries of new vaccines, there are clear advantages in partnerships that bring extra resources and targeted programmes.

However, a number of questions are also raised, especially for recipient countries, and should not be brushed aside. There are costs to aid, and some of the public–private partnerships have expected relatively high national inputs to their programmes. These costs include guaranteeing distribution networks, storing drugs at ports or airports, training health workers, and conducting trials using drugs that people may not be able to afford in the future. Such programmes do meet needs, but these needs are not determined on the basis of national priority or evidence-based assessment. In relation to drug donation programmes, Kale has argued for greater consultation with recipient countries (prior to launching), explicit cost-benefit analyses, and improved coordination between donation programmes and recipient programmes in the context of government leadership and ownership (45).

Differences in principles and values and issues of governance are therefore important, and need to be addressed. Limited representation of low-income countries in public–private partnerships raises questions of who is deciding the international policy agenda, and how much say is being given to recipient nations. The universality of multilateral institutions is diluted by partnerships, since some partners may represent a wide constituency of members, while others, such as the private sector or NGOs, may not. Furthermore, as the tables illustrate, many partnerships target specific countries. While the initiatives may need to be selective, they will primarily choose countries on the basis of the ability to get results. One value of multilateral action is its 'neutrality', which enables it to fill gaps left by the bilaterals which often support health services according to geopolitical considerations (46).

Accountability may also be interpreted in different ways by different partners. The use of private armies to protect oil pipelines by Shell in Ogoniland, Nigeria, and BP in Colombia was sharply criticized by activists both within and outside those countries. If either organization had had a partnership with a multilateral agency, the loss of perceived neutrality and legitimacy would have been significant. Many of the multilaterals have urged caution in selecting partners, but exercising that caution may be difficult. Moreover, where accountability is felt to be to shareholders or consumers rather than wider communities (or governments), conflicts of interest may occur. for example, the use of alliances within the pharmaceutical industry to fix prices may benefit shareholders but not consumers (47). It was this type of perceived conflict that aroused public concern over the UNDP Global Sustainable Development Facility partnership.

The costs for the private sector seem to be relatively small in relation to overall gains: a potential small loss of resources if programmes do nor work, but huge benefits in public relations when they succeed. For bilaterals, there are many difficult questions. For example, how far should public money be supporting hugely profitable private sector firms, in the hope of potential future gains for poor countries or poor people? In one product-development partnership (LAPDAP), WHO and the Department for International Development (DFID) are both subsidizing the pharmaceutical company SmithKline Beecham to stimulate the development of an antimalarial tablet. Although this partnership is not yet governed by any formal agreement, the parties understand that the company will retain the prerogative to set the eventual price of its drug.

Without appropriate forethought, the costs of GPPPs to the United Nations may be even larger. It is conceivable that the 'profitable' activities may be hived off to special partnerships, leaving the public organizations with the more difficult issues (e.g., supporting health systems and training personnel) for which it is harder to raise resources. It is also possible that GPPPs may serve to weaken systems of multilateral governance. This could happen as the control and authority presently vested in governing bodies is transferred to the steering groups of GPPPs, in which the private sector may have greater influence. There is an additional danger that the goals of the UN could be displaced as policies, strategies, resource allocation and activities are increasingly driven (or subject to approval) by industry instead of the organizations' governing bodies. Similarly, if the perceived neutrality of the UN is compromised by private sector involvement in its normative activities, the UN's credibility, impartiality and integrity could be undermined. Finally, traditional support for the UN could be undermined as private sector partnerships erode the goodwill of those who believe in a multilateralism in which governments, not corporations, are the decision-makers (48).

Despite claims that 'social justice' has been sought, for example through the Mectizan® donation (49), this review suggests that the promotion of social justice or equity through GPPPs may not be easy. Partnerships are highly selective in their choice of health problem. Resource allocation through partnerships may not be according to burden of disease calculations or need, but according to how a particular partnership reflects the views of its members. The donation of Zithromax® provides a case in point. Although the drug is effective against sexually transmitted infections, it was not until the discovery that Zithromax® could be used to treat trachoma that it was donated for use in some developing countries. It has been suggested that this is because public corporate involvement in the control of stigma-laden sexually transmitted infections would have caused discomfort to the shareholders, while preventing blindness had a more positive appeal.

Some GPPPs are also selective in terms of the countries in which they choose to operate. Merck's Mectizan® Donation Programme operates in all countries where onchocerciasis is endemic and, more recently, in countries where filariasis is co-endemic. Merck has also agreed to donate the drug until these diseases are eradicated. By contrast, the International Trachoma Initiative (ITI) has decided to donate Zithromax® to only five of the 16 WHO priority countries which have significant populations with trachoma, and has committed itself to only two years' donation (although the initiative may be scaled-up and extended if the trial period proves successful). Although the diseases targeted and the drugs donated through these two programmes differ and therefore entail widely different risks for the pharmaceutical companies involved, it is clear that the ITI has chosen to work in countries which are perceived to be 'less difficult'. Very poor countries, with large populations, unpopular governments or poor infrastructures may be excluded from global partnership programmes. Problems of exclusion have been raised in other forums too. Participants at a UNAIDS consultation on Bridging the Gap raised the issue of equity in terms of how countries were selected and "how other countries not involved would benefit" (50). The challenge to the development of GPPPs is to achieve a balance between harnessing the potential of partnerships while avoiding the potential negative effects.

In summary, while there are many positive aspects to the emergence of GPPPs, there remain many uncertainties and some cause for concern. Research is needed to learn more about what makes a partnership 'effective' and in particular, what organizational forms and management arrangements represent best practice for governance, accountability and representation, and what factors contribute to partnership effectiveness on the ground. Harnessing the potential and minimizing the risks of partnership relies on the systematic identification of the potential pitfalls associated with GPPPs and the use of these findings to develop appropriate guidelines, procedures and safeguards. Full advantage should be taken of the current climate of trust and goodwill between public and private sectors, not only to foster new partnership but to ensure that partnership is truly in the interests of international public health.

Acknowledgements

We would like to thank Sissel Brinchman, Joseph Cook, Tim Evans, Allan Foster, Karin Holm, Adetokunbo O. Lucas, David Mabey, Anne Mills, Michael Reich, Trudie Stubbs, Derek Yach, and staff of the Health Policy Unit, London School of Hygiene and Tropical Medicine, for sharing their views and documents with us.

Note

[a] This is not to suggest that the selection of WHO experts is perfect, but to emphasize that there are checks and balances which, for example, ensure attention to questions of representation of, say, developing countries or women.

References

1. **Mitchell-Weaver C., Manning B.** *Public–private partnerships in Third World development.* The 20th Norma Wilkinson Memorial Lecture. Geographical Paper. Reading, Reading University, 1990.
2. *Leading companies to mobilize against global AIDS epidemic.* Press Release. Geneva, UNAIDS, 23 October 1997.
3. **Chernesky M. A.** How can industry, academia, public health authorities and the Sexually Transmitted Diseases Diagnostics Initiative work together to help control sexually transmitted diseases in developing countries? *Sexually Transmitted Diseases,* 1997, **24** (2): 61–63.
4. **Ridley R., Gutteridge W. E., Currat L. J.** *New Medicines for Malaria Venture: a case study of the establishment of a public sector – private sector partnership.* Paper presented at the Third Global Forum for Health Research, 8–11 June 1999, Geneva.
5. **Berkley S., Lenton C.** *The International AIDS Vaccine Initiative.* Paper presented at the Third Global Forum for Health Research, 8–11 June 1999, Geneva.
6. **Kickbusch I., Quick J.** Partnerships for health in the 21st century. *World Health Statistics Quarterly,* 1998, **51**: 69.
7. *WHO European partnership project on tobacco dependence.* Draft document. Geneva, World Health Organization, 22 December 1998.

8. *Public-Private Partnership Programme of UNDP.* Internet communication on November 12 1999 at http:/www.undp.org/info21/business/annex3.html

9. Letter from SG Cowal, Director of External Relations, UNAIDS, to undisclosed recipient dated 19 January 1999. Geneva, UNAIDS, 1999.

10. *UNAIDS launches initiative to help bridge gap in access to HIV/AIDS-related drugs in developing world.* Press Release. Geneva, UNAIDS, 5 November 1997.

11. *Guidelines for drug donations.* Geneva, World Health Organization, May 1996.

12. **Godal T.** Fighting parasites of poverty: public research, private industry and tropical disease. *Science,* 1994, **264**: 1864–1866.

13. *Finance report of the International AIDS Vaccine Initiative: accelerating the development of preventive HIV vaccines for the world.* New York, International AIDS Vaccine Initiative, 1995.

14. *Malaria Vaccine Initiative: statement of purpose.* Seattle, WA, Program for Appropriate Technology in Health, 1999.

15. *Bristol-Myers Squibb commits $ 100 million for HIV/AIDS research and community outreach in five African countries.* Press release, Washington, DC, 6 May 1999.

16. Innovative private sector venture under way. *TDR News,* 1999, **58**: 3

17. *Roll Back Malaria: report by the Director-General to the Fifty Second World Health Assembly.* Provisional agenda item, 13 May 1999. Geneva, World Health Organization.

18. **Nunn P.** Personal communication with Head, Stop TB Initiative. London, 18 June 1999.

19. **Annan K.** Address to the US Chambers of Commerce, 8 June 1999, Washington, DC.

20. **Walt G.** International organisations in health: the problem of leadership. In: *Pocantico Retreat: Enhancing the performance of international health institutions.* Rockefeller Foundation, Social Science Research Council, Harvard School of Health, 1999.

21. **Hancock T.** Caveat partner: reflections on partnership with the private sector. *Health Promotion International,* 1998, **13** (3): 193.

22. **Lenton C.** Remarks made at parallel session number 7.1 at the Global Forum for Health Research, 8 June 1999, Geneva.

23. **Frost L., Reich M.** *Mectizan® Donation Program: origins, experiences, and relationships with co-ordinating bodies for onchocerciasis control.* Department of Population and International Health Boston, Harvard School of Public Health, 1998.

24. **Widdus R., Evans P.** *Lessons learned from the Children's Vaccine Initiative 1990–1999.* Paper presented at the Third Global Forum for Health Research, Geneva, 9 June 1999.

25. **Bellamy C.** *Public, private and civil society.* Statement of UNICEF Executive Director to Harvard International Development Conference on 'Sharing responsibilities: public, private and civil society.' Cambridge, MA, 16 April 1999.

26. **Dukes G.** The contribution of the private sector: an introduction. *Australian Prescriber,* 1997, **20** (Suppl 1): 74–75.

27. **Klein N.** UN pact with business masks real dangers. *Toronto Star,* 19 March 1999.

28. *WHO guidelines on collaboration and partnerships with commercial enterprises.* Draft discussion document dated 24 July 1999. Geneva, World Health Organization, 1999.

29. **Deen T.** UN calls for new partnership with arms industry. *InterPress Service Daily Journal,* **7** (129), 7 July 1999. Internet communication at http:/www. globalpolicy.org/reform/armsindy.htm

30. **Rosenau J. N.** Governance in the twenty-first century. *Global Governance*, 1995, **1** (1): 13–43.

31. **World Bank.** *Governance: the World Bank's experience.* Washington, DC, World Bank, 1994.

32. **Mabey D.** Personal communication, Member of Technical Expert Committee, International Trachoma Initiative, London, 28 June 1999.

33. **Haas P. M.** Do regimes matter? Epistemic communities and Mediterranean pollution control. *International Organisation*, 1989, **43** (3).

34. **Bain K.** *Building or burning bridges? The accountability of transnational NGO networks in policy alliances with the World Bank.* Paper prepared for the Conference on NGOs in a Global Future, Birmingham 1999.

35. *Bill and Melinda Gates Children's Vaccine Program: Outline for Action.* Seattle, WA, Program for Appropriate Technology in Health, 1998.

36. **Cook J.** Personal correspondence with J. Cook, Executive Director, International Trachoma Initiative, 20 May 1999.

37. **Muraskin W.** *The war against hepatitis B: A history of the International Task Force on Hepatitis B Immunization.* Philadelphia, Pennsylvania University Press, 1995.

38. *International guidelines for ethical review of epidemiological studies.* Geneva, Council for International Organizations of Medical Sciences, 1991.

39. **Khan P.** UNAIDS to publish guidelines on ethics of vaccine trials. *International AIDS Vaccine Initiative Report*, Spring 1999. New York, IAVI, 1999.

40. *Proposed programme budget for the financial period 1998–1999.* Geneva, World Health Organization, 1996.

41. **Eckholm E.** River blindness – Conquering an ancient scourge. *The New York Times Magazine*, 8 January 1989.

42. Bristol-Myers Squibb 'Secure the future' announcement and media reaction. Internet posting from the Treatment Access Forum. Internet communication, 11 May 1999 at http://www.hivnet.ch:8000/treatment-access/tdm

43. **Chetley A.** *A healthy business? World health and the pharmaceutical industry.* London, Zed Books, 1990.

44. **Lucas A.** Personal communication, 13 July 1999.

45. **Kale O. O.** *Review of disease-specific corporate drug donation programmes for the control of communicable diseases.* Paper presented at the Symposium: Drugs for Communicable Diseases – Stimulating development and availability, Paris, 15 October 1999.

46. **Drager N. et al.** What determines aid for health: an empirical analysis of bilateral aid flows. *International Conference on Macro-Economics and Health in Countries in Greatest Need.* Geneva, World Health Organization, 1992.

47. **Weber J., Barrett A.** Volatile combos: pharmaceutical alliances can boost both players' health – or drag them down. *Business Week*, 25 October 1999.

48. **Korten D.** *The United Nations and the corporate agenda.* Text circulated on the internet, July 1997. Internet communication at http://www.igc.org/globalpolicy/reform/korten.htm

49. **Foege W. H.** Ten years of Mectizan. *Annals of Tropical Medicine and Parasitology*, 1998, **92** (1): 7–10.

50. *Towards the creation of strategic partnerships: improving access to drugs for HIV/AIDS: report of a consultative meeting, 30 June–2 July 1997, World Health Organization, Geneva.* Geneva, UNAIDS, 1997.

70

PUBLIC-PRIVATE PARTNERSHIPS AND GLOBAL HEALTH EQUITY

Prospects and challenges

Augustine D. Asante and Anthony B. Zwi

Source: *Indian Journal of Medical Ethics*, 4:4 (2007), 176–80.

Abstract

Health equity remains a major challenge to policymakers despite the resurgence of interest to promote it. In developing countries, especially, the sheer inadequacy of financial and human resources for health and the progressive undermining of state capacity in many under-resourced settings have made it extremely difficult to promote and achieve significant improvements in equity in health and access to healthcare. In the last decade, public-private partnerships have been explored as a mechanism to mobilise additional resources and support for health activities, notably in resource-poor countries. While public-private partnerships are conceptually appealing, many concerns have been raised regarding their impact on global health equity. This paper examines the viability of public-private partnerships for improving global health equity and highlights some key prospects and challenges. The focus is on global health partnerships and excludes domestic public-private mechanisms such as the state contracting out publicly-financed health delivery or management responsibilities to private partners. The paper is intended to stimulate further debate on the implications of public-private partnerships for global health equity.

Introduction

Healthcare delivery is primarily the responsibility of national governments. However, in many developing countries the sheer inadequacy of financial and human resources has hampered efforts by governments to deliver healthcare to all who need it. Inefficiencies in the public sector have also undermined

303

the effective delivery of healthcare even in those countries where resources are available. With inequities in access to healthcare and essential medicines widening both within and between nations, the need for additional resources and efficient delivery strategies has never been more pressing.

Access to effective HIV/AIDS treatment, for example, remains largely inequitable worldwide. In India, a country which supplies about half of the developing world's HIV-positive population with life-saving generic anti-retroviral drugs, access to treatment is between 6 per cent and 15 per cent – well below the 28 per cent average for low- and middle- income countries (1). In many sub-Saharan African countries including Ghana, Tanzania and Democratic Republic of the Congo, access to antiretroviral drugs, despite recent improvements, remains under 20 per cent. This contrasts sharply with the situation in the developed world where over 50 per cent of patients have access to HIV medication. In Australia about 70 per cent of the 15,310 people living with HIV in 2005 had access to treatment (1, 2).

Public-private partnerships have been explored as a mechanism through which to mobilise additional resources and support for health activities, particularly in under-resourced developing countries. Over 80 such partnerships exist, many focusing on combating neglected diseases or engaged in developing new drugs or vaccines (3). The UN and its agencies have been at the forefront of engaging with the private sector in an attempt to foster collaboration that would deliver more resources for health in poorer countries (4). The World Health Organization (WHO) has identified partnerships with civil society organisations, philanthropic foundations and the for-profit private sector as key to the future of global health (5). This burgeoning collaboration with the private sector is in accordance with the United Nations' Global Compact which seeks to increase and distribute the benefits of global economic development through voluntary corporate policies and actions in the areas of human rights, labour, the environment, and good governance (6, 7).

Enthusiasts of public-private partnership such as the World Bank believe these partnerships could help address specific cost and investment challenges faced by governments and improve efficiency and quality of health services (8). Others like the WHO and several pharmaceutical companies think public-private partnerships can contribute to improving equity in access to essential drugs while enhancing research into some of the world's forgotten diseases such as trypanosomiasis, buruli ulcer, tuberculosis and malaria, all of which predominantly affect the poor (9, 10).

While public-private partnerships are conceptually appealing, many concerns exist. The structures and governance arrangements under which these partnerships operate have been critiqued, as has been their potential impact on healthcare delivery in the international context, particularly their implications for global health governance. Not so much debate, however, exists on how public-private partnerships improve or undermine global health equity. This commentary considers the viability of public-private partnerships for improving global health equity and highlights some of the key prospects and challenges. The focus is on global health partnerships and excludes domestic partnerships such as the contracting out of publicly-financed health delivery and management responsibilities to a private partner or partners. The paper is intended to stimulate debate on the implications, for global health equity, of public-private partnerships and motivate evaluative research into the equity impacts of these collaborations.

Overview of types of public-private partnership

Public-private partnerships come in diverse forms and can mean different things to different people. While the terms "public" (state-financed and con-trolled) and "private" (non-state actors operating solely for profit or on a not-for-profit basis) are less controversial, that of "partnership" is loaded with ambiguities and has no single acceptable definition. It has been used to describe a variety of collaborations between different actors. Literally, it implies the commitment to a common goal through the joint provision of resources and expertise and the sharing of risks (11). In the health sector, public-private partnership commonly refers to any partnership in global health involving government and/or inter-governmental institutions and industry (12). To some people, collaborations between government institutions, particularly ministries of health and non-governmental organisations, are good examples of public-private partnership. For purposes of the analysis in this paper, the WHO's definition which sees public-private partnership as the "means to bring together a set of actors for the common goal of improving the health of a population through mutually agreed roles and principles" appears more appropriate (13).

Lob-Levyt (14) identified three main foci for public-private partnerships in health – products, outcome and activities. Product-oriented partnerships cover efforts to increase investments in research and development into new drugs, vaccines and diagnostic tests in the face of dwindling funding for research focusing on diseases that disproportionately affect the world's poor. In these partnerships, links between public sector institutions, the pharma-ceutical industry and philanthropic foundations are considered crucial. Pharmaceutical companies usually possess the technology as well as manu-facturing and distribution expertise. These can be paired with funding from public sector partners such as governments or philanthropic foundations like the Gates Foundation to invest in vaccine and drug research and develop-ment. In order to provide incentives for the development of a particular drug, tax credits may be offered to the companies involved, or agreements may be established for advance purchases to guarantee markets for the product if it is developed. The Global Alliance for TB Drug Development involving Glaxo Smith Kline and other partners is an example of product-oriented public-private partnership.

Outcome-oriented partnerships usually involve government institutions, industry and/or private philanthropists teaming up to fight certain poverty-related diseases such as polio. A typical example is the Global 2000 initiative of Jimmy Carter, former US president, which aims at eradicating guinea worm infection (one of the world's most forgotten diseases) in endemic sub-Saharan Africa and other developing countries. The Global Alliance for Vaccines and Immunisation and the Global Programme to Eliminate Lymphatic Filariasis are other examples of outcome-oriented partnership.

Finally, activity-focused partnerships may encompass the coming together of a number of organisations to work on developing a particular drug for a particular disease. The partnership between Hoffmann La Roche and Basilea Pharmaceutica – both of Switzerland – and Fulcrum Pharma of the UK to identify next-generation oxonides that will provide a single-dose oral cure for patients with uncomplicated plasmodium falciparum malaria under the Medicines for Malaria Venture is a good example of an activity-focused partnership. An activity-focused partnership can also be one that employs private sector mechanisms in the delivery of public goods, for example, the social marketing of commodities such as condoms and bed nets.

While the above classification may serve analytical purposes, there are a plethora of collaborations in the health sector that could be described as public-private partnerships and it is not always clear how best to describe or position them.

Public-private partnerships and global health equity

Underlying the bulk of global partnerships for health is the desire to bridge the inequity gap in healthcare access between rich and poor countries, especially access to essential drugs, and to develop new vaccines for diseases of prime importance to poorer nations. In particular, partnerships involving the UN agencies consider equity a primary goal as the organisation appears to have rediscovered its core equity values in recent years. But to what extent do these partnerships seek to and actually deliver on equity? Evidence of how public-private partnerships in the health sector have affected global health equity is scarce. In addition, scepticism about the profit motives of private corporations involved in these partnerships, especially pharmaceutical companies, often leads people to overlook any of their potential equity benefits. Indeed, many have criticised what they perceive to be an "open invitation" to private corporations to play a greater role in healthcare delivery, citing the risk of exacerbating current inequities in health as a major concern.

The rest of this paper considers the prospects and challenges of public-private partnerships for improving global health equity. As noted earlier, within the international health arena there are a variety of joint initiatives that merit the description of public-private partnerships. We focus specifically on global health partnerships involving private for-profit companies, particularly those in the pharmaceutical industry.

Prospects for improving global health equity

Conceptually, health equity, irrespective of how one interprets it, requires extending access to healthcare to a broader range of citizens whether or not they have the ability to pay for the services. This seems inherently contradictory to the objectives of private companies which are established largely to make profit. So is there any evidence that global health equity has been improved through public-private partnerships?

Recent update on the HIV/AIDS pandemic by UNAIDS/WHO clearly shows an increase in access to treatment and care in low- and middle-income countries. In sub-Saharan Africa, for example, the number of people receiving HIV/AIDS treatment increased more than eight-fold from about 100,000 to 810,000 between 2003 and 2005 and more than doubled in 2005 (15). This massive improvement would not have been possible without key public-private partnerships in the HIV/AIDS sector. Partnerships such as the Accelerating Access Initiative, formed in 2000 between some UN organisations and a number of pharmaceutical companies, the Drug Access Initiative and the 3 by 5 campaign have, through price bargaining and discounting, significantly reduced prices for antiretroviral drugs in poorer developing countries, making them more affordable. Much of the HIV medications are sold today in Africa and elsewhere in the developing world at discounted prices far lower than their original prices. For example, since 2001, Abbott has been selling HIV medications in 69 least developed countries including all of Africa at $500 per patient per year; the same drug costs approximately US$7,500 per patient per year in the US (16).

In addition to the discounted prices, there have been several global donation initiatives which have enhanced equity by making HIV drugs more accessible in developing countries. The Viramune Donation Programme, for example, has since 2000 donated nevirapine for the prevention of mother-to-child transmission while the Diflucan Partnership Programme has donated fluconazole for treatment of opportunistic infections from 2001. Under the Africa Comprehensive HIV/AIDS Partnerships with the Bill & Melinda Gates Foundation, the government of Botswana receives donation of Stocrin and Crixivan from Merck to boost its HIV/AIDS treatment campaign (17).

Apart from HIV/AIDS, public-private partnerships with pharmaceutical companies have contributed significantly to combating other "neglected" diseases such as leprosy, onchocerciasis, lymphatic filariasis, malaria and tuberculosis. These diseases have debilitating effects on their victims in poorer countries where resources to fight them are significantly limited. Through public-private partnerships such as the Global Alliance for Vaccines and Immunisation, the Mectizan Donation Programme, the Global Alliance to

Eliminate Leprosy and the STOP TB initiative, there have been vaccines and considerable financial and material resources to combat some of these diseases as well as to raise their sinking profile on the global health agenda. The above examples clearly demonstrate the important role that public-private partnerships can play in improving global health equity. There are, however, several challenges that must be overcome for these partnerships to contribute effectively to enhancing global health equity.

Challenges for improving global health equity

Concerns about the viability of public-private partnerships to improve global health equity revolve around several issues including the profit motives of the private sector. Private companies seek to maintain profitability in order to survive and thrive as business entities. However, with the push to give globalisation a human face, these companies want to be seen as socially responsible in their quest for profit. While in public most of them are keen to demonstrate their "good corporate citizenship" credentials, particularly how they are helping poorer nations to access drugs at affordable prices, in private they may take actions that are largely motivated by profit and contradict claims of good corporate citizenship. Regarding access to HIV/AIDS medication, for example, although prices of antiretrovirals have dropped significantly in poorer countries, it took strong political pressure and campaign by AIDS activists for pharmaceutical companies to reduce prices.

There is evidence suggesting that several multinational drug companies still engage in policies that restrict universal access to antiretroviral drugs. For example, the World Trade Organisation recognises the importance of access to essential medicines in times of public health crisis and gives governments some freedom in the Trade-related Aspects of Intellectual Property (TRIPS) to bypass patents on drugs in emergency situations. However, several pharmaceutical companies involved in public-private partnerships have also promoted policies limiting the capacity of governments in developing countries to use TRIPS flexibility to improve drug access (17). The recent row between the government of Thailand and Merck, Abbott and Sanofi-Aventis over the planned manufacture of generic copies of the antiretrovirals Efavirenz and Kaletra and the heart drug Plavix under the TRIPS flexibility provision illustrate the desire of pharmaceutical companies to limit access in order to maximise profit. Without underestimating the importance of patent rights, such actions do not promote global health.

Another challenge regarding global health equity is the limited transparency and accountability surrounding public-private partnerships. Often, partnership arrangements with the private sector are not open to public scrutiny. The process of selecting private partners, the setting of targets to be achieved and the formulation of management guidelines are anything but transparent. Partnerships involving UN agencies, including the WHO, and private corporations usually fail to involve poorer developing nations who are often the main beneficiaries of such collaborations. The apparent lack of openness makes it difficult to assess what equity targets are set and who should be held accountable for achieving those targets, if any. It is also difficult to hold private companies accountable for failed public-private partnerships given their complex structures and governance, and the different processes of accountability within the public and private sectors. While public sector organisations are theoretically accountable to the population and could be held responsible for issues such as equity, private companies are answerable to shareholders who are typically more concerned about returns on investments than improving equity.

Competence to negotiate a mutually beneficial partnership agreement differs between the public and private sectors. Many public-private partnerships in the health sector today exist between governments of poorer developing nations and pharmaceutical companies. Most of these governments depend largely on donor funding for their healthcare provision and this may come with strings attached. Governments engaging in direct partnerships with private companies may negotiate from a weak position depending on the source of their donor support. By contrast, pharmaceutical companies have tremendous technical and financial clout and are often backed by powerful governments. The US government's aggressive defence of intellectual property rights of American pharmaceutical companies is well known (18). The massive influence of private companies could be used to dictate partnership terms and conditions to suit commercial interests and this could have severe repercussions for health equity.

Furthermore, public-private partnerships in the health sector have focused overwhelmingly on improving drug access. While this is crucial in many health systems, particularly in poorer nations, there is more to health equity than simply improving access to medicines. Equity in health, according to Sen (19), should be assessed in terms of health capabilities and achievements rather than healthcare activities. Improving drug access by cutting down prices is necessary but not sufficient to improve equity. Reasonable consensus exists among health economists that individuals have different capacities to benefit from healthcare (20) and that access to services is not synonymous with utilisation of healthcare. In sub-Saharan Africa there is ample evidence suggesting that despite improvements in access to antiretroviral drugs the bulk of people with HIV/AIDS are still without access (15). In short, equity requires adequate social arrangements that provide individuals the opportunity to achieve good health (21). It cannot therefore be effectively promoted through partnerships that focus narrowly on improving drug access; rather, it must to be pursued as part of a broader reform to strengthen health systems.

Finally, there are concerns that public-private partnerships in the health sector could threaten global health governance and derail the promotion of equity. The health sector needs strong leadership if equity objectives are to be seriously pursued. At the global level, the WHO is generally regarded as the natural leader. However, the organisation's increasing participation in partnerships with private corporations has offered the private sector a platform to actively engage in global health decision-making. There are fears that as profit-seeking corporations gain louder voice in decision-making, the WHO's leadership might be compromised and this could adversely affect the promotion of equity.

Another source of worry with regards to leadership and equity is the growing influence of the World Bank on the international health stage. Relying on its massive funding power, the World Bank has, over the past 15 years, entrenched itself as the leader in global health development. It is currently the world's largest external funder of health, committing more than $1 billion annually in new lending to improve health, nutrition and population in developing countries. In the fight against HIV/AIDS, its commitment (among the largest in the world) stands in excess of $1.3 billion, with about half of it going to sub-Saharan Africa (22). While funding from the World Bank is crucial to the efforts to improve health, there are concerns that equity considerations may suffer if neoliberals in the Bank dominate. The bank's traditional support for market mechanisms including privatisation of the health sector particularly makes many equity advocates nervous.

There are also concerns about the impact of public-private partnerships on health sector governance at country levels. In many countries, the evidence suggests that national ownership of health programmes has suffered with the increase in public-private partnerships. In Zambia and Uganda, for example, Caines and Lush (17) found little indication of national ownership of HIV/AIDS public-private partnerships programmes. Non-governmental organisations, in most cases, own and control these programmes. The limited national ownership of such programmes can potentially harm domestic policies and strategies designed to promote health equity. There is the need, however, for further research into how specific global public-private partnerships have affected health sector governance and how this in turn has enhanced or undermined equity as concrete evidence at country levels in this area remains scarce.

Conclusion

The growing inequities in health and access to healthcare worldwide require serious global attention and strong leadership from the WHO and national governments. Partnership with the private sector brings to the public health sector private financing and private sector know-how. In several instances, it has contributed to improving access to essential medicines in poorer countries and helped to mobilise additional resources and support for healthcare in the face of declining investments and rising demand for services. However, in terms of equity, public-private partnership is like a double-edged sword – it can promote as well as undermine fairness in global health. Private companies are established to generate profit and will not invest or participate in partnerships where the opportunity to make profit does not exist. The public sector stands the risk of subsidising the commercial sector with public funds if it does not go into these partnerships with well defined goals and achievable targets. It is incumbent on all governments and inter-governmental agencies engaging in partnership with the private sector to set out clear goals for improving global health equity and ensure that these goals are achieved. This should go beyond narrowly promoting equity in access to essential medicines and target improving overall equity in health by paying special attention to the determinants of ill health, the establishment of effective health systems, and improvement of access and quality of care for those worst-off.

Competing interests

The authors declare no competing interests.

References

1. WHO/UNAIDS/UNICEF. *Towards universal access: scaling up priority HIV/AIDS interventions in the health sector. Progress Report.* WHO/UNAIDS/UNICEF: Geneva; 2007 Apr.
2. National Centre in HIV Epidemiology and Clinical Research. *Annual surveillance report: HIV/AIDS, viral hepatitis and sexually transmitted infections in Australia.* NCHECR: University of New South Wales, Sydney; 2006.
3. Wemos. *Good intentions with side effects: information on global public private initiatives in health.* Wemos: Amsterdam; 2004. [Monograph on the Internet]. [Cited 2007 Jun 7]. Available from: http://www.wemos.nl
4. Buse K., Waxman A. Public-private partnerships: a strategy for WHO. *Bull World Health Organ* 2001;79:748–54.
5. Brundtland G. H. *One world: global health.* Oral presentation at the annual meeting of the American Public Health Association Atlanta, GA, USA: 2001 Oct 22.
6. United Nations Industrial Development Organisation. *Survey of small and medium enterprises in the global compact.* UNIDO; Vienna: 2004.
7. Williams M. The Global Alliance for Vaccines and Immunisation: is it a new model for effective public-private cooperation in international public health? *Am J Public Health* 2004;94:1922–5
8. Nikolic I. A., Maikisch H. *Public-private partnerships and collaboration in the health sector: an overview with case studies from recent European experience.* Discussion Paper. World Bank Health, Nutrition and Population (HNP): Washington, DC; 2006.
9. World Health Organization / Joint UN Programme on AIDS. *Accelerating access initiative: widening access to care and support for people living with HIV/AIDS.* Progress Report. Geneva: WHO/UNAIDS; 2002 Jun.

10. GlaxoSmithKline. *A Human Race*. Corporate Responsibility Report of 2006. [Cited 2007 Jun 15]. Available from: www.gsk.com/responsibility/cr-review-2006/downloads/CR-Report-2006.pdf

11. Ridley R. G. Putting the partnership into public-private partnerships. Editorials. *Bull World Health Organ* 2001;79:694.

12. Bale H. E. Reversing failure. In: Ridley R. G., Lob-Levyt J., Sachs J., Johns D., Evans T., Bale H. E., Quick J. D., et al. A role for public-private partnerships in controlling neglected diseases? Round Table Discussion. *Bull World Health Organ* 2001;79:771–7.

13. World Health Organization. *Guidelines on collaborations and partnership with commercial enterprise*. WHO: Geneva; 1999.

14. Lob-Levyt J. A donor perspective. In: Ridley R. G., Lob-Levyt J., Sachs J., Johns D., Evans T., Bale H. E., Quick J. D., et al. A role for public-private partnerships in controlling neglected diseases? Round Table Discussion. *Bull World Health Organ* 2001;79:771–7.

15. Joint UN Programme on AIDS. *Report on the global AIDS epidemic*. Geneva: UNAIDS; 2006.

16. Abbott. *Generations: Global Citizenship Report 2006*. 2007 Apr. [Cited 2007 Oct 3]. Available from: http://www.abbott.com/static/content/document/2006_gcr.pdf

17. Caines K., Lush L. *Impact of public-private partnerships addressing access to pharmaceuticals in selected low and middle income countries: a synthesis report from studies in Botswana, Sri Lanka, Uganda and Zambia*. Geneva: Initiative on Public-Private Partnerships for Health; 2004.

18. Bond P. *Against global apartheid: South Africa meets the World Bank, IMF and international finance*. Cape Town: University of Cape Town Press; 2001.

19. Sen A. *Inequality re-examined*. Oxford: Oxford University Press; 1995.

20. Culyer A. J. Equity – some theory and its policy implications. *J Med Ethics* 2001,27:275–83.

21. Sen A. Why health equity? *Health Economics* 2002;11:659–66.

22. Ruger J. P. The changing role of the World Bank in global health. *A m J Public Health* 2005;95:60–70.

71

FINANCING OF GLOBAL HEALTH

Tracking development assistance for health from 1990 to 2007

Nirmala Ravishankar, Paul Gubbins, Rebecca J. Cooley, Katherine Leach-Kemon, Catherine M. Michaud, Dean T. Jamison and Christopher J. L. Murray

Source: *Lancet*, 373:9681 (2009), 2113–24.

Summary

Background   The need for timely and reliable information about global health resource flows to low-income and middle-income countries is widely recognised. We aimed to provide a comprehensive assessment of development assistance for health (DAH) from 1990 to 2007.

Methods   We defined DAH as all flows for health from public and private institutions whose primary purpose is to provide development assistance to low-income and middle-income countries. We used several data sources to measure the yearly volume of DAH in 2007 US$, and created an integrated project database to examine the composition of this assistance by recipient country.

Findings   DAH grew from $5.6 billion in 1990 to $21.8 billion in 2007. The proportion of DAH channelled via UN agencies and development banks decreased from 1990 to 2007, whereas the Global Fund to Fight AIDS, Tuberculosis and Malaria, the Global Alliance for Vaccines and Immunization (GAVI), and non-governmental organisations became the conduit for an increasing share of DAH. DAH has risen sharply since 2002 because of increases in public funding, especially from the USA, and on the private side, from increased philanthropic donations and in-kind contributions from corporate donors. Of the $14.5 billion DAH in 2007 for which project-level information was available, $5.1 billion was for HIV/AIDS, compared with $0.7 billion for tuberculosis, $0.8 billion for malaria, and $0.9 billion for health-sector support. Total DAH received by low-income and middle-income countries was positively correlated with burden of disease, whereas per head DAH was negatively correlated with per head gross domestic product.

Interpretation This study documents the substantial rise of resources for global health in recent years. Although the rise in DAH has resulted in increased funds for HIV/AIDS, other areas of global health have also expanded. The influx of funds has been accompanied by major changes in the institutional landscape of global health, with global health initiatives such as the Global Fund and GAVI having a central role in mobilising and channelling global health funds.

Funding Bill & Melinda Gates Foundation.

Introduction

In the years leading up to the present global economic downturn, international support for improving health in low-income and middle-income countries grew substantially, which gave rise to a lively debate among global health experts on how development assistance for health (DAH) could be used effectively.[1-4] With the onset of a global recession, many expect decreases in future funding.[5-7] Surprisingly, discussions about global health financing continue to take place in the absence of a comprehensive system for tracking DAH.

The existing research on health resource flows has yielded some important estimates, but has large gaps.[8-12] The Development Assistance Committee of the Organisation for Economic Co-operation and Development (OECD) provides estimates of official development assistance by sector.[13] However, these estimates track only public sources and exclude private philanthropy, which is an important source of development assistance.[14] The OECD data also omit other important health flows, such as contributions from the Global Alliance for Vaccines and Immunization (GAVI) and core-funded activities of WHO.[13,15] Studies investigating resources for specific diseases or types of interventions[16-19] have similar disadvantages. Studies of aggregate flows provide only data from single years,[12,20] and those capturing time-series data are outdated.[21,22]

In view of the interest in DAH, why have these flows been so difficult to track comprehensively and systematically? Defining what constitutes DAH is conceptually challenging. Clarity on the scope of health resource tracking is needed, including a delineation of the types of institutions that should be tracked, what counts as health dollars and what might be health-related such as support for allied sectors, and whether assistance for all countries or just those of low and middle income should be included. Additionally, whether the quantity of interest is commitments, disbursements, or expenditure (panel) needs to be clearly defined.

Several measurement challenges make careful analysis complex, time-consuming, and at times uncertain. First, crucial variables in OECD's databases

Panel: **Definitions of terms**

Commitments
Promises of future payments made at one point in time.

Disbursements
Actual payments made against a previous commitment.

Development assistance
Funds from and activities by donor governments, multilateral agencies, and private agencies for promoting economic, social, and political development in low-income and middle-income countries.

Channels of assistance
Institutions whose primary purpose is providing development assistance to low-income and middle-income countries.

Development assistance for health (DAH)
Financial and in-kind contributions from channels of assistance to improve health in low-income and middle-income countries. DAH aims to achieve either country-specific health improvements or to finance health-related global public goods such as research and development, disease surveillance, monitoring and evaluation, and data collection. DAH does not include support for allied fields such as humanitarian assistance, food aid, water and sanitation, education, and poverty alleviation that indirectly affect health. DAH includes loans on concessional terms, which charge below-market interest rates. We distinguish gross DAH, which is the actual outflow of resources in a specific year, from net DAH, which is the gross amount minus repayments for DAH loans in previous years. Results in this Article are for gross DAH only.

Research funded by DAH channels of assistance is counted as DAH, whereas health research by other institutions whose primary purpose is not development assistance is not included.

Sources of funding
Revenue streams for the channels of assistance.

Implementing institutions
International and domestic agencies implementing health programmes for improving health in low-income and middle-income countries.

such as yearly disbursements and project descriptions are often incomplete. Second, there are no integrated databases for health-related assistance flows from private foundations and non-governmental organisations (NGOs) worldwide. Third, development assistance flows from primary funding sources through various financial intermediaries to many implementing institutions, increasing the danger of the same money being counted multiple times. Fourth, the poor quality of data from previous years makes quantification of time trends difficult. Fifth, different published sources of information for the same organisation are often inconsistent. And last, organisations use different fiscal years and accounting methods, which complicate the task of developing coherent information over time.

We aimed to tackle these challenges and develop a consistent time series of DAH from 1990 to 2007 on the basis of clear definitions and data drawn from several sources.

Methods

Conceptual framework

The first step in estimation of DAH was to identify all important public and private channels of assistance in the health sector. The webappendix p 1 shows how resources for health flow to and from these channels of assistance. In practice, some channels such as bilateral aid agencies and private foundations behave more as funding sources, whereas others such as the UN agencies and NGOs are channels of assistance as well as implementing institutions (webappendix p 2).

DAH in each year equals the sum of gross yearly disbursements on all health-sector grants and loans, and health-related programme expenditures from the channels of assistance, net of any transfers to other channels of assistance included in the study. Five points are worth noting. First, we defined health as all disease-specific support and general health-sector support, and excluded support for allied sectors such as water and sanitation, education, general budget support, and humanitarian assistance. Although development assistance to most sectors affects health, the aim of this study was to estimate direct assistance to the health sector. For comparison purposes, however, we report overall time trends in general budget support and debt relief separately. Second, we counted yearly disbursements on health-sector loans and grants rather than commitments made towards future payments. Third, DAH includes gross disbursements rather than net resource flows. Fourth, to avoid double-counting, we subtracted any flows from the channels that we were tracking to other channels also tracked by us—ie, we counted DAH from the channel most proximal to the recipient country or destination of the funds. Last, research funded by DAH channels of assistance are included in our estimate, whereas health research by institutions that do not meet our definition of a channel of assistance have been excluded.

Overview of data sources

The study tracks bilateral aid agencies in 22 member countries of the OECD Development Assistance Committee, the European Commission, WHO, the UN Children's Fund (UNICEF), the UN Population Fund (UNFPA), the Joint UN Programme on HIV/AIDS (UNAIDS), the World Bank, the Asian Development Bank, the Inter-American Development Bank, the African Development Bank, GAVI, the Global Fund to Fight AIDS, Tuberculosis and Malaria, US-based private foundations including the Bill & Melinda Gates Foundation, and US-based NGOs. Channels for which we were unable to identify robust data sources have been excluded from the analysis. We constructed two integrated databases: one reflecting aggregate flows and a second project-level database for channels that provided project-level information.

Research methods

We counted as DAH all health-related disbursements from bilateral donor agencies excluding funds that they transferred to any of the other channels tracked to avoid double-counting. We extracted this information from the OECD's creditor reporting system (CRS) database. Since donors under-reported disbursement information to the CRS before 2002, we developed a method to predict disbursements from the observed data (webappendix pp 18–24). For other grant-making and loan-making institutions, we similarly included their yearly disbursements on health grants and loans, excluding transfers to any other channels and ignoring any repayments on outstanding debts (webappendix pp 25–38 and 45–47). The yearly disbursements for grant-making and loan-making DAH institutions indicate only the financial transfers made by these agencies. Therefore, we separately estimated in-kind transfers from these institutions in the form of staff time for providing technical assistance and the costs of managing programmes (webappendix pp 53–55).

For the UN agencies, we included their yearly expenditure on health both from their core budgets and from voluntary contributions. For UNICEF, we also estimated the proportion of total expenditure that was spent on health (webappendix pp 39–44). For NGOs, we used data from US Government sources and financial documents from a sample of NGOs to estimate health expenditures by NGOs registered in the USA. The amount for 2007, which has not been released yet, was estimated on the basis of data from previous years (webappendix pp 48–52). We used data for the Bill & Melinda Gates Foundation from its tax documents, and relied on data from the

Foundation Center for all other US foundations (webappendix pp 45–47). We were unable to include NGOs and foundations registered in other donor countries because of data restrictions.

To estimate the total amounts, we carefully corrected for double-counting. For example, the global health programme at the Bill & Melinda Gates Foundation disbursed funds to several channels tracked by this study, each of which also received funds from elsewhere (webappendix p 3). We excluded the flows from the Bill & Melinda Gates Foundation to these channels from our estimate of DAH, since inclusion of those and outflows from these channels would lead to an exaggerated estimate of DAH.

We collected information about each channel's income and used it to disaggregate its contribution to DAH according to the proportion of income received from different sources. The resulting values for DAH by source are imputed rather than observed and do not indicate the total amount that the channels received from different sources.

We used the project-level database to analyse the composition of DAH by recipient country. We then assessed DAH for HIV/AIDS, tuberculosis, malaria, and health-sector budget support with keyword searches within the descriptive fields (webappendix p 56). We chose to focus on these areas in view of their relevance to present policy debates about global health finances. We separately extracted from the CRS data for general budget support and debt relief, and estimated total disbursements for both (webappendix pp 18–24). Last, we explored the relation between DAH and the burden of disease measured in disability-adjusted life-years (DALYs),[23] and between per head DAH[24] and income measured by the gross domestic product (GDP) of recipient countries.[25–27] All results are presented in 2007 US$ by first converting figures from local currencies into nominal US$ with OECD's exchange rates and then deflating these nominal dollar sequences into real 2007 US$.[25] All analyses were done in Stata (version 10.0) and R (version 2.7.1).

Role of the funding source

The funding source for this study had no role in the study design, data collection, data analysis, data interpretation, or writing of the Article. The corresponding author had full access to all data analysed and had final responsibility for the decision to submit for publication.

Results

Figure 1A shows total DAH from 1990 to 2007 in 2007 US$ disaggregated by the channel of assistance. The total amount of DAH quadrupled from $5.6 billion in 1990 to $21.8 billion in 2007. Although DAH doubled over the course of the 11 years between 1990 and 2001, it doubled again in the

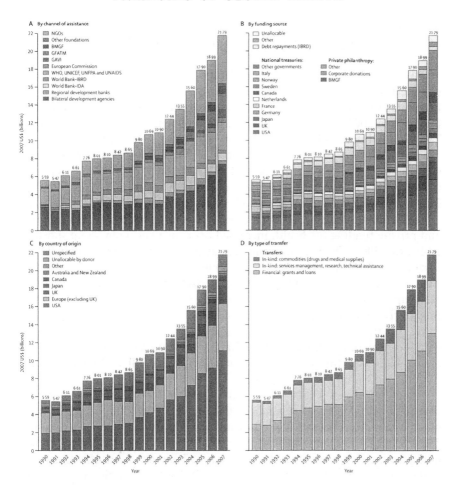

Figure 1 Development assistance for health (DAH) from 1990 to 2007 by channel of assistance (A), source of funding (B), country of origin (C), and type of assistance (D).

In B, funds from channels for which we were unable to find separated revenue information and interagency transfers from non-DAH institutions are included in the unallocable category; other refers to interest income, currency exchange adjustments, and other miscellaneous income. In C, the unallocable category includes funds such as interagency transfers from non-DAH institutions, interest income, and miscellaneous income that could not be attributed to countries. Channels for which we had no revenue information are included under unspecified. NGO=non-governmental organisation. BMGF=Bill & Melinda Gates Foundation. GAVI=Global Alliance for Vaccines and Immunization. GFATM=Global Fund to Fight AIDS, Tuberculosis and Malaria. UNICEF=UN Children's Fund. UNFPA=UN Population Fund. UNAIDS=Joint UN Programme on HIV/AIDS. IBRD=International Bank for Reconstruction and Development. IDA=International Development Association.

6 years between 2001 and 2007. The relative contributions of different channels of assistance changed substantially over time. The percentage of DAH mobilised by the UN agencies decreased from 32.3% in 1990 to 14.0% in 2007. The World Bank and regional banks accounted for 21.7% of DAH at their relative peak in 2000, which reduced to 7.2% by 2007. The share of DAH from bilateral agencies as channels of assistance decreased from 46.8% in 1990 to 27.1% in 2001, and then increased in subsequent years to 34.0% in 2007. The Global Fund and GAVI scaled up rapidly from less than 1% of DAH each in 2002 to 8.3% and 4.2%, respectively, in 2007. The Bill & Melinda Gates Foundation as a channel peaked in 2007 at 3.9% of DAH. The share of resources flowing through NGOs increased from 13.1% of DAH in 1990 to 24.9% in 2006, the last year for which we have reported data for the NGOs.

Figure 1B separates DAH by the original source of funding. Both public and private funding for health increased over time and grew more substantially after 2001. The US Government was the largest donor of public DAH during this time. The other big donors in terms of cumulative disbursements from 2002 to 2007, in decreasing order of size, were the governments of the UK, Japan, Germany, France, Netherlands, Canada, Sweden, Norway, and Italy. Private sources of funding were responsible for a growing share of DAH, up from 19.0% in 1998 to 26.7% in 2007. This peak corresponded with the entry of the Bill & Melinda Gates Foundation into the development arena. However, this graph does not capture the Bill & Melinda Gates Foundation's total disbursements.

Figure 1C shows DAH from both public and private sources, by its country of origin. The results show that the USA was the biggest contributor overall and that its share has increased over the years. This finding could be an overestimate because private contributions from citizens of other donor countries to NGOs in their countries have not been quantified due to data restrictions. The eight largest non-US NGOs for which we obtained data for some select years (webappendix pp 48–52) spent $231 million on health programmes in 2006, which is small compared with the health expenditures of US NGOs. Hence, we believe that the overall pattern is still largely as shown despite the exclusion of non-US NGOs from the study. This comparison disregards differences in national incomes across these countries. We calculated DAH as a percentage of GDP for the 22 member countries of the OECD in 2007. By this measure, the USA (0.08%) ranked fifth, behind Sweden (0.24%), Luxembourg (0.15%), Norway (0.14%), and Ireland (0.10%).

The webappendix p 4 depicts DAH by target region. The proportion of DAH for which data for target country was not available decreased from 70.6% in 1990 to 44.2% in 2007. All regions had increases in funding but the relative share of DAH for sub-Saharan Africa increased from 9.7% in 1990 to 13.8% in 2001, and then to 22.7% in 2007. This growth partly indicates the expansion of funding for HIV/AIDS.

Figure 1D disaggregates DAH into financial transfers and in-kind assistance, showing that the in-kind share of DAH is large and has grown disproportionally. Financial assistance includes all financial disbursements from DAH channels to implementing agencies and research institutions in both high-income countries and those of low and middle income. In-kind assistance has two components. The first—services management, research, and technical assistance—includes all expenditures by UN agencies on health programmes, the costs incurred by loan-making and grant-making institutions for providing technical assistance and programme management, and expenditures by NGOs net of any commodities delivered. Donated drugs and other commodities comprise the second component of in-kind transfers, and are shown separately.

Figure 2 shows DAH funding for HIV/AIDS, tuberculosis, and malaria. Disbursements for HIV/AIDS have grown, first gradually from $0.2 billion (3.4% of DAH) in 1990 to $0.8 billion (7.0%) in 2000, and then more rapidly to $5.1 billion (23.3%) in 2007. DAH for tuberculosis and malaria remained small by comparison: $0.7 billion (3.2%) and $0.8 billion (3.5%), respectively, in 2007. However, resources for malaria have substantially increased since 2005. Although donors have made arguments emphasising the importance of funds providing general health-system support that are not linked to specific programmes or diseases, the volume of these flows remained low.

Some donors, particularly the UK and the European Commission, have provided substantial general budget support. Such grants, along with debt relief, have the potential to increase resources for the health sector. The webappendix p 5 shows our estimated trend for disbursements of general budget support and debt relief, as well as the additional funds that probably

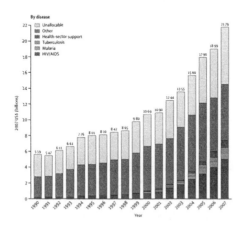

Figure 2 Development assistance for health (DAH) from 1990 to 2007 by disease. Unallocable corresponds to DAH for which we did not have project level information about disease-focus.

flowed into the health sector as a result of these streams, with the assumption that governments from low-income and middle-income countries spent 5% of the resources on health.[28] Our results show that general budget support and debt relief generated was small compared with DAH.

Figure 3 shows the composition of public DAH by channel of assistance. We used the channel of delivery code in the CRS to separate bilateral assistance from members of the Development Assistance Committee into funds going to recipient governments versus other civil society and private agencies. Contributions to GAVI and the Global Fund, as well as funds flowing to governments and civil society groups in recipient countries, have grown substantially, whereas funds flowing through the World Bank, European Commission, WHO, UNICEF, and other UN agencies have not expanded at the same pace. Since the share that flowed through unspecified channels has fallen from 1990 to 2007, these trends need to be interpreted with some caution. The webappendix p 6 shows the composition of public monies by channel for every donor country in 2007. Some countries such as France, Italy, Netherlands, and Finland have largely channelled their public funds through multilateral mechanisms. Other large donors such as the UK and the USA have channelled a substantial proportion through bilateral mechanisms or NGOs.

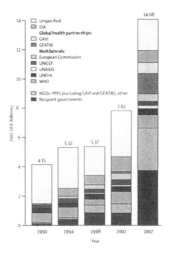

Figure 3 Publicly-financed development assistance for health (DAH) in 1990, 1994, 1998, 2002, and 2007 separated by channel.
Non-governmental organisations (NGOs), public-private partnerships (PPPs) excluding the Global Alliance for Vaccines and Immunization (GAVI) and the Global Fund to Fight AIDS, Tuberculosis and Malaria (GFATM), and other miscellaneous channels are shown together. Disbursements from the creditor reporting system when the channel of delivery code was not specified are shown here as unspecified. IDA=International Development Association. UNICEF=UN Children's Fund. UNFPA=UN Population Fund. UNAIDS=Joint UN Programme on HIV/AIDS.

The Bill & Melinda Gates Foundation is the single biggest source of private DAH. Figure 4 shows its global health commitments and disbursements. Resources for global health from the Bill & Melinda Gates Foundation have substantially risen since 2000. Since many commitments are multiyear projects, yearly disbursements are lower than the commitments. They have scaled up global health commitments substantially since 2004, reaching nearly $2 billion in both 2006 and 2007. A large share of their disbursements were transferred to other channels of assistance tracked in this study, including GAVI, the Global Fund, the World Bank, and UN agencies.

Figure 5 shows total overseas health expenditure by US NGOs included in our study from 1990 to 2007, and the proportion received from different funding sources. The share of expenditure financed through private revenues is divided into amounts from the Bill & Melinda Gates Foundation, other private financial donations, and in-kind contributions. The in-kind component, which is more than 50% in most years, included donations of drugs from pharmaceutical companies that were valued at current market prices. This accounting practice has potentially resulted in an exaggeration of the

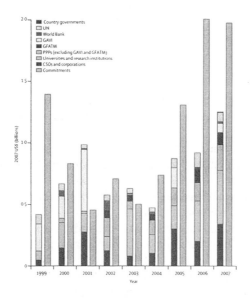

Figure 4 Bill & Melinda Gates Foundation commitments and disbursements from 1999 to 2007.
The recipients of disbursed grants, which we coded, are also shown. The category universities and research institutions includes universities, non-governmental organisations, foundations, and government institutions in all countries with a research focus. The category country governments includes all non-research oriented government agencies. GAVI=Global Alliance for Vaccines and Immunization. GFATM=Global Fund to Fight AIDS, Tuberculosis and Malaria. PPPs=public-private partnerships. CSO=civil society organisations, including non-governmental organisations and foundations.

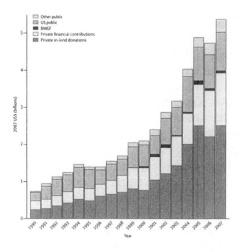

Figure 5 Total overseas health expenditure by US non-governmental organisations from 1990 to 2007.

Funds are separated by proportions of revenue received from the US Government, other public sources of funding, from the Bill & Melinda Gates Foundation (BMGF), financial donations from private contributors, and in-kind donations from private contributors. Since revenue and expenditure data for 2007 are not currently available, the overseas health expenditure for 2007 was estimated from yearly growth rates in the previous 5 years.

magnitude of resources flowing via US NGOs. The table lists the 20 US-based NGOs with the highest overseas health expenditure. Most of these NGOs with the highest percentages of revenue from in-kind contributions helped to channel drugs and medical supplies to recipient countries and partner agencies.

In view of the strong global interest in malaria, tuberculosis, and HIV/AIDS, as manifested in the Millennium Development Goals and the creation of the Global Fund, funding for these diseases are further disaggregated (figure 6) by channels of assistance. HIV/AIDS funding was strongly dominated by the US Government and the Global Fund, with other channels having a secondary but important and expanding role. By contrast, tuberculosis funding mainly flowed through grants from the Bill & Melinda Gates Foundation, the Global Fund, and WHO, with the US Government playing a small part. Despite the US President's Malaria Initiative, the pattern for malaria seemed to be similar. These results show that although the amount of DAH flowing for tuberculosis and malaria remained low as of 2007, the Global Fund and Bill & Melinda Gates Foundation have emerged as the two biggest channels of assistance for these diseases.

The share of DAH allocable by recipient country grew from 30.3% in 1990 to 56.6% in 2007. The webappendix pp 7–9 plots cumulative DAH from 2002–07 against the total burden of disease measured in DALYs for all low-income and middle-income countries. We make the comparison on a

Table 20 non-governmental organisations registered in the USA with highest cumulative overseas health expenditure from from 2002 to 2006.

	Overseas health expenditure (US$ millions)	Total overseas expenditure (US$ millions)	Revenue from private sources (%)	Revenue from in-kind contributions (%)
Food For The Poor	1492.3	3137.0	91.0%	80.4%
Population Services International	1250.3	1275.6	10.7%	0.1%
MAP International	1196.8	1210.2	99.8%	96.4%
World Vision	826.1	3150.4	73.5%	28.6%
Brother's Brother Foundation	785.8	1158.6	99.9%	99.0%
Feed The Children	706.9	2044.5	96.9%	82.6%
Catholic Medical Mission Board	699.0	746.6	99.6%	93.0%
Project HOPE	583.6	635.6	89.6%	69.2%
Medical Teams International	568.8	698.8	98.5%	89.0%
Management Sciences for Health	515.5	617.6	11.1%	0.0%
United Nations Foundation	505.9	726.9	86.1%	9.6%
Catholic Relief Services	498.1	2547.9	37.3%	2.0%
Interchurch Medical Assistance	462.6	466.6	89.6%	85.6%
Direct Relief International	431.8	507.1	99.9%	91.7%
PATH	389.5	444.1	92.2%	0.0%
The Carter Center	378.2	472.3	94.1%	45.4%
International Medical Corps	338.7	354.1	52.1%	42.8%
Pathfinder International	269.6	301.0	20.9%	0.9%
Save the Children	229.1	1229.1	48.4%	1.9%
National Cancer Coalition	226.6	242.4	100.0%	93.1%

In the case of international non-governmental organisations that have branches in several countries, the table indicates only the income and expenditure reported by their US-based branch. Expenditure is expressed in millions of real 2007 US$.

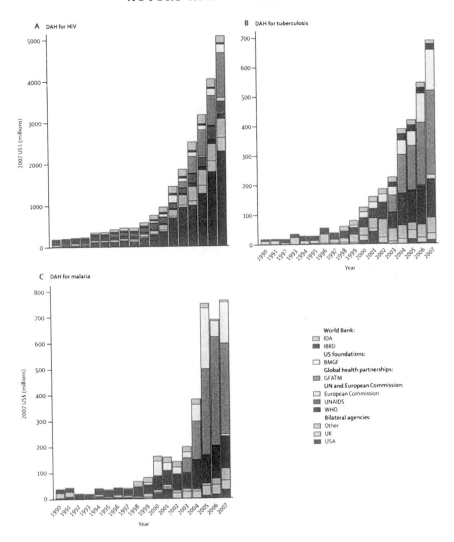

Figure 6 Development assistance for health (DAH) for HIV/AIDS (A), tuberculosis (B), and malaria (C), separated by channels of assistance, 1990–2007. IDA=International Development Association. IBRD=International Bank for Reconstruction and Development. BGMF=Bill & Melinda Gates Foundation. GFATM=Global Fund to Fight AIDS, Tuberculosis and Malaria. UNAIDS=Joint UN Programme on HIV/AIDS.

log-log scale because of the large range in amounts of DAH and DALYs across countries. Disease burden and DAH are positively correlated. However, donor assistance can greatly vary at the same level of burden; for example, there is a 33-fold difference between DAH received by Turkmenistan and Nicaragua, two countries with similar disease burden.

Some small island states such as Micronesia, Tonga, and the Marshall Islands get high levels of DAH per DALY. The correlation between health aid and disease burden has risen from 0.6 to 0.8 between 1997 and 2007. Furthermore, there is little difference in the pattern for low-income, lower middle-income, and upper middle-income countries. The correlation between per head DAH and per head GDP was near zero until the mid-1990s but has decreased steadily from -0.1 in 1999 to -0.3 in 2007, which suggests that poorer countries are receiving increasing amounts of DAH. Figure 7 shows a map of total DAH per DALY and the webappendix pp 10–12 shows disease-specific maps of DAH per DALY for HIV/AIDS, tuberculosis, and malaria. The maps show substantial variation in DAH per DALY across regions and within regions. These results suggest that country allocation of DAH is driven by many considerations, including income, burden of disease, political stability, and historical and political relations between specific donors and recipient countries.

In figure 8, the 30 countries with greatest DAH are ordered by rank in the left column, while countries are ranked in decreasing order of burden on the right. India topped both lists. Although some high-burden countries such as China, Brazil, and Bangladesh had a much higher rank on the burden list than on the DAH list, the situation was the reverse for Ethiopia, Uganda, Tanzania, Kenya, and Mozambique. Additional research into factors predicting the amount of DAH received can explain these patterns. For the ten countries receiving the most cumulative DAH and per head DAH from 2002 to 2007, the webappendix pp 13 and 14 shows the composition of DAH in terms of the channel of assistance through which these funds were received.

Discussion

This study documents what is widely recognised in the area of global health— namely, that development assistance for improving health in countries of low and middle income has expanded substantially in the past 18 years. Resources quadrupled between 1990 and 2007, and the rate of growth accelerated after 2002. The influx of resources has not only been from public sources but also from private philanthropy. Although the scale-up of global health resources from the Bill & Melinda Gates Foundation is striking, the magnitude of resources that US NGOs mobilised from other private philanthropy was greater. In particular, corporate drug and equipment donations have expanded substantially. However, the true value of

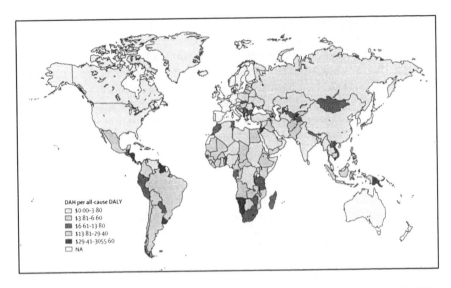

DAH per all-cause DALY
- $0·00–3·80
- $3·81–6·60
- $6·61–13·80
- $13·81–29·40
- $29·41–3055·60
- NA

Figure 7 Map showing cumulative 2002–07 development assistance for health (DAH) per all-cause disability-adjusted life-year (DALY).

The map shows international boundaries in 2006. Since DALY data were available for 2002 only, we used these data as a proxy for burden in all subsequent years. Only DAH allocable by country is shown in the map. Countries that received zero DAH over the study period and those with missing burden are not shown. DAH received is shown in millions of real 2007 $US.

these donations to recipients in developing countries might be less than the value that was recorded on US tax returns.[29]

The expansion of resources for global health especially in the past 10 years has been accompanied by a major change in the institutional landscape. Two new and large channels of resource flows, the Global Fund and GAVI, have attracted a growing share of funds, while the proportion of assistance going to UN agencies and development banks has decreased during this period. The role of NGOs in terms of spending funds from the public and private sectors has expanded tremendously, as has direct bilateral assistance to governments in low-income and middle-income countries. The shift is not only towards a smaller relative role for the UN system and the World Bank, but also for the changed status of these organisations. Over time, the share of their expenditure from voluntary contributions as opposed to assessed contributions has grown steadily (webappendix pp 39–44). To sustain their present role, the UN agencies—especially WHO and UNICEF—have to compete with recipient countries, NGOs, and other organisations for available DAH funds. This steady shift to a competitive model of funding runs the risks of undermining their crucial role as trusted neutral brokers between the scientific and technical communities on the one hand, and governments of developing countries on the other.

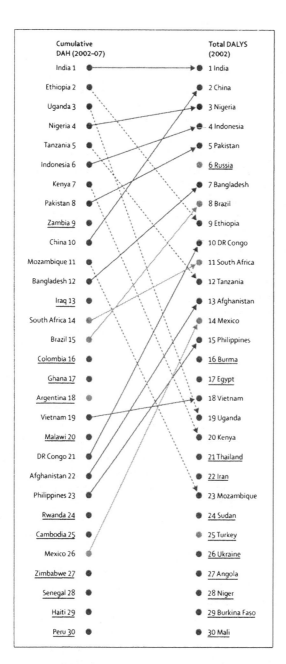

Cumulative DAH (2002–07)	Total DALYS (2002)
India 1	1 India
Ethiopia 2	2 China
Uganda 3	3 Nigeria
Nigeria 4	4 Indonesia
Tanzania 5	5 Pakistan
Indonesia 6	6 Russia
Kenya 7	7 Bangladesh
Pakistan 8	8 Brazil
Zambia 9	9 Ethiopia
China 10	10 DR Congo
Mozambique 11	11 South Africa
Bangladesh 12	12 Tanzania
Iraq 13	13 Afghanistan
South Africa 14	14 Mexico
Brazil 15	15 Philippines
Colombia 16	16 Burma
Ghana 17	17 Egypt
Argentina 18	18 Vietnam
Vietnam 19	19 Uganda
Malawi 20	20 Kenya
DR Congo 21	21 Thailand
Afghanistan 22	22 Iran
Philippines 23	23 Mozambique
Rwanda 24	24 Sudan
Cambodia 25	25 Turkey
Mexico 26	26 Ukraine
Zimbabwe 27	27 Angola
Senegal 28	28 Niger
Haiti 29	29 Burkina Faso
Peru 30	30 Mali

Figure 8 30 countries with greatest development assistance for health (DAH) from 2002 to 2007, compared with 30 countries with greatest all-cause disease burden in 2002.

Countries of low, lower-middle, and upper-middle income are shown with red, blue, and green markers and arrows, respectively. Countries in either column that received a rank lower than 30 in the other column and are, therefore, unmatched in the figure are underlined. Only DAH allocable by country is shown. DALY=disability-adjusted life-year DR=Democratic Republic.

Although HIV/AIDS, tuberculosis, and malaria account for an important part of the expansion in resources, other areas of health have also increased. While there is much discussion among donors about increasing funds transferred to developing countries through general health-sector support, the data suggest that it remains a very small part of DAH. The difference between the rhetoric and reality emphasises the value of resource tracking.

Any presentation or analysis of this type will inevitably lead to debate about the validity of the figures for all the institutions presented here. Even financial officers of the organisations that we are tracking might disagree with our figures. Although many of these differences can be accounted for on the basis of research strategies used in the study (detailed in the webappendix), we firmly believe that the best way forward will be to foster a vigorous and open debate about all the data. A broader understanding of the intricacies involved in such analysis will hopefully produce improved data in the future.

We believe that our figures provide an accurate portrayal of the reality of DAH. Nevertheless, our study has limitations. We have not included private resources raised by non-US NGOs and foundations. We obtained data for health expenditure for 1–7 years for a few large non-US NGOs for 2000–06, but were unable to include these figures in our DAH totals because we were missing data before 2000. We do not capture financial flows from low-income and middle-income countries to other such countries, and flows from non-OECD high-income countries to those of low and middle income. The most important case in this category is probably China, which is believed to be scaling up international assistance to other low-income and middle-income countries. We do not provide separate estimates for country-specific DAH and DAH for objectives such as research and development that serve many countries.[30] We have had to estimate disbursements from commitments for many donors. The validity of our results thus depends on the mapping of commitment to disbursement by donor. It would be desirable to have donors provide the full sequence of disbursements going back in time to 1990. We have also estimated health expenditures for the US NGOs. Although some of the quantities are estimated with statistical methods, we are unable to report uncertainty for our estimates at this time. These are all areas that we will work to improve in future years.

In this study we report DAH up to 2007; because of the lags in data reporting we are unable to report DAH disbursements or commitments in 2008. The 14–20 month lag in most of the data sources means that tracking trends in a timely way is very difficult at present. The current financial crisis has drawn attention to the importance of this situation. Concerns that development assistance could drop have been widely expressed.[5–7] At present, we have no real data for what is actually happening. Private foundations have lost a considerable component of their assets, which will inevitably lead to decreased donation. The key unknown is whether public monies for DAH will grow at a slower rate, stay constant, or contract. The need for timelier reporting of commitments and disbursements by institutions is reinforced in this setting of global recession and financial turmoil.

In this Article, we have not examined what happens when resources are received by an implementing government or NGO, and what proportion is spent at different points in the system. Answering these questions is essential to advance our understanding of the actual flow of resources within recipient countries. A related question asks what developing-country governments do with their own resources when they receive increased health aid. Some of the authors of this Article are engaged in research that uses DAH disbursement estimates and data for government health expenditure to investigate this crucial issue. Tracking flows for other sectors such as education, water and sanitation, and poverty alleviation, all of which affect health, will yield additional insights about development assistance to low-income and middle-income countries.

Timely and reliable information about DAH is essential for national policy making and planning. It is also needed for monitoring whether donors are honouring their commitments, to foster greater transparency in aid reporting, and as an essential component of assessments of effectiveness. As the debate on aid effectiveness intensifies,[31] careful documentation of the magnitude of DAH can be a key building block for an evidence-based discussion.

Contributors

NR managed the research project, undertook data analysis, contributed to the interpretation of the data, and drafted the Article. PG created the integrated databases, undertook data analysis, developed tools for visualisation of the results, and contributed to the interpretation of the data. RJC implemented the survey of US NGOs, undertook data collection, and coded grants from foundations. KLK compiled data for private flows and generated maps. CMM assisted with data collection and analysis. DTJ contributed to development of the conceptual basis for this research and to interpretation of the results. CJLM made key contributions to developing methods for data analysis, interpreting the data, and writing the Article.

Conflicts of interest

We declare that we have no conflicts of interest.

Acknowledgments

We thank Richard Feachem, Julio Frenk, and members of IHME's Advisory Panel on Financial Resources for Health for their advice and comments; the various people at the OECD Development Assistance Committee, The Global Fund to Fight AIDS, Tuberculosis, and Malaria, GAVI, UNICEF, WHO, UNFPA, UNAIDS, the World Bank, and several NGOs who responded to data requests and queries from us; Stanislava Nikolova for help with editing the paper; Meghan Werner for logistical support; and David Sapienza, Christina Bernard, Shannon Harris, Jennifer Berthiaume, and Haley Lee for assistance with data collection.

References

1 Farmer P., Garrett L. From "marvelous momentum" to health care for all: success is possible with the right programs. *Foreign Affairs* 2007; **86**: 155–61. http://www.foreignafrairs.org/20070301faresponse86213/paul-farmer-laurie-garrett/from-marvelous-momentum-to-health-care-for-all-success-is-possible-with-the-right-programs.html (accessed March 11, 2009).

2 Farrar J. Global health science: a threat and an opportunity for collaborative clinical science. *Nat Immunol* 2007; **8**: 1277–79.

3 Garrett L. The challenge of global health. *Foreign Affairs* 2007; **86**: 14. http://www.foreignaffairs.org/20070101faessay86103/laurie-garrett/the-challenge-of-global-health.html (accessed March 11, 2009).

4 Schieber G. J., Gottret P., Fleisher L. K., Leive A. A. Financing global health: mission unaccomplished. *Health Aff (Millwood)* 2007; **26**: 921–34.

5 Kaiser Daily HIV/AIDS Report. HIV/AIDS / global financial crisis could harm HIV/AIDS funding, Piot says. October 29, 2008. http://www.globalhealthreporting.org/article.asp?DR_ID=55258 (accessed March 11, 2009).

6 McNeil D. G. Jr. Global fund is billions short. *New York Times* (New York), Feb 2, 2009: D6. http://www.nytimes.com/2009/02/03/health/research/03glob.html?_r=2 (accessed March 11, 2009).

7 UN News Centre. Financial crisis threatens push to boost global health, says top UN official. November 12, 2008. http://www.un.org/apps/news/story.asp?NewsID=28911&Cr=financial&Cr1=crisis (accessed March 11, 2009).

8 Eiseman E., Fossum D. The challenges of creating a global health resource tracking system. Santa Monica: Rand Corporation, 2005.

9 Global Health Resource Tracking Working Group. Following the money in global health. Center for Global Development, 2005. http://www.cgdev.org/doc/ghprn/FollowingMoney_GlobalHealth.pdf (accessed March 11, 2009).

10 Levine R., Blumer K. Gaps and missing links: what do we know about resources in global health? Paper presented at Forum 8, Mexico City, November 2004. Center for Global Development. http://www.globalforumhealth.org/Forum8/Forum8-CDROM/OralPresentations/Levine%20R%20F8-358.doc (accessed March 11, 2009).

11 Powell-Jackson T., Mills A. A review of health resource tracking in developing countries. *Health Policy Plan* 2007; **22**: 353–62.

12 Sridhar D., Batniji R. Misfinancing global health: a case for transparency in disbursements and decision making. *Lancet* 2008; **372**: 1185–91.

13 Organisation for Economic Co-operation and Development. Purpose of aid charts: focus on aid to health. http://www.oecd.org/document/44/0,3343,en_2649_34469_24670956_1_1_1_1,00.html (accessed March 11, 2009).

14 Hudson Institute. The index of global philanthropy 2008. Washington, DC: Hudson Institute Center for Global Prosperity, 2008. http://www.global-prosperity. org (accessed May 12, 2008).

15 Organisation for Economic Co-operation and Development. Measuring aid to health. Paris: OECD-DAC, 2008. http://www.oecd.org/dataoecd/20/46/41453717. pdf (accessed March 11, 2009).

16 Ethelston S., Bechtel A., Chaya N., Kantner A., Vogel C. G. Progress and promises: trends in international assistance for reproductive health and population, 2004. Washington, DC: Population Action International, 2004.

17 Narasimhan V., Attaran A. Roll back malaria? The scarcity of international aid for malaria control. *Malar J.* 2003; **2**: 8.

18 Powell-Jackson T., Borghi J., Mueller D. H., Patouillard E., Mills A. Countdown to 2015: tracking donor assistance to maternal, newborn, and child health. *Lancet* 2006; **368**: 1077–87.

19 Waddington C., Martin J., Walford V. Trends in international funding for malaria control. Prepared for the Roll Back Malaria Partnership. London: HLSP Institute, 2005.

20 Kates J., Morrison J. S., Lief E. Global health funding: a glass half full? *Lancet* 2006; **368**: 187–88.

21 Michaud C. Development assistance for health: recent trends and resource allocation. Boston: Harvard Center for Population Development, 2003.

22 Michaud C., Murray C. J. External assistance to the health sector in developing countries: a detailed analysis, 1972–90. *Bull World Health Organ* 1994; **72**: 639–51.

23 WHO. WHO burden of disease data. Previous estimates: 2000–2002. Geneva: World Health Organization, 2004. http://www.who.int/healthinfo/global_burden_disease/estimates_2000_2002/en/index.html (accessed Feb 1, 2009).

24 United Nations. Population Division. World population prospects: the 2008 revision. Population database. New York: United Nations, 2008. http://esa.un.org/unpp/index.asp (accessed Aug 1, 2008).

25 International Monetary Fund. World economic outlook database. Washington, DC: IMF, 2008. http://www.imf.org/external/pubs/ft/weo/2008/02/weodata/index. aspx. (accessed Aug 1, 2008).

26 United Nations. Statistics Division. National accounts main aggregates database. New York: United Nations, 2008. http://unstats.un.org/unsd/snaama/dnllist.asp (accessed Aug 1, 2008).

27 World Bank. World development indicators online. Washington, DC: World Bank, 2008. http://web.worldbank.org (accessed Aug 1, 2008).

28 WHO. WHO national health accounts. Geneva: World Health Organization, 2009. http://www.who.int/nha/country/en/index.html (accessed March 12, 2009).

29 Reich M. R., Wagner A. K., McLaughlin T. J., Dumbaugh K. A., Derai-Cochin M. Pharmaceutical donations by the USA: an assessment of relevance and time-to-expiry. *Bull World Health Organ* 1999; **77**: 675–80.

30 Jamison D. T., Frenk J., Knaul F. International collective action in health: objectives, functions, and rationale. *Lancet* 1998; **351**: 514–17

31 Moyo D. Dead aid: why aid is not working and how there is a better way for Africa. New York: Farrar, Straus and Giroux, 2009.

72

GLOBAL HEALTH FUNDING

How much, where it comes from and where it goes

David McCoy, Sudeep Chand and Devi Sridhar

Source: *Health Policy and Planning*, 24 (2009), 407–17.

Global health funding has increased in recent years. This has been accompanied by a proliferation in the number of global health actors and initiatives. This paper describes the state of global heath finance, taking into account government and private sources of finance, and raises and discusses a number of policy issues related to global health governance. A schematic describing the different actors and three global health finance functions is used to organize the data presented, most of which are secondary data from the published literature and annual reports of relevant actors. In two cases, we also refer to currently unpublished primary data that have been collected by authors of this paper. Among the findings are that the volume of official development assistance for health is frequently inflated; and that data on private sources of global health finance are inadequate but indicate a large and important role of private actors. The fragmented, complicated, messy and inadequately tracked state of global health finance requires immediate attention. In particular it is necessary to track and monitor global health finance that is channelled by and through private sources, and to critically examine who benefits from the rise in global health spending.

Key messages

- It is frequently stated that global health funding has increased dramatically over the past decade. However, there are inadequate data to describe the precise volume of global health expenditure; the source of this funding; its management; and how it is spent.
- A detailed description of global health funding is needed to improve the efficiency, accountability, performance and equity-impact of the many actors that populate the global health landscape.
- In particular, it is necessary to track and monitor the activities of non-OECD donors as well as the funding that is sourced by and channelled through private actors.

Introduction

By most accounts, global funding for health has increased dramatically. According to the World Bank, development assistance for health grew from US$2.5 billion in 1990 to almost US$14 billion in 2005 (World Bank 2007). A recent article in *The Lancet* claimed that *official* development assistance (ODA) grew from US$8.5 billion in 2000 to US$13.5 billion in 2004 (Kates *et al.* 2006). In addition to the increase in ODA, there has been an increase in private funding for global health, which is said to now account for about a quarter of all development aid for health (Bloom 2007).

The increase in global funding for health has been accompanied by a rapid and large increase in the number of global health actors, transforming the global health landscape and making it more difficult to study. In 2004, a Global Health Resource Tracking Working Group was established to calculate the amount of funding devoted to global health. It concluded, more than 2 years later, that the task was too difficult because of: the large and diverse number of public and private sources of funding; the many types of activities and programmes that fall under the term 'global health'; the use of 'in-kind' donations of drugs and other inputs; inadequate financial management information systems; and poorly designed donor accounting structures (CGD 2007). One of its key recommendations was for better tracking and monitoring of global health financing.

This paper uses existing data on global health financing (mainly in 2006) to paint a picture of global health financing and to raise a number of policy issues and questions about 'global health'. It defines 'global health financing' as any external finance channelled towards the *health sector* of low and middle income countries (LMICs) in order to meet the needs of predominantly poor population groups. This definition excludes external finance aimed at reducing poverty, food insecurity, and the lack of access to water, sanitation and education, which are important for health, as well as emergency/humanitarian aid (e.g. in response to conflict or natural disasters), even though this includes medical care. In addition, commercial bank loans and private foreign investment directed at the health sector of LMICs are also excluded.

We mainly use publicly-available secondary data from the published literature and the annual reports of relevant actors. In addition, we quote a few unpublished data on the global health grants of some private foundations from a paper that is currently in press elsewhere. Presenting data on income and expenditure is complicated by different annual financial reporting cycles, different accounting practices and different currencies. However, we have not adjusted the data in order to standardize for a given period or time. Most of the secondary financial data were available as US dollars. Where this was not the case, we have converted currencies to US dollars based on average nominal currency exchange rates for the relevant year.

A schematic for the global health financing landscape

The schematic (Figure 1) we developed consists of three functions related to global health finance combined with a set of categories for the various actors involved in global health. The first function is labelled 'providing' and is concerned with the need to raise or generate global health funds. It consists of four main categories of actors: donor country governments; private foundations; the general public; and businesses/private corporations.

The second function is 'managing' and is concerned with the management or pooling of global health funds as well as with mechanisms for channelling funds to recipients. It has six categories of actors: the official bilateral aid agencies of donor countries such as USAID (US) and DFID (UK);

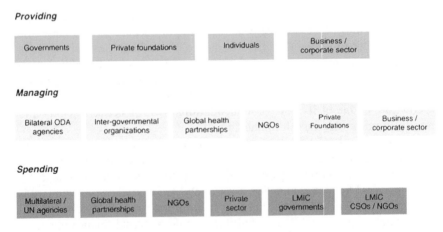

Figure 1 Schematic of the global health financing landscape.

intergovernmental organizations (IGOs) that provide grants or concessionary loans for health improvement, in particular the World Bank and European Commission; global health partnerships (GHPs) with a primary funding role such as the Global Fund to fight HIV/AIDS, TB and Malaria (Global Fund) and Global Alliance for Vaccines and Immunization (GAVI); non-governmental organizations (NGOs); private foundations; and the business/corporate sector.

The third function is 'spending' and is concerned with the expenditure and consumption of global health finance. It consists of six main categories of actors: multilateral agencies with a health focus such as the World Health Organization (WHO), UNICEF and UNAIDS; GHPs; private sector, for-profit organizations; LMIC governments; and LMIC civil society organizations (CSOs).

While this schematic reflects the appearance of an ordered global health landscape, the reality is much more chaotic. For example, several actors perform all three functions simultaneously, thus obscuring the different operational components of global health finance. In addition, the system for categorizing the different actors does not reveal the overlapping and fuzzy boundaries between them, nor the existence of hybrid organizations. Nonetheless, we believe that the schematic provides a useful framework for describing and studying global health finance. This article will now unpack and discuss each of the three functions of global health finance and their respective categories of actors, before discussing the overall picture of global health finance and various policy implications.

Providing global health finance

Governments

The official development assistance (ODA) budgets and programmes of donor country governments are a major source of global health finance. The Development Assistance Committee (DAC) of the Organisation for Economic Cooperation and Development (OECD) monitors the development assistance of 22 major donor countries[1] plus the European Commission. In 2006, the total amount of ODA disbursed by the DAC donors was US$104.4 billion, including US$7.5 billion of debt relief (OECD 2008b).

Table 1 shows DAC donor commitments and actual disbursements of ODA for 'Health' and 'Population' (which includes reproductive health care, family planning, control of sexually transmitted infections, and HIV/AIDS) in 2004, 2005 and 2006. It also provides figures for 'Water and Sanitation' and 'Emergency Response' (which covers material relief assistance and services, emergency food aid, relief co-ordination and protection services, but excludes longer term reconstruction and rehabilitation, and disaster prevention and preparedness).

Table 1 Development assistance from Development Assistance Committee (DAC) donors for selected sectors, 2004–06 (US$ millions).

	2004			2005			2006		
	H & P	*W & S*	*ER*	*H & P*	*W & S*	*ER*	*H & P*	*W & S*	*ER*
Commitments	8495	4828	6042	10 340	6031	8210	13 645	6382	6712
Disbursements	5962	2309	5283	8112	3351	8216	9577	3476	6797

Source: OECD (2008a).
Notes: H = Health; P = Population; W = Water; S = Sanitation; ER = Emergency Response.

The data show a clear rise in ODA for health and population, with disbursements increasing from US$5.96 billion in 2004 to US$9.58 billion in 2006 (about 10% of total ODA in that year). They also show a significant difference between commitments and actual disbursements of ODA to health. In 2006 for example, disbursements were more than US$4 billion less than commitments. If 'water and sanitation' are combined with 'health and population', the shortfall between what is pledged and what is actually disbursed increases to about US$7 billion.

The data also indicate that the figures quoted earlier about the increase in development assistance for health (the Lancet article estimated a figure of US$13.5 billion in 2004 and the World Bank estimated that development assistance for health had increased to almost US$14 billion in 2005) appear to be exaggerations. Actual *disbursements* of ODA for health and population by DAC donors only amounted to US$9.58 billion in 2005.

While these data represent important landmarks on the global health financing landscape, there are a number of points to note. First, increases in the volume of ODA for health may be offset by reductions in domestic spending and budget allocations. Ultimately, what matters are trends in overall health spending at the country level. Secondly, although the data from DAC covers the major donor governments involved in global health, several non-DAC countries are significant providers of ODA.

It is generally accepted that there are poor data on non-DAC ODA (Harmer and Cotterrell 2005; Brown and Morton 2008). However, the World Bank (2008) has estimated that non-DAC ODA in 2006, excluding ODA from China, amounted to US$5.17 billion. The size of China's ODA is not known with any degree of accuracy, but a general view is that China is becoming a significant player. For example, it has been reported that aid from China to Africa will reach US$1bn in 2009, over and above support for debt cancellation and training of African professionals (Manji 2008). India is also showing increased presence as a donor. India's allocation of foreign aid for 2007–08 amounted to just under US$226 million, most of which was allocated to the countries in the region, particularly Bhutan and Afghanistan (Sridhar 2008).

Although there are no data on the size of the contribution of non-DAC donors to global health, a couple of general points about non-DAC ODA might be used to estimate the size of their contribution to global health. First, many non-DAC countries provide the bulk of their ODA for emergency and humanitarian crises (Harmer and Cotterell 2005). According to one analysis, non-DAC humanitarian assistance in 2006 amounted to US$435 million (Development Initiatives 2008, p. 10). If spending on the health sector is assumed to be half that of spending on humanitarian assistance, the non-DAC contribution to global health finance would be estimated to be about US$220 million. Secondly, it seems unlikely that non-DAC countries would allocate a higher proportion of their overall ODA to 'health' compared with DAC countries. Therefore, if a relatively generous assumption is made that 10% of non-DAC ODA is allocated to health and if total non-DAC ODA amounted to about US$7 billion in 2006, our estimate of the non-DAC contribution to global health finance would be about US$700 million.

Private foundations

Data on the contribution made by private foundations towards international development are relatively limited. The World Bank stated that in 2005 private donors gave roughly US$4–4.5 billion to international development, but noted that philanthropic giving 'is significantly under-researched due to the lack of a world-wide data collection procedure' (Sulla 2006).

Private foundations have been important actors in the health sector for decades, mainly because of their ability to use funding to shape international health policy and the broader discourse around global health (Birn and Solorzano 1999; Fox 2006). However, the entry of the Bill & Melinda Gates Foundation into the global health landscape (bringing with it also the donation of US$30 billion by Warren Buffett) has taken private, philanthropic funding for international development, especially for health, to new and unprecedented heights. One estimate of the amount of private foundation spending on global health in 2005 was US$1.6 billion, much of it coming from the Gates Foundation (MacArthur 2006).

In 2006, the Gates Foundation awarded 195 global health grants amounting to US$2.25bn in total (McCoy *et al.* 2009). In terms of money paid out to global health grants, US$916 million and US$1.22 billion were disbursed in 2006 and 2007, respectively. The Foundation is now a bigger international health donor than all governments bar the United States and the United Kingdom.

Other prominent foundations operating in the health sector include the Rockefeller Foundation, the Wellcome Trust, the Ford Foundation, UN Foundation and the Aga Khan Foundation. The total expenditures of these foundations in 2006, together with an estimation of the international health grants awarded by the Wellcome Trust, the Ford Foundation and the Rockefeller Foundation, are shown in Table 2.

Table 2 Total expenditure and value of international health grants awarded by selected private foundations in 2006.

	Total expenditure 2006 (US$ million)[a]	Value of international health grants awarded in 2006 (US$ million)
Wellcome Trust	1000[b]	US$42[b]
Rockefeller Foundation	193.24	US$15.7
Ford Foundation	683.98	US$7.5
UN Foundation	306	–
Aga Khan Foundation	184.9	–

[a]*Sources*: Wellcome Trust Annual Report and Financial Statements 2006; The Rockefeller Foundation 2007 Annual Report; Ford Foundation Annual Report 2006; Aga Khan Foundation Annual Report 2006.
[b]Rough approximation, converted from UK sterling.

Finally, it should be noted that, particularly in the US, tax breaks afforded to private foundations amount to a public subsidy of their budgets and expenditure. In the US, it is estimated that 45% of the US$500 billion that foundations hold actually 'belongs to the American public' in the sense that it is money foregone by the state through tax exemptions (Dowie 2002).

The general public

The general public contributes to development finance in LMICs mainly indirectly through their tax contributions to the public budget of donor governments. They also make direct contributions, mainly through donations made to NGOs and remittances made by migrant workers. The latter source of funding, although considerable and an important source of income for many poor households in LMICs, is not usually allocated specifically to health nor considered part of the development assistance architecture, and is therefore not considered further in this paper.

There are no reliable data on the amount of money raised by private individuals to support NGO health programmes and projects in LMICs. However, we know that the amount generated for humanitarian disasters can be considerable. Voluntary contributions for humanitarian relief to the Red Cross/Red Crescent and 19 of the largest NGOs in 2006 was estimated to amount to US$2.31 billion (Development Initiatives 2008, p. 10), and about US$5 billion was raised by the general public in response to the Indian Ocean tsunami in 2004 (Tsunami Evaluation Coalition 2006).

Another way of estimating individual contributions to global health is to examine the income of international NGOs. For example, in 2006, the total income of the Medecins Sans Frontieres (MSF) international movement was approximately US$714 million (converted from Euro), of which 71.2%

came from private individuals (MSF 2006). The Rotarian Foundation is another NGO with a health focus that relies on contributions from private individuals—presently, the Rotarian movement has a target to raise US$100 million dollars over 3 years to support the international effort to eradicate polio. However, most of the wealthiest international NGOs tend to work across a range of development sectors, making it difficult to estimate the amount allocated to health specifically.

Business/corporate sector

Private companies and corporations contribute to development objectives and global health through 'corporate social responsibility' programmes, or what is referred to by some as 'corporate philanthropy'. As with private foundations, the existence of tax exemptions for some such activities means that a proportion of the expenditure consists of a public subsidy.

There are few data on 'corporate social responsibility' programmes (CGD 2007). Some papers argue that corporate donations to charities are less in aggregate than those made by private individuals (Andreoni 2001; Charities Aid Foundation 2003). As an illustration, 3.5% of MSF's income in 2006 came from private companies compared with 72.9% from individuals.

The most important corporate actors in the health sector are the large pharmaceutical companies. Although contributions to global health by pharmaceutical companies can be seen as forms of marketing and investment in business development, their dollar amounts are not insignificant. A review of the International Federation of Pharmaceutical Manufacturers & Associations (IFPMA) Health Partnerships Survey found that the industry's combined contribution to the health-related MDGs in 2006 totalled US$1.9bn (Kanavos *et al.* 2008). This included the costs of donated commodities, commodities sold at cost, cash, health care provision and training interventions.

As an example, the contributions to global health listed by Pfizer on its website include: providing 87 million treatments of azithromycin for the International Trachoma Initiative since 1998; donating US$735 million worth of fluconazole for AIDS treatment since 2000; funding 171 Pfizer Global Health Fellows (including Pfizer clinicians, epidemiologists, laboratory technicians, marketing managers and financial administrators) to work with NGOs in developing countries since 2003; and committing US$33 million to improve cancer and tobacco-related health outcomes in 2007 over 3 years.

Managing global health money

Bilateral aid agencies

About three-quarters of *disbursements* of official development assistance for health by DAC countries in 2006 were channelled bilaterally (see Table 3).

Table 3 Disbursements of official development assistance by Development Assistance Committee (DAC) donors, 2006 (US$ millions).

| | *2006* | | |
	H & P	*W & S*	*ER*
Bilateral	7173	3074	5930
Multilateral	2404	402	867
Total	9577	3476	6797

Source: OECD (2008a).
Notes: H = Health; P = Population; W = Water; S = Sanitation; ER = Emergency Response.

As far as non-DAC countries are concerned, an even higher proportion of ODA is channelled bilaterally (Harmer and Cotterrell 2005). Much of this bilateral funding is directed by donor governments through dedicated 'aid agencies', often located within Ministries of Foreign Affairs.

The biggest donor governments for global health are the United States and the United Kingdom. UK aid for international health amounted to US$1.62 billion in 2006 and was mainly managed by the Department for International Development (DFID). Foreign assistance for health from the US amounted to approximately US$4.19 billion in 2006. However, unlike the UK, the US channels its foreign assistance through multiple government agencies including USAID, PEPFAR, the President's Malaria Initiative and the Department of State (Global Health Watch 2008).

Inter-governmental organizations

Most of the ODA for health that is channelled multilaterally flows through two inter-governmental organizations: the World Bank and the European Commission (EC), the latter in the case of European donor countries.

The World Bank provides global health funding in the form of grants and concessionary loans to recipient countries through the International Development Association (IDA), which is mainly funded from the ODA budgets of donor countries. IDA spending on 'Health, Nutrition and Population' amounted to US$0.8 billion in financial year 2006 (World Bank 2007, p. 42). The Bank also makes loans for development to governments through the International Bank for Reconstruction and Development (IBRD) and for private sector development through the International Finance Corporation (IFC). Some of these monies may be directed at the health sector but do not fall into the definition of global health finance used in this paper.

As far as the EC is concerned, their role in helping to manage global health finance is smaller than the World Bank, but appears to be growing. The EC is reported to have disbursed US$421 million to 'health and population'

342

programmes in 2005 (Action for Global Health 2007), while in 2006, spending on 'health', 'population' and 'reproductive health' was said to have amounted to US$580.17 million (Action for Global Health 2008, p. 10).

Global health partnerships

The emergence of GHPs has been an important development of the global health architecture in recent years. Some have been established specifically to act as global health funding agents, two of which stand out: the Global Fund and GAVI.

Income to the Global Fund was US$2.56 billion in 2006 and US$3.15 billion in 2007; while expenditure was US$1.90 billion and US$2.71 billion in 2006 and 2007, respectively (Global Fund 2007a). GAVI's expenditure in 2006 was considerably less, at US$563.05 million (GAVI 2007). Although these two agencies are often described as *sources* of global health finance, most of their income comes from donor governments.

The Global Fund is funded by governments through bilateral channels as well as through the EC (which has pledged approximately US$1.18 billion between 2002 and 2010). Private funding to the Global Fund has been relatively small, although it increased in 2006 following a pledge of US$500 million by the Gates Foundation over 3.5 years. There has been some other private financing to the Global Fund through the (RED)™ Initiative which gets participating companies to contribute a percentage of their sales to the Fund. As of March 2008, the Initiative had contributed US$61 million. So far the Global Fund has discouraged private sector assistance in the form of in-kind contributions (Global Fund 2008b).

Donors can support GAVI in three different ways. First, through direct donations; second, by making long-term pledges to The International Finance Facility for Immunization, which effectively allows GAVI to draw down on future government donor pledges towards development assistance; and third, by making pledges to the Advance Market Commitment mechanism which supports the development and availability of a pneumococcal vaccine for developing countries.

According to GAVI Alliance Progress Reports, cumulative support to countries from 2000 to 2006 and from 2000 to 2007 amounted to about US$962 million and US$1.411 billion, respectively (GAVI Alliance 2006; GAVI Alliance 2007). From this we can infer that cumulative support to countries in 2007 was approximately US$449 million. In terms of total expenses however, the figures were US$1.216 billion and US$793 million for 2007 and 2006, respectively (GAVI 2008a).

Most of GAVI's funding comes from government donors (GAVI 2007). The US, one of GAVI's original six donors, has contributed a total of US$421.81 million over 7 years. Another of GAVI's original six donors, the UK, contributed US$121.56 million between 1999 and 2008. Canada had contributed US$148.73 million by the end of 2007, and Norway's contributions by 2007 amounted to US$291.89 million. Both the World Bank and the EC fund GAVI as well, although in relatively small amounts. But funding from the Bill & Melinda Gates Foundation is much more significant. An initial 5-year grant of US$750 million in 1999 helped establish the GAVI Fund. The Foundation pledged a further US$750 million in 2005, committing a total of US$1.51 billion to the end of 2014 (GAVI 2008b). Other foundations and individual donors contributed US$8.03 million between 1999 and 2007.

Two other actors worth mentioning are the Affordable Medicines Facility for Malaria (AMFm) and UNITAID because they exemplify the creation of global agencies charged specifically to manage the purchase of medical commodities. The AMFm was established to help purchase artemisinin-combined treatments for malaria, and is estimated to require a budget of US$1.5–1.9 billion over 5 years (AMFm 2008). UNITAID was established to provide long-term and predictable funding to purchase and help reduce the prices of drugs and diagnostics for HIV/AIDS, malaria and tuberculosis. According to its 2007 annual report, UNITAID's total expenditure from November 2006 to December 2007 was US$148 million (WHO 2008). However, it is thought that expenditure could rise to US$500m in 2009 (UNITAID 2008).

Most of the funding for the AMFm is expected to come from ODA. However, UNITAID is notable in that about 82% of its funding comes from an airline ticket levy (UNITAID 2008), pointing to the need to consider consumption taxes as a new source of global health funding.

Non-government organizations (NGOs)

As mentioned earlier, NGOs are major recipients of donations made by private individuals, effectively pooling and managing their contributions. Many NGOs also receive funding from governments and philanthropic foundations.

Over recent years, the non-government sector has grown to become a significant player in international development. An OECD-DAC Advisory Group (2008) estimated that CSOs raised US$20–25 billion in 2006, of which US$14.7 billion was raised from the ODA of DAC donor countries. It is not known what percentage of this funding is spent on health, but it is likely that the percentage is higher than the 10% of DAC ODA that is allocated to health. An estimate of 20% would mean that between US$4–5 billon was spent on global health by CSOs in 2006.

Most of the funding for international NGOs in Europe comes from private sources. For example, 87% of MSF's income comes from private donations, about two-thirds of which comes from individuals. However, the delivery of government foreign assistance through private voluntary organizations (PVOs) is a prominent feature of the United States. In FY2007, USAID channelled US$2.4 billion of ODA through PVOs (USAID 2007). The percentage of US ODA channelled through PVOs increased from 0.18% in 1980 to 6% in 2002 (OECD 2005). As a consequence, many US-based NGOs are heavily funded by the US government. For example, Care International USA receives about 60% of its income from the US government, while about a quarter of World Vision US's income comes from the US government.

NGOs also receive funding from philanthropic foundations. Some NGOs, for example, are major recipients of Gates Foundation grants. One such NGO is the Seattle-based organization PATH, which received a number of grants from the Gates Foundation between 1999 and 2007, the sum of which amounted to US$824.09 million (McCoy *et al.* 2009). Universities are also recipients of grants from the Gates Foundation and other foundations such as the Wellcome Trust. Johns Hopkins University, for example, has received US$192.32 million worth of grants from the Gates Foundation (McCoy *et al.* 2009).

Private foundations and the business/corporate sector

Private foundations and private companies can also be 'managers' of global health finance as well as 'providers' of global health finance by virtue of implementing their own programmes and projects. The budgets they manage are derived from their own income, although, as mentioned earlier, a significant amount of this income arises from public subsidies made in the form of tax exemptions.

Spending global health funding

Multilateral agencies/IGOs

UN agencies with a health mandate are one important category of recipients of global health finance. Three key agencies are the WHO, UNICEF and UNAIDS. The WHO has a budget of about US$4.2 billion for the current 2008/2009 biennium (WHO 2007a), an increase from the previous biennium budget of about US$3.3 billion. Although total income to UNICEF is greater, having risen from US$2.78 billion in 2006 to $3.01 billion in 2007 (UNICEF 2007), only a proportion of this is spent specifically on health. UNAIDS' expenditure, by comparison, is small. In 2006/07, it spent US$292 million, although US$120.7 million was transferred back to its 'cosponsors' (including WHO, UNICEF and the World Bank) to implement activities under its unified budget and workplan.

Inter-governmental organizations such as WHO and UNICEF tend to be mainly government-funded. However, private foundations are not a negligible source of funding for the WHO. In 2006, the Gates Foundation was the third equal largest funder of the WHO (Global Health Watch 2008). UNICEF also receives non-governmental funding. In 2007, while the public sector (governments and other IGOs) contributed to 65.4% of UNICEF income, private sector contributions totalled US\$868 million (28.8%), most of which was raised by local UNICEF 'national committees' that run public fundraising activities. Foundations and GHPs also contribute to UNICEF, particularly for health. For example, in 2007, the UN Foundation contributed US\$71.8 million, GAVI provided US\$47.8 million, the Global Fund granted US\$12.3 million, the Canadian Micronutrient Initiative gave US\$10.3 million, and Rotary International awarded US\$7.5 million.

While being major recipients of global health funding, WHO and UNICEF also fund other organizations, illustrating another example of the limitation of the schematic used in this paper. The WHO, for example, funds a considerable amount of technical work conducted by research institutes and universities. And similarly, UNICEF funds government and nongovernment agencies to conduct a variety of health care activities.

Global health partnerships

Unlike the Global Fund and GAVI, many GHPs are not funding agencies but are primarily implementing agencies (although some also award grants to other actors). They include the Stop TB Partnership, the Medicines for Malaria Venture, the International Trachoma Initiative, and several that have been established to develop new vaccines and medicines. Funding sources for these partnerships vary but usually include a mix of government ODA, philanthropic funding, private individual donations and in-kind contributions from the private sector. As many as seventy GHPs exist with aggregate annual expenditure running into hundreds of millions of dollars, although individually most spend less than US\$100 million per year.

The expenditure of the Stop TB Partnership in 2006 was US\$52.97 million, with 93% of this funding coming from governments, US\$2.1 million coming from foundations and Novartis contributing US\$3.2 million worth of drug donations (WHO 2007b). Income into the Medicines for Malaria Venture (MMV) was US\$76.97 million in 2007, up from US\$30.62 million in 2006 (79% of funding in 2007 came from 'private foundations and individuals', mainly the Gates Foundation) (MMV 2007). The Global Alliance for TB Drug Development spent US\$20.09 million in 2006 (TB Alliance 2007), while the International AIDS Vaccine Initiative spent US\$76.99 million and US\$87 million in 2006 and 2007, respectively (over 80% of funding coming from governments). The International Partnership for Microbicides spent about US\$72 million in 2006 (IPM 2006) and the Drugs for Neglected Diseases Initiative spent US\$8.27 million in 2006 (DNDi 2006).

Non-government organizations

International NGOs are significant spenders of global health finance. There are now a huge number of NGOs operating in the field of international

346

development and health. Their funding comes from multiple sources and it is not possible to establish an accurate figure for the amount of global health finance spent by NGOs. However, it is worth noting the budgets and expenditures of some of the larger NGOs in order to gain some perspective on the significance of their presence on the global health landscape.

Save the Children US and UK spent US$361.2 million and approximately US$280 million, respectively, in fiscal year 2007, a proportion of which would have been on child health. Care International USA and Oxfam Great Britain spent US$608 million and approximately US$426.5 million, respectively, in 2007. Total expenditure of the MSF international movement in 2006 was approximately US$700 million. The combined income of World Vision US and UK in 2007 was just over US$1 billion. The Clinton Foundation spent US$92.79 million in 2006, of which 30% was allocated to its HIV/AIDS Initiative which focuses on paediatric AIDS treatment, and 8% to its Global Initiative which funds a number of health programmes (William J. Clinton Foundation 2007). The Carter Centre's health programme expenses for 2006 were US$95.59 million.

Private sector

The private sector is also a big spender of global health finance, although a large amount of corporate contributions in the form of drug donations or discounts can effectively be viewed as money spent by those companies on themselves. In addition, a large amount of other global health spending is directed at the purchase of medicines and other commodities from private companies. For example, up to and including the Global Fund's six rounds of funding, an estimated 48% of expenditure was on commodities, products and medicines from the private sector (Global Fund 2007b). A large proportion of Gates funding is also channelled to the private sector, either to stimulate new research and development or to help purchase existing products. Similarly, a large proportion of spending by the GAVI Alliance, the Clinton Foundation, the Affordable Medicines Facility for Malaria and UNITAID will be on commodities from the private sector.

Low and middle income country (LMIC) recipients

Developing country governments are clearly important recipients of global health funds, particularly through the channels of bilateral and multilateral ODA, as well as from the Global Fund and the GAVI Alliance. Civil society organizations in LMIC countries are also recipients of global health finance from various sources. For example, developing country CSOs may receive grants directly from donor governments, northern-based international NGOs or the general public. There are, however, limited data on the amount and distribution of global health finance channelled to CSOs in LMICs.

Discussion

This paper presents a conceptual map of the contours of global health funding using a schematic that (a) differentiates the source, management and spending of global health funds, and (b) draws attention to the different categories of actors in the global health landscape. Figure 2 shows the main actors in global health finance in dollar terms for 2006 and their inter-relationships, showing the many routes by which global health funding is channelled. Given the many actors and the lack of data, the map we present is imprecise and hazy. However, this only serves to emphasize the need for a framework with which to describe and analyse the roles and relationships of the many actors operating in the messy and complex reality of global health.

A number of points stand out from Figure 2 and the earlier discussion. First, global health financing is fragmented, complicated and inadequately monitored and tracked. While the increase in number of global health actors may positively reflect the greater amount of resources and attention for global health, it may lead to an uncoordinated and competitive environment that is problematic for governments and CSOs in LMICs. Many transaction costs come attached to the proliferation of global health actors and initiatives and to the convoluted channels of financing. Ensuring adequate financial and programmatic accountability to the public of government donors, international NGOs, UN agencies and philanthropic foundations has become difficult, if not impossible.

In its latest Health, Nutrition and Population Strategy, the World Bank itself noted that having to work with so many organizations and initiatives at the global level was challenging, and that there was a need for it to be more selective over its engagement with other actors. It went on to warn that 'unless deficiencies in the global aid architecture are corrected and major reforms occur at the country level', the international community could squander the rise in attention and money directed at improving the health of the world's poor (World Bank 2007). Similarly, the UK government has described the 40 bilateral donors, 90 global health initiatives, 26 UN agencies and 20 global and regional funds working in global health as being 'over-complex' (DFID 2007). At times GHPs are established to help coordinate efforts in a particular area or aspect of health, but inevitably end up adding to the problem of an already over-complicated architecture and an over-crowded landscape.

The importance of coordination and accountability (including mutual accountability) is further heightened by the vertical and disease-based focus of many global health initiatives, together with the growing adoption of output-based performance measures that further encourages verticalization at the expense of the wider health system and country ownership. The chase for funding, success and public attention undermines efforts to ensure a more organized system of mutual accountability, coordination and cooperation (Buse and Harmer 2007).

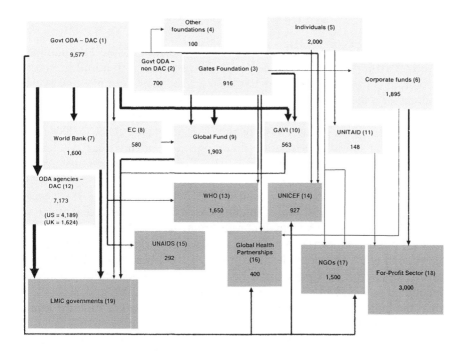

Figure 2 Overview of the main blocks of global funding for health in 2006.
Notes: (1) This figure refers to the calculation by the Development Assistance Committee (DAC) of actual disbursements made for health and population in 2006. It is expressed in 2004 dollar terms having been controlled for inflation and fluctuating exchange rates.
Source: OECD (2008a). (2) This figure is an estimate based on a guesstimate that total non-DAC official development assistance (ODA) in 2006, including China, was about US$7 billion and that health sector spending would be no more than 10% of this figure. (3) This figure represents expenditure for 2006. It is worth noting that expenditure for 2007 was US$1220 million. (4) This figure is a guesstimate based on a calculation of the grants awarded for health programmes by three of the bigger health-funding foundations: Wellcome Trust, Rockefeller Foundation and Ford Foundation (Rachlis *et al.* unpublished). (5) This figure is a guesstimate based on an assumption that voluntary contributions to health may be similar in size to voluntary contributions to humanitarian relief as estimated by Development Initiatives (2008). (6) This figure comes from the International Federation of Pharmaceutical Manufacturers & Associations (IFPMA) which estimated the size of the pharmaceutical industry's contribution to the health-related MDGs in 2006. (7) This figure represents International Development Association (IDA) spending on Health, Nutrition and Population as reported by the World Bank. (8) This figure indicates European Commission (EC) spending on 'health' and 'population and reproductive health' and comes from a report by Action for Global Health. (9) This figure represents expenditure/ disbursements for 2006. (10) This figure is the total expenses of GAVI. Source: GAVI (2007). (11) This figure comes from the UNITAID annual report. It is expected that expenditure will increase to US$ 500 million in 2009. (12) (13) This figure represents half of WHO's reported biennial budget for 2006–07. (14) This figure is a guesstimate based on the assumption that a third of UNICEF's total income in 2006 would have been spent on health. According to UNICEF's Annual Report, total expenditure through direct programme assistance on HIV/AIDS and child survival and development was US$1197 million (UNICEF 2006, p. 40). (15) This figure represents total UNAIDS expenditure for the FY 2006/07. (16) This figure is a guesstimate derived from the budgets of the global health partnerships described earlier in the text. (17) This figure is a guesstimate derived from the expenditure of Médecins Sans Frontières (MSF) and the budgets of several of the large international NGOs described earlier in the text. (18) This figure is a guesstimate derived from the data on corporate contributions to global health together with estimations of GAVI, Global Fund, UNITAID, Clinton Foundation and Gates Foundation funding of commodities. (19) According to the OECD, 96.4% of DAC funding for health was allocated to low and lower-middle income countries. From this, a spending figure of US$9230 million can be estimated for 2006 (using the same exchange rates used in Figure 3).

While the Paris Declaration on Aid Effectiveness and the International Health Partnerships are designed to improve coordination and harmonization amongst donors, success has been limited. For example, one of the findings of a recent report published by the OECD on the Paris Declaration was that many donors still insist on using their own parallel fiduciary systems even where country systems are of good quality (OECD 2008c). It also reported on 14 000 separate donor missions having been conducted in 54 recipient countries in one year, with Vietnam fielding an average of three per day.

A second point relates to the volume of global health funding. It is generally accepted that global health funding has increased over recent years as a result of a rise in ODA from donor governments and the emergence of the Gates Foundation as a major donor. However, the extent and scale of the increase in ODA for global health appears to have been inflated. Disbursements for 'health and population programmes' by DAC donor countries amounted to US$8.11 billion and US$9.58 billion in 2005 and 2006—less than the figure of US$14 billion which is commonly used to describe levels of development assistance for health.

Alarmingly, the total volume of ODA from DAC donor countries fell by 8.4% in real terms in 2007 relative to 2006 (OECD 2008b). According to a recent survey conducted by the OECD, although 102 recipient countries can expect a real increase in their aid by 2010, only 33 of them will experience an increase of US$100m or more. More worryingly, 51 recipient countries can expect a decrease in aid by 2010, while ODA to eight Least Developed Countries and four fragile states is expected to fall by over US$20bn (OECD Development Assistance Committee 2008). The current level of development assistance for health therefore falls far short of the *additional* US$22 billion required by 2007 as estimated by the WHO Commission on Macroeconomics and Health (2001). The current world financial crisis and the prospect of a worldwide recession, with donor governments cutting back further on aid budgets, present additional and serious concerns that will need to be faced.

A third issue concerns the pattern of global health spending and consumption. Global health is a multi-billion dollar industry and there are clearly competing interests amongst different actors to make use of this funding. An important question is whether global health financing is organized to suit the interests of particular actors.

For example, pharmaceutical companies appear to benefit considerably from global health programmes that emphasize the delivery of medical commodities and treatment (as well as from the positive image created by their participation in GHPs). NGOs, global health research institutions and UN bureaucracies also have an interest in increasing or maintaining their levels of income. The expanded role of NGOs is especially noteworthy. Many NGOs are now large multi-national enterprises. The MSF international movement, for example, although consisting of fairly autonomous country 'chapters', commands an annual budget of about three-quarters of a billion dollars. The income of the Seattle-based non-profit organization, PATH, in 2006 was over US$130 million (PATH 2007).

Careful attention and debate also needs to be applied to the possibility of global health funding and policy development being 'captured' by vested interests and used to support inappropriate spending on the private commercial sector, or on a large and costly global health bureaucracy and technocracy based in the North. It is important to look at not just the volume of money raised, but also how it is spent and who it benefits so as to help ensure that the needs of recipient countries are kept at the forefront.

However, the lack of data on many aspects of global health finance makes it impossible to conduct a comprehensive and detailed assessment. The gap in data and analysis on international health funding by non-DAC government donors and private foundations, and on funding that is channelled through and spent by NGOs, GHPs and the private sector, needs to be filled. Better data on the pattern and flow of global health financing would enable a more critical analysis of the performance of funders and global health actors in delivering appropriate and effective development assistance for health to LMICs.

While better data are required at the global level, what is perhaps more important are financial management and information systems in recipient countries that are capable of providing a composite picture of health expenditure that integrates external and domestic financing for health. Initiatives to strengthen budgeting and expenditure reporting systems such as the promotion of National Health Accounts and the Creditor Reporting System (CRS) of the OECD are important steps, but need to be expanded and improved. Greater use by donor governments of sector-wide or multilateral approaches to development assistance would also help considerably.

Finally, all the recommendations made above must be accompanied by the development of civil society capacity within countries to play a 'watchdog' role on how governments and external agencies are performing. An empowered and informed civil society in LMICs, including local universities and other research institutions as well as the local media, must begin to engage with the complex and fragmented supranational infrastructure of finance, actors and initiatives, and help to ensure that it impinges upon their fragile health systems in a more positive way.

Endnotes

1 Australia, Austria, Belgium, Canada, Denmark, Finland, France, Germany, Greece, Ireland, Italy, Japan, Luxembourg, Netherlands, New Zealand, Norway, Portugal, Spain, Sweden, Switzerland, United Kingdom and United States.

References

Action for Global Health. 2007. Health Warning: Why Europe must act now to rescue the health MDGs. Brussels: Action for Global Health.

Action for Global Health. 2008. Healthy Aid: Why Europe must deliver more aid, better spent to save the health Millennium Development Goals. Brussels: Action for Global Health.

Aga Khan Foundation. 2006. Annual Report 2006. Online at: http://www.akdn.org/publications/2006_akf_annual_report.pdf

AMFm. 2008. Affordable Medicines Facility – Malaria Briefing Document. Roll Back Malaria Partnership. Online at: http://www.rollbackmalaria.org/partnership/tf/globalsubsidy/080227AMFmBriefingDocument.pdf

Andreoni J. 2001. The economics of philanthropy. In: Smelser N. J., Baltes P. B. (eds.) *The International Encyclopedia of the Social and Behavioral Sciences.* London: Elsevier, pp. 11369–76. Online at: http://www.ssc.wisc.edu/~andreoni/Publications/IESBS-Andreoni.pdf

Bhattacharya A. 2008. The role of aid in a changing world. Presentation at the CIDA/North South Institute Conference, 'Does Aid Work?', 17–18 June 2008, Ottawa, Canada. Online at: http://www.nsi-ins.ca/english/events/DAW/DAWfinal_eng.pdf

Birn A.-E., Solorzano A. 1999. Public health policy paradoxes: science and politics in the Rockefeller Foundation's hookworm campaign in Mexico in the 1920s. *Social Science & Medicine* **49**: 1197–213.

Bloom D. E. 2007. Governing global health. *Finance & Development* **44**: 31–35.

Brown S., Morton B. 2008. Reforming aid and development cooperation: Accra, Doha and beyond. Policy Note. Ottawa: North South Institute. Online at: http://www.nsi-ins.ca/english/pdf/DAW_policy.pdf.

Buse K. 2004. Governing public-private infectious disease partnerships. *Brown Journal of World Affairs* **10**: 225–42.

Buse K., Harmer A. 2007. Seven habits of highly effective public-private health partnerships: practice and potential. *Social Science & Medicine* **64**: 259–71.

Charities Aid Foundation. 2003. *Payroll Giving 2001–02 Update.* Dimensions Online Briefing Paper. London: Charities Aid Foundation. Online at: http://www.cafonline.org/research.

Care International UK. 2007. CARE International UK Trustees' Report and Consolidated Financial Statements for the year ended 30 June 2007. London: Care International UK. Online at: http://www.careinternational.org.uk/download.php?id=685&utm_source=caresite&utm_medium=webpage.

Care International US. 2007. CARE USA Consolidated Financial Statements For the years ended June 30, 2007 and 2006. Atlanta, GA: Care International US. Online at: http://www.care.org/newsroom/publications/annualreports/2007/FY07_care_fin.pdf? source=170860510000 &channel=default.

The Carter Center. 2007. Carter Center Annual Report 2006–07: Strengthening lives. Atlanta, GA: The Carter Center.

CGD. 2007. *Following the Money: Toward Better Tracking of Global Health Resources.* Washington DC: Center for Global Development.

Development Initiatives. 2008. Global Humanitarian Assistance 2007/2008. Wells, UK: Development Initiatives. Online at: http://www.devinit.org/PDF%20downloads/GHA%202007.pdf

DFID (UK Department for International Development). 2007. The International Health Partnership Launched Today. News article, 5 September 2007. Online at: http://www2.dfid.gov.uk/news/files/ihp/default.asp

DNDi. 2006. 2006 Annual Report. Geneva: Drugs for Neglected Diseases Initiative. Available at: http://www.dndi.org/2008/100108/DNDi-AnnualReport-2006.pdf

Dowie M. 2002. *American Foundations: An Investigative History*. Cambridge, MA: MIT Press.

Ford Foundation. 2006. Annual Report 2006. New York: Ford Foundation. Online at: http://www.fordfound.org/pdfs/impact/ar2006.pdf

Fox D. M. 2006. Foundations' impact on health policy. *Health Affairs* **25**: 1724–9.

GAVI. 2007. Consolidated Financial Statements as of and for the years ended December 31, 2006 and 2006 (as Restated) and Independent Auditor's Report. Washington, DC: GAVI Fund. Online at: http://www.gavialliance.org/resources/GAVI_Consolidated_Financial_Statements_2006.pdf

GAVI. 2008a. Consolidated Financial Statements as of and for the years ended December 31, 2007 and 2006 (as Restated) and Independent Auditor's Report. Washington, DC: GAVI Fund. Online at: http://www.gavialliance.org/resources/GAVI_2007_financial_statements___non_A_133.pdf

GAVI. 2008b. Donor contributions and commitments. Geneva: GAVI Alliance. Online at: http://www.gavialliance.org/support/donors/index.php

GAVI Alliance. 2006. Gavi Alliance Progress Report 2006. Geneva: GAVI Alliance. Online at: http://www.gavialliance.org/resources/2006_Progress_Report.pdf

GAVI Alliance. 2007. Gavi Alliance Progress Report 2007. Geneva: GAVI Alliance. Online at: http://www.gavialliance.org/resources/2007GAVIreport.pdf

Global Fund. 2007a. Global Fund Annual Report 2007. Geneva: The Global Fund to Fight AIDS, Tuberculosis and Malaria. Online at: http://www.theglobalfund.org/documents/publications/annualreports/2007/AnnualReport2007.pdf, accessed 18 August 2008.

Global Fund. 2007b. Distribution of funding after six rounds. Geneva: The Global Fund to Fight AIDS, Tuberculosis and Malaria. Online at: http://www.theglobalfund.org/en/funds_raised/distribution/, accessed 11 December 2007.

Global Health Watch. 2008. *Global Health Watch 2: An Alternative World Health Report*. London: Zed Books.

Harmer A., Cotterrell L. 2005. Diversity in donorship: the changing landscape of official humanitarian aid. London: Overseas Development Institute Humanitarian Policy Group. Online at: http://www.odi.org.uk/HPG/papers/HPGBrief20.pdf.

IPM. 2006. Annual Report 2006: Advancing HIV-prevention options for women. Silver Spring, MD: International Partnership for Microbicides. Online at: http://www.ipm-microbicides.org/pdfs/english/ipm_publications/2007/IPM%20Annual%20Report_2006_FINAL_eng.pdf

Kanavos D., Rudisill C., Hockley T. 2008. Critical review of the IFPMA Health Partnerships Survey 2007. London: London School of Economics & Political Science. Online at: http://www.efpia.eu/content/default.asp?PageID=559&DocID=5184

Kates J., Morrison J. S., Lief E. 2006. Global health funding: a glass half full? *The Lancet* **368**: 187–8.

Kaul I. 2006. Exploring the policy space between markets and states: Global Public-Private Partnerships. In: Kaul I., Conceição P. (eds). *The new public finance: responding to global challenges*. New York: Oxford University Press for the UNDP.

Keck W. C. 2007. Cuba's contribution to global health diplomacy. Presented at Global Health Diplomacy Workshop, 12 March 2007. Online at: http://igcc.ucsd. edu/pdf/keck.pdf

MacArthur T. 2006. The scaling up of private philanthropy: implications for development outcomes. Mimeo, London: Department for International Development.

Manji F. 2008. Assessing China's role in Africa: a search for a new perspective. Presentation at conference 'The Changing Face of Global Development Finance', February 2008. Online at: http://www.halifaxinitiative.org/index.php/Speeches/1075

Marten R., Witte J. M. 2008. Transforming development? The role of philanthropic foundations in international development cooperation. GPPi Research Paper Series no. 10. Berlin: Global Public Policy Institute.

Martens J. 2007. *Multistakeholder Partnerships – Future Models of Multilateralism?* Dialogue on Globalization, Occasional Papers, No. 29. Berlin: Freidrich-Ebert-Stiftung.

McCoy D., Kembhari G., Patel J., Luintel A. 2009. The Bill and Melinda Gates Foundation's grant-making programme for global health. *Lancet* **373**: 1645–53.

McKinsey & Company. 2008. Independent External Evaluation of the Stop TB Partnership – Exhibits. Online at: http://www.stoptb.org/resource_center/assets/documents/eval2008.zip

Michaud C. 2003. Development Assistance for Health (DAH): Recent trends and resource allocation. Paper prepared for the Second Consultation of the Commission on Macroeconomics and Health, World Health Organization, Geneva, 29–30 October 2003. Online at: http://www.who.int/macrohealth/events/health_for_poor/en/dah_trends_nov10.pdf

MMV. 2007. Annual Report 2007. Geneva: Medicines for Malaria Venture. Online at: http://www.mmv.org/IMG/pdf/mmvAR07_Lrez_All.pdf

MSF. 2006. MSF International Movement Financial Report. Geneva: Médecins Sans Frontières. Online at: http://www.msf.org/source/financial/2007/MSF_Financial_Report_2006.pdf

OECD. 2005. Harmonisation, Alignment, Results: Progress Report on Aid Effectiveness. High Level Forum, Paris: OECD.

OECD. 2008a. OECD Stat Extracts. Creditor Reporting System. Online at: http://stats.oecd.org/WBOS/Index.aspx?DatasetCode=CRSNEW.

OECD. 2008b. Debt relief is down: other ODA rises slightly. 4 April 2008, News & Events, Aids Statistics, Development Co-operation Directorate (DCD-DAC), Organisation for Economic Cooperation & Development. Online at: http://www.oecd.org/document/8/0,3343,en_2649_34447_40381960_1_1_1_1,00.html

OECD. 2008c. 2008 Survey on Monitoring the Paris Declaration: Making aid more effective by 2010. Paris: OECD. Online at: http://www.oecd.org/dataoecd/58/41/41202121.pdf

OECD-DAC Advisory Group on Civil Society and Aid Effectiveness. 2008. Synthesis of findings and recommendations. Online at: http://www.oecd.org/dataoecd/61/8/41205249.pdf

OECD Development Assistance Committee. 2008. Report of 2008 survey of aid allocation policies and indicative forward spending plans. Paris: OECD. Available online at: http://www.eldis.org/cf/rdr/?doc=37313&em=050608&sub=aid

PATH. 2006. Health within reach: 2006 progress report. Seattle: PATH. Online at: http://www.path.org/files/ER_progress_rpt_2006.pdf

Renz L., Atienza J. 2006. International Grant-making Update 2006: A Snapshot of U.S. Foundation Trends. New York: US Foundation Center. Online at: http://www.cof.org/files/Documents/International_Programs/2006%20Publications/IntlUpdateOct06.pdf

Riddell R. C. 2008. The impact of aid on development objectives: Current evidence and thinking and key issues for the future. Presentation at the CIDA/North South Institute Conference, 'Does Aid Work?', 17–18 June 2008, Ottawa, Canada. Online at: http://www.nsiins.ca/english/events/DAW/Riddell.pdf

The Rockefeller Foundation. 2007. The Rockefeller Foundation 2007 Annual Report: Smart Globalization. New York. Online at: http://www.rockfound.org/library/annual_reports/2007rf_ar.pdf

Schieber G. 2006. Getting real on health financing. *Finance & Development* **43**(4). Online at: http://www.imf.org/external/pubs/ft/fandd/2006/12/schieber.htm

Sridhar D. 2008. Governance and resourcing of health: Recognizing the role of multiple stakeholders. GEG Working Paper. Oxford: Global Economic Governance Programme, Department of Politics & International Relations, University College Oxford, forthcoming.

Sulla O. 2006. Philanthropic foundations actual versus potential role in international development assistance. Mimeo, Washington, DC: World Bank Global Development Finance Report Group.

T. B. Alliance. 2007. 2007 Annual Report: Advancing the Pathway. New York: T. B. Alliance. Online at: http://www.tballiance.org/downloads/publications/TBAlliance_AnnualReport_2007.pdf

Tsunami Evaluation Coalition. 2006. Joint evaluation of the international response to the Indian Ocean tsunami: Synthesis Report. Online at: http://www.tsunami-evaluation.org/The+TEC+Synthesis+Report/Key+Messages.htm

UNAIDS. 2007. 2006 UNAIDS Annual Report: Making the money work. Geneva. Online at: http://data.unaids.org/pub/Report/2007/2006_unaids_annual_report_en.pdf

UN Foundation. 2008. About UNF: Financial Information. Online at: http://www.unfoundation.org/about/financial_info.asp, accessed 15 August 2008.

UNICEF. 2007. Annual Report 2007. New York. Online at: http://www.unicef.org/about/annualreport/files/Annual_Report_2007.pdf

UNITAID. 2008. UNITAID Budget. Geneva. Online at: http://www.unitaid.eu/index.php/en/UNITAID-budget.html

USAID. 2007. *2007 VolAg: Report of Voluntary Agencies*, Washington DC.

Wellcome Trust. 2006. Wellcome Trust Annual Report and Financial Statements 2006. Online at: http://www.wellcome.ac.uk/stellent/groups/corporatesite/@msh_publishing_group/documents/web_document/wtx035510.pdf

Wemos. 2005. Risky remedies for the health of the poor: global public-private initiatives in health. Amsterdam: Wemos Foundation. Online at: http://wemos2004.ddg22.tamtam.nl/Documents/executive%20summary%20klein%20bestand.pdf

WHO. 2007a. Proposed programme budget 2008–2009. Geneva: World Health Organization.

WHO. 2007b. The Stop TB Partnership Annual Report 2006. Geneva: World Health Organization. Online at: http://www.stoptb.org/resource_center/assets/documents/TB_annual2006_FINAL_lo.pdf

WHO. 2008. UNITAID Annual Report. Geneva. Online at: http://www.unitaid.eu/images/governance/annualreport2007.pdf

WHO Commission on Macroeconomics and Health. 2001. *Macroeconomics and health: Investing in health for economic development*. Geneva: World Health Organization.

Widdus R. 2003. Public-private partnerships for health require thoughtful evaluation. *Bulletin of the World Health Organization* **81**: 235.

William J. Clinton Foundation. 2007. Annual Report 2006. New York. Online at: http://www.clintonfoundation.org/download/?guid=16ce00b4-982c-102b-be34-001143e0d9b6

World Bank. 2007. Healthy Development: The World Bank Strategy for Health, Nutrition, and Population Results. Washington, DC: World Bank. Version: 22 February 2007.

World Bank. 2008. *World Bank Development Indicators in 2008*. Washington, DC: World Bank.

73

MULTISECTORALISM, PARTICIPATION, AND STAKEHOLDER EFFECTIVENESS

Increasing the role of nonstate actors in the Global Fund to Fight AIDS, Tuberculosis and Malaria

Garrett Wallace Brown

Source: *Global Governance*, 15:2 (2009), 169–77.

During the past ten years there has been an increased willingness by international health organizations to include multisectoral nonstate actors in their decisionmaking processes. The stated aim of expanding multisectoral involvement is to increase information flows from those on the ground, to create a sense of policy ownership by those implementing various health programs, to create a more unified front against global health priorities, and to create a more robust sense of institutional legitimacy. One such institution has been the Global Fund to Fight AIDS, Tuberculosis and Malaria, which was designed specifically to bring various stakeholders together to create a more coordinated mechanism to combat three of the world's most destructive diseases.

The purpose of this essay is to discuss the role of nonstate actors in the decisionmaking processes of the Global Fund. The aim of this discussion is not to undermine the good work of the Global Fund, but to expose certain structural weaknesses in the current way nonstate actors are incorporated into the governance process and to illustrate how these structural processes might negate their effective participation. By doing so, this exploration will help expose various deficit gaps between the stated aims of multisectoral participation within the Global Fund and its actual practice. The goal is to

encourage normative recommendations for increasing the real-world operation of stakeholder inclusiveness, ownership, partnership, and participation
within the Global Fund.

The Global Fund and its multisectoral foundations

To get a sense of the multisectoral dimension of the Global Fund, it is useful to outline some of the reasons why the Global Fund was established and
to highlight the guiding principles that underwrite its mandate. The foundations for the Global Fund were laid at a G8 summit in Okinawa, Japan,
in the year 2000. From that meeting, the G8 leaders acknowledged the need
to create a new global health partnership to respond to increasing global
health priorities. Linking effectiveness to inclusive multisectoral participation,
the G8 leaders claimed that "only through sustained action and coherent
international cooperation to fully mobilize new and existing medical, technical and financial resources, can we strengthen health delivery systems
and reach beyond traditional approaches."[1] As was further exclaimed, the
"participation of developing country partners and other stakeholders will be
essential."[2]

By linking policy effectiveness to inclusive participation, five existing failures in multilateral global health governance were recognized. First, it was
a widely held belief that there was a general lack of local expertise involved
in global health governance and the decisionmaking process. Because of this,
it was believed that global health governance failed to fully capture conditions on the ground and did not adequately reflect the particular constraints
and conditions that were involved in each recipient country. Second, because
of this lack of participatory input, it was felt that current global health
policies lacked a sense of local ownership and that this often diminished the
political will to follow through on implementation. Third, many donor countries maintained that there was a lack of institutional accountability measures
within the existing United Nations system and that this acted as a disincen-
tive for them to provide financial assistance. Fourth, it was believed that the
current United Nations system had become overly political and diffident,
so that effective global health policy and implementation could no longer
be efficiently channeled through that body. Last, it was unanimously agreed
that there was no unified and collective resource stream to fund global health
priorities and that AIDS, tuberculosis, and malaria could be effectively
managed only through a system of multisectoral cooperation, multisectoral
dialogue, and a commitment to an internationally coordinated response. As
a result, it was agreed that it was necessary to bypass the United Nations
by creating an independent institution that could tackle these global health
priorities. It was also agreed that this new institution would need to include
all the stakeholders involved and that multisectoral participation in all stages
of the process would be the most effective way to "appeal to a wide body

of donors while securing stronger commitments to the organization."[3] Thanks to this G8 summit in Japan, a 2001 United Nations Special Session on AIDS, and the establishment of a Transitional Working Group (TWG), the Global Fund was able to start its funding work in January 2002.

Through the TWG, two main normative principles were established within a Framework Document as constitutional foundations for the Global Fund. First, the Framework Document states that the Global Fund "should be a multisectoral partnership between governments, civil society, the private sector and affected communities."[4] Second, decisions of the Global Fund should represent those most in need, in that "highest priority should be given to countries and regions with the greatest need, based on the highest burden of disease and the least ability to bring financial resources to address these health problems."[5] As Article 2 of the Global Fund bylaws outline, "The purpose of the fund is to attract, manage and disburse resources through a new public-private foundation that will make a sustainable and significant contribution to the reduction of infections, illness and death, thereby mitigating the impact caused by HIV/AIDS, tuberculosis and malaria in countries in need."[6] Institutionally, to facilitate multisectoral partnership, funding decisions should be made by a multisectoral board comprising nine regional seats, six donor countries, two nongovernmental organizations (NGOs), one private foundation, one private company, a representative of those afflicted with the aforementioned diseases, and three nonvoting advisory seats representing the WHO, UNAIDS, the World Bank, and a Swiss member. Nevertheless, to facilitate broadened multisectoral partnerships locally, grant proposals should be generated by recipient countries through a multisectoral Country Coordination Mechanism (CCM). As a way to tie multisectoralism into the grant application process, CCMs are meant to be the mechanism by which local stakeholders deliberate and collectively design grant proposals, design new health programs in line with current infrastructure, and tailor program implementation strategies. In this way, the CCM process within the Global Fund specifically allows for "national ownership and respect [for] country-led formulation and implementation processes."[7]

Nevertheless, the inclusion of NGOs and other nongovernmental associations on the Global Fund board has at times been critiqued for not being a true partnership. As some have claimed, "the process seems to be dominated by those with political and economic power, leaving many representatives feeling marginalized."[8] In relation to the inclusion of health professionals, some have claimed that "the Global Fund is accountable only to donor states and there is no accountability to local health experts."[9] NGOs have at times expressed a similar concern, arguing that there is "no accountability to implementing NGO's by the Global Fund board."[10] Although the board's makeup should be reexamined to see if there are ways to foster a more robust sense of multisectoral inclusion, in many ways the views presented here can be seen as an inappropriate starting point for multisectoral change. As long as donor countries continue to finance global health initiatives on an ad hoc and piecemeal basis, the effects of economic power on the governance structure will remain. For until there are major reforms on how global health is financed, powerful countries will have an asymmetrical ability to control the decisionmaking process by dictating the terms of their financial involvement. In many ways this is not a problem specific to the Global Fund, but a problem that is endemic of current global health governance in general. Furthermore, the Global Fund's board has put into place significant formal governance procedures to encourage deliberation and consensus formation between its representatives. In this case, the problem of participation is not with the Global Fund governance procedures per se, but with disconnects that may exist between board representatives and their NGO constituents. Due to practical considerations for maintaining a workable form of decisionmaking governance, the Global Fund is forced to limit the number of participants on the board, opting to encourage multisectoral participation at the CCM level. In this regard, discussions for multisectoral partnership reform, if they are to have immediate and more pertinent results, would be most effective if focused at the CCM level.

Multisectoralism in the country coordination mechanisms

As mentioned earlier, an important level of multisectoral participation within the Global Fund is within the CCM, which is where local stakeholder partnerships are to be represented. According to the Global Fund Framework Document, the CCM process is where various stakeholders are to collectively create grant proposals, to design locally sensitive health programs, and to facilitate a corresponding implementation strategy. The CCM process is meant to ensure local ownership by allowing CCMs to design health initiatives that they deem to be most suitable to their needs. It is after the CCM has created an internally agreed upon grant proposal that it will be reviewed for feasibility by a Technical Review Panel (TRP) and submitted to the multisectoral Global Fund board for a final decision.

However, one consistent critique of the CCM process is that there are few structural safeguards to guarantee that the CCM process is in all cases multisectoral. Although the Global Fund has recently implemented six minimum requirements for CCM grant eligibility (one of which requires membership of people living with the diseases), the Global Fund has not made it a requirement for CCMs to have a certain percentage of NGO participation. Despite the fact that the Global Fund strongly *recommends* that NGOs should represent at least 40 percent of CCM membership, it does not formally *require* a minimum threshold for what should be considered a truly multisectoral grant. In other words, although the Global Fund would like all CCMs to have a genuine multisectoral complexion in order to create a sense of local cooperation and a level of inclusion by all stakeholders, it does not formally require a multisectoral condition before approving grant applications.

Historically, the Global Fund has defended this position in two ways. First, the Global Fund often claims that it is a "nonpolitical" organization in terms of policy ideology and that its primary responsibility is as a financial institution for delivering health-related funds.[11] As the Global Fund suggests, some countries will still need assistance despite the fact that authentic NGO participation would be unlikely. Because of this, the Global Fund claims that by leaving the final multisectoral complexion of CCMs somewhat fluid, the process of aid delivery can still be allowed in cases where NGO participation is difficult or impossible to manufacture. Second, the Global Fund argues that multisectoralism should include a broad conception of societal elements, which can include informally organized members of civil society such as academics, spiritual leaders, and independent medical professionals. By focusing on the inclusion of more formalized NGOs as a universal requirement, the Global Fund has suggested that it would then make unfair assumptions about what types of members are most important for every CCM, which in turn limits a sense of local ownership and self-direction.

Although these are certainly important considerations, it is important to highlight that the consequence of this policy has at times resulted in the creation of CCMs that are not multisectoral and cases where CCMs have been dominated by a core of governmental elite. As one reputable NGO related to me in South Africa in 2005, "There is a lack of honest communication and connection at the national level. This is due to political forces inside the national government and a lack of consistency within the Country Coordination Mechanism." Unfortunately, this has, in a fair number of cases, resulted in programs and CCM processes that have systematically excluded, or failed to include, various stakeholders and NGOs affected by the diseases. As one report by the London School of Hygiene and Tropical Medicine suggested, "CCM members were often ineffective at representing their constituencies and encountered obstacles in participating in CCM processes."[12] This has been mirrored by the International HIV/AIDS Alliance, which reported that "experiences varied greatly between countries," ranging from "involvement in all stages" of the CCM process, to "exclusionary marginalization."[13] Furthermore, these concerns have been echoed in a recent Global Fund report, which found that half the countries that were surveyed about NGO inclusion fell short of the Global Fund recommended target of 40 percent NGO inclusion.

Although the Global Fund has attempted to mediate this problem through the inclusion of six eligibility requirements (for example, democratic accountability, transparency, the reduction of conflict of interest, and the inclusion of people living with the diseases), it would seem that these requirements have not gone far enough to initiate meaningful inclusion by a broad contingent of stakeholder groups. This can be of critical importance, since it is often the case that NGOs are key implementing agents or, in many cases, have first-hand knowledge of conditions on the ground and thus can articulate many of the concerns of those most affected by the diseases. Furthermore, in cases where broad multisectoral cooperation has been established within a CCM, the effectiveness of grant implementation and support has generally been enhanced and significant partnerships produced. It is not surprising that many CCMs that have lacked a broad multisectoral component often suffer from ineffectiveness, incompetence, and a notable propensity for corruption.

The claim by the Global Fund that it is not a political organization is in some respects important for it to maintain. After all, the fund was established primarily to combat the three diseases, and it was crucial for the fund to try to escape the political pitfalls that were associated with the United Nations system. However, as was alluded to in the historical outline earlier, the Global Fund is not politically neutral by design: the fund was specifically established with a mission to unify and coordinate multisectoral partnerships, at both the global and local level. In this regard, the Global Fund was founded on inherently normative principles of political inclusiveness ("should be a multisectoral partnership") as well as economic distributive prioritization ("based on highest burden of disease"). Furthermore, the six eligibility requirements are in and of themselves normatively ladened with political implication, in that they focus on anticorruption, on the democratic accountability of its members, on democratic transparency, and on a transparent nomination process. What is missing, and what is critical to creating a more inclusive and effective response to these health priorities, is the additional requirement that all CCMs must meet a minimal multisectoral threshold of at least 40 percent. Although this may prevent some CCMs from obtaining grants immediately, it does not prevent them from seeking outside NGO involvement in order to fulfill the multisectoral threshold. This inclusion of outside participation has been done in the past by other CCMs, and it has been done with positive results. In addition, this does not seem out of step with the existing eligibility requirements, which already demand a certain amount of reasonable compliance with regard to the political formation of CCM bodies. Last, the Global Fund is in some ways aware of this concern, and it will be interesting to see whether the current Study Area 2 Research being conducted by the Technical Evaluation Reference Group (TERG) on partnerships and inclusion will find similar deficits and make similar CCM recommendations. Some of the general comments about partnerships and participation expressed in the Study Area 1 Research findings would suggest that CCM inclusiveness and its ability to enhance policy effectiveness will be highlighted as something in need of reevaluation by the Global Fund board.

The Global Fund as a new multisectoral alternative
to global health governance

What has always been impressive about the Global Fund is its ability to learn from critical evaluation and to rethink its institutional practice. For example, when I first began research on the Global Fund in 2002, there were large-scale complaints that it did not provide sufficient help or information on how to successfully complete grant applications. As various CCMs related (as did TERG sometime later), CCMs had no idea of what was to be included in a grant proposal or what specific questions they needed to address. However, over the past few years, the Global Fund has gone to great lengths to provide sample proposal templates and to employ dedicated staff to deal with questions from recipient countries. In addition, the Global Fund has been a self-learning and reflective organization, creating new advisory bodies and institutional mechanisms, such as TERG and the Office of Inspector General, in order for it to continually reassess its policies and to create a more effective funding mechanism. What this demonstrates is that the Global Fund is able to reformulate its institutional structures and participatory guidelines so as to bring the practice of multisectoral partnerships closer to the foundational principles outlined in its mission statement. In line with this ability for assessment and reform, my suggestion is for the Global Fund to make it a requirement that all CCMs meet a minimal standard of 40 percent multisectoral participation and NGO membership as well as to strictly monitor compliance with the existing six eligibility requirements. By doing so, I believe the Global Fund can increase a broadened sense of participation and legitimacy in four significant ways.

First, by requiring NGO inclusion, it will help legitimate CCMs by adding an additional element of broadened public deliberation, public reason giving, and power sharing. This will in effect enhance the process of internal checks and balances while also providing direct access to the decisionmaking process by those on the front line of disease-related issues. Second, by requiring NGO inclusion, it can help legitimate the funding process to wary donors that have often expressed concern about accountability, effectiveness, and the possibility of governmental corruption within CCMs. By requiring NGO participation, in line with adherence to the already existing eligibility requirements, the Global Fund can help assure donors that the CCM process does embody more than just entrenched elites and that some meaningful measure of constructive contestation will be involved in the development of local health policies. As in the case of Uganda, local and international NGOs can be effective reporting agents and anticorruption whistle-blowers. It is in this regard that NGOs will not only represent the needs of their constituencies, but also help guarantee that the CCM will be accountable to the grant process on the whole. Third, by requiring the inclusion of NGOs, especially implementing NGO agents, there is a better prospect for designing

363

complementary programs while reducing program/implementation overlap. As was the case in Russia, various experts involved with tuberculosis control were selected in order to reduce program overlap, to properly target areas of need, and to coordinate a coherent health program that would fully utilize available resources and available expertise. Fourth, by requiring the 40 percent inclusion of NGOs, the Global Fund will better mirror the normative principles of participation and partnership that underwrite its mandate; maintaining a level of consistency with its own founding principles can only help to create a sense of overarching institutional legitimacy. For as the history of the United Nations system helps to illustrate, allowing an institution to stray away from its founding principles can significantly damage the perceived legitimacy and effectiveness of that organization.

In many ways, the Global Fund offers great promise to help alleviate the destruction caused by these devastating diseases. Moreover, the Global Fund has given scholars as well as politicians an alternative model of global health governance that can help shed critical light on other traditional modes of global governance. However, its success will be based on its ability to maintain a strong and sustained sense of partnership between donor governments, recipient governments, NGOs, health professionals, and corporations. Despite the Global Fund's best efforts, both the political and financial commitments that are needed to respond to these diseases are struggling to keep pace with increased infection rates, and there are staggering statistics that we should be worried about. In 2007 alone, UNAIDS estimated that 33.2 million people were living with HIV, that 2.5 million people became newly infected, and that 2.1 million people died from AIDS. In 2005, the World Health Organization reported that 1.6 million people died of tuberculosis, while new cases of multidrug-resistant strains were alarmingly on the rise. Perhaps most depressingly, the statistics show that 500 million people become sick with malaria each year and more than 1 million people die annually from infection. What these statistics indicate, first and foremost, is that global health institutions such as the Global Fund are barely able to keep their heads above the rising tide of new infections (if not already drowning). Without renewed dedication to funding institutions like the Global Fund and an increased dedication to a truly unified multisectoral response, both globally and locally, it is my fear that global health priorities will become increasingly acute. It is for this reason that the Global Fund should reevaluate its CCM requirements so that donors as well as those affected by the diseases can feel secure that the best resources, the best minds, and the best practices available are being actively implemented.

Notes

1 G7-G8 Summit in Okinawa, 21–23 July 2000, http://ec.europa.eu/comm/external-relations/g7_g8/intro/conclusion.htm.
2 Ibid.

3 Interview with Dr. Peter Piot, director of UNAIDS and Global Fund board member, London, 8 February 2005.
4 GF Framework Document, Sec. III.
5 Ibid., Sec. VII.
6 The By-Laws of the Global Fund, Sec. I, Art. 2.
7 Framework Document, Sec. III, Subsection C.
8 Former Global Fund Board member. This interviewee wished to remain anonymous.
9 Comment made in an interview with a senior health adviser for the New Partnership for Africa's Development (NEPAD), 15 August 2005.
10 Comment made in an interview with the executive director of an implementing NGO, South Africa, 31 August 2005.
11 Framework Document, Sec. III, Subsection A.
12 Ruairi Brugha, "The Global Fund: Managing Great Expectations," *The Lancet* 364 (July 2004).
13 "NGO Participation in the Global Fund," report by the International HIV/AIDS Alliance, October 2002, p. 2, available at www.aidalliance.org/publications.

Part 12

HEALTH GOVERNANCE FRAMEWORK ISSUES

74

PUBLIC HEALTH AND THE
RIGHTS OF STATES

András Miklós

Source: *Public Health Ethics*, 2:2 (2009), 158–70.

When exercising their public health powers, states claim various rights against their subjects and aliens. The paper considers whether public health considerations can help justify some of these rights, and explores some constraints on the justificatory force of public health considerations. I outline two arguments about the moral grounds for states' rights with regard to public health. The principle of fairness emphasizes that those who benefit from public health measures ought to contribute their fair share in upholding them. Alternatively, states' rights might be justified by a natural duty of justice to uphold and not to obstruct institutions implementing public health policies. I indicate some reasons for preferring the latter justification. I further argue that the assignment of some rights to states via public health-based justification is undermined on several counts. Domestic political institutions cannot effectively perform some of their functions in protecting public health. Furthermore, transborder public health threats pose collective action problems at the global level. Finally, concerns about human rights work against the assignment of some rights to states. I conclude by arguing that these concerns call for global coordination, and that some rights claimed by states ought instead to be assigned to global institutions.

Introduction

States, when claiming political authority, do not merely assert the fact of their actual power over a number of people or over a circumscribed area. What they claim is rights of various sorts with a moral grounding. In this respect they claim to be different from other kinds of human associations that have power over persons, such as gangs of criminals. States claim authority in exercising coercive power over their subjects, and when they meet certain criteria justifying their use of coercive power, we speak of legitimate authority.

States have claimed rights to enforce requirements against persons residing on their territory, to control uses of the resources on their territory, to control movement across their borders and to exclude outsiders from the use of resources on their territory. Can public health considerations provide support for the justification of legitimate authority with these features? In this paper I will consider whether or not public health arguments can help justify some rights states have claimed, and I will explore some constraints on the justificatory force of public health considerations.

I outline two arguments about the moral grounds for states' rights with regard to public health. Some rights might be thought justified by the principle of fairness, emphasizing that those who benefit from public health measures ought to contribute their fair share in upholding them. Alternatively, states' rights might be justified by a natural duty of justice binding subjects to abide by just rules and requiring outsiders not to obstruct the working of just institutions implementing public health policies. Although I do not attempt to defend the latter position in detail, I will indicate some reasons for preferring it to the former one.

I will go on by arguing in detail, however, that the assignment of some rights to states via public health-based justification is undermined on several counts. First, it is no longer clear that domestic political institutions can still effectively perform their functions in protecting domestic public health at current levels of the international movement of persons and goods. Furthermore, transborder public health threats pose collective action problems at the global level. Finally, concerns about human rights work against the assignment of some rights to states. I conclude by arguing that these concerns call for global coordination even without postulating a general cosmopolitan duty to promote global health. Hence, some rights claimed by states ought instead to be assigned to supra- or international institutions.

The rights of territorial states

States, when claiming political authority, make a moral claim to rights of various sorts in their exercise of coercive power. We can sort these rights into three categories.[1] First, states claim rights over their subjects. They are regarded as entitled to impose and enforce legal requirements on their subjects, who in turn are thought to have a corresponding moral obligation to obey these requirements. Second, states claim rights against aliens. These include a state's right not to be interfered with in governing their subjects or their territory by other persons, groups of persons or states, and a right to control and prohibit movement across their borders, including a right to restrict immigration.[2] Finally, they claim rights over the use of their territory. These include rights such as 'rights to reasonably full control over land and resources within the territory that are not privately owned', rights to specify property by enacting a property law regime governing the acquisition and transfer of property, as well as laws in criminal law against force and fraud in seizing property, and also rights to restrict the uses of property on their territory— e.g. by zoning laws, laws regulating the exploitation of natural resources, laws restricting hazardous activities in populated areas etc. (Copp, 1999). States also claim the right to tax and regulate uses of privately owned resources on their territory.

Many of the rights states claim are relevant for public health either because public health considerations can be directly used to justify them, or because, even if not themselves based on public health grounds, some of these rights have an effect on public health within the population. Consider some examples for each type of rights.

Mandatory vaccination programs for certain infectious diseases impose a legal requirement on subjects to comply, and are one instance of states' rights over subjects.[3] Other examples include quarantine, isolation and mandatory treatment of individuals to contain epidemics, as it happened during the SARS outbreak in countries such as Hong Kong and Canada (Dawson and Verweij, 2007: 4). Finally, the legal requirement of physicians to report HIV cases by name also represents the exercise of state's right over its subjects (Bayer and Colgrove, 2002: 98–101).

With regard to rights against aliens, states claim rights to restrict travel or immigration on public health grounds, thereby restricting the freedom of movement of foreign citizens. For example, aliens may be denied admission to the United States if they cannot document their vaccination against certain vaccine-preventable communicable diseases (Fidler, 2002: 153). Also, would-be immigrants might be required to undergo detailed screening or pre-arrival treatment for a number of communicable diseases in order to be granted entry (Holland, 2007: 164).

Finally, rights over territory also have public health dimension. Laws restrict certain hazardous activities in populated areas on public health grounds. In cases of public health emergency, states claim the right to seize and appropriate private property in defense of public health; for example by using it for care, treatment and housing of patients, or by destroying contaminated materials (Gostin, 2002: 84). Laws regulating the advertising of tobacco or alcohol products and the zoning of their sales also have public health grounds. Perhaps less obviously, policies reducing socioeconomic inequalities have a public health dimension insofar as these inequalities shape the health status of a population through the social gradient of health.[4]

These public health functions are couched in terms of rights and obligations. Since these are asserted not merely as legal but also as moral rights and obligations, they are in need of moral justification. Suppose a state introduces a policy of prohibiting the immigration of people from certain parts of the world characterized by high incidence of infectious diseases, or denies entry to HIV positive persons into the country on public health grounds. The question is by what, and to what extent, are such exercises of power against

371

aliens, over subjects and over territory, justified? In what follows I will briefly outline two of the potential moral grounds for these rights and obligations, a fairness-based and a justice-based one, and indicate some reasons for preferring the second of these. In the main part of the paper I will discuss some limits to the justice-based justifications of the rights of states.

Public health measures as public goods

The fairness-based justification of the rights of states is closely related to the public good nature of public health, hence first I describe the key characteristics that make a wide range of public health measures public goods and then turn to the normative arguments underlying states' rights with regard to them. By public health I will understand throughout the paper a set of institutions, policies and actions that aim to improve or protect population health by collective means.[5]

One important function performed by states is the provision of public health for their residents. Many public health policies have been widely recognized to possess the characteristics of public goods. The benefits they provide are non-excludable and their consumption is non-rival. That is, no one within the relevant population can be excluded from the benefits provided, not even those who did not contribute to their production; on the other hand, their consumption by one person does not reduce the quantity or quality available for others.

One good example of the public good character of public health measures is creating population immunity against certain communicable diseases by mass vaccination. Population or herd immunity is a property of a group that results from the fact that a sufficient number of people within the group are immune to a disease. When population immunity exists, the likelihood of a non-vaccinated person's coming into contact with the disease drops to a very low level. This is because most people in the population who come into contact with an infected individual already have immunity and therefore will not pass on the disease.[6] The benefits of population immunity are such that people who decide not to get vaccination cannot be excluded from these.

That the provision of public goods notoriously engenders collective action problems has been regarded as central to the justification of political authority with powers of coercion. This is because their existence is made possible only through the joint effort of a significant part of the population, which is not likely to be forthcoming to a sufficient extent without coercion. Public goods can be provided only if a substantial portion of the population contributes to their production; however, contribution to their provision involves some cost for individuals. Since everyone in the public can benefit from the good whether or not one contributes, once provided, it will not be in their individual interest to contribute to it. This creates an incentive of free-riding for all those who stand to benefit from the public good in question and call for assurance that an agreement to contribute one's share is carried out. For this reason, policies and institutions involving enforcement mechanisms are frequently necessary for public good provision. This consideration seems like a good candidate for justifying the rights of states with regard to public health.

Mandatory vaccination is a case in point. Routine vaccinations in mass immunization programs entail some small risk of serious harm to the vaccinated individual and might lead to serious health damage and even death in extreme cases. On the other hand, over a certain threshold proportion of the public being vaccinated, population immunity already exists. Whether or not an individual undergoes vaccination, she will be protected from the disease. Considering the cost of individual health-risk posed by vaccination, and the fact that one is likely to be prevented from the disease by population immunity anyway, people are likely be tempted to avoid vaccination, given that the added benefit of being vaccinated may not be very significant. Mandatory vaccination might be a necessary means of bringing about and maintaining the necessary level of protection for the population. This may seem a good reason for state coercion against subjects in the field of public health. A significant public health benefit of immunity from dangerous infectious diseases cannot be provided unless there are some coercive sanctions to make it the case that people do not find it in their interest to free-ride on the effort of others and are assured that other people will also contribute their fair share.

The argument from fairness

Some public good-type public health benefits such as mandatory vaccination could not be provided without coercive measures backed up by state power. This consideration does not by itself morally justify such measures, however. One step is missing from the argument for granting states rights over their subjects with regard to mandatory public health policies. What are the moral grounds for coercing people to undergo potentially harmful treatment, even if it is necessary to provide some common benefit? An argument adapted from the literature on political obligation readily suggests itself: the argument from fairness.

The duty of fairness requires that participants deriving benefits from an ongoing practice contribute their fair share to maintaining it. Those who fail to contribute are free-riding on the effort of others and are for this reason unfair to other participants.[7] The moral requirement of fairness might in certain cases justify coercion in order to assure compliance with the cooperative practice creating and maintaining public goods. George Klosko argues that in the case of goods that are necessary for making decent lives possible, all individuals who benefit from these goods have an obligation to cooperate.[8] Since these goods are essential for living acceptable lives, so the argument goes, state coercion in securing compliance with their provision is justified.

The goods that are typically listed among these essential goods include law and order and protection from external threats, but the same description applies to public health policies as well. Without basic public health policies acceptable lives would not be possible, the benefits associated with them are provided through collective effort, and they are characterized by non-rivalrousness and non-excludability. Coercive public health measures such as mandatory vaccination may then be justified by pointing out the significant benefits citizens derive from these programs and their obligation grounded in fairness to contribute their share.

Fairness considerations have their shortcomings, however. One general reason behind these is that the argument from fairness focuses on benefits one has actually received or stands to receive from an ongoing cooperative scheme. The argument states that once one has benefited or stands to benefit from an ongoing scheme, she has an obligation to contribute her share, and if the benefits in question are essential for living acceptable lives and are provided by the state, authorities are justified in coercively enforcing this obligation. Once there is a public health program that is up and running from which one benefits, one may legitimately be required to obey the rules and shoulder part of the burden in connection with the program. Fairness considerations have nothing to say, however, about the legitimacy of establishing or extending public health policies in the first place.

Also, fairness considerations do not extend to practices that once provided benefits, but are no longer capable of doing so. Thus, the argument from fairness in the justification of states' rights over subjects is likely to be undermined by the effects of globalization. One of the argument's premises is that important public goods are being provided by states through public health policies to their subjects. As we shall shortly see, some changes described under the heading of globalization have resulted in states' diminished capacity to provide some public health benefits they could previously provide. The impact of these trends on domestic public health policies and on the argument from fairness is the following. Some public health functions previously exercised by states can no longer effectively be exercised by them. Therefore, the obligation of subjects to obey coercive public health measures is significantly weakened, or even cancelled, since the relevant public health benefits that triggered a fairness-based obligation to obey are no longer provided by the state. In the absence of an agency actually providing these public health benefits, no one has an obligation to contribute to their provision even if this were possible through alternative means.

A final shortcoming of the argument from fairness is that it cannot justify all the moral rights states claim in performing their public health functions. At best, it can justify subjects' obligation to obey; however, it has nothing to say about rights states claim against foreigners. To provide an essential public good, states must be able to enforce public health policies not only against their own citizens or residents. In many cases, the provision of some public health benefit involves coercive measures against foreigners or control over a certain territory as necessary instruments. However, aliens cannot be regarded as providers of a public benefit in the sense relevant to public goods. Even when they abide by the regulations other states impose on them, they merely refrain from interfering in the public good provision rather than being positive contributors. Even more importantly, under no plausible description can they be regarded as beneficiaries of the public health policies of other states to an extent sufficient to generate obligations of fairness to the scheme. Therefore, even if it were true that providing some public health benefit requires that states exercise power over foreign individuals, fairness considerations are insufficient to establish a moral right of states against aliens. For this and the previous reasons, I turn to a different rationale for granting states rights in public health.

Public health as a requirement of justice

Let me now outline an alternative view that stands a better chance of justifying some rights political institutions exercise over their subjects, against aliens and over their territory. The argument from fairness is neutral concerning whether or not there is a moral requirement to promote public health. It only states that once policies for the promotion of public health are cooperatively pursued, everyone benefiting from them has an obligation to contribute their fair share. We can plausibly start out from a stronger premise, however. There are good reasons for holding it as a matter of justice that public health ought to be promoted.[9] Political institutions with powers over subjects, territory and against aliens are necessary for carrying out this task.

We can justify the rights of political institutions by introducing a further premise: that every person has a natural duty of justice that requires the following things. First, all those individuals subject to a currently existing just or nearly just scheme of institutions are required to contribute their fair share to upholding it, which involves the requirement to comply with the rules of the scheme. Second, those outside an existing just or nearly just scheme must not obstruct or undermine its working. Finally, individuals must further the establishment of just institutions in case they do not yet exist.[10] The requirements following from our natural duty of justice can give a moral grounding to the rights claimed by states in protecting public health. If the provision of policies to promote public health is part of what it means to have a just scheme of institutions, state rights backed up by powers of enforcement and corresponding requirements on individuals, are morally justified by the natural duty of justice.

To illustrate, subjects might be required by their duty of justice to undergo mandatory vaccination necessary to provide the population with immunity against an infectious disease that would otherwise impose a substantial burden of disease on the population even when vaccination involves some cost to those undergoing it. In the absence of such a policy the public health function of political institutions would be seriously compromised. Furthermore, public health within a country can in some cases only be promoted by imposing certain restrictions on some freedoms of aliens, such as their freedom of movement. In these cases, political institutions may be justified in making and enforcing such restrictions against aliens, who in turn have a corresponding duty not to obstruct these rules. International travel restrictions might thus be justified in the case of the emergence of a highly contagious disease that represents catastrophic risk, and travelers are in such cases expected to abide by these restrictions.[11] Rights over territory may also be justified on public health grounds. For example, political institutions might have to restrict the movement of health-related goods across borders in defense of the health care system serving the relevant population, if free imports would undermine some important public health aims.[12]

Whether such public health policies are justified is to a large extent an empirical question. The justifiability of mandatory vaccination policy for a contagious disease, for example, depends on a number of facts about the character of the epidemic and the organization of society. It might be the case that voluntary vaccination programs result in higher participation rates than mandatory programs do. However, under certain circumstances mandatory vaccination might be the only way to go. If mandatory vaccination is the only available means to sustain population immunity, one might argue that individuals have a duty of justice to undergo vaccination and states have an obligation to establish a mandatory vaccination policy.[13]

The limits of state sovereignty: the erosion of state capacities, global public goods

The rights states have in promoting the public health within their borders are not without limits, however. Not all the rights states have historically claimed are justifiable. There are several reasons why nation-states in their current form might not be the appropriate bearers of at least some of these territorial rights, hence why the state-system as we know it may need to be supplemented or replaced by some alternative global political regime. These considerations significantly constrain the justification of specific institutional arrangements capable of performing the functions necessary for promoting public health.

In what follows, I will look at two such constraints on states' rights: the need for global coordination due to the erosion of state capacities and the prospect of achieving better health outcomes on one hand, and concern about human rights on the other hand.

Let me first outline some public health-based considerations that have made some territorial rights usually associated with states outdated in the sense that, due to modern developments, either most states are no longer capable of exercising certain functions that could be used to justify these rights, or it is desirable that functions previously exercised by territorial states be transferred to supranational institutions. Recent institutional, social, economic, ecological and technological developments have brought about both the demand for supranational coordination in many areas and also the capacities that were lacking in previous institutional arrangements. This applies to public health too.

Some of the most pressing current public health issues have taken a global dimension. Recent epidemics such as HIV/AIDS, cholera, ebola, SARS and avian flu all presented or threatened with global public health problems with potentially catastrophic consequences. States' capacity to protect public health by exercising their rights has been significantly diminished by changes in social networks, the global economy, ecology and technological developments, such as the increase in the volume of the movement of persons, goods and ideas. In turn, improved domestic health outcomes are now possible by better global coordination that involves removing some elements of state sovereignty and granting additional rights to other entities, such as supranational institutions. These changes have undermined the moral rationale for granting some of the rights states have claimed for themselves.

This process can take several forms. One obvious case relates to the movement of persons such as travel and migration. Infectious diseases can spread across populations more rapidly than ever, due to the rapid speed of travel enabled by modern technology and the increasing numbers of people traveling. Early detection of and response to some dangerous infectious diseases on the state level is made difficult or impossible by the relatively short travel time of even the longest international flights compared to the incubation period of these diseases. Not only is the transmission of existing strains of infectious diseases facilitated, their mutation and development of new strains is also made easier by the same changes. These changes have decreased the capacity of individual states to effectively prevent or contain the spread of communicable diseases.

Moreover, potential responses to these global public health issues suffer from similar collective action problems to what we saw characterizing domestic public health policies. Global coordination is necessary to effectively promote public health in most societies; however, such cooperation may not be forthcoming or may not be efficient due to some built-in problems. Increased global travel and trade volume facilitating the spread of infectious diseases is made a global collective action problem by the incapacity of individual states to achieve the globally desirable outcome by acting alone.

Consider the example of the role of antibiotics in facilitating the emergence of resistant strains. It is now well known that the overuse of antibiotics contributes to the emergence of drug resistant strains such as multidrug resistant tuberculosis, creating negative externalities for countries with responsible drug-policies. Suppose country A is aware of the threats of drug misuse and decides to restrict the use of antibiotics by imposing strict regulations on their prescription. This means that it has to incur substantial costs and to forgo some potential minor benefits of a more liberal use of antibiotics in order to prevent the emergence of resistant strains. For example, it has to devote resources to monitoring patients' drug use, patient support and quick introduction of alternative drug regimens when resistance begins to emerge (Kremer, 2006: 32). Suppose, however, that other countries are less strict in regulating the use of antibiotics and for this reason multidrug resistant forms of a disease emerge. Given the rapidity of the movement of persons across borders, country A will no longer be able to benefit from its more restrictive regulations, while still bearing its costs. Without international cooperation the desired aim cannot be reached.[14]

Control of the use of antibiotics is one case of global public goods in public health that present global collective action problems; however, there are other important cases too. Let us see a brief list of these.

Eradication efforts

In the case of communicable diseases that are close to eradication, like polio today, a global public good can be created by efforts targeted at its final eradication. In the case of polio, the benefits of its eventual eradication would be mostly enjoyed by rich countries, which at the moment have to expend considerable resources on vaccinating their population. The costs would, however, have to be borne disproportionately by poorer countries, which otherwise have other priorities, considering some more pressing public health problems they face and the low prevalence of polio in these countries (Kremer, 2006).

Disease surveillance

Early information gained from global surveillance is necessary for controlling the spread of some communicable diseases. However, individual countries have an incentive to free-ride by benefiting from the efforts of neighboring and other countries without contributing their share. Disease reporting might be costly for them, for example, because of the economic effects of adverse publicity or travel bans or recommendations by other countries or WHO.

Medical knowledge generation and dissemination

Medical research is usually costly; on the other hand, the benefits generated from it are sometimes enjoyed also by countries that did not contribute their share of the costs. In economic terms this means that there is a tendency to underinvest by rich countries and private companies into R&D on vaccines and drugs targeting diseases in poorer countries, for example into developing vaccines for schistosomiasis or malaria, since they cannot recover the costs.

One main reason is that patent protection, which is the main safeguard in rich countries for pharmaceutical companies to recover the costs of their investment into research and development, is less comprehensive in developing countries that have chosen to limit patent protection for drugs. This has resulted in underinvestment in R&D for drugs most needed by low- and middle-income countries. This problem can be overcome by devising and financing programs that encourage the provision of R&D in pharmaceutical research into drugs that can most effectively reduce the burden of disease in poor countries.[15]

In addition to providing incentives for R&D in drugs and vaccines for neglected diseases, the establishment of public health norms and standards is also an important form of medical knowledge generation. WHO already performs this function for a range of activities, such as diagnosis, treatment, prevention, surveillance and health information. These norms and standards, such as the International Classification of Diseases and Injuries and the Essential Drugs List developed by WHO, also constitute important global public goods because, once they exist, most people will benefit from their application.

These are examples of potential global public health measures that would bring about better health outcomes in many countries, which, however, require global cooperation due to the public good nature of these benefits. They provide us with a further reason to think that states should give up some rights they have claimed for themselves, which should instead be assigned to transnational bodies. If justice requires the effective provision of public health for a given population or within a given territory, political institutions ought to be so organized as to carry out this task on pain of injustice. Global collective action problems impose significant limits on what states can achieve by way of public health policy. On one hand, they reduce capacities states formerly had in protecting public health. On the other hand, they prevent potential improvements in public health outcomes states cannot individually achieve. These constraints can be overcome only by greater global coordination, which is then required by justice.

Justice then requires the provision of global public goods in public health because these goods enable the promotion of public health for any given population or territory. The fact that there are available mechanisms to provide global public goods that promote public health make it the case that people have a duty to implement these mechanisms and abide by their rules.[16]

Notice that the normative force of a requirement to establish these policies and institutions need not be stemming from a commitment to global justice, which requires the promotion of global public health by the relevant agents. For the argument to go through, it suffices if we recognize the importance of promoting domestic public health. Assuming that domestic justice requires the promotion of public health within society, and that the only way to do so is by overcoming the global collective action problems outlined above, global public health institutions and policies are required even on what are essentially domestic justice grounds. Thus the justification of global public health measures can be premised on the more modest requirement to promote domestic public health.

The limits of state sovereignty: human rights

In addition to the erosion of state capacities and the need for global coordination, the human rights of citizens and aliens as well limit state sovereignty in public health protection. These considerations emphasize that, due to the importance of some other values, not all the rights states have claimed may be justified even by considering the public health benefits they would yield, and thus some of them are to be rejected. The reason is that they might be in conflict with the requirements of human rights enshrined in various international human rights documents, guiding the working of international institutions.

Under the concept of human rights, persons possess a universally valid claim to certain rights, regardless of race, gender or nationality. Although the foundations and nature of human rights are a contested issue, there is sufficient consensus about the content of a minimal list of human rights that allows for prescribing some limits on the rights of states against their citizens and aliens. This list is likely to include rights such as rights against violence, enslavement, coercion and torture, and also rights to freedom of conscience and expression and to free movement. When acknowledging an internationally accepted list of human rights, I do not include a human right to health on this list. It remains questionable whether it is even conceptually coherent to talk about a human right to health as such, nor does this right command wide acceptance internationally. There is, however, convergence on a narrower list that significantly constrains the rights of states.[17]

One way to see the doctrine of human rights is that there is a minimum content of political morality that must constrain any setup of political institutions. Initially it emphasized the significant limit posed by human rights to what states may do to their subjects. It is now widely accepted that states ought not to violate the basic human rights of their subjects in imposing and enforcing their institutions and policies. On the other hand, more recently there has been a growing consensus that in addition to the human rights of citizens, the rights of outsiders as well place a limit on state sovereignty. The lives of outsiders are directly or indirectly significantly affected by the way states operate, hence the rights states have against aliens are subject to assessment from the point of view of the interests of outsiders as well. For example, states' right to prohibit movement across their borders is significantly qualified by the aliens' right to free movement, or their right to seek asylum. A blank denial of entry to residents of certain countries on public health grounds can be hard to justify, for example, in the face of the fact that some of these immigrants are persecuted in their home country, or cannot fulfill even their basic needs due to crushing poverty. The strength of considerations supporting denial of entry is also much weaker in the case of epidemics that unfold relatively slowly over years, such as HIV and tuberculosis, than it is in the case of rapidly progressing epidemics because the urgency of the problem is smaller. Travel or immigration restrictions cannot be justified across the board, only in some well-circumscribed cases: factors such as the speed of disease transmission, the risk entailed and the harm potentially afflicting the would-be immigrants in the case of denial of entry also need to be taken into account. We can convincingly claim that prohibiting immigration in some such cases would violate human rights, thus states do not have an unqualified right to do so. Even when some restrictions may be allowed in the interest of public health, the existence of other considerations entail that these can be in effect only temporarily.[18]

Human rights have stronger force than mere normative aspirations. Not only do they act as normative constraints on the moral justifiability of rights claimed by states, but as legal rights they can also successfully limit state powers. That human rights impose limits on what states are entitled to do to their subjects and aliens has been recognized by the various fundamental human rights documents that have become part of international law in the second half of the twentieth century, such as the Universal Declaration of Human Rights, or the International Covenant on Economic, Social and Cultural Rights. These legally binding covenants have been ratified by many governments, and the rights they embed often substantially limit state sovereignty. In addition to being incorporated in international law through the various human rights documents, human rights have also entered global governance through the working of international institutions, networks and NGOs, which have employed human rights standards either in defining their aims or in limiting the permissible means to achieving their aims. Such entities, even though not created through international human rights documents, have explicitly or implicitly made reference to human rights norms in their working, with an effect on health outcomes. One notable example is the WHO's new International Health Regulations. Countries subject to IHRs are required to cooperate in preventing international public health emergencies. However, in applying the regulations, states are required to respect human rights and fundamental freedoms of persons, notably they should 'treat travellers with respect for their dignity, human rights and fundamental freedoms' (WHO, 2005).

Other international and regional institutions have also incorporated human rights norms in their public health-relevant policies. At the international level, the United Nations Joint Programme on HIV/AIDS (UNAIDS) and United Nations Development Program (UNDP) have explicitly adopted human rights norms into their health strategies and policy guidance. Regionally, the Pan American Health Organization (PAHO) addressed human rights issues in the treatment of HIV-infected persons.

Human rights considerations are relevant for delimiting the rights of states in public health even if we do not think there is a human right to health, or that a focus on human rights would provide us with the best means of promoting global public health. Instead of defining the aims of public health policies, human rights act as important constraints on the promotion of public health, whether it is domestic or global. Since in some cases they conflict with the rights claimed by states in promoting public health, the transfer of public health powers from state to global institutions is required if the transfer can resolve this conflict.

The rights of states and global governance in the face of global public health challenges

Returning to the rights of states, we need to see what follows from the above considerations. We saw earlier that states have claimed some rights against their subjects, against aliens and over their territory, which can be justified by pointing out that state powers are necessary for performing public health functions that ought to be discharged as a matter of justice. I further argued, however, that there are good reasons why political institutions are not entitled to all the rights traditionally associated with territorial states.

Some non-public-health-based considerations such as human rights standards constrain the justification and the exercise of state powers, and even public health considerations must respect them. On the other hand, the need for global coordination necessary for the provision of public health domestically has undermined the justification of granting some of the rights to states.

The diminishing of state powers, however, does not defeat the justice-based argument for public health promotion as it would fairness-based arguments. Whereas in the absence of effective public health policies there would be no requirement of fairness to set up such policies, our natural duty of justice requires the establishment of institutions and policies capable of effectively performing public health functions. Since states with their traditional territorial rights do not necessarily represent the best currently available institutional setup, justice considerations with regard to public health may call for the establishment of alternative institutional schemes capable of effectively performing public health functions.

One might object here that the mere existence of weak states does not provide an argument for moving away from state authority. One might conclude instead that state powers should be strengthened, especially in light of the fact that states might be reluctant to waive parts of their sovereignty. However, there are compelling reasons to resist this conclusion. First, I have argued that this might not be possible because global collective active problems in public health provision impose significant limits on what nation-states can achieve by way of public health policy. In these cases there is simply no way to strengthen states to cope with these problems, and global coordination is required. Second, in other cases it is not morally desirable to strengthen nation-states: for example if doing so would undermine or violate some human rights. Therefore, there seems to be no viable alternative to setting up transnational institutions and actors.[19]

Such reforms are facilitated by the fact that, in addition to creating new problems, recent changes provide new opportunities for achieving better health outcomes worldwide. The current global institutional setup already provides new instruments for promoting public health and represents a departure from the nation-state system. A large number of non-state actors have appeared as competitors challenging territorial governance by states on the domain of public health as well. For instance, an increasing number of functionally defined, non-territorial institutions are already in place. Territorial political authority has in practice already been supplemented by a horizontally dispersed, functionally defined system of global governance. As a result, some of the nation-states have in fact already given up a substantial part of their sovereignty.

The current global setup of health-related institutions is extremely complex. One significant player with global reach in public health is the WHO. The WHO is an international organization with 192 member states, with global, regional and national offices, responsible for some aspects of public health globally. Its primary aim is global health promotion, with functions in setting health policy positions and norms, monitoring their implementation, managing information and promoting R&D, facilitating national and global health cooperation and promoting the development and testing of new technologies and practices for disease control, health care delivery and risk reduction. In some cases it is entitled to pursue its objectives even without the mediation of national government agencies, which makes it capable of overcoming some global collective action problems in public health promotion.

For example, prompted by the need for increased global cooperation in infectious disease surveillance and response, the new International Health Regulations (IHRs) adopted in 2005 grant the WHO substantial authority to obtain information about outbreaks from sources other than national authorities, which sometimes have incentives to defer reporting or to downplay the scope of the problem. In performing its role in preventing the global spread of communicable diseases the WHO now collects information from local media reports and the Internet, which it uses for issuing travel recommendations. It does so by sometimes sidestepping government channels of the countries concerned, e.g. by scanning Internet reports about suspicious outbreaks. This works against states' traditional rights over their territory, however, it makes it easier to overcome one of the global collective action problems outlined earlier. It enables improved global infectious disease surveillance and as a result, it helps prevent the global spread of infectious diseases, such as SARS. On the other hand, the IHRs also enable governments to perform their domestic public health functions by providing for them advance notice to prepare for an outbreak on their territory, for example by obtaining the necessary vaccines. The IHRs also grant WHO the authority to take action in response to outbreaks. It may in some cases issue travel bans or invoke quarantine even in the face of protests by some individual countries concerned.[20] It also has the authority to allocate stockpiles of vaccines in public health emergencies. These competences enable the WHO to contribute to the global provision of a number of health-related public goods.

Other transnational institutions and bodies also play a role in promoting public health. Some of these have other primary objectives than health promotion, however, their working has a public health dimension and sometimes public health is an explicit consideration in their policies. For example, WTO regulation in the context of free trade requires adherence to public health criteria. It grants the right to officials from importing states to inspect and test goods within the territory of the exporting country to prevent health risks potentially affecting their residents by importing diseases through commerce (Fidler, 2002: 154). Another transnational organization, the World Bank commits substantial part of its lending each year for health, nutrition and population projects in developing countries where it has been one of the largest supporters of HIV/AIDS programs. A further example of an international body with public health relevance is shown by the role of UNICEF in providing vaccines for child immunization worldwide: it supplies about 40 per cent of the world's vaccines for children (Kremer, 2006: 28).

Other institutions have less than global scope, still they transcend national boundaries in the application of their policies affecting public health. For example, regional development banks such as the Inter-American Development Bank and African Development Bank also provide funds for combating communicable diseases.

Yet another form of transnational institutions in the public health domain is represented by specialized agencies or public–private partnerships that have a limited scope of competence in public health promotion, typically extending to some well-circumscribed set of diseases. The Joint United Nations Programme on HIV/AIDS (UNAIDS) plays a role in extending antiretroviral treatment to an ever larger number of people living with AIDS in developing countries, following the '3 by 5' initiative targeting the provision of ARV treatment to three million patients by the end of 2005. The Global Fund to Fight AIDS, Tuberculosis and Malaria funds investments in the local public health infrastructure and the scale up of prevention and treatment of these diseases. The Global Alliance for Vaccines and Immunization (GAVI) aims to increase children's access to vaccines in developing countries by funding immunization services.

Finally, non-governmental organizations have an increasing impact on global public health. The most notable example is the Gates Foundation that has committed large funds to battling HIV/AIDS, tuberculosis, malaria and other neglected diseases that have a large share in the global disease burden. Other philanthropic foundations include the Rockefeller Foundation, which has supported R&D to improve global health. Another NGO, ProMED-mail, developed an electronic disease surveillance and early warning system that worked in competition with those operated by states and international organizations like WHO. NGOs influence global health not only by expending funds and providing care, but also by influencing policymaking by states and international organizations. For example, NGOs featured prominently alongside states and international organizations in the debates about intellectual property regulation applying to antiretrovirals in the TRIPS negotiations. The campaign lead by Medecins Sans Frontieres on improving access to antiretrovirals played a major role in shaping the intellectual property rights regime governing the working of pharmaceuticals in developing countries (Fidler, 2002: 158). Thus, in addition to the effects of international institutions, NGO activism in global health has considerably affected global public health and constrained state territorial sovereignty. They successfully challenged some territorial rights of states on grounds of better global health outcomes that could be achieved with an alternative scheme.[21]

This proliferation of initiatives, actors, interests, norms, processes and funding streams in global public health has had two effects. First, as some observers have noted, the importance of health in world politics has grown in the last ten years (Fidler, 2007: 3). This is partly because health has come to feature as an issue in a range of other policy areas such as security, trade, environmental protection, development or human rights. Second, the elements of this complex system do not constitute a coherent structure of governance. Competences are overlapping. Some agencies channel resources through domestic institutions, others have their own permanent staff in countries. NGOs and multinational corporations are involved in making domestic and international health regulation and in implementing health policy, for example by drafting regulations or participating in public–private partnerships. As a result, these institutions, initiatives, NGOs and multinational corporations constrain states' exercise of public health sovereignty by reducing exclusive control of states over their subjects and their territory. They grant some rights over a state's subjects and territory to other states, international organizations and non-state actors, thereby reducing the potential sphere of rights states are capable of exercising over their own subjects and territory.

Critics have claimed that the lack of coordination between various actors in global health has had adverse effects on health justice globally. For example, given the focus of many of these initiatives on a small number of diseases, especially on HIV/AIDS, priorities get skewed.[22] If this is so, this would mean that in addition to solving some problems in global public health, the proliferation of global health initiatives gives rise to some additional problems that need to be tackled on the global level, as they cannot be solved by individual states. These problems can also take the 'tragedy of the commons' form, with non-state actors appearing as yet another group of agents whose pursuit of their own aims leads to collectively suboptimal global health outcomes. For example, the entry of NGOs like the Gates Foundation into the health care sector in developing countries has been claimed to cause an internal 'brain-drain' due to the substantial differences in incomes between health workers in the public sector and NGO-financed projects (Daniels, 2008: 330). This in turn might hinder the scaling up of other health-promoting projects in the same countries. This illustrates how lack of coordination can lead to worse health outcomes even among institutions that aim at promoting health.

Nevertheless, this multilayered system does have an effect on global health, even though it might not be optimal and might not resemble domestic health systems. It contrasts with the traditional territorial nation-state model, being rather a mixture of various levels and forms of governance making up a system with 'criss-crossing lines of authority' (Kis, 2001: 223). Jurisdictions within it are not clear-cut, but often competing or overlapping, 'generating ambiguities about the principal location of authority and political responsibility'. (Held and McGrew, 2002: 10) Some of the institutions making up this system have powers of enforcement, others operate on the basis of voluntary self-regulation. Some norms are incorporated in international law as 'hard law', others are followed as 'soft law' by state and non-state actors on other grounds, such as in view of positive incentives. Some institutions are functionally rather than territorially defined, and even in the case of those with territorial jurisdiction, authority is often not located at the level of nation-states. Some of these institutions perform a limited set of functions, others have a wider scope of authority (Kis, 2001: 223). This is a complex, multilayered scheme of institutions performing supra- and transnational, regional and local governance with a mixture of functionally and territorially defined authority.

Should we applaud this trend toward non-state-level public health activities? If we think justice requires adequate public health policies for a given population or within given territory, political institutions ought to be so organized as to carry out this task. The empirical considerations showing emerging global public health threats and available new non-state instruments demonstrate, on one hand, that nation-states' capacity to carry out this function has diminished, and, on the other hand, that there are available alternative actors and institutions capable of bringing about improved public health outcomes. Therefore, justice requires the application of these new instruments, even if its requirements hold only within a restricted population or territory.

Conclusion

The numerous initiatives and actors that affect global health now constitute a system that is substantially different from the model of the nation-state system where units have final and exclusive authority over a fixed territorial space. The elements of this new scheme have been set up for a variety of reasons. Considerations of the value of health or of justice may not figure very prominently behind many of these. However, the justice-based requirement to promote public health, as well as the requirement to respect human rights, prompt us in the direction of relying on some of the existing elements, reforming others so that they better fit human rights and more effectively promote public health, and establishing new ones, rather than returning to the system of territorially defined nation-states. Considerations of public health and focus on the capacities provided by this new institutional setup support the claim that, for a range of human activities, nation-state-based territorial governance may not be a good, or the best, way of regulation.

Acknowledgements

I would like to thank Angus Dawson, Bruce Jennings, Michael Selgelid, Jurgen de Wispelaere and participants of the Manchester Political Theory Workshop on Public Health for comments on an earlier draft of this paper. Work on this paper was supported by the Harvard University Program in Ethics and Health.

Notes

1 I borrow this typology from Copp (1999: 18, 22–23) and Simmons (2001: 302–306).
2 In including the right to control and prohibit movement across the state's borders under this category, I diverge from the categorization provided by Simmons (2001: 306).
3 There is a continuum between voluntary choice about immunization and mandatory immunization. States sometimes make some prospective benefits conditional on receiving immunization, such as when they make school enrolment conditional on proof of the child's vaccination. See Holland (2007: 138). However, mandatory vaccination is considered and used as a policy instrument in some cases.
4 See the rich literature on the social determinants of health. One place to start is Marmot (2004).
5 This is not intended as a precise definition, and I am fully aware of the complexities the demarcation of the field of public health engenders. In the paper I am concerned with measures that I take to be relatively uncontroversially falling within the domain of public health. For a rich exploration of the concept of public health, see Verweij and Dawson (2007).
6 See Dawson (2007). Dawson, following Paul (2004), distinguishes between herd protection and herd immunity, where the former is taken to refer to the diminished likelihood of someone's contracting a disease because of other persons' being immune to it, and the latter means acquiring individual immunity through the secondary spread of the agent used in the immunization. I do not follow this terminology in this paper, but I would like to point out that population immunity in my usage corresponds to herd protection in that terminology.
7 The principle was first suggested by Hart (1955). The most elaborate and influential defense of the principle with regard to political obligation is provided by Klosko (1992).
8 Some additional criteria must also be fulfilled: the goods in question must be worth their costs and must be fairly distributed (Klosko, 1992: chap. 2).
9 I do not have the space here to defend this claim. For one convincing detailed argument, see Daniels (1985) and Daniels (2008). For the purposes of this paper,

however, I want to remain neutral about the grounds for viewing public health as a matter of justice, without committing to Daniels's equality of opportunity-based version of the defense.

10 John Rawls argues that we have a natural duty of justice that 'requires us to support and comply with just institutions that exist and apply to us', and 'it also constrains us to further just arrangements not yet established, at least when this can be done without too much cost to ourselves.' (Rawls, 1999: 99). My characterization of this duty is more expansive in that it requires outsiders not to undermine just institutions. This can plausibly be seen as a natural extension of Rawls's formulation.

11 For one such proposal, see Epstein (2006).

12 The fairness-based and justice-based arguments I have outlined are of course not exhaustive of the list of potential justifications of state rights on public health grounds. Notably, I do not discuss here justifications based on the no-harm principle. For reasons I do not have the space to go into here, I believe that that principle cannot be successfully invoked in defense of a wide spectrum of public health measures that are characterized by public good properties.

13 I thank an anonymous referee of this journal for raising this point.

14 For the history of the emergence of MDRTB and some ethical issues raised by its global spread, see Selgelid (2008: 10–20, 2007: 218–229).

15 See the proposals by Michael Kremer and Thomas Pogge. For Kremer, see Glennerster and Kremer (2004). For Pogge, see Hollis and Pogge (2008).

16 An interesting question arises in connection with global public goods about the legitimacy of transnational coercive mechanisms that might be necessary for the creation and maintenance of cooperation yielding global public goods. What criteria of legitimacy do these structures have to meet? Do they call for a global democracy or egalitarian global distributive requirements? One can plausibly argue that at the very least these structures trigger requirements to include affected parties in the decision-making mechanisms determining their distribution. Similarly, if these mechanisms enable wealthy states to advance their interests in health promotion, but leave poor countries with no or little benefits, then the interests of all have not been adequately taken into account in decision-making, if significantly greater benefits could be gained by the worst-off states at little sacrifice by others. However, transnational coercive mechanisms may generate more demanding requirements too. One might argue that global public goods in health ought to be distributed equally. For example, if we can show that the current global intellectual property rights regime incentivizing pharmaceutical research and development primarily benefits affluent countries, and these can be replaced or supplemented by some alternative regime that enables better health outcomes in poor countries, rich countries may have a duty to reform the existing scheme (Hollis and Pogge, 2008). Lack of space prevents me from giving a detailed account of the legitimacy-grounding conditions of global cooperation.

17 For the purposes of the paper's argument, I need not take a stance on the controversial issue of global socioeconomic justice. Regardless of whether requirements of socioeconomic justice apply across countries, it suffices here to acknowledge that there are some human rights that can successfully constrain the rights of states in public health.

18 This is not to say that many states do not in fact impose stricter regulations on immigration. It is arguable, however, that in these cases they violate human rights, both as moral rights and as legal rights embedded in international legal documents.

19 I thank an anonymous reviewer of this journal for raising this point.
20 In the case of the SARS epidemic in 2003, this is what happened when China and Canada lobbied against WHO's recommendations against traveling in these two countries.
21 It was suggested to me by Bruce Jennings that these forms of global cooperation might be thought to give rise to fairness-based obligations for the individual countries benefiting from them to contribute their share. This may be so, but even in this case this point would not undermine the justice-based justification of global public health measures. Rather, the two types of obligation—i.e. fairness-based and justice-based—would be mutually reinforcing. The justice-based obligation would hold even in cases when no such cooperation exists, prescribing the establishment or extension of public health policies. On the other hand, fairness-based obligations, alongside justice-based obligations, would be triggered when public-good-generating cooperation already exists.
22 Between 1996 and 2005, annual spending on AIDS programs in developing countries increased from $300 million to $8 billion, in contrast with the $2 billion share allocated to malaria and tuberculosis together that jointly account for a comparable part of the global disease burden. See Cohen (2006). For a comprehensive critique of the anarchical nature of global health initiatives, see Garrett (2007).

References

Bayer, R. and Colgrove, J. (2002). Bioterrorism, Public Health, and the Law. *Health Affairs*, **21**, 98–101.

Cohen, J. (2006). The New World of Global Health. *Science*, **311**, 162–167.

Copp, D. (1999). The Idea of a Legitimate State. *Philosophy and Public Affairs*, **28**, 3–45.

Daniels, N. (1985). *Just Health Care*. New York: Cambridge University Press.

Daniels, N. (2008). *Just Health*. New York: Cambridge University Press.

Dawson, A. (2007). Herd Protection as Public Good. In Dawson A. and Verweij M. (eds), *Ethics, Prevention, and Public Health*. Oxford: Oxford University Press, pp. 160–178.

Dawson, A. and Verweij, M. (2007). Introduction. In Dawson A. and Verweij M. (eds), *Ethics, Prevention, and Public Health*. Oxford: Oxford University Press, pp. 1–12.

Epstein *et al.* (2006). Controlling Pandemic Flu and the Value of International Travel Restrictions. Working Paper, Brookings Institution.

Fidler, D. (2002). A Globalized Theory of Public Health Law. *Journal of Law, Medicine and Ethics*, **30**, 150–161.

Fidler, D. (2007). Architecture Amidst Anarchy. *Global Health Governance*, January **1**, 1–17.

Garrett, L. (2007). The Challenge of Global Health. *Foreign Affairs*, **86**, 14.

Glennerster, R. and Kremer, M. (2004). *Strong Medicine: Creating Incentives for Pharmaceutical Research on Neglected Diseases*. Princeton, NJ: Princeton University Press.

Gostin, L. (2002). Public Health Law in an Age of Terrorism. *Health Affairs*, **21**, 79–93.

Hart, H. L. A. (1955). Are There Any Natural Rights? *Philosophical Review*, **64**, 175–191.

Held, D. and McGrew, A. (2002). Introduction. In *Governing Globalization*. Cambridge: Polity Press, pp. 1–24.

Holland, S. (2007). *Public Health Ethics*. Cambridge: Polity Press.

Hollis, A. and Pogge, T. (2008). The Health Impact Fund: Making New Medicines Accessible for All.

Kis, J. (2001). Nation-Building and Beyond. In Will, K. and Magda, O. (eds), *Can Liberal Pluralism be Exported?* Oxford: Oxford University Press, pp. 220–242.

Klosko, G. (1992). *The Principle of Fairness and Political Obligation*. Oxford: Rowman and Littlefield.

Kremer, M. (2006). Global Public Goods in Communicable Disease Control. International Task Force on Global Public Goods: *Expert Paper One: Infectious Disease*. Stockholm.

Marmot, M. (2004). *The Status Syndrome*. New York: Owl Books.

Paul, Y. (2004). Letter: 'Herd Immunity and Herd Protection'. *Vaccine*, **22**, 301–302.

Rawls, J. (1999). *A Theory of Justice*, rev. edn. Cambridge, MA: Harvard University Press.

Selgelid, M. (2007). Ethics and Drug Resistance. *Bioethics*, **21**, 218–229.

Selgelid, M. (2008). Ethics, Tuberculosis and Globalization. *Public Health Ethics*, **1**, 10–20.

Simmons, A. John. (2001). On the Territorial Rights of States. *Philosophical Issues*, **35**, 300–325.

Verweij, M. and Dawson, A. (2007). The Meaning of 'Public' in 'Public Health'. In Dawson A. and Verweij M. (eds), *Ethics, Prevention, and Public Health*. Oxford: Oxford University Press, pp. 13–30.

World Health Organization. (2005). International Health Regulations, Geneva. Quoted in Lance Gable: The Proliferation of Human Rights in Global Health Governance. *Journal of Law, Medicine & Ethics*, **35**, 534–544.

75

THE POLITICS OF DISEASE

Governance and emerging infections

Elizabeth M. Prescott

Source: *Global Health Governance*, 1:1 (2007), 1–8.

Infectious disease outbreaks demand a timely and proportional response. The responsibility for this action falls to those with the power to harness the processes and systems by which a society operates in order to effect the changes necessary to limit transmission of an illness. Controlling emerging and reemerging infectious diseases can require extreme actions and coordination between many national and international actors making the ability to respond a reflection of the capacity of a governing system. In the absence of good governance, opportunities are created for disease to emerge, while at the same time, an aggressive response is often hindered. Failures in governance in the face of infectious disease outbreaks can result in challenges to social cohesion, economic performance and political legitimacy. Overall, the need for coordination of actions despite a high degree of uncertainty and high costs makes curtailing infectious disease a challenge in the absence of good governance.

Introduction

According to the World Bank, "a country's governance system comprises the full array of state institutions and the arrangements that shape the relations between the state and society. [...] Public sector governance refers to the way the state acquires and exercises the authority to provide and manage public goods and services—including both public capacities and public accountabilities."[1] Many societal problems must be addressed through coordinated efforts. Populations look to those with political authority to confront these challenges and harness institutional resources in a manner proportionate to the societal burden. The nature of the efforts needed to contain and control a communicable pathogen put emerging and reemerging infectious disease (ERID) into the category that requires concerted action. Therefore, characteristics of ERIDs create unique political challenges requiring effective governance to coordinate and mount the appropriate response.

ERIDs are highly variable in their pathogenic characteristics. These difference help define the impact the disease will have on society. By looking at specific characteristics of ERIDs and taking examples from past outbreaks, this paper will examine the impact of emerging infectious disease on social cohesion, economic performance and political legitimacy. This analysis demonstrates significant implications of ERIDs beyond short-term health impacts as the spread of ERIDs expose preexisting failures of governance at the national and international level. Focusing on this link demonstrates the need for good governance by national and international authorities to best prepare for combating emerging diseases.

Emerging and reemerging infectious diseases and governance

An infectious disease is an illness caused by an organism that enters the body then grows and multiplies in cell, tissue or cavities of the body.[2] Infectious diseases are the leading cause of death worldwide and novel pathogens continue to emerge and reemerge as the ecosystems in which they interact with human hosts evolve.[3] The necessary public health response to contain an infectious pathogen depends on the nature of the agent and characteristics of disease progression. Infections can be acute – such as influenza – with the disease occurring in a short duration and being contagious for a short period of time.[4] Alternatively, infectious diseases can be chronic – such as Hepatitis B and C – with a longer duration of communicability due to continual reproduction of the pathogen.[5] Identification of the causative agent of an infectious illness is critical to determining how to counter the health challenge. Novel or emerging pathogens – such as SARS in China in 2003 – are often difficult to quickly identify. As many illnesses have overlapping symptoms, close examination by trained public health professionals is critical to diagnosis of re-emerging or novel pathogens. Provision of this level of public health expertise requires time and resources making ERID a difficult challenge to maintaining the health of any population.

When functioning properly, an effective public health infrastructure requires close and timely coordination between knowledgeable professionals who are able to craft and implement what is deemed an appropriate response to the identified challenge. Rarely is there perfect information about the nature of an emerging disease. Tolerance for uncertainty and trust in the aptitude of public health professionals by political authorities is critical to implementation of the recommended response. Additionally, in most cases, the actions deemed necessary to counter a growing disease epidemic can be costly and require implementation with minimal deliberation without consensus.[6] These characteristics demand political dexterity that is difficult to achieve.

The response to an outbreak of infectious disease is primarily a domestic government function. Maintaining the capacity to respond to a plethora of pathogens is a costly goal for governments. Recognizing that pathogens do not respect political borders, international resources are made available to help combat infectious diseases with the aim of minimizing negative health impacts in a specific country as well as preventing further geographic spread.[7] However, international organizations such as the World Health Organization (WHO) have limited ability to respond to outbreaks of infectious disease without explicit invitation by the local government where an outbreak occurs.[8] As such, a government is responsible for addressing domestic public health challenges but is forced to recognize and publicly admit when capacity is insufficient and international assistance is necessary. Achieving this balance of domestic sovereignty over health issues and international responsibility to prevent further transmission is challenging and requires effective domestic governance.

For this reason, an outbreak of an ERID can be indicative of and exacerbated by ineffective governance at the national and international levels. Domestic ability to respond to an emerging pathogen requires effective information gathering and dissemination to appropriately trained individuals who are able to assess the data. Pathogens that are not commonly encountered often require broad consultation with the international health community to effectively identify. In the case of SARS, China delayed disclosure of atypical illness to the international community until the disease attracted international attention as a global problem.[9] Soon after international disclosure, the global scientific community sought to understand the pathogen, engaging experts in the field of coronaviruses – mostly from animal health – critical to elucidating characteristics of the human disease.[10] The absence of transparency by the Chinese government early in the SARS epidemic is attributed with fueling the global spread of disease, demonstrating the role poor transparency can play in exacerbating an infectious disease challenge.[11]

Dissemination of information within governments can also hinder disease response. Many ERIDs are zoonotic in origin meaning that they are passed from animals to humans, inducing disease.[12] As such the appropriate response to an epidemic can require actions to control the pathogen in animals concurrent with interventions in the human population. This is demonstrated in the ongoing battle against avian influenza and has complicated the response to the human health challenge. The expansion of the virus to the bird populations forced countries to find mechanisms for collaboration between ministries of health and agriculture. The varied mandates of these ministries can make an uncomfortable fit for information sharing and concerted action. The ability to function collaboratively within governments can determine the success in responding to an ERID making effective intra-governmental interaction critical.

Effective allocation of critical resources is also necessary for responding to the dynamic threat posed by infectious disease. In some cases assets can be re-deployed from other governmental functions. As seen in the SARS outbreak, governments in Asia were able to utilize the military to perform basic public health functions such as taking temperatures at transit centers and tracing contacts for sick patients.[13] Unfortunately, resources do not always exist to be redeployed to public health functions, resulting in the need for quick and responsive international assistance. If there are global resources available to dedicate to a pathogen when it emerges, a surge in funds could localize the outbreak. In the case of a pandemic of influenza, however, all countries will need assistance simultaneously taxing international organizations such as the WHO. In this scenario, resources will need to be prioritized making their allocation less of a humanitarian effort than a strategic diplomatic tool.

Additionally, the capacity to take decisive and costly actions in the face of imperfect information can challenge many governments. In acute public health challenges expediency is critical to an effective response so the problem can be countered before it grows too large to contain with available resources. Leaders who are capable of committing to high-risk decisions based on informed scientific opinion are at an advantage. Evidence suggests that the actions taken by the Vietnamese government in response to SARS, – which were aggressive and costly – were also responsible for extinguishing a growing epidemic in that country.[14] In relation to avian influenza, the delay in identification and response to the arrival of the virus into the bird populations in Nigeria resulted in transmission to other countries in the region.[15] The absence of a rapid and comprehensive response to the pathogen in the early days of introduction in Africa leave the international animal health community highly concerned that avian influenza will become endemic, increasing the challenge for eradication. What these examples highlight is the need for governments to identify an emerging disease challenge, devise a realistic plan for containment, and execute the strategy in a consistent and comprehensive manner. All of these functions rely heavily on effective systems of governance.

Disease disruption

Infectious disease epidemics have plagued society throughout recorded history leading to high levels of disruption when large portions of a population become incapacitated as the epidemic unfolds.[16] For an individual, health is a critical component for active participation in civil society. From a societal perspective, individual engagement in civil society is critical for the economy and politics to function. This connection exacerbates the impact of disease beyond the affect on an individual's health. As such, ERIDs pose a challenge to social cohesion, economic performance and political legitimacy. All of these implications from ERIDs underscore the need for effective governance.

Social cohesion

To achieve social cohesion the majority of citizens must respect the rule of law, human rights and share a commitment to social order. Members of society need to feel as if their interests are best served by maintaining the legal processes that enable conflict resolution through democratic and institutional processes. These systems function with a normal level of social strain but are susceptible to disruption when faced with heightened levels of societal stress.

An epidemic, by definition, results in more cases of disease than normally experienced.[17] With emerging diseases, outbreaks are unlikely to have been predicted and preemptively allocated resources. When they occur there is an increase in demand for resources creating an opportunity for societal strain. This can lead to scarcity of resources and disruption to social cohesion. Historically, epidemics have been known to induce shortages of critical commodities requiring controlled allocation of resources or occasionally rationing of available supplies.[18] In acute epidemics, the need to allocate available resources requires decision-making in a time frame not conducive to consensus. Confronted with limited resources, increasing demand and the need for selective allocation, individuals may abandon previously accepted social norms in an effort to acquire finite commodities perceived to preserve their wellbeing.

The fear of infection and possible blame from transmission of communicable diseases can add to social tension in an expanding epidemic. In the case of ERIDs, the source and mode of disease transmission is often poorly understood preventing convincing reassurances from the public health community. As fear of contracting a disease grows, the pressure increases on individuals to make decisions that previously may have seemed unfathomable. During the influenza pandemic of 1918, many deaths were attributed to breakdowns in basic social assistance that was commonplace in absence of a deadly pathogen.[19] Neighbors were not providing even basic provisions such as food and water out of fear of contracting the disease.[20] Nurses, otherwise dedicated to service in a high-risk work environment, refused to report for duty.[21] In a climate where the basic safety of an individual is in question, social norms can be quickly undermined without a strong and coordinated government effort to inform and assist the population.

Economic performance

In economic terms, an epidemic is an exogenous shock that forces a rapid response from governments and markets. The impact of ERID on economic performance can be seen at many levels. The specific characteristics of disease progression and availability of treatments will have a significant impact on the health care cost associated with containing an epidemic. Chronic infections or those diseases with expensive treatment options can consume significant health care resources. ERIDs are often unbudgeted forcing governments to reallocate resources that might otherwise have been used more productively, further straining budgets and future economic growth.

The human capital cost associated with disease can be substantial. While the loss of a single life to infectious disease is tragic from a humanitarian perspective, a disease that kills or permanently debilitates individuals early in life will have a high societal cost through lost productivity. Early analysis of the economic impact of HIV/AIDS in Southern Africa suggests substantial current and projected costs associated with the growing pandemic.[22] The overall impact on a society will vary by many factors including the degree to which human capital has been diversified through training. For example, in economies with a high degree of specialized labor the loss of an individual can create a gap in skill set that may be costly to replace. In economies with less differentiated labor pool, the ability to easily substitute people who can perform the most critical functions could minimize economic disruption. If the labor pool is tight – with little unemployment – even a small loss in human productive capacity could be significant as the price for acquiring human capital increases. High fatality epidemics such as the Black Death in the 14th Century – resulting in the death of at least a third of European population – can cause labor markets to tighten thereby increasing the value of human capital.[23] In case of the Black Death, the shortage of labor is thought to have changed the balance of power between the elite and the peasant classes while also spurring the development of innovations that improved productivity of human capital, laying a foundation for the Renaissance.[24]

Further, uncertainty surrounding an outbreak forces individuals and organizations to reevaluate economic decisions. At the individual level, this can manifest in changes to planned purchases or delay in activities perceived to be more risky. During the SARS outbreak, despite extensive messaging from US public health authorities about the near absence of risk, there were reports of Americans avoiding Chinese food restaurants in North America.[25] Negative economic impacts were seen as companies sourced from alternate suppliers or cancelled business travel to the affected region.[26] The SARS outbreak also resulted in economic impacts as companies reevaluated the geographic diversity of suppliers or international facilities to prevent being completely incapacitated from another regional shutdown.[27] The diversion of foreign direct investment in the region was substantial during and immediately after the outbreak.[28]

The long-term economic implications of a specific ERID outbreak is more difficult to establish and will depend on whether the disease causes an outbreak that is acute or chronic. The SARS outbreak in 2003 was a single shock that quickly receded allowing normal activities to resume. Had the pathogen returned in the winter of 2004 as some feared, the associated cost would have been more significant.[29] In contrast, the chronic AIDS pandemic is unfolding over generations accumulating long-term societal and economic costs that can only be estimated at this point in history.[30]

Political legitimacy

The ability of an ERID to impact political legitimacy depends on factors inherent in the disease as well as the social and political environment in which the disease emerges. Outbreaks of ERIDs are, by their nature, unpredictable and not easily controlled. Over time, a slow trickle of new pathogens appears on the global stage attracting varying degrees of attention.[31] Many quickly become integrated into societal expectation of disease burden without ever entering the political sphere while others such as Bovine Spongiform Encephalopathy (BSE) or HIV/AIDS, are propelled into the headlines with lingering political implications.[32]

The fundamental characteristics of a pathogen also impact the degree of strain a society experiences. A disease that emerges but has few negative health consequences – causing only mild social or economic disruption – poses little risk to the legitimacy of the governing regime. Occasionally, however, a pathogen emerges that has significant negative health impacts causing disruption to society and potentially threatening political legitimacy. When a pathogen first emerges it is often difficult to predict the full trajectory of an outbreak suggesting that all ERIDs be looked at for their ability to destabilize society.

The arrival of an ERID with significant health impacts presents a societal challenge for a governing authority. A substantial outbreak of disease can make individuals more vulnerable and highlight weaknesses in the provision of governmental services. As more people seek access, government services may not be able to meet expectations generating the perception of failure to meet societal needs. Further, as the response is devised and implemented, an anxious population will critique the judgment and effectiveness of the regime. In absence of the epidemic these weaknesses might have gone undetected. When presented with the inability of the regime to meet expectations for responding to an outbreak, legitimacy may be undermined.

Societal expectation for a government's responsibility for the provision of health is also a critical factor when determining the degree to which a disease can threaten political legitimacy. Control of an emerging pathogen requires actions that are coordinated, something governing authorities may be in the best position to provide. In some cases, however, the population may not hold a political authority directly responsible for the failure to contain infectious disease. In order for responsibility to be attributed to those that govern, a population must trust that a government has the capability and willingness to respond in the face of disaster. If the population does not have the expectation that a government will address a health challenge – do to lack of desire or ability – the political impact of a mishandled response may be minimized.

An example of this can be seen in the outbreak of Japanese encephalitis in northern India in 2005.[33] Despite the existence of a prophylactic vaccine, this vector borne disease aggressively infected children in the 2005 monsoon season leaving over 1000 dead and many more brain damaged. Domestic production of a Japanese encephalitis vaccine was minimal but importation of a vaccine from China was an option. Instead, daily reports of children dying met with political promises to do a better job next year. Failure to secure the vaccine to protect children from the disease did not seem to impact political legitimacy. The affected population, persistently plagued by infectious disease, had little expectation of governmental protection from disease thereby diminishing the impact an outbreak could have on political legitimacy. In contrast, shortages of influenza vaccine in the US in the fall of 2004, well in advance of any detected negative health impacts, resulted in significant popular and political attention. Blame was attributed broadly but the effectiveness of political leadership was questioned.[34] The American population has high expectations that political leaders will make available plentiful health care goods when they are needed. Failure to provide influenza vaccines was seen as a failure to meet these expectations, and therefore worked to undermine confidence in those that were viewed as being responsible.

Conclusion

Emerging and reemerging infectious diseases can undermine the social, economic and political functions of a society. As an outbreak spreads, governments are forced to respond to an unpredicted crisis requiring costly decisions made on imperfect information. The ability to implement and coordinate the necessary actions is reflective of effectiveness governance. An ERID outbreak can magnify preexisting weaknesses resulting in politically visible failures that might otherwise have gone undetected. Further, the spread of infectious disease can reflect the absence of an effective public health system, necessary for basic health maintenance.

Ultimately, the political impact of an outbreak of an ERID depends on the governing capability of the country concerned as well as the credibility the country has with its own population. The potential political impact from an ERID in a country which is known to have good governance and whose population trusts the institutional ability to respond to an outbreak will be higher if the country is unable to meet the challenge effectively. Similarly the inverse holds true.

Interestingly, this interrelationship might present disincentives for a government to raise expectation for their ability to deal with the overall burden of disease. As a population becomes more accustomed to protection from common diseases, expectations could increase for protection from every infectious disease. Therefore, a high level of public health provision in a population could make a regime more susceptible to the politically destabilizing effects of an ERID. While there are many social and economic benefits from minimizing the burden of infectious disease, this suggest a regime could be made more politically vulnerable to an emerging pathogen if the societies overall health is high and a government is viewed as being capable of responding to a novel challenge.

Notes

1 World Bank Global Monitoring Report 2006, Available at www.worldbank.org (accessed on May 21, 2006).
2 "Infectious Disease" Complete Medical Encyclopedia. Eds J. Leikin & M. S. Lipsky. American Medical Association. Random House 2003. pp 721.
3 *ibid.*
4 *ibid.*
5 *ibid.*
6 Erik Millstone and Patrick van Zwanenberg. "Mad Cow Disease – painting policy-making into a corner". September 2004. Available at *http://www.merrea. org/Updates/BSE/BSE%20Preliminary%20Report.pdf* (last accessed 9/17/06).
7 In the UN, the World Health Organization (WHO) deals with human health, the Food and Agriculture Organization (FAO) and the World Organization for Animal Health (OIE) assists with animal health. Many other non-governmental and philanthropic organizations also work in this arena.
8 In 2005 the WHO amended the International Health Regulations to minimize obstacles to the formal notification process necessary when identifying epidemics. More information on these changes can be found at: http://www.who.int/csr/ihr/en/. (Last accessed 4/23/06)
9 Tony Saich, "Is SARS China's Chernobyl or Much Ado About Nothing." *SARS in China: Prelude to Pandemic?* Eds Arthur Kleinman and James Watson, Stanford University Press, Stanford, CA 2006. pp 71–104.
10 "Learning from SARS: Preparing for the Next Disease Outbreak. Workshop Summary." The Institute of Medicine, National Academy of Sciences. Released: January 27, 2004.
11 Tony Saich, "Is SARS China's Chernobyl or Much Ado About Nothing." *SARS in China: Prelude to Pandemic?* Eds Arthur Kleinman and James Watson, Stanford University Press, Stanford, CA 2006. pp 71–104.
12 "Zoonosis" Complete Medical Encyclopedia. Eds J. Leikin & M. S. Lipsky. American Medical Association. Random House 2003. pp 1310.
13 "How Singapore Fights SARS" Diana Tan. ThingsAsian Article published 5/4/03. Available at http://www.thingsasian.com/goto_article/article.2223.html (last accessed on 4/19/06).
14 "Severe Acute Respiratory Syndrome (SARS): Status of the Outbreak and Lessons for the Immediate Future" WHO, 2003. and "How Vietnam beat the bug", CNN, April 28, 2003. Available at http://www.cnn.com/2003/WORLD/asiapcf/east/04/28/sars.vietnam/index.html. (Last accessed: 4/19/06)
15 "Avian flu outbreak in Nigeria yields worrisome scenario" by Elisabeth Rosenthal, Donald G. McNeil Jr., New York Times, Sunday, February 12, 2006.
16 Jared Diamond, "Guns, Germs, and Steel: The Fates of Human Societies", (New York, NY: W.W. Norton and Company). pp 195–214.
17 "Epidemic" Complete Medical Encyclopedia. Eds J. Leikin & M. S. Lipsky. American Medical Association. Random House 2003. pp 515.
18 John Kelly. "The Great Mortality: An intimate History of the Black Death, the Most Devastating Plague of All Time," (New York, NY: HarperCollins. 2005).

19 John M. Barry. "The Great Influenza: The Epic Story of the Deadliest Plague in History". (Penguin. 2004)

20 *ibid.*

21 *ibid.*

22 Erica Barks-Ruggles, Tsetsele Fantan, Malcom McPherson, and Alan Whiteside. "The Economic Impact of HIV/AIDS in Southern Africa". Brookings Institution Conference Report. September 2001. Available at http://www.brookings.edu/comm/conferencereport/cr09.pdf (last accessed 9/17/06).

23 John Kelly. "The Great Mortality: An intimate History of the Black Death, the Most Devastating Plague of All Time," (New York, NY: HarperCollins. 2005).

24 *ibid.*

25 "SARS Fears Hurting Chicago's Chinatown: Businesses Feeling The Pinch Of Virus" April 21, 2003. Available at http://www.nbc5.com/news/2148938/detail.html (last accessed on 4/22/06).

26 Thomas Rawski, "SARS and China's Economy." *SARS in China: Prelude to Pandemic?* Eds Arthur Kleinman and James Watson, (Stanford, CA: Stanford University Press, 2006). pp 105–121.

27 Unpublished personal communication with CEO of biotechnology company

28 Jong-Wha Lee and Warwick J. McKibbin "Globalization and Disease: The Case of SARS." Asian Economic Papers, Winter 2004, Vol. 3, No. 1, Pages 113–131

29 *ibid*

30 Clive Bell, Shantayanan Devarajan and Hans Gersbach. "The Long-run Economic Costs of AIDS: Theory and an Application to South Africa" June 2003. Available at http://www.globalprogressiveforum.org/files/0/gpf/world_bank_long_run_economic _costs_of_aids.pdf (last accessed on 4/22/06).

31 "Microbial Threats to Health: Emergence, Detection, and Response" Institute of Medicine, National Academy of Sciences. Released on March 18, 2003. Available at http://www.iom.edu/CMS/3783/3919/5381.aspx (Last accessed on 4/22/06.)

32 Tony Barnett. "The long-wave event. HIV/AIDS, politics, governance and 'security': sundering the intergenerational bond?", *International Affairs*, 82, 2(2006) pp 297–313 and Erik Millstone and Patrick van Zwanenberg. "Mad Cow Disease – painting policy-making into a corner". September 2004. Available at *http://www. merrea.org/Updates/BSE/BSE%20Preliminary%20Report.pdf* (last accessed on 9/17/06).

33 "Brain disease takes a thousand lives in India" by Shaoni Bhattacharya, 30 September 2005, NewScientist.com. Available at http://www.newscientist.com/article.ns?id=dn8084 (last accessed on 4/22/06).

34 "With Few Suppliers of Flu Shots, Shortage Was Long in Making" By DENISE GRADY, October 17, 2004. Available at: http://www.nytimes.com/2004/10/17/health/17flu2.html?ei=5090&en=917f53168745994c&ex=1255665600&partner=km arx&pagewanted=print&position=(Last accessed on 4/22/06).

76

HAGGLING OVER VIRUSES

The downside risks of securitizing infectious disease

Stefan Elbe

Source: *Health Policy and Planning*, 25:6 (2010), 476–85.

This article analyses how the 'securitization' of highly path-ogenic avian influenza (H5N1) contributed to the rise of a protracted international virus-sharing dispute between develop-ing and developed countries. As fear about the threat of a possible human H5N1 pandemic spread across the world, many governments scrambled to stockpile anti-viral medications and vaccines, albeit in a context where there was insufficient global supply to meet such a rapid surge in demand. Realizing that they were the likely 'losers' in this international race, some developing countries began to openly question the benefits of maintaining existing forms of international health coop-eration, especially the common practice of sharing national virus samples with the rest of the international community. Given that such virus samples were also crucial to the high-level pandemic preparedness efforts of the West, the Indonesian government in particular felt emboldened to use international access to its H5N1 virus samples as a diplomatic 'bargaining chip' for negotiating better access to vaccines and other benefits for developing countries. The securitized global response to H5N1 thus ended up unexpectedly entangling the long-standing international virus-sharing mechanism within a wider set of political disputes, as well as prompting governments to subject existing virus-sharing arrangements to much narrower calcul-ations of national interest. In the years ahead, those risks to international health cooperation must be balanced with the policy attractions of the global health security agenda.

Key messages

- Indonesia's decision in December 2006 to cease sharing its H5N1 virus samples with the international public health community has prompted widespread consternation in the West, as well as eliciting considerable support from many developing countries.
- The resulting international virus-sharing controversy has persisted for 4 years and has since become enmeshed in a broader set of complex legal, political and economic issues that make the disagreement very difficult to resolve.
- The securitization of highly pathogenic avian flu contributed to the emergence of this international virus-sharing dispute, showing that a securitized response to infectious disease management can also have downside risks in terms of complicating international health cooperation.

Introduction

Amidst pressing international concern that the world was on the cusp of a renewed human influenza pandemic, the Indonesian government took the controversial decision in December 2006 to cease sharing its H5N1 virus samples with the international community. It did so after discovering that the virus samples it had been forwarding freely to the World Health Organization (WHO) through the long-standing Global Influenza Surveillance Network (GISN) were being passed on to pharmaceutical companies in the West, where they were being used to develop lucrative new vaccines. Indonesia pointed out that this violated the WHO's own guidelines according to which virus samples should not be distributed outside of the WHO network without prior consent of originating countries (WHO 2005b: 2). Western pharmaceutical companies subsequently also offered those novel vaccines back to the Indonesian government at commercial rates, which Indonesian authorities deemed unaffordable in light of the country's large population of more than 220 million people.

Indonesia's decision to stop this 'exploitative' process by withholding its virus samples split opinion within the international community. Many governments and medical researchers in the West expressed consternation and even anger at a decision they claim is recklessly endangering international public health and global health security. Yet Indonesia's position has also won considerable support, especially amongst many developing countries who feel similarly unable to afford vaccines at market rates. The resulting international dispute over virus sharing has now lasted for 4 years, and marks one of the most substantial setbacks in international health cooperation of the past decade.

The precise causes of this virus-sharing controversy are difficult to pin down, not least because both sides in the dispute have engaged in a fair bit of diplomatic mud-slinging regarding each other's motives. At the time, the Indonesian health minister Siti Fadilah Supari levied outlandish accusations at the United States government, including that the latter was ciphering off virus samples in order to develop biological weapons at Las Alamos National Laboratories (Supari 2008: 19), a charge she reiterated in more general and country non-specific terms as recently as March 2009 when she stated publicly that 'I'm truly afraid the world will use our viruses or DNAs to create a mass biological weapon that may be used to attack us' (*Jakarta Globe* 2009). During that same period, some policy-maker in the West similarly sought to tarnish the reputation of the Indonesian health minister, with opinion pieces written in influential newspapers and internet blogs disparaging of her attempts to locate Indonesia's health policies within wider anti-Western struggles, and openly speculating about more selfish or other political reasons for her position on virus sharing (Holbrooke and Garrett 2008; Leavitt 2008).

Nor was the decision to withhold virus samples from the international public health community uncontroversial within Indonesia itself. Certainly the position of the health minister was endorsed at the time by the country's president, and throughout her term of office (which ended in 2009) Supari remained a popular political figure frequently featured in Indonesian lifestyle magazines. Yet dissenting voices within Indonesia were also not difficult to find. Interviews carried out with Indonesian officials by Paul Forster during 2008 revealed that some thought she was mostly using the issue of virus sharing as a way of deflecting attention from other political failures. Others cited the wider popularity within Indonesian politics of standing up to the West, and also noted that her line would appeal to Islamist and nationalist parties. Others still indicated that her motivation ultimately remained a mystery and that there may also be other psychological factors involved (Forster 2009: 47–49). Those interviewees further pointed to tensions within the Indonesian Ministry of Health, where the virus-sharing dispute was seen to be distracting from other crucial items of business and complicating relations with the WHO (Forster 2009: 48). The course of events leading up to the international virus-sharing dispute is therefore complex, and is also likely to include a range of factors associated with Indonesian domestic politics. Even with the benefit of hindsight, the emergence of the international virus-sharing dispute cannot be readily reduced to a single factor.

Yet one important aspect of that virus-sharing controversy that analysts have so far overlooked is the contributing role played by the initial 'securitization' of highly pathogenic avian influenza. That securitized international response to H5N1 had two fateful consequences. First, the considerable fear of an imminent human pandemic provoked a competitive rush amongst governments around the world (including Indonesia) to secure access to pharmacological counter-measures for reducing the spread of H5N1. In a global context where there were insufficient global supplies to meet that sudden surge in demand, it did not take long for some developing countries to become acutely aware that a profound conflict of interest exists between developed and developing countries when it comes to maintaining existing forms of international health cooperation. The international virus-sharing mechanism may work well for developed countries that possess their own pharmaceutical manufacturing base, but the material benefits accruing from such cooperation for developing countries are far less evident.

Second, the high-level concern about H5N1 in the West suddenly also rendered the viruses circulating in Indonesia's territorial borders very 'valuable'. At the time the West needed unencumbered and legal access to samples of those viruses in order to track the global evolution of the virus and to develop pharmacological treatments against the threat. Without such access, the West would not be able to maintain a set of comprehensive and up-to-date medical interventions to protect their populations—even if they had the manufacturing capacity to do so (unless Western countries were able to obtain such samples through channels other than the GISN). Amidst the occasionally frenzied efforts of the West to shore up its defences against the impending H5N1 threat, and the political pressure it consequently put on developing countries where human cases of H5N1 infection were already occurring, the Indonesian government in particular came to realize that it now controlled access to what was in fact a very precious 'resource'—and one which it, in turn, could deploy as a diplomatic bargaining chip on the international stage for negotiating greater access to vaccines and other benefits for developing countries.

Both effects of the securitization of H5N1 have ultimately made the virus-sharing dispute more difficult to resolve: the first has embroiled the long-standing international virus-sharing mechanism in a much wider set of North–South disputes, whilst the second has rendered international health cooperation a matter of more narrow and calculated national interest. A key lesson to emerge from the international virus-sharing controversy is therefore that a securitized response to infectious disease management can also have unanticipated consequences in terms of further complicating international health cooperation. In the years ahead, those downside risks associated with a securitized response to global public health will need to be balanced with the evident benefits of the global health security agenda, especially in terms of mobilizing political leadership and resources for the management of emerging and re-emerging infectious diseases.

Method

This article undertakes a case study analysis of the international response to the emergence of human infections with highly pathogenic avian influenza

A viruses of the subtype H5N1 (hereafter simply H5N1). Specifically, the article analyses how the securitized nature of that global response to H5N1 contributed in recent years to the rise of a protracted international virus-sharing dispute between developed and developing countries. The study draws upon securitization theory as its conceptual framework, which was initially developed in the non-medical disciplines of International Relations and Critical Security Studies. Securitization theory is principally concerned with discerning how issues are responded to differently in national and international policy circles when they become widely perceived or 'framed' as pressing existential threats. Crucially, and as a constructivist social theory, securitization theory does not try to establish whether any particular issue 'really' constitutes a security threat or not; instead it mostly comes into play once an issue has already been securitized, and forms a useful conceptual tool for studying the political consequences of such a securitization process. Based on an extensive analysis of a wide range of different international issues that have become securitized over the past two decades, securitization theory has been able to identify a set of policy advantages and drawbacks that can accrue once issues are securitized.

Taking an interdisciplinary approach and bringing securitization theory to bear directly on the international response to highly pathogenic avian influenza is useful in that H5N1 too became widely perceived as constituting such a pressing existential threat in international policy circles (especially throughout 2005 and 2006). Indeed, H5N1 marks one of the most prominent international health issues to have become securitized over the past decade. H5N1 can thus serve as a pertinent case study for tracing how the effects of securitization unfold specifically in the field of global health. The following study analyses those political consequences in relation to the international virus-sharing dispute, and shows those effects to be consistent with the wider trends witnessed in a range of other securitization processes that have already occurred outside of the health sector.

The empirical material for this study on the international politics of virus sharing was drawn from a variety of different sources. Those sources include more than a dozen semi-structured, one-to-one background interviews carried out with key participants in the international virus-sharing dispute. The article also took into account a range of policy papers, background papers, working papers and articles on virus sharing generated by international organizations, governments, think tanks and newspapers (secondary data), as well as scholarly articles and books published on the virus-sharing controversy (tertiary data). Those sources were located through library searches, scholarly databases in public health and international relations, internet searches using a commercial search and contacts in the international academic and policy communities.

Results and discussion

The securitization of H5N1

What exactly does it mean to say that an issue has become 'securitized'? Scholars of international politics succinctly define securitization as the political process through which an issue is 'presented as an existential threat requiring emergency measures and justifying actions outside the normal bounds of political procedure' (Buzan *et al.* 1998: 23–24). The decisive factor in identifying a securitization process is therefore not whether the word 'security' is directly invoked, but rather whether an issue is presented according to the aforementioned logic of an existential threat (Buzan *et al.* 1998: 33). Such existential threats can be military in nature, as is frequently the case when one state declares war on another. Yet such securitization processes can also unfold in response to issues that are essentially non-military in character. In fact one of the most notable features of the international security agenda over the past decade is the growing number of broader social issues that have been discussed as pressing existential threats, ranging from climate change and the 'war' on drugs, through to migration and the progressive merging of security and development in many parts of the world. As a rapidly evolving literature now documents, infectious diseases have become the latest in a long line of non-military issues to be securitized in such a manner (Elbe 2006; McInnes and Lee 2006; Ingram 2007; Kelle 2007; Davies 2008; Fidler and Gostin 2008; Leboeuf and Broughton 2008; Scoones and Forster 2008).

In the case of H5N1, the manifestations of that securitization process are already too numerous to recount in full; but a few examples will suffice to illustrate the point. Writing in the *New York Times* in 2005, two senators from the US Senate Foreign Relations Committee warned their readers that we usually think about national security threats in terms of nuclear proliferation, rogue states and terrorism, but that 'another kind of threat lurks beyond our shores, one from nature, not humans — an avian flu pandemic. An outbreak could cause millions of deaths, destabilize Southeast Asia (its likely place of origin), and threaten the security of governments around the world' (*New York Times* 2005). One of the two Senators sounding that alarm was—at the time—a junior Democrat from the state of Illinois, who had just been elected to Senate the previous year, and who would later go on to become President of the United States of America, Barak Obama. In his view, H5N1 was not just another infectious disease to be dealt with by routine international public health measures, but a new and grave global threat requiring a much more urgent policy response. That same year, across the Atlantic, the Civil Contingency Secretariat in the United Kingdom echoed that avian flu is 'as serious a threat as terrorism' (Lean 2005).

In 2006 the National Security Strategy of the United States (Office of the President of the United States 2006) then directly acknowledged the threat posed by 'public health challenges like pandemics (HIV/AIDS, avian influenza) that recognize no borders'. The 2006 World Economic Forum held in Davos, Switzerland, similarly identified H5N1 as the primary threat preoccupying global business and political leaders. Noting limited supplies of anti-viral drugs, its report warned that in the worst case scenario there could even be 'rioting to gain access to scarce supplies of anti-virals and vaccines; a collapse of public order; partial de-urbanization as people flee population centres; the extinction of trust in governments; decimation of specific human skill sets; and forced, large-scale migration, associated with the further collapse of already weak states' (World Economic Forum 2006: 9). In retrospect, 2005 and 2006 thus emerge as the 2 years in which the securitization of highly pathogenic avian influenza reached its highest level, in terms of H5N1 being widely perceived as a pressing existential threat demanding an urgent and sustained international response.

That concern with the acute existential threat posed by H5N1 would continue well into 2007 and 2008, although there is some evidence that the threat perception began to decline in the course of 2008, and attention also rapidly shifted to the emergence of influenza A (H1N1) in the spring of 2009 (World Bank 2008). Yet in 2007 the WHO still referred to avian flu as 'the most feared security threat' (WHO 2007: 45), whilst in 2008 pandemic threats remained salient enough to be officially incorporated into the United Kingdom's National Security Strategy, both because of their ability to directly affect the country and because they could potentially undermine international stability (Cabinet Office 2008: 3). That same year the World Bank warned in one of its reports that even though the incidence of human cases of infection was declining in many countries, 'the virus remains a substantial threat to global public health security' (World Bank 2008: 10).

It is possible, then, to trace how highly pathogenic avian influenza has become 'securitized' over the past 5 years. During this time, H5N1 was elevated from a technical public health issue that could be dealt with through the routine procedures of public health institutions and scientific experts, to something perceived as posing a much more existential threat to populations, economic systems and even political structures. The international response to the threat of H5N1, in short, emerges as a classic example of a securitization process, and that also makes it an ideal case study for analysing the kinds of policy advantages and drawbacks that accrue when issues become securitized specifically in the field of global health.

Turning first to the policy advantages, the securitization of H5N1 has undoubtedly raised political awareness about the virus around the world, and has persuaded policy-makers to formulate a range of pandemic preparedness plans. A survey carried out by the United Nations System Influenza Coordination Unit suggests that over 140 countries have now developed national pandemic preparedness plans, although their extent varies significantly between countries and many of the plans still remain untested in practice

(World Bank 2008: 52). The threat associated with H5N1 has also freed up resources to address the issue, with US$2.7 billion having been pledged globally (US$1.5 billion disbursed) for pandemic preparedness efforts (World Bank 2008: 8). A 2008 World Bank report thus found that 'the threat posed over the last 5 years has mobilized an unprecedented coming together of the animal health, human health, disaster preparedness and communication sectors to work in a cross discipline, cross sector and cross boundary way' (World Bank 2008: 8). Moreover, such preparations were undoubtedly helpful in making governments feel more prepared when dealing with the outbreak of new human infections with influenza A (H1N1) in the course of 2009. All of those developments also confirm a core insight witnessed in relation to a range of other securitization processes, namely that they can have policy benefits in terms of mobilizing resources and garnering greater political attention for important issues (Buzan et al. 1998: 29).

Those benefits notwithstanding, however, international efforts to prepare the world for a possible human H5N1 pandemic have also encountered at least one very significant setback when the Indonesian government decided unexpectedly at the end of 2006 that it would no longer share its H5N1 virus samples with the rest of the international community. That move threw a sizeable spanner into the global pandemic preparedness machinery because Indonesia was, in many ways, at the 'forefront' of a possible H5N1 pandemic, reporting the highest numbers of human cases and deaths of H5N1 infection up to that point in time. Without access to the viruses circulating within Indonesia's territorial borders, it was no longer possible for the international public health community to acquire comprehensive surveillance data about how the virus was evolving, nor to develop stockpiles of up-to-date candidate vaccines based on the more virulent Indonesian virus strands.

With emotions running high on both sides, the stand-off between the West and Indonesia (backed vocally by many other developing countries such as Thailand, Brazil, India as well as the Third World Network) has become known in the international public health community as the 'virus-sharing controversy'. That dispute has now lasted for 4 years and, despite some limited progress being made, fundamental disagreements persist amongst the core parties in this dispute. As we shall see below, the securitized response to H5N1 contributed to that critical setback in international public health cooperation in at least two ways, and in a manner that is consistent with the wider effects of securitization processes previously witnessed in other policy areas and sectors outside the domain of global health.

The international scramble for anti-virals and vaccines

One effect of securitization processes observed more generally is that when issues become securitized, governments often resort to emergency measures and engage in 'extraordinary defensive moves' in order to meet that perceived threat (Buzan *et al.* 1998: 204). That was certainly the case in relation to H5N1 as well. As bird flu came to be perceived as a pressing global security threat, many governments around the world embarked upon a frenzied race to acquire special medical counter-measures to meet this impending threat.

In the case of H5N1 there are actually many different ways in which governments could respond to a possible pandemic, including a range of non-pharmacological interventions such as isolation, quarantine and contact tracing, through to traveller screening, and implementing social distancing measures that minimize public gatherings by closing schools and cancelling mass spectator events. In fact, when it comes to seasonal flu many developing countries do not routinely resort to medical countermeasures such as mass vaccination or prescribing anti-virals—an understandable public health strategy in light of competing budgetary pressures and a range of other health issues that also need to be urgently addressed.

Yet given the perceived level of the H5N1 threat, most governments rapidly concluded that confronting H5N1 required more than just the usual public health responses to communicable diseases, not least because the considerable international anxiety around H5N1 created immense domestic pressures for governments to be seen to be taking the strongest possible action to protect citizens against a pending pandemic. Many governments decided that in the event of a pandemic the best line of defence would be the extensive use of pharmacological interventions like anti-virals and new vaccines. Manufacturers of anti-virals like oseltamivir (brand name Tamiflu) claim that the drug can be used both to treat those infected with H5N1 (if taken within 48 hours of the onset of symptoms) and as a prophylactic given to those who have been in contact with people who have been infected. In addition to anti-virals, a 2005 report by the WHO also observed that 'vaccines are universally regarded as the most important medical intervention for preventing influenza and reducing its health consequences during a pandemic' (WHO 2005a: 45). Amongst the considerable anxiety that a human H5N1 pandemic was imminent, anti-virals and vaccines thus quickly became seen as the 'magic bullet' or 'gold standard' for countries to defend themselves against the looming threat. Not surprisingly, the serious concern about the threat posed by H5N1 ended up stimulating immense international demand for those pharmacological products, not least because many governments around the world felt that the only way to adequately protect their populations was to take the extraordinary step of pro-actively stockpiling those medicines (especially anti-virals) to ensure availability of supplies for rapid dispersal in the event of a pandemic materializing.

Yet from a global public health perspective that intense focus on acquiring medical counter-measures also had one significant drawback: there was insufficient international manufacturing capacity to meet such a sudden surge in demand. As the 2005 WHO report went on to note, 'the greatest problem is inadequate production capacity. Demand will unquestionably outstrip supply, particularly at the start of a pandemic' (WHO 2005a: 46). Put differently, in the event of pandemic transmission of H5N1 there would inevitably be 'winner' and 'loser' populations. There would be those countries which would benefit from the protection afforded by pharmacological interventions (or at least do so before the majority of other countries), and those that would have to settle for a more 'low-tech' approach probably associated with higher rates of morbidity and mortality.

Who were the likely loser populations going to be? It was not difficult for several developing countries to deduce that it was likely to be them, as they were facing a double disadvantage. First, manufacturing capacity—especially in terms of vaccines—was geographically concentrated in developed countries (Australia, Europe, Japan and North America) giving those countries a distinct advantage in terms of securing access to medicines for their populations (WHO 2005a: 47). Second, under market conditions where demand outstrips supply, the factor most likely to determine who would secure those treatments would be price; and here too it would be difficult for developing countries to compete with their wealthier counterparts.

Such global inequalities are certainly not new. Many developing countries have in fact long been aware of how the market dynamics of supply and demand have frequently not worked to their advantage in the area of public health. In many cases such free market conditions also do not exist in the first place, because the allocation of medical counter-measures are often agreed between governments and commercial companies through pre-purchase agreements long in advance of a pandemic actually materializing. Moreover, related concerns about global inequalities were already simmering amongst developing countries amidst the extensive changes negotiated to the International Health Regulations, the rise of new international surveillance mechanisms (Calain 2007), as well as the wider (and controversial) discussions about global health security (Aldis 2008: 373–4). Yet as the world was confronted with the spectre of an impending H5N1 pandemic, those inequalities crystallized in quite a stark manner, and in a way that could not be easily ignored by anyone who cared to take a closer look. If a pandemic was coming, there would be huge disparities in the medical defences available to countries around the world.

The realization of that profound inequality provoked deep frustrations about existing forms of global health governance. In fact, some developing countries were so dismayed at the possibility of having to confront an imminent pandemic without access to such medical interventions that they began to openly question the value of maintaining existing forms of international health cooperation which appeared to be mostly benefitting developed countries. Those developing country frustrations feature particularly prominently in the account of the virus-sharing dispute advanced by the Indonesian Health Minister Siti Supari in her book *It's Time for the World to Change* in which she describes her experiences and views on the international virus-sharing dispute (Supari 2008). Although the English translation of the book was officially withdrawn by her in February 2008 (due to what she claims were inaccuracies in the translation), the book nonetheless provides a useful insight into her overall reasoning and decision-making.[1]

In the book Supari recounts an early but formative encounter with this scarcity problem specifically in relation to anti-virals. When in 2005 she was finally able to find some resources from other government budgets to purchase Tamiflu for treating early human cases of H5N1 infection that had emerged in Indonesia, she claims that she could not obtain supplies because the medicine was being pre-emptively stockpiled by Western countries, which at that point did not even have any human cases of infection with H5N1. She was concerned that it may have proved impossible for Indonesia to acquire the medicines at that time, had it not been for the willingness of Australia and Thailand to share their supplies with Indonesia (Supari 2008: 5–6).

That episode occurred early on in the securitization of H5N1, and the international production of Tamiflu has expanded considerably since that time, including production in generic form. Nevertheless, that early experience with the limited availability of Tamiflu clearly left a lasting impression on Supari, especially in relation to the eventual development of a vaccine, for which production capabilities would initially remain similarly insufficient to meet demand:

> "The incident of the sweeping out of the *Tamiflu* stock by developed countries that had no cases of the disease was [sic] really made a deep wound in my heart. . . . Just imagine that when human pandemic of avian flu strikes developing or even poor countries and than [sic] because of the scarceness of the medicine they have to witness their people die. A thought flashed into my mind. Whenever they find vaccine for human pandemic of avian flu, I was certain that the rich countries with lots of money will be the first priority, even though the materials of the vaccines, i.e. the viruses come from the affected countries."
>
> (Supari 2008: 5–6)

That fear would become partially realized in 2006 when she was informed by a journalist from the Australian Broadcasting Corporation that an Australian company was trying to develop a vaccine on the basis of the Indonesian strain that it had shared with the international community through the GISN.

This problem of the uneven international distribution of medical counter-measures also continues today in relation to accessing H5N1 vaccines. A report released in March 2009 by the international management consulting firm Oliver Wyman, which was commissioned by the Bill and Melinda Gates Foundation, estimates that the most likely scenario in the event of a H5N1 pandemic would be an international production capacity of 2.5 billion doses of pandemic vaccine in the first 12 months (after the production strain is received), which would still require 4 years to meet global demand (Oliver Wyman 2009). New developments in cell-based vaccines may change that overall equation in coming years, but that is still some time off. Moreover, and as also became clear in relation to H1N1 in 2009, because vaccines usually need to be virus specific, developed countries too would have to wait several months before the first mass-produced vaccines became available. Nevertheless, those inequalities remain an important and enduring feature of global health governance, much to the dissatisfaction of many developing countries.

So frustrated and disillusioned was the Indonesian government in par-ticular, that it took the controversial decision in December 2006 to withdraw from the mechanism by ceasing to share its H5N1 virus samples with the international community unless the viruses were formally recognized as Indonesian (by signing a formal Material Transfer Agreement), and until greater access to vaccines and other benefits derived from the virus-sharing mechanism were secured for developing countries. As Siti Supari put it in a March 2007 speech at the High Level Meeting on Responsible Practices for Sharing Avian Influenza Viruses and Resulting Benefits, 'it is time to change the mechanism of the GISN because it is not in favour of the avian flu affected countries' (Supari 2008: 52). Indonesia, in other words, would no longer cooperate with the long-standing virus-sharing mechanisms unless the concerns of developing countries about access to vaccines and other benefits were systematically addressed first. That crucial decision effectively triggered the international virus-sharing dispute.

With the benefit of hindsight, then, it is possible to trace how the securitized response to H5N1 provoked a chain of events that would end up putting substantial new pressure on existing forms of international public health cooperation. The immense fear surrounding H5N1 compelled governments around the world to protect their populations by undertaking emergency defensive measures like seeking stockpiles of anti-virals and new vaccines. Yet because there is insufficient supply capacity at international level for meeting this demand, that proved very difficult for developing countries to achieve. The latter quite understandably became disillusioned with the merits of maintaining existing forms of public health cooperation like the international virus-sharing mechanism and began openly questioning its legitimacy. From their perspective, those forms of international health cooperation may work well for developed countries that possess their own pharmaceutical manufacturing base, but the material benefits accruing from such cooperation for developing countries are far less evident.

All of this also fundamentally changed the prospects of continuing inter-national health cooperation between developed and developing countries. Whereas hitherto the international virus-sharing mechanism was largely seen as a routine system of functional public health cooperation between countries around the world, its operation now became a heavily politicized North–South issue that eventually also attracted the support of the 112 member strong Non-Aligned Movement (in May 2008). By this point in time the international virus-sharing mechanism was no longer just a technical or functional issue between Indonesia and the WHO, but a political contest between developed and developing countries. After operating for more than half a century, the GISN now faced one of its most significant political challenges to date (Brammer *et al.* 2007: 254–55). That is one significant vector though which the securitized global response to H5N1 has unexpectedly ended up politically complicating an important and long-standing mechanism of international health cooperation.

Turning lethal viruses into diplomatic bargaining chips

A second effect frequently associated with securitization processes is that they also tend to encourage greater and more high-level state involvement in the handling of an issue (Buzan *et al.* 1998: 29). That is because of the historical role of the state in terms of being the main provider of security, and the view that providing that security is also one on if its core duties. As issues become securitized they thus tend to attract much closer and high-level attention from governments. Evidence of this wider tendency can similarly be found at play in the case of H5N1. However, in the latter case that high-level state involvement too ended up further complicating international health cooperation as some states suddenly began to subject the international virus-sharing mechanism to much narrower calculations of national interest, and even attempted to use virus samples as diplomatic bargaining chips for pursuing their national interest.

The Indonesian government in particular recognized that the securitized international response to H5N1, with all of its frenzied pandemic preparedness activities, also offered positive political opportunities for exploiting the virus-sharing mechanism in the pursuit of the country's national interest. The Indonesian government knew at least three things. First, all the high-level attention on H5N1 made it clear to the government how pressing a political concern H5N1 was in the West, and how much political pressure there was to protect populations against this threat. In the United States, for example, the growing concern about the threat posed by H5N1 had even led to the extraordinary creation of a new high-level position within the US State Department—the Special Representative on Avian and Pandemic Influenza. Protecting their populations against a possible H5N1 pandemic was evidently one of the top political priorities of many Western governments at the time.

Secondly, because Western countries initially had no human cases of H5N1 infection occurring within their own territories, they could only make the vaccines necessary to protect their populations by getting access to wild viruses from other countries, such as Indonesia, where human infections were already occurring (Supari 2008: 10). Without legal and open access to these virus samples, Western governments would struggle to maintain up-to-date surveillance and medical interventions for H5N1 (unless they obtained virus samples by other means). Virus samples were thus a crucial 'resource' for Western governments as they scrambled to protect their populations against the prospect of an imminent pandemic.

Thirdly, because it was eventually confirmed that the Indonesian virus strand was more virulent than other strands, a vaccine based on the Indonesian strand would be the most desirable in terms of offering protection (Supari 2008: 25–27). Describing her realization that the Indonesian virus was distinct and more virulent (and thus of immense interest to those tracking the evolution of the virus and making vaccines), Supari actually felt 'happy' because for Indonesia that now meant 'bargaining power!' (Supari 2008: 27). Supari, in other words, realized at this crucial moment that access to Indonesian virus samples could form new diplomatic leverage for the Indonesian government in its attempts to secure greater access to medical countermeasures for Indonesia. The Indonesian health minister described her thinking in the following, candid terms: 'I had to change the paradigm. How? I had nothing. My country is not a superpower. I am only a Health Minister with 240 million people to serve . . . I had to do something . . . the main variable . . . is the wild virus. So I had to stop the virus sharing with the WHO-CC [World Health Organization Collaborating Centers]' (Supari 2008: 163). As Indonesia began to assert its 'viral sovereignty' over H5N1 viruses circulating in its territory, those viruses now became transformed from mere biological materials to key political 'bargaining chips' in the diplomatic arsenal of the Indonesian state, which it would use to further its own national interest on the international stage.

Going down this path was a high-risk strategy, of course, in that this would only work as long as the Indonesian government could actually maintain tight control over the viruses circulating in its territories, and prevent outside countries from obtaining virus samples from Indonesia through other channels. Presumably this is part of the reason why the Indonesian health minister later also expressed her desire to evict the US Naval Laboratory (NAMRU-2) from the country, which she suspected at the time as being a back channel for virus samples leaving her country. NAMRU-2 has since been closed down and has been replaced by a new civilian facility. It is probably also for that same reason that before leaving office, Supari further instructed laboratories and researchers in Indonesia not to accept foreign donations any more, as she feared that those funding streams could be accompanied by other demands from foreign donors. Although the future status of a military facility by a foreign country, or indeed foreign aid, is not something which would not normally be seen to fall within the portfolio or remit of a health minister, these are issues she began to take a very keen interest in, presumably because if viruses were to be transferred out of the country through military facility or other links, that would seriously—and perhaps fatally—undermine her bargaining position on virus sharing.

Yet armed with those new 'bargaining chips', Supari also felt sufficiently emboldened to hold out for more than just a few concessions made by the West, and to push for a fundamental transformation of the virus-sharing mechanism. When, for example, she was approached by the WHO with offers of a laboratory upgrade and as much vaccine as they needed in February 2007, she turned those offers down. The reason she cites for this decision is that she did not want Indonesia to be dependent upon the charity of other countries, insisting that 'by recognizing our right over the viruses, we can obtain whatever we need respectfully, because we own something precious to give' (Supari 2008: 41).

Rather than simply accepting those offers of material support, and resolving the dispute there and then, the Indonesian health minister instead formulated a much stronger demand that made Indonesia's resumption of virus sharing conditional upon a more fundamental reformation of the whole virus-sharing mechanism. Her underlying position, which she subsequently advanced at the intergovernmental meeting in November 2007, became: 'Number One: Virus sharing is a sovereign right of a country and not to be compromised. Number Two: Benefits sharing is a consequence of virus sharing, which instead of a charity from the developed country to the country where the virus originated, it is the right of the latter' (Supari 2008: 116–7). Today the negotiations around virus sharing are therefore no longer simply about re-integrating Indonesia into the GISN, but have now become about fundamentally transforming that entire virus-sharing mechanism. Moreover, even though Supari is no longer in office, her position continues to be defended by Indonesian officials, as can be seen by the more recent assertion of a member of the Indonesian Democratic Party of Struggle that 'Jakarta should not succumb to pressure from the West. I agree with the position of our former health minister [Siti Supari] who has been firmly defending our national interest' (Budianto 2010).

In the end, Supari's stronger demand for fundamental transformation of the system may bring future benefits for developing countries. Already the WHO has taken some steps to accommodate the demands of Indonesia and other developing countries, including the development of a system for tracking the movement of shared H5N1 virus samples, and exploring the feasibility of creating a stockpile of vaccines that developing countries could draw on. However, the core demand for a more fundamental transformation of the international virus-sharing mechanism has not been achieved to date. That is because developed countries are currently not prepared to agree to such a fundamental transformation, which—in turn—would not be in their national interest.

Indeed, countries like the United States are very hesitant to agree to a deeper reform of a system that has been operating (in their view very successfully) for more than half a decade. As former US Secretary of Health and Human Services, Mike Leavitt, indicated in his blog from 14 April 2008, he thought Indonesia was ultimately working on a principal of 'share samples, get paid' (Leavitt 2008). That may seem like a terse formulation, but it is the underlying principle of whether benefits sharing should be formally tied to virus sharing that now divides both sides and that now makes progress so difficult to achieve. From the perspective of the United States virus sharing should not be linked to benefit sharing in a formal way. Leavitt did acknowledge at the time that 'the issues of the availability of vaccines and the sharing of samples are both legitimate ones, and we must deal with them both, but we should not link. World health should not be the subject of barter' (Leavitt 2008). In his view such formal linking would 'begin to erode our ability to make vaccines at all, because once the practice of free and open sharing of viruses stops, the slope is slippery, and there will be no end to the demands' (Leavitt 2008). Yet it should not go amiss that this position also favours the national interest of the United States, in that it would be the best system for ensuring that Western countries continue to have unfettered access to samples of new viruses irrespective of where on the planet they first emerge.

In either case, the United States government will no doubt be encouraged by the fact that other developing countries have not followed Indonesia's more drastic step of ceasing to share virus samples (though vocally support-ing Indonesia). It will have further noted that the more recent concern about an influenza A (H1N1) pandemic did not spark any additional attempts to withhold virus samples. The United States government thus continues to make the promotion of global health security one of its key objectives in meeting biological threats (National Security Council 2009), with the result that a deep diplomatic gulf thus remains between the core parties in the dispute. Indeed, today the issue of virus and benefit sharing is still unresolved, with diverging views on several core issues, and remains subject to further discussion in an open-ended working group (World Health Assembly 2010).

Here too, then, it is possible in retrospect to trace how the securitized response to H5N1 eventually began to put new pressures on the international virus-sharing mechanism and international health cooperation. As a result of the much closer and high-level governmental attention on H5N1, the entire issue of virus sharing suddenly and unexpectedly became subject to much more narrow calculations of state interest. The Indonesian government in particular realized that it was in the United States' national interest to secure and maintain access to these samples, and Indonesia in turn could use the granting of access to these samples as a way of furthering its own national interest of achieving greater benefits from sharing its viruses. Whilst that strategy may bring advantages to developing countries in the long run (which still remains to be seen), the push for a more fundamental transforma-tion of the virus-sharing system has also raised the political stakes in the dispute further still, and ultimately culminates in a more difficult stand-off between the supporters of the GISN mechanism and those states like Indonesia pushing for fundamental reform. In that process the entire virus-sharing mechanism became transformed from a largely low-level, habitual and routine system of functional public health cooperation, to something that was subject to much narrower considerations of state interests, and would effectively become a bargaining chip in high-level diplomatic negotiations between states pursuing competing national interests. This too forms an important vector through which international health cooperation has, in the end, been complicated by the securitized international response to H5N1.

Conclusion

What wider lessons about the securitization of infectious diseases can be drawn from the case of H5N1? Those lessons need to be teased out with considerable care. Not only is it very difficult to generalize from a single case study, but we have also already noted that there are undoubtedly a variety of different factors involved in the emergence of the international virus-sharing dispute, including factors particular to Indonesian politics. It is also noteworthy that besides Indonesia, no other country (including those vocally supporting the Indonesian position) has undertaken a similar, formal refusal to share virus samples. Nor, for that matter, has such a refusal manifested itself in the more recent case of the influenza A (H1N1) pandemic.

That said, there is a wider and important lesson that can be learned from the virus sharing episode. Scholars of securitization processes usefully remind us that 'one has to weigh the always problematic side effects of applying a mind-set of security against the possible advantages of focus, attention, and mobilization' (Buzan *et al.* 1998: 29). In the case of H5N1 we have seen there were certainly benefits to a securitized response to global health that can be discerned, especially in terms of resources and political mobilization. However, in many ways the more important lesson to emerge from the ongoing international virus-sharing dispute, and one that has still not been sufficiently appreciated in international policy circles, is that there can also be unanticipated downside risks associated with responding to health issues in a securitized mode. In the case of H5N1, the securitized international response has also had a range of less salient effects in terms of entangling the long-standing virus-sharing mechanism in a wider set of non-technical and non-medical disputes in international politics. Indeed, the securitized response to H5N1 ended up inadvertently provoking an intense re-politicization of international virus sharing where the latter is no longer seen to be of mutual benefit, but as a bargaining chip used by countries like Indonesia to fundamentally reform the virus-sharing mechanism.

None of the foregoing analysis is to imply that things inevitably had to turn out this way, or to detract from the responsibilities of the key parties involved in the dispute. Nor is it to deny that the prospect of a future H5N1 pandemic associated with high human mortality and morbidity was indeed a very disquieting prospect. Yet as an important instance in which a health issue did become prominently securitized in international policy circles, the case of H5N1 does demonstrate very clearly that a securitized response to infectious diseases can also structure global health debates in ways that are not conducive to achieving higher levels of international health cooperation. That is an important insight and cautionary note worth retaining for the future when it comes to dealing with emerging infectious diseases. After all, one of the most salient features of global health over the past decade has been precisely the tendency by many policy makers to try to deliberately shift global health from the mould of 'low' politics, and to make global health a more pressing concern of 'high' politics, by actively seeking the securitization of health through the agenda on global health security.

Funding

The research conducted for this article was supported by a grant from the British Academy on Health Security (BARDA-47928).

Note

1 I would like to thank Paul Forster from the STEPS Centre in the Institute of Development Studies at the University of Sussex for his assistance in locating a copy of this book.

References

Brammer L., Postema A., Cox N. 2007. Seasonal and pandemic influenze surveillance. In: M'ikanata M., Lynfield R., van Beneden C., de Valk H. (eds). *Infectious Disease Surveillance*. Oxford: Blackwell.

Budianto L. 2010. RI pushes for fair virus sharing scheme despite Obama visit. *Jakarta Post*. 10 February.

Buzan B., Wæver O., de Wilde J. 1998. *Security: A New Framework for Analysis*. Boulder, CO: Lynne Rienner.

Cabinet Office. 2008. *The National Security Strategy of the United Kingdom: Security in an Interdependent World*. London: Cabinet Office.

Calain P. 2007. From the field side of the binoculars: a different view on global public health surveillance. *Health Policy and Planning* 22: 13–20.

Davies S. 2008. Securitizing infectious disease. *International Affairs* 84: 295–313.

Fidler D., Gostin L. 2008. *Biosecurity in the Global Age: Biological Weapons. Public Health and the Rule of Law*. Stanford, CA: Stanford University Press.

Forster P. 2009. *The Political Economy of Avian Influenza in Indonesia*. STEPS Working Paper 17. Brighton: STEPS Centre.

Holbrooke R., Garrett L. 2008. 'Sovereignty' that risks global health. *Washington Post*. 10 April.

Ingram A. 2007. HIV/AIDS, security and the geopolitics of US-Nigerian relations. *Review of International Political Economy* **14**: 510–34.

Jakarta Globe. 2009. Minister wary of foreign 'Attack'. *Jakarta Globe*. 21 May.

Kelle A. 2007. Securitization of international public health: implications for global health governance and the biological weapons prohibition regime. *Global Governance* **13**: 217–35.

Lange J. E. 2007. Pandemic flu: towards an effective global preparedness policy. Remarks at Chatham House, London, United Kingdom, October 17.

Lean G. 2005. Bird flu 'as grave a threat as terrorism'. *The Independent*. 26 June. Online at: http://www.independent.co.uk/environment/bird-flu-as-grave-a-threat-as-terrorism-496608.html.

Leavitt M. 2008. Indonesia. Entry into Secretary Mike Leavitt's Pandemic Influenza Blog, 14 April. Online at: http://archive.hhs.gov/secretarysblog/my_weblog/pandemic _planning/index.html.

Leboeuf A., Broughton E. 2008. Securitization of health and environmental issues: process and effects. A research outline. Working Paper. Paris: Institut Français des Relations Internationales. May 2008.

McInnes C., Lee K. 2006. Health, security and foreign policy. *Review of International Studies* **32**: 5–23.

National Security Council. 2009. *National Strategy for Countering Biological Threats*. Washington, DC: White House: November.

Office of the President of the United States. 2006. *The National Security Strategy of the United States*. Washington, DC: White House.

New York Times. 2005. Grounding a pandemic. *New York Times*. 6 June.

Scoones I., Forster P. 2008. *The International Response to Highly Pathogenic Avian Influenza: Science, Policy and Politics*. STEPS Working Paper No. 10. Brighton: STEPS Centre.

Supari S. 2008. *It's Time for the World to Change*. Jakarta: PT. Sulaksana Watinsa Indonesia.

World Economic Forum. 2006. *Global Risks 2006*. Geneva: World Economic Forum.

World Health Assembly. 2010. Pandemic Influenza Preparedness: sharing of influenza viruses and access to vaccines and other benefits. Resolution of the World Health Assembly, WHA63.1, 19 May. Online at: http://apps.who.int/gb/ebwha/pdf_files/ WHA60/A60_R28-en.pdf.

WHO. 2005a. *Avian Influenza: Assessing the Pandemic Threat*. Geneva: World Health Organization.

WHO. 2005b. *Guidance for the Timely Sharing of Influenza Viruses/Specimens with Potential to Cause Human Influenza Pandemics*. Geneva: World Health Organization.

WHO. 2007. *The World Health Report 2007 – A Safer Future: Global Public Health Security in the 21st Century*. Geneva: World Health Organization.

World Bank. 2008. *Responses to Avian Influenza and State of Pandemic Readiness*. Fourth Global Progress Report. Washington, DC: World Bank.

Wyman O. 2009. *Influenza Vaccine Supply and Demand*. Summary of Key Findings. Online at: http://www.oliverwyman.com/ow/pdf_files/InfluenzaVaccineSupplyDem andMar09.pdf.

77

AIDS AND INTERNATIONAL SECURITY IN THE UNITED NATIONS SYSTEM

Simon Rushton

Source: *Health Policy and Planning*, 25:6 (2010), 495–504.

Two assumptions underpin much of the literature that has examined the links between HIV/AIDS and security: (1) that HIV/AIDS is now firmly established as an international security issue; and (2) that Resolution 1308, adopted by the UN Security Council in July 2000, was the decisive moment in the securitization process. This article questions both of those assumptions. It argues that even within the Security Council, HIV/AIDS' status as a bona fide threat to international peace and security is not entirely secure. Despite the fact that the Resolution was adopted unanimously, there is considerable doubt over the extent to which the Council members were persuaded that HIV/AIDS is genuinely a threat to international peace and security. Furthermore, the Council's subsequent actions suggest a retreat from the issue. The article moves on to examine statements made in and by some of the other key UN System bodies grappling with HIV/AIDS. Focusing in particular on the General Assembly, the Economic and Social Council and UNAIDS, it is argued that the international security framing of HIV/AIDS has not generally achieved a great deal of traction within these bodies. Alternative framings, in particular international development and human rights, occur far more frequently. This raises issues for our understanding of both securitization theory and the global governance of HIV/AIDS.

Key messages

- It is widely assumed that HIV/AIDS is now firmly established as an international security issue and that UN Security Council Resolution 1308 was the defining moment in the 'securitization' of the pandemic.
- In fact, however, HIV/AIDS can best be understood as an example of a partial—or even perhaps a failed —securitization.
- If we look beyond the Security Council to the wider UN System, it becomes apparent that alternative framings of HIV/AIDS, in particular international development and human rights, are far more prevalent.
- This has implications both for securitization theory and for our understanding of the global governance of HIV/AIDS.

Introduction

The idea that infectious diseases can and should be treated as security threats has gained ground rapidly over the last decade, and the transformation of HIV/AIDS into an issue of international peace and security has been particularly widely discussed. Opinion has been divided over whether 'securitization' is to be welcomed or to be feared in this case, but almost everyone agrees that it has happened and that it represents a significant development in the global politics of the pandemic. The generally accepted version of the securitization story rests upon two key assumptions: (1) that HIV/AIDS is now firmly established as an international security issue; and (2) that Resolution 1308, adopted by the UN Security Council in July 2000, was the decisive moment in the securitization process.

This article critically examines both of these assumptions. First, it discusses the process that led to the adoption of Resolution 1308 and scrutinizes both the text of the Resolution itself and the Security Council's subsequent actions. Whilst in some ways it is true that the Council's statement that HIV/AIDS represents 'a threat to international peace and security' was a significant moment, it is argued that it was in reality less decisive than the bald headline suggests. Resolution 1308 was certainly the result of a concerted attempt, spearheaded by the USA, to promote the HIV–security linkage, but that does not in itself constitute solid evidence of a successful securitization. Sustaining the claim that securitization has been successful would require evidence of a much broader acceptance of the claims made about the security dimensions of the disease. It is argued that even within the Council—often presented as being at the centre of the securitization story—HIV/AIDS' status as a bona fide threat to international peace and security is not entirely secure.

The article then moves on to examine how widespread the framing of HIV/AIDS as an international security issue has been within the wider UN System. If securitization has indeed been successful it would be reasonable to expect this to be reflected in the discourse of other UN organs and agencies. Three UN bodies that have engaged with HIV/AIDS are examined: the General Assembly, the Economic and Social Council (ECOSOC) and UNAIDS. A decade after Resolution 1308, the article finds that international security issues have only been evident to a limited extent in statements on HIV/AIDS made in and by these other UN System bodies. HIV/AIDS *is* sometimes discussed as a security issue, but far more commonly as a matter of international development or human rights.

Overall, then, the article questions whether the received wisdom over the securitization of HIV/AIDS stands up to scrutiny. Whilst it was clearly the case that the backers of Resolution 1308, in particular key figures in the US government, were deliberately making a 'securitizing move' (Buzan *et al.* 1998: 25), the result may best be seen as an example of a failed, or at best a partial, securitization. In the immediate aftermath of Resolution 1308 it seemed reasonable to assume that securitization had been successful: the picture now is far less certain. This finding has implications for our understanding of both securitization theory and the global governance of HIV/AIDS. For the former it points to a need for greater research into securitization processes, particularly cases of failed and partial securitization. How does persuasion operate in this process and how far can power explain outcomes? How can we empirically determine the point at which an issue has been successfully securitized? In what institutional settings does security carry a particular weight, and what alternative framings are privileged elsewhere?

In terms of the global governance of HIV/AIDS, the argument here raises a number of questions and highlights some areas where further research is needed. There is a clear need for a better understanding of the ideas that shape the approaches adopted by the various actors and institutions engaged in tackling the pandemic. Are the various ways in which different agents understand and respond to 'the AIDS problem' compatible? How do the hierarchies and relationships between these bodies operate? How much does security thinking really matter, and where?

Methods

A literature review using a number of online databases was conducted to identify scholarly work that has examined the links between HIV/AIDS and security, focusing in particular on those works that have discussed the national/international security dimensions of the pandemic. Like a large proportion of this existing work, the theoretical underpinnings of this article are taken from the model of securitization developed by the 'Copenhagen School' (Buzan *et al.* 1998).

422

This article critically analyses the empirical claims about Resolution 1308 that have been made in the literature, comparing those claims with information contained in the official UN records of the relevant Security Council sessions (available through the UN's Official Document System at http://documents.un.org/) and contemporary news sources. This was supplemented by Freedom of Information requests made to the UK Foreign & Commonwealth Office and the US Department of State for material relating to the adoption of Resolution 1308. One notable result of these requests was the release of telegrams exchanged between the UK Mission to the UN in New York and the Foreign & Commonwealth Office in London and between the US Mission to the United Nations (USUN) in New York and the State Department in Washington, DC. Both sets of documents provide a number of valuable insights into the background to the adoption of Resolution 1308.

In order to gauge the extent to which international security-based discussions of HIV/AIDS have been in evidence across the wider UN System, the article examines three other UN bodies: the General Assembly (specifically its adoption of the Millennium Development Goals in 2000 and the 2001 Special Session on HIV/AIDS); the Economic and Social Council (which founded UNAIDS and which has passed a number of Resolutions on the topic since 2000); and UNAIDS, the body charged with coordinating the UN System's response. These particular bodies and events have been selected because they, along with Resolution 1308, have been perceived within and outside the UN as particularly notable in the UN System's engagement with the pandemic (UNAIDS 2009). These sections of the article again make use of official UN Records, published reports and speeches by key personnel. A textual analysis of speeches, resolutions, decisions and reports was carried out in order to show the prevalence of an international security-based framing of HIV/AIDS, and a comparison is made with international development and human rights, two of the principal alternative frames.

Defining the HIV–security linkage

As William Aldis (2008) argued in a recent article in *Health Policy and Planning*, the field of 'health security' has been characterized by a variety of often incompatible definitions, with little agreement over who is being secured or from what. This is not unique to health, and reflects broader definitional and conceptual contestation over the meaning of 'security', a phenomenon that is well-recognized within Security Studies (Baldwin 1997) and which has led to security being described as an 'essentially contested concept' (Buzan 1991). In recent years HIV/AIDS has been presented as a security threat at a variety of levels of analysis: human security (Fourie and Schonteich 2001); national security (Ostergard 2002); regional security (Gebretensae 2004); international security (Singer 2002); and global security (Prins 2004). It has also been linked to a number of other 'securities', including food security (de Waal and Whiteside

2003) and reproductive health security (Pallikadavath and Stones 2003). It is, therefore, obviously important to be explicit about the type of security being discussed in this article. The focus here, as it was in the Security Council, is on international security. Whilst HIV/AIDS has been linked with other kinds of security—perhaps most notably the concept of 'human security'—this article concerns itself with the attempted construction of HIV/AIDS as a threat to international peace and security (and, by extension, regional and national security).

In practice, as has been rightly pointed out on many occasions (e.g. Feldbaum *et al.* 2006; McInnes 2006), attempts to present HIV/AIDS as an international security threat have been characterized by three major claims.

(1) That HIV is a threat to the stability of states or regions. A variety of ways in which the disease can contribute to instability have been proposed: the 'hollowing out' of state institutions through illness and premature death (Garrett 2005: 41); the economic and social consequences of lost productivity (Fox and Kassalow 2001: 1555); the creation of AIDS orphans, which could fuel the child soldier problem (Singer 2002: 151); illness and premature death having a detrimental impact upon the effectiveness of the military and security services charged with maintaining order (Ostergard 2002: 342–4).

(2) That the threat posed by HIV will increasingly be a global one. Although to date attention has largely focused on sub-Saharan Africa, much of the same logic could apply in other regions, including Asia where prevalence rates in the 'next wave' of states (including emerging powers seen as critical to regional and global security such as China and India) are on the rise (National Intelligence Council 2002; Schneider and Moodie 2002; Thompson 2004; Hunter 2005). As Alan Dupont (2001: 225) has argued:

> "If HIV continues to proliferate in East Asia, as seems likely, the virus will undermine civil society, slow the democratisation process and intensify poverty, resource scarcity and conflict, directly affecting the national security interests of afflicted states, the region's collective security interests and the lives of millions of people. What is especially worrying about the AIDS pandemic is that even though Asia has already overtaken Africa as the epicentre of the disease, its full impact will not be felt for perhaps another decade because of HIV's lengthy incubation period."

(3) That HIV/AIDS is detrimental to the effectiveness of international peace-keeping forces in those areas of the world where stability has already broken down. Furthermore, there have been concerns that UN peace-keeping troops could actually be vectors for the spread of HIV in the

host population (Prins 2004: 942; Tripoldi and Patel 2002). Clearly these issues were particularly troubling to the UN Security Council.

Thus, the types of securitizing claims in question reflect traditional international security concerns: instability, armed conflict, military effectiveness and international peacekeeping operations.

The overwhelming view in the literature (especially the International Relations literature) is that these claims have become a widely accepted basis for understanding and responding to HIV/AIDS; that the pandemic has been successfully securitized and that Security Council Resolution 1308 was the most high-profile symbolic manifestation of that process (e.g. Prins 2004; Elbe 2005; McInnes 2006; Fidler 2007).

It is certainly true that some do approach HIV/AIDS, at least in part, as an international security issue. The USA is the clearest example. It was within the US intelligence agencies that the idea that HIV/AIDS is a threat to security was first incubated (CIA 1987; National Intelligence Council 2000). To some extent this has fed through into US policy responses, with the President's Emergency Plan for AIDS Relief (PEPFAR) being partly a response to security concerns, alongside economic, humanitarian and religious rationales for action (Garrett 2005; Feldbaum 2009: 5). Whilst it is impossible to quantify the extent to which security as opposed to these other concerns has motivated US action, there are some clear examples of activities that do have an explicitly security-oriented focus, not least the Department of Defense's HIV/AIDS Prevention Program, which focuses on reducing the incidence of HIV/AIDS in (particularly African) militaries (Department of Defense 2010; McInnes and Rushton 2010: 240–2). As Ingram (2005) has noted, however, in this respect the US approach is often divergent from those of other states (Ingram contrasts US policy with UK policy).

The key question, then, is the extent to which the HIV–security linkage has been accepted and adopted by other actors. This is a crucial point for the Copenhagen School, who are careful to distinguish between a 'securitizing move' and successful securitization. The latter would require the audience to be persuaded that HIV genuinely is a security issue (Buzan *et al.* 1998: 25). They also dismiss the idea that securitization is a binary either/or state, with Ole Waever (2003) having called for more attention to be paid to partial and failed examples of securitization. For the majority of commentators, however, HIV/AIDS is a case of successful securitization and Resolution 1308 is viewed as powerful empirical evidence that the audience (in that case the 15 members of the Council who adopted the Resolution unanimously) were persuaded (e.g. Elbe 2005: 403–4; Prins 2004: 941–2; McInnes 2007: 93–4). In the next section this article subjects that claim to greater scrutiny, arguing that there is in fact good reason to doubt the extent to which real persuasion took place.

The article then moves on to examine the extent to which a security-based discourse of HIV/AIDS has been evident in other parts of the UN System in the decade since Resolution 1308. Although this article focuses solely on the UN System, it is clearly true that many non-UN bodies are important actors in the global governance of HIV/AIDS, including international funding mechanisms such as the Global Fund to Fight AIDS, TB and Malaria; bilateral programmes; NGOs and civil society groups; and private foundations such as the Bill & Melinda Gates Foundation (Cohen 2002). Nevertheless, there are good reasons for focusing the analysis here within the UN System. First, through its various fora, agencies and funds, the UN has been at the forefront of debates around appropriate global responses to HIV/AIDS since the establishment of the World Health Organization (WHO)'s Global Programme on AIDS in 1987. Secondly, given the widespread identification of the Security Council, in many ways the senior organ of the UN, as a crucial actor in the securitization of HIV, if the international security discourse was to gain traction anywhere it is within the UN System that we could most obviously expect to see it. How far has the splash created by 1308 rippled out across the UN System?

Findings

The Security Council

It is difficult to think of a body more qualified than the Security Council to make a judgement on whether an issue constitutes a threat to international peace and security, and no doubt this is one of the reasons that Resolution 1308 has been so widely interpreted as proof of the securitization of HIV/AIDS. Yet there is room for considerable doubt over whether it was actually the culmination of a successful securitization process. Three issues in particular call this interpretation into question.

Firstly, despite the fact that Resolution 1308 was adopted unanimously by the Security Council, there are doubts over whether the members of the Council at the time—not to mention others outside the Council—ever fully accepted the case that HIV/AIDS should be addressed as a threat to international peace and security. The Council's seizure of the issue was the result of concerted efforts by key individuals in the Clinton Administration to highlight the international peace and security dimensions, particularly in sub-Saharan Africa. Richard Holbrooke, at the time the US Ambassador to the UN, was the driving force behind this process, placing the issue on the Council's agenda, convincing key colleagues in the Clinton Administration—not least Vice-President Gore—to actively support the Council's discussion of the issue, and later persuading his fellow Council members to adopt the Resolution. Although the degree to which this was a contested process has largely been ignored (e.g. David 2001: 561) there is ample evidence that the issue was controversial behind the scenes. A number of accounts of the negotiation process refer to the necessity of convincing reluctant Council members that

HIV/AIDS fell within the Council's remit (Holbrooke 2000: 1; Sternberg 2002). Those states that initially had serious reservations included three of the permanent five members: Russia, China and France (Prins 2004: 941). The report on the negotiations sent by the US Mission in New York to the State Department included a comment specifically focusing on the difficulty of persuading the Chinese and Russians to back the resolution (and also noting the debates with France, which was pushing for an international conference or a General Assembly Special Session on HIV/AIDS):

> "USUN pushed the Russians and Chinese as far as they could go to get this Resolution passed. If we are going to follow this up with additional Council measures—as many other Council members support—we should expect opposition from Russia and China, as well as trouble with the French on the conference idea."
>
> (USUN 2000: para 10)

In addition to this, many of the major peacekeeping troop contributors were unhappy about the Resolution (UK Mission to the UN 2000; USUN 2000: para 7). Even the UK—the USA's strongest ally in getting the Resolution through the Council—had private qualms about whether HIV should be on the Security Council agenda at all (Foreign & Commonwealth Office 2000a; 2000b).

Ultimately, as we know, Holbrooke was successful in steering the Resolution through the Council despite these various sources of opposition. But being persuaded to support the Resolution is not necessarily the same as being persuaded by the securitization claims: Council members are required to weigh up a wide range of interests in deciding whether or not to vote in favour of a Resolution. In this case this undoubtedly included the political and reputational costs of opposing a Resolution addressing such a major human tragedy in addition to the usual US influence over the Council. If the other 14 Council members were genuinely persuaded, we might expect them to repeat the securitizing claims in other contexts. As will be shown below in the examination of the General Assembly's Special Session on HIV/AIDS in 2001, there is little evidence that they are particularly prone to do so.

Secondly, the Resolution focuses on HIV as an international peace and security threat in only a limited sense, conforming to what Barnett and Prins (2005: 11) refer to as the 'narrow construction' of HIV/AIDS as a security issue. The January 2000 Security Council debate had been couched in a somewhat broader manner, but the Resolution that was eventually passed in July was a far more tightly focused document. The changes in the nature of the debate over those 7 months have not been widely flagged up in the literature, but this is an important shift which again gives an indication of the controversy that surrounded the issue, with USUN documents noting that:

"The Russian delegation made it clear that they had instructions from Moscow (A) to link the Resolution as closely as possible to peacekeeping operations only, (B) to weaken or remove language declaring that AIDS was already a global threat, and (C) to work with the United States delegation to find common ground . . ."

(USUS 2000: para 10)

Although Resolution 1308's preamble does indeed rehearse many of the claims about the link between HIV/AIDS and international security outlined above, these are couched in relatively soft language—for example, 'the HIV/AIDS pandemic, *if unchecked, may* pose a risk to stability and security' (emphasis added). As Michael C. Wood (1998: 86–7) states, the preambles to Council resolutions 'need to be treated with caution since they tend to be used as a dumping ground for proposals that are not acceptable in the operative paragraphs'. When we look at the operative paragraphs we find that they focus solely on HIV/AIDS in relation to peacekeeping personnel. This is an important subject, no doubt, but a very specific one, which falls clearly and uncontroversially within the Security Council's remit. So, far from indicating a unanimous acceptance of the broader claims about the potential security consequences of the pandemic, the fact that they appear only in the preamble may in fact show the opposite.

Thirdly, the Council's subsequent treatment of HIV/AIDS can be seen as a retreat from Resolution 1308 and a return, post-9/11, to a more 'traditional' security agenda. Some concrete actions did follow from the Resolution, in particular UNAIDS' work with the UN's Department of Peacekeeping Operations (UNAIDS 2005), but far from becoming a major player in the global governance of HIV/AIDS (as many predicted in 2000), the issue seems to have dropped off the Council's agenda. The failure of UNAIDS and other key movers behind securitization to produce hard evidence to substantiate the securitizing claims seems to have been one of the key reasons for the Council dropping it. Indeed, in preparation for the planned Council meeting in September 2005, UNAIDS commissioned Tony Barnett and Gwyn Prins of the LSE to produce a report that would represent, in Peter Piot's words, 'part of UNAIDS' effort to provide the Security Council with an evidence base about the AIDS-security nexus' (Barnett and Prins 2005: 5). Yet the report Barnett and Prins produced was not what UNAIDS was expecting at all, and indeed was scathing about the quality of evidence upon which many of the claims about the military and HIV/AIDS in particular were based. They noted that 'asserted statistics about high prevalence rates tended to be recycled from one secondary source to another', and that much of the literature is based upon 'Factoids'—'soft opinions that have hardened into facts'—that are 'the intellectual viruses of quick and dirty synthetic studies'. They bemoaned 'the failure to recognise the gaps [in the evidence] and therefore a willingness to engage in extrapolations with weak anchorage' (Barnett and Prins 2005: 7). Whilst the report did not deny the potential impact of HIV/AIDS on peacekeepers and other uniformed services, its tone was hardly likely to enthuse the Council members to devote further time to the issue, particularly if they had not previously been fully persuaded that it belonged on the agenda at all. Far from bolstering the securitization case the Barnett and Prins report contributed directly to HIV/AIDS dropping off the Council's agenda. The biannual pattern established by the Council's 2001, 2003 and 2005 meetings on HIV/AIDS has not continued: there has been no formal Council discussion of HIV/AIDS since 2005, although a Council meeting on the subject is apparently scheduled for autumn 2010.

One of the great hopes of securitization is that it can bring an issue to the top of the political agenda (e.g. Altman 2003). HIV/AIDS, however, was already clearly established on the international political agenda prior to July 2000, so to attribute its profile to securitization is highly problematic. Neither can the Council be given the credit for the huge increase in resources that have been devoted to tackling HIV since the turn of the millennium. There has been no major effort by the Council to improve global responses (although some of the individual Council members, particularly the USA, have spent heavily). Indeed, UNAIDS points to the Declaration of Commitment on HIV/AIDS (discussed below) rather than Resolution 1308 as the turning point in global financial commitments (see Figure 1).

If the Council's actions provide a less than solid basis for asserting that HIV/AIDS has been transformed into an international security issue, does the linking of HIV/AIDS and security in other key parts of the UN System suggest that we have witnessed a successful case of securitization? Here the article moves on to examine some key statements made in and by three other UN bodies—the General Assembly, ECOSOC and UNAIDS— and attempts to judge the prevalence of the international security framing in relation to two prominent alternatives: international development and human rights.

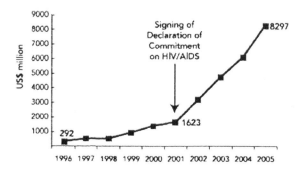

Figure 1 Estimated total annual resources available for AIDS, 1996–2005.

The General Assembly

Although it is derided by some as a mere 'talking shop' the General Assembly has in fact made a number of significant interventions on HIV/AIDS. Three of these—and the ideas that underpinned them—are worthy of particular attention.

The first was the adoption of the Millennium Development Goals (MDGs), Goal 6 of which commits states to reverse the tide of HIV infection. Although what became the MDGs had been under discussion within the OECD and the UN System since at least 1996 (OECD DAC 1996; Vereker 2002: 135; Hulme 2007), it was at the General Assembly's Millennium Summit in September 2000 that they were formally adopted. There has been a good deal of scepticism over whether the targets will be achieved by 2015, but the MDGs have at least focused international attention on those challenges included in the goals and have heightened the political costs of failure to at least make progress on achieving them. Doing so may, of course, have relevance to a security agenda in the indirect sense that development might reduce the likelihood of conflict and increase international security (High-level Panel on Threats, Challenges and Change 2004). In terms of the ideas underpinning the MDGs, however, it was clearly international development itself rather than international security, which was the primary motivation.

Perhaps the most high-profile General Assembly event to focus exclusively on HIV/AIDS was the June 2001 three-day 'UN General Assembly Special Session' (UNGASS) devoted to the issue. These special sessions are used relatively sparingly and it was held at a high political level (many of those representing their countries were heads of state or government, or in some cases Ministers of Health or Development), showing the importance that member states attached to the issue. As is characteristic of such occasions, most countries were keen to take the opportunity to speak: 182 state representatives made speeches over the 3 days, along with Secretary-General Kofi Annan, UNAIDS Executive Director Peter Piot, and representatives of some 20 international organizations, civil society groups, regional organizations and UN agencies.

What is striking when one examines the speeches made at the UNGASS is that mentions of the link between HIV/AIDS and international security were surprisingly rare. Of the 182 states that made statements, only 33 (just over 1 in 6) referred to the disease in terms of national or international security.[1] Where they did so, those references tended to be brief and bland statements noting that, amongst other things, HIV/AIDS represents a potential threat to state stability. This example, taken from the statement of Nigeria, is typical of the genre:

> "Nigeria welcomes the convening of this United Nations special session to set the agenda for meeting the immense challenges posed

by a disease so deadly that it has become one of the greatest obstacles to human development and security."

(UN General Assembly 2001a: 14)

In fact, statements focused overwhelmingly on alternative discursive framings of the pandemic: HIV/AIDS as a public health problem of course, but also as an international development challenge and as a human rights issue. Despite coming only a year after Resolution 1308, the international security dimensions were only a minor feature of discourse at the UNGASS. Resolution 1308 itself was scarcely mentioned.[2] International security concerns did not even feature prominently in the statements made by those states that had been on the Council at the time Resolution 1308 was adopted: only four of those 15 states (Bangladesh, France, Mali and the USA) mentioned international security issues. The other 11 were silent on international security. This might further add to the doubts expressed above over the extent to which the Council members in July 2000 were genuinely persuaded by the US-led securitizing move.

The culmination of the UNGASS was the adoption of a 'Declaration of Commitment on HIV/AIDS' (UN General Assembly 2001c), a declaration that has, like the MDGs, been both heralded as a major achievement in its own right (e.g. Parker 2002) and used as a yardstick against which to judge progress made. The Declaration made little reference to international security at all. It did highlight the fact that conflict and disasters can contribute to the spread of HIV (UN General Assembly 2001c: paras 75 and 76), and called on states to take action to reduce rates amongst their uniformed services (paras 77 and 78) but did not make the claim that HIV can contribute to bringing about instability and conflict. Neither did it make reference to Resolution 1308.

Four years later a second high-level meeting on HIV/AIDS was held with the primary aim of measuring progress on the commitments made in the 2001 Declaration and MDG 6. Once again in the statements made in the plenary sessions there were relatively few references to the international security implications of HIV/AIDS. Again the overwhelming emphasis was on international development and human rights. This time the text adopted by the Assembly (the so-called 'Political Declaration on HIV/AIDS') did note that 'HIV/AIDS constitutes a global emergency and poses one of the most formidable challenges to the development, progress and stability of our respective societies and the world at large' (UN General Assembly 2006: 1), but it emphasized human rights (e.g. paras 11, 12) and international development (e.g. para 13) far more than security.

In short, the international security-based framing of the pandemic seems to have had only a limited impact within the General Assembly. It is international development and human rights, not security, which have largely defined the Assembly's treatment of HIV/AIDS.

431

ECOSOC

The UN Charter sets out the area of ECOSOC's competence as 'international economic, social, cultural, educational, health and related matters' (Article 62) as well as human rights. One of its key tasks is coordinating the work of the UN System's various specialized agencies, funds, commissions and other subsidiary bodies. As such, it would in many ways appear to be the 'natural home' for HIV/AIDS amongst the organs of the UN, and it is clear that at least some of the states who opposed the Security Council's involvement in the issue believed that HIV/AIDS 'belonged' in ECOSOC.[3] Despite this, ECOSOC's treatment of HIV/AIDS has gone almost entirely unexamined in the academic literature. Indeed, other than dutiful sections in the UN textbooks, which cover it largely for the sake of completism, ECOSOC scarcely receives any academic attention at all.

The establishment of UNAIDS was ECOSOC's most significant contribution to date to the global response. Although there was widespread agreement that the UN System's efforts in this area needed to be improved, the process of designing the new coordinating mechanism was a difficult and drawn-out one (Knight 2008). ECOSOC Resolution 1994/24 marked the formal establishment of UNAIDS, although the new body did not begin work until January 1996. In terms of the ideas underpinning UN responses this was an interesting historical moment: the creation of UNAIDS was in part a reaction against the narrower medical/public health-based approach of the WHO and a recognition of the multisectoral and multi-faceted nature of the problem (Parker 2000: 43). This, however, predated the securitizing move made by the USA in 2000. It should not be surprising, therefore, that Resolution 1994/24 referred to the particular challenges HIV/AIDS posed in developing countries and to the necessity of the UN System working with other development partners, but made no reference to international security.

But even post-2000, ECOSOC has not seriously addressed the security dimensions of the pandemic. There have been three relevant ECOSOC Resolutions passed in this period. Two of these have concerned the work of UNAIDS. The first, in 2005 (UN ECOSOC 2005), reaffirmed the outcomes of the UNGASS and the Millennium Declaration, but made no mention of the Security Council (or, indeed, international security) noting only that HIV/AIDS 'Exacerbates poverty and poses a major threat to economic and social development and to food security in heavily affected regions'. The second (UN ECOSOC 2007) directly quoted the General Assembly's Political Declaration of 2005, repeating the phrase: 'HIV/AIDS constitutes a global emergency and poses one of the most formidable challenges to the development, progress and stability of societies and the world at large . . .'. It did not expand upon this statement. The third post-2000 ECOSOC Resolution on HIV/AIDS (UN ECOSOC 2004) was quite different in character, dealing specifically with HIV/AIDS in prisons and correctional facilities. As such it treated HIV primarily as a human rights issue, specifically the rights of prisoners.

As in the General Assembly, then, development and human rights have been foregrounded by ECOSOC. Security has scarcely figured at all, other than in the ritualistic quotation of other declarations.

UNAIDS

The story with UNAIDS is somewhat different. From the outset one of its explicit purposes was to increase the profile of the disease as an international political issue (UN ECOSOC 1994). As the Executive Director Peter Piot stated in 1999, 'In the coming year, the UNAIDS Secretariat and Cosponsors will need to intensify their advocacy with the most senior policy makers and opinion leaders' (UNAIDS 1999: 34–5). The Copenhagen School suggest that securitization is an excellent way of achieving this and it seems fitting that UNAIDS was involved from an early stage in the attempt to get the issue on the Security Council agenda. UNAIDS Executive Director Peter Piot played a central role, seizing the opportunity to get increased attention (and, he no doubt hoped, resources) for the battle against AIDS. As Richard Holbrooke (2006) recalled:

"I didn't know Peter Piot very well until the Security Council session, but he was excited by it. He realized that the world was going to pay more attention. We were breaking the issue out of the field of health specialists and into the international consciousness as a security issue. Peter told me later that it was the best day of his first four years as head of the UNAIDS."

Piot has himself spoken about the benefits that he sees as accruing from presenting AIDS as a security issue, saying in 2005 that:

"When we look at the history of the fight against AIDS, there is no doubt that resolution 1308 (2000) is a milestone in the response to the epidemic. By underscoring the fact that the spread of HIV/AIDS, if unchecked, may pose a risk to stability and security, the Security Council . . . has transformed how the world views AIDS. I say "transformed" because many now view AIDS as a threat to national security and stability, in addition to being a threat to development and public health alone."

(UN Security Council 2005: 5)

No doubt because of Piot's involvement—unlike in the General Assembly or ECOSOC—the security discourse gained a reasonably high level of traction within UNAIDS. Furthermore, in terms of practical responses UNAIDS has been at the forefront of working on some of the security-related aspects, in particular with national militaries and UN peacekeeping forces (UNAIDS 2005).

Even within UNAIDS, however, international security has not been the dominant way in which HIV/AIDS is framed. Rather, the securitizing move was one way in which UNAIDS sought to build a sense of emergency. Other framings—international development and human rights again being the most prominent—have also been deployed as ways of encouraging governments and donors to do more. Although not a scientific test, some persuasive support for this claim can be seen in the frequency of the security framing of HIV/AIDS in the biannual UNAIDS/WHO *Report on the Global AIDS Epidemic*. These reports are the most high-profile of UNAIDS' publications, and thus are a key part of its strategy for increasing international attention. Although they have on occasion included discussions of HIV/AIDS as a national/international security issue, this has not by any means been the primary frame. The development and human rights aspects of HIV/AIDS dominate the reports, dwarfing the number of references to security (see Figure 2).

So whilst UNAIDS has played a role in promoting the security dimensions of HIV/AIDS, it would be impossible to conclude that it is the dominant frame within the reports. Rather what we can see is a willingness to frame HIV in any (or all) of the available ways. Security is one weapon in the armoury, but only one amongst several.

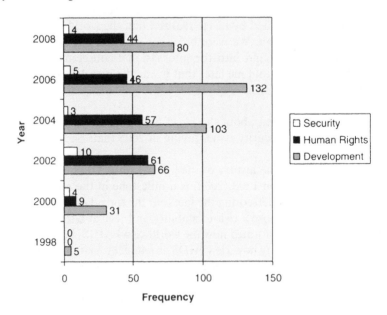

Figure 2 Frequency of terms 'security', 'human rights' and 'development' in UNAIDS Global Reports 1998–2008. Includes 'security' in the limited sense of 'international security' (i.e. excluding 'food security', 'economic security', etc.); includes 'development' in the limited sense of 'international development'.

Conclusions

In short, it has been argued here that the securitization of HIV/AIDS has been far less successful than is often supposed. Even the Security Council—identified frequently as the key actor in the securitization process—agreed only reluctantly to pass what was, after all, a relatively non-committal resolution, and has subsequently seemed to back away from the issue. A securitizing move was certainly made, but the result may best be understood as a partial—or perhaps even a failed—case of securitization. If we look beyond the Council to the wider UN System we find that the international security dimensions of HIV/AIDS are evident in the discourse, but only to a limited extent. Alternative framings are given far more weight. Although some states (the USA being the clearest example) continue to view HIV in part as a security threat, there is certainly no unanimity on this. These findings have implications both for securitization theory and for our understanding of the global governance of HIV/AIDS.

For one, the HIV/AIDS case demonstrates the difficulty in determining whether the securitization threshold has been crossed. On the face of it a Security Council Resolution would seem to be powerful evidence that it has, and in the early–mid 2000s there were good reasons for believing in a successful securitization. A decade after Resolution 1308 the picture looks somewhat different. Yet the mere existence of a Resolution may give a false impression of consensus: divisions often lie beneath the surface.

It also calls into question whether security is always a trump card. In fact different approaches are required in different fora and for different audiences. In large part this is about institutional agendas, and this can be seen extremely clearly in the UN System context. The Security Council is primarily concerned with threats to international peace and security, and thus constructing HIV/AIDS in those terms was a prerequisite to getting it on the Council agenda. But security does not seem to override other concerns in the same way elsewhere in the UN family. The dominance of the G77 within the General Assembly has made international development one of the key buttons for states to push in that forum. ECOSOC's work is in areas such as human rights and development. It should come as no surprise, then, that the discourse within these fora reflects these biases. For those seeking to raise the profile of an issue, then, it is a case of horses for courses.

This has obvious implications for our understanding of the global governance of HIV/AIDS. Whilst a lot of attention in the academic literature has centred on the actions of the Council, the Assembly's commitments on HIV/AIDS seem to have done far more to increase the resources available. This points to a need for further research into which bodies have the biggest impact on global responses, how the relationships between them work, and what ideas and concepts underpin their engagements.

The debate around AIDS and security has recently moved on in a positive way, with work such as that emanating from the Netherlands-backed 'AIDS,

Security and Conflict Initiative' (ASCI) beginning to set out some important and promising new research agendas (e.g. de Waal 2010; de Waal *et al.* 2009). We must certainly remain alert to evidence of the potentially troubling side-effects of securitizing HIV (Elbe 2006), but also to the implications of different understandings of the nature of the HIV problem (and consequently the appropriate way of responding). It is far from certain that the demands of international security, economic development and human rights can be reconciled. There is thus a need for a holistic view of global responses to the pandemic and the ways in which the international community seeks to deal with what is, after all, at its heart a human tragedy.

Acknowledgements

This work was supported by the European Research Council under the European Community's Seventh Framework Programme [Ideas Grant Ref. 230489-GHG]. All views expressed remain those of the author.

Earlier drafts of this article were presented at the International Studies Association Annual Convention in 2009 and the conference on 'Unhealthy Governance: Securitising Infectious Diseases in Asia' held at the University of Hong Kong in May 2009. I am grateful to the participants in those events and also to Colin McInnes, Huw Williams and the reviewers of *Health Policy and Planning* for their helpful comments and suggestions.

Notes

1 Those that did so were (in the order in which they addressed the Assembly): Botswana, Mozambique, Nigeria, Portugal, Rwanda, Norway, USA, Pakistan, Algeria, Mali, Thailand, Barbados, France, Mexico, Germany, Panama, Monaco, Brunei, Bolivia, Yemen, Nepal, Congo, Antigua & Barbuda, United Arab Emirates, Swaziland, Belize, Saint Lucia, Cyprus, Bangladesh, Fiji, Lebanon, Sierra Leone, D.R. Congo.
2 Thailand was an exception to this (UN General Assembly 2001b: 7).
3 USUN noted that during the negotiations a number of developing countries 'said HIV/AIDS was only minimally within the Council's competence and ascribed lead roles to ECOSOC and the General Assembly' (USUN 2000: para 7).

References

Aldis W. 2008. Health security as a public health concept: a critical analysis. *Health Policy and Planning* 23: 369–75.
Altman D. 2003. AIDS and security. *International Relations* 17: 417–27.
Baldwin D. A. 1997. The concept of security. *Review of International Studies* 23: 5–26.
Barnett T., Prins G. 2005. *HIV/AIDS and Security: Fact, Fiction and Evidence—A Report to UNAIDS*. London: LSEAIDS. Online at: http://www.lse.ac.uk/collections/DESTIN/publink/barnett/Barnett%20and%20Prins%20Fact%20Fiction%20and%20Evidence%20REPORT.pdf.

Buzan B. 1991. *People, States and Fear: An Agenda for International Security Studies in the Post-Cold War Era*. 2nd edn. London: Harvester Wheatsheaf.

Buzan B., Waever O., de Wilde J. 1998. *Security: A New Framework for Analysis*. Boulder, CO: Lynne Rienner.

CIA. 1987. *Sub-Saharan Africa: Implications of the AIDS Pandemic. SNIE 70/1–87*. Washington, DC: Central Intelligence Agency.

Cohen J. 2002. Gates Foundation rearranges public health universe. *Science* **295**: 2000.

David M. 2001. Rubber helmets: the certain pitfalls of marshalling Security Council resources to combat AIDS in Africa. *Human Rights Quarterly* **23**: 560–82.

de Waal A. 2010. HIV/AIDS and the challenges of security and conflict. *The Lancet* **375**: 22–3.

de Waal A., Klot J. F., Mahajan M. *et al.* 2009. *HIV/AIDS, Security and Conflict: New Realities, New Responses*. New York/The Hague: Social Science Research Council/Clingendael Institute). Online at: http://www.ssrc.org/workspace/images/crm/new_publication_3/{e2090d2b-72a8-de11-9d32-001cc477ec70}.pdf.

de Waal A., Whiteside A. 2003. New variant famine: AIDS and food crisis in southern Africa. *The Lancet* **362**: 1234–7. Department of Defense. 2010. DoD HIV/AIDS Prevention Program. Online at: http://www.med.navy.mil/SITES/NHRC/DHAPP/Pages/default.aspx.

Dupont A. 2001. *East Asia Imperilled: Transnational Challenges to Security*. Cambridge: Cambridge University Press.

Elbe S. 2005. Aids, security, biopolitics. *International Relations* **19**: 403–19.

Elbe S. 2006. Should AIDS be securitized? The ethical dilemmas of linking HIV/AIDS and security. *International Studies Quarterly* **50**: 119–44.

Feldbaum H. 2009. *U.S. Global Health and National Security Policy: A Report of the CSIS Global Health Policy Center*. Washington, DC: Center for Strategic and International Studies. Online at: http://csis.org/files/media/csis/pubs/090420_feldbaum_usglobalhealth.pdf.

Feldbaum H., Lee K., Patel P. 2006. The national security implications of HIV/AIDS. *PloS Medicine* **3**: 774–8.

Fidler D. 2007. A pathology of public health securitism: approaching pandemics as security threats. In: Cooper A. F., Kirton J. J., Schrecker T. (eds). *Governing Global Health: Challenge, Response, Innovation*. Aldershot: Ashgate, pp. 41–64.

Foreign & Commonwealth Office. 2000a. Telegram from the FCO to the UK Mission to the UN in New York, 13 July 2000. Released to the author under the Freedom of Information Act 2000.

Foreign & Commonwealth Office. 2000b. Telegram from the FCO to the UK Mission to the UN in New York, 14 July 2000. Released to the author under the Freedom of Information Act 2000.

Fourie P., Schonteich M. 2001. Africa's new security threat: HIV/AIDS and human security in Southern Africa. *African Security Review* **10**: 29–42.

Fox D. M., Kasalow J. S. Making health a priority of US foreign policy. *American Journal of Public Health* **91**: 1554–6.

Garrett L. 2005. *HIV and National Security: Where Are the Links?* New York: Council on Foreign Relations.

Gebretensae G. B. 2004. HIV/AIDS and Regional Security in Africa: Principles for Incorporating HIV/AIDS into the Common African Security and Defense Policy and Establishing HIV/AIDS Guidelines for the African Standby Force London: Justice Africa. Online at: http://www.justiceafrica.org/wp-content/uploads/2006/07/Tsadkan_Draft_Principles.pdf.

High-level Panel on Threats, Challenges and Change. 2004. *A More Secure World: Our Shared Responsibility*. New York: United Nations.

Holbrooke R. 2000. Remarks at UN Headquarters on Implementation of Security Council Resolution 1308 on HIV/AIDS, 22 December 2000 USUN Press Release #213 (00).

Holbrooke R. 2006. Interview, PBS *Frontline* Online at: http://www.pbs.org/wgbh/pages/frontline/aids/interviews/holbrooke.html.

Hulme D. 2007. *The Making of the Millennium Development Goals: Human Development Meets Results-based Management in an Imperfect World*. BWIP Working Paper 16. Manchester: Brooks World Poverty Institute.

Hunter S. S. 2005. *AIDS in Asia: A Continent in Peril*. Houndmills, Basingstoke: Palgrave Macmillan.

Ingram A. 2005. Global leadership and global health: contending meta-narratives, divergent responses, fatal consequences. *International Relations* **19**: 381–402.

Knight L. 2008. *UNAIDS: The First 10 Years*. Geneva: UNAIDS.

McInnes C. 2006. HIV/AIDS and security. *International Affairs* **82**: 315–26.

McInnes C. 2007. HIV/AIDS and national security. In: Poku N., Whiteside A., Sandkjaer B. (eds). *AIDS and Governance*. Aldershot: Ashgate, pp. 93–114.

McInnes C., Rushton S. 2010. HIV, AIDS and security: where are we now? *International Affairs* **86**: 225–45.

National Intelligence Council. 2000. *The Global Infectious Disease Threat and its Implications for the United States*. NIE 99-17D. Online at: http://www.dni.gov/nic/PDF_GIF_otherprod/infectiousdisease/infectiousdiseases.pdf.

National Intelligence Council. 2002. *The Next Wave of HIV/AIDS: Nigeria, Ethiopia, Russia, India, and China*. ICA 2002–04 D, September 2002. Online at: http://www.dni.gov/nic/PDF_GIF_otherprod/HIVAIDS/ICA_HIVAIDS20092302.pdf.

OECD DAC. 1996. *Shaping the 21st Century: The Contribution of Development Co-operation*. OECD: Paris. Online at: http://www.oecd.org/dataoecd/23/35/2508761.pdf.

Ostergard R. 2002. Politics in the hot zone: AIDS and national security in Africa. *Third World Quarterly* **23**: 333–50.

Pallikadavath S., Stones R. W. 2003. Women's reproductive health security and HIV/AIDS in India. *Economic and Political Weekly* **38**: 4173–81.

Parker R. 2000. Administering the epidemic: HIV/AIDS policy, models of development, and international health. In: Whiteford L. M., Manderson L. (eds). *Global Health Policy, Local Realities*. Boulder, CO: Lynne Rienner.

Parker R. 2002. The global HIV/AIDS pandemic, structural inequalities, and the politics of international health. *American Journal of Public Health* **92**: 343–7.

Piot P. Transcript of meeting on 'HIV & Security', Council on Foreign Relations, 18 July 2005. Online at: http://www.cfr.org/publication/8428/hiv_and_national_security.html.

Prins G. 2004. AIDS and global security. *International Affairs* **80**: 931–52.

Schneider M., Moodie M. 2002. *The Destabilizing Impacts of HIV/AIDS*. Washington, DC: Center for Strategic and International Studies. Online at: http://www.csis.org/media/csis/pubs/0205_destimp.pdf.

Singer P. 2002. Aids and international security. *Survival* **44**: 145–58.

Sternberg S. 2002. Former diplomat Holbrooke takes on global AIDS. *USA Today*. 10 June.

Thomspon A. 2004. International security challenges posed by HIV/AIDS: implications for China. *China: An International Journal* **2**: 287–307.

Tripoldi P., Patel P. 2002. The global impact of HIV/AIDS on peace support operations. *International Peacekeeping* **9**: 51–66.

UK Mission to the UN. 2000. Telegram from the UK Mission to the UN in New York to the Foreign & Commonwealth Office, 17 July 2000. Released to the author under the Freedom of Information Act 2000.

UNAIDS. 1999. Programme Coordinating Board: Report of the Executive Director. UNAIDS/PCB(8)/99.2. Geneva.

UNAIDS. 2005. *On the Front Line: A Review of Policies and Programmes to Address AIDS among Peacekeepers and Uniformed Services*. New York: UNAIDS.

UNAIDS. 2006. *Report on the Global AIDS Epidemic*. Geneva: UNAIDS.

UNAIDS. 2009. Goals, United Nations Declarations and Resolutions on AIDS. Online at: http://www.unaids.org/en/AboutUNAIDS/Goals/default.asp.

UN ECOSOC. 1994. Resolution 1994/24. Online at: http://www.un.org/documents/ecosoc/res/1994/eres1994-24.htm.

UN ECOSOC. 2004. Resolution 2004/35. Combating the spread of HIV/AIDS in criminal justice pre-trial and correctional facilities. Online at: http://www.un.org/en/ecosoc/docs/2004/resolution%202004-35.pdf.

UN ECOSOC. 2005. Resolution 2005/47. Joint United Nations Programme on HIV/AIDS (UNAIDS). Online at: http://www.un.org/en/ecosoc/docs/2005/resolution%202005-47.pdf.

UN General Assembly. 2001a. Special Session on HIV/AIDS, A/S-26/PV.1. 25 June 2001.

UN General Assembly. 2001b. Special Session on HIV/AIDS, A/S-26/PV.2. 25 June 2001.

UN General Assembly. 2001c. *Declaration of Commitment on HIV/AIDS*. New York: United Nations.

UN General Assembly. 2006. Political Declaration on HIV/AIDS. A/RES/60/262.

UN Security Council. 2000. Security Council Resolution 1308. S/RES/1308. 17 July 2000.

UN Security Council. 2005. Security Council 5228th Meeting. S/PV.5228. 18 July 2005.

UN Security Council. 2007. Security Council 5749th Meeting S/PV.5749 (25 September 2007).

USUN. 2000. Telegram from the United States Mission to the United Nations, New York to the Secretary of State, Washington DC, July 2000. Declassified 20 July 2005. Released to the author under the Freedom of Information Act on 8 February 2007.

Waever O. 2003. Securitisation: Taking stock of a research programme in Security Studies Unpublished manuscript. Online at: http://media.fpn.bg.ac.yu/nacionalnai-globalnabezbednost/03%20Socio%20konstruktivisticke%20teorije/03%20Literatura/Waever_2003__Securitisation_Taking_stock_of_a_research_programme_in_ Security _Studies.doc.

Vereker J. 2002. Blazing the trail: eight years of change in handling international development. *Development Policy Review* **20**: 133–40.

Wood M. C. 1998. The interpretation of Security Council Resolutions. *Max Planck Yearbook of United Nations Law* **2**: 86–7.

78

DIPLOMACY AND THE POLIO IMMUNIZATION BOYCOTT IN NORTHERN NIGERIA

With scientific evidence and pressure from political allies and religious authority figures, a Nigerian polio vaccine boycott was brought to an end

Judith R. Kaufmann and Harley Feldbaum

Source: *Health Affairs*, 28:4 (2009), 1091–101.

Abstract

The boycott of polio vaccination in three Northern Nigerian states in 2003 created a global health crisis that was political in origin. This paper traces the diplomatic actions that were taken by the Global Polio Eradication Initiative, the United Nations, and the U.S. government, to restart polio vaccination and resolve the crisis. The polio vaccination boycott in Northern Nigeria provides a useful case study of the practice of global health diplomacy.

In August 2003 the political leadership of several Northern Nigerian states responded to community pressure and banned federally sponsored polio immunization campaigns. The stoppage was justified by "evidence" that the polio vaccine was contaminated with antifertility drugs intended to sterilize young Muslim girls. The suspension in Northern Nigeria, particularly in Kano State, led to a global outbreak of polio; the disease spread into twenty countries across Africa, the Middle East, and Southeast Asia and caused 80 percent of the world's cases of paralytic poliomyelitis during the stoppage.

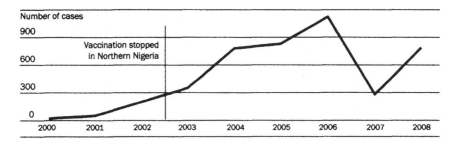

Exhibit 1 Cases Of Wild Poliovirus in Nigeria, 2000–December 2008.
Source: World Health Organization/Global Polio Eradication Initiative, "Wild Poliovirus 2000–2009," April 2009, http://polioeradication.org/content/general/casecount.pdf (accessed 10 April 2009).

The vaccine boycott eventually led to costs of more than US$500 million to control the polio outbreak, and it essentially ended hopes of eradicating polio in this decade (Exhibit 1).[1]

The solution to this global health crisis, caused by internal Nigerian political forces, was not typical: not only was epidemiological information required, but also diplomatic action. Previous literature has examined the political and public health background to the crisis, and the public health response to the vaccination stoppage.[2] What has not been previously reported is how international diplomatic tools were mobilized to end the formal political boycott. There has been much discussion recently of "health diplomacy," but few case studies or little historical examination of how diplomacy and health interact.[3] By examining the diplomatic response to the polio boycott in Nigeria, this paper provides a case study in the use of traditional diplomacy to support global health efforts—an important component of health diplomacy.

This case study is based on a literature review, examination of previously unavailable Global Polio Eradication Initiative (GPEI) and U.S. government documents, and thirteen in-depth interviews with people involved in the crisis. Interviews were used to go beyond published accounts of the crisis and to illuminate the experiences, perspectives, and interests of both policymakers and institutions.

Origins of the vaccine boycott

Historical political, ethnic, and religious tensions in Nigeria were exacerbated after the April 2003 election, when retired General Olusegun Obasanjo, a born-again Baptist from the southern part of Nigeria, was elected to a second term as president over retired General Muhammadu Buhari, a Muslim northerner. Reflecting and exacerbating these tensions were regional disparities in the provision and use of health services, with poorer health outcomes found in the North.[4]

The *Weekly Trust*, an important northern newspaper, reported that the formal suspension began at a 21 July 2003 meeting of the Jama'atul Nasril Islam (JNI, a northern umbrella group of Muslim organizations):

> One of the Emirs presented a memo on the concerns and apprehensions of his people on the allegations that the polio vaccination campaign was being used for the purpose of depopulating developing countries, and especially Muslim countries. . . . Although some of the more senior Emirs tried to dismiss the observation as mere rambling by their subjects, the Supreme Council on Sharia implementation in Nigeria led by a respected Kano-based medical doctor, Dr Datti Ahmed brought the apprehensions into full public glare when . . . he told newsmen that his council had reasons to suspect contamination of the polio vaccines with HIV/AIDS virus, anti-fertility substances and other dangerous elements.[5]

According to then U.S. Ambassador to Nigeria John Campbell, the boycott "was about fear and disaffection at the popular level that fastened on immunization as a precipitant. . . . Once the safety of the vaccines became a popular issue, which leaders could not control, they gave in with some reluctance." He continued by saying, "This was not really about technical issues. The issue was Northern Nigeria's thorough disaffection with the Obasanjo government."[6]

A source who has worked closely with the Nigeria polio program said, "This was one of the clearest examples of a public health issue being hijacked for political reasons. . . . The bulk of people were sincerely concerned, but clearly the leadership and the encouragement to continue was political." The global polio vaccination campaign had become enmeshed in local Nigerian politics, with northern political leaders ceasing polio immunizations in their states.[7]

Early response to the vaccine boycott

Rumors about safety have plagued many immunization programs, including in the United States, where there are groups and Web sites devoted to theories about the links between immunizations and conditions such as autism.[8] As the United Nations Children's Fund (UNICEF) notes, "Occasionally rumours arise such as a link between immunization and family planning or that vaccination could cause HIV/AIDS. While these rumors are groundless, when they spread, they can severely damage immunization efforts."[9] Generally speaking, local leaders with influence in the community are most effective in countering rumors when they arise.[10]

When rumors about tainted vaccine first began to circulate in Nigeria in 2003, the initial assumption by those involved was that these rumors would be shortlived and that tools and lessons learned from other regions would be sufficient to convince those involved to recommit to the campaign.[11] Gianni Murzi, the UNICEF Nigeria director at the time, explained:

> Our own Western-oriented . . . background tells us if vaccine is found to be good, then it's scientifically good, that's it. . . . Instead, the population who rejected it was thinking in other terms, and we didn't realize the power of that and how disruptive that could have been. . . . We didn't see it coming, and unfortunately that is quite normal.[12]

The United Nations envoy

Simultaneously, but completely separately, then U.S. Secretary of State Colin Powell and UNICEF headquarters suggested to United Nations (UN) Secretary-General Kofi Annan that he send Ibrahim Gambari, the secretary-general's senior adviser for African affairs, to Nigeria as the secretary-general's special envoy. Normally, the UN Secretariat would not send a national of a country to negotiate in his or her country of origin, for fear of conflict of interest or pressure being put on the individual. However, in this case, most felt that Gambari was uniquely qualified. Gambari's father was a Muslim northerner and Emir of Ilorin, and his mother was a southerner. Gambari has served under virtually all of the surviving former Nigerian presidents, including those with presumed influence in the North, and had managed President Obasanjo's 1991 campaign to be UN secretary-general.

Gambari met with President Obasanjo and the federal minister of health in early 2004. According to Gambari, President Obasanjo approved visits to the Sultan of Sokoto, the Emir of Kano, traditional leaders of the Muslim communities, and former presidents, including General Buhari, saying, "You get to where I find it difficult to get to. They will probably listen to you more than they will listen to me, and you will have access."[13] Gambari presented letters from the secretary-general, appealing for their help and their intervention to resolve the boycott.[14] He spent four hours in heated debate with Datti Ahmed, the doctor who had first called for the suspension of the polio immunization campaign.

Sokoto demonstrated the complexity of the situation. The Sultan of Sokoto is traditionally a spokesman for the region's Muslims on important issues.[15] He is also the head of the JNI. However, the JNI secretary-general was an opponent of polio immunization. Thus, although Gambari felt that the sultan was convinced by the plea that the boycott was hurting children and giving Nigeria a bad name, others within the religious establishment continued to support the boycott.

The sultan did join President Obasanjo at the kick-off of the polio immunization campaign in neighboring Zamfara State in March 2004, and Gambari left Sokoto with assurances from the governor that he would support immunization and would work to convince his colleague, the governor of Kano.

The trip to Kano was, according to Gambari, the most difficult. Gambari describes Kano this way: "Kano has always gone the opposite way politically from the rest of the country. . . . Then, of course, they like to give trouble to the central government on an issue where the central government is vulnerable, religion."

Because the governor was of General Buhari's party, it was in his political interest to make things difficult for President Obasanjo. To both the governor and Dr. Ahmed, Gambari's message was simple: "Suppose you are wrong. . . . You are going to condemn a whole people to this life of misery. At least consider you may be wrong." Although not immediately successful, Gambari felt that he had created some doubts. Murzi said of Gambari's visit, "With his ability to work in the North, he succeeded in helping us establish a dialogue up North. That visit was instrumental. It opened up the doors for increased conversation."

The GPEI and the organization of the Islamic Conference

In 2003 the GPEI Secretariat, headquartered at the World Health Organization (WHO) in Geneva, began contact with the Organization of the Islamic Conference (OIC), "an inter-governmental organization grouping fifty-seven States [whose mission is] to safeguard and protect the interests of the Muslim world in the spirit of promoting international peace and harmony among various people of the world."[16] The rationale was that the six remaining polio-endemic countries at the time (Nigeria, Niger, Egypt, India, Pakistan, and Afghanistan) either were majority Muslim or had large Muslim populations, especially in the endemic areas.[17] All but five of the fifty-seven OIC members were polio-free, thanks to advice and support from the GPEI—including advice on choice of vaccines—and could thus counter questions about the efficacy and safety of the polio vaccine and the aims of the eradication initiative.

Anand Balachandran, GPEI interagency coordinator and a social scientist, saw that "the OIC, being a political body, was a platform . . . important to defusing the idea that the GPEI and WHO were controlled by Western donors."[18] The secretariat first built a relationship with the OIC ambassador in Geneva, a Senegalese, who played a key role in getting the ambassadors of the OIC countries in Geneva engaged. The GPEI secretariat then briefed these ambassadors in Geneva, London, and New York. The briefings moved the polio crisis and eradication issues beyond ministers of health to gain broader diplomatic and political support.

The Nigerian boycott, and the continued spread of polio outside Nigeria's borders, made the approach to the OIC more urgent. With the Tenth Islamic Conference scheduled for 16–17 October 2003 in Malaysia, David Heymann, the newly appointed special envoy on polio of the WHO director-general, contacted the Malaysian minister of health, with whom he had worked on severe acute respiratory syndrome (SARS) earlier. The minister and the government of Malaysia put polio on the summit agenda, which was, as Heymann describes it, "quite unusual, particularly in a politically charged atmosphere."[19]

The resolution at the OIC summit urged the remaining polio-endemic OIC countries, including Nigeria, to accelerate their efforts and called on the international community, including OIC members and philanthropic organizations in the Islamic world, to fund the effort.[20] The GPEI continued to share information with the OIC through the ambassadors in Geneva, including evidence on the safety and efficacy of the vaccines.

Quietly, with support from the GPEI, the OIC secretariat and the regional director for WHO's Eastern Mediterranean Regional Organization (EMRO) worked to get religious leaders to speak out on polio. Ultimately, a number of fatwas, or Islamic religious rulings, were issued on polio vaccination.[21] These were important in countering the argument that the vaccine was a Western plot to wipe out Muslims. They also gave, according to Balachandran, "space and options for the political decision makers to move the issue from one of religion concern to the political realm, where they could come up with a deal."[22]

Heymann says of the outreach to the OIC and to other regional organizations, "The most valuable thing was getting the OIC involved and they were helpful in many, many ways as was the African Union. . . . Plus getting some Islamic interpretation through the [Islamic] Fiqh [Academy], which was helpful in understanding . . . that the vaccine was safe. We had great help from the Islamic community." Such help took concerted and coordinated outreach by the GPEI.

The U.S. government

Polio was already on the policy radar screen in the United States in 2003–2004. The U.S. government had decided to make closing the GPEI funding gap a goal of the 2004 G8 Sea Island Summit. One U.S. government official recalls that the U.S. view was that eradicating polio fit perfectly with U.S. interests. The United States was already the largest donor to the GPEI, and the goals of closing the funding gap and eradicating polio by 2005 seemed achievable. Also, the GPEI was a public-private partnership, in line with U.S. government policy preference.

The Centers for Disease Control and Prevention (CDC) had personnel in Nigeria. They reported their concerns about the immunization efforts and the vaccine boycott to the U.S. Department of Health and Human Services (HHS), which suggested to the National Security Council in October 2003 that President George W. Bush send a letter to President Obasanjo, urging him to move forward with the immunization campaign. Others felt that too overt an intervention by the United States could exacerbate the problem in Northern Nigeria, where the war in Iraq had eroded support for the United

States and where the polio immunization campaign was seen as a Western plot.[23]

At the same time, the State Department's small office of International Health Affairs (IHA) suggested to the Bureau of African Affairs (AF) an action plan for diplomatic action on polio. Although sympathetic, AF had other priorities. Nigeria was playing an important role in peace-keeping efforts in Sierra Leone and Liberia and had provided safe haven to former Liberian President Charles Taylor, to help end the civil war in that country. The United States had economic interests as well; Nigeria was the fifth-largest supplier of crude oil to the United States, so AF did not focus intently on the polio issue.

However, in January 2004 Secretary of State Powell raised the boycott in a staff meeting and asked for more information. To respond to the request with specific action items, IHA asked for suggestions from the CDC, the U.S. Agency for International Development (USAID), and GPEI. Ellyn Ogden of USAID said that even with all of her experience, including being a part of the team working on the G8 summit, she didn't know what diplomatic tools were available:

> I was having a hard time making that transition from a technical person in epidemiology to what tools did State have. . . . I didn't know what to ask for. I didn't know about demarches, I didn't know about briefing notes or cables. I didn't know what State could bring.[24]

William Steiger, the head of the HHS Office of Global Health Affairs, emphasizes the importance of giving policymakers specific actions that can be taken:

> You need to break the situation down into very understandable pieces, preferably with specific outcomes or specific steps to get senior policymakers to agree or to have their buy-in. If we had just said polio is a disaster but we don't know what to do about it, I don't think we would have gotten anywhere. We were able to say, OK, we have a problem, we think we have a several things that we'd like to have you do. . . . It made everybody understand more easily how we could play a role.[25]

Following up on the suggestions, then HHS secretary Tommy Thompson sent a letter to his Nigerian counterpart and made polio a part of his visits to Pakistan, India, and Afghanistan in April 2004. HHS deputy secretary Claude Allen raised the polio issue on a previously scheduled trip to Nigeria, using information from the GPEI to suggest approaches to non-Nigerian Islamic leaders who might be helpful. Secretary Powell met with his Nigerian counterpart in New York and raised the issue of polio, as did senior officials of State when they visited the Middle East and Pakistan. The State Department complemented GPEI efforts with the African Union (AU). In July 2004 Assistant Secretary of State for African Affairs Constance Newman delivered to former president of Mali, Alpha Oumar Konaré, the head of the AU, a letter from Secretary Powell urging action on polio at the 3–6 August Addis Ababa (Ethiopia) summit.

Instructions were sent to the U.S. Embassy in Nigeria, which established a task force to ensure coordination. The chargé d'affaires met with the governor of Kano to urge an end to the boycott. U.S. embassies in the region were asked to discuss polio with their counterparts and to urge host governments to do what they could to turn around the situation in Northern Nigeria.

The end game?

It is hard to know precisely why the governor of Kano finally ended the boycott. Many of those interviewed for this paper believe that there may have been an internal Nigerian deal. Others say "no," arguing that any deal would have become public knowledge and thus would have threatened the governor's reputation. What is known is that the governor of Kano, by April of 2004 the sole government official opposing immunization, was under increasing pressure. The diplomatic efforts described above ensured that the governor understood the cost to his and Kano State's reputation if the boycott continued. The WHO was able to provide evidence that 80 percent of global cases of polio paralysis in the world originated in Kano. Or it may simply be that the official boycott had outlived its political usefulness for the Kano government.

Some people feel that another technical action, albeit one with diplomatic ramifications, might have contributed to the resolution. By 2004, countries around the world were asking the WHO and the GPEI, in their technical advisory role, for advice on what steps should be taken "to prevent or limit the international spread of wild poliovirus."[26] While the WHO had been asked by countries for advice, Heymann said that an explicit goal was to make sure that Saudi Arabia understood the potential spread of polio and the role of vaccine in stopping outbreaks, particularly during the January 2005 Hajj (the annual pilgrimage to Mecca, in Saudi Arabia). The WHO sent a *note verbale* to all WHO members outlining the recommendations that were included in the *Weekly Epidemiological Record* of 6 August 2004.[27] The WHO Representative in Nigeria, among others, made certain that the governor of Kano was aware that travelers from Kano might have to be vaccinated at the airport to travel elsewhere, including to the Hajj. The possibility of Saudi Arabia's instituting WHO recommendations on polio vaccinations undercut the contention that polio immunization was a Western plot to sterilize Muslims.

At the same time, the CDC was looking into whether similar restrictions on travels to the United States were advisable. U.S. Ambassador Campbell told the CDC that he was prepared to support such restrictions, if they were scientifically based and necessary for the protection of the U.S. public. He made sure that officials in Nigeria knew of the possibility that the United States would follow the WHO recommendations to require vaccination before travel.

On 30 June 2004, in the same media release in which it announced the consultative process with experts to "evaluate additional measures that might be required to prevent the further international spread of wild poliovirus from Northern Nigeria," the WHO announced that it had been informed by the governor of Kano of "the intention to resume polio immunizations campaigns there in early July."[28]

Other discussions helped achieve a face-saving way to withdraw. Heymann's conversations with the governor of Kano in summer 2004 suggested the use of a panel of pediatricians to recommend restarting vaccination. In addition, UNICEF's ability to quietly divert shipments of polio vaccine produced in Indonesia, a Muslim country, for use in Nigeria allowed the face-saving claim that a safer vaccine was to be used for vaccination (Indonesian-manufactured vaccine had been used for years in Nigeria, even before the boycott began). The idea of supplying vaccine from a Muslim country chosen by the health officials in the North had first surfaced during Gambari's visit.

The boycott began with parents who were disgruntled with the lack of health services. The governor of Kano's decision to allow the resumption of immunization campaigns removed only one barrier to polio eradication in Nigeria. Work remains to be done in convincing communities to allow their children to be immunized.

Global health diplomacy lessons

One person who worked with the GPEI to resolve the boycott said, "The greatest lesson is for the public health community that we are dealing with a political thing."[29] This case study holds a number of lessons for global health and insights into the practice of health diplomacy.

Diplomacy as a useful global health tool   Diplomacy can be a useful tool in pursuing global health efforts. This is particularly true when the challenges to global health efforts are political, rather than scientific, as they were in this case. Resolving problems such as the vaccine boycott, or the sharing of influenza virus samples, will increasingly rely on diplomatic action. However, diplomacy is not a panacea and could not greatly alter the regional health-status disparities in Nigeria that contributed to the boycott.

Global, complex undertakings   Both health and health diplomacy are global and are characterized by great complexity and a highly diverse constellation of actors. This crisis began at the subnational level in Nigeria; affected a global eradication effort supported by other nations, international organizations, and nongovernmental organizations (NGOs); and was only resolved by using diplomacy across these levels to restart vaccinations (Exhibit 2). This global environment makes operationalizing health diplomacy a complex endeavor, because diplomacy may involve numerous and nontraditional actors (such as the OIC) in responding to global health problems.

Need to generate action   The need for actionable suggestions is critical to engaging governments; simply saying that the vaccine boycott was a problem did not generate action To enact such suggestions, public health professionals need to learn how to approach diplomats and ministries of foreign affairs. Similarly, diplomats require greater training on the role that health can play in foreign policy. Only then will the problems of coordination on global health issues, both within countries and between nations and international institutions, begin to be solved.

Science and politics   Although scientific evidence on the spread of polio was useful in pressuring Kano State to rescind the boycott, the flexibility to address political perceptions of the situation was also critical. Suggesting the use of a panel of pediatricians to give the governor of Kano political cover to retreat from the boycott and diverting vaccine shipments from Indonesia to Nigeria to address Nigerian Muslims' perceptions of the vaccine were unusual but effective actions in restarting vaccination. Notifying the governor of Kano that Saudi Arabia would institute vaccination requirements for the Hajj and enlisting Islamic scholars and fatwas are further examples of well-targeted diplomatic pressure in service of global health.

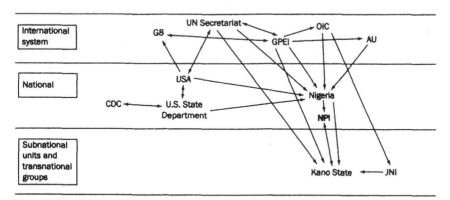

Exhibit 2 Interactions Between Global Actors Working To Resume Polio Eradication In Kano State, Nigeria.
Source: Authors' analysis.
Notes: UN is United Nations. G8 is Group of Eight. OIC is Organization of the Islamic Conference. GPEI is Global Polio Eradication Initiative. AU is African Union. CDC is U.S. Centers for Disease Control and Prevention. NPI is National Program on Immunization. JNI is Jama'atul Nasril Islam (Nigeria's umbrella Muslim organization).

Despite the obvious good done by diplomatic efforts, it is important to realize that it was a combination of local and international, technical and diplomatic efforts that eventually led to a resolution of the formal Kano boycott. The end was not quick, and it is hard to ascribe success to any single action. Flexibility; coordination among multiple actors; and a willingness to mix politics, public health, and diplomacy were all a part of the effort. All must be part of the toolbox to address future global health challenges.

Notes

The authors gratefully acknowledge the funding provided by the Bill and Melinda Gates Foundation. They thank Scott Barrett and Joshua Michaud of the Global Health and Foreign Policy Initiative, Duza Baba for his help with Exhibit 2, and Anand Balachandran for help with the timeline (in the online appendix, see Note 7 below).

1 L. Roberts, "Infectious Disease: Vaccine-Related Polio Outbreak in Nigeria Raises Concerns," *Science* 317, no. 5846 (2007): 1842.

2 See, for example, M. Yahya, "Polio Vaccines—'No Thank You!' Barriers to Polio Eradication in Northern Nigeria," *African Affairs* 1067, no. 423 (2007): 185–204; A. S. Jegede, "What Led to the Nigerian Boycott of the Polio Vaccination Campaign?" *PLoS Medicine* 4, no. 3 (2007): e73; and E. Renne, "Perspectives on Polio and Immunization in Northern Nigeria," *Social Science and Medicine* 63, no. 7 (2006): 1857–1869.

3 I. Kickbusch et al., "Global Health Diplomacy: Training across Disciplines," *Bulletin of the World Health Organization* 85, no. 12 (2007): 971–973; V. Adams, T. E. Novotny, and H. Leslie, "Global Health Diplomacy," *Medical Anthropology* 27, no. 4 (2008): 315–323; and M. Chan, J. G. Store, and B. Kouchner, "Foreign Policy and Global Public Health: Working Together towards Common Goals," *Bulletin of the World Health Organisation* 86, no. 7 (2008): 498.

4 Jegede, "What Led to the Nigerian Boycott?"

5 "Nigeria Polio Vaccine: Controversy Over or Renewed?" *Weekly Trust*, 6 March 2004.

6 John Campbell, ambassador to Nigeria, interview, 26 November 2007.

7 A timeline of these events is available in an appendix, online at http://content. healthaffairs.org/cgi/content/full/28/3/1091/DC1.

8 See, for example, the National Vaccine Information Center (NVIC) home page, http://www.nvic.org, and the Global Vaccine Awareness League (GVAL) home page, http://www.gval.com.

9 UNICEF, "Engaging Communities," http://www.unicef.org/immunization/index_ communities.html (accessed 10 April 2009).

10 For example, when rumors about the polio vaccine circulated among Coptic Christians in Alexandria, Egypt, in 2002, vaccinations were done in the churches, to counter the rumors. See B. Hiel, "Egypt Remains Committed as It Closes In on Becoming Polio-Free," *Pittsburgh Tribune-Review*, 3 April 2005.

11 United Nations Children's Fund, Eastern and Southern Africa Regional Office, *Combatting Antivaccination Rumours: Lessons Learned from Case Studies in East Africa*, http://www.path.org/vaccineresources/files/Combatting_Antivac_Rumors_ UNICEF.pdf (accessed 16 January 2009).

12 Gianni Murzi, UNICEF, personal communication, 8 January 2008.

13 Ibrahim Gambari, UN special envoy, interview, 6 December 2007.

14 Press Release, Ibrahim Gambari, 17 March 2004 (received from the GPEI).

15 M. Plaut; "Obituary: The Sultan of Sokoto," 29 October 2006, http://news.bbc. co.uk/2/hi/africa/6096858.stm (accessed 10 April 2009).

16 Organization of the Islamic Conference, "About OIC," http//www.oic-oci.org/page_detail.asp?p_id=52 (accessed 10 April 2009).
17 Since then, two countries, Egypt and Niger, have gone at least a year without a case of indigenous polio.
18 Anand Balachandran, GPEI, interviews, 10 and 12 December 2007, and subsequent e-mail correspondence.
19 David Heymann, World Health Organization, interview, 10 December 2007.
20 UNICEF, "Joint Press Release: Global Polio Eradication Initiative Welcomes OIC Decision to Step Up Effort to Eradicate Polio," http://unicef.org/media_15021.html (accessed 10 April 2009).
21 Fatwas on polio vaccination were issued in late 2003 and early 2004 by Dr. Mohamed Sayed Tantawi, Grand Imam of El Azhar Al Sharif; the Islamic Fiqh Academy (circulated by the OIC); Muhammed Abdul Alim, Grand Mufti of Egypt; and, Abdul Aziz Ibn Abdullah Ibn Baaz, Grand Mufti of Saudi Arabia and president, Committee of Muslim Scholars.
22 Balachandran, personal communication, 21 February 2008.
23 Obasanjo was well known in Washington and appreciated for his commitment to health issues. He stood at President Bush's side when the latter announced the first governmental contribution to the as yet nonexistent Global Fund to Fight AIDS, Tuberculosis, and Malaria, in May 2001.
24 Ellyn Ogden, USAID, interview, 14 November 2007.
25 William Steiger, HHS Office of Global Health Affairs, interview, 17 January 2008.
26 World Health Organization, *Weekly Epidemiological Record*, 32, no. 79 (6 August 2004), pp. 289–290, http://www.who.int/wer/2004/en/wer7932.pdf (accessed 10 April 2009).
27 A *note verbale* is a memorandum, written in the third person and unsigned, used to convey information to a representative of a government.
28 WHO, "Kano, Nigeria, Informs WHO of the Intention to Resume Polio Immunization Campaigns," Press Release, 30 June 2004, http://www.who.int/mediacentre/news/notes/2004/np16/en (accessed 10 April 2009).
29 Anonymous, interview, 12 December 2007.

Part 13

INSTITUTIONS AND PROTECTIONS

79

GLOBAL PUBLIC HEALTH SURVEILLANCE UNDER NEW INTERNATIONAL HEALTH REGULATIONS

Michael G. Baker and David P. Fidler

Source: *Emerging Infectious Diseases*, 12:7 (2006), 1058–65.

The new International Health Regulations adopted by the World Health Assembly in May 2005 (IHR 2005) represents a major development in the use of international law for public health purposes. One of the most important aspects of IHR 2005 is the establishment of a global surveillance system for public health emergencies of international concern. This article assesses the surveillance system in IHR 2005 by applying well-established frameworks for evaluating public health surveillance. The assessment shows that IHR 2005 constitutes a major advance in global surveillance from what has prevailed in the past. Effectively implementing the IHR 2005 surveillance objectives requires surmounting technical, resource, governance, legal, and political obstacles. Although IHR 2005 contains some provisions that directly address these obstacles, active support by the World Health Organization and its member states is required to strengthen national and global surveillance capabilities.

On May 23, 2005, the World Health Assembly adopted the new International Health Regulations (IHR 2005) (*1*) as an international treaty. This step concluded the decade-long effort led by the World Health Organization (WHO) to revise the old regulations (IHR 1969) to make them more effective against global disease threats. Originally adopted in 1951 (*2*) and last substantially changed in 1969 (*3*), IHR 1969 had lost its effectiveness and relevance by the mid-1990s, if not earlier (*4*).

The resurgence of infectious diseases noted in the first half of the 1990s showed IHR 1969's limitations. For example, after smallpox was eradicated in the late 1970s, IHR 1969 only applied to the traditionally "quarantinable" diseases of cholera, plague, and yellow fever. In addition, IHR 1969 restricted surveillance to information provided only by governments, lacked mechanisms for swiftly assessing and investigating public health risks, contained no strategies for developing surveillance capacities and infrastructure, and failed to generate compliance by WHO member states. WHO began revising IHR 1969 in 1995 (5), and IHR 2005's adoption completed the modernization of this important body of international law on public health.

IHR 2005 departs radically from IHR 1969 and represents a historic development in international law on public health (6). IHR 2005 expands the scope of the regulations' application, strengthens WHO's authority in surveillance and response, contains more demanding surveillance and response obligations, and applies human rights principles to public health interventions. The most dramatic of these changes involves a new surveillance system that far surpasses what the IHR 1969 contained. After reviewing key surveillance concepts and frameworks, this article describes IHR 2005's surveillance regime and assesses its likely performance. It concludes by discussing obstacles that could prevent IHR 2005 from becoming an effective global public health surveillance system and addressing how these obstacles might be overcome.

Key surveillance concepts and evaluation framework

Public health surveillance has been defined as "the ongoing systematic collection, analysis, and interpretation of outcome-specific data for use in the planning, implementation, and evaluation of public health practice" (7). A surveillance system requires structures and processes to support these ongoing functions (7).

The Centers for Disease Control and Prevention (CDC) developed guidelines that identify the essential elements and attributes for an effective public health surveillance system (8). According to these guidelines, evaluating surveillance systems involves 2 main steps: 1) describing the purpose, operation, and elements of the system and 2) assessing its performance according to key attributes. This article uses this 2-step approach to evaluate the global public health surveillance system prescribed by IHR 2005.

Surveillance system specified in IHR 2005

In the CDC framework, describing a surveillance system includes 4 main elements: 1) health-related events under surveillance and their public health importance, 2) purpose and objectives of the system, 3) components and processes of the system, and 4) resources needed to operate it (8).

Health-related events under surveillance

IHR 2005 identifies health-related events that each country that agrees to be bound by the regulations (a "state party") must report to WHO. In terms of health-related events that occur in its territory, a state party must notify WHO of "all events which may constitute a public health emergency of international concern" (article 6.1). These events include any unexpected or unusual public health event regardless of its origin or source (article 7). IHR 2005 also requires state parties, as far as is practicable, to inform WHO of public health risks identified outside their territories that may cause international disease spread, as manifested by exported or imported human cases, vectors that may carry infection or contamination, or contaminated goods (article 9.2).

IHR 2005 provides guidance to assist state parties' compliance with these obligations in 4 ways. First, IHR 2005 defines a "public health emergency of international concern" (PHEIC) as "an extraordinary event which is determined [by the WHO Director-General] . . . (i) to constitute a public health risk to other States through the international spread of disease and (ii) to potentially require a coordinated international response" (article 1.1). Unlike IHR 1969's limited scope of application to just 3 communicable diseases (*3*), IHR 2005 defines disease as an illness or medical condition that does or could threaten human health regardless of its source or origin (article 1.1). This scope therefore encompasses communicable and noncommunicable disease events, whether naturally occurring, accidentally caused, or intentionally created.

Second, IHR 2005 contains a "decision instrument" (annex 2) that helps state parties identify whether a health-related event may constitute a PHEIC and therefore requires formal notification to WHO (Figure 1). The decision instrument focuses on risk assessment criteria of public health importance, including the seriousness of the public health impact and the likelihood of international spread.

Third, IHR 2005 includes a list of diseases for which a single case may constitute a PHEIC and must be reported to WHO immediately. This list consists of smallpox, poliomyelitis, human influenza caused by new subtypes, and severe acute respiratory syndrome (SARS). A second list of diseases exists (Figure 1) for which a single case requires the decision instrument to be used to assess the event, but notification is determined by the assessment and is not automatic. Finally, IHR 2005 also encourages state parties to consult with WHO over events that do not meet the criteria for formal notification but may still be of public health relevance (article 8).

IHR 2005's expansion of the range of public health events under surveillance and the use of risk assessment criteria in deciding what is reportable is possibly the single most important surveillance advance in IHR 2005. This change greatly enhances effective surveillance of emerging infectious diseases, which are "infections that have newly appeared in a population or have existed but are rapidly increasing in incidence or geographic range" (*9*). IHR 2005's surveillance strategy, especially the decision instrument, has been specifically designed to

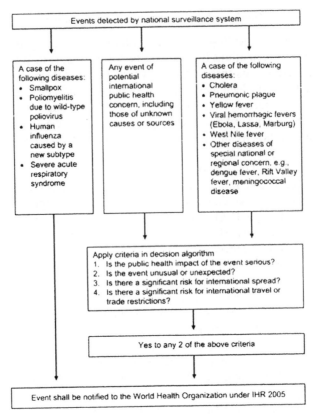

Figure 1 International Health Regulations (IHR) 2005 decision instrument (simplified from annex 2 of IHR).

make IHR 2005 directly applicable to emerging infectious disease events, which are usually unexpected and often threaten to spread internationally.

In addition to events that may constitute a PHEIC, IHR 2005 also requires state parties to report the health measures (e.g., border screening, quarantine) that they implement in response to such events (article 6). State parties are also specifically required to inform WHO within 48 hours of implementing additional health measures that interfere with international trade and travel, unless the WHO Director-General has recommended such measures (article 43).

Purpose and objectives of surveillance under IHR 2005

IHR 2005's purpose is to prevent, protect against, control, and facilitate public health responses to the international spread of disease (article 2), and IHR 2005 makes surveillance central to guiding effective public health action against cross-border disease threats. The regulations define surveillance as "the systematic ongoing collection, collation and analysis of data for public health purposes and the timely dissemination of public health information for assessment and public health response as necessary" (article 1.1). Surveillance is central to IHR 2005's public health objectives, which explains why IHR 2005 requires all state parties to develop, strengthen, and maintain core surveillance capacities (article 5.1). This obligation goes beyond anything concerning surveillance in IHR 1969, which did not address surveillance infrastructure and capabilities beyond a general requirement for a state party to notify WHO of any outbreak of a disease subject to the regulations.

Components and processes of IHR 2005 surveillance

IHR 2005 describes key aspects of the surveillance process from the local to the global level. As part of IHR 2005's core surveillance and response capacity requirements, each state party has to develop and maintain capabilities to detect, assess, and report disease events at the local, intermediate, and national levels (article 5.1, annex 1). Officials at the national level must be able to report through the national IHR focal point to WHO when required under IHR 2005 (articles 4.2 and 6). The regulations also mandate that WHO establish IHR contact points that are always accessible to state parties (article 4.3). Connecting these levels produces the surveillance architecture illustrated in Figure 2.

Requiring that a national IHR focal point be established is another surveillance initiative in IHR 2005. The focal point is designed to facilitate rapid

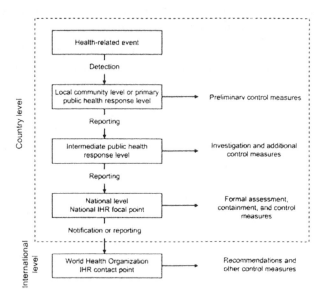

Figure 2 Public health surveillance structures and processes specified in International Health Regulations (IHR) 2005.

sharing of surveillance information because it is responsible for communicating with the WHO IHR contact points and disseminating information within the state party (article 4.2). By linking national IHR focal points through WHO, IHR 2005 establishes a global network that improves the real-time flow of surveillance information from the local to the global level and also between state parties (article 4.4).

Resources needed to operate IHR 2005's surveillance system

Building and maintaining the surveillance system envisioned in IHR 2005 will require substantial financial and technical resources. State parties will be primarily responsible for providing resources needed to develop their core surveillance capacities. Each state party has to assess its ability to meet the core surveillance requirements by June 2009. In addition, each state party has to develop and implement a plan for ensuring compliance with core surveillance obligations (articles 5.1 and 5.2, annex 1).

WHO is obliged to assist state parties in meeting their surveillance system obligations (article 5.3), but this provision does not allocate any WHO funds for this purpose. State parties are required to collaborate with each other in providing technical cooperation and logistical support for surveillance capabilities and in mobilizing financial resources to facilitate implementation of IHR 2005 (article 44.1).

Evaluating the IHR 2005 surveillance system's attributes and potential performance

Key attributes of effective surveillance systems identified by CDC are usefulness, sensitivity, timeliness, stability, simplicity, flexibility, acceptability, data quality, positive predictive value, and representativeness. Of these attributes, usefulness, sensitivity, timeliness, and stability will be most critical to the success of the IHR 2005 surveillance system. Simplicity, acceptability, and flexibility will affect the establishment and sustainability of the surveillance system. Data quality, positive predictive value, and representativeness are central to accurately characterizing health-related events under surveillance. Table 1 summarizes these attributes, provides commentary on their relevance to effective surveillance under IHR 2005, and assesses the likely performance of the IHR 2005 surveillance system for each attribute. The following paragraphs concentrate on assessing IHR 2005 with respect to the key attributes of usefulness, sensitivity, timeliness, and stability.

Usefulness of the surveillance system

The central premise of IHR 2005 is that rapidly detecting PHEIC will support improved disease prevention and control both within and between state parties.

Table 1 International Health Regulations (IHR 2005) assessed according to attributes of public health surveillance systems (adapted from [8]).

Attribute	Attribute details	Relevance to IHR 2005
Usefulness	Contribution to prevention and control of adverse health-related events	Design and scope imply improved usefulness compared with IHR 1969, but attribute must be evaluated after IHR 2005 has operated for a period
Sensitivity	Proportion of true events detected by system and ability to detect outbreaks	Specifies notification of all potential public health emergencies of international concern (**PHEIC**) and provides multiple pathways to increase sensitivity
Timeliness	Speed between steps particularly from event onset to response	Specifies assessment within 48 h and reporting within 24 h by state parties and prescribes immediate reporting of events at local and intermediate levels within state parties
Stability	Reliability and availability of surveillance system	All state parties must notify all potential **PHEIC** from June 2007 and establish capacity to detect, assess, and report events by 2012, with potential extensions to 2016
Simplicity	Simplicity of structure and ease of operation	Architecture of surveillance system is streamlined and transparent, especially at international level
Flexibility	Ability to adapt to changing information needs and operating conditions	Use of risk assessment criteria means that surveillance applies to new as well as established disease threats
Acceptability	Willingness of persons and organizations to participate	Establishment of surveillance in international law represents commitment by state parties to participate
Data quality	Completeness and validity of recorded data	Specifies information to be reported and includes provisions for validation and assessment of all reports to separate rumors from real events
Positive predictive value	Proportion of reported events that are true events	Oriented toward high sensitivity with correspondingly low specificity and positive predictive value, so **WHO** will not declare most notified events to be **PHEIC**
Representativeness	Ability to describe events over time and their distribution by place and person	Likely to be increased after validation and assessment, as for data quality

Ample evidence shows that delayed recognition and response to emerging diseases may result in adverse consequences in terms of illness and death, spread to other countries, and disruption of trade and travel (10). The usefulness of surveillance under IHR 2005 represents the sum of all the critical system attributes and can only be assessed after the system is in operation, so this attribute is not discussed here. However, for the future sustainability and development of IHR 2005, we must evaluate its overall usefulness and document its contribution to prevention and control of adverse health events. IHR includes mechanisms to review and, if necessary, amend its provisions and in particular requires periodic evaluation of the functioning of the decision instrument (article 54).

Sensitivity of the surveillance system

The IHR 2005 surveillance provisions imply 100% sensitivity as a standard, namely the reporting of all events that meet notification requirements. The use of risk assessment criteria (Figure 1) also allows for higher sensitivity for PHEIC than would be possible with a list of predetermined disease threats (as in IHR 1969). To test the potential sensitivity of the decision instrument proposed in drafts of the revised IHR in 2004, investigators in the United Kingdom applied the then-proposed decision instrument to all events (N = 30) that were important enough to have been published in the national surveillance bulletin for England and Wales during 2003 (11). According to this method, 12 of the 30 events would have been reportable under the decision instrument. These events included all those that were considered potential PHEIC. Investigators concluded that the decision instrument was highly sensitive for selecting outbreaks and incidents that require reporting under the proposed IHR revision.

The sensitivity of the IHR 2005 surveillance system will probably be affected by 2 factors. First, in all likelihood, inadequate capacities at the local and intermediate levels within state parties will limit the system's sensitivity more than capacities at the national level. Second, state parties may not always be willing to comply with their reporting obligations in the face of possible adverse political and economic consequences that may result from alerting the world to a disease event in their territories. Fear of such adverse consequences undermined reporting obligations in IHR 1969.

IHR 2005 incorporates strategies to address these potential limitations. First, as noted above, IHR 2005 requires state parties to build and maintain core local, intermediate, and national surveillance capabilities (article 5.1, annex 1). Fulfillment of this obligation will improve surveillance capacity vertically, from local to national levels, which should support higher sensitivity.

Second, IHR 2005 permits WHO to improve sensitivity by collecting and using information from multiple sources. IHR 1969 only allowed WHO to use information provided by state parties (3), and failure of state parties to abide by their reporting obligations adversely affected WHO surveillance activities (5). Under IHR 2005, WHO can collect, analyze, and use information gathered from governments, other intergovernmental organizations, and nongovernmental organizations and actors (article 9.1). By permitting WHO to cast its surveillance network beyond information it receives from governments, IHR 2005 creates opportunities for WHO to improve the sensitivity of the surveillance system and avoid being blocked by governmental failure to comply with reporting requirements.

Timeliness of the surveillance system

Public health practitioners understand how timely notification of public health risks is necessary for effective intervention strategies (12,13), lessons reiterated in the SARS pandemic (14). Timely surveillance is also stressed in connection with strategies to deal with pandemic influenza (15,16). Timeliness may be the most important attribute that IHR 2005 will have to demonstrate to be effective.

IHR 2005 contains several provisions that relate to timeliness. National-level assessments with the decision instrument must be completed within 48 hours (annex 1, part A, 6[a]). State parties must then notify WHO within 24 hours of assessing any event that may constitute a PHEIC or that is unexpected or unusual (articles 6.1 and 7). The same 24-hour requirement applies to reporting public health risk outside a state party's territory that may constitute a PHEIC (article 9). State parties must also respond within 24 hours to all requests that WHO makes for verification of health-related events in their territories (article 10.2).

Timeliness of reporting is likely to be affected more by actions taken at local and intermediate levels than national-level provision of information to WHO. In this regard, IHR 2005 includes the core surveillance capacity that local and intermediate public health entities must be able to carry out their reporting responsibilities immediately (annex 1).

WHO's ability to draw on a wide array of sources of information, including the Internet and nongovernmental organizations and actors, may enhance the timeliness of the IHR 2005 surveillance system (13,17). In countries that have less well-developed local, intermediate, and national surveillance systems, nongovernmental sources of information can often provide information faster than governments. Accessing this type of information early and often helps WHO contact countries sooner, which increases the chances of more effective interventions.

Stability of the surveillance system

The obligations each state party has to build and maintain core capacities in surveillance at the local, intermediary, and national levels, combined with the responsibilities for surveillance WHO has globally, should construct a global surveillance system that will be stable and reliable over time. Recognizing that core capacities at the national level and below will not develop overnight, IHR 2005 gives state parties until June 2012 to develop these capacities (article 5.1). State parties can obtain a 2-year extension on this deadline by submitting a justified need and an implementation plan and can request an additional 2-year extension, which the WHO Director-General has the discretion to approve or deny (article 5.2).

The 5-year grace period, and the possibility of 2-year extensions, was a necessary compromise and reflects the difficulties many developing states will have in improving their surveillance systems. The stability and reliability of the IHR 2005 surveillance system are designed to increase steadily as the grace period and any extensions come to an end.

Potential obstacles to achieving IHR 2005 surveillance system objectives

Continued lamentations about the weaknesses of public health surveillance nationally and globally (*18*) illustrate that achieving useful, sensitive, timely, and stable surveillance through IHR 2005 will be a challenge for states and the international community. Several potential obstacles, including technical, resource, governance, legal, and political concerns, will complicate and frustrate efforts to improve national and global surveillance capabilities. Table 2 summarizes these potential barriers and possible responses.

Technical issues

Emerging infectious diseases often create technical challenges for surveillance, even for the most technologically advanced and well-resourced countries. The sensitivity of surveillance systems for new pathogens has historically been limited, particularly if such pathogens presented themselves in unusual or unexpected ways. Recent modeling has shown that the ability to control the spread of a new pathogen is influenced by the proportion of transmission that occurs before the onset of overt symptoms or through asymptomatic infection (*19*). This property explains why diseases such as influenza and HIV may be more difficult to control than smallpox or SARS.

Consequently, surveillance needs to be sufficiently sensitive to detect infectious agents that have not yet resulted in large numbers of diagnosed cases. One approach to this challenge is syndromic surveillance (*20*), but such surveillance has not been effective in detecting emerging infectious diseases early (*21*). In fact, WHO abandoned syndromic surveillance as a strategy for the revised IHR after pilot studies demonstrated that it was not effective (*22*). Improved diagnostic technologies may also help public health authorities identify new pathogenic threats (*23*). Strategies for enhancing reporting processes have been well described (*24*).

Table 2 Barriers to International Health Regulations (IHR) 2005 surveillance effectiveness, and potential responses.

Barrier	Description	Potential responses
Technical	Difficulty detecting previously unrecognized pathogens, especially those with asymptomatic transmission	Specialized surveillance approaches such as syndromic surveillance; improved diagnostic technologies; training and support for epidemiology, laboratory, and other staff
Resource	Limited resources for public health surveillance, particularly in developing countries	Systematic global strategy for assessment and development of surveillance and response capacities, particularly in developing countries
Governance	Lack of awareness about limitations of existing surveillance and lack of governance capabilities to develop and manage sophisticated systems	Training and support for public health professionals and managers; periodic surveillance system evaluations; performance monitoring focusing on attributes such as sensitivity and timeliness
Legal	Potential for countries to make reservations to some obligations in IHR 2005 and concerns it may not be consistent with domestic law in some countries	Formulation of reservations to ensure minimal effects on public health surveillance; development of "model" public health legislation that can be adapted for use in many countries
Political	Concern about potential negative effects on trade and tourism from reporting disease events	Strategies to limit excessive responses; fostering a collaborative, measured response to public health emergencies of international concern; awareness of self-defeating effects of withholding information

Resource issues

The demands of IHR 2005 surveillance obligations will confront many countries, particularly developing countries, with resource challenges. IHR 2005 does not include financing mechanisms, which leaves each state party to bear the financial costs of improving its own local, intermediate, and national level surveillance capabilities. The obligation on state parties and WHO to collaborate in mobilizing financial resources (article 44) is a weak obligation at best. The lack of economic resources will, if not more vigorously addressed as recommended by the UN Secretary-General (*25*), retard progress on all aspects of the upgraded surveillance system. WHO, in conjunction with the United Nations and the World Bank, could consider developing a global strategy to support the development and maintenance of core surveillance capacities.

Governance issues

Governance obstacles include managerial and administrative weaknesses in countries from the local to the national level. Few countries have conducted a systematic review of their surveillance systems, and thus most lack detailed knowledge of gaps and limitations in their surveillance infrastructures and how to address these problems (*26*). Only a few states have assessed their ability to detect and respond to emerging disease threats, such as those posed by bioterrorism agents (*27*). The IHR 2005 requirement that each state party assess the condition of its public health surveillance within 2 years of the regulations' entry into force should help countries improve their national governance for surveillance purposes. Again, many states will need external assistance with such work.

Legal issues

State parties may face legal complications in implementing IHR 2005 within their national legal and constitutional systems. For example, the United States has indicated that requirements of US federalism may affect its compliance with IHR 2005 (*28*). The US position suggests that other countries may also wish to formulate reservations to IHR 2005 to account for the demands of their national constitutional structures and systems of law (*29*). Whether such reservations will undermine the IHR 2005 surveillance system cannot be assessed, but this concern has to be monitored closely as countries determine whether reservations are required under their national constitutional systems. IHR 2005 also specifies that domestic legislation and administrative arrangements be adjusted fully with IHR 2005 by June 2007, or by June 2008 after a suitable declaration to the WHO Director-General (article 59.3). Helping state parties update their public health law may be technical assistance that industrialized countries can provide.

466

Political issues

Questions remain about the level of political commitment countries will demonstrate in implementing IHR 2005. IHR 1969 suffered because state parties frequently failed to report notifiable diseases and routinely applied excessive trade and travel restrictions (*4*). The relevance of such trade and travel concerns was most recently illustrated during the SARS pandemic through China's initial fears that disclosing the pandemic would harm its economy and foreign trade (*30,31*). WHO's access to nongovernmental sources of surveillance information reduces the incentives that state parties once had to hide disease events, as was demonstrated during the SARS pandemic (*32*). In addition, IHR 2005 includes provisions that require WHO to recommend, and state parties to use, control measures that are no more restrictive than necessary to achieve the desired level of health protection (articles 17, 43). Uncertainty lingers, however, as to whether these obligations will fare better in terms of state party compliance than similar ones in IHR 1969.

Conclusion

Establishing effective global public health surveillance is at the heart of IHR 2005. Evaluating the surveillance system specified by IHR 2005 is necessary to understand the potential for this new set of international legal rules to contribute to global health governance. IHR 2005 prescribes essential elements of a surveillance system and seeks to achieve the critical attributes of usefulness, sensitivity, timeliness, and stability. These features resonate with other aspects of IHR 2005 that make it a seminal development for global health governance. In May 2006, the World Health Assembly adopted a resolution urging WHO member states to comply immediately, on a voluntary basis, with IHR 2005 in light of the threat posed by avian influenza (*33*).

The task of turning the IHR 2005 vision of an effective global public health surveillance system into reality is daunting. Of the obstacles complicating this challenge, lack of financial resources to upgrade surveillance systems, especially in developing countries, will be the most difficult to overcome. In IHR 2005, public health has been given a governance regime unlike anything in the history of international law on public health. Turning the blueprint detailed in IHR 2005 into functional architecture that benefits all is one of the great public health challenges of the first decades of the 21st century.

References

1. World Health Assembly. Revision of the International Health Regulations, WHA58.3. 2005 [cited 2006 May 2]. Available from http://www.who.int/gb/ebwha/pdf_files/WHA58-REC1/english/Resolutions.pdf
2. United Nations. International Sanitary Regulations, 175 UN Treaty Series 214. 1951.

3. World Health Organization. International Health Regulations (1969). 3rd ed. Geneva: The Organization; 1983.

4. Fidler D. International law and infectious diseases. Oxford: Clarendon Press; 1999.

5. World Health Organization. Global crises—global solutions: managing public health emergencies through the revised International Health Regulations. Geneva: The Organization; 2002.

6. Fidler D. From international sanitary conventions to global health security: the new International Health Regulations. Chinese J International Law. 2005;4:325–92.

7. Thacker S. B. Historical development. In: Teutsch S. T., Churchill R. E., editors. Principles and practice of public health surveillance. New York: Oxford University Press; 2000. p. 1–16.

8. Centers for Disease Control and Prevention. Updated guidelines for evaluating public health surveillance systems: recommendations from the guidelines working group. MMWR Morb Mortal Wkly Rep. 2001;50:1–36. Available from http://www.cdc.gov/mmwr/preview/mmwrhtml/mm5030a5.htm

9. Morse S. S. Factors in the emergence of infectious diseases. Emerg Infect Dis. 1995;1:7–15.

10. Heymann D. L., Rodier G. Global surveillance, national surveillance, and SARS. Emerg Infect Dis. 2004;10:173–5.

11. Morris J., Ward J. D., Nicoll A. Proposed new International Health Regulations 2005—validation of a decision instrument (algorithm). Euro Surveill. 2004;9:66–7. Available from http://www.eurosurveillance.org/eq/2004/04-04/pdf/eq_12_2004_66-67.pdf

12. Jajosky R. A., Groseclose S. L. Evaluation of reporting timeliness of public health surveillance systems for infectious diseases. BMC Public Health. 2004;4:29.

13. Grein T. W., Kamara K. B., Rodier G., Plant A. J., Bovier P., Ryan M. J., et al. Rumors of disease in the global village: outbreak verification. Emerg Infect Dis. 2000;6:97–102.

14. Reflections on SARS. Lancet Infect Dis. 2004;4:651.

15. Ferguson N. M., Cummings D. A., Cauchemez S., Fraser C., Riley S., Meeyai A., et al. Strategies for containing an emerging influenza pandemic in Southeast Asia. Nature. 2005;437:209–14.

16. Longini I. M. Jr, Nizam A., Xu S., Ungchusak K., Hanshaoworakul W., Cummings D. A., et al. Containing pandemic influenza at the source. Science. 2005; 309:1083–7.

17. Samaan G., Patel M., Olowokure B., Roces M. C., Oshitani H.; World Health Organization Outbreak Response Team. Rumor surveillance and avian influenza H5N1. Emerg Infect Dis. 2005;11:463–6.

18. Butler D. Disease surveillance needs a revolution. Nature. 2006;440:6–7.

19. Fraser C., Riley S., Anderson R. M., Ferguson N. M. Factors that make an infectious disease outbreak controllable. Proc Natl Acad Sci U S A. 2004;101:6146–51.

20. Mandl K. D., Overhage J. M., Wagner M. M., Lober W. B., Sebastiani P., Mostashari F. Implementing syndromic surveillance: a practical guide informed by the early experience. J Am Med Inform Assoc. 2004;11:141–50.

21. Weber S. G., Pitrak D. Accuracy of a local surveillance system for early detection of emerging infectious disease. JAMA. 2003;290:596–8.

22. Revision of the International Health Regulations. Progress report. Wkly Epidemiol Rec. 2001;76:61–3.

23. Cockerill F. R., Smith T. Response of the clinical microbiology laboratory to emerging (new) and reemerging infectious diseases. J Clin Microbiol. 2004;42:2359–65.

24. Silk B. J., Berkelman R. A review of strategies for enhancing the completeness of notifiable disease reporting. J Public Health Manag Pract. 2005;11:191–200.

25. Secretary-General of the United Nations. In larger freedom: towards development, security and human rights for all: report of the secretary-general, A/59/2005. New York: United Nations; 2005.

26. McNabb S. J., Chungong S., Ryan M., Wuhib T., Nsubuga P., Alemu W., et al. Conceptual framework of public health surveillance and action and its application in health sector reform. BMC Public Health. 2002;2:2.

27. Bravata D. M., McDonald K. M., Smith W. M., Rydzak C., Szeto H., Buckeridge D. L., et al. Systematic review: surveillance systems for early detection of bioterrorism-related diseases. Ann Intern Med. 2004;140:910–22.

28. Statement for the record by the Government of the United States of America concerning the World Health Organization's revised International Health Regulations. 2005 May 23 [cited 2006 May 2]. Available from http://usinfo.state.gov/usinfo/Archive/2005/May/23-321998.html

29. Wilson K., McDougall C., Upshur R. The new International Health Regulations and the federalism dilemma. PLoS Med. 2006;3:e1.

30. Hesketh T. China in the grip of SARS. BMJ. 2003;326:1095.

31. Liu Y. China's public health-care system: facing the challenges. Bull World Health Organ. 2004;82:532–8.

32. Fidler D. SARS, governance, and the globalization of disease. Basingstoke (UK): Palgrave Macmillan; 2004.

33. World Health Assembly. Application of the International Health Regulations (2005). WHA59.3. 26 May 2006 [cited 2006 June 1]. Available from http://www.who.int/gb/ebwha/pdf_files/WHA59/WHA59_2-en.pdf

80

EXPLORING THE INTERNATIONAL ARENA OF GLOBAL PUBLIC HEALTH SURVEILLANCE

Philippe Calain

Source: *Health Policy and Planning*, 22 (2007), 2–12.

Threats posed by new, emerging or re-emerging communicable diseases are taking a global dimension, to which the World Health Organization (WHO) Secretariat has been responding with determination since 1995. Key to the global strategy for tackling epidemics across borders is the concept of global public health surveillance, which has been expanded and formalized by WHO and its technical partners through a number of recently developed instruments and initiatives. The adoption by the 58th World Health Assembly of the revised (2005) International Health Regulations provides the legal framework for mandating countries to link and coordinate their action through a universal network of surveillance networks. While novel environmental threats and outbreak-prone diseases have been increasingly identified during the past three decades, new processes of influence have appeared more recently, driven by the real or perceived threats of bio-terrorism and disruption of the global economy. Accordingly, the global surveillance agenda is being endorsed, and to some extent seized upon by new actors representing security and economic interests. This paper explores external factors influencing political commitment to comply with international health regulations and it illustrates adverse effects generated by: perceived threats to sovereignty, blurred international health agendas, lack of internationally recognized codes of conduct for outbreak investigations, and erosion of the impartiality and independence of international agencies. A companion paper (published in this issue) addresses the intrinsic difficulties that health systems of low-income countries are facing when submitted to the ever-increasing pressure to upgrade their public health surveillance capacity.

Key messages

- The core argument over global surveillance has moved from public health concerns toward foreign and security policies, and economic interests.
- The impartiality and independence of the WHO Secretariat are at stake in this process.
- These elements challenge the sovereignty of WHO Member States and their commitment to abide by the revised (2005) International Health Regulations.

Purpose and methodology

The original idea and thematic areas framing this and a companion article (Calain 2007) arose from the author's observation of a significant gap between: (1) the rhetoric and momentum entertained around the concept of global public health surveillance (introduced in the next three sections), and (2) the difficulties and resistance of national actors toward implementing public health policies prioritized under the (2005) International Health Regulations (IHR).

In an attempt to expose and understand this gap, two complementary perspectives were considered. Firstly, the international agencies (individuals, groups, organizations, nations) that have shaped and promoted the concept of global surveillance were explored to analyse influences acting beyond the strict realm of public health. This is the topic of this first article. Secondly, from the 'recipient's' side of international policies, the implementation of a global surveillance agenda is imposing new constraints and programmatic priorities upon developing countries, often relayed through development agencies. This country perspective is further analysed and illustrated in the companion article.

The methodology of both papers is based on an insider's perspective, from which the author could initiate the mapping of thematic categories that encompass different influences revolving around the concept of global surveillance. This mapping has two dimensions: historical and vertical (hierarchical). The author's past experience as a bystander of some key outbreak events pointed to the need for an historical (retrospective) component of the analysis. On the other hand, the vertical dimension of the problem became obvious from personal observations made at three levels of assignments (international, regional and national), mostly but not exclusively under World Health Organization (WHO) mandates. While an insider's access has inspired both the mapping of thematic categories and personal views on how they articulate with each other, supporting data (secondary research) have been exclusively selected from the public domain, essentially peer-reviewed articles or web-based documents.[1]

As shown in further sections, data and discourse analysis around global public health surveillance lead to the two key observations, that: (1) WHO's impartiality and independence are strained by domestic political interests of influential Member States or economical forces, and (2) security and public health agendas interfere and create ambiguity over roles and mandates. I hypothesize that these two facts underpin perceived threats to sovereignty occurring in the process of abiding by the revised IHR. Primary research directly addressing individual views of country stakeholders involved in global surveillance networks would add further weight and present another facet to the analysis of the problem presented in this paper. Both approaches would be complementary however, since they would involve different perspectives and suffer from qualitatively different limitations in the retrieval of information.

In the centre of the arena: the WHO secretariat and the revision of international health regulations

In May 2005, the 58th World Health Assembly adopted a much overdue revision of the IHR, referred to as the IHR(2005) (WHO 2005a). Compared with the 1969, 1973 and 1981 versions of the IHR, the revised regulations expand considerably the scope of internationally notifiable epidemic diseases, they accommodate criteria for novel epidemic events and they set out conditions for involvement of the international community in outbreak response. In May 1995, the 48th World Health Assembly had already adopted two resolutions calling, respectively, for a revision of the IHR and for the establishment of a comprehensive programme to tackle new, emerging and re-emerging infectious diseases (WHO 1995a). Accordingly, in October 1995, a new unit was established at WHO as the Division of Emerging Viral and Bacterial Diseases Surveillance and Control (EMC) (WHO 1995b), to be later renamed successively as the Department of Communicable Diseases Surveillance and Response (CSR) and the Department of Epidemic and Pandemic Alert and Response (EPR). In 2000, under the operational support of CSR team members, a Global Outbreak Alert and Response Network (GOARN) was created to coordinate technical resources involved worldwide in combating outbreak-prone diseases (Enserink 2004). The apparent success of GOARN and collaborating technical partners in limiting the international spread of SARS in 2003 (Heymann and Rodier 2004) has vindicated efforts led by WHO to put the control of emerging or re-emerging diseases high on the global health agenda.

Next to giving itself the necessary legal instruments (through the revised IHR) and putting itself in a position to coordinate international response to outbreaks (through the GOARN), the WHO Secretariat has crystallized around the CSR/EPR Department a considerable amount of expertise in capacity building, in preparation for deliberate epidemics and in promoting public health surveillance at all levels. Inspired by a model developed from the early ages of the United States Centers for Disease Control and Prevention (US-CDC), WHO has become the flagship of the concept of global surveillance of communicable diseases (Heymann and Rodier 1998). Since 2003, a limited pandemic of SARS first, soon followed by the fearsome expansion of epizootic avian H5N1 influenza from South-East Asia to the entire Old World, have been putting this concept to the test. The SARS and avian influenza epidemics have certainly helped in facilitating the acceptance of the new IHR, through their combined health and economic impacts. Avian influenza H5N1 is now in the limelight of international health concerns by being seen as a possible precursor of an upcoming human pandemic (WHO 2005b). Since the end of 2005, several high profile meetings in Geneva, Ottawa, Tokyo and Beijing have tried to mobilize the international community to shift health priorities and financial resources toward preparedness against the anticipated influenza pandemic (Health Canada 2005; World Bank 2005; WHO 2005c; WHO Regional Office for the Western Pacific 2005). In May 2006, the 59th World Health Assembly called upon Member States to speed up the implementation of the IHR(2005), or at least of the provisions that are deemed relevant to the hazards posed by avian influenza and pandemic influenza (WHO 2006).

Historical landmarks of public health surveillance

Public health surveillance applied to outbreak detection and monitoring is not a new idea. During the plague of London in 1665, parish clerks compiled weekly bills of mortality detailing about 40 different causes of death (Naphy and Spicer 2001). In a recent era, the most influential character was Alexander Langmuir who established and popularized the modern concepts of disease surveillance, following the footsteps of the 19th century statistician William Farr (Thacker and Gregg 1996).[2] A public health epidemiologist by training, Langmuir pursued an academic career in parallel with holding high-level positions in committees of the US Department of Defense overseeing biological warfare programmes during the World War II and the Cold War periods (Fee and Brown 2001). In 1949, he was recruited to the US-CDC, to become its chief epidemiologist. Building upon the US experience of malaria and poliomyelitis eradication programmes, he designed a remarkably successful national system of disease reporting and created the Epidemic Intelligence Service.

The 1990s saw the rise of the 'emerging diseases worldview', a post-colonial concept rooted in new biomedical concerns as much as in perceived threats from a 'de-territorialized' world.[3] A landmark 1992 report of the US National Academy of Science (Institute of Medicine 1992) formalized the definitions of 'emerging' and 're-emerging' diseases and explicitly discussed their global implications. The social, humanitarian, economic and political fallout of (re)-emerging diseases became obvious, first in 1991 when cholera reappeared in South America (Sánchez and Taylor 1997) and next in April 1994 when plague broke out in Surat, India (Garrett 2001). The latter circumstance showed how panic and lack of leadership can lead to unnecessary impacts on national economies and on local communities (Cash and Narasimhan 2000). In April 1995, an outbreak of highly fatal cases of haemorrhagic fever in Kikwit in the Bandundu Province of DRC (former Zaire) came to the attention of the international health community through a network of informal and rather delayed channels, before it could be confirmed as the re-emergence of an Ebola virus. It attracted an unusual amount of press coverage and scientific attention worldwide, partly justified by concerns over international spread. Lessons from the outbreak in Kikwit (Heymann *et al.* 1999) led to surveillance being put at the core of CSR activities, and to the revival of interest in the International Health Regulations.[4]

Precursor regimes of international governance on communicable diseases actually date back to the first International Sanitary Conference of 1851. Under their successive formats, they already incorporated mixed concerns over public health as well as related trade and political issues (Fidler 2003). Their impact seems, however, to have been rather limited. In contrast, the widespread interest in international health regulations seen at the present time reveals new dimensions to the global public health debate, as well as far-reaching implications of global surveillance.

Semantic ambiguities

When Alexander Langmuir (1963, 1971) redefined surveillance to fit his own public health purposes, he departed from a former meaning which restricted the term to *individuals*, i.e. typically contacts who had to be followed up for signs of disease without restricting their movements by isolation or quarantine.[5] Instead of individuals, Langmuir's (1963) modern view of surveillance applies to *diseases*, as defined by:

> 'the continued watchfulness over the distribution and trends of incidence through the systematic collection, consolidation and evaluation of morbidity and mortality reports and other relevant data. Intrinsic in the concept is the regular dissemination of the basic data and inter-pretations to all who have contributed and to all others who need to know.'

With some prophecy, Langmuir anticipated future problems and cautioned that: 'the actual performance of the research study should be recognized as a function separate from surveillance'. The blurred boundary between research and surveillance is a critical issue that was later emphasized by Stephen Thacker, a succeeding senior epidemiologist at the US-CDC.[6] Thacker noted the ambiguities carried under 'disease surveillance' and 'epidemiologic surveil-lance', and he advocated the term 'public health surveillance' to avoid confusion with epidemiologic research (Thacker and Gregg 1996). Directly inspired by Thacker's definition, the WHO definition of public health surveillance proposed under resolution WHA58.3 (WHO 2005a) is clear enough to avoid confusion with research activities:

'Surveillance means the systematic ongoing collection, collation and analysis of data for public health purposes and the timely dissemination of public health information for assessment and public health response as necessary.'

Despite its clear merits, however, the latter definition carries two sources of ambiguity, which were further reflected during the international consultation process and in the drafting of advanced versions of the revised IHR(2005). These ambiguities relate to (1) the scope of health events targeted by surveillance, and (2) the sort of 'public health action' in which the international community – through WHO experts – will find itself involved by virtue of the IHR(2005) mandate. Shared concerns by some experts and policy makers over the scope of the new IHR appear in successive versions of a decision instrument annexed to the IHR(2005) (WHO 2004a). Initially designed exclusively as a criteria-based algorithm, the final version of the annex ultimately includes as well a number of specific diseases, leaving it open to frequent updates as new pathogenic agents become identified. In the same line, it is not explicit whether the IHR(2005) have regulatory authority over programme evaluation as well as detection of epidemics, both being classical components of communicable diseases surveillance.[7] In a conceptual framework endorsed by members of the CSR team (McNabb et al. 2002), the two related components of 'public health action' (acute 'epidemic-type' response and planned 'management-type' response) are explicitly considered as complementary outputs of 'public health surveillance'. What will be missing in some cases of new epidemic threats, especially when the risk assessment is inconclusive, is a gauge of the degree of urgency from which international action is legitimate. These issues have some relevance obviously in terms of national sovereignty.

More recently, WHO has been promoting, developing and implementing in several countries the relatively new concept of Early Warning Systems (EWARS) for outbreak surveillance (WHO 2005d). Direct reference to EWARS would perhaps have lifted some ambiguities carried by too loose a definition of surveillance and would have better clarified the scope of the IHR(2005) and their derived requirements for Member States.

Of equal relevance to the scope of the IHR(2005) is the lack of conceptual clarity over the term 'global health security' (Aginam 2005; McInnes and Lee 2006). 'Global health security' features prominently in WHO policy documents (for an example see WHO 2001) to summarize the overall strategy covered by epidemic alert and response activities. Other international alliances (Global Health Security Initiative 2006) use the term with a clear orientation toward the public health response to the specific threats of international biological, chemical and radio-nuclear terrorism.

Sovereignty and ethical standards

How and if Member States of WHO will abide by the IHR(2005) (which are to become legally binding in June 2007) will obviously depend on a delicate balance between perception of threats from specific health events (public health effects *per se*, or political or economical consequences), incentives set up by interested parties and any consideration of national sovereignty.

Sovereignty has been one of the main matters of discussion during successive consultations leading to resolution WHA58.3 (WHO 2004a). The issue has an additional level of complexity for countries with federal governments, where authority over public health is generally devolved to regional jurisdictions (Wilson *et al.* 2006). The IHR(2005) do not include a sanctions regime for States that fail to comply with their provisions (WHO 2005e). Several jurists (Plotkin and Kimball 1997; Fidler 2003) have stressed the marginal role of former versions of the IHR compared with other international regimes, notably the World Trade Organization[8] and its related multilateral agreements dealing in a more direct way with factors causing the emergence of communicable diseases. It is, however, likely that the new IHR will become more influential than their precursor versions of 1969, 1973 and 1981, for several reasons: (1) the broader scope of health events under consideration, (2) a more active and better defined role for WHO in the response phase, and (3) more flexible mechanisms for WHO to circulate information critical to control public health threats (including information from nonofficial sources or about non-compliant state parties). Despite the latter opportunity embedded in the new IHR, it will remain as difficult as ever for WHO to exercise its handling of sensitive information, especially in a world where the press and the public are the driving forces behind increased transparency.

The 2003 SARS epidemic illustrates better than anything else how early disclosure of public health events can be felt as a threat to sovereignty by national authorities. The first known case of SARS was identified retrospectively in Guangdong province, China, as early as 16 November 2002 (Zhong *et al.* 2003). Although rumours of a worrying epidemic had obviously been circulating earlier (Rosling and Rosling 2003), it took until 11 February 2003 for Chinese authorities to acknowledge the gravity of the problem and to notify officially the international community and WHO of severe cases of respiratory diseases in Guangdong.[9] Later, in April, China's health minister made official statements grossly understating the extent of the epidemic, which had by then reached the capital Beijing.[10] The ultimate but delayed disclosure of accurate public health information by Chinese officials had in this case an obviously positive impact, but also a high political price (BBC

News, 5 April 2003). Had the IHR(2005) already entered into force by that time, it is not clear how WHO could have exercised more intrusive powers toward a sovereign state in this affair.

Two months later, on 23 April, WHO issued a travel advisory based on sound and definite epidemiological criteria (Rodier 2003). Accordingly, travellers were advised to consider postponing all but essential travel to Beijing and Shanxi Province in China, and to Toronto, Canada. This resulted in an outcry by Canadian politicians and local health experts who assumed that the outbreak in Toronto was well under control (Gray 2003). The issue here was not a lack of transparency, but conflicting opinions between national and international experts about appropriate public health measures. Again, it is a matter of speculation if enactment of the IHR(2005) would have eased tensions in this second example of perceived national interference through WHO authorities. Such political contretemps might appear superficially as the misguided exercise of sovereignty, but reasons can be more complex than a mere display of power, political achievements or national pride by jealous community leaders. The revised IHR(2005) directly or indirectly cover issues of national sovereignty arising during a 'health emergency of international concern', notably through articles 9–13 and 47–49 (WHO 2005a). However, they do not address problems of national sovereignty when there are legitimate concerns from Member States about the misuse of the multilateral privileges granted to WHO experts under the regulations. Issues at stake here are confidentiality of information, conflicts of interest and intellectual property.

Confidentiality of patients' personal information from the mass media has been an issue during outbreak investigations involving international teams of experts who worked in the same environment as members of the press.[11] Beside such cases of external intrusions, insiders of international outbreak response teams can themselves be involved in breaches of codes of conduct when global surveillance points its beam toward a novel health event of international importance. In fact, Langmuir's view that public health surveillance and scientific investigations must be kept distinct is no longer tenable. Nowadays, especially when unspecified microorganisms are suspected to be causing emerging diseases, field scientific research is a necessary ally to the public health response. Prompt collection and analysis of both epidemiological data and laboratory specimens by research institutions have been critical to the understanding of recent outbreaks such as SARS and H5N1 avian influenza. In similar contexts, foreign scientific experts seconded to the field are often working in a legal and ethical limbo, or in ignorance of local regulations. They should thus find it difficult to face the essential questions of confidentiality of information, conflicts of interest and intellectual property arising as they proceed in their investigations on foreign territory. Some of them see, rightly or not, the advance of their research agenda as a legitimate compensation for their voluntary participation in an international emergency. Regardless, the emergency of some situations is no excuse for misconduct, which could sometimes amount to looting of national data or scientific assets.

One paper (Heymann *et al.* 2001) indicates that: 'WHO has also revised its guidelines for the behaviour of foreign nationals during and after field operations in the host country'. A WHO website lists a series of 'Guiding principles for international outbreak alert and response', quoting among them a commitment that: 'All network responses will proceed with full respect for ethical standards, human rights, national and local laws, cultural sensitivities and traditions' (WHO 2005f). This is a timely and most useful initiative. It is unfortunate though that those guiding principles have not had a wider public audience for debate, and are not explicitly included among the binding obligations attached to the IHR(2005). Through their article 45, the IHR(2005) cover only one ethical issue relevant to surveillance, namely the treatment of personal data. A much broader range of ethical questions to be addressed by surveillance practitioners have been reviewed by Snider and Stroup (2000). Given past conflicting experiences, and the regular involvement of partners with different cultural and national backgrounds, there should be more elaboration on what ethical standards should apply internationally in the process of collecting 'outbreak intelligence', ideally with consultation with professionally trained ethicists.

Impartiality and independence

One of the strengths of the IHR(2005) is the fact that they were initiated, developed and endorsed under the authority of an international organization acting through its Secretariat as an impartial and independent body.[12] Compliance with the operational requirements of the IHR(2005), and acceptance by Member States of a necessary trade-off from their national sovereignty, will depend on how impartial and independent the WHO Secretariat is seen by technical and political players in countries affected by any 'public health emergency of international concern'.

As far as global surveillance and international assistance are concerned, real or perceived imbalances in WHO's impartiality and independence arise from the influence of hidden agendas (e.g. scientific or political) and of funding sources, respectively. These two points are developed below.

WHO field operations authorized under the IHR(2005) have been a contentious topic where some states perceived draft provisions as violations of their national sovereignty (Tucker 2005). Articles 47–49 of the IHR(2005) put under the authority of the Director-General the appointment of an 'IHR roster of experts' and of an 'Emergency committee'. The latter is mandated with advising on 'whether an event constitutes a public health emergency of international concern; the termination of a public health emergency of international concern; and the proposed issuance, modification, extension or termination of temporary recommendations' (WHO 2005a). The text is explicit about a fair nomination process 'with due regard to the principles of equitable geograph-ical representation'. But as far as the public health response is concerned, the relevant section (Article 13) is less explicit about selection criteria. It simply tasks WHO with ' . . . the mobilization of international teams of experts for on-site assistance'. Here again, GOARN's 'Guiding principles for international outbreak alert and response' should be taken as more than a declaration of intention when the claim is made that: 'There is fair and equitable process for the participation of Network partners in international responses'.

For Member States enjoying the position of providing experts for assistance through WHO, there might be a genuinely altruistic motivation to join and help in international public health responses. There is no doubt, however, that national interests are at play as well: international visibility, opportunities for training and experience, access to publishable data, control over the response process, and of course concerns over disease spread to their own territory. Through the US-CDC's technical supremacy over all components of outbreak investigation, the US has gained a most privileged access to WHO's surveil-lance and response networks. This privileged partnership is reflected in the Global Pathogen Surveillance Act (GPSA), a bill that has been introduced during each of successive sessions of the US Congress since 2002 (United States Senate 2002; Congressional Record: US Senate 2002, 2003 and 2005). Through the provision of assistance in the form of fellowships, in country training and laboratory rehabilitation, the GPSA includes strong incentives for developing nations to link up with WHO's global surveillance network. It also sets out a number of important conditions attached to eligibility. Section 4 of the GPSA stipulates that:

'In General . . . assistance may be provided to an eligible developing country under any provision of this Act only if the government of the eligible developing country (1) permits personnel from the World Health Organization and the Centers for Disease Control and Pre-vention to investigate outbreaks of infectious diseases within the borders of such country; and (2) provides pathogen surveillance data to the appropriate agencies and departments of the United States and to international health organizations.'

The US-CDC's key relationship toward WHO is further defined in a 2002 Strategy Paper:

'As an international entity, WHO is a critical partner in opening doors to U.S. scientists, facilitating U.S. participation in international efforts to identify new threats and contain potential pandemics.'
(Centers for Disease Control and Prevention 2002,
cited under 'WHO and CDC: Collaboration
on International Outbreak Assistance')

In the same document, the US-CDC's ambitious 'Vision for the Future' is described as:

> 'Regional and disease-specific surveillance and response networks will increase in number and geographical area until they cover all parts of the world and monitor all infectious diseases of regional or global importance. The networks will link up with each other and evolve into a global 'network of networks' that provides early warning of new health threats . . . and increased capacity to monitor the effectiveness of public health control measures.'

Similar intentions, although perhaps less explicit, are certainly on the agenda of other governmental GOARN partners.[13]

Beside above-mentioned national interests, economic forces are equally at work to promote global public health surveillance. Development agencies, such as the World Bank, have been gaining in influence over global and regional health policies since the 1980s (Walt 2001). Recently, they have felt the urge to strengthen regional programmes addressing surveillance and response to emerging diseases. This pattern of influence has been boosted by the combined effects of the SARS epidemic in 2003 and the recent re-emergence of H5N1 avian influenza, both threatening global markets in general and Asian economies in particular. As a major development agency in countries affected by those events, the Asian Development Bank (ADB) has recently launched a new funding initiative for communicable disease control in the Greater Mekong Subregion, granting a combined total of US$30 millions to governments of Vietnam, Cambodia and Laos (Asian Development Bank 2005a). In July 2005, the ADB and the Heads of States of Greater Mekong Subregion nations officially endorsed this programme as part of broader resolutions on common economic and social development expressed in the 'Kunming Declaration' (Asian Development Bank 2005b).

This illustrates how a development agency has taken the initiative in setting up a new health agenda at sub-regional level, building upon the pervasive discourse on global surveillance. This further illustrates just one among several parallel donor-driven initiatives on regional surveillance, where the WHO Secretariat has entered into partnership as an implementing agency, essentially under terms of technical assistance (Asian Development Bank 2004, 2005a), and regardless of the disruptive effects that such initiatives might have on health systems (Calain 2007). As pointed out by Smith (2005),

> 'the argument [for overseas funding] has subtly shifted from one of the recipient countries well-being to the donor countries well-being, under the argument of the global public good. In this regard,

infectious disease . . . has been the primary driver of health-related global public good arguments.'

Blurred boundaries between global security and global public health surveillance

Whether the threat posed by the deliberate release of biological agents has actually been increasing during the last few years, compared with the Cold War era, is still a matter of debate (Fee and Brown 2001), which will only be settled by history. The fact is that the intentional dissemination of anthrax spores in the US in 2001 (a minor event from a pure public health perspective) has had a major psychological impact, and has nurtured the ground for an international consensus over the importance and the acuity of the problem. It has also somewhat shifted the focus from state-sponsored activities (a legacy of the Cold War) to the dystopian, fear-appealing concept of global, ubiquitous and sustained terrorist threats. At first glance, it would seem logical that the mechanisms set up for outbreak surveillance and response by WHO through its GOARN resources would be used irrespective of the origin of the initial contamination—natural or deliberate. Actually, the issue of WHO being involved in 'bioterror investigations' has been a heated one during debates surrounding the 2005 revision of the IHR (Anonymous 2005a,b; Tucker 2005; Woodall 2005; Fidler and Gostin 2006), to the point that the final version of the document eliminates any mention of deliberate epidemics.

The origin of the difficulties is probably to be found in recent developments surrounding the implementation of the (1972) Biological Weapons Convention (BWC), which is still lacking an effective mechanism to monitor compliance by Member States and to punish violators (Tucker 2004). This gap in international enforcement regimes is an anomaly that contrasts with the existence of two related conventions pertaining to the deliberate release of chemical agents or radio-nuclear materials, and whose watchdog agencies are, respectively, the Organisation for the Prohibition of Chemical Weapons and the International Atomic Energy Agency. Similar efforts to create a multilateral enforcement mechanism to the BWC derailed in July 2001 during its Fifth Review Conference (Tucker 2004). Through a new interim process pending on the next (6th) Review Conference scheduled in 2006, Member States have convened a number of technical meetings, to which WHO, the Food and Agriculture Organization (FAO) and the Office International des Epizooties (OIE) were granted observer status. Topics of the preparatory 'Meeting of Experts' in July 2004 (United Nations 2004) and of the ensuing 'Meeting of States Parties' in December 2004 were directly relevant to WHO's surveillance and capacity building activities. Through remarkably non-committing language, the States Parties' final report simply commends WHO's efforts to strengthen global surveillance (United Nations 2006), although some country representatives were more vocal during the debates. Brazil, for example, expressed the view that:

> 'The WHO or other specialized international bodies should not be used as substitutes for a proper multilaterally negotiated and legitimate verification regime within the scope of the BWC',

adding further that:

> 'Security issues and the investigation of possible violations of the BWC are not included in the mandate of these organizations, and it should so remain.'
>
> (quoted in Department of Peace Studies,
> University of Bradford 2004)

At about the same time, higher pressure was put on WHO by the submission to the UN General Assembly of a 'report of the UN Secretary General's High-Level Panel on Threats, Challenges and Changes' (Tucker 2005), recommending that the Security Council's authority be engaged to 'support the work of WHO investigators or to deploy experts reporting directly to the Council . . .' and to 'mandate greater compliance . . . if existing International Health Regulations do not provide adequate access for WHO investigations and response coordination'.

In any case, bio-security issues are clearly tainting WHO's efforts to implement global surveillance, and might to some extent jeopardize compliance by WHO Member States to the IHR(2005) regime. As put forward by an analyst of the BWC (Woodall 2005):

> 'If countries should perceive WHO staff or consultants as intelligence agents with a dual responsibility to investigate treaty violations as well as health matters, the result could be unwillingness to report outbreaks at their onset and reluctance to request the help of WHO or permit its entry. These reactions would seriously impede efforts to control the global spread of disease.'

To some extent, WHO is resisting any involvement in monitoring activities that fall outside its health mandate. In a programme of work for 2004–05 (WHO 2004b), WHO kept a distance from the BWC, with the statement that:

> 'The disarmament and non-proliferation dimensions of the BWC are clearly outside the public health mandate of WHO. This explains why the primary emphasis of WHO's work on deliberately caused diseases is on the public health preparedness and response to the deliberate use of biological agents that affect health.'

Further illustrating the ambiguity of WHO's position on global health security, Aginam (2005) has pointed out the contrast between recognized mandates of the Organization, with respect to the proliferation of biological and chemical weapons on the one hand and the legality of nuclear weapons on the other.

Misperceptions of blurred mandates between security and public health issues have been further entertained on the occasion of public-private partnerships or of privileged relationships with Member States. This can be illustrated by two examples. In December 2002, WHO welcomed the establishment of a much-needed contingency fund for the prompt response to public health emergencies. Funding was obtained through a partnership between WHO and the Nuclear Threat Initiative (NTI), a prominent and authoritative US charitable organization 'working to reduce the threats from nuclear, biological and chemical weapons'. Former Senator Sam Nunn, co-chair of NTI, was unequivocal in justifying the partnership by dual objectives, and declared:

'. . . The fight against infectious diseases has always been a moral imperative. Today, it is also a security imperative.'

(WHO 2002)

The US Global Pathogen Surveillance Act mentioned in the previous section offers further illustration of an ambivalent instrument under which WHO finds itself committed. Although when enacted the GPSA will definitely benefit countries in need of technical assistance and help broaden public health surveillance networks, its purpose is clearly dual, as summarized by Senator Helms, one of its proponents:

'While we are supportive of the public health benefits of this Act, we should not lose sight of the intent of this legislation—to combat bioterrorism and enhance U.S. national security.'

(Congressional Record: US Senate 2002)

The latest version of the GPSA (Congressional Record: US Senate 2005) incorporates a new section (number 13) requesting the President to 'establish the Office of Foreign Biological Threat Detection and Warning within either the Department of Defense, the Central Intelligence Agency, or the Centers for Disease Control and Prevention with the technical ability to conduct event detection and rapid threat assessment related to biological threats in foreign countries'.

The links between health, foreign policy and security policy are increasingly recognized and they relate to the blurring of boundaries between domestic and foreign agendas, an outcome of globalization (Owen and Roberts 2005). As demonstrated by McInnes and Lee (2006), the relationship between global public health on one hand, and foreign and security policies on the other is currently set on unequal terms. The agenda is dominated by the interests of the foreign and security communities, and it is skewed in favour of national interests instead of global public health. Moreover, this imbalance of influences leads to prioritizing those epidemic hazards perceived as significant risks for the West, at the expense of the far more prevalent diseases affecting the developing world. The two examples given above – the Nuclear Threat Initiative and the US Global Pathogen Surveillance Act – are perfect illustrations of this policy shift from health concerns to foreign and security agendas, centred on national interests.[14] More importantly, they indicate that the WHO Secretariat, willingly or not, provides some legitimacy to such a trend. Fidler and Gostin (2006) have shown how the revised IHR(2005) contain 'an international legal regime unprecedented in the history of the relationship between international law and public health' and how they establish important new powers for WHO. Fidler (2004) also asserts that WHO had already exercised extra-legal and extra-ordinary authority over states during the SARS outbreak, well before the new IHR would become binding for Member States. Such an increase in power granted by the international community to an international organization, linked with some intrusive authority, should call for stricter adherence to independence and impartiality.

Conclusions

The understanding that epidemic diseases spread without boundaries is no longer a matter of interest restricted to public health specialists and epidemiologists. Recent events of international dimensions like the SARS pandemic, the ongoing avian influenza epizootic and the alleged threats of deliberate epidemics have brought together in the same arena public health, economy and security communities to forge a comprehensive surveillance agenda. Although the trade and political dimensions of epidemic diseases were already reflected in former legal regimes of international collaboration, the revised IHR(2005) broaden the scope of interference by UN bodies and open the door to intrusive interventions where public health would not necessarily be the main incentive.

In this respect, it is significant that some of the most heated debates around the revision of the IHR were ignited by issues such as national sovereignty and investigations of bio-terrorism events. Despite official endorsement of the new document by all WHO Member States, it is likely that the same issues and related misperceptions will come back on the agenda and affect future compliance with the regulations.

One could argue that—to a large extent—there is enough convergence between public health, economy and security interests in the control of communicable diseases to allow for a global surveillance agenda to encompass a broader range of activities and actors. Such a view carries the risk of seeing public health priorities being hijacked as Trojan Horses for other international agendas, leading to further decline in trust about international institutions, their impartiality and their independence.

As illustrated in this article, WHO has occasionally been engaged in ambiguous partnerships with new actors in the surveillance arena, representing security interests (e.g. non-proliferation lobbies) and economic interests (e.g. regional development banks). Misperceptions about the rationale for global surveillance generated by such conflicts of interest or blurred agendas will probably fuel further concerns about their sovereignty among Member States when it comes to enacting the revised IHR. If WHO wants to act as an influential and independent institution, it should reclaim authority and initiative in setting an independent agenda for public health surveillance, emphasizing the precedence of health issues over economic or security interests. By demonstrating more political independence toward influential Member States and by exercising caution over the boundaries of 'public health surveillance' and 'global health security', WHO would make gains in credibility and efficiency over the control of communicable diseases affecting the majority of the world's population. Endorsement or participation in regional or global surveillance initiatives should not be systematic, or entertained for the sake of funding or political opportunities. If the way forward is through 'integrated surveillance' (discussed in Calain 2007), this is an additional reason for an international institution to exercise independent authority and to assert the flaws of any supranational surveillance initiative that would be redundant or overlapping with existing national systems or priority programmes.

In addition to a clear stance on its independence and impartiality, there are three more processes in which WHO should engage more actively to avoid perceived threats to national sovereignty being generated by the recourse to the IHR(2005). First, the concept of Early Warning Systems should be clarified as the sole component of public health surveillance covered by the IHR(2005) and their binding articles. Secondly, the issue of scientific investigations bound to international outbreak responses should be formally addressed in terms of intellectual property, ownership and direct benefits for countries receiving technical support. Finally, there is a need to establish and formalize an internationally accepted code of conduct for public health surveillance and outbreak investigations.

Such conditions would serve better the cause of low-income nations, and give credibility to the IHR(2005), an otherwise remarkable document which represents more than 10 years of achievements by WHO and its technical partners.

Acknowledgements

I wish to express my gratitude to Professor Gill Walt for inspiring discussions on health systems in developing countries, and for her encouragement to publish on policy issues around global public health surveillance. Both of my papers published in this journal issue have benefited from substantial improvements following very helpful suggestions by anonymous reviewers.

The views expressed in this paper are the sole responsibility of the author and do not necessarily reflect those of the World Health Organization or other organizations. The manuscript was conceived and written at a time when the author was an independent researcher.

Notes

1 Three key primary sources of information were identified from medical datasets and retrieved systematically: MEDLINE (key word: 'International health regulations' and 'Outbreak surveillance'), the entire collection of the journal 'Emerging Infectious Diseases' and all documents published on the EPR (former CSR) website of WHO. Additional references and links quoted in these primary sources were further explored and retrieved as needed. Key public statements identified in this way were submitted to further analysis and selected when they shed light on stakeholders' intentions.

2 In the 19th Century, William Farr, superintendent of the Statistical Department of the Registrar General's Office in England and Wales, routinely collected mortality data to describe the impact of epidemic influenza in 1847 (Langmuir 1976) and set new public health surveillance standards on the occasion of a cholera epidemic in 1848–49 (Langmuir 1963).

3 For a comprehensive historical and political review of the emergence of this concept, see King (2002).

4 Earlier, essential elements of global public health surveillance (including the role of WHO as a coordinating body) were reviewed at the 'Technical Discussions' forum of the 21st World Health Assembly in 1968 (WHO 1968).

5 This outdated meaning of 'surveillance' is now officially captured under the definition of 'public health observation' (WHO 2005a: Part I, Article 1 Definitions).

6 Thacker broadened the use of public health surveillance beyond the restricted field of communicable diseases, he conceptualized the three classical goals of surveillance data analysis (estimation of morbidity and mortality, detection of epidemics and programme evaluation) (Thacker et al. 1989), and he defined classical indicators used for the evaluation of surveillance systems (Thacker et al. 1988).

7 In the historical context in which the idea of revising the IHR had taken place, their earlier promoters obviously had in mind the control of rapidly evolving emergencies such as outbreaks of haemorrhagic fevers or cholera. But given the broad 'Purpose and scope' stated in the IHR(2005) ('. . . a public health response to the international spread of diseases'), one wonders how, for instance, the new regulations would have applied in the late 1980s to HIV/AIDS when its spread, albeit slow, became already a matter of urgent international concern.

8 The World Trade Organization (created in 1995) administers 29 multilateral agreements, two of which are particularly relevant to preventing the spread of communicable diseases across borders: the General Agreement on Tariffs and Trade (GATT) and the Agreement on the Application of Sanitary and Phytosanitary Measures (SPS agreement). For an analysis of their mechanisms, see Plotkin and Kimball (1997).

9 For detailed accounts of the initial events of the SARS epidemic in China, see Heymann (2006) and Annex B in Bartlett et al. (2006).

10 What now appears as a cover-up operation by high-level Chinese authorities was quickly revealed publicly by Dr Jiang Yanyong, a prominent military surgeon and party member. Dr Jiang's courageous posture is now acknowledged as an important contribution to halt the spread of SARS (Kahn 2004; Ramon Magsaysay Award Foundation 2004).

11 A typical example has been well documented during the outbreak of Ebola haem-orrhagic fever in Kikwit in 1995 (Heymann *et al.* 1999; Garrett 2001: 77).

12 Article 37 of the Constitution of the World Health Organization, 1946 (WHO 1994).

13 Building around the evolving concept of territoriality, King (2002) has proposed an outstanding historical perspective on global disease information networks.

14 Fidler (2005) also sees this policy shift as pertaining to the particular issue of sur-veillance: '... the United States' interest in improving global infectious disease surveillance views improved global surveillance as a means to increase national and homeland security against bioterrorism, not as a vehicle for improving global health. Any constructive health consequences for other countries that spill over from improved global surveillance represent a positive externality but are not the primary foreign policy objective.'

References

Aginam O. 2005. Bio-terrorism, human security and public health: can international law bring them together in an age of globalisation? *Medicine and Law* **24**: 455–62.

Anonymous. 2005a. Global health agency split over potential antiterrorism duties. *Nature* **434**: 686.

Anonymous. 2005b. WHO sets health rules but ducks bioterror issue. *Nature* **435**: 550.

Asian Development Bank. 2004. Technical assistance to the Kingdom of Cambodia, Lao People's Democratic Republic, and Socialist Republic of Viet Nam for preparing the Greater Mekong Subregion Regional Communicable Diseases Control Project. Online at: [http://www.adb.org/Documents/TARs/REG/tar-oth-37621.pdf], accessed 9 October 2006.

Asian Development Bank. 2005a. Report and Recommendation of the President to the Board of Directors on a Proposed Grant to the Kingdom of Cambodia, the Lao People's Democratic Republic, and the Socialist Republic of Viet Nam for the Greater Mekong Subregion Regional Communicable Diseases Control Project. Online at: [http://www.asiandevbank.org/Documents/RRPs/LAO/37604-LAO-RRP.pdf], accessed 9 October 2006.

Asian Development Bank. 2005b. Kunming Declaration: 'A stronger GMS Partner-ship for Common Prosperity'. News release. Online at: [http://www.adb.org/Media/Articles/2005/7879_Greater_Mekong_Subregion_declaration/], accessed 9 October 2006.

Bartlett C. L. R., Kickbusch I., Coulombier D. 2006. UK Government's Foresight project, Infectious Diseases: preparing for the future. Supporting paper D4.3: cultural and governance influence on detection, identification and monitoring of human disease. Online at: [http://www.foresight.gov.uk], accessed 9 October 2006.

BBC News. 5 April 2003. China 'sorry' for slow bug response. Online at: [http://news.bbc.co.uk/go/pr/fr/-/l/hi/health/2919967.stm], accessed 9 October 2006.

Calain P. 2007. From the field side of the binoculars: a different view on global public health surveillance. *Health Policy and Planning* **22**: 13–20.

Cash R. A., Narasimhan V. 2000. Impediments to global surveillance of infectious diseases: consequences of open reporting in a global economy. *Bulletin of the World Health Organization* **78**: 1358–66.

Centers for Disease Control and Prevention. 2002. *Protecting the Nation's Health in an Era of Globalization*. CDC's Global Infectious Disease Strategy. Atlanta, GA:

Centers for Disease Control and Prevention. Online at: [http://www.cdc.gov/globalidplan/4-introduction.htm], accessed 9 October 2006.

Congressional Record: US Senate. 2002, 2003 and 2005. Global Pathogen Surveillance Act. Online at: [http://thomas.loc.gov/home/search.html], accessed 21 March 2006. Successive versions have been passed by the US Senate under the following records: Senate Bill S. 2487 (107th Congress, 2002), Senate Bill S. 871 (108th Congress, 2003), and Senate Bill S. 2170 (109th Congress, 2005).

Congressional Record: US Senate. 2002. Record of the session of August 01, 2002: page S8024. Global Pathogen Surveillance Act of 2002. Online at: [http://thomas.loc.gov/home/r107query.html], accessed 9 October 2006.

Department of Peace Studies, University of Bradford. 2004. The Biological and Toxin Weapons Convention: Inter Review Conference Meetings. 2004 Meeting of Experts: 19–30 July 2004. Other Statements and Presentations by State Parties: Brazil. Online at: [http://www.opbw.org/new_process/mx2004/other_pres/brazil-statement.pdf], accessed 18 October 2006.

Enserink M. 2004. A global fire brigade responds to disease outbreaks. *Science* **303**: 1605–6.

Fee E., Brown T. M. 2001. Preemptive biopreparedness: can we learn anything from history? *American Journal of Public Health* **91**: 721–6.

Fidler D. 2003. Emerging trends in international law concerning global infectious disease control. *Emerging Infectious Diseases* **9**: 285–90.

Fidler D. P. 2004. Germs, governance, and global public health in the wake of SARS. *Journal of Clinical Investigation* **113**: 799–804.

Fidler D. P. 2005. Health as foreign policy: between principle and power. *The Whitehead Journal of Diplomacy and International Relations* **6**: 179–94.

Fidler D. P., Gostin L. O. 2006. The new International Health Regulations: an historic development for international law and public health. *Journal of Law, Medicine and Ethics* **34**: 85–94.

Garrett L. *Betrayal of trust: the collapse of health systems.* Oxford: Oxford University Press.

Global Health Security Initiative. 2006. GHSI background. Online at: [http://www.ghsi.ca/english/background.asp], accessed 9 October 2006.

Gray J. 2003. SARS taints Toronto's image. BBC News, 24 April 2003. Online at: [http://newsvote.bbc.co.uk/mpapps/pagetools/print/news.bbc.co.uk/2/hi/americas/2973803.stm], accessed 9 October 2006.

Health Canada. 2005. International activities – global pandemic influenza readiness. Online at: [http://www.hc-sc.gc.ca/ahc-asc/intactiv/pandem-flu/index_e.html], accessed 9 October 2006.

Heymann D. L. 2006. SARS and emerging infectious diseases: a challenge to place global solidarity above national sovereignty. *Annals Academy of Medicine Singapore* **35**: 350–353.

Heymann D. L., Rodier G. R. 1998. Global surveillance of communicable diseases. *Emerging Infectious Diseases* **4**: 362–5.

Heymann D. L., Rodier G. 2004. Global surveillance, national surveillance, and SARS. *Emerging Infectious Diseases* **10**: 173–5.

Heymann D. L., Barakamfitiye D., Szczeniowski M., *et al.* 1999. Ebola hemorrhagic fever: lessons from Kikwit, Democratic Republic of the Congo. *Journal of Infectious Diseases* **179**(Suppl. 1):S283–6.

Heymann D. L., Rodier G. R. and the WHO Operational Support Team to the Global Outbreak Alert and Response Network. 2001. Hot spots in a wired world:

WHO surveillance of emerging and re-emerging infectious diseases. *The Lancet Infectious Diseases* 1: 345–53.

Institute of Medicine. 1992. *Emerging infections: microbial threats to health in the United States*. Lederberg J., Shope R. E. and Oaks S. C. (eds). Washington, DC: National Academies Press.

Kahn J. 2004. China releases the SARS whistle-blower. *The New York Times*, 21 July 2004.

King N. B. 2002. Security, disease, commerce: ideologies of postcolonial global health. *Social Studies of Science* 32: 763–89.

Langmuir A. D. 1963. The surveillance of communicable diseases of national importance. *New England Journal of Medicine* 268: 182–92.

Langmuir A. D. 1971. Evolution of the concept of surveillance in the United States. *Proceedings of the Royal Society of Medicine* 64: 681–4.

Langmuir A. D. 1976. William Farr: founder of modern concepts of surveillance. *International Journal of Epidemiology* 5: 13–18.

McInnes C., Lee K. 2006. Health, security and foreign policy. *Review of International Studies* 32: 5–23.

McNabb S., Chungong S., Ryan M., *et al.* 2002. Conceptual framework of public health surveillance and action and its application in health sector reform. *BMC Public Health* 2: 2. Online at: [http://www.biomedcentral.com/1471-2458/2/2], accessed 9 October 2006.

Naphy W. G., Spicer A. 2001. *The Black Death: a history of plagues, 1345–1730*. Stroud, UK and Charleston, SC: Tempus; 2001.

Owen J. W., Roberts O. 2005. Globalisation, health and foreign policy: emerging linkages and interests. *Globalization and Health* 1: 12. Online at: [http://www.globalizationandhealth.com/content.1/1/12], accessed 9 October 2006.

Plotkin B. J., Kimball A. M. 1997. Designing an international policy and legal framework for the control of emerging infectious diseases: first steps. *Emerging Infectious Diseases* 3: 1–9.

Ramon Magsaysay Award Foundation. 2004. The 2004 Ramon Magsaysay Awardee for Public Service. Citation for Jiang Yanyong. Online at: [http://www.rmaf.org.ph/Awardees/Citation/CitationJiangYan.htm], accessed 9 October 2006.

Rodier G. R. M. 2003. Why was Toronto included in the World Health Organization's SARS-related travel advisory? *Canadian Medical Association Journal* 168: 1434–5.

Rosling L., Rosling M. 2003. Pneumonia causes panic in Guangdong province. *British Medical Journal* 326: 416. Sánchez J. L., Taylor D. N. 1997. Cholera. *The Lancet* 349: 1825–30.

Smith R. D. 2005. *Infectious disease and risk: lessons from SARS*. London: The Nuffield Trust; 2005.

Snider D. E., Stroup D. F. 2000. Ethical issues. Chapter 9. In: Teutsch S. M., (ed). *Principles and practice of public health surveillance*. Oxford: Oxford University Press; 2000.

Thacker S. B., Gregg M. B. 1996. Implementing the concepts of William Farr: the contributions of Alexander D. Langmuir to public health surveillance and communications. *American Journal of Epidemiology* 144: S23–8.

Thacker S. B., Parrish R. G., Trowbridge F. L. and Surveillance Coordination Group. 1988. A method for evaluating systems of epidemiological surveillance. *World Health Statistics Quarterly* 41: 11–18.

Thacker S. B., Berkelman R. L., Stroup D. F. 1989. The science of public health surveillance. *Journal of Public Health Policy* 10: 187–203.

Tucker J. B. 2004. The BWC new process: a preliminary assessment. *The Nonproliferation Review* **11**: 26–39.

Tucker J. B. 2005. Updating the International Health Regulations. *Biosecurity and Bioterrorism: Biodefense strategy, practice, and science* **3**: 338–47.

United Nations. 2004. Secretariat of the BWC Meeting of Experts. Press document 02.08.04, Biological weapons convention expert meeting concludes. Online at: [http://www2.unog.ch/news2/documents/newsen/dc04029e.htm], accessed 9 October 2006.

United Nations. 2006. Biological Weapons Convention. Report of the 2004 Meeting of States Parties 6–10 December 2004. Document BWC/MSP/2004/3. UN Department for Disarmament Affairs, Weapons of Mass Destruction Branch. Online at: [http://disarmament2.un.org/wmd/bwc/annualmeetings/listofdocs-2004%20States%20Parties%20mtgs.html], accessed 21 March 2006.

United States Senate. 2002. Biden introduces bill to defend against bioterror and improve disease tracking. Press release, May 9, 2002. Online at: [http://biden.senate.gov/newsroom/details.cfm?id=182660], accessed 9 October 2006.

Walt G. The international arena. Chapter 7 in: *Health Policy: an introduction to process and power*. 5th edn., London: Zed Books.

WHO. 1968. The surveillance of communicable diseases. Final report of technical discussions of the 21st World Health Assembly, May 1968. *WHO Chronicle* **22**: 439–44.

WHO. 1994. Constitution of the World Health Organization, 1946. World Health Organization Basic Documents, 40th edition. Geneva: World Health Organization.

WHO. 1995a. Resolutions and decisions of the 48th World Health Assembly: Revision and updating of the International Health Regulations, WHA48.7; Communicable diseases prevention and control: new, emerging, and re-emerging infectious diseases, WHA 48.13. Geneva: World Health Organization.

WHO. 1995b. Press release WHO/75, 17 October 1995. Geneva: World Health Organization.

WHO. 2001. World Health Assembly Resolution 54.14: Global health security: epidemic alert and response. Geneva: World Health Organization.

WHO. 2002. WHO-NTI establish global emergency outbreak response fund. Joint press release, 2 December 2002. Online at: [http://www.who.int/mediacentre/news/releases/pr92/en], accessed 9 October 2006.

WHO. 2004a. Intergovernmental working group on revision of the international health regulations (Provisional agenda item 2): Summary report of regional consultations. Document A/IHR/IGWG/2. Online at: [http://www.who.int/gb/ghs/pdf/IHR_IGWG_2-en.pdf], accessed 9 October 2006.

WHO. 2004b. Preparedness for deliberate epidemics: programme of work for the biennium 2004–2005. Document WHO/CDS/CSR/LYO/2004.8. World Health Organization, Department of Communicable Disease Surveillance and Response. Online at: [http://www.who.int/csr/resources/publications/deliberate/WHO_CDS_CSR_LYO_2004_8/en/], accessed 9 October 2006.

WHO. 2005a. Revision of the International Health Regulations. Fifty-eighth World Health Assembly. Document WHA58.3. Online at: [http://www.who.int/gb/ebwha/pdf_files/WHA58/A58_4-en.pdf], accessed 9 October 2006.

WHO. 2005b. Avian influenza: assessing the pandemic threat. Document WHO/CDS/2005.29. Online at: [http://www.who.int/csr/disease/influenza/H5N1-9reduit.pdf], accessed 9 October 2006.

WHO. 2005c. Joint News Release, WHO/FAO/OIE/World Bank. Global Influenza Meeting 9 November 2005. Online at: [http://www.who.int/mediacentre/news/releases/2005/pr58/en/index.html], accessed 9 October 2006.

WHO. 2005d. Early warning systems. Online at: [http://www.who.int/csr/labepidemiology/projects/earlywarnsystem/en/print.html], accessed 9 October 2006.

WHO. 2005e. Frequently asked questions about the International Health Regulations. Online at: [http://www.who.int/csr/ihr/howtheywork/faq/en/print.html], accessed 9 October 2006.

WHO. 2005f. Guiding principles for international outbreak alert and response. Online at: [http://www.who.int/csr/outbreaknetwork/guidingprinciples/en/print.html], accessed 9 October 2006.

WHO. 2006. World Health Assembly Resolution 59.2: Application of the International Health Regulations (2005). Online at: [http://www.who.int/gb/ebwha/pdf_files/WHA59/WHA59_2-en.pdf], accessed 9 October 2006.

WHO, Regional Office for the Western Pacific. 2005. Japan-WHO joint meeting on early response to potential influenza pandemic. Online at: [http://www.wpro.who.int/sites/csr/meetings/mtg_20050112–13.htm], accessed 9 October 2006.

Wilson K., McDougall C., Upshur R., *et al.* 2006. The new international health regulations and the federalism dilemma. *PloS Medicine* **3**: 30–4.

Woodall J. P. 2005. WHO and biological weapons investigations. *The Lancet* **365**: 651.

World Bank. 2005. International Pledging Conference on Avian and Human Influenza, Beijing, 17–18 January 2006. Online at: [http://www.worldbank.org/avianflu], accessed 9 October 2006.

Zhong N. S., Zheng B. J., Li Y. M., *et al.* 2003. Epidemiology and cause of severe acute respiratory syndrome (SARS) in Guangdong, People's Republic of China, in February. *The Lancet* **362**: 1353–8.

81

THE NEW INTERNATIONAL HEALTH REGULATIONS

Considerations for global public health surveillance

*Jessica L. Sturtevant, Aranka Anema
and John S. Brownstein*

Source: *Disaster Medicine and Public Health Preparedness*, 1:1 (2007), 117–21.

Abstract

Global public health surveillance is critical for the identification and prevention of emerging and re-emerging infectious diseases. The World Health Organization recently released revised International Health Regulations (IHR) that serve as global legislation and provide guidelines for surveillance systems. The IHR aim to identify and prevent spread of these infectious diseases; however, there are some practical challenges that limit the usability of these regulations. IHR requires Member States to build necessary infrastructure for global surveillance, which may not be possible in underdeveloped countries. A large degree of freedom is given to each individual government and therefore different levels of reporting are common, with substantial emphasis on passive reporting. The IHR need to be enforceable and enforced without impinging on government autonomy or human rights. Unstable governments and developing countries require increased assistance in setting up and maintaining surveillance systems. This article addresses some challenges and potential solutions to the ability of national governments to adhere to the global health surveillance requirements detailed in the IHR. The authors review some practical challenges such as inadequate surveillance and reporting infrastructure, and legal enforcement and maintenance of individual human rights.

Emerging and reemerging infectious diseases represent an increasingly important public health threat.[1-3] In 2000, infectious diseases were responsible for 22% of all deaths and 27% of disability adjusted life-year (DALYs) worldwide.[4] Developing countries are particularly affected. In Africa in 2000, for example, infectious diseases accounted for 50% of mortality and 52% of DALYs.[4] A multitude of factors contribute to this situation, including a decline in control efforts, drug and pesticide resistance, unsuccessful vaccine development, urbanization, and increased population growth and mobility.[1-3,5] Increases in international trade of food and pharmaceuticals, and environmental changes in climate, water supply, and forestation also have had an enormous impact on the globalization of infectious diseases.[4] Public health surveillance plays a critical role in controlling infectious diseases and requires dynamic, international solutions that address complex interactions among pathogens, vectors, hosts, and the environment.[2,4,6,7]

In 2005 the World Health Organization (WHO) released its revised global legislation pertaining to infectious disease outbreaks, the International Health Regulations (IHR).[8,9] The IHR, which became effective on June 15, 2007, require the WHO's 193 Member States to develop and maintain effective global health surveillance systems for the early detection, confirmation, timely response, and reporting of infectious disease outbreaks. The IHR represents an important step in achieving global health security by promoting the prevention and control of communicable diseases within and across international borders.

This article addresses some challenges and potential solutions to the ability of national governments to adhere to global health surveillance requirements detailed in the IHR. Specifically, we briefly review some practical challenges such as inadequate surveillance and reporting infrastructure, and legal enforcement and maintenance of individual human rights.

International Health Regulations

The IHR was developed in 1969 and focused on monitoring only a select few infectious diseases, including cholera, plague, and yellow fever.[6,10] The IHR was even amended in 1981 to exclude smallpox after its eradication in the late 1970s.[11,12] The 2005 revision has expanded its focus to include any disease with potential global public health threat. The IHR requires WHO Member States to investigate and report on any event that constitutes a public health emergency of international concern,[9] including communicable infectious diseases and noncommunicable etiologies, such as chemical or radiological incidents (Figure 1). The IHR stipulates that national governments must assess the severity of an outbreak within 48 hours of initial detection and report to the WHO within 24 hours of confirmation. Reporting must include information about case definitions, laboratory findings,

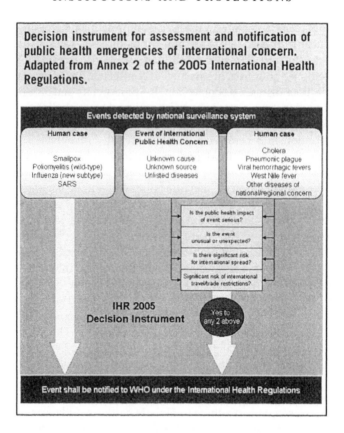

Figure 1 Decision instrument for assessment and notification of public health emergencies of international concern. Adapted from Annex 2 of the 2005 International Health Regulations.

incidents of morbidity and mortality, communicable risk factors, and public health response.[13]

Effective June 15, 2007, the IHR have called upon national ministries of health and foreign affairs departments to jointly establish a National Focal Point for health security monitoring and plan of action for infectious disease detection, confirmation, response, and reporting. National Focal Points must adhere to WHO Guiding Principles for International Outbreak Alert and Response.[13,14] These principles include establishing strong technical leadership during field responses, building local capacity for future epidemics, and ensuring respect for legal, human rights, and cultural sensitivities. By June 15, 2009, WHO expects that Member States will have met the necessary infrastructural requirements to fully implement global health surveillance systems, as stipulated by the IHR.

494

Challenges in global health surveillance infrastructure

The IHR requires national governments to implement and maintain outbreak surveillance systems at local or primary, state or intermediate, and national public health agency levels. This poses a formidable challenge to under-developed nations, which may not have adequate infrastructural capacity.[6,15,16] Ensuring appropriate surveillance infrastructure is particularly important in these contexts because developing countries have been the source of new diseases, including Marburg hemorrhaghic fever in Zimbabwe,[17] Ebola virus in the Democratic Republic of Congo,[18] Lassa fever in west Africa,[19] *Vibrio cholerae* 0139 in India,[20] and HIV in central Africa.[21] Moreover, it is recognized that the majority of the global infectious disease burden remains concentrated among the poorest 20% of the world's population and often occurs in rural areas of developing countries where people have limited access to health care and clinical surveillance systems.[4]

The IHR does not tell nations how to conduct surveillance but rather tells them what results surveillance should produce. Although this offers national governments a great deal of freedom to determine their own contextually and economically appropriate surveillance mechanisms, it may also lead to passive public health reporting systems that have typically been insensitive and unreliable for early detection of infectious disease outbreaks. In a resource-scarce environment, clinical and syndromic surveillance methods may be favored over laboratory reporting. Potentially more timely, these data sources may, however, lack the required specificity for outbreak confirmation.[22] National governments would benefit from having explicit standards and guidelines to support the infrastructural development of their national infectious disease surveillance systems. This is especially important for developing countries that have limited infrastructural capacity and that may need support to establish these systems for the first time.

Countries with current or recent armed conflict may require additional support to establish sustainable national surveillance systems due to the destruction of health care and other basic infrastructure. In Ivory Coast, for example, it is estimated that 80% of health care facilities were destroyed or looted during conflict, and 90% of health professionals abandoned their posts.[23] Twenty years of conflict in the Democratic Republic of Congo have rendered the health care system incapable of providing basic health care services to its citizens.[24] National organizations and national nongovernmental organizations (NGOs) can play an important role in strengthening the epidemiological surveillance capacities of national governments. Many international humanitarian aid organizations, such as the United Nations High Commissioner for Refugees, Doctors Without Borders, and Save the Children survey emerging and reemerging infectious diseases as part of their program planning. Lack of epidemiological expertise among some NGOs has led, however, to methodologically inaccurate surveillance analyses and reporting. NGOs assisting national governments in infectious disease surveillance would benefit from receiving standardized training to ensure that their surveillance methodologies are scientifically sound and reproducible.[25]

The WHO has suggested that international and national military forces may also be well positioned to strengthen infectious disease surveillance in conflict settings, given their logistic capacity and increasing involvement in peacekeeping and humanitarian relief operations. Successful examples of military involvement in public health surveillance have been noted in Peru and Thailand.[26-28] In Peru, the national navy implemented the Ministry of Health's national public health surveillance system, contributing to the identification of 31 disease outbreaks, including Peru's first confirmed cyclosporiasis epidemic. In Thailand, technical assistance from the US Army enabled the national government to define risk factors for HIV infection, assess the impact of HIV prevention efforts on lowering incidence, and understand the natural history of epidemics.

Internet-based global systems can also provide valuable information for early detection of infectious disease outbreaks, especially in areas invisible to day-to-day global public health efforts.[29] This was demonstrated by the early identification via the Internet of the severe acute respiratory syndrome (SARS) outbreak in Guangdong Province, China.[30,31] A number of public and private global surveillance initiatives aggregate unstructured data from Internet-based discussion sites, news outlets, and blogs.[2,32,33] These initiatives include the Program for Monitoring Emerging Disease,[7,34-37] the Public Health Agency of Canada's Global Public Health Intelligence Network,[31,38] and other Internet-based global systems such as HealthMap,[39,40] MediSys,[41] and Epispider.[42] The WHO's Global Outbreak Alert and Response Network depends largely on unstructured data to inform populations of outbreak verification activities.[2,32] The increased uptake of unstructured Internet data by these organizations suggests that the public has an increasingly important role to play in global disease surveillance.[43]

Despite the growing importance of these unstructured information sources for monitoring emerging infectious diseases, Internet-based reporting of infectious disease outbreaks is limited in developing countries due to lack of affordability, access, and education. The increasing digital divide between countries is demonstrated by huge variations in Internet access within and between countries.[44] Economic challenges associated with the expansion of information and communications technology has been demonstrated in India. Increasing access to some 550,000 villages in India would cost the government 12.5% of its gross domestic product, diverting resources from other basic health interventions.[45] Developing countries will require increased multilateral support to effectively report and communicate information about emerging and reemerging infectious diseases to the public.

While developing countries with limited resources work toward strengthening their public health surveillance systems with assistance from international organizations, the military, and the public, emerging diseases may be also tracked by national sentinel surveillance and tourists returning home. A review of 60 sentinel sites in 29 countries by the Alumni for Global Surveillance network found that sentinel surveillance efficiently uncovered infectious diseases of international importance, including large numbers of influenza and dengue fever.[46] A review of *Shigella dysenteriae* serotype 1 (Sd1) incidence among European travelers suggests that this may be a viable method of alerting international public health officials to new outbreaks.[47]

These systems have the potential to generate increased, yet spurious and potentially inaccurate alerts. Countries that incorporate unstructured data in their national surveillance systems need to be cautious about publicly reporting information that has not been verified[48,49] because it can invite significant economic, social, and political damage on a country.[12,15] The negative consequences of premature, inaccurate reporting were illustrated in 1991 in Peru, when inflammatory reports of a cholera epidemic led national governments to boycott foodstuffs and issue travel warnings, incurring economic losses of US$770 million in trade.[15] A similar incident occurred in 1994 in India, when government officials declared an outbreak of plague before laboratory confirmation. Unfounded and premature outbreak reporting resulted in overreaction by the international community, stigmatization by media, and a loss of more than US$2 billion in tourist- and trade-based revenue.[15,49]

Challenges in legal enforcement of the IHR

The current system of global surveillance relies heavily on individual government participation and information. Government corruption and instability can have a negative impact on the effectiveness of a global surveillance system.[46] Some countries may not see the benefit of IHR compliance, especially if disease reporting has the potential to cause economic damage.[12,15,16,50] Other member states may be negatively affected due to travel or trade restrictions. There need to be guidelines for seeking compensation. In the recent outbreaks of avian influenza in Asia, some countries were hesitant to share the viral sequence with global authorities and vaccine manufacturers because they believed that they would never benefit from the development of a vaccine.[51]

Inadequate infectious disease reporting mechanisms can also hamper the ability of governments to respond to real emerging health threats in a timely manner.[52] In Myanmar (Burma), delayed reporting of the avian flu virus to the public may have undermined government efforts to contain the epidemics because citizens unknowingly engaged in high-risk transport and sale of animals.[53] In China, the months of delay in the reporting of the SARS outbreak precluded implementation of an effective and timely international public health intervention.[12]

At the same time, there is no legal mandate requiring these systems to exist or specify the required quality of surveillance. The WHO has no formal means by which to enforce the IHR.[8,50] These new regulations state that countries are "obliged" to report public health emergencies to the WHO (IHR 2005)[9]; however, compliance is voluntary and largely influenced by the reporting country's ability to detect and respond to possible public health situations.[15] International law is difficult to enforce and has been largely disregarded.[54] The HIV/AIDS pandemic has been a clear example of the limitations of the IHR, for which countries have developed exclusionary policies openly violating provisions of the health regulations.[55]

Another level of ethical concern regarding global surveillance is the individual right. Although obtaining and sharing personal medical information in the context of a global emergency is necessary to ensure timely contact tracing, quarantine, or other public health measures,[12] privacy of patient information is also important to ensure patient security.[8,51] The delicate balance between individual and public rights and public health surveillance was demonstrated in the recent example of an American man who traveled on several flights while infected with extensively drug-resistant tuberculosis. Failures to enforce a no-fly alert and detain the passenger led to dangerous public exposure to the virulent tuberculosis strain, and demonstrated the clear need for adherence to the IHR.[56] Due to media release of information there was a failure to maintain patient confidentiality, which has led to extreme stigmatization of the man in question.

Conclusions

As the new IHR entered into force on June 15, 2007, questions remained as to whether compliance with the IHR will be feasible given the significant challenges associated with infrastructural capacity, reporting mechanisms, multilateral coordination, and legal enforcement. Developing countries will require additional support to establish surveillance infrastructure; NGOs and the military may play important roles, especially in countries affected by armed conflict. The Internet could also play an important role in promoting early detection of outbreaks. These benefits must be carefully balanced with the adverse consequence of premature and/or inaccurate public infectious disease reporting. Legal enforcement of the IHR remains problematic in the absence of sanctions and in the context of maintaining individual human rights.

Authors' disclosure

This work was supported by the National Library of Medicine (R21LM009263-01), the National Institutes of Health, and the Canadian Institutes of Health Research.

References

1. Feldmann H., Czub M., Jones S., et al. Emerging and re-emerging infectious diseases. *Med Microbiol Immunol.* 2002;191:63–74.

2. Heymann D. L., Rodier G. R. Hot spots in a wired world: WHO surveillance of emerging and re-emerging infectious diseases. *Lancet Infect Dis.* 2001;1(5): 345–353.

3. Lederberg J., Shope R. E., Oats S. C., eds. *Emerging Infections: Microbial Threats to Health in the United States.* Washington, DC: Institute of Medicine, National Academy Press; 1992.

4. Saker L., Lee K., Cannito B., Gilmore A., Campbell-Lendrum D. *Globalization and Infectious Diseases: A Review of the Linkages.* Geneva: UNDP/World Bank/WHO Special Programme for Research and Training in Tropical Diseases; 2004.

5. Wilson M. E. Travel and the emergence of infectious diseases. *Emerg Infect Dis.* 1995;1:39–46.

6. Heymann D. L., Rodier G. R. Global surveillance of communicable diseases. *Emerg Infect Dis.* 1998;4:362–365.

7. Woodall J. P. Global surveillance of emerging diseases: the ProMED-mail perspective. *Cad Saude Publica.* 2001;17 Suppl:147–154.

8. Gostin L. O. International infectious disease law: revision of the World Health Organization's International Health Regulations. *JAMA.* 2004;291:2623–2627.

9. 58th World Health Assembly. Revision of the International Health Regulations. 2005. *http://www.who.int/csr/ihr/IHRWHA58_3-en.pdf.* Accessed July 8, 2007.

10. How is WHO responding to global public health threats? *PLoS Med.* 2007;4:e197.

11. Baker M. G., Fidler D. P. Global public health surveillance under new international health regulations. *Emerg Infect Dis.* 2006;12:1058–1065.

12. Gostin L. O., Bayer R., Fairchild A. L. Ethical and legal challenges posed by severe acute respiratory syndrome: implications for the control of severe infectious disease threats. *JAMA.* 2003;290:3229–3237.

13. World Health Organization. The Designation or Establishment of National IHR Focal Points. *http://www.who.int/csr/ihr/English2.pdf.* Accessed July 15, 2007.

14. World Health Organization. Guiding Principles for International Outbreak Alert and Response. *http://www.who.int/csr/outbreaknetwork/guidingprinciples/en/index. html.* Accessed July 15, 2007.

15. Cash R. A., Narasimhan V. Impediments to global surveillance of infectious diseases: consequences of open reporting in a global economy. *Bull WHO.* 2000;78:1358–1367.

16. Gostin L. O. Pandemic influenza: public health preparedness for the next global health emergency. *J. Law Med Ethics.* 2004;32:565–573.

17. Gear J. S., Cassel G. A., Gear A. J., et al. Outbreake of Marburg virus disease in Johannesburg. *BMJ* 1975;4:489–493.

18. Johnson K. M., Lange J. V., Webb P. A., Murphy F. A. Isolation and partial characterisation of a new virus causing acute haemorrhagic fever in Zaire. *Lancet.* 1977;1:569–571.

19. Frame J. D., Baldwin J. M. Jr, Gocke D. J., Troup J. M. Lassa fever, a new virus disease of man from West Africa: I. Clinical description and pathological findings. *Am J Trop Med Hyg.* 1970;19:670–676.

20. Ramamurthy T., Garg S., Sharma R., et al. Emergence of novel strain of *Vibrio cholerae* with epidemic potential in southern and eastern India. *Lancet*. 1993; 341:703–704.

21. Sharp P. M., Bailes E., Chaudhuri R. R., Rodenburg C. M., Santiago M. O., Hahn BH. The origins of acquired immune deficiency syndrome viruses: where and when? *Philos Trans R Soc Lond B Biol Sci*. 2001;356:867–876.

22. Mandl K. D., Overhage J. M., Wagner M. M., et al. Implementing syndromic surveillance: a practical guide informed by the early experience. *J Am Med Inform Assoc*. 2004;11:141–150.

23. ART on the frontline PlusNews Special. Cote D'Ivoire: Access to HIV/AIDS treatment in rebel north precarious. *Irin News*. January 9, 2007.

24. Van Herp M., Parque V., Rackley E., Ford N. Mortality, violence and lack of access to healthcare in the Democratic Republic of Congo. *Disasters*. 2003;27:141–153.

25. Spiegel P. B. HIV behavioural surveillance surveys in conflict and post-conflict situations: A call for improvement. *Global Public Health*. 2006;1:147–156.

26. Chretien J. P., Blazes D. L., Coldren R. L., et al. The importance of militaries from developing countries in global infectious disease surveillance. *Bull WHO*. 2007;85:174–180.

27. Sharp T. W., Luz G. A., Gaydos J. C. Military support of relief: a cautionary review. In: Leaning J., Briggs S., M., Chen L. C., eds. *Humanitarian Crises: The Medical and Public Health Response*. Cambridge, MA: Harvard University Press;1999:273–291.

28. Torres-Slimming P. A., Mundaca C. C., Moran M., et al. Outbreak of cyclosporiasis at a naval base in Lima, Peru. *Am J Trop Med Hyg*. 2006;75:546–548.

29. Woodall J. Official versus unofficial outbreak reporting through the Internet. *Int J Med Inform*. 1997;47:31–34.

30. Heymann D. L., Rodier G. Global surveillance, national surveillance, and SARS. *Emerg Infect Dis*. 2004;10:173–175.

31. Mawudeku A., Blench M. Global Public Health Intelligence Network (GPHIN). 7th Conference of the Association for Machine Translation in the Americas. *www.mt-archive.info/MTS-2005-Mawudeku.pdf*. Accessed April 26, 2007.

32. Grein T. W., Kamara K. B., Rodier G., et al. Rumors of disease in the global village: outbreak verification. *Emerg Infect Dis*. 2000;6:97–102.

33. M'Ikanatha N. M., Rohn D. D., Robertson C., et al. Use of the internet to enhance infectious disease surveillance and outbreak investigation. *Biosecur Bioterror*. 2006;4:293–300.

34. Chase V. ProMED: a global early warning system for disease. *Environ Health Perspect*. 1996;104:699.

35. Hugh-Jones M. Global awareness of disease outbreaks: the experience of ProMED-mail. *Public Health Rep*. 2001;116 Suppl 2:27–31.

36. Woodall J., Calisher C. H. ProMED-mail: background and purpose. *Emerg Infect Dis*. 2001;7(3 Suppl):563.

37. Madoff L. C., Woodall J. P. The internet and the global monitoring of emerging diseases: lessons from the first 10 years of ProMED-mail. *Arch Med Res*. 2005;36:724–730.

38. Mykhalovskiy E., Weir L. The Global Public Health Intelligence Network and early warning outbreak detection: a Canadian contribution to global public health. *Can J Public Health*. 2006;97:42–44.

39. Brownstein J. S., Freifeld C. HealthMap: Global Disease Alert Map. *www. healthmap.org*. Accessed August 29, 2007.

40. Larkin M. Technology and public health: Healthmap tracks global diseases. *Lancet Infect Dis*. 2007;7:91.

41. Health Threats Unit at Directorate General Health and Consumer Affairs of the European Commission. MedISys (Medical Intelligence System), *http://medusa. jrc.it*. Accessed September 14, 2007.

42. Tolentino H. Scanning the Emerging Infectious Diseases Horizon: Visualizing ProMED Emails Using EpiSPIDER. Paper presented at International Society for Disease Surveillance Annual Conference; Baltimore, 2006.

43. Keystone J. S., Kozarsky P. E., Freedman D. O. Internet and computer-based resources for travel medicine practitioners. *Clin Infect Dis*. 2001;32:757–765.

44. Brodie M., Flournoy R. E., Altman D. E., Blendon R. J., Benson J. M., Rosenbaum M. D. Health information, the Internet, and the digital divide. *Health Aff (Millwood)*. 2000;19:255–265.

45. Bhatnagar S., Schaware R. *Information and Communication Technology in Development: Cases from India*. Thousand Oaks, CA: Sage Publications; 2000.

46. Arita I., Nakane M., Kojima K., Yoshihara N., Nakano T., El-Gohary A. Role of a sentinel surveillance system in the context of global surveillance of infectious diseases. *Lancet Infect Dis*. 2004;4:171–177.

47. Guerin P. J., Grais R. F., Rottingen J. A., Valleron A. J. Using European travellers as an early alert to detect emerging pathogens in countries with limited laboratory resources. *BMC Public Health*. 2007;7:8.

48. Bloom B. R. Lessons from SARS. *Science*. 2003;300:701.

49. Deodhar N. S., Yemul V. L., Banerjee K. Plague that never was: a review of the alleged plague outbreaks in India in 1994. *J Public Health Policy*. 1998;19:184–199.

50. Fidler D. P. Emerging trends in international law concerning global infectious disease control. *Emerg Infect Dis*. 2003;9:285–290.

51. Schuklenk U., Gartland K. M. Confronting an influenza pandemic: ethical and scientific issues. *Biochem Soc Trans*. 2006;34 (Pt 6):1151–1154.

52. Butler D. Disease surveillance needs a revolution. *Nature*. 2006;440:6–7.

53. Beyrer C., Suwanvanichkij V., Mullany L. C., et al. Responding to AIDS, tuberculosis, malaria, and emerging infectious diseases in Burma: dilemmas of policy and practice. *PLoS Med*. 2006;3:e393.

54. Koh H. Why do nations obey international law? *Yale Law J*. 1997;106:2599–2659.

55. Fidler D. P. Globalization, international law, and emerging infectious diseases. *Emerg Infect Dis*. 1996;2:77–84.

56. Tanne J. H. Tuberculosis case exposes flaws in international public health systems. *BMJ*. 2007;334:1187.

82

INTERNATIONAL ORGANISATIONS AND THEIR ROLE IN HELPING TO PROTECT THE WORLDWIDE COMMUNITY AGAINST NATURAL AND INTENTIONAL BIOLOGICAL DISASTERS

B. Vallat, J. Pinto and A. Schudel

Source: *Revue Scientifique et Technique*, 25:1 (2006), 163–72.

Summary

Preventing the spread of disease through international movements is one of the key objectives of the World Organisation for Animal Health (OIE). One of the ways it seeks to achieve this is by publishing international standards and guidelines aimed at, *inter alia*, preventing the importation of pathogens that are dangerous for animals and humans and strengthening Veterinary Services so that they can improve their surveillance and response systems. The OIE works in close partnership with the Food and Agriculture Organization of the United Nations (FAO), and together the two organisations have developed a joint initiative – the Global Framework for the Progressive Control of Transboundary Animal Diseases (GF-TADs). Member Countries of these organisations could increase their capacity to manage the risks of disease occurrences, whether natural or deliberately introduced, if they would all strictly implement existing OIE international standards. Compliance with these standards greatly depends on the political willingness of national policy-makers and on a successful transfer of resources to developing countries in support of good governance and appropriate policy implementation. A United Nations Resolution obliging its Member Countries to implement OIE standards could prove invaluable in this respect.

Introduction

Preventing the spread of animal diseases and zoonoses through international movements is one of the key objectives of both the World Organisation for Animal Health (OIE) and the Food and Agriculture Organization of the United Nations (FAO). The OIE seeks to accomplish this by establishing international standards and guidelines aimed at preventing the importation of pathogens that are dangerous for animals and humans (while avoiding unjustified sanitary barriers) and through the surveillance, notification and control of diseases.

The OIE was founded in 1924, well before the creation of the United Nations. Initially, 28 countries united with a mandate to share information on animal disease outbreaks to allow Member Countries to take the appropriate control measures to protect themselves and to prevent further spread of the disease. There are now 167 OIE Member Countries. Providing a mechanism for prompt reporting of disease outbreaks/occurrences is still one of the primary roles of the OIE, but the organisation is also recognised as the international standard-setting agency in the area of animal health. OIE standards include:

– procedures for surveillance and prompt reporting of outbreaks of animal diseases and zoonoses
– requirements to be met by Veterinary Services for surveillance, notification, early warning and response, and the chain of command
– requirements that should be met for a country or zone to be defined as free from certain infectious animal diseases and zoonoses
– recommendations for the safe importation of animals, animal products, semen, and embryos
– procedures for the inactivation of infectious agents
– the general provisions that countries should meet reduce the risk of the spread of infectious animal diseases and zoonoses, including standards on the quality of national Veterinary Services.

These standards are included in various OIE publications, such as the *Terrestrial Animal Health Code* (*Terrestrial Code*), the *Aquatic Animal Health Code* (*Aquatic Code*), the *Manual of Diagnostic Tests and Vaccines for Terrestrial Animals* (*Terrestrial Manual* [3]) and the *Manual of Diagnostic Tests for Aquatic Animals* (the *Aquatic Manual* [2]), the contents of which will be described in more detail later.

The FAO is one of the largest of the specialised United Nations Agencies, the mission of which is to develop agriculture, animal production, fisheries and forestry. In the field of animal production, the FAO Animal Health Service focuses its activities on assisting developing country members to control infectious and parasitic diseases, and to prevent their spread to other countries or regions. Livestock are important in supporting the livelihoods of poor livestock keepers, consumers, traders, and labourers throughout the developing world. Diseases affecting livestock can have a significant impact on animal productivity and production, on trade in live animals, meat and other animal products, on human health (through diseases transmissible from animals to humans), and, consequently, on the overall process of economic development. The activities of the FAO Animal Health Service include the provision of relevant and up-to-date information on:

– selected animal and zoonotic diseases
– the means of, and basic requirements for, the control and management of major animal diseases
– the increasingly important area of safeguarding humans from diseases originating from livestock and/or transmitted through the consumption of animal products.

More recently, the OIE and FAO have been strongly committed to convincing national policy-makers and international donors that the cost of strengthening Veterinary Services so that they can provide better surveillance, early warning systems and management of epizootics, including zoonoses, is negligible compared with the economic losses resulting from the accidental or intentional introduction of infectious animal diseases and zoonoses.

This paper briefly describes the shared objectives of the two organisations before discussing the systems they have in place to achieve these aims and providing details of the standard-setting work of the OIE.

Common objectives of the OIE and the FAO

The OIE and FAO have certain key objectives in their work for the prevention and control of infectious animal diseases and zoonoses; these main areas of activity are discussed below.

Transparency in the animal disease situation worldwide

Each OIE Member Country is committed to providing reports to the OIE Animal Health Information Department on its health status regarding significant animal diseases and diseases transmissible to humans; the OIE then disseminates the information to all Member Countries to enable them to take appropriate action and to protect themselves. The FAO stipulates that notification to the OIE is obligatory and provides tools for data capture and reporting. Non-member countries are encouraged to report.

Collection, analysis and dissemination of veterinary scientific information

Using the FAO network and its own network of internationally recognised scientists, Collaborating Centres and Reference Laboratories, the OIE collects, analyses and publishes the latest scientific information on the control and prevention of important animal diseases, including those transmissible to humans. The FAO serves as a source of expert advice to OIE groups and committees.

Strengthening of international coordination and cooperation in the control of animal diseases

The FAO implements and/or contributes to the implementation of country or regional projects and programmes to prevent and control animal diseases by strengthening capacities and emergency preparedness for disease detection, analysis, and reaction. With OIE support, the FAO provides technical expertise to Member Countries (particularly developing countries) requesting assistance with animal disease control and eradication programmes. These activities are performed in coordination with other regional and international organisations, donor countries, and agencies responsible for supporting and funding the control of infectious animal diseases and zoonoses.

World trade in animals and animal products: protecting animal and human health while avoiding unjustified sanitary barriers

The OIE develops standards for use by its Member Countries to enable them to protect themselves against disease incursions as a result of trade in animals and animal products, while avoiding unjustified sanitary barriers. These standards are developed by experts from the Member Countries and from the OIE network of 170 Collaborating Centres and Reference Laboratories and in collaboration with FAO and FAO/IAEA (International Atomic Energy Agency) Joint Division experts.

In 1995 the standards developed by the OIE were recognised by the Agreement on the Application of Sanitary and Phytosanitary Measures (SPS Agreement) of the World Trade Organization (WTO). In order to harmonise SPS measures and remove unjustifiable sanitary restrictions to international trade, the Agreement states that Governments should use these international standards, guidelines and recommendations. Its goal is to minimise the risk of importing pathogens and to remove unjustified restrictions to international trade. The Agreement states that while it is the sovereign right of a country to provide an appropriate level of animal and public health protection at its borders, this right is not to be misused for protectionist purposes. An importing country can only apply sanitary measures to imports if a similar level of protection is applied internally and to all imports. Members Countries may introduce standards providing a higher level of protection than that provided by the OIE standards if there is a scientific justification, but these standards must be based on science-based risk analysis.

The FAO is in charge of assisting its Member Countries, particularly the developing countries, to implement international animal health standards.

It has undertaken several studies on the cost of complying with the standards established by world bodies and has developed mid- and long-term policy options that countries can use to implement such standards. Moreover, the FAO is committed to developing a systems approach, through national capacity building and performance indicators, to assist countries to attain compliance and improve trade opportunities.

Towards greater transparency in the animal health situation worldwide

The OIE is the worldwide observatory for animal health. It is supported in this mandate by the FAO. Its key mission is to keep national Veterinary Services and international organisations informed of the appearance and course of epizootics in any country in the world that represent a threat to animal or public health (zoonoses). The system is based on official animal disease information reports that the Veterinary Services of Member Countries have an obligation to submit to the OIE. The use of standard reporting forms ensures that the system is fed with the required data in a standardised format. The strength of the OIE Animal Disease Information System is its 'legal' basis as defined in Chapters 1.1.2 and 1.1.3 of the OIE *Terrestrial Code* and in Chapters 1.1.3 and 1.2.1 of the OIE *Aquatic Code* (6, 7).

The OIE Animal Health Information System has procedures for gathering weekly, annual and biannual animal health data from around the world (the International Monitoring System) and procedures for collecting more urgent information (the International Early Warning System). The International Early Warning System consists of an alert procedure to warn of exceptional epidemiological events (natural or intentional) occurring in Member Countries. Information is aimed at decisionmakers and other stakeholders to enable them to take necessary preventive measures. Under this system, the occurrence of a disease, including zoonoses, or any exceptional epidemiological event must be reported as soon as possible (within 24 hours) to the OIE Central Bureau, which then quickly redistributes the information through a variety of channels. Follow-up reports are provided weekly to allow end-users to follow the epidemiological situation as it develops.

To improve the transparency of animal health information, the OIE is also working with the FAO to develop a verification procedure for non-official information from various sources on the existence of disease outbreaks that have not yet been officially notified to the OIE. These processes use different sources of information such as diagnostic results from OIE or FAO Reference Laboratories, scientific papers, field projects, newspapers, the internet, Global Public Health Intelligence (GPHIN), and ProMed.

In addition, in order to improve the control of highly contagious diseases, the FAO and OIE have recently developed a new initiative: the Global Framework for the Progressive Control of Transboundary Animal Diseases

(GF-TADs), which is based on a regional approach to animal disease control. The GF-TADs will improve both the quality and quantity of disease information and epidemiological intelligence. An integral aspect of the GF-TADs programme is the Global Early Warning System (GLEWS), which is due to be developed jointly by the FAO, the OIE and the World Health Organization (WHO) as an instrument to assist stakeholders and the international community to predict and prevent livestock animal disease threats through epidemiological analysis and the integration of additional factors that may have an impact on the occurrence and spread of such diseases (e.g. economic factors, civil unrest, climatic changes). The success of this initiative will rely heavily on the sharing of information on animal health and zoonoses in humans among the three organisations. Results of disease information tracking systems will be shared and compared for verification purposes. Through its own Animal Disease Information System the OIE will verify information with the Government representatives of the various Member Countries, thus significantly improving the quality of official information. Similarly, the FAO, through projects and activities in its Member Countries, will also verify the reliability of information and work towards improving transparency. The WHO will also share information gathered by its Global Alert and Response Team and other parties working in the area of zoonotic diseases and veterinary public health.

The expected activities of the GLEWS can be summarised as follows:

– use of designated OIE/FAO Collaborating Centres/Reference Laboratories for specific analysis and modelling trends;
– dissemination of information that complements the OIE Information System;
– dissemination of early warning messages that concentrate on predicting livestock animal disease threats through epidemiological analysis and the integration of additional factors that may have an impact on the occurrence and spread of such diseases;
– design of control strategies;
– development of coordinated responses to animal health and zoonotic emergencies. If consultation among the OIE and FAO shows that an onsite assessment of the situation would be valuable, an urgent field mission may be considered, in consultation with the WHO when relevant. This joint mission would engage the country authorities, especially those of the Ministries of Health and of Agriculture, to obtain a better appreciation of the situation and offer assistance in the formulation of urgent intervention strategies. The joint mission experts would be responsible for briefing supervisors and suggesting a course of action.

While every effort is being made to improve the OIE Animal Health Information System, the major difficulty encountered, as with any international activity, is the quality of the information received, especially information from countries where the Veterinary Services do not comply with OIE standards and do not have adequate resources (e.g. lack of trained veterinarians and epidemiologists, poor equipment and laboratory facilities, inadequate involvement of farmers and other stakeholders in national surveillance systems, and absence of disease control programmes and emergency preparedness plans). In such countries, potentially dangerous situations might go unnoticed or not be dealt with promptly, thereby increasing the risk of disease spreading to other countries.

The OIE has a limited source of emergency funds for use in rapidly assisting Member Countries faced with exceptional epidemiological situations. Typically, these funds are used to immediately send experts from OIE Reference Laboratories or Collaborating Centres to assess the epidemiological situation in the field, and advise national authorities and other international organisations.

The FAO has a well-defined mandate to provide assistance to countries in the field of animal health. One of the key tools it uses to achieve this is its Emergency Prevention System-Livestock (EMPRES-Livestock) programme, which became fully operational in 1994. This system promotes the containment and control of the most serious epizootic diseases of livestock (transboundary animal diseases – TADs), and their progressive elimination on a regional and ultimately a global basis, through international cooperation, involving early warning, early reaction, research, and coordination. EMPRES capitalises on the information provided by the Global Livestock Production and Health Atlas (GLiPHA: www.fao.org/ag/againfo/resources/en/glipha/default.html), which depicts animal population densities, production systems, soil use, and other quantitative information that aids in disease intelligence, ecological understanding, and the development of intervention measures. The EMPRES-Livestock programme focuses on the major epizootic diseases – rinderpest, avian influenza, contagious bovine pleuropneumonia, foot and mouth disease, peste des petits ruminants, Rift Valley fever, Newcastle disease, lumpy skin disease, classical swine fever, and African swine fever. Early warning messages with trend analyses and the potential implications of the disease are posted on the web and distributed via the EMPRES-Livestock mailing list. EMPRES provides training assistance to national epidemiologists and advises on the development of surveillance programmes in the least developed countries.

In the event of a disease emergency and at the request of an FAO Member Country EMPRES can intervene to assist in combating diseases through the FAO's Technical Cooperation Division. Currently, technical cooperation projects (TCPs) are ongoing in over 40 countries, some with regional approaches to disease surveillance and control. While efforts are being made to build capacities in some least-advanced countries, what has been achieved so far has to be further strengthened to better respond to the real needs of many countries, e.g. the need for assistance in improving their national surveillance and monitoring systems and in bringing their contingency plans up to an acceptable level. Furthermore, the available resources must be dramatically increased for tackling emergency situations and to avoid the spread of TADs to other countries.

The warning system operated by the OIE Central Bureau allows Member Countries to react rapidly if the need arises. Member Countries must report any of the following incidents to the OIE Central Bureau within 24 hours:

– the first outbreak of an OIE listed disease
– the re-occurrence of a listed disease following a report declaring that the outbreak has ended
– the first occurrence of a new strain of a pathogen
– the sudden and unexpected increase in the distribution, incidence, morbidity or mortality of a disease prevalent within the country
– an emerging disease with significant morbidity and mortality or zoonotic potential
– evidence of change in the epidemiology of a listed disease (including host range, pathogenicity, strain).

This information is immediately relayed to the other Member Countries as follows:

– by fax or e-mail to countries directly threatened
– through the weekly publication *Disease Information*, available on the OIE website or by mail using the OIE distribution list.

Subsequent to any of the above notifications, Member Countries should send weekly reports by fax or e-mail to provide further information on the evolution of the incident that justified urgent notification.

The FAO obtains additional information from its networks: extensive field activities, Reference Laboratories, rumour-tracking (e.g. GPHIN, ProMed). This information and the resulting analyses are communicated to Member Countries and the OIE either directly or through various channels (FAO-AGA website, EMPRES Bulletin, etc.). As previously mentioned in the above discussion of the GLEWS, a cooperative approach to the information systems is currently being developed between the OIE, FAO and WHO.

These warning systems will provide an improved worldwide surveillance network for the early detection and rapid reporting of any suspicious disease occurrence that is natural or could have its origin in an act of agroterrorism/ bioterrorism, i.e. an intentional introduction of pathogens.

Through the International Early Warning System all OIE Member Countries receive alert messages on disease outbreaks, or suspicion thereof, via fax or e-mail. In addition, the OIE annual publication entitled *World Animal Health* provides a wide variety of information on the animal health situation world-wide and reports on the disease control methods Member Countries apply. A selection of all this information is integrated into the World Animal Health Information Database (WAHID) – a regularly updated computerised database available on the OIE website (www.oie.int).

Scientific information is disseminated through other publications, including the OIE *Scientific and Technical Review* (and similar FAO publications), which contains research articles and guidelines of the very highest standard for animal disease control. The FAO also publishes manuals on specific disease recognition, guides on contingency planning, participatory approaches to epidemiology, and booklets on sample collection and submission.

By collecting, processing and disseminating data on animal diseases through-out the world, the OIE and FAO endeavour to ensure transparency in the animal health situation worldwide for the benefit of its Member Countries. The information thus generated is essential for the success of national and regional disease control programmes, for reducing the health risks arising from international movements, and for the early detection of disease attributable to the escape or deliberate introduction of pathogens from acts of bioterrorism.

Towards improved health safeguards in international trade

The smooth flow of animals and animal products requires:

- the development and adoption by the international community of animal health standards aimed at avoiding the risk of importing and spreading diseases and pathogens transmissible to animals and humans
- the harmonisation, strict implementation, and greater transparency of national animal health regulations applicable to trade in animals and their products so as to avoid unjustified sanitary barriers.

OIE standards

The WTO Agreement on the Application of Sanitary and Phytosanitary Measures advocates the use of standards developed under the auspices of the OIE. Various normative works, approved by the OIE International Committee (the OIE's highest authority; every Member Country is represented), are designed to promote the harmonisation of regulations applicable to trade and animal disease control, these are:

- the *Terrestrial Code*
- the *Aquatic Code*
- the *Terrestrial Manual*
- the *Aquatic Manual.*

The *Terrestrial Code* for mammals, birds and bees is developed by the Terrestrial Animal Health Standards Commission, and the *Aquatic Code* is developed by the Aquatic Animal Health Standards Commission (see section entitled Specialist Commissions). The *Codes* contain the requirements for the international movement of animals and animal products and also provide guidelines for disease reporting (see chapters 1.1.2 and 1.1.3 of the *Terrestrial Code* and chapters 1.1.3 and 1.2.1 of the *Aquatic Code* [6, 7]). Both these publications are updated annually and are available in paper and electronic versions (www.oie.int).

The *Terrestrial Manual*, developed by the Biological Standards Commission, and the *Aquatic Manual*, developed by the Aquatic Animal Health Standards Commission, presents standard methods for diagnostic tests and vaccine production to be applied notably in the context of international trade and national animal disease control programmes. Both texts constitute the reference standards for the international harmonisation of the diagnosis of animal diseases and vaccine control; they also contain specific chapters on the following topics:

- sampling methods
- the packaging and transport of samples
- quality management and the biosecurity of veterinary laboratories
- tests for sterility and freedom from contaminants
- human safety in the veterinary microbiology laboratory
- veterinary vaccine production
- disinfection and inactivation procedures
- laboratory methodologies for bacterial antimicrobial susceptibility testing.

In addition to the standards that appear in the *Manuals* the OIE publication *Quality Standard and Guidelines for Veterinary Laboratories: Infectious Diseases* (1) describes standards for the management and biosecurity of laboratories conducting tests for infectious diseases. It contains technical requirements for these laboratories and includes specific details with respect to test method validation, reference reagents, and laboratory proficiency testing.

The FAO plays a prominent role in providing expertise to the OIE and assisting countries to meet OIE standards through various activities such as national expert capacity building, field projects, and the transfer of technologies and expertise.

OIE activities

As well as publishing standards and disseminating disease information reported by Member Countries, the OIE now takes a proactive approach to disease reporting and will also report information on confirmed positive results provided by OIE Reference Laboratories (4) or from unofficial sources, such as scientific publications, ProMed and lay publications, after the information has been verified by the Member Country.

In addition to reporting disease occurrence the OIE, through the work of the Scientific Commission for Animal Diseases, develops and updates lists of countries recognised as being free from some serious diseases, most notably foot and mouth disease, bovine spongiform encephalopathy, rinderpest and contagious bovine pleuropneumonia. These lists make a substantial contribution to the health security of international movements.

Towards objective and impartial expertise in animal health

The International Agreement of 25 January 1924 establishing the OIE made it responsible for promoting and co-ordinating research on the surveillance and control of animal diseases throughout the world. This objective has been attained by the creation of a worldwide animal health network, involving the establishment of Specialist Commissions and Working Groups, the designation of Collaborating Centres and Reference Laboratories, the organisation of meetings of experts and the continuing publication of scientific articles.

Specialist commissions

The four Specialist Commissions study problems of animal disease surveillance and control and questions relating to the harmonisation of international regulations. Members are elected by the representatives of all OIE Member Countries (the International Committee).

The Terrestrial Animal Health Standards Commission contributes to the development, in collaboration with other Specialist Commissions, of the generic and specific chapters in the *Terrestrial Code*. In addition, it promotes the adoption by the International Committee of standards on animal health (including zoonoses), animal welfare, and animal production food safety. It also promotes harmonised surveillance methods and disease control regulations and proposes guidelines and recommendations concerning the trade or international movement of mammals, birds and bees and their products.

The Scientific Commission for Animal Diseases contributes to the development of better strategies and methods for animal disease surveillance and control. The Commission convenes groups of specialists of the highest standard, particularly in the event of an animal health emergency, to verify or evaluate the status of Member Countries in terms of specific animal diseases.

The Biological Standards Commission harmonises methods for the diagnosis of animal diseases and the control of biological products, especially vaccines used for veterinary purposes. The Commission coordinates a programme to develop standard reagents aimed at standardising diagnosis.

The Aquatic Animal Health Standards Commission collects all available information on disease control methods for fish, molluscs and crustaceans.

The Commission harmonises rules governing trade in aquaculture products and recommends the optimum diagnostic methods. It also organises scientific meetings on these topics.

All the standards proposed by the various specialist Commissions must be approved by the International Committee before publication. All the standards, recommendations and guidelines of the OIE relating to animal health, zoonoses and international trade in animals and animal products are recognised by the WTO.

OIE reference laboratories and collaborating centres

These OIE Reference Laboratories and Collaborating Centres, of which there are 170, covering 92 diseases and topics and located in 31 different countries, provide OIE Member Countries with support and scientific advice on all matters relating to the surveillance and control of animal diseases. This support can take many forms, such as the provision of experts (over 150 world-renowned scientists), the preparation and supply of diagnostic kits or standard reagents, and the organisation of seminars, courses, and scientific meetings.

Working groups

Three OIE Working Groups are currently active:

– wildlife diseases
– animal welfare
– animal production food safety.

These Working Groups meet to review progress made in their field and to ensure that the information is made available rapidly to all OIE Member Countries. They also contribute to the organisation of scientific meetings, seminars, workshops and training courses.

The OIE Working Group most concerned with biosafety and biosecurity is the Working Group on Wildlife Diseases (WGWD). This Group collects information on wildlife diseases from Member Countries and urges Member Countries to recognise the importance of wild animals as potential reservoirs (and even as possible targets of deliberately introduced biological agents) when planning responses to outbreaks of disease, exotic or otherwise.

The WGWD has determined that relatively few countries have developed plans for responding to any disease incursions that may affect wild animals. In order to assist OIE Member Countries that may wish to undertake such planning, the WGWD will, in the course of the next 3 years, review preparedness and response plans that already may have been prepared. From these plans the Group will identify the essential major components and information requirements for this planning.

National preparedness for the possible incursion of exotic diseases must include both the preparedness of all the relevant public authorities and stakeholders to intervene and the assembly of up-to-date information on the population size, demography and susceptibility of indigenous wild animal species. It should also include the development of feasible procedures for the early recognition and diagnosis of a disease outbreak, the subsequent prevention of disease transmission between wildlife and domestic livestock and the spread of disease within wild animal populations. Effective planning for responses to an exotic disease incursion must accord to wildlife the same degree of attention that is now given solely to domestic livestock. A national consultative network of wildlife expertise needs to be created and deployed in order to develop a range of techniques that can be used to reduce the risk of transmission of disease from livestock to wildlife (and *vice versa*) in the event of an exotic disease outbreak. These actions will establish the necessary databases, lines of communication and science-based plans to achieve a high level of preparedness to deal with an exotic disease incursion into a national wildlife population.

The OIE Working Group on Animal Production Food Safety, established between the OIE and high level representatives of the Codex Alimentarius Commission, is responsible for hazards to consumers that are likely to occur during animal production (on the farm). This Working Group also covers intentional actions likely to occur on a farm, e.g. the introduction of zoonotic agents.

During the 72nd General Session of the OIE International Committee in 2004, Member Countries recognised that zoonotic diseases are emerging and re-emerging with great frequency. They indicated their overwhelming support for a greater OIE role in confronting the challenges of such zoonoses. They also recognised the need to co-ordinate activities horizontally, among animal and public health officials and organisations, and vertically, through national, State, and local groups. For this purpose a Resolution (Resolution No. XXIX) was adopted during the 72nd General Session which encouraged further consideration of the OIE's thinking and commitment regarding emerging and re-emerging zoonoses; more specifically, it advocated the following:

- active consideration of this issue as part of the development of the fourth OIE strategic plan (2005–2010)
- the creation of an Ad hoc Group on Emerging Diseases which would work closely with members of the Working Group on Wildlife Diseases, the Working Group on Animal Production Food Safety, the Ad hoc Group on Epidemiology, OIE Reference Laboratories and other relevant bodies or experts (5).

There appears to be little possibility of preventing bioterrorist attacks on domestic animals and the subsequent spill-over into wildlife populations.

There is also the risk that wildlife could be the initial target of covert bio-attacks and that infection could then spread into contiguous domestic livestock. Consequently, interdisciplinary and international efforts to increase surveillance and identification of disease pathogens and improved mechanisms for interagency and intergovernmental co-operation and collaboration will be necessary to combat the threat of disease agents likely to be used as a bioweapon.

Conclusions

If they are correctly implemented the tools currently available through the OIE and FAO can do a lot to increase the ability of Member Countries and of the International Community to protect themselves against the threat of a bioterrorist incident. However, such protection depends on the diligence with which Member Countries follow the existing guidelines and recommendations. The livestock development programmes of the FAO Animal Production and Health Division include recommendations on animal production, health and policy, all of which are invaluable in preparing an effective response to a biological disaster. If these recommendations are implemented alongside OIE guidelines the better prepared a country can be. The OIE guidelines and the benefits they bring can be summarised as follows:

- the OIE standards designed to control disease and to prevent the accidental or intentional introduction of pathogens provide a basis for the harmonisation of national legislation
- the OIE guidelines relating to the biosecurity of laboratories (based on expertise provided from researchers in human and animal health), provide advice on the safe management of biological agents used in those laboratories
- the OIE guidelines, standards and recommendations (and EMPRES principles) relating to surveillance and prompt notification of diseases of domestic livestock and wild animals (including zoonoses) encourage transparency of disease information
- the OIE standards on the quality and evaluation of Veterinary Services can be used to improve the quality and efficiency of Member Countries Veterinary Services, thereby guaranteeing increased vigilance in disease monitoring and surveillance. Compliance with these standards leads to improved early warning and early detection systems, thus ensuring a timely and rapid response to any emergency.

It is plain therefore that effective global biosecurity can only be achieved if all OIE and FAO Member Countries conscientiously comply with the standards and guidelines of the OIE, effectively train stakeholders and ensure the availability of adequate human and material veterinary resources.

515

Many countries share a common concern about the natural occurrence or deliberate misuse of biological pathogens that can affect public health, food and animal production. Existing methods of disease prevention and containment, regulations, international guidelines and standards are being extended at both national and international levels to improve the ability of countries to prevent, manage and recover from natural, accidental or deliberate introduction of animal diseases. In this regard there are, at present, substantial differences among countries in the perception of national threat from the deliberate use of pathogenic biological agents. However, significant progress would be made if all Member Countries would strictly implement existing OIE international standards. This is dependent on the political willingness of all national policy-makers and the transfer of resources from developed countries to developing countries in order to support good governance and appropriate policies based on the implementation of existing standards. A Resolution on this voted by the United Nations would provide great support in this respect.

References

1. World Organisation for Animal Health (OIE) (2002). – OIE Quality Standard and Guidelines for Veterinary Laboratories: Infectious Diseases, 1st Ed. OIE, Paris.
2. World Organisation for Animal Health (OIE) (2003). – OIE Manual of Diagnostic Tests for Aquatic Animals, 4th Ed. OIE, Paris.
3. World Organisation for Animal Health (OIE) (2004). – OIE Manual of Diagnostic Tests and Vaccines for Terrestrial Animals, 5th Ed. OIE, Paris.
4. World Organisation for Animal Health (OIE) (2004). – Resolution XXVIII: Proposed change to the mandate for OIE Reference Laboratories. In Proc. 72nd General Session of the OIE International Committee, 23–28 May 2004, Paris. OIE, Paris, 149–150.
5. World Organisation for Animal Health (OIE) (2004). – Resolution XXIX: Emerging and re-emerging zoonotic diseases – challenges and opportunities. In Proc. 72nd General Session of the OIE International Committee, 23–28 May 2004, Paris. OIE, Paris, 151–152.
6. World Organisation for Animal Health (OIE) (2005). – OIE Aquatic Animal Health Code, 8th Ed. OIE, Paris.
7. World Organisation for Animal Health (OIE) (2005). – OIE Terrestrial Animal Health Code, 14th Ed. OIE, Paris.
8. World Organisation for Animal Health (OIE) (2005). – Report of the meeting of the OIE Working Group on Wildlife Diseases, 14–16 February 2005. In Proc. 73rd General Session of the OIE International Committee, 22–27 May 2005, Paris. OIE, Paris (73 SG/13/GT).

83

THE WORLD HEALTH ORGANIZATION AND THE TRANSITION FROM "INTERNATIONAL" TO "GLOBAL" PUBLIC HEALTH

Theodore M. Brown, Marcos Cueto and Elizabeth Fee

Source: *American Journal of Public Health*, 96:1 (2006), 62–72.

The term "global health" is rapidly replacing the older terminology of "international health." We describe the role of the World Health Organization (WHO) in both international and global health and in the transition from one to the other. We suggest that the term "global health" emerged as part of larger political and historical processes, in which WHO found its dominant role challenged and began to reposition itself within a shifting set of power alliances.

Between 1948 and 1998, WHO moved from being the unquestioned leader of international health to being an organization in crisis, facing budget shortfalls and diminished status, especially given the growing influence of new and powerful players. We argue that WHO began to refashion itself as the coordinator, strategic planner, and leader of global health initiatives as a strategy of survival in response to this transformed international political context.

Even a quick glance at the titles of books and articles in recent medical and public health literature suggests that an important transition is under way. The terms "global," "globalization," and their variants are everywhere, and in the specific context of international public health, "global" seems to be emerging as the preferred authoritative term.[1] As one indicator, the number of entries in PubMed under the rubrics "global health" and "international health" shows that "global health" is rapidly on the rise, seemingly on track to overtake "international health" in the near future (Table 1). Although universities, government agencies, and private philanthropies are all using the term in highly visible ways,[2] the origin and meaning of the term "global health" are still unclear.

We provide historical insight into the emergence of the terminology of global health. We believe that an examination of this linguistic shift will yield important fruit, and not just information about fashions and fads in language use. Our task here is to provide a critical analysis of the meaning, emergence, and significance of the term "global health" and to place its growing popularity in a broader historical context. In particular, we focus on the role of the World Health Organization (WHO) in both international and global health and as an agent in the transition from one concept to the other.

Let us first define and differentiate some essential terms. "International health" was already a term of considerable currency in the late 19th and early 20th century, when it referred primarily to a focus on the control of epidemics across the boundaries between nations (i.e., "international"). "Intergovernmental" refers to the relationships between the governments of sovereign nations—in this case, with regard to the policies and practices of public health. "Global health," in general, implies consideration of the health needs of the people of the whole planet above the concerns of particular nations. The term "global" is also associated with the growing importance of actors beyond governmental or intergovernmental organizations and agencies—for example, the media, internationally influential foundations, nongovernmental organizations, and transnational corporations. Logically, the terms "international," "intergovernmental," and "global" need not be mutually exclusive and in fact can be understood as complementary. Thus, we could say that WHO is an intergovernmental agency that exercises international functions with the goal of improving global health.

Table 1 Number of articles retrieved by PubMed, using "International Health" and "Global Health" as search terms, by decade: 1950 through July 2005.

Decade	International Health[a]	Global Health[a]
1950s	1 007	54
1960s	3 303	155
1970s	8 369	1 137
1980s	16 924	7 176
1990s	49 158	27 794
2000–July 2005	52 169[b]	39 759[b]

[a]Picks up variant term endings (e.g. "international" also picks up "internationalize" and "internationalization"; "global" also picks up "globalize" and "globalization").
[b]Number for 55 months only.

Given these definitions, it should come as no surprise that global health is not entirely an invention of the past few years. The term "global" was sometimes used well before the 1990s, as in the "global malaria eradication program" launched by WHO in the mid-1950s; a WHO Public Affairs Committee pamphlet of 1958, *The World Health Organization: Its Global Battle Against Disease*[3]; a 1971 report for the US House of Representatives entitled *The Politics of Global Health*[4]; and many studies of the "global population problem" in the 1970s.[5] But the term was generally limited and its use in official statements and documents sporadic at best. Now there is an increasing frequency of references to global health.[6] Yet the questions remain: How many have participated in this shift in terminology? Do they consider it trendy, trivial, or trenchant?

Supinda Bunyavanich and Ruth B. Walkup tried to answer these questions and published, under the provocative title "US Public Health Leaders Shift Toward a New Paradigm of Global Health," their report of conversations conducted in 1999 with 29 "international health leaders."[7] Their respondents fell into 2 groups. About half felt that there was no need for a new terminology and that the label "global health" was meaningless jargon. The other half thought that there were profound differences between international health and global health and that "global" clearly meant something transnational. Although these respondents believed that a major shift had occurred within the previous few years, they seemed unable clearly to articulate or define it.

In 1998, Derek Yach and Douglas Bettcher came closer to capturing both the essence and the origin of the new global health in a 2-part article on "The Globalization of Public Health" in the *American Journal of Public Health*.[8] They defined the "new paradigm" of globalization as "the process of increasing economic, political, and social interdependence and integration as capital, goods, persons, concepts, images, ideas and values cross state boundaries." The roots of globalization were long, they said, going back at least to the 19th century, but the process was assuming a new magnitude in the late 20th century. The globalization of public health, they argued, had a dual aspect, one both promising and threatening.

In one respect, there was easier diffusion of useful technologies and of ideas and values such as human rights. In another, there were such risks as diminished social safety nets; the facilitated marketing of tobacco, alcohol, and psychoactive drugs; the easier worldwide spread of infectious diseases; and the rapid degradation of the environment, with dangerous public health consequences. But Yach and Bettcher were convinced that WHO could turn these risks into opportunities. WHO, they argued, could help create more efficient information and surveillance systems by strengthening its global monitoring and alert systems, thus creating "global early warning systems." They believed that even the most powerful nations would buy into this new globally interdependent world system once these nations realized that such involvement was in their best interest.

Despite the long list of problems and threats. Yach and Bettcher were largely uncritical as they promoted the virtues of global public health and the leadership role of WHO. In an editorial in the same issue of the Journal. George Silver noted that Yach and Bettcher worked for WHO and that their position was similar to other optimistic stances taken by WHO officials and advocates. But WHO, Silver pointed out, was actually in a bad way: "The WHO's leadership role has passed to the far wealthier and more influential World Bank, and the WHO's mission has been dispersed among other UN agencies." Wealthy donor countries were billions of dollars in arrears, and this left the United Nations and its agencies in "disarray, hamstrung by financial constraints and internal incompetencies, frustrated by turf wars and cross-national policies."[9] Given these -realities. Yach and Bettcher's promotion of "global public health" while they were affiliated with WHO was, to say the least, intriguing. Why were these spokes-men for the much-criticized and apparently hobbled WHO so upbeat about "global" public health?

The World Health Organization

The early years

To better understand Yach and Bettcher's role, and that of WHO more generally, it will be helpful to review the history of the organization from 1948 to 1998, as it moved from being the unquestioned leader of international health to searching for its place in the contested world of global health.

WHO formally began in 1948, when the first World Health Assembly in Geneva, Switzerland, ratified its constitution. The idea of a permanent institution for international health can be traced to the organization in 1902 of the International Sanitary Office of the American Republics, which, some decades later, became the Pan American Sanitary Bureau and eventually the Pan American Health Organization.[10] The Rockefeller Foundation, especially its International Health Division, was also a very significant player in international health in the early 20th century.[11]

Two European-based international health agencies were also important. One was the Office Internationale d'Hygiène Publique, which began functioning in Paris in 1907; it concentrated on several basic activities related to the administration of international sanitary agreements and the rapid exchange of epidemiological information.[12] The second agency, the League of Nations Health Organization, began its work in 1920.[13] This organization established its headquarters in Geneva, sponsored a series of international commissions on diseases, and published epidemiological intelligence and technical reports. The League of Nations Health Organization was poorly budgeted and faced covert opposition from other national and international organizations, including the US Public Health Service. Despite these complications, which limited the Health Organization's effectiveness, both the Office Internationale d'Hygiène

Publique and the Health Organization survived through World War II and were present at the critical postwar moment when the future of international health would be defined.

An international conference in 1945 approved the creation of the United Nations and also voted for the creation of a new specialized health agency. Participants at the meeting initially formed a commission of prominent individuals, among whom were René Sand from Belgium, Andrija Stampar from Yugoslavia, and Thomas Parran from the United States. Sand and Stampar were widely recognized as champions of social medicine. The commission held meetings between 1946 and early 1948 to plan the new international health organization. Representatives of the Pan American Sanitary Bureau, whose leaders resisted being absorbed by the new agency, were also involved, as were leaders of new institutions such as the United Nations Relief and Rehabilitation Administration (UNRRA).

Against this background, the first World Health Assembly met in Geneva in June 1948 and formally created the World Health Organization. The Office Internationale d'Hygiène Publique, the League of Nations Health Organization, and UNRRA merged into the new agency. The Pan American Sanitary Bureau—then headed by Fred L. Soper, a former Rockefeller Foundation official—was allowed to retain autonomous status as part of a regionalization scheme.[14] WHO formally divided the world into a series of regions—the Americas, Southeast Asia, Europe, Eastern Mediterranean, Western Pacific, and Africa—but it did not fully implement this regionalization until the 1950s. Although an "international" and "intergovernmental" mindset prevailed in the 1940s and 1950s, naming the new organization the *World* Health Organization also raised sights to a worldwide, "global" perspective.

The first director general of WHO, Brock Chisholm, was a Canadian psychiatrist loosely identified with the British social medicine tradition. The United States, a main contributor to the WHO budget, played a contradictory role: on the one hand, it supported the UN system with its broad worldwide goals, but on the other, it was jealous of its sovereignty and maintained the right to intervene unilaterally in the Americas in the name of national security. Another problem for WHO was that its constitution had to be ratified by nation states, a slow process: by 1949, only 14 countries had signed on.[15]

As an intergovernmental agency, WHO had to be responsive to the larger political environment. The politics of the Cold War had a particular salience, with an unmistakable impact on WHO policies and personnel. Thus, when the Soviet Union and other communist countries walked out of the UN system and therefore out of WHO in 1949, the United States and its allies were easily able to exert a dominating influence. In 1953, Chisholm completed his term as director general and was replaced by the Brazilian Marcolino Candau. Candau, who had worked under Soper on malaria control in Brazil was associated first with the "vertical" disease control programs of the Rockefeller Foundation and then with their adoption by the Pan American Sanitary

Bureau when Soper moved to that agency as director.[16] Candau would be director general of WHO for over 20 years. From 1949 until 1956, when the Soviet Union returned to the UN and WHO, WHO was closely allied with US interests.

In 1955, Candau was charged with overseeing WHO's campaign of malaria eradication, approved that year by the World Health Assembly. The ambitious goal of malaria eradication had been conceived and promoted in the context of great enthusiasm and optimism about the ability of widespread DDT spraying to kill mosquitoes. As Randall Packard has argued, the United States and its allies believed that global malaria eradication would usher in economic growth and create overseas markets for US technology and manufactured goods.[17] It would build support for local governments and their US supporters and help win "hearts and minds" in the battle against Communism. Mirroring then-current development theories, the campaign promoted technologies brought in from outside and made no attempt to enlist the participation of local populations in planning or implementation. This model of development assistance fit neatly into US Cold War efforts to promote modernization with limited social reform.[18]

With the return of the Soviet Union and other communist countries in 1956, the political balance in the World Health Assembly shifted and Candau accommodated the changed balance of power. During the 1960s, malaria eradication was facing serious difficulties in the field; ultimately, it would suffer colossal and embarrassing failures. In 1969, the World Health Assembly, declaring that it was not feasible to eradicate malaria in many parts of the world, began a slow process of reversal, returning once again to an older malaria control agenda. This time, however, there was a new twist; the 1969 assembly emphasized the need to develop rural health systems and to integrate malaria control into general health services.

When the Soviet Union returned to WHO, its representative at the assembly was the national deputy minister of health. He argued that it was now scientifically feasible, socially desirable, and economically worthwhile to attempt to eradicate smallpox worldwide.[19] The Soviet Union wanted to make its mark on global health, and Candau, recognizing the shifting balance of power, was willing to cooperate. The Soviet Union and Cuba agreed to provide 25 million and 2 million doses of freeze-dried vaccine, respectively; in 1959, the World Health Assembly committed itself to a global smallpox eradication program.

In the 1960s, technical improvements—jet injectors and bifurcated needles—made the process of vaccination much cheaper, easier, and more effective. The United States' interest in smallpox eradication sharply increased; in 1965, Lyndon Johnson instructed the US delegation to the World Health Assembly to pledge American support for an international program to eradicate smallpox from the earth.[20] At that time, despite a decade of marked progress, the disease was still endemic in more than 30 countries. In 1967, now with the support of the world's most powerful players, WHO launched the Intensified Smallpox Eradication Program. This program, an international effort led by the American Donald A. Henderson, would ultimately be stunningly successful.[21]

The promise and perils of primary health care, 1973–1993

Within WHO, there have always been tensions between social and economic approaches to population health and technology- or disease-focused approaches. These approaches are not necessarily incompatible, although they have often been at odds. The emphasis on one or the other waxes and wanes over time, depending on the larger balance of power, the changing interests of international players, the intellectual and ideological commitments of key individuals, and the way that all of these factors interact with the health policymaking process.

During the 1960s and 1970s, changes in WHO were significantly influenced by a political context marked by the emergence of decolonized African nations, the spread of nationalist and socialist movements, and new theories of development that emphasized long-term socioeconomic growth rather than short-term technological intervention. Rallying within organizations such as the Non-Aligned Movement, developing countries created the UN Conference on Trade and Development (UNCTAD), where they argued vigorously for fairer terms of trade and more generous financing of development.[22] In Washington, DC, more liberal politics succeeded the conservatism of the 1950s, with the civil rights movement and other social movements forcing changes in national priorities.

This changing political environment was reflected in corresponding shifts within WHO. In the 1960s, WHO acknowledged that a strengthened health infrastructure was prerequisite to the success of malaria control programs, especially in Africa. In 1968, Candau called for a comprehensive and integrated plan for curative and preventive care services. A Soviet representative called for an organizational study of methods for promoting the development of basic health services.[23] In January 1971, the Executive Board of the World Health Assembly agreed to undertake this study, and its results were presented to the assembly in 1973.[24] Socrates Litsios has discussed many of the steps in the transformation of WHO's approach from an older model of health services to what would become the "Primary Health Care" approach.[25] This new model drew upon the thinking and experiences of nongovernmental organizations and medical missionaries working in Africa, Asia, and Latin America at the grassroots level. It also gained saliency from China's reentry into the UN in 1973 and the widespread interest in Chinese "barefoot doctors," who were reported to be transforming rural health conditions. These experiences underscored the urgency of a "Primary Health Care" perspective that included the training of community health workers and the resolution of basic economic and environmental problems.[26]

These new approaches were spearheaded by Halfdan T. Mahler, a Dane, who served as director general of WHO from 1973 to 1988. Under pressure from the Soviet delegate to the executive board, Mahler agreed to hold a major conference on the organization of health services in Alma-Ata, in the Soviet Union. Mahler was initially reluctant because he disagreed with the Soviet Union's highly centralized and medicalized approach to the provision of health services.[27] The Soviet Union succeeded in hosting the September 1978 conference, but the conference itself reflected Mahler's views much more closely than it did those of the Soviets. The Declaration of Primary Health Care and the goal of "Health for All in the Year 2000" advocated an "inter-sectoral" and multidimensional approach to health and socioeconomic development, emphasized the use of "appropriate technology," and urged active community participation in health care and health education at every level.[28]

David Tejada de Rivero has argued that "It is regrettable that afterward the impatience of some international agencies, both UN and private, and their emphasis on achieving tangible results instead of promoting change . . . led to major distortions of the original concept of primary health care."[29] A number of governments, agencies, and individuals saw WHO's idealistic view of Primary Health Care as "unrealistic" and unattainable. The process of reducing Alma-Ata's idealism to a practical set of technical interventions that could be implemented and measured more easily began in 1979 at a small conference—heavily influenced by US attendees and policies—held in Bellagio, Italy, and sponsored by the Rockefeller Foundation, with assistance from the World Bank. Those in attendance included the president of the World Bank, the vice president of the Ford Foundation, the administrator of USAID, and the executive secretary of UNICEF.[30]

The Bellagio meeting focused on an alternative concept to that articulated at Alma-Ata—"Selective Primary Health Care"—which was built on the notion of pragmatic, low-cost interventions that were limited in scope and easy to monitor and evaluate. Thanks primarily to UNICEF, Selective Primary Health Care was soon operationalized under the acronym "GOBI" (Growth monitoring to fight malnutrition in children, Oral rehydration techniques to defeat diarrheal diseases, Breastfeeding to protect children, and Immunizations).[31]

In the 1980s, WHO had to reckon with the growing influence of the World Bank. The bank had initially been formed in 1946 to assist in the reconstruction of Europe and later expanded its mandate to provide loans, grants, and technical assistance to developing countries. At first, it funded large investments in physical capital and infrastructure; in the 1970s, however, it began to invest in population control, health, and education, with an emphasis on population control.[32] The World Bank approved its first loan for family planning in 1970. In 1979, the World Bank created a Population, Health, and Nutrition Department and adopted a policy of funding both stand-alone health programs and health components of other projects.

In its 1980 *World Development Report*, the Bank argued that both malnutrition and ill health could be countered by direct government action—with World Bank assistance.[33] It also suggested that improving health and nutrition could accelerate economic growth, thus providing a good argument for social sector spending. As the Bank began to make direct loans for health services, it called for more efficient use of available resources and discussed the roles of the private and public sectors in financing health care. The Bank favored free markets and a diminished role for national governments.[34] In the context of widespread indebtedness by developing countries and increasingly scarce resources for health expenditures, the World Bank's promotion of "structural adjustment" measures at the very time that the HIV/AIDS epidemic erupted drew angry criticism but also underscored the Bank's new influence.

In contrast to the World Bank's increasing authority, in the 1980s the prestige of WHO was beginning to diminish. One sign of trouble was the 1982 vote by the World Health Assembly to freeze WHO's budget.[35] This was followed by the 1985 decision by the United States to pay only 20% of its assessed contribution to all UN agencies and to withhold its contribution to WHO's regular budget, in part as a protest against WHO's "Essential Drug Program," which was opposed by leading US-based pharmaceutical companies.[36] These events occurred amidst growing tensions between WHO and UNICEF and other agencies and the controversy over Selective versus Comprehensive Primary Health Care. As part of a rancorous public debate conducted in the pages of *Social Science and Medicine* in 1988, Kenneth Newell, a highly placed WHO official and an architect of Comprehensive Primary Health Care, called Selective Primary Health Care a "threat . . . [that] can be thought of as a counter-revolution."[37]

In 1988, Mahler's 15-year tenure as director general of WHO came to an end. Unexpectedly, Hiroshi Nakajima, a Japanese researcher who had been director of the WHO Western Pacific Regional Office in Manila, was elected new director general.[38]

Crisis at WHO, 1988–1998

The first citizen of Japan ever elected to head a UN agency, Nakajima rapidly became the most controversial director general in WHO's history. His nomination had not been supported by the United States or by a number of European and Latin American countries, and his performance in office did little to assuage their doubts. Nakajima did try to launch several important initiatives—on tobacco, global disease surveillance, and public—private partnerships—but fierce criticism persisted that raised questions about his autocratic style and poor management, his inability to communicate effectively, and, worst of all, cronyism and corruption.

Another symptom of WHO's problems in the late 1980s was the growth of "extrabudgetary" funding. As Gill Walt of the London School of Hygiene and Tropical Medicine noted, there was a crucial shift from predominant reliance on WHO's "regular budget"—drawn from member states' contributions on the basis of population size and gross national product—to greatly increased dependence on extrabudgetary funding coming from donations by multilateral agencies or "donor" nations.[39] By the period 1986–1987, extrabudgetary funds of $437 million had almost caught up with the regular budget of $543 million. By the beginning of the 1990s, extrabudgetary funding had overtaken the regular budget by $21 million, contributing 54% of WHO's overall budget.

Enormous problems for the organization followed from this budgetary shift. Priorities and policies were still ostensibly set by the World Health Assembly, which was made up of all member nations. The assembly, however, now dominated numerically by poor and developing countries, had authority only over the regular budget, frozen since the early 1980s. Wealthy donor nations and multilateral agencies like the World Bank could largely call the shots on the use of the extrabudgetary funds they contributed. Thus, they created, in effect, a series of "vertical" programs more or less independent of the rest of WHO's programs and decisionmaking structure. The dilemma for the organization was that although the extrabudgetary funds added to the overall budget "they [increased] difficulties of coordination and continuity, [caused] unpredictability in finance, and a great deal of dependence on the satisfaction of particular donors,"[40] as Gill Walt explained.

Fiona Godlee published a series of articles in 1994 and 1995 that built on Walt's critique.[41] She concluded with this dire assessment: "WHO is caught in a cycle of decline, with donors expressing their lack of faith in its central management by placing funds outside the management's control. This has prevented WHO from [developing] . . . integrated responses to countries' long term needs."[41]

In the late 1980s and early 1990s, the World Bank moved confidently into the vacuum created by an increasingly ineffective WHO. WHO officials were unable or unwilling to respond to the new international political economy structured around neoliberal approaches to economics, trade, and politics.[42] The Bank maintained that existing health systems were often wasteful, inefficient and ineffective, and it argued in favor of greater reliance on private-sector health care provision and the reduction of public involvement in health services delivery.[43]

Controversies surrounded the World Bank's policies and practices, but there was no doubt that, by the early 1990s, it had become a dominant force in international health. The Bank's greatest "comparative advantage" lay in its ability to mobilize large financial resources. By 1990, the Bank's loans for health surpassed WHO's total budget, and by the end of 1996, the Bank's cumulative lending portfolio in health, nutrition, and population had reached $13.5 billion. Yet the Bank recognized that, whereas it had great economic strengths and influence, WHO still had considerable technical expertise in matters of health and medicine. This was clearly reflected in the Bank's widely influential *World Development Report, 1993: Investing in Health*, in which credit is given to WHO, "a full partner with the World Bank at every step of the preparation of the Report."[44] Circumstances suggested that it was to the advantage of both parties for the World Bank and WHO to work together.

WHO embraces "global health"

This is the context in which WHO began to refashion itself as a coordinator, strategic planner, and leader of "global health" initiatives. In January 1992, the 31-member Executive Board of the World Health Assembly decided to appoint a "working group" to recommend how WHO could be most effective in international health work in light of the "global change" rapidly overtaking the world. The executive board may have been responding, in part, to the Children's Vaccine Initiative, perceived within WHO as an attempted "coup" by UNICEF, the World Bank, the UN Development Program, the Rockefeller Foundation, and several other players seeking to wrest control of vaccine development.[45] The working group's final report of May 1993 recommended that WHO—if it was to maintain leadership of the health sector—must overhaul its fragmented management of global, regional, and country programs, diminish the competition between regular and extrabudgetary programs, and, above all, increase the emphasis within WHO on global health issues and WHO's coordinating role in that domain.[46]

Until that time, the term "global health" had been used sporadically and, outside WHO, usually by people on the political left with various "world" agendas. In 1990, G. A. Gellert of International Physicians for the Prevention of Nuclear War had called for analyses of "global health interdependence."[47] In the same year, Milton and Ruth Roemer argued that further improvements in "global health" would be dependent on the expansion of public rather than private health services.[48] Another strong source for the term "global health" was the environmental movement, especially debates over world environmental degradation, global warming, and their potentially devastating effects on human health.[49]

In the mid-1990s, a considerable body of literature was produced on global health threats. In the United States, a new Centers for Disease Control and Prevention (CDC) journal, *Emerging Infectious Diseases*, began publication, and former CDC director William Foege started using the phrase "global infectious disease threats."[50] In 1997, the Institute of Medicine's Board of International Health released a report, *America's Vital Interest in Global Health: Protecting Our People, Enhancing Our Economy, and Advancing Our International Interests*.[51] In 1998, the CDC's *Preventing Emerging Infectious Diseases: A Strategy for the 21st Century* appeared, followed in 2001 by the Institute of Medicine's *Perspectives on the Department of Defense Global*

Emerging Infections Surveillance and Response System.[52] Best-selling books and news magazines were full of stories about Ebola and West Nile virus, resurgent tuberculosis, and the threat of bioterrorism.[53] The message was clear: there was a palpable global disease threat.

In 1998, the World Health Assembly reached outside the ranks of WHO for a new leader who could restore credibility to the organization and provide it with a new vision: Gro Harlem Brundtland, former prime minister of Norway and a physician and public health professional. Brundtland brought formidable expertise to the task. In the 1980s, she had been chair of the UN World Commission on Environment and Development and produced the "Brundtland Report," which led to the Earth Summit of 1992. She was familiar with the global thinking of the environmental movement and had a broad and clear understanding of the links between health, environment, and development.[54]

Brundtland was determined to position WHO as an important player on the global stage, move beyond ministries of health, and gain a seat at the table where decisions were being made.[55] She wanted to refashion WHO as a "department of consequence"[55] able to monitor and influence other actors on the global scene. She established a Commission on Macroeconomics and Health, chaired by economist Jeffrey Sachs of Harvard University and including former ministers of finance and officers from the World Bank, the International Monetary Fund, the World Trade Organization, and the UN Development Program, as well as public health leaders. The commission issued a report in December 2001, which argued that improving health in developing countries was essential to their economic development.[56] The report identified a set of disease priorities that would require focused intervention.

Brundtland also began to strengthen WHO's financial position, largely by organizing "global partnerships" and "global funds" to bring together "stakeholders"—private donors, governments, and bilateral and multilateral agencies —to concentrate on specific targets (for example, Roll Back Malaria in 1998, the Global Alliance for Vaccines and Immunization in 1999, and Stop TB in 2001). These were semiautonomous programs bringing in substantial outside funding, often in the form of "public–private partnerships."[57] A very significant player in these partnerships was the Bill & Melinda Gates Foundation, which committed more than $1.7 billion between 1998 and 2000 to an international program to prevent or eliminate diseases in the world's poorest nations, mainly through vaccines and immunization programs.[58] Within a few years, some 70 "global health partnerships" had been created.

Brundtland's tenure as director general was not without blemish nor free from criticism. Some of the initiatives credited to her administration had actually been started under Nakajima (for example, the WHO Framework Convention on Tobacco Control), others may be looked upon today with some skepticism (the Commission on Macroeconomics and Health, Roll Back Malaria), and still others arguably did not receive enough attention from her administration (Primary Health Care, HIV/AIDS, Health and Human Rights, and Child Health). Nonetheless, few would dispute the assertion that Brundtland succeeded in achieving her principal objective, which was to reposition WHO as a credible and highly visible contributor to the rapidly changing field of global health.

Conclusion

We can now return briefly to the questions implied at the beginning of this article: how does a historical perspective help us understand the emergence of the terminology of "global health" and what role did WHO play as an agent in its development? The basic answers derive from the fact that WHO at various times in its history alternatively led, reflected, and tried to accommodate broader changes and challenges in the ever-shifting world of international health. In the 1950s and 1960s, when changes in biology, economics, and great power politics transformed foreign relations and public health, WHO moved from a narrow emphasis on malaria eradication to a broader interest in the development of health services and the emerging concentration on smallpox eradication. In the 1970s and 1980s, WHO developed the concept of Primary Health Care but then turned from zealous advocacy to the pragmatic promotion of Selective Primary Health Care as complex changes overtook intra and interorganizational dynamics and altered the international economic and political order. In the 1990s, WHO attempted to use leadership of an emerging concern with "global health" as an organizational strategy that promised survival and, indeed, renewal.

But just as it did not invent the eradicationist or primary care agendas, WHO did not invent "global health"; other, larger forces were responsible. WHO certainly did help promote interest in global health and contributed significantly to the dissemination of new concepts and a new vocabulary. In that process, it was hoping to acquire, as Yach and Bettcher suggested in 1998, a restored coordinating and leadership role. Whether WHO's organizational repositioning will serve to reestablish it as the unquestioned steward of the health of the world's population, and how this mission will be effected in practice, remains an open question at this time.

Contributors

All authors contributed equally to the research and writing.

Acknowledgments

The authors are grateful to the Joint Learning Initiative of the Rockefeller Foundation, which initially commissioned this article, and to the Global

Health Histories Initiative of the World Health Organization, which has provided a supportive environment for continuing our research.

References

1. A small sampling of recent titles: David L. Heymann and G. R. Rodier, "Global Surveillance of Communicable Diseases," *Emerging Infectious Diseases* 4 (1998): 362–365; David Woodward, Nick Drager, Robert Beaglehole, and Debra Lipson, "Globalization and Health: A Framework for Analysis and Action," *Bulletin of the World Health Organization* 79 (2001): 875–881; Gill Walt, "Globalisation of International Health," *The Lancet* 351 (February 7, 1998): 434–437; Stephen J. Kunitz, "Globalization, States, and the Health of Indigenous Peoples," *American Journal of Public Health* 90 (2000): 1531–1539; *Health Policy in a Globalising World*, ed. Kelley Lee, Kent Buse, and Suzanne Fustukian (Cambridge, England: Cambridge University Press, 2002).

2. For example, Yale has a Division of Global Health in its School of Public Health, Harvard has a Center for Health and the Global Environment, and the London School of Hygiene and Tropical Medicine has a Center on Global Change and Health; the National Institutes of Health has a strategic plan on Emerging Infectious Diseases and Global Health; Gro Harlem Brundtland addressed the 35th Anniversary Symposium of the John E. Fogarty International Center on "Global Health: A Challenge to Scientists" in May 2003; the Centers of Disease Control and Prevention has established an Office of Global Health and has partnered with the World Health Organization (WHO), the World Bank, UNICEF, the US Agency for International Development, and others in creating Global Health Partnerships.

3. Albert Deutsch, *The World Health Organization: Its Global Battle Against Disease* (New York: Public Affairs Committee, 1958).

4. Randall M. Packard, " 'No Other Logical Choice': Global Malaria Eradication and the Politics of International Health in the Post-War Era," *Parassitologia* 40 (1998): 217–229, and *The Politics of Global Health, Prepared for the Subcommittee on National Security Policy and Scientific Developments of the Committee on Foreign Affairs, US House of Representatives* (Washington, DC: US Government Printing Office, 1971).

5. For example, T. W. Wilson, *World Population and a Global Emergency* (Washington, DC: Aspen Institute for Humanistic Studies, Program in Environment and Quality of Life, 1974).

6. James E. Banta, "From International to Global Health," *Journal of Community Health* 26 (2001): 73–76.

7. Supinda Bunyavanich and Ruth B. Walkup, "US Public Health Leaders Shift Toward a New Paradigm of Global Health," *American Journal of Public Health* 91 (2001): 1556–1558.

8. Derek Yach and Douglas Bettcher, "The Globalization of Public Health, I: Threats and Opportunities," *American Journal of Public Health* 88 (1998): 735–738, and "The Globalization of Public Health, II: The Convergence of Self-interest and Altruism," *American Journal of Public Health* 88 (1998): 738–741.

9. George Silver, "International Health Services Need an Interorganizational Policy," *American Journal of Public Health* 88 (1998): 727–729 (quote on p. 728).

530

10. *Pro Salute, Novi Mundi: Historia de la Organización Panamericana de la Solud* (Washington, DC: Organización Panamericana de la Salud, 1992).

11. See John Farley, *To Cast Out Disease: A History of the International Health Division of the Rockefeller Foundation* (1913–1951) (Oxford: Oxford University Press, 2003); Anne-Emmanuelle Birn, "Eradication, Control or Neither? Hookworm Versus Malaria Strategies and Rockefeller Public Health in Mexico," *Parassitologia* 40 (1996):137–147; *Missionaries of Science: Latin America and the Rockefeller Foundation*, ed. Marcos Cueto (Bloomington: Indiana University Press, 1994).

12. *Vingt-Cinq Ans d'Activité de l'Office Internationale d'Hygiène Publique, 1909–1933* (Paris: Office Internationale d'Hygiène Publique, 1933); Paul F. Basch, "A Historical Perspective on International Health," *Infectious Disease Clinics of North America* 5 (1991): 183–196; W. R. Aykroyd, "International Health—A Retrospective Memoir," *Perspectives in Biology and Medicine* 11 (1968): 273–285.

13. Frank G. Bourdreau, "International Health," *American Journal of Public Health and the Nation's Health* 19 (1929): 863–878; Bourdreau, "International Health Work," in *Pioneers in World Order: An American Appraisal of the League of Nations*, ed. Harriet Eager Favis (New York: Columbia University Press, 1944), 193–207; Norman Howard-Jones, *International Public Health Between the Two World Wars: The Organizational Problems* (Geneva: WHO, 1978); Martin David Dubin, "The League of Nations Health Organisation," in *International Health Organisations and Movements, 1918–1939*, ed. Paul Weindling (Cambridge, England: Cambridge University Press, 1995), 56–80.

14. Thomas Parran, "The First 12 Years of WHO," *Public Health Reports* 73 (1958): 879–883; Fred L. Soper, *Ventures in World Health: The Memoirs of Fred Lowe Soper*, ed. John Duffy (Washington, DC: Pan American Health Organization, 1977); Javed Siddiqi, *World Health and World Politics: The World Health Organization and the UN System* (London: Hurst and Co, 1995).

15. "Seventh Meeting of the Executive Committee of the Pan American Sanitary Organization," Washington, DC, May 23–30, 1949, Folder "Pan American Sanitary Bureau," RG 90–41, Box 9, Series Graduate School of Public Health, University of Pittsburgh Archives.

16. WHO, "Information. Former Directors-General of the World Health Organization. Dr Marcolino Gomes Candau," available at http://www.who.int/archives/wh050/en/directors.htm, accessed July 24, 2004; "In memory of Dr M. G. Candau," *WHO Chronicle* 37 (1983): 144–147.

17. Randall M. Packard, "Malaria Dreams: Postwar Visions of Health and Development in the Third World," *Medical Anthropology* 17 (1997): 279–296; Packard, "No Other Logical Choice" *Parassitologia* 40 (1998): 217–229.

18. Randall M. Packard and Peter J. Brown, "Rethinking Health, Development and Malaria: Historicizing a Cultural Model in International Health," *Medical Anthropology* 17 (1997): 181–194.

19. Ian and Jennifer Glynn, *The Life and Death of Smallpox* (New York: Cambridge University Press, 2004), 194–196.

20. Ibid, 198.

21. William H. Foege, "Commentary: Smallpox Eradication in West and Central Africa Revisited," *Bulletin of the World Health Organization* 76 (1998): 233–235; Donald A. Henderson, "Eradication: Lessons From the Past," *Bulletin of the World Health Organization* 76 (Supplement 2) (1998): 17–21; Frank Fenner,

Donald A. Henderson, Issao Arita, Zdenek Jevek, and Ivan Dalinovich Ladnyi, *Smallpox and its Eradication* (Geneva: WHO, 1988).

22. *The New International Economic Order: The North South Debate*, ed. Jagdish N. Bhagwati (Cambridge, Mass: MIT Press, 1977); Robert L. Rothstein, *Global Bargaining: UNCTAD and the Quest for a New International Economic Order* (Princeton, NJ: Princeton University Press, 1979).

23. Socrates Litsios, "The Long and Difficult Road to Alma-Ata: A Personal Reflection," *International Journal of Health Services* 32 (2002): 709–732.

24. Executive Board 49th Session, WHO document EB49/SR/14 Rev (Geneva: WHO, 1973), 218; *Organizational Study of the Executive Board on Methods of Promoting the Development of Basic Health Services*, WHO document EB49/WP/6 (Geneva: WHO, 1972), 19–20.

25. Socrates Litsios, "The Christian Medical Commission and the Development of WHO's Primary Health Care Approach," *American Journal of Public Health* 94 (2004): 1884–1893; Litsios, "The Long and Difficult Road to Alma-Ata."

26. John H. Bryant, *Health and the Developing World* (Ithaca, NY: Cornell University Press, 1969); *Doctors for the Villages: Study of Rural Internships in Seven Indian Medical Colleges*, ed. Carl E. Taylor (New York: Asia Publishing House, 1976); Kenneth W. Newell, *Health by the People* (Geneva: WHO, 1975). See also Marcos Cueto, "The Origins of Primary Health Care and Selective Primary Health Care," *American Journal of Public Health* 94 (2004): 1864–1874; Litsios, "The Christian Medical Commission."

27. See Litsios, "The Long and Difficult Road to Alma-Ata," 716–719.

28. "Declaration of Alma-Ata, International Conference on Primary Health Care, Alma-Ata, USSR, 6–12 September, 1978," available at http://www.who.int/hpr/NPH/docs/declaration_almaata.pdf, accessed April 10, 2004.

29. David A. Tejada de Rivero, "Alma-Ata Revisited," *Perspectives in Health Magazine: The Magazine of the Pan American Health Organization* 8 (2003): 1–6 (quote on p. 4).

30. Maggie Black, *Children First: The Story of UNICEF, Past and Present* (Oxford: Oxford University Press; 1996), and *The Children and the Nations: The Story of UNICEF* (New York: UNICEF, 1986), 114–140. UNICEF was created in 1946 to assist needy children in Europe's war ravaged areas. After the emergency ended, it broadened its mission and concentrated resources on the needs of children in developing countries.

31. UNICEF, *The State of the World's Children: 1982/1983* (New York: Oxford University Press, 1983). See also Cueto, "Origins of Primary Health Care."

32. Jennifer Prah Ruger, "The Changing Role of the World Bank in Global Health in Historical Perspective," *American Journal of Public Health* 95 (2005): 60–70.

33. *World Development Report 1980* (Washington, DC: World Bank. 1980).

34. *Financing Health Services in Developing Countries: An Agenda for Reform* (Washington, DC: World Bank, 1987).

35. Fiona Godlee, "WHO in Retreat; Is It Losing Its Influence?" *British Medical Journal* 309 (1994): 1491–1495.

36. Ibid, 1492.

37. Kenneth Newell, "Selective Primary Health Care: The Counter Revolution," *Social Science and Medicine* 26 (1988): 903–906 (quote on p. 906).

38. Paul Lewis, "Divided World Health Organization Braces for Leadership Change," *New York Times*, May 1, 1988, p. 20.
39. Gill Walt, "WHO Under Stress: Implications for Health Policy," *Health Policy* 24 (1993): 125–144.
40. Ibid, 129.
41. Fiona Godlee, "WHO in Crisis," *British Medical Journal* 309 (1994):1424–1428; Godlee, "WHO in Retreat"; Fiona Godlee, "WHO's Special Programmes: Undermining From Above," British *Medical Journal* 310 (1995):178–182 (quote on p. 182).
42. P. Brown, "The WHO Strikes Mid-Life Crisis," *New Scientist* 153 (1997): 12; "World Bank's Cure for Donor Fatigue [editorial]," *The Lancet* 342 (July 10, 1993): 63–64; Anthony Zwi, "Introduction to Policy Forum: The World Bank and International Health," *Social Science and Medicine* 50 (2000): 167.
43. World Bank, *Financing Health Services in Developing Countries.*
44. *World Development Report, 1993: Investing in Health* (Washington, DC: World Bank, 1993), iii–iv (quote on pp. iii–iv).
45. For a full account, see William Muraskin, *The Politics of International Health: The Children's Vaccine Initiative and the Struggle to Develop Vaccines for the Third World* (Albany: State University of New York Press, 1998).
46. Bo Stenson and Göran Sterky, "What Future WHO?" *Health Policy* 28 (1994): 235–256 (quote on p. 242).
47. G. A. Gellert, "Global Health Interdependence and the International Physicians' Movement," *Journal of the American Medical Association* 264 (1990): 610–613 (quote on p. 610).
48. Milton Roemer and Ruth Roemer, "Global Health, National Development, and the Role of Government," *American Journal of Public Health* 80 (1990): 1188–1192.
49. See, for example, Andrew J. Haines, "Global Warming and Health," *British Medical Journal* 302 (1991): 669–670; Andrew J. Haines, Paul R. Epstein, and Anthony J. McMichael, "Global Health Watch: Monitoring Impacts of Environmental Change," *The Lancet* 342 (December 11, 1993): 1464–1469; Anthony J. McMichael, "Global Environmental Change and Human Population Health: A Conceptual and Scientific Challenge for Epidemiology," *International Journal of Epidemiology* 22 (1993): 1–8; John M. Last, "Global Change: Ozone Depletion, Greenhouse Warming, and Public Health," *Annual Review of Public Health* 14 (1993): 115–136; A. J. McMichael, *Planetary Overload, Global Environmental Change and the Health of the Human Species* (Cambridge, England: Cambridge University Press, 1993); Anthony J. McMichael, Andrew J. Haines, R. Sloof, and S. Kovats, *Climate Change and Human Health* (Geneva: WHO, 1996); Anthony J. McMichael and Andrew Haines, "Global Climate Change: The Potential Effects on Health," *British Medical Journal* 315 (1997): 805–809.
50. Stephen S. Morse, "Factors in the Emergence of Infectious Diseases," *Emerging Infectious Diseases* 1 (1995): 7–15 (quote on p. 7).
51. Institute of Medicine, *America's Vital Interest in Global Health: Protecting Our People, Enhancing Our Economy, and Advancing Our International Interests* (Washington, DC: National Academy Press, 1997).
52. *Emerging Infections: Biomedical Research Reports*, ed. Richard M. Krause (San Diego: Academic Press, 1998); *Preventing Emerging Infectious Diseases: A Strategy*

for the 21st Century (Atlanta: Centers for Disease Control and Prevention, 1998); *Perspectives on the Department of Defense Global Emerging Infections Surveillance and Response System*, ed. Philip S. Brachman, Heather C. O'-Maonaigh, and Richard N. Miller (Washington, DC: National Academy Press, 2001).

53. For example, Laurie Garrett, *The Coming Plague: Newly Emerging Diseases in a World Out of Balance* (New York: Farrar, Straus and Giroux, 1994).

54. Lawrence K. Altman, "US Moves to Replace Japanese Head of WHO," *New York Times*, December 20, 1992, p. 1.

55. Ilona Kickbusch, "The Development of International Health Priorities—Accountability Intact?" *Social Science & Medicine* 51 (2000): 979–989 (quote on p. 985).

56. Commission on Macroeconomics and Health, *Macroeconomics and Health: Investing in Health for Economic Development* (Geneva: WHO, 2001); see also Howard Waitzkin, "Report of the WHO Commission on Macroeconomics and Health: A Summary and Critique," *The Lancet* 361 (February 8, 2003): 523–526.

57. Michael A. Reid and E. Jim Pearce, "Whither the World Health Organization?" *The Medical Journal of Australia* 178 (2003): 9–12.

58. Michael McCarthy, "A Conversation With the Leaders of the Gates Foundation's Global Health Program: Gordon Perkin and William Foege," *The Lancet* 356 (July 8, 2000): 153–155.

84

ARE EXISTING GOVERNANCE STRUCTURES EQUIPPED TO DEAL WITH TODAY'S GLOBAL HEALTH CHALLENGES – TOWARDS SYSTEMATIC COHERENCE IN SCALING UP

Devi Sridhar, Sanjeev Khagram and Tikki Pang

Source: *Global Health Governance*, 2:2 (2008/2009), 1–25.

The global financial crisis and a new political era shaped by the new US administration have led to a revival of interest in effective global health governance, and provide an opportunity to review existing mechanisms in the context of contemporary global health challenges. On the underlying premise that "global governance is actually global problem solving" it is proposed that the primary objective of good global health governance is to strengthen healthcare delivery systems in the developing world with an emphasis on the importance of primary health care. In order to achieve this objective, innovations which take into account new global political and economic realities are needed. A multi-level, multi-party and multi-purpose partnership framework of global health governance (global, regional, national) is put forward which includes all the key players and attempts to integrate the key functions needed to achieve an inclusive, equitable, flexible, democratic and sustainable mechanism. Based on shared values of solidarity, democracy and equity, and fully acknowledging the sovereignty of countries and other stakeholders, the proposed framework consists of a multilateral governance platform coordinated by the World Health Organization supported by high-level political commitment and policy coherence, and ultimately operationalised by effective implementation mechanisms through global action networks (GANs). GANs are a mode of governance involving authoritative negotiations between state and non-state players which have interests and capacities to influence and shape outcomes in specific issue areas.

Introduction: the challenge of global health

In order to improve health and health equity, especially in the developing world, effective, equitable and sustainable mechanisms of global health governance (GHG)[1] are needed to deal with the complex and diverse challenges facing health today. On the underlying premise that "global governance is actually global problem solving" it is proposed that the primary objective of good global health governance is to strengthen healthcare delivery systems in the developing world with an emphasis on the importance of primary health care. In recent times, the GHG field has been driven by the influences of globalization[2], and health policy has had to take into account a range of global issues including pandemic disease, human migration, conflict, urbanization, travel, global trade, health care financing, information and communications technology, role of civil society, health law, health diplomacy and climate change. The risks to health and development caused by globalization disproportionately affect populations living in the developing world, as exemplified by the potential health impacts of climate change and global warming.[3]

Most recently, there are fears that the current global financial crisis will have a negative impact on global health through, for example, cuts in the health budgets of resource-limited countries as well as reduced aid flows from OECD countries.[4] Health, as well as education, are often the first victims of budget cuts in times of limited funding and competing priorities, and the crisis is likely to place increased pressure on publicly-funded healthcare delivery systems. As the crisis originated in the now debt-ridden developed world, overseas development aid in health may be similarly affected and will, in particular, impact on countries where external resources make up a significant proportion of national health budgets. Although global health aid accounts for only 0.3 percent of total expenditures on health globally (6.5 percent in sub-Saharan Africa), in some countries like the Solomon Islands and Mozambique, for example, 82 percent and 66 percent of the national health budgets respectively come from external sources.[5] WHO estimates that 23 countries have over 30 percent of their total health expenditures funded by donors.

In terms of disease challenges, threats of epidemics and pandemics continue as demonstrated by recent outbreaks of cholera in Zimbabwe, Ebola virus in Angola and increased activity associated with avian influenza. The threat of an entirely new pathogen emerging was illustrated with the appearance of a new influenza A (H1N1) virus in 2009 and the detection of a new arenavirus in 2008 which caused a fulminant haemorrhagic fever, killing 4 out of 5 people it infected[6] – amid other concerns that a strain of Ebola virus may have moved from pigs to humans.[7] Murray *et al* have estimated that an influenza pandemic occurring today may kill 51–81 million people with 96 percent of the deaths occurring in the developing world.[8] Developing countries also have to deal with the additional burden of chronic diseases and injuries, estimated to make up 70 percent of the global disease burden by 2020.[9]

It is against this background of contemporary global health challenges that we examine whether the current mechanisms and structures in GHG are equipped to deal with the global health challenges facing us today. We start by describing what the current global health landscape looks like.

Global health landscape

The essential functions of GHG are generally agreed upon and include convening, defining shared values, ensuring coherence, establishing standards and regulatory frameworks, providing direction (e.g. setting priorities), mobilizing and aligning resources, and promoting research.[10] Dodgson *et al* have reviewed the conceptual meaning and defining features of global health governance (GHG), emphasizing that globalization is an important force behind the emergence of the GHG concept.[11] They consider that GHG has several essential elements including its trans-national and cross-border nature, its need to see health determinants from a multi-sectoral perspective and the desirability to be inclusive of all key actors and stakeholders. They have attempted to identify and map the key actors and their possible positions at a given time in the GHG framework. This mapping places international organizations (e.g. WHO, World Bank) at the centre but complemented by a cluster of state and non-state players "fanning" outwards and dealing with specific health issues.

By Dodgson *et al*[12] and others[13], the main institutions have been identified as ranging from multilateral organizations (e.g. WHO, UNAIDS, UNFPA, UNICEF, World Bank), multi-country networks (e.g. G8, G20, G24), regional entities (EC/EU, ASEAN), partnerships (e.g. Global Fund, GAVI, International Health Partnership+, UNITAID, MMV, GABTD, IAVI), bilateral (e.g. UK DFID, Germany's GTZ, USAID, PEPFAR) initiatives and agencies, philanthropies (e.g. the Bill & Melinda Gates Foundation, Carso Foundation) and the private sector (e.g. Unilever) and civil society (e.g. People's Health Movement, Oxfam, MSF).

A general trend over the past two decades involving a number of these institutions has been an unprecedented increase in the number and available resources for global health initiatives aimed at improving health in the developing world. It is estimated that there are more than 40 bilateral donors, 26 UN agencies, 20 global and regional funds, and 90 global health initiatives active at the moment.[14] These initiatives have been accompanied by significant resources. Prah Ruger has estimated that global financial investments in health doubled from US$6 billion in 2000 to nearly US$14 billion in 2005[15], and this figure may reach US$20 billion in 2008. With the caveat that some overlaps exist between various initiatives, another analysis suggests that more than US$40 billion have been pledged, committed or spent by 9 initiatives launched between 1998–2005.[16] In the most recent example, the UK has announced a new strategy called "Health is Global" which sets a course for increasing financing to strengthen health systems with an emphasis on universal coverage, health workforce, access to essential interventions, patient safety, non-communicable diseases and injuries, and sexual, reproductive and maternal health.[17] This largesse at the global level has also been accompanied by increased national spending on health in many middle-income developing countries, e.g. India and China.[18]

Despite this financial windfall, and in spite of the articulation of a set of principles for more effective and equitable aid delivery, in the form of the Paris and Accra Declarations on Aid Effectiveness[19], it is disconcerting to note that the current landscape is characterized by fragmentation, lack of coordination and even confusion as a diverse array of well-funded and well-meaning initiatives descend with good intentions on countries in the developing world.[20] Many of these initiatives are narrowly focused on specific diseases (e.g. HIV/AIDS, malaria and TB) rather than systems-wide strengthening, tend to be "top-down" in nature and are largely driven by donor agendas rather than the country's own needs and priorities. Many of the initiatives also lack mechanisms of accountability, transparency and evaluation in the way they operate within countries[21], and tend to focus on short-term results – thus raising a real question about future sustainability. Internal brain drain, as manifested by loss of health workers from the public sector to better funded initiatives and NGOs offering better remuneration, has been highlighted as a particularly serious problem. Although some efforts are ongoing (e.g. in relation to the Global Fund to Fight HIV/AIDS, TB and Malaria which has started to fund health worker costs) much more needs to be done on evaluating the impact of multiple initiatives on national health systems.[22]

Many of these initiatives pose a real burden on the capacities of countries to absorb the health aid and, "instead of representing prioritized contributions to sustainable change, funds are simply fueling an 'aid industry' of fragmented assistance."[23] In 2008, a group of former ministers of health and senior health officials from developing countries identified three current challenges in global health financing and governance arrangements[24]: too many initiatives – donors need to learn to "stay the course"; national strategies are being weakened by parallel priorities and implementation directed largely by donors; and limited transparency and information on activities and inadequate reporting on the part of donor agencies. Anecdotally, it has been reported, for example, that a district medical officer in Tanzania spends 25 full days per quarter writing reports for various agencies which provide development aid to the health sector.[25] Health improvement in the developing world is arguably not just about throwing more and more money at the problem although some such as Jeffrey Sachs might contest this. It is rather about how to use the money most effectively to improve health in a sustainable manner. There is thus a consensus among academics and policy-makers that current models and mechanisms are inadequate to meet the challenges and, arguably, represent a failure of governance arrangements. Such concerns have been expressed since the late 1990s when Lee[26], for example, stated that "we must rethink the goals and activities of present institutions" and more recently by Sridhar[27] who stated that GHG needs to deal with three significant changes in the global health system in the past two decades, characterized as being "too many players, too many initiatives", "go-it-alone bilateral aid," and the "Gates empire."

Accordingly, it has been pointed out that there is a "growing demand for new governance architecture for global health," and that the "desire for governance reform is widespread, if not epidemic"[28]. The call for review and rationalization has also been extended to the field of global health research governance.[29] Amidst questions such as "do we have the architecture for health aid right?"[30], and calls for a "Bretton Woods II" summit, there has been no shortage of vigorous debate and discussion in this field in terms of possible options and alternatives for better GHG, often drawing on the subject of global governance more generally.

Innovations

A variety of different models and mechanisms have been proposed as possible improvements or as complements to current modes of governance. These range from informal to formal, from conceptual to pragmatic and from "soft" to "hard" instruments with many permutations and combinations in between. Some examples will be highlighted.

Within the WHO, the leading international health agency, there has been an increasing use of "harder" instruments[31] e.g. the revised International Health Regulations (IHR) and the Framework Convention on Tobacco Control (FCTC) which both came into force in 2005.[32] In spite of ongoing challenges in the implementation of these international legal instruments[33] there continues to be interest in this approach as exemplified by a proposed role for global administrative law[34] and, in the public health field, a proposal for a Framework Convention on Global Health.[35] Both the IHR and the FCTC represent the outcome of extensive inter-governmental processes coordinated by the WHO which reflects the strong interest of sovereign states in global health issues, and a desire on their part to have a voice in the development and implementation of appropriate governance mechanisms and instruments.

Most recently, the ongoing Intergovernmental Meeting on Pandemic Influenza Preparedness: Sharing of Influenza Viruses and Access to Vaccines and Other benefits (PIP-IGM) is attempting to deal with fair and equitable sharing of influenza vaccines.[36] In the recently concluded 124th Session of the WHO Executive Board, counterfeit medicines, migration of health personnel, and health partnerships were other examples of important global issues where WHO Member States expressed a desire for a stronger voice through a more inclusive consultative process, including the possibility of formal mechanisms such as formal consultations and inter-governmental working groups.

In addition to the WHO, the role of major global institutions, in particular the World Bank and the G8 has been the subject of recent interest.[37,38] in the post-Wolfowitz era, there appears to be some enthusiasm for the World Bank's new strategy for health, population and nutrition which seems to focus on the institution's strengths and comparative advantage in terms of its established relationship with developing country governments. In its annual summit in 2008 in Tokyo, the G8 gave prominence to global health issues but it has been criticized as being unrepresentative in that eight countries controlling 65 percent of world output represent only 13 percent of the world's population.[39] To make it more representative and reflective of current realities, it has been suggested that a new G8 could be formed by Brazil, China, the European Union, India, Indonesia, Japan, Russia and the USA, or perhaps there should be a move towards the G20 forum.[40]

Taking a more regional approach, Kickbusch and Matlin have proposed the idea of establishing a European Council on Global Health which "would seek to influence policy and improve practice through advocacy-based evidence and analysis."[41] They envisage that such a council could become part of an alliance of similar councils in different parts of the world. This idea has recently obtained funding from the UK's new "Health is Global" strategy.[42] The regional approach is also reflected in the idea of trans-governmental networks, which focus on relationship building to collectively solve important issues.[43] Examples of such regional platforms could include ASEAN, the European Community, MERCOSUR and the newly formed UNASUR in Latin America.[44]

Moving from a geopolitical to a more issue-based approach, the influential World Economic Forum has proposed the formation of "Global Agenda Councils" for each major world challenge which will provide objective and expert advice, objective situational assessments and recommend solutions to major global problems.[45] Such councils would act to support and advise existing governance structures and would not aim to replace them. More recently, the governments of Germany and France propose the convening of a Berlin Evolution of Medicine Summit which are envisaged "to inform and advice governments, policy makers, health-care professionals, and business leaders worldwide."[46]

In an attempt to provide a unified structure, and taking into account the clear links between health, poverty and development – and acknowledging the increasingly global and inter-sectoral nature of health problems – Horton has proposed the creation of a World Development Organization as a form of GHG.[47] The purpose of such an organization would be as an advocate for further attention and funding as well as a scientific and technical agency for human development which would set standards for development work and coordinate bilateral and multilateral development aid and programmes.

In acknowledgement of the important role of market forces, Kaul has suggested that a new system of global governance should be composed of a series of issues or global public goods-centred policy "loops" which stretch from the national to the international level and back to the national level.[48] Kaul's view seems to support the importance of taking advantage of market dynamics as a one of the key "drivers" of governance which should be supported by promoting innovative financing mechanisms such as the advance market commitment (AMC) and the International Finance Facility for Immunization (IFFIm). Continuing along the vein of "techno-fixes", but focusing on the increasing scientific capacity of developing countries like India, Brazil and China, Mahoney and Morel propose that a global health innovation system could represent a novel GHG model to plan, coordinate, conduct and support efforts to develop and deliver new technologies for diseases which primarily affect the poor in the developing world.[49]

In contrast to the models and mechanisms described so far, Fidler questions the preoccupation with structures (and the use of the term "architecture", stating that that "the architecture metaphor begins to look inapt") and, in the context of "unstructured plurality" which characterizes GHG today, proposes that global health should instead adopt a "source code".[28] The challenge for GHG is to effectively apply the "source code" in various areas affecting health, with the efforts in each "then inform(ing) the evolution of the source code, producing an expanding network of actors, processes, ideas, and initiatives that shape global health governance". Similar sentiments have been expressed by Walt[50] who argues that the architecture analogy is misplaced "because it draws our attention to structures and global level discourses, and away from actors, interests and values, and country level implementation".

Two recent GHG innovations are also worth a mention. First, and in the context of market failures to develop drugs for the poor[51], an attempt has been made at developing a global, market-based, systemic solution to health challenges faced by the world's poor. The recently launched Health Impact Fund is presented as "an optional mechanism that offers pharmaceutical innovators a supplementary reward based on the health impact of their products, if they agree to sell those products at cost."[52] The proposed Fund would be financed mainly by governments. Second, UNITAID, "a laboratory for innovative financing," has collected over $600 million in less than 2 years mainly through an air travel tax, has reduced the price of anti-retrovirals by 40 percent and is also funding the supply of diagnostics and treatments in 38 developing countries.[53]

Attempts at coordination: the WHO and IHP+

It would be fair to state that the models and mechanisms described above are not mutually exclusive and overlaps exist but the plethora of diverse initiatives point clearly to the lack of coordination, direction and account-ability as three of the key challenges facing GHG today.

Given the lack of coordination and accountability among numerous global health initiatives, Garrett has suggested that "the only organization with the political credibility to compel cooperative thinking is the WHO."[54] Strong leadership is urgently needed and as the leading international public health agency representing 193 sovereign states, WHO "is uniquely positioned to provide this leadership by virtue of its role in setting evidence-based norms on technical and policy matters, highlighting best practices that improve health globally, and monitoring and coordinating action to address current and emerging global health threats."[55] This statement from a recent Institute of Medicine Report advising the new US administration on global health, goes on to state that "the US President should demonstrate support for the WHO as a leader in global health."

However, and as pointed out by many, a number of factors have eroded WHO's ability to be the lead institution in GHG.[56] It is perceived to be bureaucratic and inefficient, subject to political pressure from its more powerful Member States, and lacking clear priorities among a multitude of programmes. There is also a perception that the organization has not been able to deal with the challenges posed by globalization and, as a result, others have stepped into the void. Importantly, it suffers from inadequate resources and the reality that nearly 80 percent of its budget now come from external donors, rather than from assessed contributions from Member States, has brought into question WHO's neutrality and independence. A disjoint has also been highlighted in the way the Organization allocates its resources with budget allocations heavily skewed towards infectious diseases (87 percent) with non-communicable diseases and violence and injuries receiving only 12 percent and 1 percent respectively.[57]

However, and despite reservations of the role and effectiveness of international organizations, the WHO, in the view of some, should be "reinvented" and not be the victim of "early retirement".[58] in the GHRG field, WHO has been involved, for example, in improving transparency and access to the results of clinical trials globally through the establishment of an International Clinical Trials Registry Platform (ICTRP).[59] It played a critical coordinating role during the SARS outbreak in 2003 and the new influenza A (H1N1) crisis in 2009, and has been the main driver behind the success of two GHG instruments (the IHR and the FCTC). It is also a key player in convening the International Health Partnership and Related Initiatives (IHP+).

An earlier initiative to establish better coordination and alignment of GHI's, referred to as the H8[60], has now been extended to the IHP+.[61] The IHP+ is an attempt to bring 23 countries, 13 organizations and civil society to work together in partnership to improve health outcomes through a single, harmonized in-country implementation strategy. At the centre of this strategy is the "country compact" where development partners work in the context of existing in-country mechanisms through a single, costed, results-oriented national health plan with the objective of scaling-up effective coverage as a means of achieving the targets set by the health-related MDG's. To date Ethiopia, Mozambique, Nepal, Rwanda and Uganda have signed the country compact and other countries are in the process of doing so. In terms of the financial stream, the IHP+ recently launched a High-level Task Force on Innovative International Financing for Health Systems with the UK government, for example, pledging a £500 million contribution.

Global Action Networks

An additional model for coordination are cross-sectoral Global Action Networks (GANs).[62] Described as a mode of governance involving authoritative negotiations between state and non-state players which have interests and capacities to influence and shape outcomes in specific issue areas, GANs usually start with a focus on "techno fixes" around small, centrally structured networks but they then develop and shift their focus to building social relationships and effecting deeper change, subsequently evolving into decentralized, polycentric networks. GANs have been described as "functional responses to gaps generated by processes of globalization that states and the extant inter-state system cannot fill," and also possess the ability to bring into the picture other key players.

GANs are an innovation that have the potential of robustly filling the ever widening gaps in global governance. In theory and increasingly in practice, GANs seize the opportunities to address global problems in an increasingly interconnected world that international agencies, governments, businesses and civil society organizations acting separately have proven unable or unwilling to meet. Filling this "global governance as global problem solving deficit" lies at the functional core of their missions.

Since the end of the Cold War which created a major window of opportunity for global governance experimentation, and particularly over the last decade, more than five dozen GANs were established and new ones are being created in virtually every issue area. Prominent examples of initiatives in the global health field that can be categorized as GANs include the Global Fund, GAVI, GAIN, the Stop TB campaign among others. The Global Fund, despite its numerous problems, is arguably one of the most innovative cross-sectoral financing arrangements in global health of the past two decades and has dramatically increased the resources directed towards addressing HIV/AIDS, tuberculosis and malaria worldwide.

Not all global partnerships focused on health or in other fields aspire to be or will become GANs. GANs as an ideal type share a set of strategic principles:

- Being truly global and multi-level (working transcontinentally if not worldwide across the local, national, regional and international levels of governance and bridging extant divides such as North-South, cultures, nations, sectors, ethnicities, genders).

- Implementing interdisciplinary action-learning and reflective action to produce otherwise unattainable results by attaining synergies between knowledge and practice (through a range of strategies including agenda setting, knowledge generation/sharing, capacity building, resource mobilization, conflict resolution, public education, and certification among others).
- Building enduring yet nimble multi-stakeholder and cross-sectoral, interorganizational *networks* (linking international agencies, governments, businesses, civil society organizations and other actors while still utilizing hierarchies or markets as appropriate)

GANs are innovations whose legitimacy is being forged by optimizing democratic imperatives (transparency, participation and accountability) and effectiveness (adaptability, efficiency, and scalability). The underlying theory of change of GANs is animated by a view that effectiveness in global problem solving requires all legitimate and consequential actors to be coherently linked in order to scale impact and generate the systemic changes that are needed.

GANs must be understood as having two levels of outcomes. One is a collectively defined goal or goals that all participating organizations can buy into. It derives from the fundamental rationale for founding a GAN – the need to bring together distinctive competencies and resources on a global scale. This first level of outcome may be called a "system-organizing" goal – GANs can be thought of attempts to organize diffuse activities of many organizations into a new global "system". For example, the Global Reporting Initiative aims to bring together diverse stakeholders to create a global system of corporate reporting.

This over-arching goal is seemingly broad, but it must support the particular objectives that lead organizations to participate in order for the GAN to be successful and sustainable. Unilever and Walmart participate in the Marine Stewardship Council not only to develop sustainable fisheries, but to develop those that will also be profitable for it. Success in a GAN is determined by collective commitment to both the over-arching goals, and to support for individual stakeholders to reach at least some of their own objectives. This emphasizes the importance of clearly articulating these two different sets of goals and ensuring collective commitment to them.

Three initiating paths for GANs can be distinguished. One emphasizes a period of two to three years of consultation with the various stakeholders followed by an initiating meeting of some sort, in a sense like a constitutional convention. A second group of GANs have begun out of the imagination and usually as a program of one or a couple of organizations. The third path is appropriate when there is already a relatively well-developed "global space" for the participants. For example, global conferences on the topic of water issues were organized from time-to-time which led to the realization that more formal and permanent organizational arrangements would be valuable.

This led to the formation of the Global Water Partnership and the World Water Council.

In general, successful GANs follow a development path from a centralized model where the role of a "Secretariat" dominates to a polycentric network with many dispersed hubs of activity communicating with each other. However, in some cases, the centralized model may be simply a conscious and strategic choice; for example, when the principal function involves distribution of funds as with the Global Fund and the International Youth Foundation. In some cases the GANs get "stuck" at a development phase with a centralized model; this reflects the difficulty of shifting to the higher development stage which demands a new way of thinking about organizing.

GANs also change their focus in addition to their structure. As the diverse stakeholders work together, new ways of thinking about the issue emerge – one of the most remarkable examples is the shift from defining climate change as an outgrowth of overpopulation of the South, to defining it as an environmental impact footprint of people living in the North. Participants generally start out with a "techno-fix" or specific operational improvements as the goal. For example, leading participants often come from a problem-solving perspective and think about their issue in terms of developing appropriate solutions and getting others to buy into the solution they have developed. They think of the challenge as creating the "right" code of ethics, or the "right" physical technology to respond to a question such as energy and climate change, or the "right" way to build human capacities. Only as they work together do they start to understand that the critical challenge is also about creating social relationships and processes where they can work effectively together in the face of dynamically changing circumstances, challenges and opportunities.

This is certainly a challenge GANs are still facing as they often try to bring together policy makers, scientists/specialists, community activists and business people, among many others. Although the evidence-based promise of GANs is significant, their legitimacy and effectiveness nevertheless remains constrained. On the one hand, their ability to realize their development potential is being limited by a need for more broad-based understanding, support and engagement by the full range of stakeholder groups. On the other hand, the human competencies and institutional capacities to develop the full potential of GANs need to be greatly strengthened. GANs correspondingly may be likened to the same stage of the development of the multinational corporations in the mid-19th century, or international organizations in the aftermath of World War II. Another continual challenge for most GANs is to ensure the equal involvement of and "ownership" by stakeholders from the global south across sectors: government, civil society and the private sector. In the field of global health, this is largely the case. Nevertheless, GANS have been an important innovation in recent years in global governance.

Possible future global governance architectures

Before turning to what a global health governance architecture might look like, it is useful to turn to global governance more broadly. At least seven possible global governance architectures compete for ideological hegemony if not institutional pre-eminence in the contemporary world.[63] These models include: 1) multilateralism, 2) market governance, 3) grassroots globalism, 4) multiple regionalisms, 5) world statism, 6) networked governance, and 7) institutional heterarchy. These models are clearly internally diverse, by no means fully articulated, nor mutually exclusive or necessarily exhaustive. The overview below offers an initial survey of these models for further refinement and debate: all can be seen to be at work in the field of global health governance.

Multilateralism is by far the easiest global governance architecture to see and various versions of it are arguably the most discussed, advocated, and practically applied today. In its minimal desirable form, this model entails truly functioning and formally equal "sovereign" states covering the planet, all fulfilling more or less rule of law procedural standards internally. Through transparent, participatory, and accountable processes of principal-agent delegation and monitoring from citizens to states to inter-state organizations (IOs) embedded in well articulated regional or worldwide inter-state regimes (IRs – norms, rules, decision-making structures and processes), challenges and opportunities facing the world society of states (and their citizens) are addressed fairly, effectively and efficiently.

Multilateralism has two generic sub-types. The first is what might be called state-centric multilateralism. In this case global governance is primarily shaped by the agreements and coordinated behavior of national states. The primary mechanisms for this form are the various G's – the G8, G20, G24 and G77 for example. In this variant, inter-state organizations (IOs) play primarily a supportive and secondary role to national states. In the second form of multilateralism on the other hand, IOs play much more of a lead role. The more central position of IOs might be the result of greater delegation by national states, greater legitimacy and capacity on the part of the IO or IOs in that field, or both. This sub-model thus might be called IO-centric multilateralism.

Market governance is predicated on either the assumption that well functioning and unfettered global markets are the best allocation mechanisms for a globalizing world. More often than not, it is argued, governance through markets will produce progress and order through innovation and competition. A slightly more nuanced justification for the market governance model is that market imperfections even when they occur are still more desirable forms of governance than state intervention because of the even greater likelihood and pernicious effects of state failure. In other words, a world governed by somewhat imperfect markets is certainly better than a world governed by widespread state failures.

But the theory and practice of market governance is not always seen in opposition to states. Many scholars and policy-makers argue that the primary role of states (with their IOs and IRs) is to foster and catalyze better functioning markets. States should also utilize market mechanisms rather than command and control mechanisms if and when regulation is required and to promote social and environmental goals that are not automatically delivered by markets. Finally, other actors such as private sector firms and civil society organizations can, do and should promote market governance through voluntary corporate citizenship efforts and forms of regulation that often can bypass the state altogether.

Grassroots globalism involves at least the extreme de-centering of territorial bureaucratic national states and extant IOs and IRs, and replaces them with peoples organizing anew in self-governing local communities. It entails radical decentralization of authority relations to the "local" level through processes of direct participation in all spheres of political, economic, and social life. This deep democratization is also predicated on eliminating the centrality of markets and multinational corporations in favor of modes of production, distribution and consumption that combine the best features of socialist, solidarity and ecologically embedded economies. Dynamism would be ensured through empowered citizen participation for the continual reinvigoration of societies, especially through the cyclical emergence and waning of transgressive social movements (feminist, ecological, etc.) from time to time.

Moving to a higher governance level than the local, one could imagine a world of *multiple* cooperative regionalisms. One key notion in this model is that the pre-dominant locus of authority would not be national states but rather at various regional collectivities of political units (states or other forms) and societies. An important facet of this model is that these regional collectivities would not primarily or all be states themselves just governing larger geographical territories. The regions could be territorially smaller or larger, organized differently or similarly, but all would meet minimum thresholds of democratic decision-making and institutional capacity. The regions could be more or less self-contained but would cooperatively interact with each other to the extent that trans-regional problems or opportunities arose. One could also imagine the emergence of inter-regional organizations and regimes in a world of multiple cooperative regionalisms.

There also remains the enduring possibility of a world state, more or less legally constituted and governed. The range of possible institutional arrangements of a world state is potentially limitless and can draw heavily on the long traditions of theorizing and experimenting with "sub-planetary" sovereign territorial political regimes. At the center of the notion of a world state would, however, be the notion that citizens would acquire their ultimate rights and owe their ultimate responsibilities to a global, formal, and centrally organized authority with worldwide reach.

A world state would require a planetary military-security establishment with a "monopoly of force", unless the possibility of complete demilitarization is

547

achieved. Even then, some form of police force with worldwide reach would certainly be needed. It would also have a universal tax collecting agency for it to be a considered a state in the most minimal sense. The Universal Declaration of Human Rights, along with the set of ratified, international treaties could likely be the base constitutional framework for a world state. This world state could have a planetary assembly, planetary executive, planetary court, planetary bank, etc. One could imagine various forms of democracy (parliamentary, presidential, etc.), and forms of federalism with subsidiary territorial units (either homogenously or heterogeneously) assembled together or constituted anew. Alternatively, or in some mixed form, functional domains (a planetary corporatism?) could be the organizing basis of this world state. And various permutations could be imagined.

Models of networked governance come in two versions – the trans-governmental and the multi-stakeholder or cross-sectoral. Proponents of both espouse that networks can provide the appropriate balance between the efficiency of decentralized markets, the authority of hierarchical states, and the accountability of democratic systems required for a complex, high-paced and deeply interconnected world. These networks are likely to cross levels of governance but can be either ad-hoc or institutionalized. The key difference between the two types is the nature of the actors that constitute the networks – in the transgovernmental image it is primarily state governmental and bureaucratic agencies (although not just from central states), whereas in the multi-stakeholder variant it is state engaged with non-state actors from various sectors (e.g. private sector firms, civil society organizations).

In the trans-governmental image, horizontal and vertical networks of governmental officials and agents (e.g. central bankers, judges, legislators, ministers, generals) from disaggregated states share information, increase capacity and coordinate activity to manage global affairs. In the multi-stakeholder variant, networks of relevant actors from across sectors (public governmental, private business and private non-profit/non-governmental in particular) join together in dynamic institutional arrangements to address global challenges and seize global opportunities in different domains of social life. Global Action Networks (GANs) that combine the comparative advantage of groups from across multiple sectors and are themselves potentially linked together fill critical gaps in global governance. States and inter-state organizations are still important but varyingly and not always predominantly so.

Institutional heterarchy involves a world of multiple types, forms and levels of authoritative political organizations and units (communities, religions, interest associations, epistemic communities, companies, states, inter-state organizations, social movements, regions, transnational or global networks of various kinds, etc.), and various types and levels of governance. Individuals or groups would simultaneously participate and consider themselves members and/or citizens of several of these. All individuals and collectivities would be subject to an evolving but not overriding global constitutional and legal framework.

Another way of thinking about institutional heterarchy is to imagine a legitimized and formally combined multi-layered (MLG) and poly-centric (PCG) set of territorial and functional governance arrangements. 'MLG can be defined as an arrangement for making binding decisions that engages a multiplicity of politically independent but otherwise interdependent actors – private and public – at different levels of territorial aggregation in more or less continuous negotiation/deliberation/ implementation, and that does not assign exclusive policy competence or assert a stable hierarchy of political authority to any of those levels." In contrast, "PCG can be defined as an arrangement for making binding decisions over a multiplicity of actors that delegates authority over functional tasks to a set of dispersed and relatively autonomous agencies that are not controlled – *de jure* or *de* facto – by a single collective institution."

While other possible global governance architectures are analytically possible and worth considering, this initial mapping above offers a continuum of potential futures that have been espoused as desirable by actually existing groups and coalitions. Empirical traces of each of these seven clusters are more or less in existence in the contemporary historical period with grassroots globalism and world statism being the least empirically discernible – and certainly in the area of global health. But no one of them is fully consolidated and unequivocally legitimated. Rather these models are hotly contested.

Criteria for good global health governance

Reflecting on the global governance more broadly, and informed by experiences with existing GHG and GHRG arrangements, some criteria may be defined for improved mechanisms of GHG. Regardless of what model is most appropriate or effective, and assuming that "no one size fits all" will be the rule, it is proposed that future mode(s) of good GHG should possess six key criteria.

First, GHG has to be the outcome of a series of balancing acts between the needs of national and global governance, including consideration of regional needs. On this point, it has been stated that ". . . . global governance cannot replace the need for good governance in national societies; in fact, in the absence of quality local governance, global and regional arrangements are bound to fail or will only have limited effectiveness".[64] It also has to achieve a balance between formal and informal mechanisms, and between market forces and demands for social justice and equity.

Other balancing acts are needed. Between a focus on specific diseases of immediate public health concern and a holistic, systems strengthening approach, and between legitimacy, democracy, participation on one hand, and effectiveness on the other as well as between ideas and theories of governance, and the realities of implementation, i.e. the need to actually "make it work". Between learning from past successes (and failures), and acknowledging the need for innovation on future governance needs in the context of a new political era and continued pressures from globalization, both positive and negative.

Second, GHG has to be inter- and trans-sectoral in nature and adopt a multi-sectoral and multi-disciplinary approach. Global health governance cannot exist in isolation within the health sector and must be cognizant of, and linked to, other initiatives – it should aim for "health in all governance", embracing other key sectors including trade, agriculture, diplomacy, labour, law and environment.

Third, it has to be inclusive and embrace the diversity of interested parties and stakeholders, and be able to "listen to wider voices". It has to be sensitive to local context, needs, capacities and knowledge and how these fit within the wider framework of global norms and standards. As pointed out by Fidler, the current diversity and plurality of actors, interests, norms and financing modes may actually possess future governance potential.[65] Listening to wider voices also means acknowledging the contributions of local knowledge and experiences in governance, as exemplified by preparedness for epidemics and pandemics, as well as in building stronger health systems.[66]

Fourth, GHG has to agree on and define the roles and responsibilities of various players based on a shared set of substantive norms and values including ethics, equity, solidarity, democracy and the right to health – and adopt the principles contained in the Paris Declaration on Aid Effectiveness in order to better harmonize and align health development aid.

Fifth, ideally, it has to have a transparent and accountable system of checks and balances and must monitor and evaluate its performance and impact, and give due consideration to issues of sustainability. While this might seem impractical given that the various institutions involved in governance have their own systems of accountability, it is an ideal worth striving towards given the universal benefits.

Sixth, GHG must harness the power of information and evidence to guide its actions by striving for "evidence-informed governance" including promoting research into the topic of GHG itself. This is a relatively neglected research field which faces conceptual, analytic and design challenges and has to sometimes deal with the political nature of the issues.[67] GHG should also creatively utilize advances in information and communications technologies to gather information and data important for good governance in various areas. The recent reported use of the internet search engines, Yahoo and Google, for influenza surveillance illustrates this point[68], as well as UNITAID's creative use of on-line ticketing to collect a levy on international airline tickets mentioned previously.

A multi-level approach to governance

What is the way forward? It has been proposed that several factors should be taken into account: strengthening mechanisms to hold donors accountable for their actions, a focus on developing national plans and strengthening national leadership, and promoting south-south collaboration.[69] Based on consideration of the above criteria, future needs and current realities, and the fairly obvious need for a flexible and inclusive model, a GHG partnership framework model which is based on a multi-level, multi-purpose and multi-stakeholder perspective where the different layers perform distinct but mutually supportive functions is proposed (Figure 1). The layers can be envisaged as performing several key functions, including "summitry"-advocacy-coherence, governance-accountability, and technical-operational, and is based on a set of shared values of inclusiveness, democracy, solidarity and equity.

First and foremost, the partnership framework should have high level political commitment, visibility and policy coherence. In this regard, and in the current context of the global financial crisis, the G8, despite its limitations, may have a particularly important role to play in helping to influence and change the global health agenda and its priorities.[70] Ullrich has also proposed that the G8 may be able to provide a "cure" for GHG by providing much needed multi-level policy coherence within the GHG system through three unique governance mechanisms: mutual accountability, delegation to other institutions, and the "ratchet effect" around convergence of annual meetings of key players (e.g. the World Bank, OECD, IMF).[71] The G8 Summit of 2008 in Tokyo placed health high on the agenda, making commitments to strengthen health systems, improve maternal, newborn and child health, and strengthen countermeasures against infectious diseases.[72] It is also noteworthy that the MDGs have remained on the agenda for the G8's 2009 Summit to be hosted by Italy in July 2009.[73] However, it is worth noting that in financial regulation and economic governance, the G8 has waned in importance to the G20 as a decision-making and consensus-building forum. A similar shift is occurring in global health governance.

Supporting and complementing the high level entities such as the G8 and G20, a supporting role is envisaged for regional, high-level trans-governmental platforms such as ASEAN, the European Community and MERCOSUR and USASUR in Latin America. These forums could enrich the framework by providing additional, diplomacy-style relationship-building types of mechanisms and processes, both formal and informal, which complement the more traditional, western-oriented normative approaches. Regional platforms based in the developing world could also play an important role in promoting south-south collaborations for health improvement as has been seen, for example, with Cuban doctors working in Africa and the close collaboration among ASEAN countries after the 2003 tsunami.

At the next level, and linked to its delegation mechanism, the G8, or possibly G20, should ensure the presence of a strong backbone for the partnership framework in the form of an effective, inclusive, and transparent governance mechanism with some form of formal executive "power". The WHO, as the leading international health agency could provide such a governance platform

– "while it is far from perfect, there seems little doubt that the WHO should be the leader, and given certain reforms, it could manage the chaotic and crowded landscape and play a key role as coordinator".[74] Despite the prevailing sentiment that the WHO could not take on such a political task, perhaps this is an opportune time to revisit the issues, especially in the renewed interest for reform expressed in the recent IOM advisory to the new US administration.[75] WHO can arguably play a central role in ensuring that the potential for positive synergies which exist between health systems, research for health and the global health initiatives are vigorously exploited by all stakeholders to ensure maximum, mutual added value. In this regard, the proposal for the formation of a Committee C of its World Health Assembly[76], which will aim to improve "consistency of global health action and coordination", is worth considering.

In terms of a possible mechanism, the establishment of a "Committee C" of the World Health Assembly (WHA) could take a step towards achieving this objective. Article 18 of the WHO constitution gives the Organization a legitimate role to "ensure more transparency and debate between global health players." Committee C would complement the existing Committees A (which deals with programmatic-technical matters) and B (which deals with budget and managerial matters). The proposed committee would bring together WHO Member States, major global health initiatives and other key stakeholders (e.g. civil society) in an annual, formal platform to strive for better coordination, alignment and harmonization. It would, in the standard *modus operandi* of the WHA, operate through proposing resolutions for adoption but "to explicitly welcome within such resolutions commitments independently taken by other partners that would be annexed to the resolution."[77] Critically, however, and to overcome major concerns over such a structure disempowering developing countries[78], the voting power to pass resolutions should be solely vested in the Member States, thus preserving their autonomy and independence in the governance of WHO. While Committee C would not address the underlying problem of the WHO which is that it is heavily reliant on voluntary contributions and thus vulnerable to donor priorities, it would take a step forward at addressing the democratic deficit within the WHO, as well as provide a platform for the various global health actors to meet annually. While the actual form of "Committee C" needs much more discussion and reflection, what it is ultimately attempting to address is the chaos in the global health system and the leadership role the WHO could assume.

At the technical-operational level, the most appropriate conceptual framework are the GANs due to their flexibility, their focus on building social relationships, their inherent iterative learning capacity, and their potential for catalyzing needed change. The areas in which GANs should be active could be discussed and agreed upon at the Committee C of the WHO and their actual, in-country implementation would then depend on a broad spectrum of implementing instruments including public sector agencies, private sector entities (including public-private partnerships) and civil society-NGOs. The function of the GANs is therefore to define a broad mission, e.g. ". . . to save children's lives and protect people's health by increasing access to immunization in poor countries" (for GAVI), and the mission would, in turn, define the types of possible implementing modes at the national level. One could also envisage different GANs defining different missions across the spectrum of contemporary health challenges, with the concept being especially suited to having an inter-sectoral focus, e.g. addressing the social determinants of health.

Three important directions should be taken in relation to GANs to improve the field of global health problem solving and global governance. The first is to support the further development of global health GANs that already exist such as the Global Fund towards the strategic goals of being truly global, action-learning oriented and truly inter-organizational, cross-sectoral networks. The second is the creation and support of new global health GANs such as around the issue of building and strengthening health delivery systems in countries where they are weak or non-existent. The third is to seize opportunities to partner with GANs in other issues areas that are directly linked to key global health problems and goals. For example, working with the Global Water Partnership on issues of water and health, with the Microcredit Summit Campaign around micro-finance opportunities to improve health access and outcomes, with the Global Knowledge Partnership on improving Information and Communications Technology systems related to health goals, or with the Global Partnership for the Prevention of Armed Conflict to re-frame ending mass violence as at least partly a global health issue.

GANs can also benefit in future from the UN Reform initiative, "Delivering as One."[79] This pilot initiative is being tested in eight countries (Albania, Cape Verde, Mozambique, Pakistan, Rwanda, Tanzania, Uruguay and Viet Nam) and its aim is to determine how the UN family – with its many and diverse agencies – can deliver in a more coordinated way at country level. The objective is to ensure faster and more effective development operations and accelerate progress to achieving the Millennium Development Goals. The success of this initiative will depend on overcoming barriers to effective cooperation that exist within the UN, demonstrated by the difficulties that UNAIDS has experienced.[80]

In the context of broader models and categories of global governance, the proposed partnership framework (Figure 1) probably fits what has been described as "institutional heterarchy"[81] which involves a variety of "multiple types, forms and levels of authoritative political organizations and units and various types and levels of governance." In our view, the proposed framework addresses and satisfies some of the key criteria for good GHG. It acknowledges sovereignty (of both Member States and other key stakeholders)[82], diversity and multiple layers of governance; it is inclusive, transparent and has shared

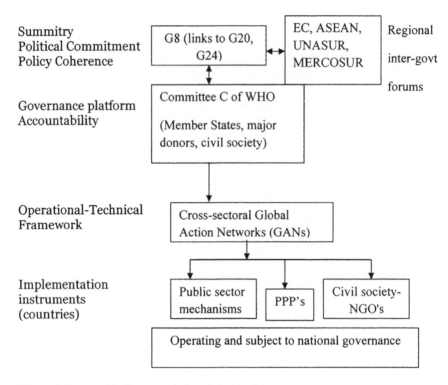

Summitry
Political Commitment
Policy Coherence

G8 (links to G20, G24)

EC, ASEAN, UNASUR, MERCOSUR

Regional

inter-govt

forums

Governance platform
Accountability

Committee C of WHO

(Member States, major donors, civil society)

Operational-Technical
Framework

Cross-sectoral Global
Action Networks (GANs)

Implementation
instruments
(countries)

Public sector
mechanisms

PPP's

Civil society-
NGO's

Operating and subject to national governance

Figure 1 Partnership framework for global health governance.

values and, above all, it provides a single, democratic and inclusive coordination platform with an accountability element, arguably two critical requirements in today's complex landscape. Importantly, and rather than creating totally new structures, it makes use of existing institutions and their current mandates. It is also important that emphasis is placed on obtaining results. Something akin to a global public health "scorecard"[83] should perhaps be developed for GHG.

Ultimately, however, the success of the proposed framework must be predicated on the development of a shared overarching vision which focuses more on the "why" and less on the "how". The functions of governance has been outlined and debated extensively, and the nuances, permutations and mechanisms of various governance models are a fertile field of academic study in and of itself. But what is ultimately important is that "global health governance is about global problem solving"[84] and its "why" is primarily about developing good national governance in order to strengthen health care delivery systems in the developing world. When global health governance has, and embraces, a shared "why", it can bear with and accommodate almost any "how"[85] in its quest to deliver health and health equity to disadvantaged populations in the developing world.

Notes

1 Defined as the formal and informal institutions, norms and processes which govern or directly influence global health policy and outcomes.

2 Kelley Lee, "A dialogue of the deaf? The health impacts of globalization", *Journal of Epidemiology and Community Health* 55, no.9, (2001): 619; D. Bettcher and Kelley Lee, "Globalization and public health," *Journal of Epidemiology and Community Health* 56, no. 1, (2002): 8–17; T. Pang and E. G. Guindon, "Globalization and risks to health," *EMBO Reports* 5, no. S1 (2004): S11–S16; Dr Margaret Chan, Director-General of WHO, "Globalization and health," Remarks at the UN General Assembly, October 24, 2008 (http://www.who.int/dg/speeches/2008/20081024/en/index.html).

3 M. St. Louis and J. Hess, "Climate change: impacts on and implications for global health," *American journal of Preventive Medicine* 35, no. 5, (2008): 527–538.

4 World Health Organization, *The Financial Crisis and Global Health, Report of a High-Level Consultation*, Geneva, 19 January 2009, Available online PDF [18p.] at: http://www.who.int/mediacentre/events/meetings/2009_financial_crisis_report_en_.pdf; Richard Horton, "The global financial crisis: an acute threat to health", *The Lancet* 373 no. 9661 (2009): 355–356.

5 World Health Organization, *World Health Statistics*, 2008.

6 Claire Keeton, "South African doctors move quickly to contain new virus," *Bulletin of the World Health Organization* 86, no.12 (2008): 912–913.

7 Dennis Normile, "Scientists Puzzle over Ebola-Reston Virus in Pigs," *Science* 323, no. 5913 (2009): 451; "Four more Filipinos infected with the Ebola-Reston virus," *The International Herald Tribune*, January 30, 2009 (http://www.iht.com/articles/ap/2009/01/30/asia/AS-Philippines-Ebola-Reston.php).

8 Christopher J. L. Murray, Alan D. Lopez, Brian Chin, Dennis Feehan, and Kenneth H. Hill, "Estimation of potential global pandemic influenza mortality on the basis of vital registry data from the 1918–20 pandemic: a quantitative analysis." *The Lancet* 369, no. 9554 (2006): 2211–2218.

9 World Health Organization, *Preventing Chronic Diseases–A Vital Investment*, Geneva, 2005.

10 Obijiofor Aginam, *Global Health Governance*, University of Toronto Press, 2005; David Bloom, "Governing global health," *Finance and Development* 44, no. 4, (2007): 31–35.

11 Richard Dodgson, Kelley Lee, Nick Drager, "Global Health Governance: A Conceptual Review," Centre on Global Change & Health Dept of Health & Development, London School of Hygiene World Health Organization & Tropical Medicine, and Department of Health and Development, World Health Organization Discussion Paper No. 1, Feb 2002.

12 Richard Dodgson, Kelley Lee, Nick Drager, "Global Health Governance: A Conceptual Review," Centre on Global Change & Health Dept of Health & Development, London School of Hygiene World Health Organization & Tropical Medicine, and Department of Health and Development, World Health Organization Discussion Paper No. 1, Feb 2002.

13 Devi Sridhar, "Post-Accra: Is their space for country ownership in global health?," *Third World Quarterly* 30, no.7 (2009).

14 Karen McColl, "Europe told to deliver more aid for health," *The Lancet* 371, no. 9630 (2008): 2072–2073.

15 Jennifer Prah Ruger, "Global health governance and the World Bank," *The Lancet* 370, no. 9597 (2007): 1471–1474.

16 Jon Cohen, "The New World of Global Health," *Science* 311, no. 5758 (2006): 162–167.

17 Dawn Primarolo, Mark Malloch-Brown, Ivan Lewis, on behalf of the Interministerial Group for Global Health, "Health is global: a UK government strategy for 2008–13," *The Lancet* 373, no. 9662 (2009): 443–445.

18 Winnie Yip and Ajay Mahal, "The Health Care Systems of China and India: Performance and Future Challenges," *Health Affairs* 27, no. 4 (2008): 921–932.

19 The Paris Declaration on Aid Effectiveness http://www1.worldbank.org/harmonization/Paris/FINALPARISDECLARATION.pdf

20 Laurie Garrett, "The challenge of global health," *Foreign Affairs* 86 (January/February 2007): 14–38; Devi Sridhar, "Global health – who can lead?", *The World Today 65, no. 2*, February 2009, Chatham House.

21 Devi Sridhar and Rajaie Batniji, "Misfinancing global health: a case for transparency in disbursements and decision making," *The Lancet* 372, no. 9568 (2008): 1185–1191.

22 AHPSR, The impact of global health initiatives on health systems (http://www.who.int/alliance-hpsr/researchsynthesis/project3/en/index.html)

23 The money flows, the boy dies," *International Herald Tribune*, April 25, 2007. (http://www.iht.com/articles/2007/04/25/opinion/eduganda.php)

24 Global Economic Governance Programme, University of Oxford, "Setting a developing country agenda for global health," Report of a high-level working group (http://www.globaleconomicgovernance.org/docs/Workingpercent20Group percent 20Report percent20May percent202008.pdf).

25 Michael D. Conway, Srishti Gupta, and Srividya Prakash, "Building better partnerships for global health," *McKinsey Quarterly* 2006; December: 1–8.

26 Kelley Lee, "Shaping the future of global health cooperation: where can we go from here?", *The Lancet* 351, no. 9106 (1998): 899–902.

27 Sridhar, "Global health-who can lead?".

28 David Fidler, "Architecture amidst anarchy: global health's quest for governance," *Global Health Governance* 1, no. 1 (2007): 1–17.

29 John-Arne Røttingen, Paulo Marchiori Buss, Sally Davies, and Oumar Touré, "Global health research architecture-time for mergers?" *The Lancet* 373, no. 9659 (2009): 193–105; "The state of health research worldwide," *The Lancet* 372, no. 9649 (2008): 1519.

30 Tore Godal, "Do we have the architecture for health aid right? Increasing global aid effectiveness," *Nature Reviews Microbiology* 3, no. 11 (2005): 899–903.

31 Ian Smith, "State-Centered Approaches to Global Health Governance," IOM Committee on the US Commitment to Global Health, Washington, DC, June 26, 2008 (http://www.iom.edu/Object.File/Master/55/687/Smith.pdf)

32 The International Health Regulations (IHR) are an international legal instrument that is binding on 194 countries across the globe, including all the Member States of WHO. Their aim is to help the international community prevent and respond to acute public health risks that have the potential to cross borders and threaten people worldwide. The IHR, which entered into force on 15 June 2007, require countries to report certain disease outbreaks and public health events to WHO. Building on the unique experience of WHO in global disease surveillance, alert and response, the IHR define the rights and obligations of countries to report public health events, and establish a number of procedures that WHO must follow in its work to uphold global public health security. The Framework Convention on Tobacco Control (FCTC) is a treaty adopted by the 56th World Health Assembly on May 21, 2003. It became the first World Health Organization treaty adopted under article 19 of the WHO constitution. The treaty came into force on February 27, 2005. It had been signed by 168 countries and is legally binding in 163 ratifying/accessioned countries representing over 3 billion people. There are currently 32 non-parties to the treaty (14 which has not signed and 18 which have signed but

not ratified). The objective of the treaty is "to protect present and future generations from the devastating health, social, environmental and economic consequences of tobacco consumption and exposure to tobacco smoke." To this end, the treaty provides a framework of national, regional and international tobacco control measures, including the setting of broad limits on the production, sale, distribution, advertisement, taxation, and government policies towards tobacco.

33 "Implementation of tobacco control policies proves hard to do," *The Lancet* 369, no. 9580 (2007): 2133.

34 Simon Chesterman, "Globalization rules: accountability, power, and the prospects for global administrative law", *Global Governance* 14, no. 1 (2008): 39–52.

35 Larry O. Gostin, "Meeting the survival needs of the world's least healthy people – a proposed model for global health governance", *Journal of the American medical association* 298, no. 2, (2007): 225–228. Lawrence O. Gostin and Allyn L. Taylor, "Global health law: a definition and grand challenges", *Public Health Ethics* 1, no. 1, (2008): 53–63

36 World Health Organization, Intergovernmental Meeting on Pandemic Influenza Preparedness; Sharing of Influenza Viruses and Access to Vaccines and Other benefits (http://www.who.int/gb/pip/)

37 Jennifer Prah Ruger, "Global health governance and the World Bank," *The Lancet* 370, no. 9597 (2007): 1471–1474.

38 Heidi Ullrich, "Global health governance and multi-level policy coherence: can the G8 provide a cure?," Working Paper No. 25, Centre for International Governance Innovation, Ontario, Canada, 2008; Michael R. Reich and Keizo Takemi, "G8 and strengthening of health systems: follow-up to the Toyako Summit," *The Lancet* 373, no. 9662 (2009): 508–515.

39 Rhona Macdonald and Richard Horton, "Global health and the G8 – is power just too sweet to share?," *The Lancet* 372, no. 9633 (2008): 99–100

40 Krzysztof Rybinski, "Global Governance," *The Economist*, July 26, 2008, 22.

41 Ilona Kickbusch and Stephen Matlin, "A European Council on Global Health", *The Lancet* 371, no.9626 (2008): 1733–1734.

42 Dawn Primarolo, Mark Malloch-Brown, Ivan Lewis, on behalf of the Inter-ministerial Group for Global Health, "Health is global: a UK government strategy for 2008–13," *The Lancet* 373, no. 9662 (2009): 443–445.

43 Anne-Marie Slaughter, *A New World Order* (Princeton: Princeton University Press, 2004).

44 http://www.comunidadandina.org/sudamerica.htm

45 Klaus Schwab, "No more top-down leadership", *Newsweek*, November 17, 2008. (http://www.newsweek.com/id/167740).

46 Mazda Adli, Sabine Kleinert, and Antoine Lafont et al., "Shaping future health: Berlin Evolution of Medicine Summit," *The Lancet* 373, no. 9663 (2009): 519–520.

47 Richard Horton, "The case for a global development organisation," *The Lancet* 360, no. 9333, (2002): 582–583.

48 Inge Kaul, "Global Governance in the Making: An Exploration of Change and Innovation in International Cooperation Practices and Concepts," Paper presented at the ST Lee Project Conference on Global Governance, Singapore, December 4–6, 2008; Inge Kaul, Isabelle Grunberg and Marc Stern, eds., *Global Public Goods: International Cooperation in the 21st Century* (New York: Oxford University Press, 1999): 450–507.

49 Richard T. Mahoney and Carlos M. Morel, "A global health innovation system (GHIS)," *Innovation Strategy Today* 2, no. 1, (2006): 1–12.

50 Gill Walt, personal communication and seminar at Oxford University, Feb 13, 2009.

51 Pierre Chirac and Els Torreele, "Global framework on essential health R&D," *The Lancet* 367, no. 9522 (2006): 1560–1561.

52 Incentives for Global Health, "The Health Impact Fund: Making New Medicines Accessible for All" (http://www.yale.edu/macmillan/igh/)

53 UNITAID URL; The (voluntary) tax is collected directly when travelers purchase tickets on the internet and varies from 1–4 Euros for economy class to 10–40 Euros for business and first class. http://www.unitaid.eu/

54 Laurie Garrett, "The challenge of global health," *Foreign Affairs* 86, no. 1 (2007): 14–38.

55 Institute of Medicine, *The US Commitment to Global Health: Recommendations for the New Administration*, National Academic Press, Washington, 2009 (http://www.nap.edu/catalog/12506.html)

56 Kelley Lee, *The World Health Organization* (Oxford: Routledge 2009).

57 David Stuckler, Lawrence King, Helen Robinson, Martin McKee, "WHO's budgetary allocations and burden of disease: a comparative analysis," *The Lancet* 372, no. 9649 (2008): 1563–1569.

58 Kelley Lee, Seminar on "WHO at sixty: a time for reinvention rather than early retirement," University of Oxford, November 21, 2008 (http://www.globaleconomicgovernance.org/events_old.php)

59 World Health Organization, International Clinical Trial Registry Platform (http://www.who.int/ictrp/en/)

60 H-8 refers to GAVI, Bill & Melinda Gates Foundation, Global Fund to Combat HIV AIDS-TB-Malaria, UNAIDS, UNICEF, WHO, World Bank, UN Population Fund.

61 IHP+ (http://www.internationalhealthpartnership.net/)

62 Sanjeev Khagram, "Possible Future Architectures of Global Governance: A Transnational Prospective/Perspective," *Global Governance* 12, no. 1 (2006): 97–117.

63 Steve Waddell and Sanjeev Khagram, "Multi-Stakeholder Global Networks: Emerging Systems for the Global Common Good," in Pieter Glasbergen, Frank Biermann, Arthur P. J. Mol, eds., *Partnerships, Governance and Sustainable Development: Reflections on Theory and Practice* (UK: Edward Elgar Press, 2007), Sanjeev Khangram. "Transnational Transformations: From Government Centric International Regimes to Multi-Actor, Multi-Level Global Governance?," with Saleem Ali, in Ken Conca et al (eds.), *Sustainable Global Governance* (New York: Routledge, 2008).

64 Raimo Vayrynen, *Globalization and Global Governance* (New York: Rowman & Littlefields, 1999).

65 David Fidler, "Architecture amidst anarchy: global health's quest for governance," *Global Health Governance* 1, no. 1 (2007): 1–17.

66 Dennis Normile, "Indonesia Taps Village Wisdom to Fight Bird Flu," *Science* 315, no. 5808 (2007): 30–33; Barry S. Hewlett and Richard P. Amola, "Cultural contexts of Ebola in Northern Uganda," *Emerging Infectious Diseases* 9, no. 10, (2003): 1242–1248; Andrew Cornwall and Alex Shankland, "Engaging Citizens: Lessons from Building Brazil's National Health Systems," *Social Science and Medicine* 66, no. 10 (2008): 2173–2184.

67 Alliance for Health Policy and Systems Research, *Neglected Health Systems Research: Governance and Accountability*. October 2008. (http://www.who.int/alliance-hpsr/ AllianceHPSR_ResearchIssue_Governance.pdf)

68 Philip M. Polgreen, Yiling Chen, David M. Pennock, and Forrest D. Nelson, "Using internet searches for influenza surveillance," *Clinical Infectious Diseases* 47, no. 11 (2008): 1443–8.

69 Devi Sridhar, "Post-Accra: Is their space for country ownership?," *Third World Quarterly* 30, no. 7, (2009).

70 Richard Horton, "The global financial crisis: an acute threat to health", *The Lancet* 373, no. 9661, (2009): 355–356.

71 Heidi Ullrich, "Global health governance and multi-level policy coherence: can the G8 provide a cure?," Working Paper No. 25, Centre for International Governance Innovation, Ontario, Canada, 2008

72 G8 Hokkaido Toyako Summit, Health-Section 1.1, (http://www.mofa.go.ip/policy/economy/summit/2008/doc/pdf/20080929_02.pdf)

73 G8 Summit, La Maddalena, Italy, July 2009, http://www.g8italia2009.it/G8/Home/IlContesto/G8-G8_Layout_locale-1199882116809_ObiettiviMillennio.htm; Kiyoshi Kurokawa, Yoshiro Banno, Seigo Hara and James Kondo, "Italian G8 Summit: a critical juncture for global health," *The Lancet* 373, no. 9663 (2009): 526–527.

74 Sridhar, "Global health – who can lead?".

75 Institute of Medicine, *The US Commitment to Global Health: Recommendations for the New Administration*, National Academic Press, Washington, 2009 (http://www.nap.edu/catalog/12506.html)

76 Gaudenz Silberschmidt, Don Matheson and Illona Kickbush, "Creating a Committee C of the World Health Assembly," *The Lancet* 371, no. 9623 (2008): 1483–1486.

77 *Ibid.*

78 Rajaie Batniji, "Coordination and accountability in the World Health Assembly," *The Lancet* 372, no. 9641 (2008): 805.

79 United Nations Development Group, Delivering as One Pilots (http://www.undg.org/?P=7)

80 Devi Sridhar, Danielle Kuczynski and Kristie Latulippe, "Background Report for the UNAIDS Leadership Transition Working Group" Center for Global Development and GEG, available at http://www.cgdev.org/doc/UNAIDS_Leadership_11_03_08.pdf.

81 Sanjeev Khagram, "Possible Future Architectures of Global Governance: A Transnational Prospective/Perspective," *Global Governance* 12, no. 1 (2006): 97–117.

82 Defined as the responsibility of a state to protect the dignity of its own citizens and extends to a state's responsibility to other states to follow through on their commitments, and for the global effects of its domestic policies.

83 Robert Beaglehole and Ruth Bonita, "Global public health: a scorecard," *The Lancet* 372, no. 9654 (2008): 940–049.

84 Sanjeev Khagram, ST Lee Project Conference on Global Governance, Singapore, December 4–6, 2008.

85 Viktor E. Frankl, *Man's Search for Meaning* (London: Rider Publishing, 2004).

SARS IN SINGAPORE— CHALLENGES OF A GLOBAL HEALTH THREAT TO LOCAL INSTITUTIONS

Giok Ling Ooi and Kai Hong Phua

Source: *Natural Hazards*, 48 (2009), 317–27.

Abstract

SARS (Severe Acute Respiratory Syndrome) has been declared by WHO (World Health Organisation) as a global health threat. Within a period of four to five months in 2003, the disease infected some 8,000 people in more than 25 countries and left 774 dead. The many studies that have been done on the spread of SARS in Asia as well as countries as far flung as Germany and Canada have focused on the global dimension of the infectious disease as well as the speed of its spread upon emergence in southern China and then Hong Kong. Less attention has been paid to its spatial distribution at the national and local scales. This discussion focuses on the spread of SARS at the national and local spatial scales. In the process, the study presents the management of a hazard, in this case, an emerging infectious disease by national health care institutions such as the hospitals that ultimately proved to have been wholly unprepared for coping with at least the health aspects of the outcome of a globalised national agenda for growth and economic progress.

1 Introduction

When SARS was identified in Singapore, both hospitals and the health-care delivery system appeared to have been caught unprepared despite being key institutions in a city–state that has been increasingly seeking integration with the global economy. Singapore has regularly topped indices comparing the most globalised economies in the world and had been among the most successful cities competing for MICE (meetings, incentive travel, conferences, and exhibitions) both in the region and internationally (Ooi and Shaw 2004). Not only does the international airport and port in Singapore see a throughput of high numbers of travellers but Singaporeans themselves are among the most travelled people in the region, if not the world.

Globalisation challenges not only local businesses and cultures but also institutions as well as social and political processes including those concerning governance and in turn, public administration. Questions have been raised about diminished social obligations as government involvement appear to have receded in the face of international economic integration (Rodrik 1997). Studies about the impact of economic globalisation have generally focused on the relevance of the nation–state (Strange 1996) as well as local industry and enterprises in an increasingly integrated world. Cultural globalisation has equally been of concern in terms of its homogenising influence on lifestyles and consumption patterns particularly among the young (Fellman et al. 2003; Watson 1997). Indeed, tensions generated by conflicts between local identities and the cultural changes influenced by cultural globalisation appear as an inevitable outcome in countries seeking closer integration with the world economy (Keohane and Nye 2001; Meyer et al. 1997).

Globalisation implies the multiplicity of linkages and interconnections between the states and societies that make up the modern world system. It describes the process by which events, decisions and activities in one part of the world can come to have significant consequences for individuals and communities in quite distant parts of the globe. Globalisation has two distinct dimensions: scope (or stretching) and intensity (or deepening) (McGrew 1992, p. 23). Indeed, the concept of 'time–space compression' advanced by Harvey (1989) has been cited regularly in accounts of how physical distance has been replaced with speed distance. In other words, globalisation highlights the need for responses to address the speed at which activities, information and influences can reach across the globe. There has been, relatively speaking, a neglect in the consideration of the need for institutional changes and responses particularly in the health sector with globalisation. Attention however, has been focused on environmental concerns such as the shifting of environmental stresses to developing countries with economic globalisation (Sachs 1999). Contemporary threats, both environmental and health-related, do not appear to respect borders as SARS illustrated amply. The analysis of the way in which Singapore institutions managed ultimately to organise its fight against SARS suggests the failure of both institutions and institutional processes particularly in their response to the implications and outcomes of economic globalisation. While the crisis was addressed, '. . . The public service rallied together, putting aside turf rivalries, for a prompt and comprehensive SARS response. . . . mistakes were made. Like the failure to enforce infection-control measures at all hospitals, which allowed the virus to spread. . . . errors in judgement . . . Like the failure to isolate some SARS cases early enough' (Chua

2004, p. 21). Some 74.8% of the cases in Singapore were infected in hospitals and nursing homes (Teo et al. 2005).

Specifically in the case of SARS, the responses of the health-care institutions —hospitals, private clinics and their general practitioners, the health ministry and its agencies including laboratories—highlighted the neglect in studying the impact of globalisation and global environmental change on health care needs. Vulnerability was an issue because the readiness of health institutions and personnel was not a matter being given special attention. In particular, there has been little attention paid to the establishment of a system of institutional processes to help hospitals and health personnel respond collectively to the threat of the emerging infection diseases that have been seen increasingly in different parts of the world today. In the following discussion, the evidence of the rapid spread of the disease highlights the lack of preparedness among the local health institutions in relatively globalised cities such as Singapore, to face a global health threat. This was particularly in terms of information networking and sharing nationally and regionally. There was however, greater success in the action taken by the national government to respond to the containment and then isolation of the disease once it was identified and its nature better communicated and understood. In many ways, the highly centralised regime of governance in Singapore helped to put in place public health measures that resulted in the containment of the disease including infection control procedures in key health institutions.

2 Globalisation and health hazards

The rapid transmission of SARS through global travel to cities across the world has prompted epidemiologists and public health specialists to observe that the world faces increasing risk from such emerging infectious diseases. The World Health Organisation has already identified more than 30 such emerging or re-emerging infectious diseases including the West Nile virus and HIV among others (WHO 1996). SARS is considered a global health threat and has wreaked havoc in what the world has known as countries with highly efficient institutions as well as health care delivery systems that were equally well-regarded. Singapore was one of these countries where health care institutions and personnel were caught off-guard by a global outbreak that they did not appear prepared to take on at the time SARS struck in 2003.

Epidemiological studies and those of public health response have highlighted the growing rise in contacts that stems from contact between human and animal reservoir populations such as in the case of SARS. In the case of the so-called nipah virus epidemic in Malaysia over the period of 1998–1999, the fruit bat population that was dislocated because of habitat fragmentation and destruction due to economic development, then went on to infect the pig population in nearby farms. These pigs further infected human pig-handlers in the process (Chua et al. 2000; Lam and Chua 2002) including at least one such human handler in Singapore. Transmission of the disease was facilitated by poor farming practices. The emergence of the nipah virus was considered to have been induced by humans and human actions particularly in habitat degradation.

A number of factors have been identified with the emergence of highly infectious diseases which included SARS. These comprise agricultural development and urbanisation involving massive land clearance as well as deforestation, population migration, biodiversity loss and habitat fragmentation, air and water pollution, climatic changes and hydrological alterations, such as the building of dams (Patz and Confalonieri 2004). 'Multiple factors, including economic development and land use, human demographics and behaviour, and international travel and commerce, contribute to the emergence and re-emergence of infectious diseases' (Fauci 2005, p. 1079; Morse 1995). In the case of SARS, there is particular concern with the growth of the market in wildlife trade. Such trade results in disease-carrying hosts in wild game markets that abound in cities, such as Guangdong in China. This implies increased exposure of human handlers and consumers to animal reservoirs of novel micro-organisms. These markets are, in addition, a tourist attraction with large numbers of international and domestic visitors brought in daily to tour them. While in the past, such wild game markets have been small in scale and localised in terms of the clientele, there has been rapidly growing demand resulting in the development of regional networks and an increase in wildlife hunting (Bell et al. 2004).

SARS however, struck Singapore through international travel and travellers, namely Singaporeans who had travelled to Hong Kong and stayed in the same hotel as a doctor who had been infected in Guangzhou in southern China. Failure of the institutional practices in the health care delivery system was one of the factors that would have led to the rapid transmission of the diseases or at least the failure at arresting and containing the spread of the infectious disease. Another factor that is a regional concern is the lack of an information network among health care as well as public health institutions that are located in globalising cities that are increasingly integrated in the world system of international travel and other business connections. Indeed, there have been allegations of cover up and unwillingness to share information among China's authorities that in turn affected the way in which the disease was managed in cities such as Hong Kong and countries including Vietnam, Taiwan and Singapore.

Infected travellers to affected countries caught the disease through human to human transmission and travelled unawares to countries that had previously not been affected. (Hawkey et al. 2003). In Singapore, the infected patients spread the disease to health workers in hospitals and other patients as well as their visitors. These in turn were infected and also spread the disease to their friends and family members as well as the public and community at large. The disease started in the Guangdung Province in southern China at the end of 2002 but by 2003, when the global outbreak was finally ended, the SARS virus had affected a total number of 8,000 people or more in some 25 countries. SARS killed 774 people during this global outbreak. Thirty-three of them were in Singapore.

3 Institutional preparedness and ineptitude in responding to global forces

Emerging infectious diseases or EIDs have been identified as a prospective new scourge because of their global dimension (Morse 1995). SARS was an emerging infectious disease that confounded national governments and hospital management in both Asia and a number of other countries around the world.

In Singapore, as in other places around the world, the WHO identified 'super-transmission' events involving the infection of more than 10 people by one patient infected with SARS (WHO 2003). The first person to be identified with SARS and who had been hospitalised, transmitted the disease to a chain of at least 90 people including members of her family and her church.

The spread of SARS in terms of its geographical distribution in Singapore is important in establishing the soundness of the initiatives and practices that eventually led to the end of the transmission and the outbreak in the city–state. Stricken patients checked into varying government restructured hospitals. Major hospitals had their share of cases before isolation and quarantine procedures were put in place. Singapore was placed on WHO's list of affected countries for which it issued travel advisories, alerts and restrictions.

In all, Singapore saw 238 cases among which 14% or 33 patients died. This was over a period shorter than three months from February to May 2003 with the first case identified on 25th February (see Table 1). The first case of SARS in Singapore to be seen in a hospital had spread the disease to both her parents, two grandparents, an uncle and her pastor within the period of 3 weeks or so between end February 2003 and March. The patient lost both her parents and two grandparents during the time. The pastor also eventually died from SARS. This first patient also transmitted her illness to another patient in the same ward who would eventually spread the virus to another hospital as well as to a family member working in a food whole-sale centre in Singapore. In all, this patient transmitted the virus to 12 people before she was isolated a fortnight later.

The rapid spread of the virus among patients and their family members as well as visitors highlights the state of alertness and awareness of health institutions and health personnel to the prospects of emerging infectious diseases the spread of which can be aided by global links. A chain of trans-mission has been described (Goh et al. 2006) in which the major hospitals

Table 1 Probable SARS cases—estimated figures around the world.

Areas	Cumulative number of cases			Median age (range)	Number of deaths[a]	Case fatality ratio (%)	Number of imported cases (%)	Date onset first probable case	Date onset last probable case
	Female	Male	Total						
Australia	4	2	6	15 (1–45)	0	0	6 (100)	26-Feb-03	1-Apr-03
Canada	151	100	251	49 (1–98)	43	17	5 (2)	23-Feb-03	12-Jun-03
China	2,674	2,607	5,327[b]	Not available	349	7	Not applicable	16-Nov-02	3-Jun-03
China, Hong Kong special administrative region	977	778	1,755	40 (0–100)	299	17	Not applicable	15-Feb-03	31-May-03
China, Macao special administrative region	0	1	1	28	0	0	1 (100)	5-May-03	5-May-03
China, Taiwan	218	128	346[c]	42 (0–93)	37	11	21 (6)	25-Feb-03	15-Jun-03
France	1	6	7	49 (26–61)	1	14	7 (100)	21-Mar-03	3-May-03
Germany	4	5	9	44 (4–73)	0	0	9 (100)	9-Mar-03	6-May-03
India	0	3	3	25 (25–30)	0	0	3 (100)	25-Apr-03	6-May-03
Indonesia	0	2	2	56 (47–65)	0	0	2 (100)	6-Apr-03	17-Apr-03
Italy	1	3	4	30.5 (25–54)	0	0	4 (100)	12-Mar-03	20-Apr-03
Kuwait	1	0	1	50	0	0	1 (100)	9-Apr-03	9-Apr-03
Malaysia	1	4	5	30 (26–84)	2	40	5 (100)	14-Mar-03	22-Apr-03
Mongolia	8	1	9	32 (17–63)	0	0	8 (89)	31-Mar-03	6-May-03

Table 1 (cont'd)

Areas	Cumulative number of cases			Median age (range)	Number of deaths[a]	Case fatality ratio (%)	Number of imported cases (%)	Date onset first probable case	Date onset last probable case
	Female	Male	Total						
New Zealand	1	0	1	67	0	0	1 (100)	20-Apr-03	20-Apr-03
Philippines	8	6	14	41 (29–73)	2	14	7 (50)	25-Feb-03	5-May-03
Republic of Ireland	0	1	1	56	0	0	1 (100)	27-Feb-03	27-Feb-03
Republic of Korea	0	3	3	40 (20–80)	0	0	3 (100)	25-Apr-03	10-May-03
Romania	0	1	1	52	0	0	1 (100)	19-Mar-03	19-Mar-03
Russian Federation	0	1	1	25	0	0	Not available	5-May-03	5-May-03
Singapore	161	77	238	35 (1–90)	33	14	8 (3)	25-Feb-03	5-May-03
South Africa	0	1	1	62	1	100	1 (100)	3-Apr-03	3-Apr-03
Spain	0	1	1	33	0	0	1 (100)	26-Mar-03	26-Mar-03
Sweden	3	2	5	43 (33–55)	0	0	5 (100)	28-Mar-03	23-Apr-03
Switzerland	0	1	1	35	0	0	1 (100)	9-Mar-03	9-Mar-03
Thailand	5	4	9	42 (2–79)	2	22	9 (100)	11-Mar-03	27-May-03
United Kingdom	2	2	4	59 (28–74)	0	0	4 (100)	1-Mar-03	1-Apr-03
United States	13	14	27	36 (0–83)	0	0	27 (100)	24-Feb-03	13-Jul-03
Vietnam	39	24	63	43 (20–76)	5	8	1 (2)	23-Feb-03	14-Apr-03
Total			8,096		774	9.6	142		

[a] Includes only cases whose death is attributed to SARS.

[b] Case classification by sex is unknown for 46 cases.

[c] Since 11 July 2003, 325 cases have been discarded in Taiwan, China. Laboratory information was insufficient or incomplete for 135 discarded cases, of which 101 died.

and nursing homes featured prominently as the locations for the transmission of the disease. The implication was that 1 week's delay in the implementation of infection control measures could triple the size of the epidemic and increase its duration to 4 weeks (Tai 2006; Wallinga and Teunis 2004). There appears to be a gap that needs to be addressed between the speed at which economies are globalising and the state of preparedness of their institutions for such global integration. Certainly, the health care delivery system in Singapore was highly vulnerable, from the point of view of preparedness, to the onslaught of rapid infection and fatality that the SARS virus brought. It took authorities one week between the death from SARS of a worker from a wholesale market and the closure of the market as well as the start of contact tracing to ensure that all who had been in contact with the worker would be quarantined (Chua 2004). http://www.who.int/csr/sars/country/table/en/index.html (Access on 26 March 2007).

The spread of the SARS virus was chiefly among locals in Singapore (see Table 1 above). Only 8 or 3% of the cases had been imported from affected countries. In the case of a large number of European countries, 100% of the cases were imported, hence implying that the transmission among the locals was contained. In Singapore, the overwhelmingly large proportion of cases resulted from local transmission. While it is noted that the infectiousness of SARS has not been uniform, the discussion is about the lack of infection control measures to contain its spread among locals. In many instances, the transmission was among cases that had been hospitalised. Fatalities included medical doctors and nursing staff. The pattern was similar to that of most East Asian countries beginning with China and including cities like Hong Kong. Taiwan too was equally struck. Here, the challenge to the implementation of quarantine procedures was evident: health workers threatened to jump out of hospital windows, thereby defying their quarantine orders. This was an event widely covered by international media.

The end of the global outbreak was possible because institutions in affected countries subsequently worked with WHO to manage cases as well as establish infection control measures. Measures taken included a travel advisory to affected countries to keep travellers better informed about the progress made towards containing the disease. Quarantine of travellers particularly from the affected countries and suspected cases were instituted. Several ministries in Singapore participated in the establishment of the control measures and procedures that were put into place. Throughout Singapore, temperature monitoring was also introduced. Singapore also eventually established procedures for contact tracing. Places including schools as well as a wholesale market were vacated and closed with the detection of suspected cases. Screening at port and airport was set up, focussing particularly on travellers returning from China and Hong Kong (Tambyah 2003).

The seriousness of the outbreak in terms of institutional responses could be gauged by the difficulty facing both the Ministry of Education and Ministry of Health to require schools that were due to start after a stretch of holidays to remain closed. Neither ministries required schools to remain closed after the holidays ended and SARS cases remained on the rise. Nevertheless the decision to close schools had to be taken in the end, in part to allay fears of further infections by children who might have travelled abroad with their families during the holidays. The state of unpreparedness of the hospitals to face the challenges posed by SARS was seen in the toll on hospital patients who were being treated for other complaints including serious illnesses such as cancer. The Singapore General Hospital SARS debrief report noted that 'There were many victims of the SARS crisis in Singapore who never had SARS at all who were just sick patients who didn't get the care that they needed due to the many constraints that came along with the SARS crisis and all the attendant measures needed to combat the outbreak' (Chua 2004, p. 67).

Lack of information from China as well as knowledge of how to contain and stop the transmission of the disease plagued the Singapore hospitals and government agencies involved. This institutional lapse and the failure on the part of the Chinese authorities to inform the rest of the region was reflected in the number of cases seen in the countries with close travel and business links to both China and Hong Kong. Ultimately, the committee established to manage the isolation and quarantine procedures for cases was chaired by the Minister of Home Affairs. Ultimately, the Ministry of Health managed the isolation and quarantine system while the Minister of Home Affairs chaired a multi-agency committee to ensure smooth coordination of government policies and activities. Quarantine procedures were implemented with cases placed under 24 h camera surveillance and policing was introduced to ensure that suspected cases particularly among members of the public served out their quarantine orders.

4 Discussion

The intervention recommended by WHO is instructive mainly because of the implications that globalisation in the future would signal for cities as well as countries seeking closer integration with global economy and networks. For the management of SARS at the international level, the WHO has recommended a surveillance plan that spans a variety of geographical zones. One of these geographical zones encompasses the sources or original starting points for SARS in Guangdung in southern China with high potential for species transfer of the virus. This is the zone with a potential for the re-emergence of the disease. Other zones comprise the countries and cities affected because of import through travellers from the potential zone of re-emergence of SARS. Indeed, the links between these two types of geographical zones identify a territorial swathe connected through business and tourism as well as migration. In brief, globalisation has been a force in paving the way for the recent outbreak of SARS and its geographical distribution in terms of transmissions, patients and fatalities.

Apart from the two geographical zones linked by the potential for a re-emergence of the disease mainly because of the global business and travel connecting the zones affected in the last outbreak, the remaining zones comprise areas facing relatively low risk from SARS and its spread. At the local level and institutionally, the emphasis is on early detection and management of the cases. Institutional processes of contact tracing and the sharing of databases of such infectious diseases and patients among health institutions and workers also appear crucial should the disease re-emerge in the future. Public health control measures were applied at three fronts—prevention and control within healthcare settings, community and at the borders (James et al. 2006, p. 20). These measures included a designated hospital for the treatment of SARS patients as well as stringent entry and exit checks at port and airport to screen and control importation as well as exportation of new cases. 'The rapid containment of the outbreak was due to the strong political leadership, effective command, control and coordination at all levels, prompt and coordinated interagency response, high level of professionalism and dedication of HCWs (Health care workers), and strong community support' (Goh et al. 2006, p. 309; also see Chua 2004; Menon and Goh 2005).

Among all the public sector hospitals, only one was spared from the onslaught of SARS which meant that the virus spread to all the rest. The then Health Minister, Mr Lim Hng Kiang, suggested that the hospitals lapsed because of the mind set that 'I'm the tertiary hospital, I know what to do. Why are you telling me what to do? Infection control, these are all basic things. So this is where they messed up unfortunately. . . . SGH (Singapore General Hospital) was a disappointment' (Chua 2004, p. 65). The Minister had noted that a regimental sergeant-major (RSM) type of CEO would do well during SARS because this CEO would have been able to maintain tight discipline in infection control measures. 'In the army, we call it battle discipline. I don't need generals, I told the hospitals. I need RSMs' (Chua 2004, p. 65). In other words, the Minister for Health during the SARS epidemic in Singapore was commenting on the readiness of hospitals to contain infection and arrest the spread of the virus.

Other lapses highlighted the need for a system for contact-tracing. This would be a system to enable quarantining measures to be taken once people who had been in contact with patients had been traced. Not only was contact-tracing stretching to the limits the resources of the hospitals but the subsequent system that was established failed to put such tracing into place when relevant public sector agencies were in the process of shutting down facilities and isolating them because of a SARS case that had been identified. Such contact-tracing became crucial in ensuring quarantine measures were put into place effectively. The Ministry of Health found that it was unable to cope with the sheer scale of the contact-tracing effort. Neither was it able to maintain an effective quarantine system nor provide information to the public at the same time. Both the Ministry of Defence and Singapore Armed Forces were needed to support the effort of the Ministry of Health with software to maintain the database necessary for contact-tracing, a call centre to help members of the public and also people serving their quarantine.

In many ways, the SARS outbreak in Singapore highlighted the need for a patient-centric process of case-management particularly by the health care delivery system that is in place. Briefly, institutions in the health care delivery system will have to establish a case profile that recognises other institutional intervention or institutions involved in the management of cases or patients that all hospitals can share. Currently the system relies mostly on patients to carry their case history, particularly the hospitals or clinics where they have been, to the next hospital they are visiting. Such transfers of patients among hospitals led to the rapid spread of the virus to the hospitals where the largest clusters, that is, numbers of people and health workers, were infected.

An important implication arising from the way in which SARS spread among Singapore health institutions is the need for greater connectivity among agencies and workers in the health-care delivery system. Institutions need to put in place, processes in terms of cooperative procedures for information sharing and co-management of cases particularly that of emerging infectious diseases such as, SARS. An urgent need for open and transparent collaboration among countries has been highlighted (Heymann 2006). Indeed, such collaboration led to the interruption of human-to-human transmission of SARS at all sites within six months. The SARS crisis was a tragic way of showing up the gaps in the institutional processes of health agencies in Singapore for effective response to hazards, such as emerging infectious diseases, that global travel can bring.

Nonetheless, Singapore has been praised by WHO and others for the establishment of public health control measures involving cross-sectional inter-ministerial collaboration and coordination (James et al. 2006). These were the measures that eventually led to the containment of the spread of the disease.

The economic costs of SARS were high. Singapore's open economy is highly dependent on the use of its airport and port as well as its airlines such as Singapore Airlines. In addition, the hotel industry and related activities were highly dependent on tourism as well as international business travel. Much of the tourism sector came to a standstill and shoppers stayed away from eateries and other commercial outlets. Globally, Smith (2006, p. 3114) cites sources that estimated the macro-economic impact of SARS at US$30–100 billion or around US$3–10 million/case. In a rather macabre twist, a number of the hotels served as quarantine centres for staff of a mental health institute where another fever cluster had been identified during the original SARS outbreak. While it proved to be a false alarm, it was a decision taken to quarantine health workers of the institute in hotels because the institute itself had no facilities to accommodate the staff. The measure taken underscores the limits to which the institutions of Singapore and in particular, its health delivery system as well as public health processes were stretched during the SARS crisis.

References

Bell D., Robertson S., Hunter P. R. (2004) Animal origins of SARS coronavirus: possible links with the international trade in small carnivores. Philos Trans R Soc Lond B Biol Sci 359(1447):1107–1114

Chua K. B. (2000) Nipah virus: a recently emergent deadly paramyxovirus. Science 288:1432–1435

Chua L. H. (2004). A defining moment—how Singapore beat SARS. Institute of Policy Studies and Ministry of Communications, Information and the Arts, Singapore

Fauci A. S. (2005) Emerging and re-emerging infectious diseases: the perpetual challenge. Acad Med 80:1079–1085

Fellmann J., Getis A., Getis J. (2003) Human geography—landscapes of human activities. 7th edn, Wm. C. Brown Publishers, Dubuque, Iowa (USA)

Goh K.-T., Cutter C., Heng B.-H., Ma S., Koh B. K. W. Kwok C. (2006) Epidemiology and control of SARS in Singapore. Ann Acad Med 35:301–316

Harvey D. (1989) The condition of postmodernity. Blackwell, Oxford

Hawkey P. M., Bhagani S. Gillespie S. H. (2003) Severe acute respiratory syndrome (SARS): breath-taking progress. J Med Microbiol 52:609–613

Heymann D. (2006) SARS and emerging infectious diseases: a challenge to place global solidarity above national sovereignty. Ann Acad Med Singapore 35:350–353

James L., Shindo N., Cutter J., Ma S. Chew S. K. (2006) Public health measures implemented during the SARS outbreak in Singapore, 2003. Public Health 26:20–26

Keohane R. O., Nye J. S. (2001) Power and inter-dependence. Addison-Wesley

Lam S. K., Chua K. B. (2002) Nipah virus encephalitis outbreak in Malaysia. Clin Infect Dis 34(Suppl 2):S48–S51 McGrew A. G. (1992) Conceptualising global politics. In: McGrew A. G., Lewis P. G. (eds) Global politics: globalisation and the nation-state. Polity Press, Cambridge, pp 1–28

Menon K. U., Goh K. T. (2005) Transparency and trust: risk communications and the Singapore experience in managing SARS. J Commun Manage 9:375–383

Meyer J. W., Boli J., Thomas G. M., Ramirez F. O. (1997) World society and the nation-state. Am J Sociol 103(1):144–175

Morse S. S. (1995) Factors in the emergence of infectious diseases. Emerg Infect Dis 1:7–15

Ooi G. L., Shaw B. J. (2004) Beyond the port city—development and identity in 21st century Singapore. Pearson-Prentice-Hall, Singapore

Patz J., Confalonieri U. (2004) Human health: infectious and parasitic diseases. In Millennium ecosystem assessment: conditions and trends. Island Press, Washington, DC

Rodrik D. (1997) Has globalisation gone too far? Institute for International Economics, Washington, DC

Sachs W. (1999) Planet dialectics: explorations in environment and development. Zed Books, London

Smith R. D. (2006) Responding to global infectious disease outbreaks: lessons from SARS on the role of risk perception, communication and management. Soc Sci Med 63:3113–3123

Strange S. (1996) The retreat of the state: the diffusion of power in the world economy. Cambridge University Press, Cambridge

Tai D. Y. H. (2006) SARS: how to manage future outbreaks? Ann Acad Med Singapore 35:368–373

Tambyah P. A. (2003) SARS: responding to an unknown virus. Eur J Clin Microbiol Infect Dis 23(8):589–595

Teo P., Yeoh B. S. A., Ong S. N. (2005) SARS in Singapore: surveillance strategies in a globalising city. Health Policy 72:279–291

Wallinga J., Teunis P. (2004) Different epidemic curves for severe acute respiratory syndrome reveal similar impacts of control measures. Am J Epidemiol 160:509–516

Watson J. L. (1997) Golden arches east: McDonald's in east Asia. Stanford University Press, Stanford

World Health Organisation, WHO (1996) World Health Report 1996: fighting disease, fostering development. World Health Organisation, Geneva

World Health Organisation, WHO (2003) Weekly epidemiological record, No. 14, April

Website. http://www.who.int/csr/sars/country/table/en/index.html (accessed on 26 March 2007)

Part 14

CIVIL SOCIETY AND
HEALTH GOVERNANCE

86

THE ROLE OF NON-GOVERNMENTAL ORGANIZATIONS AND THE PRIVATE SECTOR IN THE PROVISION OF HEALTH CARE IN DEVELOPING COUNTRIES

Andrew Green

Source: *International Journal of Health Planning and Management*, 2:1 (1987), 37–58.

Summary

A major component of total health care in many developing countries is that provided by organizations outside the state sector. Analysis of the relationships between the state and non-state sectors and explicit government policies towards the non-state sector have, however, often been neglected. Within many developing countries, there is heterogeneity rather than homogeneity within the non-state sector, making the task of developing consistent and workable policies difficult. In order for such policies to be developed, a clear understanding of the characteristics and roles of the various non-governmental and private health care providers is needed. This, in turn, requires the development of analytical tools and evaluative criteria. This article outlines and discusses issues requiring consideration in the formulation of policies, and sets a preliminary agenda for research action.

Introduction

For many developing countries, health care provided by organizations outside the state sector is a major constituent in the total sum of health care provision. Indeed, in many countries, such non-state health care accounts for the majority of all health care. Paradoxically, however, until recently there has been markedly little attention paid to the role of this sector by the governments of many of these countries, by international agencies, or by academic researchers.

This situation is now changing, with greater recognition and interest in this area by governments and some international agencies, particularly the Christian Medical Commission, the World Health Organization (WHO) at its assembly in 1986, and the World Bank. There are various reasons for this increased awareness, but two stand out as being of particular importance. Firstly, the emergence of the philosophy of primary health care, which, *inter alia*, stresses the need for multi-sectoral and multi-agency collaboration. Secondly, the recent and continuing global recession, and its effects on the public financing of social, and in particular health, services, has prompted interest in alternative funding arrangements. Linked to this second point has been increased interest in the development of methodologies to determine the nature, sources and scale of existing health care finance.

However, the burgeoning recognition of the size, and hence potential effects (whether helpful or harmful) of the non-state sector, has not, in general, led to concomitant policy action on the part of the sector itself, governments, nor international development agencies. This paper attempts to set out the major issues that require exploration and research, in order that such policies can be more fully formulated.

The paper, firstly, examines the characteristics that distinguish and differentiate non-governmental organizations (NGOs) and the private sector, from each other and from state-provided services. For analysis to be made of their relative roles, it is important that their prime distinguishing characteristics be identified.

The next section then looks briefly at the existing evidence on the role and importance of NGOs in the field of health care. What little literature there is, is often characterized by either underplaying the extent of both NGOs and the private sector, or by gross generalizations about their actual or potential role. Such generalizations, it is argued, are both inaccurate and unhelpful, in a field where heterogeneity, rather than homogeneity, is the order of the day. Various criteria are then suggested as both descriptive and analytical tools, and which highlight this heterogeneity.

The arguments surrounding the public/private mix for health care are then addressed, noting that: (a) even the most ardent 'marketeers' have accepted the need for some public sector provision, and that hence the debate focuses on the *optimal* extent of this provision; (b) the theoretical debate has not yet been, and indeed may never be, concluded; (c) even in the more industrial countries of the West, where the debate has existed as a mainstream activity in the fields of health planning and economics, there are wide differences of opinion as to the optimum mix, and equally wide sources of contradictory evidence.

The final section looks at the area of policy formulation and the optimal strategy for any government in the mix of service provision and regulatory controls. The article concludes by urging that urgent research attention should be focused on tools and criteria that can be used to formulate appropriate policies.

NGOs, the private sector and the state

Analysis of the respective roles of, and comparative advantages between, the state, NGOs and the private sector requires a prior definition of these three terms. Presently, literature uses a variety of terms to describe health care organizations, including: government, state, public sector, social security, voluntary, non-governmental, charity, mission, private-non-profit, and private-for-profit.

For the purpose of this article, a working definition is chosen which accords with common usage. This definition uses two criteria—whether an organization is directly managed by and accountable to the state; and, whether its stated aims are explicitly in pursuit of profit maximization. Under such criteria, NGOs are defined as non-profit-making organization, outside direct state control, and the private sector is defined as profit-maximizing non-state activites.

Though such a definition is adequate for present purposes, in practice the demarcation is more ambiguous. Three examples illustrate this diversity. Firstly, organizations such as district designated hospitals in Tanzania, managed by the church, but heavily subsidized and controlled by the state, occupy an uneasy position between being an NGO and being part of the state sector. Secondly, the term 'private' is often used to denote the opposite to 'public' rather than profit-maximizing. Thus, for example, the Private Hospital Association of Malawi is made up largely of church organizations. Thirdly, the term *state* is deliberately chosen in many countries to include, in addition to ministry of health (central government) activities, health services managed by local authorities, or other ministries and quasi-governmental activities, such as the large social insurance organizations typical of Latin America. However, several of these display organizational characteristics (for example, a degree of autonomy) similar to NGOs.

The development of tools by which one can describe, categorize and analyse the different health organizational forms, is of much more than academic interest. The development of policy guidelines is dependent upon the ability to describe and delineate such organizations, for which further research is required. Such research would be able to draw upon the experience of health sectors within developed countries and non-health sectors in the developing world (such as education) where policies in this area may be further advanced.

The importance of NGOs and the private sector in health and hospital care in developing countries

Until recently the role in terms of both size and nature of the non-state sector within the health field, was not given due recognition by governments or international agencies. Government development plans were often characterized by a failure to mention, let alone take account of, in anything more than a cursory fashion, the existence and role of such organizations. Similarly, international aid agencies concentrated their efforts on the government sector. (To some degree this was due to a failure to differentiate sufficiently between the dual role of government health agencies as responsible both for national health policy, and for major service provision and funding.) Furthermore, where recognition *was* given, there was often little distinction made between NGOs and the private sector. The World Bank *Health Sector Policy Paper* of 1975, for example, makes no such distinction (World Bank, 1975).

This situation is, however, for many countries, now changing with a more explicit recognition of the extent and importance (wheher negative or positive) of the non-state sector. At least two explanations can be identified. Firstly, the acceptance of the philosophy of primary health care has, to varying degrees, forced upon governments and others involved in health care, a recognition of the need to appraise critically the workings of *all* health care providers, through its stress on multi-agency collaboration, appropriate health care and equity. Closely allied to this has been a push in many countries to a more decentralized system of health care, placing greater emphasis on a planning, management and coordinating role at the local (district) level.

Secondly, the financial crisis, in part the result of a global recession, which has been evident in many developing countries over the last decade, has forced a closer look at means of expanding (or in some cases maintaining) health care provision with minimal implications for government expenditure. This has led to greater interest in the non-state sector as one possible way of achieving this strategy. Financing surveys, whose importance in providing planning information is gradually being recognized, have been an important source of comprehensive information on the overall size of the different sectors. For instance, comparative information has been compiled (de Ferranti, 1985) on the level of total private expenditure in 37 developing countries, showing a range, as a percentage of total health expenditure, of between 12% for Lesotho to 87% for Bangladesh and Korea.

The evidence that is readily available (Cumper, 1986; Abel-Smith, 1985) would appear to show that: between countries there is a wide variation in the size and composition of the non-state sector; and, that there are methodological difficulties in making comparative estimates compounded by the lack of a single survey/accounting system.

Types and characteristics of the NGO/private sector

Analysis of both NGOs and the private sector suffers from broad generalizations. NGOs have been described variously as being autonomous, flexible, innovative and cost-effective; or, alternatively, as failing to meet national health needs, unplanned, duplicative or inefficient (WHO, 1985). Whilst any of these descriptions may be justifiable when applied to particular NGOs, they are inaccurate and unhelpful when applied to the sector as a whole. Similarly, the debate on the role of the private sector has often polarized (Roemer *et al*, 1984). For the development of policy, it is first essential that a clear understanding be developed of both the *types* and the *characteristics* of individual NGOs in a country.

Main NGO/private sector types

Seven broad groupings of non-state organizations involved in the health field can be identified:

Religious organization   Possibly the longest established organizations are those which are church-related. They are often major providers of health care alongside other social development services including, most commonly, education. Whilst their connection with the church has always implied a religious motive for this work, this has manifested itself in different ways with different religious and denominations, some seeing health services as a vehicle for proselytization, and others seeing them as an end in themselves.

The motivations of any particular church-based health service have implications for both its approach to health care and its desire to work with other NGOs and with government. To some degree a gradual overall shift away from a proselytizing motive can be discerned, resulting perhaps from the reduced availability of external funding, and from a parallel localization of church-related activities. However, wide variations still exist. Church-related health services are often multi-dimensional, and involve hospital-based services with outreach satellite clinics, of either a mobile or permanent nature. The church has also often been associated with particular disease programmes of a vertical nature — such as leprosy. Many church-related services have had extensive involvement in training staff, usually in the first instance for their own purposes, but often for government and other sectors as well. Attitudes to government vary from organizations that are committed to working within the government structure and which may see their long-term future as part of government, to those anxious to maintain their autonomy.

International (social welfare) NGOs   Various international NGOs, usually based in developed countries, are involved in the provision of health care. The relationship between the central office and the country-based office varies, with some being seen as outreach branches carrying out central policy (e.g. Oxfam) to those who have an affiliated relationship (e.g. Red Cross and Red Crescent Societies). The scope of activities of such NGOs varies. Although originally an explicit and well-defined target listed (e.g. Red Cross — disaster/ emergency relief; Save the Children — children's welfare; International Planned Parenthood Federation — family planning), this has, depending on the periphery-to-centre relationship, commonly broadened out. Thus the Red

579

Cross, for example, is, in many countries, increasingly active in the primary health care field. The degree of decentralization of such NGOs depends largely on the dependence of local branches on central funding. One specific subgroup of international NGOs are the service clubs such as Lions and Rotary, which have commonly shared international aims, but local organization. They differ from other international NGOs in that they are primarily involved in fund-raising activities rather than direct service provision.

Locally based (social welfare) NGOs In contrast to the international NGOs there are a variety of locally based NGOs operating within the social welfare field. Two subgroups are identifiable — NGOs dealing with broad community development issues, and often geographically focused, and NGOs which are more issue specific.

Within the first group fall traditional social groupings and women's groups. The second group focuses on specific issues and may have as much a pressure group role as a service delivery role. The impact of both such groups is extremely variable. Their restricted funding base implies that the majority are unlikely to be involved in the direct provision and management of health and, in particular hospital, care; but, through their pressure group activities, they may be highly influential in general policy formulation.

Unions and trade and professional associations A fourth group comprises organizations whose primary motive is the protection and promotion of their constituents, including trade unions and trade associations. Whilst their present role within the field of health activities is limited, there is a potential, particularly on the demand-side, for an expansion of their role. The present extent and strength of such groups is still generally small, though within Latin America the role of union activity in this field has been recognized for some time. Professional health-related associations are, of course, important for specific reasons on the supply-side.

Other non-profit making organizations A fifth group of non-government organizations comprises services provided outside the public sector, but with access limited to certain groups or individuals on non-financial grounds. Occupational health services, for example, often have a substantive input to the overall health sector, and may be regarded as non-profit making in themselves.

Non-profit making (but pre-paid) health care This sector, comprising organizations modelled on American group health care, such as Health Maintenance Organizations (HMOs), is still relatively rare in many developing countries, requiring a minimum concentrated population base of adequate income. However, it is likely that this sector will grow. One example of this is Latin America, where urban concentrations of skilled labour have led to a growth in this sector. ISAPRES in Chile, for example, perform similar roles to

HMOs in the USA; in 1984 the 17 ISAPRES had a total of over 852 000 enrollees out of a total population of approximately 11.2 million (Scarpaci, 1985).

Private sector   The last group comprises the for-profit organizations, which may be locally based, or part of a wider international corporate structure. Though this sector as a whole is presently a major element in the total health care system of many developing countries, the main emphasis lies in the area of individual private medical and nursing practices, and the provision of drugs, rather than in the organization of hospital care. Of considerable importance in many developing countries, however, is the use of public facilities, in a *private, profit-seeking manner*, by either state-employed physicians or private practitioners. Such use may or may not be officially condoned or used as a fringe benefit to government medical employees.

Characteristics

A number of characteristics can be examined which further demonstrate the diversity in the nature of the non-state sector, and are important in analysing the role of such institutions within the health sector. These major character-istics are outlined, and their importance discussed, below.

Motivational

The influence of an organization's objectives on its performance is a field that is fraught with difficulty. Studies relating to hospitals within industrialized countries have looked at a variety of variables within both the for-profit and not-for-profit sectors, to explain performance; such variables coming from both economic schools of thought (via the theory of the firm) and from beha-vioural schools of though (McGuire, 1985). Despite the depth of debate, no clear view on which are the key determining variables has emerged. In part this is the result of the difficulty in analysing the role within organizations of health professionals and, in particular, doctors. It has been argued (Majone, 1984), for example, that there is a convergence of interests between non-profit-making organizations and professionals, and that as such NGOs are highly suitable organizations for the delivery of health care. However, though in spe-cific instances this may be the case, it cannot be held, *a priori*, that *all* NGOs are more suited, either in comparison to the private sector or to the state sector. Furthermore, it is by no means clear that the interests of health professionals converge with the health care needs of the community.

Proselytization was originally an important motive for many religious health services, and such motives may have led to an unduly curative bias, as a means of attracting patients. Whilst proselytization as the *sole* motive is now rare, the religious culture of some church health services can on occasion be a source of tension between them and other organizations, and in particular government health services. An example of an often contentious area can be found in the field of family planning (and most particularly abortions), where strong attitudinal differences may exist. A more general problem may be found in the area of personnel management. Where staff are expected to identify themselves with the organization's religious motive, this may be *positive* resulting in higher commitment; or, *negative*, when for example schemes to allow staff transfers between government and NGOs are arranged or training is carried out for government staff by NGOs. Motivation is often cited as a cause for perceived quality differences between government, NGOs and the private sector; however, even where such quality differences can be demonstrated, it is difficult to single out motivation as the prime variable.

A second tension may exist between those NGOs that are issue specific, or those that are primarily involved in fund-raising, where different views of priorities may exist. This may be particularly difficult where the NGO has a pressure group role, within a system where lobbying balances between uses of resources are weak.

Between the NGOs themselves there may be sufficient differences in philosophy leading to an atmosphere of competition rather than collaboration. For example, many religious NGOs are located in close proximity to each other as a result of earlier competitive proselytization. Whilst there are some circumstances where competition may be regarded as healthy, situations are still common where there is unnecessary duplication of facilities, or where inefficient and possibly dangerous dualistic supervisory or referral mechanisms exist within an area served by two NGOs, or an NGO and government.

The interests of other than religious NGOs are again different. Organizations involved in the provision of employment-related health care, are primarily motivated to demonstrate that such services affect profits or productivity through either decreasing employee absenteeism, increasing worker productivity, or enhancing the payment package in fields of skill shortage. The last of these may give rise to an unduly curative approach, with expensive, high-technology health care as a conspicuous end in itself.

The effect of profit-maximization as an organizational objective, on the type of health care provided, has been well documented in the literature on industrialized countries and is unlikely to be very different in shape in developing countries. Of crucial importance on the scale and type of health care is the means of financing (and particularly fee-for-service and insurance) and the degree and type of regulation. Also of great importance to the for-profit sector, though its importance is not confined to this sector, is the form of payment to the doctor (Glazer, 1970).

Types of health service

Within the non-state sector, there is a wide diversity, as has already been shown, of types of activities within the health field including fund-raising, lobbying, and service provision. Even within these activities, wide variations are possible. Examination of just one of these activities — the provision of hospital care, illustrates wide variations in (a) *location*: many NGOs (though certainly not all, as is sometimes argued) are rurally based; whereas private hospitals are almost entirely based in the larger towns and cities, as are industrial health services (though some mines/plantation/agrobusiness-related hospitals may be rural); (b) *activity*: differences exist as to the type of hospital care — whether specialist or general — and the degree of identification with primary health care through, for example, referral mechanisms, preventive activities, or community development activities. Private hospitals, for example, are likely to cater for short-term, acute cases, as being the most profitable; (c) *form of provision of service*: even between similar activities, differences often exist as to the way in which services are provided, as a result of the technology used, including staffing mix, equipment, form of buildings, and plant, and the degree of innovation.

Internal organizational characteristics

The characteristics of the organizational structure of non-state sector organizations differ tremendously. They can be contrasted with the state sector which usually has, within any one country, similar organizational structures between institutions of the same type, such as hospitals. Differences are likely to emerge, as a result of a number of factors including: (a) *motivational differences*. Firstly, NGOs that have a strong proselytizing tradition may be heavily influenced by either the local or international church. Secondly, within industrial health care the decision-making process is likely to reflect the management style of the industry it services. Lastly, the degree of divergence between the professionals and the profit recipients in a for-profit institution will influence the relative strengths of the medical profession *vis-a-vis* the adminstrative cadres; (b) *size*, both in terms of the hospital itself, and (where applicable) in terms of its size in relation to its parent organization; (c) *accountability* — the degree to which formal structures of accountability have been set up and are adhered to; (d) *strength of the medical and nursing professions* generally within the country, and their ability to exploit this within the context of a specific administrative framework; (e) *staffing policies* — the extent to which the particular organization is staffed and run by expatriates, and the degree of participation in management by the workforce.

External relationships

The relationships that NGOs/private health services have with other agencies are extremely varied, and are documented in Figure 1. Examples of factors that influence the relationship are given in the body of the matrix, and include: historical antecedents; motivational considerations; considerations of trust, often as a result of information sharing; legal/bureaucratic barriers; existing

FACTORS AFFECTING RELATIONSHIP WITH OTHER INSTITUTION IN AREAS OF:

RELATIONS WITH:	Policy/Planning/ information sharing	Medical referrals/ policies and supervision	Shared support services including training and supplies
Other institutions run by the same parent body	Degree of centralization of parent body Location of facilities		
Other non-state sector services	Existence/effectiveness of central coordinating body[1] Historical factors Perceptions of competition vs complementarity		
Government services	Representation on government bodies and vice versa; degree of formal integration of NGOs[2]	Complementarity of types and location of services	Degree of national training/manpower planning; size of central procurement system
	Funding arrangement Legal framework		

[1] Such as the Voluntary Health Association of India; Private Hospital Association of Lesotho.
[2] Varying as between subvention provision to formal designation as district hospitals (as in Tanzania).

Figure 1 The combination of relationships possible between an NGO/private health service with other agencies.

service patterns throughout the country; and, lastly, the degree of government or external financing.

The nature of such relationships is key to the future development of efficient health care. Whilst there may be a place for different organizational types within any country's health system, the ability of such a network to work efficiently is greatly constrained by the lack of clear, open relationships *within* the network; coordinating mechanisms may either exist, in the first instance, outside of government, with government then collaborating with non-state institutions *through* an intermediary body; or may exist within government, with itself then providing the coordinating mechanism. There would appear to be no clear evidence as to which model is likely, *a priori*, to be most effective.

Funding base

The means of financing the non-state sector again varies tremendously from country to country. Figure 2 shows the possible permutations that are possible.

During the 1970s a major form of NGO health care — the religious/charity sector — began increasingly to face financial difficulties. This can be traced, in general, to three factors. Firstly, a reduction in overseas recurrent cost support. In part this may be a result of a declining interest in, and priority given by many denominations to, mission work. In common with official government aid (bilateral or multilateral), international NGO aid has often been directed at capital expenditures — thereby worsening the financing situation, through incurring greater future recurrent commitments. Other factors are, secondly, the impact of world inflation, particularly in the area of pharmaceuticals; and, lastly, an increasing divergence in fee levels between comparable government agencies and NGOs.

An many cases the situation has become critical, particularly where government policies had been to restain or freeze their own user charges. In such situations, the NGOs that relied on user charges (which can often be as high

FORMS OF FUNDING SOURCE

PROVIDER	User charges	Voluntary insurance	Employment related	Compulsory insurance	Tax revenue	Donations/ grant/aid
State	x			x	x	Community, international aid
NGO	x	x			As grants/ subsidy	Community, international aid
Occup-ational health	x		x		As subsidy	
Private sector for profit	x	x			As subsidy	

Figure 2 Major forms of funding of different health care providers.

as 70% (Kolobe and Pekeohe, 1980)) as a source of finance fell back onto a strategy of increasing them, often to a point where utilization rates began to decline, as users either could not afford services or chose to travel to the nearest government facility. Such a strategy often compounded the problem. In some countries this situation led to demands for (increased) government subventions, prompting the Ministry of Health to review policies towards NGOs. Alongside such government policy reviews, the NGOs themselves, faced with a common problem, recognized in a number of countries the need for a common policy and formed coordinating mechanisms. To the extent that governments have accepted a need to increase subventions, this has carried the potential (not always exploited) for closer integration of such NGOs into the state sector. The extent of overseas funding and hidden subsidies is often unknown, so that withdrawal of overseas support creates unexpected difficulties. Examples of this include donations in kind (for example, of drugs) and the deployment of volunteer staff.

Government-explicit subsidies may take a variety of forms, ranging from: a straight annual grant (in some cases linked to factors such as the operating size or budget); to payment for particular services (such as treatment for communicable disease); or, reimbursement for particular items of expenditure (such as salaries or drugs).

Elements of the non-state sector that relied on health insurance as a main source of funding appear to have been less affected by the global economic recession, which may have hit higher income groups and hence their clients less severely. Within the NGO sector, there is, in some cases, the development of 'private' facilities, charging commercial rates, which are provided alongside their usual services, and are used to cross-subsidize such services.

One area that is of clear importance for the development of government policy is the degree to which both NGOs and the private sector receive hidden subsidies from government in the form of, amongst others, tax relief, training, access to cheaper or even free medical supplies, and the use of government facilities either directly or indirectly (Segall, 1983). Information of such hidden subsidies is rarely carried in conventional accounting systems, and yet is essential to obtain a comprehensive picture of the funding characteristics of the non-state sector.

Manpower training and usage

Manpower may include both externally recruited expatriates and citizens trained either within the particular employing organization or outside. There are a number of major issues to be addressed here, involving the relationship between government and the non-state sector, as regards training and employment policies. These include: (a) *Standardization and coordination of training*: individual NGOs may provide a variety of different training programmes mainly

devised for their own needs. This is most obvious in auxiliary training programmes where national licensing and curriculum standards are relatively
undeveloped. Where such training *is* nationally recognized, NGOs have often
had a lead role in determining national curricula. The general relevance of
such curricula then depends of the degree to which the training organization is
effectively integrated with or collaborates with government. The private sector
is rarely involved in training, with resultant hidden subsidies for this sector. (b)
Staff transferability and deployment: as a result of either different training levels
of bureaucratic barriers (such as the non-recognition of experience) transferability of staff between institutions within the non-state sector, or between
the non-state sector and government, may be difficult. Furthermore, pay-scale
differentials between the private sector and the state sector are often a cause
of staff movement between sectors, or of pressure within the state sector to
move towards unrealistic private sector levels of pay. Conversely, the NGO
sector may be unable to meet even state sector pay levels, leading to recruitment difficulties (McGilvray, 1974). In a number of countries, the government
has responded either through coercive policies such as bonding, or by incentive
policies such as allowing state doctors to practise privately, in some cases
using government facilities, thereby effectively increasing their real income.
Further major differences between NGOs and government agencies stem
from their ability to attract volunteers and to employ part-time staff. The
motivational differences between government and NGOs, and the often wide
activity base of NGOs, appear to give them a substantial comparative advantage over the use of volunteers (Rankin, 1985). Even where government agencies
have made deliberate efforts to involve communities in the planning of local
services, and as resources to provide the services, their success rate would
appear to have been low compared to NGOs. This seeming advantage can,
however, on occasion, become a sourse of tension, where volunteers are
being used as substitutes for paid staff. (c) *Appropriate manpower mixes*:
utilization of different types of staff would appear to vary between organizations, having implications for their cost-effectiveness. This can either be
relative (for example ratio of doctors to nurses) or absolute (for example
doctors per head). An example of the latter is given by Gish (1971), who
compares a 100-bedded women's wing in a public hospital in Tehran, with
a 30-bedded private hospital. The former has four part-time and one full-time
doctors, the latter has six part-time and four full-time doctors. (d) *Localization
policies*: the ability of some NGOs to recruit expatriates at subsidized rates
may be a deterrent to localization policies. One example of where this may be
difficult is the not uncommon situation of expatriate spouses holding unpaid
positions, thereby reducing local employment opportunities. (e) *Manpower
planning*: all the above have implications for the ability of government to
perform effectively manpower planning, which is often further constrained
by the lack of *information* on both the demand for, and supply of manpower
from the non-state sector, and in particular the private sector.

Degree of innovation

One argument that is frequently put forward in favour of NGOs, and to a lesser extent the private sector, relates to their apparent innovativeness. Innovation may in this context occur either in the form of technology adopted, or the form of organization. Within the private sector, the former may manifest itself in a replication of the latest high-technology medical care practised in the more industrialized countries. In addition, in some countries, the private sector has introduced new forms of organization. (Scarpaci, 1985). Many NGOs pride themselves on the use of more appropriate technology and on their degree of innovation in service delivery. The degree to which this is generally true merits investigation, though certainly NGOs have been involved in path-breaking work such as the Flying Doctor Service in East Africa by AMREF. The ability and need to innovate is generated, it is suggested, through an historically lower funding rate, motivational differences and a flexibility of operation. Whilst many governments recognize the usefulness of NGOs in this respect, and indeed may use them to circumvent their own organizational constraints, such individualistic, unplanned and often unevaluated innovation can result in extremely heterogenious services whose prime characteristic is not necessarily *better* health care, but *different* health care, with implications for planning and coordination.

Evaluating the non-state sector

The preceding section outlined a number of characteristics that differentiate NGOs and the private sector from government, and between themselves. As a result of certain of these differing characteristics, arguments are employed that purport to demonstrate the comparative advantage of one sector over another, and hence the need for policies to encourage or discourage parts of all of the sector. This section accepts as a premise, the provision by the state of certain forms of (particularly public) health care. Such as assumption is commonly accepted, with the debate focusing rather on *how* comprehensive such state provision should be. Figure 3 outlines the arguments which are now discussed in greater detail in the test below. The arguments, though often interlinked, are grouped into five sets of issues:

— Does the existence of the non-state sector lead to *additional net resources?*
— Are organizations within the non-state sector more or less *efficient* at providing (certain types of) health care?
— Are there differences in *quality* between the state and non-state health care?
— Does the existence of a variety of organizations within the non-state sector alongside a state sector, have implications for the *planning and*

Arguments for NGOs/private sector	Arguments against NGOs/private sector
Resource mobilization	
Can tap additional sources of funds.	Use of user charges creates inequities.
Can release public sector resources by syphoning off demand.	The extent of additional real resources is less than apparent, due to:
	(a) hidden subsidies;
	(b) less efficient use of resources.
Efficiency	
More efficient in use of resources due to motivation/management structure	Less efficient due to inabilities to exploit economies of scale.
	Duplicates service provision.
Service quality	
Provides high quality of service.	Creates unrealistic expectations in the public sector.
	Lack of regulatory mechanisms may reduce quality of service below acceptable minimum.
Planning/coordination	
Is autonomous, innovative, 'loyal opposition'.	Duplicates services.
	Is unplanned in national terms.
Equity	
NGOs locate services in rural areas.	Private sector located in urban areas.
Existence of alternative provision provides freedom of choice.	Access to health care dependent on financial status of patient.
More responsive to consumers through market mechanism.	Less responsive to community needs.
	Not democratically controlled.

Figure 3 Summary of the main arguments for/against the non-state sector.

coordination of health services, and ultimately for the efficiency of the health sector as a whole?

— What are the *equity* implications of the existence of difference sectors?

Resource mobilization

One of the central issues surrounding the non-state sector is whether or not the existence of this sector increases the total share of resources available for health care, from either internal or external sources. External resources may be available through tapping different aid channels such as international NGOs, in which case it is particularly useful as a source of foreign exchange. Internal resources may be seemingly generated by shifting the demand of certain groups from the public sector to the private/NGO sector, thereby releasing public sector resources for other purposes.

Counter arguments focus on two themes. Firstly, that the level of additional *real* resources generated may, in net terms, be less than is at first sight apparent—either because subsidies of various kinds are borne centrally, or becuase it results in a less efficient use of overall resources. A second argument is that expressed in terms of equity. It is argued that for demand for private services to exist alongside the public sector, there must be a (perceived at least) difference between either the coverage or quality of service provision of the public sector and the private sector, which may be a result of either the hotel aspects of the service, or of the treatment itself. To the degree to which fees charged in the private sector are prohibitive for a large section of the population, this is a continuing source of inequity.

Efficiency

A second set of arguments focuses on whether resources are likely to be used more efficiently in the state or the non-state sector. Arguments for the non-state sector are based on neo-classical economic arguments that competition will (under certain circumstances) achieve an optimal allocation of resources. Though such proponents recognize that in the field of health care, such perfect conditions do not pertain, they argue that effort should be directed to creating such conditions or substitutes for such conditions, rather than providing alternative publicly operated systems. However, it is worth noting that the basic premise for competitive markets — profit maximization — not only does not apply to the not-for-profit sector, including NGOs, but may also not apply to the for-profit sector, where research has suggested a number of other maximands, rather than profit (McGuire, 1985).

Arguments as to the comparative advantage of the NGO sector, the state sector, or the private sector are complex and, to a large degree, untested, with perceptions being largely based on anecdotal evidence (Brown and Tenn, 1985). Inefficient or unnecessary medical practice in terms of the treatment used, may occur in private practice where consumer information may be limited (this may be a particular problem in developing countries) as a result of profit motivation and fee-for-service payment systems; flexible management *may* be the hallmark of some NGOs/private organizations, free from government bureaucratic encumberances; conversely, poor management may occur in other NGOs or private health care, where specialist management training is unavailable or where medical interests dominate. The potential for exploiting economies of scale in areas such as drug purchasing, which are open to large public sector purchasers, may not be available (though through group purchasing could be) to individual non-state organizations acting alone.

In addition to the above questions, which clearly need empirical investigation, and which are primarily concerned with the technical efficiency of individual organizations, are arguments that relate to the non-state sector and its effect on the overall efficiency of the health sector. Some of these arguments relate to the present uncoordinated nature of the health sector in many countries, with the inefficient duplication of resources and activities. Other arguments are concerned with allocative efficiency and the use to which resources are put. Thus, scarce health resources may be used (albeit with technical efficiency) by the private sector on services which are not regarded in community health terms as of high priority. Such inefficiency is often compounded by its ability to raise unrealistic expectations/public pressure for similar provision by the state. Such issues are further explored below.

It is clear that research into general indicators of efficiency, and the relative cost-effectiveness of various organizational modes, is a vital pre-requisite of policy formulation. It is important to note, however, that because of the multiplicity of factors that impinge on the efficiency of a particular organization, much of this research will be country-specific; it is possible that only the research methodology itself will be more widely applicable.

Quality of service

Clearly linked to the last point is the set of arguments that concern the relative quality of services provided by the state and non-state sectors. There are two main issues — the first related to the provision of 'over-high quality' care, and the second to ensuring provision of minimum standards of care. One perception of NGOs is their ability to provide a higher quality of health care. Within developing countries this has rarely been tested: partly due to methodological difficulties in finding institutions whose ownership or management can be compared; and, partly due to difficulties in measuring quality itself, particularly in developing countries (Eldar, 1983). Such perceptions may arise through observation of the lower occupancy rates prevailing in NGO and private sector hospitals. However, the opportunity cost of this particular indicator of quality is likely to be a reduction in accessibility or coverage.

To the extent that service provision in NGOs, and more particularly the private sector, is determined by clinicians, it is reasonable to hypothesize that policies regarding resource allocation may be biased towards individualistic clinical viewpoints, at the expense of the wider community health. Such phenomena are well-reported and are the cause of tension in many health organizations (Majone, 1984). At the other end of the spectrum is the inability or unwillingness of the state, in many developing countries, to devote scarce resources to the regulation and inspection of non-state services to ensure that *minimum* standards are maintained.

Planning and coordination role in primary health care

In terms of the planned provision of care, arguments for the non-state sector range from the viewpoint that the market is the best planner, or that NGOs are as a result of their community links, or that the private sector is as a result of its responsiveness to demand, to a viewpoint that a regulatory form of government planning and/or government funding of services is possible without necessarily the involvement of the state in the actual *provision* of services. Emerging interest in the decentralization of health care management is also used as an argument for the non-state sector. Arguments against focus on *efficiency* criteria, as discussed above, with, for example, the claim that the absence of planning leads to: a duplication of services (Schulpen, 1975); and the lack of referral mechanisms or standardization of medical practice; and, on *equity*, to the belief that planning is a mechanism for determining needs-based services, rather than demand-responsive services.

Private health care based on a medical model, it has been argued earlier, is less likely to be concerned with wider issues of community health or primary health care, and as such, where its existence is permitted at all, requires close regulation. NGOs, on the other hand, have, in many instances, been at the forefront of innovative primary health care activities, particularly those with links into other sectors or activities, such as broader community development. Governments may, in addition, welcome the existence of NGOs, not just as potential innovative pilots, but as agencies providing specific services whose importance the government recognizes but which are politically too sensitive for it to provide; for example family planning services. In some countries NGOs may also act as a 'ginger group' or as loyal opposition; they may also be used by ministries of health to bypass their own government bureaucratic constraints, through contracting-out service provision. Acceptance of the need for state *planned* health care does not necessarily imply or require state *provision* of health care. However, it does imply the need for knowledge of the particular activities of non-state health care, their strengths and weaknesses, and the ability, where necessary, to regulate them. Such information and regulatory mechanisms are at present conspicuous by their absence in many developing countries; research in this area would clearly be beneficial.

Equity/social justice

Health care may be viewed as either an investment or a consumption good. In the former case, its allocation is not related to issues of equity but rather to those of productivity. Proponents of this view of health care argue that health care should be targeted at certain groups; and that equity losses in the short-term are worth such overall development gains. Roemer, arguing for social insurance, has made this point strongly (Roemer, *et al*, 1984); the same could be argued for occupational health care and its subsidization by the state. Proponents of the consumption good view of health care are concerned rather that health care is available in relation to need and not on any other criteria. As such it is difficult to reconcile the two views.

Arguments couched in terms of equity and social justice are of four types, the first two concerned with access to services. Firstly, those concerned with the location of facilities point, on the one hand, to the concentration of private hospital care in urban areas, and on the other to the location of many NGO facilities in rural areas. Secondly, where access is restricted through financing mechanisms, namely reliance on user charges, or high insurance premiums/copayment charges, there are clear implications for equity in terms of utilization of services in relation to need. Thirdly, there are arguments which relate to the degree of subsidization of private services by public monies. Lastly, there is the libertarian view that argues for freedom of choice. How such arguments are assessed and concluded will depend on a government's understanding of, and commitment to, equity; and, hence, on the ideological standpoint of the government.

For many countries, other than those with a clear socialist ideology, an evaluation of the non-state sector as a whole is unlikely to lead to unambiguous answers: value judgements will be required as to the trade-off between equity and resource mobilization. The two research questions that need answering are:

— Do organizations within the non-state sector release or tap additional resources (either through efficiency or resource mobilization)?
— If so, do any equity losses outweigh any benefits gained from the additional resources?

Implications for policy

Preceding sections have examined the size and characteristics of the non-state sector, and argued that, in many countries, it is a significant force in the health care field. The last section concluded that, for many countries with a non-Socialist ideology, it is not possible to make generalized evaluative comments about the non-state sector. Rather, country-specific and organization-specific evaluations are needed, as a precursor to policy formation.

Perhaps because of the very real difficulties in making such assessments, health care policy formulation for many countries appears to have avoided looking too closely at this sector. Yet, as a significant component within the health sector, it is clear that such a situation cannot continue. Indeed, increasingly, governments are being forced, often through their own financial crises, or those of the NGO sector, to formulate policies in this field; however, this is often in the absence of a workable policy-making framework that asks the right questions and provides the methodology to find the answers.

This concluding section, therefore, suggests a range of policy options open to governments in this area and identifies areas of research that are needed to improve policy selection.

The state has two potential roles within the field of health care — as a *provider* and as a *regulator*. Policy development within this area needs to disentangle these two functions, if the full range of options available are to be adequately assessed. Figure 4 shows the possible range of positions open, in broad terms, to governments. Any country can be represented by a position on the diagram which shows the particular mix of service provision and regulatory controls prevailing.

The optimal strategy for any particular country at a certain time and under particular circumstances may change, as external circumstances or political

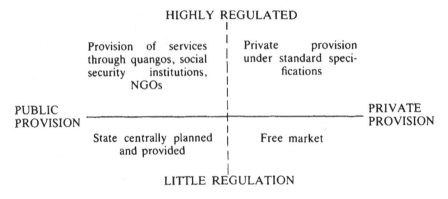

Figure 4 Mix of service provision and regulatory controls.

assumptions and social values change. In addition, policies may be markedly different towards the different organizations, or towards NGOs compared to the private sector. It has been argued, for example (de Ferranti, 1985), that it may be more sensible in the long term for governments to support private insurance than employer-based health care for firms. Similarly, it would be perfectly consistent for governments to contract-out and fund certain types of service provision to certain NGOs, and yet withdraw all subsidies from the private sector. What is required is a means of continuously assessing the options available, and determining the best route of attaining the chosen position. Figure 5 sets out a variety of such options.

For the development of coherent government policies towards the non-state health sector, research is required that will assist governments: (a) in determining their long-term goals in terms of a public/private mix, through identification of the specific implications and effects of different systems; (b) to determine and analyse their own present country position, and, in the absence of specific policy interventions, its likely future course; (c) to identify and assess feasible short- and medium-term options to attain their long-term goals.

Similarly, NGOs themselves need to determine their long-term role and strategy. The Christian Medical Council of the World Council of Churches has, in a number of countries, provided support and advice in such deliberations. For many church-related NGOs, such reviews provide the impetus to rethink the rationale and hence character of their work. Some, as a result of such reviews, have concluded that their involvement should be terminated and the health facility handed over to government; others have looked towards strategies for working more closely with government whilst maintaining a separate identity; some have taken the opportunity to increase *local* control of church policy.

Industrial health services fall into a different category, in that their future is likely to be as strong or as tenuous as the industry to which they are linked. However, their wider role in the health care system does need a similar review.

MEASURE	RESOURCE IMPLI-CATIONS	DEGREE OF REGULATION/CONTROL
Nationalization — the take-over and continual operation, with or with out compensation, of facilities	Major resource implications	Would allow complete integration into national system
Increase or decrease in subsidy/subvention — either on a general basis, or specific to certain items or functions	Resource implications either positive or negative	Provides an opportunity for closer coordination of services without total integration; can be used to encourage provision of certain services
Designation of hospitals as government agents	May require funding, through subventions or through agreed fees for service	Allows integration into the government planning system, without total management responsibilities
Fiscal Policy	Revenue earner/loser	Can be linked to specific factors
Direct regulatory action	Minimal funding requirements other than regulatory mechanism and inspectorate	May be difficult to enforce; can be applied on costs or quality (including type of technology adopted)
Encourage collaborative	Minimal	Reciprocal participation on decision-making bodies; encouragement of central coordinating bodies, etc
Foreign exchange controls	May have positive economic benefits	Can be used to control drugs, and importation of equipment
Manpower controls	Minimal direct implications	Through bonding, licensing, licensing etc
Central drug supply controls	Minimal	Central drug policies
Legislative prohibition of certain categories of health care	May require funding to provide replacement services	May drive such activities as private care under-ground

Figure 5 Selected policy options open to government.

MEASURE	RESOURCE IMPLI-CATIONS	DEGREE OF REGULATION/ CONTROL
Provide seed money for initiatives (through subventions, grants or fiscal incentives)	Resource requirements in short term	May be used to underwrite new, innovatory forms of organization
Legislative requirement for industrial health care	Minimal government; may affect industrial profits	Problems of implementation

Figure 5 (cont'd)

In order to assist organizations to carry out such reviews, which should form an important input into the formulation of government policy, research is needed which assists NGOs to: identify their preferred long-term and medium-term role within the health sector (this may differ from their present role); determine the true costs of current operations; identify areas of ineffi-cient operation (both within and between organizations); identify medium- and long-term strategies; and, identify means to improve efficiency. Furthermore, research is required that results in evaluative techniques, and indicators of output and efficiency, which can be *easily* used by NGOs.

Conclusion

A number of themes have run through this article. Firstly, the heterogeneity of organizations operating in the health sector (both *between* countries and *within* them); secondly, the present and potential impact of the non-state sector; thirdly, the present incomplete state of the art relating to the economics of the public/private mix; fourthly, the different social objectives between countries on which policy is made; and lastly, the lack, in many countries, of a clear framework for policy formulation in this field. On that last point, however, there would appear to be little justification for global blanket policies about NGOs, in the absence of specific country analysis, and an understand-ing of each particular NGO. There may be more justification for broad policies towards the private-for-profit sector where more homogeneity is exhibited, and where the negative effects are apparent.

Three main types of institution are involved in policy formulation in this field — the national governments in developing countries, NGOs and the private sector institutions themselves, and aid agencies. Whilst each of these is likely to have different policy objectives, they share much common ground in their need for information and analytical tools on which to formulate their policy actions, and it is in this area — the development not of policies them-selves, but rather of tools and criteria that can be used to formulate policies, that, it is argued, urgent research attention should be focused. The following summarizes the main questions which need to be addressed in each country in order for robust and relevant policies to be formulated.

Firstly, basic question that needs to be answered for each country concerns the present size of the non-state health sector, both in aggregate terms (by facility, resource and expenditure) and by type. Where financing or comprehensive sector reviews surveys have been carried out, this information may be available; in other countries, research may be required to determine this basic picture. Some further attention also needs to be given to develop definitions that describe accurately the different types of organization.

Secondly, not only is country-specific information required as to the current size of the non-state sector, but information is needed that describes past trends, and projects into the future, in the absence of policy changes, the future size of the sector. Thirdly, a number of possible characteristics on non-state sector hospitals have been set out in this article, the precise configuration of which will vary as a result of the country or organization context. Tools need to be developed to allow the analysis of such characteristics.

Finally, this article has reviewed a series of issues that relate to the effects that the non-state sector have on the availability and utilization of resources. These issues have been identified as a series of questions, for the answer to which evaluative tools need developing. The size and potential impact of the non-state sector upon health care and upon health itself strongly suggest that policy development and, hence, research in this area should be seen as a priority.

Acknowledgements

This article is based on work completed in 1986 on behalf of the World Bank, whose support is hereby acknowledged. The views expressed within the paper do not, however, necessarily reflect World Bank policies, nor is the World Bank responsible for its content.

The author would like to thank Carol Barker, Nuffield Centre for Health Services Studies, University of Leeds, and Ann Mills, London School of Hygiene and Tropical Medicine, for comments on an earlier draft.

References

Abel-Smith, B. (1985). Global perspectives on health service financing. *Social Science and Medicine* **21** (9), 957–963.

Brown G., Tenn, W. (1985). Management in church hospitals. *International Hospital Federation, Official Yearbook*, IHF.

Cumper, G. (1986). *Health Sector Financing: Estimating Health Expenditure in Developing Countries*. EPC Publication No. 9. London: London School of Hygiene and Tropical Medicine.

de Ferranti, D. (1985). *Paying for Health Services in Developing Countries: An Overview.* World Bank Staffing Working Paper No. 721. World Bank.

Dunlop, D. (1983). Health care financing: recent experience in Africa. *Social Science and Medicine* **17** (24), 2017–2025.

Eldar, R. (1983). Quality assessment and assurance in hospitals of developing countries. *Public Administration and Development* **5** (1), 13–24.

Gish, O. (1971). *Doctor Migration and World Health.* Occasional Papers in Social Administration, No. 43. London: bell.

Glazer, W. A. (1970). *Paying the Doctor: Systems of Renumeration and Their Effects.* Baltimore: John Hopkins.

Kolobe, Pekeohe. (1980). A survey of the financial status of the private health association of Lesotho's hospital. Private Health Association of Lesotho, estimate 70% of recurrent expenditure by private hospitals is recovered from user charges. Quoted in: Prescott, N., Warford, J., Economic appraisal in the health sector. In: Lee, K., & Mills, A., (Eds). (1983). *The Economics of Health in Developing Countries.* Oxford: Oxford University Press.

McGilvray, J. (1974). An exercise in the development of health care priorities. Christian Medical Commission. McGuire, A. (1985). The theory of the hospital: a review of the models. *Social Science and Medicine* **20** (11), 117–184.

Majone, G. (1984). Professionalism and non-profit organisations. *Journal of Health Politics, Policy and law* **8** (4), 639–659.

Rankin, J. P. (1985). Volunteers in primary health care: problems and possibilities. *World Health Forum* **6**, 24–26. Roemer, M. I. *et al.* (1984). Private medical practice: obstacle to health for all. Round Table Discussion. *World Health Forum* **5**, 195–210.

Scarpaci, J. L. (1985). Restructuring health care financing in Chile. *Social Science and Medicine* **21** (4), 415–431. Schulpen, T. W. J. (1975). *Integration of Church and Government Medical Services In Tanzania: Effects at District Level.* African Medical and Research Foundation, Nairobi: AMREF.

Segall, M. (1983). Planning and politics of resource allocation for primary health care: promotion of meaningful national policy. *Social Science and Medicine* **17** (24), 1947–1960.

WHO. (1985). Collaboration with non-governmental organisations in implementing the global strategy for Health for All. *Background document for the Technical Discussions at the 38th World Health Assembly.* Geneva: WHO.

World Bank. (1975). *Health Sector Policy Paper.* Washington: World Bank.

87

CIVIL SOCIETY ORGANISATIONS AND GLOBAL HEALTH INITIATIVES

Problems of legitimacy

Cathal Doyle and Preeti Patel

Source: *Social Science & Medicine*, 66:9 (2008), 1928–38.

Abstract

Civil society organisations (CSOs) have a prominent role in global health initiatives such as The Global Fund to Fight AIDS, Tuberculosis and Malaria (the Global Fund) and, in the United States, the President's Emergency Plan for AIDS Relief (PEPFAR). They are increasingly consulted by international organisations and, in some cases like the Global Fund, are involved in decision-making. They are also increasingly seen as crucial agents in delivering health interventions on the ground. Some donors prefer to channel funds through CSOs in developing countries than through perceived to be corrupt or inefficient government agencies. This paper examines this growing role and the arguments put forward to justify their increasing influence, particularly in HIV/AIDS initiatives. It analyses the main challenges to CSOs' legitimacy and outlines key responses to these challenges. It concludes by suggesting a number of research priorities that might help to evaluate the impact of CSOs in global health initiatives.

Introduction

Civil society organisations and global health governance

Civil society organisations (CSOs) include nonprofit making or 'public-interest' organisations established by citizens to improve health. CSOs typically involved in global health include non-governmental organisations (NGOs) or community-based organisations (CBOs) that either deliver health interventions or lobby for change in policy to tackle global health problems (advocacy NGOs). These are distinct from 'private-interest' organisations established by corporations with a purely commercial or profit-making agenda. This distinction is important as around half of the bodies registered as CSOs at the United Nations are affiliated with business interests and representatives of commercial companies, including many Public Relations front organisations (Rowson, 2005).

In recent years, civil society organisations (CSOs) have played an increasingly important role in global health governance. Global health governance can be defined as "governance efforts among states and non-state actors for purposes of protecting and promoting human health" (Fidler, 2005). The term 'governance' refers to the way in which groups including CSOs work together towards shared goals and to find solutions to identified social problems. It is 'global' in the sense that such cooperation transcends national boundaries. CSOs are formally consulted by health-related international organisations such as the World Health Organisation (WHO), the Joint United Nations Program on HIV/AIDS (UNAIDS) and the United Nations Children's Fund (UNICEF). They are seen as key partners in recently established global health initiatives (GHIs) such as the Global Fund to Fight HIV/AIDS, Tuberculosis and Malaria (Global Fund), President's Emergency Plan for AIDS Relief (PEPFAR), GAVI (The Global Alliance for Vaccines and Immunization) and the World Bank's Multi-Country HIV/AIDS Program.

Despite this escalating prominence of CSOs, few questions are asked about the legitimacy of their growing role. Legitimacy in this context implies the validity or justification of an organisation's claim to represent the interests of a group of people. For political parties in democracies, for example, the source of legitimacy is primarily the ballot box. Trade unions argue they receive their legitimacy from the authority provided by their members' choosing to join them and paying membership fees. Not all voters or union members want the same thing and a political party or trade union will make decisions against the interests of some of its members. Nevertheless, such democratic procedures enable representatives to validly claim legitimacy. The source of legitimacy for CSOs is not so clear. But without such legitimacy what justification is there for including CSOs in decision-making that affects the health of millions of people? Some advocacy CSOs argue their legitimacy comes from their role in giving a voice to the concerns of people who have been marginalized or ignored in the political process. Others claim that their legitimacy is based on their technical ability and track record in tackling diseases. But little research has been conducted to test the assumptions underlying these claims. Current monitoring and evaluation of CSO activity in GHIs is superficial, concentrating mainly on variables that are easily measurable, such as attendance at meetings. This article examines these claims to legitimacy and discusses some of the problems that they raise for evaluating the effectiveness of global health interventions, particularly in the area of HIV/AIDS.

Methodology

This paper is based on qualitative academic literature, Internet resources and press articles. Search terms such as 'Civil Society', 'Civil Society Organisations', 'non-governmental organisations', 'NGOs', 'global health initiatives', 'governance', 'global governance' and 'global health governance,' were entered into medical and social science databases such as IBSS, Ovid, PubMed, Embase and Medline. These revealed several articles on global governance and NGOs more broadly and the ones relevant to health and CSOs have been reviewed in this paper. Taking a multi-disciplinary approach to the analysis, this paper reflects both theoretical and empirical studies from international relations, development studies, sociology, political science and public health.

Results

Increased financial resources for CSOs through global health initiatives

As Table 1 illustrates, expenditure on various global health initiatives from public and private sources has increased considerably in recent years resulting in more resources for CSOs (Science Magazine, 2006). This scale of funding can be compared, for example, to an annual program budget for the World Health Organisation in 2004–2005 of US$901 million (World Health Organisation, 2005).

Significant resources from this funding have been directly channelled to CSOs. For example, Chart 1 shows the breakdown of funding allocated by the Global Fund to fight AIDS, Tuberculosis and Malaria with almost 50% allocated to non-government agencies in May 2006 (The Global Fund to Fight AIDS, 2006a).

Table 2 shows that under PEPFAR, government agencies receive only in the region of 15% of funding allocated to the top 10 'prime partners' (partners that receive funding directly from the US Government) for the fiscal year 2005 (Avert, 2006), with 43% going to nonprofit organisations and a further 10% going to faith-based organisations.

A single grant of $11.7 million to an NGO-led initiative in Senegal allocated under the Global Fund can be compared to an annual overall government expenditure on health of $90 million in 2004 (The Global Fund to Fight AIDS, 2006a; World Health Organisation, 2006). The scale of these resources allocated to CSOs emphasises the call for closer scrutiny of their effectiveness and legitimacy as partners in GHIs.

The inclusion of CSOs in global health governance organisations is usually justified on one of two grounds (1) their involvement enhances democracy and (2) they have a comparative advantage in delivering health interventions. Both these aspects are analysed below.

Table 1 Illustrative selection of new global health efforts since 1998.

Organisation	Focus	Year launched	Donors	Pledged, committed or spent funds
Bill and Melinda Gates Foundation	Global health	2000	Bill and Melinda Gates	$6.2B
The Global Fund to Fight AIDS, Tuberculosis and Malaria	Financing treatment and prevention	2002	Governments, foundations, corporations	$8.6B
President's Emergency Plan for AIDS Relief (PEPFAR)	Financing and delivery of HIV/ AIDS prevention and treatment	2004	U.S. government	$15B
International Finance Facility for Immunization	Financing vaccine delivery/GAVI	2005	U.K., France, Italy, Spain, Sweden	$4B
Multi-Country HIV/AIDS Program	Financing scale-up of existing government and community prevention and treatment efforts	2000	World Bank	$1.1B
Global Alliance for Vaccin es and Immunization (GAVI)	Financing and delivery of childhood vaccines	1999	Gates Foundation, governments	$3B
Public-Private Partnerships	Drugs, vaccines, microbicides, diagnostics	n/a	Philanthropists, governments, industry	$1.2B
Anti-Malaria Initiative in Africa	Cut malaria incidence in half by 2010 in 15 countries	2005 (proposed)	U.S. government	$1.2B
United Nations Foundation	Children's and women's Health	1998	Ted Turner	$360M

Source: Science Magazine (2006). "The New World of Global Health." Science Magazine 311.

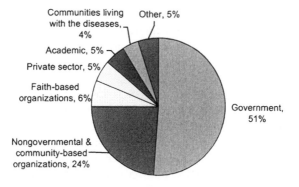

Chart 1 Breakdown of funding allocated by the Global Fund by implementing agency
– May 2006.
Source: The Global Fund to Fight AIDS (2006a). Monthly Progress Update – 27 July 2006.

Table 2 Breakdown of Funding to PEPFAR Top 10 Prime Partners 2005.

Partner	Type	Total Amount (US$ million)
Family Health International	Nonprofit	103,375
Government departments	Government	83,281
John Snow, Inc.	Commercial	71,483
Elizabeth Glaser Pediatric AIDS Fund	Nonprofit	61,639
Catholic Relief Services	Faith-based	52,973
Management Sciences for Health	Nonprofit	44,447
Harvard University	University	37,728
Columbia University	University	34,675
Johns Hopkins University	University	24,639
Population Services International	Nonprofit	22,208

Source: Avert (2006). PEPFAR prime partners in fiscal year 2005, www.avert.org.

Justification 1 – CSO's involvement enhance democracy

Some argue that CSOs, through their membership of consultative or decision-making bodies of international health-related organisations, act as public representatives and help to make global health governance policy-making more transparent, accountable and democratic. This is evidence, some would argue, of a growing 'global civil society' where groups of citizens participate in debate and action to further the interest of a global citizenry (Anheier, Glasius, & Kaldor, 2001). While globalization has a number of negative impacts on health such as the global spread of HIV/AIDS, transnational drug-trafficking, the spread of non-communicable 'lifestyle' diseases to developing countries and global panics around SARS and avian flu (Lee, 2003), it has also had positive consequences, such as increased opportunities for

603

communication and networking which has facilitated greater empathy and a growing recognition of common interests in tackling disease. This, it is argued, provides a foundation for trust and solidarity between citizens in different countries and sows the seeds for an emerging global civil society determined to address health problems.

Global networks of health-related CSOs in developed and developing countries tackle problems such as HIV/AIDS, creating advocacy and 'epistemic' groups or 'communities' sharing knowledge on health problems and devising potential solutions that constitute global policy-making. For example, links between national and global NGOs were vital in persuading the South African government to make anti-retroviral drug treatment more widely available for HIV/AIDS treatment (Seckinelgin, 2003). The International HIV/AIDS Alliance and the International Council of AIDS Service Organisations build links between CSOs in developed and developing countries, providing support for NGOs and CBOs in developing countries to tackle the disease at a community level.

Advocates argue that CSOs are responding to democratic deficits both at global and national levels and are working to create democratic foundations where these are lacking. The absence or lack of democratic legitimacy in international organisations necessitates the involvement of CSOs, opening up their decision-making to scrutiny and debate. CSOs ensure that the voices of populations affected by global health problems (such as HIV/AIDS, Tuberculosis and Malaria) are heard and their needs reflected in global policies. They scrutinise the operations of international organisations and challenge the elitist 'club model' of global governance in operation since the end of the Second World War (Keohane & Nye, 2001). Scholte (2004), for example, argues:

"... inputs from civil society groups can bring helpful information and insights to policy processes, including data and perspectives that are missing in official circles. Discussions with civil society bodies can also provide global governance agencies with an important gauge of the political viability of existing and contemplated policy measures. And, so many people presume, well conducted relationships with civil society associations could enhance the democratic legitimacy of global governance arrangements with increased public participation and public accountability."

(Scholte, 2004, p. 215)

CSOs help to build a democratic culture where citizens participate in public debate, where there is access to information about the consequences of different policy choices and where there is transparency of and accountability for decision-making. This enables communities to articulate their needs, to mediate differences between different groups, to make decisions about the allocation of scarce resources, and to create sustainable interventions for tackling disease. As the social, cultural and economic determinants of poor health are best understood by communities themselves, the input of CSOs, it is argued, is essential for the success and sustainability of interventions to tackle disease (Barnett & Whiteside, 2002). Hsu describes the lack of local civil society participation or 'low-level' democracy in some developing countries as the 'missing link in building disease-resistant societies' (Hsu, 2004).

Justification 2 – CSOs have an advantage in delivering health interventions

It is often argued that the legitimacy for CSOs partnership role in global health governance is justified by their practical contribution to health and wellbeing. Their history of achievement, community knowledge and efficiency, give these organisations a *comparative advantage* in delivering health interventions, especially to hard-to-reach or vulnerable populations. Many donors, therefore, prefer to channel funds directly to CSOs, bypassing what they think are inefficient, ineffective and sometimes corrupt public sector agencies (Kamat, 2004).

The Global Fund to fight AIDS, Tuberculosis and Malaria, for example, describe CSOs as:

> ". . . . the foundation upon which effective responses to the three diseases of AIDS, tuberculosis and malaria are being built. Civil Society (Organisations) are the advocates who in many countries stimulated the first recognition and response to HIV and AIDS. It is Civil Society who is the critical implementers of support, prevention and care programmes particularly to the most vulnerable and hard to reach communities."
>
> (The Global Fund to Fight AIDS, 2006b)

Let us consider more closely both of these widely held justifications as they incorporate assumptions that are largely unexamined within health research. Despite their growth in funding and growing profile within governance structures, evidence to illustrate that CSOs are either more effective at delivering health interventions than other agencies, or that they make health governance more democratic is lacking. Below we discuss some of the challenges to these widely held assumptions in more detail.

Challenges to the legitimacy of CSOs' role in global health governance

'There is no such thing as global civil society'

Many question the very existence of a 'global civil society' as presented by political theorists such as Held (2003) and Kaldor (2003). Some argue that 'global civil society' is a hollow analogy of 'real' civil society, an entity built on a history of trust or coexistence between people living in physical proximity and sharing a common culture. They see civil society and the organisations that stem from them as both the product of and a foundation for a territorially bound democratic society. It consists of a set of organisations with frequently competing agendas that achieve their objectives (be it serving the practical interests of their members or promoting an ideological viewpoint) by influencing public opinion, pressurising political representatives or holding decision-makers to account through scrutiny. They invigorate the party political process and demand accountability from government agencies. From a health perspective, this would explain, for example, the power of CSOs representing older people successfully preventing cuts in the Medicare federal health insurance program in the United States or patient-group CSOs promoting the national availability of drugs to treat Alzheimer's disease in the National Health Service (NHS) in the United Kingdom.

Tensions between demands of different CSOs are contained within national political systems that, by and large, are considered legitimate by the citizens they govern. But this model of civil society, it is argued, "is not scalable up to the whole planet" (Anderson & Rieff, 2004, p. 34). The absence of trust and solidarity beyond national boundaries, a reflection of our tribal instincts, makes the development of a 'transnational political community' that would bolster the legitimacy of global governance agencies unlikely (Zurn, 2004).

'Global civil society' is for some a dishonest attempt to create an idealised space where a vast collection of individuals and organisations are assumed to be pooling their interests to secure the optimal outcome (Amoore & Langley, 2004). Divorced from the reality of governance and underplaying differences between CSOs, some argue that the term confers spurious legitimacy on the actions of international agencies and the Western donor countries that support CSO activity. Discussing global health initiatives to tackle HIV/AIDS, Seckinelgin argues that the use of the term 'global civil society' confers an undeserved democratic legitimacy on policy decisions:

> "In the absence of people's voices, their (patients') needs and expectations are assumed to be addressed in the activities of the metaphorical civil society that is NGOs".
>
> (Seckinelgin, 2003, p. 114)

Critics argue that rhetoric about the 'representative' role of global civil society assumes a consensus between CSOs that does not always exist. The conflicting agendas of different CSOs is often underplayed. In the case of health, to argue that such a diverse number of organisations involved in GHIs are working towards a common purpose is problematic. CSOs frequently have conflicting agendas and disagree on how to tackle global health problems.

For example, sexual abstinence programs favoured by some faith-based CSOs as a response to HIV/AIDS (and favoured, in particular by PEPFAR) and condom distribution programs favoured by secular programs are the subject of bitter ideological disputes (Epstein, 2005a). Obscuring the differences between different types of CSOs prevents a critique of their relationships both with each other and with international agencies and donor countries upon which they depend for their funding and long-term sustainability. Some argue that since the 1980s, CSOs have been 'depoliticised' and 'professionalised' through reliance on Western donor funding, making them passive agents of the neoliberal agenda. CSOs that challenge this agenda and compete with national and international agencies to influence policy have been sidelined. Seckinelgin argues that it is by *not* challenging the international policy frameworks that NGOs have a significant role (Seckinelgin, 2005).

Also, unequal power relations between CSOs in developed countries and those in developing countries undermine the idea of global civil society. The ability of CSOs in developing countries to participate effectively in a networked global civil society is hampered by limited resources and, in some cases, political repression within their own country. Talk of 'partnership', some commentators argue, obscures such logistical and political obstacles.

'Global civil society' rhetoric disguises agenda of bypassing governments

Rhetoric about the representative role of CSOs, some argue, disguises what they see as the real agenda of many global health governance agencies and Western donor countries – the use of CSOs to deliver health interventions directly, bypassing government agencies where possible. Some see this policy as a practical necessity, given the poor state of health systems in many developing countries and the ability of CSOs to deliver interventions to 'hard-to-reach' populations. Some donors, concerned about corruption, also view CSOs as a safer and more effective aid-delivery mechanism. Others characterise it as ideologically driven, with CSOs helping to impose a neoliberal or free-market model of development that view government institutions as inherently inefficient. Decreased state spending in developing countries on health as a result of structural adjustment policies imposed by the World Bank and the International Monetary Fund since the 1980s has gone hand-in-hand with increased funding for CSOs (Kamat, 2004).

Whether this channelling of resources by GHIs via CSOs is driven by pragmatism or ideology, a large growth in the 'marketplace' for CSOs intervention in health has occurred (as illustrated by Chart 1 and Table 2). Some believe this CSO-led approach and the bypassing of government agencies has had a number of negative effects that either undermines claims of CSOs to be enhancing democracy or undermines the potential effectiveness of global health interventions. These arguments are analysed below.

Elevation of CSOs undermines democracy within countries

Dahl argues that efforts by CSOs to hold global governance agencies to account are doomed to failure as these organisations are by their very nature undemocratic. This is an inevitable consequence of sovereignty stopping at national borders (Dahl, 2003). Others argue that even if these agencies are amenable to democratic reform, CSOs will not bring this about. There are no popular elections to endorse CSO 'representatives' and without this endorsement, critics argue, claims that CSOs help to democratise global governance are unfounded (Anderson & Rieff, 2004). Governments in some developing countries argue that the claims of global CSOs to be the voice of their citizens are diluting the influence of their national representatives within international organisations like the United Nations and undermining one of the few levers they have to influence the decision-making of international organisations (Keohane & Nye, 2001).

On a national level, where CSOs deliver health interventions directly to populations and bypass national agencies, governments' ability to build their own democratic legitimacy within their borders is undermined. As Parkhurst suggests, health interventions should be seen as political actions, with implications for sovereignty and the control governments have over domestic policy (Parkhurst, 2005). Delivering (and being seen to deliver) health services on the ground is an important way for governments to build legitimacy and depriving them of this opportunity undermines their credibility in the eyes of their population. Palmer illustrates how the bypassing of government in health interventions in post-conflict Afghanistan could potentially undermine the government's ability to build legitimacy (Palmer, Strong, Wali, & Sondorp, 2006). By contrast, Parkhurst argues that the Ugandan government used its response to HIV/AIDS to construct national legitimacy, working with NGOs under a government umbrella that enabled them to retain some control of the process and claim credit for achievements (Parkhurst, 2005).

CSOs' legitimacy is undermined by their own lack of accountability and transparency

Some suggestions have been made that the legitimacy of CSOs' representative role is undermined by a lack of accountability from within that potentially contributes to rather than challenges international and national democratic deficits. Scholte (2004), for example, argues:

"Regrettably, most civil society groups have operated very limited and unimaginative accountability mechanisms in relation to their own activities. At best, the organisations have tended to have no more than loose oversight by a board (often composed largely of friends, who are in some cases paid), periodic elections of officers (with low rates of participation and sometimes dubious procedures),"

(Scholte, 2004, p. 230)

Goodin (2003) claims that it needs to be clearer who CSOs are accountable to, what precisely they are accountable for and, how (or by what mechanism) they make themselves accountable. CSOs often do not provide sufficient information about their operations, funding sources and expenditures (Benner, Reinicke, & Witte, 2004). The tendency to judge CSOs on their commitment to a 'good cause,' or on their claims to be 'representing' people is no longer adequate (Anderson & Rieff, 2004). They need to be more accountable for their competence in pursuing their objectives and the results or 'outputs' of their actions than they have been to date (Goodin, 2003). From a health perspective, CSOs can be evaluated, for example, on whether they have reduced the prevalence of a particular disease or been successful at lobbying for a policy-change that benefits health. Examples of the latter include campaigns for free anti-retrovirals by the Treatment Action Campaign in South Africa, Medicine San Frontiers and other CSOs globally.

The unclear relationship between global CSOs and community-based organisations

Advocates argue that the work of CSOs at a community level to improve health provides legitimacy for CSO involvement in global health governance. But sceptics question how and to what extent smaller community-based CSOs undertaking health work on the ground connect with larger global CSOs that play a representative role within global health governance structures. Epstein argues that global CSOs working on HIV/AIDS initiatives in South Africa use their resources to take over rather than cooperate with community-based organisations (Epstein, 2005a, 2005b). She describes an example of an American NGO, Hope Worldwide, that received a grant from PEPFAR of $8 million to support 165,000 'AIDS orphans' in South Africa. Under pressure to meet this ambitious target she argues Hope Worldwide attempted to coopt a small community organisation in order to count the children they were helping. Rau argues that international organisations have little trust in the professionalism of community-led initiatives and use their funding power to shape CSO-led interventions, merely 'adopting the language of collaboration' without relinquishing bureaucratic or technical control (Rau, 2006). Community-based CSOs, it is argued, have been crowded out by a growing number of 'operational' NGOs with few links to the communities they serve, undermining local ownership and stewardship (Seckinelgin, 2005).

The creation of a 'marketplace' for CSO interventions undermines claims to comparative advantage

Sceptics argue that the supposed comparative advantage of CSOs in delivering health interventions is overstated. Many argue that the dependence of the majority of CSOs on donor funding and the pressure to achieve quick results has led to bureaucratisation, homogenization and perverse incentives that undermine the potential advantage of CSOs in addressing health problems.

Market mechanisms such as competitive tendering, short-term renewable contracts and performance measurement, has led to a preoccupation with organisational survival and a willingness to deliver programs regardless of their utility. This market model also creates incentives to underplay project difficulties and exaggerate benefits. In the search for 'one size fits all' solutions, standardised or homogenised tools and programs to tackle disease are replicated across the globe. The pressure for quick results encourages the 'scaling-up' of interventions that, although successful in some settings, are inappropriate in others.

Using the example of HIV/AIDS programs, the pressure to survive in this market environment is creating short-term, unsustainable interventions, which create distrust in communities (Seckinelgin, 2003). Each country has a unique set of complex social, economic and psychological determinants of a disease like HIV/AIDS (Barnett & Whiteside, 2002). But critics would argue that tools used for HIV/AIDS interventions are replicated without an under-standing of how to use them in a particular context. Seckinelgin argues that tools successful in developed countries in the 1980s and 1990s tend to fail in developing countries:

> ". . . most efforts are anchored in cyclical campaigns with homo-genised tools that center on the distribution of posters, condoms or information . . . (that) . . . create profound fatigue among the infected and the affected. People are constantly told that they are facing a grave disease and that to save themselves they should be loyal to one partner, use condoms or abstain from having sex. Also, many are tired of being subjects of workshops and training programs, only to be told these things again and again."
>
> (Seckinelgin, 2005, p. 360)

Donors' interest in hasty demonstrable 'results' reinforces this homogenised approach, favouring interventions that can be easily measured (such as number of condoms distributed, training workshops organised, and numbers of people counselled). These concentrate on inputs rather than outcomes measuring, for example, changes in sexual behaviour. Interventions are usually short-term and the long-term benefits of these actions beyond a program or budget cycle are rarely considered. As one commentator argues:

"the most effective responses to HIV/AIDS are those which emerge from within societies; and they tend to be long-term, complex and difficult to evaluate. These are precisely the strategies which donors, despite their best intentions, find most difficult to support."

(Panos Institute, 2003, p. 4)

Rau argues that international agencies lack the credibility and trust within communities that would make 'ownership' of HIV/AIDS programs more sustainable. Community-based organisations on the other hand have the trust of the communities but are often treated with scepticism by international technical experts (either because of technical shortcomings or because they are seen as a threat to their professional influence).

National health systems undermined by preference for CSOs

Cooley suggests that if there was a unified 'global civil society' working in the interests of populations in developing countries, then CSOs would cooperate by pooling resources and sharing information (Cooley & Ron, 2002). But the current 'market model' increases competition between CSOs within countries and the duplication of CSO-led interventions drains precious resources from health systems. To secure funding for several projects, government staff need to process separate sets of paperwork and other population health priorities such as vaccination and routine health duties outside of the remit of the intervention, are often sidelined (Brugha et al., 2004). Competition leads CSOs to concentrate their interventions in countries or areas where it is easier to achieve results quickly – picking 'low lying fruit' – further marginalising vulnerable and difficult-to-reach populations, especially in rural areas or countries affected by conflict and poor governance.

The channelling of funds through NGOs to support primary health care can destabilise a fragile health infrastructure and undermine local control of health programs. In Mozambique in the 1990s, the huge influx of NGOs with large budgets and lucrative incentives to conduct contract work and attend capacity-building sessions pulled local health workers away from routine health system work. This led to:

". . . reduced mobile vaccination brigades, poorer treatment of patients by demoralized health workers, pharmaceutical shortages, loss of skilled personnel, under-the-table payments for free services, absenteeism from regular duties, and a host of other systemic dysfunctions have clearly undermined NHS effectiveness in significant ways that may have offset much of foreign aid's positive impact."

(Pfeiffer, 2003, p. 734)

Furthermore, the achievements of short-term projects can evaporate when CSOs leave due to inadequate training or a lack of resources in local health institutions.

Discussion

The remainder of this article will suggest a number of research priorities that might help to evaluate the role of CSOs in global health initiatives.

Rosenau argues that we will only be able to understand governance on a global scale through incisive descriptions of the agents that sustain it (Rosenau, 2000). If global civil society really is a conduit for representing people's interests then advocates need to give more precise descriptions of how this happens. Current descriptions tend to list organisations and actors that are assumed to constitute a coherent force for 'good' (Amoore & Langley, 2004). But many health-related CSOs have different aims and different roles within health interventions – sometimes conflicting, sometimes complementary – and the growing number of CSOs makes it difficult to see how they fit into the model of an integrated networked global civil society working to improve health.

If advocates claim that networks are connecting global CSOs to local CSOs, thereby creating a health-promoting global civil society, then convincing descriptions of how these complex networks operate are vital. Mapping of the different types of CSOs involved in health, their connections with each other and an assessment of how their interests clash or coincide is also necessary. For example, the links between CSOs delivering health interventions at a local level and 'advocacy' CSOs operating globally need to be clearly differentiated and participants' perspectives on these networks need to be analysed. Descriptions of consultative or representative mechanisms would help clarify how (or whether) the interests at a community level are represented at a global level. Tensions and power imbalances within these networks should also be analysed. Participants' views on the relationships between Northern and Southern CSOs and on the extent to which 'Southern' concerns are being represented in global health governance institutions need to be researched. The 'participation gap' due to inequities of material, intellectual and other resources needs to be examined and the effectiveness of efforts to address current power imbalances through networking also needs to be evaluated (Whitman, 2002). The selection process of CSOs that participate in these networks and an evaluation of those that have been excluded should also be considered.

One hypothesis emerging from this article is that CSOs' ability to change global health policy for the benefit of the public is undermined by their 'co-option' by international organisations and donor agencies. If independent advocacy CSOs that challenge how health policies are framed are being shunned in favour of more subservient 'service delivery', NGOs then one of their claims to legitimacy is undermined. This hypothesis needs to be tested and the power of CSOs compared to other government or private sector representatives in global health governance structures needs to be closely examined.

The hypothesis that community-based 'bottom-up' programs to tackle disease are more effective and sustainable than 'top-down' 'homogenised' programs needs to be tested through systematic research. So too does the hypothesis that CSOs merely roll out inappropriate homogenised tools developed by their Western donors. Evidence to support or refute such hypotheses is currently severely lacking (Rau, 2006). Indeed the assumption that clear distinctions can be made between 'bottom-up' and 'top-down' approaches is questionable. Some programs may be hybrids of externally designed tools 'adapted' to local circumstances through community action (Swidler, 2006). Studies of the content, mode-of-delivery and effectiveness of programs and comparative analyses of their effectiveness in different settings are necessary. If the local context of an intervention is all-important then analysis of the different geographical, cultural, political, social and cultural variables that may prevent or promote success in different settings is also crucial. It is not all that surprising that some interventions are more successful in some settings than others. It would be more surprising, however, if there was no scope for interventions to 'travel'. If every community is unique and there is no scope to scale-up interventions, then the very idea of a global solution to global health problems is problematic.

Opportunity costs also need to be considered. Comparisons of the time taken by community-based programs and 'top-down' programs to get started and reach optimum efficiency are crucial. If an externally imposed program gets results quicker (albeit imperfect ones) then, at least from the perspective of reducing mortality and morbidity, it may be preferable.

Research suggests that bypassing government agencies to deliver interventions directly to communities can undermine the ability of national health systems to address their health problems. Brain drain, staff neglecting routine health duties, competition between CSOs, and a reluctance to coordinate their activities on the ground places an enormous strain on limited resources (Pfeiffer, 2003; Walt, Pavignani, Gilson, & Buse, 1999). More research on the impact of the recent growth of CSOs on developing countries' health infrastructure is needed. Comparisons of the programmatic effectiveness of CSO-delivered intervention that work in partnership with state health services against those that bypass these health services are also crucial for policy-mapping. Longer-term evaluation of the impacts of programs on population health and assessments of health services' ability to sustain programs in the long run are also needed.

It is inevitable that as CSOs become more influential actors in global health governance and increase their role in service delivery there will be tensions between their claims to be representing people with poor health and their obligations to other stakeholders. Demands for accountability will multiply – from beneficiaries, donors, staff, network partners, the media and others (Brown & Moore, 2001).

To maintain their credibility and legitimacy, CSOs delivering health interventions need to reconcile these tensions and complex demands. Workable systems of accountability that balance the different allegiances of CSOs are also necessary. Theoretical models used in social science may prove useful in teasing out what accountability means for a health-related CSO and how more effective accountability mechanisms can be implemented. Goodin suggests starting with three simple questions – who are CSOs accountable to, for what and how do they make themselves accountable (Goodin, 2003)? Benner et al. (2004) for example, call for a 'pluralistic system of accountability' involving financial, legal, professional, peer and reputational accountability.

The process by which CSOs are chosen to participate in GHIs both at a global and national level and their accountability to the populations targeted by those interventions should be made more transparent. Tayler (2006), for example, argues that national or regional CSOs chosen to participate in global HIV/AIDS initiatives in some countries have close links with national political representatives or civil servants that can undermine their credibility.

It is important for CSOs to be able to demonstrate how those affected by interventions are involved in decision-making. The United Nations Economic and Social Council laid down the following preconditions for the inclusion of NGOs in United Nations consultations:

> "The organization shall have a representative structure and possess appropriate mechanisms of accountability to its members, who shall exercise effective control over its policies and actions through the exercise of voting rights or other appropriate democratic and transparent decision-making processes".

> (United Nations, 1996)

Similar preconditions could be laid down for global health governance agencies and CSOs. Many CSOs are aware of this vulnerability and have initiated efforts to address shortcomings. For example, 10 of the leading global CSOs produced an 'Accountability Charter' in 2006 to promote transparency and accountability (Consumers' International, 2006). Research into new emerging models of accountability and debates on how they can be applied or adapted by health-related CSOs would be useful.

Conclusion

CSOs play a prominent role in the delivery of GHIs. The arguments of both advocates and sceptics of CSOs should be applied to GHIs. Failure by advocates to respond to the sceptical arguments put forward here may weaken the legitimacy of CSO involvement in GHIs. A response based on more detailed research into the role that CSOs play within global health interventions and governance structures and the consequences (intended and unintended) of their involvement is needed. The theoretical models of CSO legitimacy such as those developed by Benner et al. (2004), Goodin (2003) and others could be adapted and applied to the role of CSOs in GHIs. If health research can clarify how different CSOs operate in different contexts it could help to identify those variables that promote or impede the success of health interventions in different settings globally.

References

Amoore, L., & Langley, P. (2004). Ambiguities of global civil society. *Review of International Studies, 30*(1), 89–110.

Anderson, K., & Rieff, D. (2004). 'Global civil society': a sceptical view. In H. Anheier, M. Glasius, & M. Kaldor (Eds.), *Global civil society 2004/5*. London: Sage.

Anheier, H., Glasius, M., & Kaldor, M. (2001). Introducing Global civil society. In H. Anheier, M. Glasius, & M. Kaldor (Eds.), *Global civil society 2001*. Oxford: Oxford University Press.

Avert. (2006). *PEPFAR prime partners in fiscal year 2005*. Avert. Available from: <www.avert.org/media/pdfs/pepfar-partners.pdf>.

Barnett, T., & Whiteside, A. (2002). *AIDS in the twenty-first century*. Palgrave: Macmillan.

Benner, T., Reinicke, W. H., & Witte, J. M. (2004). Multisectoral networks in global governance: towards a pluralistic system of accountability. *Government and Opposition, 39*(2), 191–210.

Brown, L. D., & Moore, M. H. (2001). *Accountability, strategy and international non-governmental organisations*. [Working Paper No. 7]. Hauser Center for Nonprofit Organizations, Kennedy School of Government, Harvard University. Available from: <http://www.institut-gouvernance.org/docs/accountability.strategy.and.international. ngos.pdf>.

Brugha, R., Donoghue, M., Starling, M., Ndubani, P., Ssengooba, F., & Fernandes, B., et al. (2004). The Global Fund: managing great expectations. *Lancet, 364*(9428), 95–100.

Consumers' International. (2006). *NGOs lead by example: World's international NGOs endorse accountability charter*. Consumers' International. Available from. <http:// www.consumersinternational.org/Shared_ASP_Files/UploadedFiles/1D54BD8F-71CC-409C-9488-C1E7F6035EBA_AccountabilityCharterpressrelease.doc>.

Cooley, A., & Ron, J. (2002). The NGO scramble: organisational insecurity and the political economy of transnational action. *International Security, 27*(1), 5–39.

Dahl, R. A. (2003). Can international organizations be democratic? A skeptic's view. In D. Held, A. McGrew, D. Goldblatt, & J. Perraton (Eds.), *The global transformations reader* (pp. 530–541). Cambridge: Polity Press.

Epstein, H. (2005a). God and the fight against AIDS. *New York Review of Books, 52*(7).

Epstein, H. (2005b). The lost children of AIDS. *New York Review of Books, 52*(17).

Fidler, D. (2005). Health, globalization and governance: an introduction to public health's 'new world order'. In K. Lee, & J. Collin (Eds.), *Global change and health* (pp. 161–177). London: Open University Press.

Goodin, R. E. (2003). Democratic accountability: the distinctiveness of the third sector. *Archives Europeennes De Sociologie, 44*(3), 359–396.

Held, D. (2003). Cosmopolitanism: taming globalization. In D. Held, A. McGrew, D. Goldblatt, & J. Perraton (Eds.), *The global transformations reader* (pp. 500–513). Polity Press.

Hsu, L. N. (2004). *Building dynamic democratic governance and HIV-resilient societies.* United Nations Development Programme: Oslo Governance Centre. Available from: <www.undp.org/oslo-centre/docs05/LeeNahHsu_final.pdf>.

Kaldor, M. (2003). Global civil society. In D. Held, A. McGrew, D. Goldblatt, & J. Perraton (Eds.), *The global transformations reader* (pp. 559–563). Polity Press.

Kamat, S. (2004). The privatization of public interest: theorizing NGO discourse in a neoliberal era. *Review of International Political Economy, 11*(1), 155–176.

Keohane, R., & Nye, J. (2001). The club model of multilateral cooperation and problems of democratic legitimacy. KSG Working Paper No. 01-004. Available from: <http://ssrn.com/abstract=262175>.

Lee, K. (2003). *Health impacts of globalization.* Basingstoke: Palgrave Macmillan.

Palmer, N., Strong, L., Wali, A., & Sondorp, E. (2006). Contracting out health services in fragile states. *British Medical Journal, 332*, 718–721.

Panos Institute. (2003). *Missing the message? 20 years of learning from HIV/AIDS.* London: Panos Institute. Available from: <www.panos.org.uk/PDF/reports/MissingTheMessage.pdf>.

Parkhurst, J. O. (2005). The response to HIV/AIDS and the construction of national legitimacy. *Development and Change, 36*(3), 571–590.

Pfeiffer, J. (2003). International NGOs and primary health care in Mozambique: the need for a new model of collaboration. *Social Science & Medicine, 56*(4), 725–738.

Rau, B. (2006). The politics of civil society in confronting HIV/AIDS. *International Affairs, 82*(2), 285–295.

Rosenau, J. N. (2000). Change, complexity and governance in a globalizing space. In J. Pierre (Ed.), *Debating governance: Authority, steering, and democracy* (pp. 167–200). Oxford: Oxford University Press.

Rowson, M. (2005). Health and an emerging civil society. In K. Lee, & J. Collin (Eds.), *Global change and health* (pp. 195–211). Open University Press.

Scholte, J. A. (2004). Civil society and democratically accountable global governance. *Government and Opposition, 39*(2), 211–233.

The new world of global health. *Science Magazine, 311*, 2006.

Seckinelgin, H. (2003). Time to stop and think: HIV/AIDS. In H. Anheier, M. Glasius, & M. Kaldor (Eds.), *Global civil society 2002/3.* London: Sage.

Seckinelgin, H. (2005). A global disease and its governance: HIV/AIDS in sub-Saharan Africa and the agency of NGOs. *Global Governance, 11*, 351–368.

Swidler, A. (2006). Syncretism and subversion in AIDS governance: how locals cope with global demands. *International Affairs, 82*(2), 269–284.

Tayler, L. (2006). *Corruption and AIDS – An overview of the issue.* HLSP Institute. Available from: <http://www.hlspinstitute.org/>.

The Global Fund to fight AIDS, Tuberculosis and Malaria. (2006a). Progress Report. <http://www.theglobalfund.org/en/funds_raised/reports/>. (Accessed 27.07.06).

The Global Fund to fight AIDS, Tuberculosis and Malaria (2006b). [Civil society website] Available from: <http://www.theglobalfund.org/en/partners/ngo/>.

United Nations. (1996). *ECOSOC Resolution 1996/31 – Arrangements for consultation with non-governmental organizations.* United Nations. Available from: <habitat.igc.org/ngo-rev/>.

616

Walt, G., Pavignani, E., Gilson, L., & Buse, K. (1999). Health sector development: from aid coordination to resource management. *Health Policy and Planning, 14*(3), 207–218.

Whitman, J. (2002). Global governance as the friendly face of unaccountable power. *Security Dialogue, 33*(1), 45–57.

World Health Organisation. (2006). *National Health Accounts Data.* World Health Organisation. Available from: <http://www.who.int/nha/country/MLI.xls>.

World Health Organization. (2005). *Proposed programme budget for 2004–2005.* World Health Organization. Available from: <www.who.int/gb/ebwha/pdf_files/WHA56/ea5651.pdf>.

Zurn, M. (2004). Global governance and legitimacy problems. *Government and Opposition, 39*(2), 260–287.

88

THE POTENTIAL OF HEALTH SECTOR NON-GOVERNMENTAL ORGANIZATIONS

Policy options

Lucy Gilson, Priti Dave Sen, Shirin Mohammed and Phare Mujinja

Source: *Health Policy and Planning*, 9:1 (1994), 14–24.

Non-governmental organizations (NGOs) have increasingly been promoted as alternative health care providers to the state, furthering the same goals but less hampered by government inefficiencies and resource constraints. However, the reality of NGO health care provision is more complex. Not only is the distinction between government and NGO providers sometimes difficult to determine because of their operational integration, but NGOs may also suffer from resource constraints and management inefficiencies similar to those of government providers. Some registered NGOs operate as for-profit providers in practice. Policy development must reflect the strengths and weaknesses of NGOs in particular settings and should be built on NGO advantages over government in terms of resource mobilization, efficiency and/or quality. Policy development will always require a strong government presence in co-ordinating and regulating health care provision, and an NGO sector responsive to the policy goals of government.

Introduction

The World Bank's 1993 World Development Report, *Investing in Health*, calls for public policies which promote diversity and competition in health care provision, giving particular emphasis to non-governmental organizations (NGOs). This call, like its predecessors, is based on the expectation that NGOs have significant advantages over government in the provision of health care. Do NGOs live up to these expectations? This paper throws light on current practices and future opportunities, in order to inform the process of policy development with respect to the incorporation of NGOs within health systems.

Current practice

Defining characteristics and motivation

Green's 1987 paper defines NGOs as non-profit-maximizing and, at most, indirectly managed by, or accountable to, the state. Although expected to ensure that funds received from government are not misused and are used for health care provision, NGOs are rarely subjected to more detailed monitoring of resource use. Implicit in this basic definition is a key perceived strength of NGOs: that, like health professionals, they are primarily motivated by humanitarian concern. However, some NGOs do pursue profits. For example, after the abolition of private for-profit care in Tanzania in 1977 some medical practitioners continued to operate on a for-profit basis, 'under the umbrella of voluntary agencies' (Mujinja et al. 1993, p.4). In Bombay, India, almost all non-public hospitals are registered under the Charitable Trust Act and so are eligible for certain tax benefits. The only requirement of registration is that they provide free services to 12.5% of their in-patients. The profits that they earn are defined as 'surplus' and are supposedly re-invested in the hospital, but there is little regulation of this practice (Yesudian 1993).

Concern has also been expressed that even non-profit-maximizing NGOs are not motivated solely by humanitarian ideals. They are often perceived as most interested in proselytizing their faith (Green 1987) – the reluctance of the Roman Catholic Church to allow the provision of family planning services is seen as a weakness of care and cited as an example of inappropriate motivations.

Finally, failure to develop national capacity to operate health and other services and continued strong connection to an external 'parent' organization is seen as indicating a lack of commitment to the country of operation (Cumper 1986). Even local churches may be perceived as essentially external organizations when they receive substantial external funding and when their health services are primarily managed by expatriate staff. Such organizations may appear to be unaccountable to the state.

The motivations of the NGO sector are, therefore, more heterogenous than commonly perceived and their lack of direct accountability to government may only exacerbate concern about their 'true' motivation.

Contributions, diversity and importance

Green (1987) identifies six groups of NGOs operating in the health sector: religious organizations, international (social welfare) NGOs, locally based (social welfare) NGOs, unions and trade and professional associations (interested in the protection and promotion of their members), other non-profit-making organizations (such as occupational health services) and non-profit-making (but pre-paid) health care (such as health maintenance organizations).

Overall, NGOs have four health sector functions:

Service provision   providing comprehensive services from health facilities or addressing a particular problem (e.g. tuberculosis, blindness or AIDS). NGOs have also, traditionally, been important because they have served the most vulnerable populations, improving access and coverage. In Zimbabwe 80%, and in Tanzania 90%, of church hospitals are in rural areas initially less favoured by other health care providers; but in other countries NGOs also work with urban slum dwellers, tribal groups, women and children.

NGOs, especially churches, represent a particularly important element of health care provision in Africa (Table 1). Green (1987) suggests that unions and trade and professional organizations and non-profit-making (but pre-paid) health care may have most relevance to Latin America, and, of the countries represented at the workshop, only in Mexico were there examples of NGOs other than religious groups involved in health care provision. However, in Asia a variety of medical foundations have played important roles within the health sector.

Social welfare activities   In Nepal local NGOs are involved in care for the disabled, and international NGOs such as the Save the Children Fund and CARE undertake a range of development-related activities (Gurung and Olsen 1993). In Pakistan, of the 8000 active NGOs, two-thirds predominantly have a social welfare orientation (Aga Khan University 1993). Zambian experience also suggests that African NGOs are involved in such activities, having particular concern for groups such as the disabled, children, youth and women (DiS 1992).

Table 1 Indicators of the volume of health care provision by NGOs.

Country (organization)	% of total no. of hospitals/hospital beds	% of total services/ no. of contacts/ population coverage	% of health sector expenditure
Ghana (church)		40% (population)	
Malawi (church)		30% (services)	12%
Mexico (social welfare)		> 6% (contacts)	
Nepal (church)	19% (hospitals) 26% (beds)		
Tanzania (church)	40% (hospitals)		37–43% (1976)
Uganda (church)	20% (beds)		
Zimbabwe (church)		40% (contacts)	

Source: Country background papers for 1993 LSHTM workshop.

Support activities Church organizations in Africa usually train some/all of their own nursing staff with varying degrees of government regulation. In Tanzania the government sets the training syllabi, certifies the qualifications of church training schools and may even subsidize their activities, but elsewhere the government has not subjected church training institutions to close scrutiny.

NGOs have also sometimes taken responsibility for drug supply. In India two organizations, 'low cost drugs' and the 'community development medicinal unit', supply essential, generic drugs to a range of non-profit organizations. In Uganda, the Joint Medical Stores for NGOs is operated by the Catholic and Protestant Boards on behalf of member organizations. It obtains drugs either through import or through Uganda Pharmaceutical Ltd (a parastatal), or drugs are purchased through donations from external sources.

Research and advocacy The role of international and local NGOs in developing and promoting the primary health care concept, community health workers and community financing approaches are the most well-known examples of the innovative action-research of NGOs which, complemented by advocacy and lobbying at national and international levels, has informed policy-making (Cumper 1986).

Although making a small contribution to health care provision, NGOs in India, for instance, have provided examples of 'good practice' for government to emulate. They have also been valued internationally for their grass-roots advocacy, raising the aspirations of local communities and empowering them to demand better government services. However, NGOs' usefulness as models for national systems has been limited by their small size and peculiar characteristics – making replication of their activities on a national scale unlikely (e.g. with respect to community health workers: Walt 1990).

NGOs are, therefore, not only providers of health care but also community activists, managers, trainers, development workers and international lobbyists. In all these roles, whatever their size or nature, they make an important contribution to the health sector.

Financing structure and problems

Overt government support for NGO health care includes financial grants, donations in-kind, such as drugs and supplies, and grants tied to specific types of health expenditure, particularly salaries. In Ghana and Malawi the salaries of all church health staff are paid by government, whilst in Uganda staff are seconded to church health facilities from government. More covert forms of government support are provided through tax subsidies and exemptions: in Malawi, church organizations affiliated to the Christian Association of Malawi (CHAM) are able to purchase drugs from the Central Medical Stores at subsidized rates; the Ghanaian members of the equivalent organization (CHAG) are exempted from paying import duties on drugs, dressings, equipment and other items; and in Nepal some NGOs receive tax exemptions for goods and services on the recommendation of the national NGO co-ordinating body.

The extent of the Papua New Guinean government subsidization of church health care results in these services being seen 'as part of the public health sector' (Thomason 1993, p.5). Similarly, in Tanzania government seconds staff to NGO-owned hospitals designated as district hospitals and provides 'bed grants' to them (Tsh 1000, just over $2, per approved bed); even some church dispensaries operate with staff seconded from government. In Ghana, 'agency' hospitals were built by the government but are managed by NGOs, and receive equipment and drugs from government in addition to financial support.

The problems of government support have included: delays in disbursement, lack of flexibility in use (tied to particular items of expenditure), or unacceptable conditions (e.g. in Zimbabwe, government-prescribed fee levels are thought to be too high for the clients served by church facilities). Moreover, as governments have themselves faced economic constraints this source of funding has become less stable, causing particular problems for those NGO facilities closely allied with government.

International support for local NGOs comes from churches, private trusts and international NGOs. Multilateral and bilateral agencies have also shown increasing interest in supporting the sector since the 1980s. Yet international support has a variety of problems: it is often project-specific, leaving NGOs

Table 2 Financing NGO health care.

Country	Source of funding		
	government	*other*[1]	*fees*
Ghana	45%	5%	50%
India		+	+ + +
Malawi	40%	20–30%	30–40%
Mexico			+ + +
Nepal	0%	87%	13%
Pakistan		+ + +	
PNG	+ + +		
South Africa			+ + +
Tanzania[2]	33%	33%	33%
Uganda	10%	10–20%	70–80%

Source: Country background papers for 1993 LSHTM workshop.
Notes: + + + = major source; + = minor source
[1] mostly local/external donations.
[2] More detailed evaluation has shown that 20–80% of NGO hospital expenses are covered through external donations, that fees can represent up to 100% of dispensary funding and 50–100% of hospital funding (Mujinja et al. 1993).

with difficulties in meeting core organizational costs; it is usually available only for limited periods; and international donors are often interested only in supporting capital or start-up costs, or projects they themselves perceive as important. In addition, receipt of overseas support can compromise sovereignty and independence. In Nepal the dominance of international donor support for NGOs has serious implications for the long-term sustainability of their activities (Gurung and Olsen 1993). International support provided to NGOs may also be seen by governments as a threat to national sovereignty because, by their nature, NGOs are outside direct government control. Channelling international support to NGOs without consultation with government may, therefore, only exacerbate pre-existing concern about motivations and activities.

Many local church health care providers are, however, currently facing a funding crisis as overseas contributions diminish in the face of global recession and declining developed country domestic support (Green 1987). In South Africa the number of beds provided by charity and welfare hospitals has decreased by more than 26% since 1983 as a result of the escalating costs of maintaining the facilities, and static or declining resources (Booysen 1993).

Other, smaller sources of finance include commercial activities. A Bangladeshi NGO, for example, runs a printing press and uses the proceeds to subsidize health care (Streefland and Chowdhury 1990). More commonly, as in Bombay, private hospital beds are charged at full-cost prices to cross-subsidize use by the poor. Even so, the fees of NGO hospitals in Bombay are at least five times lower than those of for-profit hospitals (Yesudian 1993).

Community resources have become a particularly important source of finance for NGOs since the late 1970s, as a result of the decline in other support. They are most often tapped through user fees retained at the point of collection, but a variety of community financing mechanisms, based, for example, on pre-payment or drug revolving funds, have also been used. Thus, in Nepal the Lalitpur Community Development and Health Programme has been run on the basis of a health insurance scheme since 1978 (Gurung and Olsen 1993). A ticket system entitles each family to get treatment at health posts and, if necessary, to be referred to the main hospital (but as the ticket is often not bought until the family needs treatment, it often functions more like a user fee system).

The experience of community financing is, however, mixed. The volume of revenue that NGOs can raise from local resources may be constrained by the limited capacity of the typically poor surrounding community, and by the organizations' desire to provide services to all regardless of ability to pay. A Tanzanian study of 42 NGO health facilities, for example, found that only 9% did not use an exemption mechanism (Mujinja et al. 1993). In Ghana, CHAG issues guidelines concerning the minimum and maximum charges and suggests that as much flexibility as possible is given to poorer patients (Dakpallah and Adusei 1993). The consequence of protecting the poor may be seen in the Nepalese experience where reliance on external funding is a direct result of the continued provision of free services to marginalized groups (given that government gives no financial support to these organizations).

The growing economic crisis facing NGOs appears to be starting to force the organizations to revise their fees upwards to meet their overall funding shortfall. Such actions may not only have negative consequences for equity but may initiate NGOs into the vicious cycle of falling resources, rising prices, lower quality, lower utilization, falling resources. These problems would certainly undermine the potential of NGOs to tap the community resources not available to poorly perceived government services.

Efficiency and quality of provision

A major justification for the promotion of NGO services is that they are more efficient and of higher quality than either government or for-profit providers (World Bank 1987, 1993). However, available evidence is limited and variable.

The perceived quality of NGO providers is often better than that of government (Asamoa-Baah et al. 1992). One survey in Tanzania found that 45% of respondents always preferred to use an NGO health facility and that consumers preferred NGO facilities because of their availability of drugs and good services (Mujinja et al. 1993). Other Tanzanian surveys have found that the functioning of NGO facilities was better than that of government, particularly their regular availability of drugs (Andersson-Brolin et al. 1991), and that NGO health staff had greater technical skills than government staff (Kanji 1992).

In contrast, a fourth Tanzanian study (Gilson 1992) identified weaknesses which included: few outreach activities; greater cold chain failures in NGO than government facilities; health worker performance of duties at levels below the generally poor level of government facilities, especially for antenatal consultations; employment of untrained, or inadequately trained, staff. A PNG study pointing to better church structural quality found that this performance was dependent on the greater level of resources and range of services available in church units; controlling for these factors indicated that there was no difference in the performance of government and church units (Garner et al. 1990).

The evidence on technical efficiency is even more limited. If better perceived quality leads to higher utilization than in government units, technical efficiency may also be better in NGO facilities (if increased utilization leads to lower average/marginal costs without impairing quality). However, poorly perceived 'value for money' and relatively low utilization may lead NGO services to be of lower technical efficiency than government services (Gilson 1992). Better

NGO technical efficiency is thought to result partly from managerial efficiency, as NGOs are not, by definition, constrained by government bureaucracy. They should, for example, be able to react quickly to changing needs, making decisions at the health facility level without reference to a higher authority and using funds and human resources flexibly. Such potential advantages have resulted in church units being designated as district hospitals in Malawi.

Management flexibility may, however, encourage inefficiency. Anecdotal and other reports abound about the lack of management systems in NGO facilities (Asamoa-Baah et al, 1992; DiS 1992) and planning is often weak (Andersson-Brolin 1991; DiS 1992). Problems can also arise because NGOs focus on the needs of the local community rather than on national needs, and may have different concepts of service provision to those of national policy (Asamoa-Baah et al. 1992). They may, thus, build health facilities in inappropriate locations, of inappropriate size, using technology that is too sophisticated relative to local needs and national plans, and provide an unbalanced service mix whilst using an unbalanced manpower mix (Green 1987).

The two factors most critical to the management performance of any organization are organizational structure and skills. The independence of NGOs and their reliance on a variety of funding sources places NGO health care providers within a complex organizational structure, with links to their own 'parent' organization, to the various branches of government responsible for health care in any country, to the local community and, possibly, to a number of external organizations (Andersson-Brolin et al. 1991; Asamoa-Baah et al. 1992; DiS 1992). Such complexity can undermine accountability, particularly where leadership is not rooted in a local, viable organizational structure, and can tax the management skills of NGO managers (e.g. because different supporting bodies demand different accounting procedures and returns). A review of the health services provided by the Roman Catholic Church in Zambia found that sisterhood 'managing agencies' (groups of nuns responsible for health facilities) are the critical group of health care managers, and expressed concern that these agencies are being transferred to Zambian leadership before adequate management training has been provided. "The non-Catholic groups are even more vulnerable . . . most personnel in leadership positions are expatriate . . . Some of the non-church organisations visited had very unstable organisational structures, with person-based leadership, little formalised accountability and little real participation by the target groups" (DiS 1992, p. 44).

Evidence of NGO inefficiency or of quality failures indicates the importance of government action to regulate and monitor NGO provision of health care.

Co-ordination with government planners and providers

Although only indirectly accountable to government, interaction between NGOs and government is inevitable. At a minimum, NGOs must register with governments and obtain licences for operation. In Tanzania the state has the power to influence the location and size of NGOs, the types of staff employed and even to fix the fee ceiling of certain services through the 1977 Private Hospital Act No.6.

National umbrella groups (Table 3) are seeking to improve co-ordination between individual NGOs, and NGOs and government, in a range of countries. In Malawi, CHAM seeks both to serve its members' interests in negotiations with the government and to ensure collaboration and communication between its members. There are similar bodies in Ghana (CHAG) and India (the Voluntary Health Association of India); in Uganda, there are medical bureaux for each of the major religious groups (Catholic, Protestant, Muslim); and, in Nepal, there is an overall NGO co-ordinating body, the Social Services National Co-ordinating Council (SSNCC), as well as an umbrella church organization known as the United Mission to Nepal (UMN).

Umbrella organizations can facilitate cooperation between NGOs by providing technical support to their membership, promoting information sharing, negotiating with the state, and encouraging cost-effective practices (such as bulk

Table 3 Current patterns of co-ordination between NGOs and government.

Country	District/local co-ordination	National co-ordination
Ghana	district-designated hospitals; DHMT[1] liaises with local churches	NGOs register with Private Hospitals and Maternity Homes Board; staff register with Medical and Dental Council and Nurses and Midwives Board; submit health statistics; CHAG co-ordinates
Malawi	soon to introduce cross-referral of patients and CHAM institutions to be given responsibility for district health system management	consultation in policy formulation through CHAM; approval of new facilities required from government
Nepal	one experiment of district-designated hospital; cross-referral; co-ordination through the district public health office and district medical officer	registered with SSNCC or, as UMN, work directly with government; government licenses and regulates; joint policy-making groups for planning, budgeting etc.
Tanzania	district-designated hospitals; DHMTs formally responsible for liaison with churches	licensed and regulated; no effective umbrella organization
Uganda	district authorities officially responsible for co-ordination	umbrella organizations; limited interaction between government and NGOs

Source: Country background papers for 1993 LSHTM workshop.
Note: [1] DHMT = district health management team.

drug purchasing and supply). They may also be well-placed to participate in national policy-making and planning. CHAM formulates operational policies in the interests of its member organizations, in consultation with the Ministry of Health. The Medical Council of Malawi (MCM), established through the 1987 Medical Practitioners and Dentists Act, is composed of nine members, at least two of whom should be from the private sector in order to allow 'for the incorporation of the interests of the many NGOs' (Ngalande Banda and Simukonda 1993, p.11). The MCM has been charged with the critical responsibilities of licensing private practice, regulating the training of medical personnel, and controlling and regulating the medical profession and practice.

At the district level, health management teams and planning activities can directly involve NGO representatives. Swaziland's 1986 decentralization guidelines, for example, gave a direct role to NGOs in regional health planning, even in discussion of resource allocations (GOS 1986). Co-operation between NGOs and government may be even closer, for example when NGO facilities function as district referral hospitals (district-designated) or benefit from staff seconded from government. In such cases there are generally specific mechanisms for co-ordination; for example, district-designated hospitals in Tanzania are managed by a Board composed of church and government representatives. In Nepal one UMN hospital has been district-designated and consequently receives 2.6% of its running costs from government (Gurung and Olsen 1993). In Malawi the creation of health delivery areas will allow CHAM hospitals to become responsible for all services in their areas, whether government or CHAM-owned. It is hoped that this integration of CHAM and government facilities will improve overall management of the health system allowing, for example, cross supervision between government and NGO providers (Ngalande Banda and Simukonda 1993).

However, it is not clear how effective such mechanisms are in bringing about co-ordination or in assuring quality. In Uganda, 'the government cannot directly interfere with the running of the [church] hospitals provided these operate within the policy guidelines outlined for the whole country' (Asiimwe and Lule 1993 p.25). It is difficult to co-ordinate fees between government and church health facilities in Malawi because fees are not uniform within CHAM, and there is a policy of non-interference between member organizations. A further area of continuing poor performance in co-ordination in some countries is that of information provision, as in Tanzania and Uganda.

Responsibility for poor co-ordination is often evenly divided, NGOs may not be prepared to discuss their own policy or financial health, and may fail to see the importance of local accountability. At the same time, governments in Africa often unfairly distrust church organizations because of their colonial past, continuing links to parent churches, and apparent unwillingness to adopt national policies such as family planning. State systems themselves also suffer from management weaknesses. In Uganda the NGOs complain of the 'bureaucratic delays they experience when trying to clear their matters with the Ministry of Health, the lack of clear national health policy guide-lines, and the absence of grants in aid . . . the government has never defined the role of NGOs and only 'hopes' that NGOs will automatically fall into the National Health System' (Asiimwe and Lule 1993, p.12).

Green (1987) suggests that the influences over the NGO/government relation-ship vary between the three functions of policy making and planning, medical referrals, and shared support services (training and supplies). For the first two, the funding arrangements of NGOs and the legal framework within which they operate are important. Policy/planning co-ordination is also influenced by NGOs' representation on government bodies and vice versa, and by the degree of formal integration of NGOs with government services. Med-ical referrals are affected by the complementarity and location of services. Relationships over shared support services are influenced by the degree of national training and manpower planning and/or the size of the central drug procurement system. Overall, therefore, the role of government in determining the context of the relationship is critical to the effectiveness of co-ordination between NGOs and government at both national and district levels.

Policy strategies and requirements for NGO provision of health care

Four broad policy strategies exist with respect to NGO provision of health care: restrict their operations; maintain the current level of service provision and existing, limited, government regulation; regulate, co-ordinate and super-vise; and actively promote (Asamoa-Baah et al. 1992). Table 4 considers the potential of each of these options for four of the countries represented at the LSHTM workshop. The following discussion draws on these specific examples in identifying more general policy lessons.

Where NGOs are major providers of health care, as in Africa, restriction is unlikely to be a viable policy option because of the strengths of NGOs and the resource constraints facing government (Table 4). The Tanzanian Minister of Health, for example, noted in his 1985 budget speech, that 'the government does not only need NGOs but wants them as partners' (Mujinja et al. 1993, p.19). However, simply maintaining the status quo, in terms of levels of service provision and government regulation, would not address existing NGO weak-nesses and might even exacerbate them. Ensuring effective use of all health care resources requires the government to consider ways of regulating and super-vising NGOs, given concern about their ability to sustain revenue generation, their efficiency and quality of care, and their co-ordination with government.

Discussion of NGO sustainability in Zambia identified three critical fac-tors: organizational capacity (e.g. ability to mobilize and manage resources, ability to solve problems and respond to new needs), activity profile (e.g. range of services, level of care, volume of care, technology) and contextual factors (e.g. government policy framework, socio-economic conditions, health

Table 4 Policy options and their potential.

Country	Policy strategy with respect to NGO health care provision			
	restrict	maintain status quo	regulate and supervise	actively promote
Ghana	no: important to health system, government in difficulties	no: mechanisms for co-ordination exist, potential contribution great	yes: build on umbrella organization; further develop central MOH and district management	yes: for management improvement in whole system
India	no: sector too small to justify restriction	no: encourage as potential examples of good practice	yes	yes: promote provision for specified populations in natural field 'laboratories'
Mexico	no: sector too small to justify restriction	no: encourage as potential examples of alternative models	yes	yes: promote experimentation with new models of care provision
Tanzania[1]	no: important to health system, government in difficulties	maybe: MOH weak, ineffective NGO umbrella organization	maybe: build on existing close links e.g. district-designated hospitals	no: mechanisms for co-ordination too weak

Note: [1] Two policy options appear to exist for Tanzania because although there is limited to operation at the national level between NGOs, and between NGOs and government, at a local level closer co-ordination results from the practice of designating church hospitals as district hospitals.

needs, availability of other services) (DiS 1992). These indicate that there are two pre-requisites for either of the remaining two policy options.

The first is a national MOH sufficiently strong to, at the minimum, set guidelines for NGO operations, monitor their implementation and provide the necessary support and co-ordination. The second is an NGO sector that is able to initiate and sustain resource mobilization, without over-reliance on external sources, and that has the capacity for efficient resource management, using transparent management systems that ensure accountability for resource use. External NGOs must have a commitment to the development of local capacity and all NGOs must be prepared to interact with government and other partners in health care, accepting the need for some adjustment in activities, and for some regulation and co-ordination.

Where external resources are available to such organizations it is also important that their use is open to government inspection. It might be even better if their use is agreed through discussion between government and NGOs. In South Africa, for example, international and national funding for local NGOs is currently channelled through trusts managed by trustees from different interest groups, including government. The trusts are politically neutral and ensure co-ordination among the various interested parties.

Where NGOs do not play a major role in health care provision, as in Asia and Latin America, it is still important to develop mechanisms for co-ordination to ensure that their experimentation and achievements are used within the development of the wider health system. Such co-ordination requires, first, that government provides an enabling environment for NGOs, drawing out and implementing the relevant lessons. Second, a supportive and flexible NGO sector is necessary, experimenting in ways that have lessons for the wider health system.

A key lesson from current NGO experience is that co-ordination among NGOs themselves can facilitate the tasks of government. If sufficiently strong, NGO umbrella organizations might even take over some of the tasks otherwise undertaken by government: self-regulation and/or channelling funds from external sources. Such organizations can certainly promote mutual understanding and collaborative policy development. Further research might, therefore, evaluate the bureaucratic efficiency of umbrella organizations, and individual NGOs, to assess their potential for further development.

Regulate, co-ordinate and supervise

Regulation is discussed in detail by Bennett et al. (in this volume). The degree and nature of NGO regulation will differ from that of for-profit providers to the extent that NGOs are prepared to work with government and are motivated by similar concerns.

However, as with for-profit providers, current experience suggests that the stick of regulation is best tempered by the carrot of incentives. Regulation of facility location, catchment areas, service mix or personnel mix is, thus, currently most often undertaken where resources are provided by government to NGOs. Other incentives for co-operation include close connections and consultation with government. As the Nepalese experiment with the Lalitpur Community Development and Health Programme indicates, it is helpful to supplement formal regulatory procedures with mechanisms for ensuring functional co-ordination, where roles can be defined and agreed, and through which the NGOs' potential for flexibility, innovation and health promotion can be stimulated (Gurung and Olsen 1993). Moreover, whatever the doubts about NGO motivations, their importance within health systems indicates that policy action must build trust between governments and NGOs.

Actively promote

NGOs might be promoted as health care providers (with responsibility for managing and operating either specific interventions or all services within an area), as trainers (managing and developing training programmes), as managers of support systems (such as drug supply), or as examples of good management practice. However, current experience suggests that NGO involvement in health care should only be promoted where:

- they have a long-term and sustained comparative advantage both in provision (in terms of better performance relative to standards) and in financing (i.e. long-term access to resources not available to government);
- they can meet a need not otherwise met and can make a positive contribution to the health system (e.g. by improving coverage through the extension of health services to areas previously without access, or introducing more efficient management procedures);
- they will use an untapped potential (e.g. health promotion or community mobilization through their congregations/members) (Asamoa-Baah et al. 1992).

In Zambia, for example, evaluation suggested that NGOs do not have potential for expanding coverage and need to improve their facilities to government standards rather than increase the volume and care level provided. However, they do have potential 'as partners to government at the district level for ensuring the delivery of a 'basic care package' . . . [and] . . . as partners with MOH in capacity building at district level' (DiS 1992, p.57).

Where the above requirements are met, promotion will still require financial incentives and the maintenance and development of supporting structures which ensure co-ordination and supervision. Block grants from government to NGOs might be given for an agreed package of services to be provided either within a geographical area or specific facility. In India, under the Integrated Child Development Programme, all the health facilities of several districts in Gujarat

State, including the government staff, have been handed over to an NGO. Government provides a grant for these activities and is then responsible for monitoring the services provided. In other words, government has 'contracted out' service provision to NGOs (see McPake in this volume for further discussion of the potential for contracting in relation to public provision of health care).

Alternatively, appropriate activities (i.e. activities important to government health policy objectives and in which NGOs have a competitive advantage) might attract a subsidy from government, or enhance organizations' eligibility for tax exemptions. Secondment of government health care managers or other health professionals might also promote health care provision by NGOs in areas where they have other advantages, such as a capacity for resource mobilization or a previously untapped potential for health promotion activities.

In every case the role of the government must also be strengthened. A block grant system, for example, should only be introduced if government skills in negotiating and setting contracts are sufficiently strong. The range and nature of government action may, however, vary with the importance and functions of NGOs. Where NGOs contribute little to the health system, local level controls may be adequate; where they are significant contributors (as in Africa), stronger, more wide-ranging government action is required.

Where the above pre-requisites for promotion of NGOs as health care providers are not met, NGOs may still be encouraged to be innovators and advocates of alternative health care strategies. Promotion in these cases may perhaps require only an enabling environment, but may also benefit from financial support and a co-ordinating mechanism.

Summary and conclusions

The strengths of NGO care can be characterized as: their motivational force (where humanitarian concerns are paramount); their willingness to serve in relatively remote areas; their non-bureaucratic and flexible style of operation; their often close relationship with the community served; their ability to experiment and innovate in patterns of provision and financing; and their provision of high quality care at low cost in some areas. However, their weaknesses include: a vulnerable financial base resulting in a growing reliance on fees and on fee levels beyond that affordable by all members of the community; isolated operation, often with little regard to the wider health system and with little or no participation in national and district planning; reluctance to adopt national policy-guidelines where they conflict with other concerns (e.g. in family planning); poor information systems and sometimes weak management capacities.

Given these strengths and weaknesses, the research required to support policy formulation with respect to NGOs includes:

- strategies for strengthening and developing MOH capacity to co-ordinate and regulate at national and local levels
- structures/mechanisms for coordination between NGOs and between NGOs and government
- evaluation of relative NGO efficiency in provision and management, and of factors influencing efficiency
- evaluation of the potential functions for NGOs in different circumstances (e.g. provision versus training versus research)
- the development of quality monitoring procedures and tools.

The current, mixed performance of NGOs in relation to health care provision indicates that policy development with respect to the health sector role of NGOs should be cautious, building on the strengths whilst recognizing the weaknesses. It is particularly important to clarify the relative roles of government and NGOs in service delivery and management, and government's role in planning and regulation. Government capacity to implement its defined functions must be strengthened, whilst NGOs require a stronger, more stable financial base and improved co-ordination amongst themselves. Finally, mutual trust and willingness to coordinate is required for the development of the NGO sector towards national policy goals.

Acknowledgements

The authors thank their colleagues at the January 1993 workshop on the 'public/private mix for health' for their contributions. The paper also draws on the discussions of the November 1992 consultation on district health systems held in Dakar, Senegal, to assist with the development of the 1993 World Development Report. Final responsibility for the paper remains, however, with the authors. The Health Economics and Financing Programme is funded by ODA.

References

Aga Khan University. 1993. Public/private mix for health care country paper, Pakistan. Paper prepared for January 1993 workshop on the public/private mix, LSHTM, London.

Andersson-Brolin L., Ole-Memiri B. L., Michanck E. and Ndagala D. 1991. *The art of survival: a study of sustainability in health projects.* Stockholm: SIDA.

Asamoa-Baah A., Gilson L., Kerker M., Mogedal S. and Pangu K. A. 1992. The public private mix at the district level. Report of working group: consultation on district health systems, Dakar, Senegal, November 1992.

Asiimwe D. and Lule J. G. 1993. The public/private mix in the financing and provision of health services in Uganda. Paper prepared for January 1993 workshop on the public/private mix, LSHTM, London.

Booysen M. 1993. The public/private health care mix in South Africa. Paper prepared for January 1993 workshop on the public/private mix, LSHTM, London.

Cruz C., Zurita B. and Zapata O. 1993. Public/private mix background paper: the case of Mexico. Paper prepared for January 1993 workshop on the public/private mix, LSHTM, London.

Cumper G. 1986. The changing role of NGOs: no longer the eunuch in the harem? *Health Policy and Planning* **1**(4): 335–44.

Dakpallah G. F. and Adusei J. 1993. The public/private mix in health care delivery in Ghana. Paper prepared for January 1993 workshop on the public/private mix, LSHTM, London.

DiS. 1992. *NGOs as partners in health care, Zambia: a review of sustainability.* Oslo: DiS.

Garner P., Thomason J. and Donaldson D. 1990. Quality assessment of health facilities in rural Papua New Guinea. *Health Policy and Planning* **5**(1): 49–59.

Gilson L. 1992. Value for money?: the efficiency of primary health facilities in Tanzania. PhD thesis, University of London.

Government of Swaziland (GOS). 1986. *Guidelines for future operation of health services in Swaziland.* Mbabane: GOS.

Green A. 1987. The role of non-governmental organisations and the private sector in the provision of health care in developing countries. *International Journal of Health Planning and Management* **2**: 37–58.

Gurung M. S. and Olsen I. T. 1993. The public/private mix in health care, Nepal. Paper prepared for January 1993 workshop on the public/private mix, LSHTM, London.

Kanji N. Kilima P. M. and Munishi G. M. 1992. Quality of care in primary curative care in Dar es Salaam. London: Health Policy Unit, London School of Hygiene and Tropical Medicine.

Mujinja P. G. M., Urassa D. and Mnyika K. S. 1993. The Tanzanian public/private mix in national health care. Paper prepared for January 1993 workshop on the public/private mix, LSHTM, London.

Ngalande Banda E. E. and Simukonda H. P. M. 1993. The public/private mix in the health sector in Malawi. Paper prepared for January 1993 workshop on the public/private mix, LSHTM, London.

Streefland P. and Chowdhury M. 1990. The long-term role of national non-government development organisations in primary health care: lessons from Bangladesh. *Health Policy and Planning* **5**(3): 261–6.

Thomason J. 1993. Papua New Guinea country paper, Paper prepared for January 1993 workshop on the public/private mix, LSHTM, London.

Walt G. (ed). 1990. *Just another pair of hands?: CHWs in national programmes.* Milton Keynes, UK: Open University Press.

World Bank. 1987. *Health Care Financing: An Agenda for Reform.* Washington DC: World Bank.

World Bank. 1993. *Investing in Health: the World Development Report.* Washington DC: World Bank.

Yesudian C. 1993. The nature of private health services in Bombay. Paper prepared for January 1993 workshop on the public/private mix, LSHTM, London.

89

IGO–NGO RELATIONS AND HIV/AIDS

Innovation or stalemate?

Christer Jönsson and Peter Söderholm

Source: *Third World Quarterly*, 16:3 (1995), 459–76.

In 1981 the symptoms later labelled acquired immunodeficiency syndrome (AIDS) were encountered for the first time among five homosexual men in Los Angeles, California. Few people, if any, at that time could possibly have foreseen the consequences of the diagnosis. By the end of 1994 over one million AIDS cases had been reported to the World Health Organization (WHO). Taking under-reporting into account, WHO estimates that about 4.5 million men, women and children are now suffering from AIDS (see Figure 1).

Projections into the future indicate that we have witnessed only the beginning of the pandemic. Over 14 million persons are carriers of HIV, the virus that causes AIDS. The average incubation time of 10 years, with asymptomatic carriers continuously spreading the virus, leads to estimates ranging from 40 million to 100 million HIV-infected individuals by the year 2000.[1]

In little more than a decade, AIDS has provoked responses on an unprecedented scale in the history of health. A gradual realisation that AIDS was not confined to certain high-risk groups, but was affecting every corner of the world, provoked calls for international action. The United Nations (UN) system, with its reputation and expertise in health as well as social and economic development, was soon compelled to mount a response to the disease. The UN, it was thought, could substantially help mobilise governments and international organisations to develop policies to prevent and control HIV/AIDS, and to mitigate the economic and social consequences resulting from the virus.

A global offensive was launched in 1987, 'the year of global AIDS mobilization'.[2] In May of that year WHO initiated its Special Programme on AIDS, later known as the Global Programme on AIDS (GPA). In October AIDS was discussed by the UN General Assembly, the first time a specific disease was considered

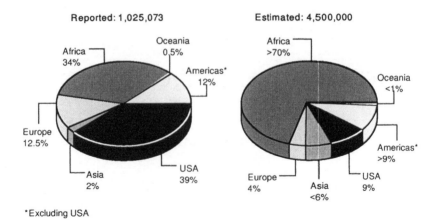

Reported: 1,025,073   Estimated: 4,500,000

*Excluding USA

Figure 1 Total number of AIDS cases in adults and children from the late 1970s until
late 1994.
Source: WHO Global Programme on AIDS GPA/SERSG 95009 12 January 1995.

by that forum. Another watershed was the January 1988 world summit of
health ministers, attended by delegates from 148 countries, which issued the
so-called London Declaration on AIDS Prevention. Endorsing the WHO GPA,
the document called for 'the involvement of all relevant governmental sectors
and nongovernmental organizations in creating the supportive social environment
needed to ensure the effective implementation of AIDS prevention programmes
and humane care of affected individuals'.[3]

The stage was thus set for global collaboration by a broad range of organisational actors. This paper draws on a collaborative study, more fully reported
elsewhere, which uses an interorganisational approach to trace the emergence of transnational cooperative structures in response to AIDS.[4] Of chief
concern here are the efforts at creating and maintaining links among and
between intergovernmental organizations (IGOs) in the UN system and the many
heterogeneous organisations usually lumped together under the NGO label.
After a discussion of the nature of the AIDS issue, we focus on two aspects
of IGO–NGO relations: various ways of framing the AIDS issue, which tend to
empower and disempower different sets of organisational actors; and the
conscious efforts by GPA to coordinate IGO and NGO activities. In conclusion,
we identify some lessons and insights of broader applicability emanating
from the AIDS case.

The nature of AIDS

Several characteristics of the AIDS issue are germane to understanding organisational responses. First, AIDS provides a graphic illustration of the degree
of interdependence and mutual vulnerability among peoples. It involves

so many different actors that it cannot be dealt with effectively by a single organisation—whether a national government, international organisation, multinational business corporation or nongovernmental organisation.[5] 'AIDS cannot be stopped in any single country unless it is stopped in all countries.'[6]

Second, AIDS typifies an issue that spans global and community levels, in which penetrating societies is of utmost importance. It is an issue for which community and global connections are arguably more important than the national ones.[7] Global cooperation and community-based treatment, care, and education are the indispensable components of an effective AIDS strategy.

Third, efforts to prevent or halt the spread of AIDS encroach upon the private and personal spheres that are normally beyond the purview of states. AIDS is a fatal infection that spreads through behaviour considered private or even taboo, such as premarital sexual relationships, extramarital sex, commercial sex, sex between men and needle sharing when injecting drugs. Though present, these practices are seldom openly acknowledged in any society. Some governments even choose to deny them altogether.

Fourth, the long incubation period of HIV/AIDS, combined with the fact that young adults, the most productive and reproductive members of the population, are primary targets, makes this the first epidemic in medical history for which the infected have formed articulate and well-informed consumer lobbies. Impatient with bureaucratic responses, various coalitions of People with AIDS (PWAS) have demanded respect for those who are ill, and access to treatment for them. This has been said to represent a revolution in public health, a dramatic rupture with the past, with repercussions beyond the AIDS issue.[8]

These traits combine to challenge the orthodox state-centric view of international relations. States, either alone or collaborating in IGOs, cannot halt the spread of AIDS. Only through the interaction of states, IGOs and NGOs can care and education reach into societies. Only through interaction can a global policy that is responsive to the demands of those affected by the epidemic be formulated. In the next section, we analyse to what extent NGOs and IGOs have assumed prominent roles in the transnational processes triggered by the HIV/AIDS pandemic.

Framing the issue

Problem definition, or framing, is a crucial aspect of agenda-setting. Problems do not exist 'out there', but are the result of subjective interpretations of certain perceived conditions and events. Most of what we generally recognise as international problems can be framed in a variety of ways. The importance of framing a problem has been recognised in different research traditions. Prospect theory, for example, asserts that the way people frame a problem determines in part how they see the consequences of choice.[9] And cognitive scientists have shown that categorisation is not independent of who is doing the categorising. Categories do not exist in the world but have to do with the world as we interact with it.[10] Framing, in short, is a highly political process. Goals of organisations and systems of organisations are subordinated to the goals of those who control the categorisation process.[11] Moreover, different ways of framing an issue mobilise and empower different types of actors at the expense of others.

AIDS *as a medical problem*

The most obvious and orthodox way of framing AIDS is in terms of medical science. Within the biomedical paradigm, the causes of ill health are located within the body, and AIDS is conceptualised in an elaborate scientific vocabulary.[12] This framing of HIV/AIDS mobilised and empowered actors traditionally engaged in health-related activities such as epidemiological surveillance, biomedical research and health care.

Associated with a medical understanding are a set of practices established as a social institution. The social institution public health entails standard operating procedures understandable to those well versed in its discourse. Thus, a search for the causative agent of AIDS constituted the reflexive response by medical research institutes. As the Center for Disease Control (CDC) in Atlanta received the first reports from doctors in California and New York about homosexual men developing a rare form of skin cancer and pneumonia, the research apparatus at CDC's disposal was immediately set in motion, reports were disseminated, articles submitted for publication and public hearings arranged. Also, CDC reported the new strange medical condition to the WHO epidemiological surveillance unit, which started to compile information and to disseminate it around the world. Long-established international cooperative structures in the field of health were activated.

As discovery was followed by a search for the cause, the number of actors grew. Quasi-governmental organisations were given resources to start research. For example, the National Institutes of Health (NIH) in Maryland as well as the Pasteur Institute in Paris became engaged. As results accumulated, yet other nongovernmental actors were involved in the form of publishers of medical journals and professional organisations for public health specialists. Furthermore, as possibilities for vaccines and drugs were explored, pharmaceutical companies saw potential profits and began to think about new products and markets.

Medical experts were also the first to bring AIDS to the international agenda in earnest. In August 1983 the Panamerican Health Organization (PAHO), in cooperation with the US NIH and CDC, convened a regional meeting of scientists and public health workers in Washington, DC to exchange information on the occurrence of AIDS. Two months later a similar meeting in Aarhus, Denmark focused on AIDS in Europe. It was co-organised by the Danish Cancer Society, WHO and the European Organization for Cooperation in Cancer Prevention Studies.

The First International Conference on AIDS was convened in Atlanta in April 1985 and may be considered the beginning of worldwide mobilisation of the scientific community. The Atlanta conference, organised by CDC and co-sponsored by the US Department of Health and WHO, was attended by scientists and health authorities from 50 countries. International AIDS conferences have since become annual—since 1994, biennial—events, furnishing opportunities for exchange of viewpoints between specialists and for raising public awareness. Although their topics and participants have gradually expanded, medical framing remains the predominant approach. The International AIDS Society, a voluntary association of scientific interest groups and a co-sponsor of the annual AIDS conferences, is a principal NGO within this frame.

However, a medical understanding of the pandemic is far from simple. Traditional medical solutions to epidemics—a drug that would cure the disease, a vaccine that would prevent infection—have remained beyond reach. In this respect, AIDS is a medical problem thus far without a medical solution. Moreover, any approach to preventing or controlling AIDS needs to be informed by the particularities of the epidemiological patterns and the routes of infection. In short, medical framing tends to hide other aspects of the pandemic.

Jonathan Mann, former executive director of GPA, coined the notion of three epidemics to highlight its multifaceted nature. The first epidemic is the silent and unnoticed infection by HIV that began spreading from continent to continent in the 1970s. The global manifestations of the infection, the spread of AIDS cases, represents the second wave. The third epidemic concerns the social, economic, political and cultural reactions to, and consequences of, the first two epidemics. This includes social disruption as individuals, families, groups and societies are affected; the economic consequences of expensive health care and loss of income, families' losses of breadwinners and societies' losses of entire generations of workers; and the stigmatisation of and discrimination against those infected by the virus. The third epidemic, says Mann, is 'as central to the global AIDS challenge as the disease itself' and can be 'as destructive as the preceding ones'. It 'threatens increasingly to overshadow and overwhelm the epidemics of HIV and AIDS'.[13]

AIDS as a problem of human rights

The notion of a third epidemic implies several possible framings in addition to the medical one. Blame and stigmatisation represent one alternative conceptualisation, not only in the general public but also among policymakers. AIDS is understood not in biomedical and scientific terms but in moral and sometimes even theological terms. The disease is viewed not primarily as the result of infection by a micro-organism but as a social, moral or spiritual affliction.[14] This includes calls for quarantine and other exclusionary policies as a response to the actual mode of transmission and also to the felt need to establish a boundary between 'us' and 'them'. In the mid-1980s several countries, including the USA, passed legislation restricting the entry of HIV-infected individuals. Aided by the discovery of the AIDS virus in 1983 to 1984 and the subsequent development of diagnostic tests, policy-makers were often prodded into such action by religious and conservative organisations.

An antithetical framing is in terms of human rights. Discrimination and violations of the human rights and dignity of HIV-infected people then become key aspects, and refinement of legal instruments and international conventions become the preferred solution. The human rights conceptualisation to a certain extent stands in stark contrast to the medical framing. Surveillance of the epidemic invokes practices that may raise questions of human rights. These practices include involuntary testing of high-risk groups, such as prostitutes, prisoners, intravenous drug users and homosexuals; users of health services, such as pregnant women and patients with sexually transmitted diseases; migrants or travellers; and certain occupation groups, such as military and health personnel. Notifying health authorities of cases of AIDS, ostensibly only a technical public health measure, also raises the human rights issues of confidentiality and anonymity.

Homosexual men in the USA and Europe were the first known AIDS victims and also the first to organise a response. People with AIDS reacted to what they perceived as grave injustices, such as loss of employment and housing, occupational restrictions, for example in health care and food handling, or social ostracism. Organisation was facilitated because homosexual communities, especially in the USA, were already well organised as a result of the struggle for respect and non-discrimination dating back to the civil rights era of the late 1960s. AIDS mobilised these gay organisations and provided them with a target for their frustration. They were relatively well equipped with organisational resources, such as office space, committed and educated staff and, not least, established contacts with policy-makers within city, state and national authorities. On the one hand, this mobilisation spawned numerous AIDS service organisations (ASOs) engaged in providing basic health care and counselling for the sick. Around the world, ASOs mushroomed and became institutional vehicles of volunteer, community-based AIDS prevention and care efforts. On the other hand, public advocacy and activist organisations, such as Gay Men's Health Crisis in the USA, quickly rose to prominence. ACT-UP (the AIDS Coalition to Unleash Power) is a prominent activist organisation that stages direct action, including civil disobedience, to target institutions that impede AIDS research or discriminate against HIV-infected people. Starting as a local activist group in New York's Greenwich Village, ACT-UP now has chapters in several countries around the world.

It is noteworthy that the first intergovernmental body to address the epidemic was a human rights organisation. In 1983 the Council of Europe pointed to the human rights aspects of the epidemic in a couple of remarkable resolutions.[15] The involvement of the Council of Europe at an early moment, when denial and dim recognition of the AIDS problem prevailed, may seem surprising. Human rights issues are traditionally given high priority on the organisation's agenda, but the various Council of Europe institutions have a conservative record. The council's action on a very sensitive issue can be attributed to the pre-existence of a specialised committee concerned with safe blood products and the precedent of a 1981 resolution on discrimination against homosexuals which, in turn, reflected a history of lobbying by homosexual activists.

Several international organisations, IGOs as well as NGOs, have established an elaborate set of practices and a discourse for dealing with human rights. However, the worlds of public health and human rights seldom meet. Yet human rights became a crucial element of GPA's global AIDS strategy. This reflected Jonathan Mann's growing consciousness of the human rights aspects of AIDS, developed in conversations with a handful of intellectuals. Not only did Mann accept that human rights of PWA/HIV should be respected because it was right, he also found a public health rationale for respecting them. If AIDS was a reason for discrimination, he argued, effective prevention campaigns would not reach the targets; the problem would be driven underground and allowed to fester undisturbed by public intervention.

GPA officials hosted consultations with human rights and AIDS-related NGOs in Geneva and New York in May 1988 and requested the British-based human rights NGO, Rights and Humanity, to prepare an internal briefing document on how to involve UN agencies in human rights aspects of AIDS. Attention to these aspects gradually gained momentum, as NGOs pressed for incorporation of human rights aspects of the AIDS pandemic in the annual international AIDS conferences, co-sponsored by WHO. An International Consultation on AIDS and Human Rights was convened in Geneva in July 1989 in collaboration with the UN Centre on Human Rights. Four dozen participants from a wide variety of professional fields and representing an array of international, regional and national civic-based and public organisations exchanged ideas and concerns. Although instrumental in clarifying issues, this meeting also unveiled organisational constraints. Specifically, GPA and the UN Centre on Human rights represented divergent organisational cultures and working habits. Their relations remained strained, and little result was achieved in the further development of policies at the intersection of AIDS and human rights.

AIDS *as a socioeconomic problem*

Yet another framing defines the epidemic as a socioeconomic problem. AIDS was initially perceived to be a 'disease of affluence' confined to the Western industrialised countries, but it has become ever more evident that AIDS is a 'disease of poverty'. In a global perspective, AIDS becomes a North–South problem, epitomising the gap between developed and developing countries. Foreign aid then constitutes the time-honoured response.

WHO's active involvement with AIDS coincided with the realisation that the epidemic was spreading rapidly in the Third World. Support to developing countries in providing health for all has been a mainstay of WHO's work since the late 1970s. It is therefore natural that WHO's growing involvement brought the North–South aspects of the AIDS problem into focus. By the same token, development NGOS also became potential actors.

WHO GPA assumed a coordinating role in providing AIDS-related foreign aid to the Third World. For many donor countries, channelling financial resources through WHO offered a convenient way out of a political quandary. WHO Director-General Halfdan Mahler put it succinctly during an informal meeting on AIDS in connection with the 40th World Health Assembly in May 1987: 'A number of major bilateral donors have stated clearly that their bilateral efforts to combat AIDS have been constrained by political sensitivities, and inadequate knowledge, expertise, experience, and financial and human resources . . . That is why [they] have decided to complement WHO's programme and centrally-funded activities.'[16]

One limitation in WHO's ability to fulfil its coordinating role in foreign assistance results from having governmental agencies as its national counterparts. In the Third World, health ministries are notoriously weak and inefficient. GPA therefore first turned to UNDP to improve its access in developing countries, forming the 'WHO–UNDP Alliance to Combat AIDS' in March 1988. The purpose was to take advantage of UNDP's socioeconomic expertise and presence in most Third World countries. UNDP resident representatives were authorised to coordinate all external assistance to national AIDS programmes at the country level. The idea of combining the strengths of WHO and UNDP, while sound in theory, worked less well in practice. The envisaged collaboration was encumbered by duplication and turf battles.

In short, socioeconomic framing became predominant with WHO's involvement. At the same time, the very definition of AIDS as a North–South issue contributed to a gradual erosion of WHO's role as lead agency because donor countries and development IGOS and NGOS came to question WHO's competence. In the absence of medical solutions, development had to focus on education and behaviour change. The burden of design then passes from medical to social science. WHO's traditional partners in member states and among NGOS have primarily medical expertise. Although the number of NGOS in official relations with WHO is impressive, very few deal with development and hardly any deal with health service and education in rural settings.

As this brief account shows, there exists a confounding variety of framings of, and proposed solutions to, the AIDS problem—all with their concomitant sets of interested organisational actors. In the following section, we trace the efforts by WHO GPA to forge links with NGOS from various sectors in hammering out a global AIDS policy.

Forging IGO–NGO links

After the initiation of GPA, WHO's role as lead agency in AIDS-related international cooperation was endorsed by states and by a host of intergovernmental organisations. WHO's interest in NGOs increased as the implications of its ambitious Global Strategy for Health for All by the Year 2000 took hold.[17] That strategy represented a redirection of WHO towards a broader focus on health care and its role in development; and it required a partnership among governments, WHO and NGOs. Thus, when WHO developed its responses to HIV/AIDS, it acquired the potential to become a focal point for transnational NGO activity.

From the beginning of his tenure as head of GPA, Jonathan Mann demonstrated an enthusiastic, if initially lonely, conviction that cooperation with NGOs would prove to be essential. He and newly-recruited colleagues built up contacts and insights into the NGO world, while an increasing number of NGO representatives sought information and cooperation from GPA.

By the end of 1987, GPA had recruited Robert Grose, an experienced hand with NGO relations who came from the Overseas Development Administration of the United Kingdom. Grose's task included not merely direct contact with NGOs but the creation of an organised structure for that line of contacts. By that time, it had become obvious that a few NGOs were taking an interest in and occasionally carrying out loud and dramatic demonstrations at the international AIDS conferences that GPA was co-sponsoring. Other NGOs were becoming involved in the growing number of National AIDS Programs (NAPs) that GPA promoted.

However, most GPA staff had little experience in working with NGOs outside the public health and medical sectors; no consensus existed within GPA concerning the degree of influence that NGOs should be given in GPA policy and programme discussions. One group wanted NGOs to help GPA with the execution of programmes and with information gathering. NGOs, it was argued, 'do not possess an overall appreciation of the AIDS pandemic and all its manifestations and, moreover, usually represent a specific interest group and hence possess only a specific or limited orientation toward the dilemma as a whole'.[18] Another group, including Mann and Grose, wanted to include ASOs and AIDS-related NGOs in all aspects of the policy process. They proposed and started to build 'a small informal working group composed of those persons and organizations with whom we feel comfortable, to strategize and map out a framework'.[19]

The informal GPA-centred network included individuals who were nodes in regional networks and who multiplied discussions. Among them were key Red Cross officials in Geneva, a creative and bold homosexual man responsible for the AIDS activities of the Norwegian Red Cross and a Canadian physician and human rights activist plugged into the North American ASOs.

On the whole, the picture began to emerge of a fairly small group of people in regular contact with each other.

Many ASOs pressed for official acknowledgement of their legitimacy and competence and for representation on AIDS-related bodies. In addition, they sought material support. Both as a matter of policy and of legal capacity, IGOs have been cautious in directly supporting NGOs. GPA sought an indirect route via national governments and the GPA-sponsored National AIDS Programs. In 1991 GPA officially recommended that NAPs commit at least 15% of the funds channelled through WHO to support NGO AIDS activities. In reality, however, collaboration between national programmes and NGOs remained limited, and resource flows to NGOs through the NAPs were small.[20] GPA also initiated a Partnership Program to distribute 'seed' grants directly to NGOs for specific projects. To qualify, projects had to be carried out jointly by transnational and local NGOs and required the approval of both national governments and national programmes.

An international NGO forum

Several leading AIDS activists lobbied GPA, requesting assistance in setting up an umbrella organisation to group the new ASOs and other NGOs. Ken Morrison of the Canadian AIDS Society recalls the early history:

> Early in 1988, the Canadian AIDS Society (CAS) wrote to WHO to request assistance in setting up an international forum. This was followed by more and more concrete proposals from CAS. Richard Rector, wandering American, was working hard in and out of WHO lobbying for such a forum. In Brazil, Walter Almeida, behind his computer, his telephone and fax machine, churned out proposals. The Canadian Council for International Co-operation, an umbrella organization of international development agencies, also put together a proposal for an international AIDS project.[21]

Grose and Mann encouraged these plans. Such a structure would explicitly recognise the role of NGOs, while at the same time responding to demands from within the WHO structure and elsewhere for more bureaucratic tidiness. After several informal consultations between GPA officials and a small group of NGO representatives, the first international meeting of ASOs was held in Vienna in late February 1989. Another ASO conference took place in Montreal in June the same year, just before the Fifth International AIDS Conference. Representatives of more than 100 AIDS-related NGOs participated. A task force of representatives from nine regions was established to develop the organisational structure and a programme of action for a proposed International Council of ASOs (ICASO).

Ratification was to take place at the Second International AIDS NGO Conference, set to coincide with the Sixth International AIDS Conference in San

Francisco in 1990. As a result of a widespread boycott of the San Francisco conference because of US legislation restricting entry of HIV-infected travellers, the NGO conference was moved to Paris and convened in early November 1990. Ratification of ICASO proved to be controversial, since proponents of the new umbrella organisation had failed to involve counterparts at the local and regional level.

Africans took the lead in opposing ICASO. During the first African caucus session, three-fourths of the participants argued that they had never heard of ICASO. The sole African member of the ICASO planning committee claimed she had never been asked to contribute during the drafting process. Attitudes among the participants from other regions were mixed. Many felt that the structure of ICASO was being forced on them without prior consultation. The conference ended with the ICASO ratification left in suspense. In the end, the conferees agreed that the organisational development process was to go forward but opted for a more decentralised and regionalised structure, which was confirmed in 1991.

Formal representation of NGOs became an issue in connection with the GPA Global Management Committee (GMC), the highest policy-making body of GPA. Because almost all GPA funding derives from voluntary contributions by governments, their representatives sought an appropriate supervisory device. GMC consists of representatives of all governments making unearmarked contributions to the GPA budget. Other members represent WHO regions and the six IGOs that have cooperated most intensely with GPA. NGOs were at first limited to observer status at GMC meetings but, as early as January 1988, some NGOs requested representation in GMC. GMC anticipated success in the plans to create an umbrella organisation, and accepted one NGO representative as a full member. With the controversial nature of ICASO, it has become difficult to represent the varied perspectives and interests of NGOs, and the presence of a full NGO member has been postponed while a growing number of NGOs participate as observers.

Informal networking

Annual international AIDS conferences have been forums for informal networking. The earliest NGO meetings, as we have seen, were held in conjunction with these larger conferences. Since then, they have provided ample opportunities for contact among various NGOs and the establishment of *ad hoc* coalitions and networks.

For several years, non-medical issues played a subordinate role in official conference programmes. The 1992 conference in Amsterdam, by contrast, reflected a commitment by the organisers to bring social issues into a new balance with biomedical science and public health. The planners also made a special effort to involve People with AIDS and local organisations from the Third World. The conference programme reflected an integrated approach, and NGOs played an unprecedented role in the planning as well as the proceedings. A series of workshops were specifically aimed at empowering small organisations to grow and connect to other similar organisations. Skills such as producing newsletters, communicating with authorities and organising workshops were taught; and HIV-net, a computerised bulletin board connecting several organisations, was set up. Subsequent conferences have not matched the precedent set by Amsterdam concerning NGO involvement.

The Amsterdam conference included the prominent presence of a new organisation, Global AIDS Policy Coalition (GAPC), which was started by Mann from his new post at Harvard University, where he went after leaving WHO. It has assembled outstanding researchers, policy analysts, practitioners and community workers from around the world. A special area of interest is the nexus of AIDS, health and human rights issues. From his Harvard position and as head of GAPC, Mann has been able to stay at the forefront of the global policy process, despite his abrupt exit from WHO after a dispute with the director-general.

NGOS *and* AIDS-*related foreign assistance*

One particular area where NGOs have played an operational role, alone, or in collaboration with IGOs, is AIDS-related foreign assistance. From the outset, most multilateral aid was channelled through GPA. From 1987 to 1990, donors increased their funding annually, so that GPA's financial resources increased from $29.8 million in 1987 to $79.3 million in 1990.[22]

NGOs had a comparative advantage in the multilateral aid effort. Efficient AIDS programmes demanded sustained community commitment. In order to play a role in such programmes, GPA needed to establish credibility and trust among organisations with documented results in health service delivery and sex education. Without such contacts, little rationalisation could exist for using GPA for channelling resources from major donors. Naturally, GPA staff were aware of how donors like the US Agency for International Development (US AID) and the Swedish International Development Agency (SIDA) were enthusiastic about NGOs in general.

In November 1989 the bilateral donors and UN agencies represented on the GPA Global Management Committee decided to commission an external review of GPA. Although it conformed to WHO's usual practice, there were other signs of dissatisfaction with the way GPA performed its coordinating role. By 1990 there was a shift towards bilateral funding. Moreover, in 1991 for the first time contributions to GPA declined at the same time as total contributions (bilateral and multilateral) for AIDS prevention and care in the Third World decreased.[23]

The review criticised the deficient coordination among UN agencies, citing 'duplication of effort and territorial rivalries'.[24] In addition, the review pointed to problems in GPA's relations with NGOs. While praising the farsightedness of recognising the importance of NGOs in early policy documents, the review also stated that 'a number of NGOs felt that GPA was attempting to mediate and control their initiatives'.[25] Problems of NGO coordination were noted at the national level as well:

> During visits to countries, the ERC [External Review Committee] noted that NGOs (where they exist) receive few funds through NAPs [National AIDS Programs], and that collaboration appears to be a low priority. Donors have attempted to channel funds directly to NGOs through their own institutional mechanisms. In addition, some have begun to explore new ways of channeling technical and financial assistance to NGOs: needs are being assessed and a range of possible measures will be explored.[26]

The review recommended that a new structure for coordination be formed at the global level, and called for stronger interagency coordination at country level, with special emphasis on NGO participation.[27] Succeeding designs for new coordination bodies were drafted by various *ad hoc* committees, only to be rejected. At the GMC meeting in November 1992, an informal working group managed to produce a proposal that was adopted unanimously. The proposal called for a GMC Task Force consisting of three representatives each from recipient governments, donor governments, the UN family and NGOs.

The task force idea originated from Nils-Arne Kastberg, a member of the Swedish mission in Geneva who had not previously dealt with cooperation on AIDS. Primarily a development expert, he had prior experience in UN coordination issues, had participated in the Nordic UN Project to reevaluate development efforts, and had taken an active part in the reorganisation of UN disaster relief. Kastberg was appointed chairperson of the task force and came to play a prominent role in informal interagency consultations that eventually resulted in a joint and co-sponsored UN programme on HIV/AIDS, endorsed by ECOSOC in July 1994.

While this new programme primarily concerns coordination within the UN family, it envisages NGO participation in a programme coordinating board and in the secretariat. Whereas the original plan for a joint and co-sponsored program called for collaboration with 'nongovernmental organizations, community-based organizations and groups of people living with HIV and AIDS',[28] this to date has received scant attention in the interagency bargaining process. Confronted with a *fait accompli*, NGOs have generally been wary of the new coordination scheme.

In sum, AIDS has raised several questions concerning IGO–NGO relations but provided few answers. For all the efforts at collaboration, a persistent element of mutual mistrust can be discerned. NGOs have feared that GPA wants control rather than coordination, and have balked at a too close identification with IGOs. At the same time, GPA has had to struggle with the confounding variety of NGOs, not all of which are seen as responsible partners. NGOs and GPA have remained 'reluctant partners'.[29]

Lessons and conclusions

Several lessons of broader applicability can be derived from the experience of IGO–NGO links in this specialised yet diffuse and elusive issue. In keeping with our interorganisational approach, we shall concentrate on five inter-related aspects: the problems of NGO representation and representativeness; the advantages and disadvantages of formal versus informal coordination; the costs of network building; the varying degrees of organisation among interested actors; and the kind of expertise needed in network building.

Representation

Problems of representation are inescapable facts of international coordination. IGOs face perennial discussions of representation. The dividing line typically separates the principle of one state, one vote and representation qualified by some special attribute of the state considered essential for the implementation of the organisation's task. In the case of the task force, for instance, donor countries agreed that their three members would represent the countries of the European Community (now Union); the countries of Scandinavia and the European Free Trade Association (EFTA); and North America, Japan and Australia. This division was obviously based on con-tributions to AIDS-related assistance.

NGO representation presents special difficulties. According to the GMC decision, the selection of three NGO representatives for the task force was to be made by 'appropriate NGO coordinating bodies'.[30] In the absence of an official, commonly accepted NGO forum, this deliberately vague formulation left open the selection procedure. The actual choice of the Amsterdam-based AIDS Coordination Group, the Senegal-based ENDA-Tiers Monde and the Global Network of People Living with HIV/AIDS was made through an informal consultation process involving established NGO networks. As network theory would predict, these selections depended on trusted persons rather than organisations as such. From the Amsterdam group, Maria de Bruyn had a central role in European development-orientated networks. From ENDA-Tiers Monde, El Hadj As Sy was the pivotal person linking African ASOs, although his organisation, founded in 1972 with support from the UN Environment Program (UNEP), had little claim to be a key actor in the AIDS field.

It is still unclear how a few organisations might represent the hetero-geneous NGO community—in the task force or in any other contemplated coordination body. Whereas the task force symbolises official recognition of

NGO access to decision-making and coordination, difficult questions concerning constituency and representation remain.[31] Representation problems, in short, arise in any formalisation of IGO–NGO links, and informal solutions are as valid as more formalistic procedures to elect participants.

Formal versus informal coordination

The case of AIDS illustrates the common tendency to search for formal mechanisms whenever a need for international coordination is perceived. Yet there are indications that informal network-like arrangements have certain advantages when it comes to complex coordination tasks. For example, Ernst Haas recommends that international organisations 'resist an overt reordering and centralization of authority', 'minimize hierarchies and regulations' and 'minimize the importance of the boundary between the organization and its environment'.[32] Proceeding from a study of the coordination of regional transport in the San Francisco Bay area, Donald Chisholm arrives at similar conclusions: 'While I do not quarrel with the contention that interdependence requires coordination, I strongly dispute the reflexive assumption that coordination is inexorably tied to centralized arrangements such as comprehensive plans and consolidated agencies'.[33]

Formalisation raises a host of problems, one of which is representation, as discussed above. Formal coordination structures inevitably limit the number of organisations represented, whereas informal coordination among many independent, partly overlapping organisations provides more points of access to the decision-making process.[34] Another problem is that formalisation normally introduces an element of hierarchy. And even hints of centralisation tend to invite controversy. To wit, everyone wants coordination but no one wants to be coordinated.

In the case of AIDS, the designation of WHO as the lead agency injected elements of hierarchy and centralisation from the outset. The degree of conflict and the variety of agencies concerned with AIDS were probably underestimated, but they became obvious in the process. The joint and cosponsored UN programme differs in that it aims to create a new structure between rather than above existing agencies. Explicitly seeking to avoid verticalisation, the UN programme promotes a multisectoral approach. Furthermore, one of the lessons learned from developing a joint and co-sponsored UN programme pertained to the participating organisations' need to preserve their identities, which are often endangered by hierarchical coordination designs.

Informal coordination structures also tend to be more flexible and adaptable than formal ones. Roles and definitions of tasks are determined not by a single authority but by the participating agencies themselves. Roles can be continuously redefined and specific tasks renegotiated. Moreover, information tends to flow more freely through informal structures than through formal channels, which are often ineffective when information is sensitive or politically charged. In effect, the informal yet crucial role played by the *ad hoc* task force, with representatives of IGOs and NGOs as well as donor governments, is an example of the advantages of informal coordination. The task force served as a clearinghouse for exchange of information and views among key actors in the institutional bargaining process. It would hardly have been able to transmit information to and from constituencies and forward comments and views to the involved agencies so freely had it been part of a formal, hierarchical coordination structure.

In international cooperation generally, and concerning AIDS in particular, the lack of trust among governments and between IGOs and NGOs is an irritant. One important advantage of informal over formal organisation is that it provides an opportunity for mutual mistrust gradually to be broken down and replaced by confidence.

Of course, informal organisation should not be idealised. There are disadvantages associated with informal channels based on personal relationships. They are extremely vulnerable to high rates of turnover among personnel, especially when they result in departures from the interorganisational system instead of movements within the system.[35] This is especially relevant in connection with AIDS, where high staff turnover and burnout occur at the managerial level of national AIDS programmes, and where people with HIV/AIDS—who are more susceptible than others to exhaustion, sickness and death—are often key links in national and international networks.[36] Thus, informal organisation is not a substitute for, but rather an important complement to, formal organisation.

Costs of network building

There is a variety of costs associated with network building. First, transaction costs, to borrow a term from economists, can be formidable for small and especially for poor NGOs. Face-to-face contacts constitute the foundation of transnational networks, which usually require generous travel funds. In the field of AIDS, this represents a significant obstacle to universal representation at international gatherings, since the participation of Third World NGO representatives has overwhelmingly depended on funding from industrialised countries. Financial dependencies stay in the way of closer IGO–NGO links in other issue areas as well.

In addition to these tangible costs, there are other, less material but equally significant ones. For many NGOs, opposing and criticising government policies have been traditional. To collaborate with governments and IGO in networks and to formulate and implement joint programmes may imply a profound change in identity with concomitant costs: 'Their *autonomy* is challenged: by engaging in coordinated programmes, NGOs surrender a certain degree of autonomy over their own actions and the external factors that might affect them. Finally, their *cohesion* is weakened, as new tensions emerge within the NGO.'[37]

It is obvious that anticipation of these kinds of costs contributed to the reluctance among NGOs for full-fledged cooperation with WHO's AIDS strategy.

Finally, individual leadership—a crucial ingredient in effective transnational networks—entails notable costs. The example of Jonathan Mann is illustrative. During his years as director of GPA, Mann provided vital leadership. He was an active network builder; his background in public health made him well equipped to integrate medical professionals and other AIDS activists; he made important contributions to the formulation of the goals of global AIDS cooperation; and in his travels around the world, he was in constant interaction with the work. In the process, he apparently failed in the internal functions pertaining to his constituent organisation, WHO; in 1990 he was replaced by a long-standing WHO official. As this and other examples indicate, successful leadership in a transnational network may endanger the leader's position within his or her home organisation, whether governmental, intergovernmental or nongovernmental. Leadership implies a readiness to depart from narrow organisational roles and to base initiatives on a conception of collective goals, however controversial.

Degree of organisation

One factor working against the creation of a tightly knit AIDS network is the varying degree of organisation among relevant actors. Among affected groups, homosexual men are incomparably the best organised. In several Western countries, they constitute influential pressure groups; they have been able to mobilise and articulate political demands; and they have developed well-functioning international networks. As the AIDS epidemic developed across the globe, it became apparent that this was not a disease restricted to the gay community. In fact, three-quarters of all adults with HIV in the world today have been infected through heterosexual transmission. Yet homosexual men remain key actors in transnational networks. Other affected groups—such as prostitutes, intravenous drug users, haemophiliacs, women or children—have few or no organisations to look after their interests; they thus play a peripheral role in transnational cooperation.

There are great geographical variations as well. The degree of organisation in the Third World and Eastern Europe is low compared with North America and Western Europe. The networking that goes on tends to link English-speaking representatives of industrialised countries. Even when it comes to addressing AIDS problems in the Third World, some of the most influential organisations are based in the industrialised world, such as the UK NGO AIDS Consortium for the Third World in London and the National Council for International Health in Washington. Lack of funding is a major obstacle to better organisation in the Third World. In Eastern Europe, in addition, there is a lack of experience of working in grassroots organisations and a heritage of distrust. After several decades of compulsory membership in voluntary organisations, volunteerism has a negative connotation.

Expertise

The popular notion that epistemic communities—knowledge-based networks of experts—play a key role in international policy coordination finds little support in our study of AIDS. Close informal relationships among individuals representing organisations appeared at crucial junctures in every instance of cooperation we found. However, they did not usually fit neatly with the notion of epistemic communities. Rather, the networks were looser in both intention and composition.

Our study suggests that international cooperation in a specialised issue area requires not only know-how but also 'know-who'. Expert knowledge of an issue such as AIDS needs to be combined with knowledge of the relevant organisational and individual actors who might contribute to a solution to the problem: who are they? Under what restraints do they work? How can they be accessed? This is precisely the kind of knowledge that is necessary for successfully building networks.

Among AIDS activists there has often been insufficient understanding of the workings and vagaries of international organisations, especially of the UN system. Conversely, the most successful network builders have developed expertise about organisational actors. It is also noteworthy that a person with absolutely no AIDS expertise but with solid knowledge of the UN system and other actors on the North–South arena assumed a central position in recent efforts at coordinating assistance to the Third World.

In sum, an interorganisational perspective on IGO–NGO links in the global response to AIDS reveals possibilities as well as limitations. NGOs are necessary partners, since they represent the victims of the epidemic, can span the local and global levels, and are better equipped than government authorities to deal with the sensitive, private issues involved in AIDS prevention. NGO representatives also have assumed central positions in informal transnational networks. Yet mutual mistrust, turf battles and the tendency to search for formal coordination mechanisms have stood in the way of closer links and greater efficiency in combating AIDS.

Notes

1 Jonathan Mann, Daniel J M Tarantola & Thomas W Netter, *AIDS in the World: A Global Report*, Cambridge, MA: Harvard University Press, 1992, p 3.
2 Jonathan Mann as quoted in Panos Institute, *AIDS in the Third World*, London: Panos Institute, 1988, p 94.
3 The text of the document can be found, eg in WHO/GPA, *Global Programme on AIDS: Progress Report Number 4*, WHO/GPA/GEN/88.3, Geneva, October 1988, pp 87–88.

4 Leon Gordenker, Roger A Coate, Christer Jönsson & Peter Söderholm, *International Cooperation in Response to AIDS*, London: Pinter Publishers, 1995.

5 Such issues have been variously labelled 'global indivisibilities', 'interdependence issues', or 'international physical externalities'. See respectively, James A Caporaso, 'International Relations theory and multilateralism: the search for foundations', *International Organization*, 46, 1992, p 599. James N Rosenau, *Turbulence in World Politics*, London: Harvester Wheatsheaf, 1990, p 106; Mark W Zacher, 'The decaying pillars of the Westphalian temple: implications for international order and governance', in James N. Rosenau & Ernst-Otto Czempiel (eds), *Governance without Government: Order and Change in World Politics*, Cambridge: Cambridge University Press, 1992, pp 76–80.

6 WHO/GPA, *Special Programme on AIDS: Progress Report Number 1*, WHO/SPA/GEN/87.2, Geneva, April 1987, p 5.

7 Jonathan Mann, 'Pandemic disease, NGOs and the future of public health', address to the Second International Conference of AIDS-related NGOs, Paris, 3 November 1990.

8 Interview with Jonathan Mann, 'SIDA: Une révolution dans la santé', *L'Autre Journal*, 5, October 1990, pp 89–101.

9 Daniel Kahneman & Amos Tversky, 'The psychology of preferences', *Scientific American*, 246, 1982, pp 160–173.

10 George Lakoff, *Women, Fire, and Dangerous Things: What Categories Reveal about the Mind*, Chicago, IL: University of Chicago Press, 1987.

11 Robert W Cox, 'Problems of global management', in Toby T Gati (ed), *The US, the UN, and the Management of Global Change*, New York: New York University Press, 1983, p 64.

12 Ken Plummer, 'Organizing AIDS', in Peter Aggleton & Hilary Homans (eds), *Social Aspects of AIDS*, London, The Falmer Press, 1988, p 23.

13 Panos Institute, *AIDS and the Third World*, p 69.

14 Plummer, 'Organizing AIDS', p 28.

15 Council of Europe, *R(83)8 and Resolution 812:1983*, Strasbourg, 1983.

16 Halfdan Mahler quoted in WHO, *Report of the External Review of the World Health Organization Global Programme on AIDS*, GPA/GMC(8)/92.4, Geneva, 1992, p 4.

17 The strategy was set out in World Health Assembly resolution WHA 34.36, 1981. See also Leon Gordenker, 'The World Health Organization: sectoral leader or occasional benefactor?', in Roger A Coate (ed), *US Policy and the Future of the United Nations*, New York: The Twentieth Century Fund Press, 1994, pp 171–172.

18 WHO/GPA, Memorandum from Terry Mooney to Jonathan Mann, 7 March 1988.

19 Ibid.

20 WHO, *External Review*, p 19.

21 *Opportunities for Solidarity*, final report of the Montreal Meeting of NGOs involved in community AIDS service, Montreal 2–4 June 1989, p 6.

22 WHO, *1991 Progress Report: Global Program on AIDS*, Geneva: WHO, 1992, Annex 8.

23 Mann *et al, AIDS in the World*, pp 511–12, 519.

24 WHO, *External Review*, p 39.

25 Ibid, p 35.

26 Ibid.

27 Ibid, pp 42–43, 47.

28 WHO, *Executive Board document*, EB93/INF.DOC/5, Geneva, 1993, p 2.

29 Compare John Farrington & Anthony Bebbington, *Reluctant Partners: Non-Governmental Organizations, the State and Sustainable Agricultural Development*, London: Routledge, 1993, p 26.

30 WHO/GPA, *Extraordinary Meeting of the Management Committee 23–25 November 1992: Conclusions and Recommendations*, GPA/GMC(E)92.7, Geneva, 1992, Annex 2.
31 The reference to 'nongovernmental organizations, community-based organizations and groups of people living with HIV and AIDS' in the *Study of a joint and cosponsored United Nations programme on HIV/AIDS*, WHO, EB93/INF.DOC./5, represents one attempt to distinguish different groups or constituencies.
32 Ernst B Haas, *When Knowledge is Power: Three Models of Change in International Organizations*, Berkeley, CA: University of California Press, 1990, pp 201, 206, 207.
33 Donald Chisholm, *Coordination Without Hierarchy: Informal Structures in Multiorganizational Systems*, Berkeley, CA: University of California Press, 1989, p 13.
34 Ibid, pp 173–182.
35 Ibid, pp 29, 142.
36 Mann *et al.*, *AIDS in the World*, pp 301–305.
37 Farrington & Bebbington, *Reluctant Partners*, p 49.

90

HEALTH PROGRAMS IN FAITH-BASED ORGANIZATIONS

Are they effective?

Mark J. DeHaven, Irby B. Hunter, Laura Wilder,
James W. Walton and Jarett Berry

Source: *American Journal of Public Health*, 94:6 (2004), 1030–6.

Objectives. We examined the published literature on health programs in faith-based organizations to determine the effectiveness of these programs.

Methods. We conducted a systematic literature review of articles describing faith-based health activities. Articles (n=386) were screened for eligibility (n=105), whether a faith-based health program was described (n=53), and whether program effects were reported (28).

Results. Most programs focused on primary prevention (50.9%), general health maintenance (25.5%), cardiovascular health (20.7%), or cancer (18.9%). Significant effects reported included reductions in cholesterol and blood pressure levels, weight, and disease symptoms and increases in the use of mammography and breast self-examination.

Conclusions. Faith-based programs can improve health outcomes. Means are needed for increasing the frequency with which such programs are evaluated and the results of these evaluations are disseminated. (*Am J Public Health.* 2004;94:1030–1036)

There is a sizable multidisciplinary literature describing the health-related activities of religious or faith-based organizations (FBOs). Studies have described the features of successful health promotion programs and partnerships in churches[1,2] and the importance of the church as an ally in efforts to provide preventive health and social services to at-risk populations.[3] In addition, the interconnections between public health, health education, and FBOs have been examined,[4] and the possible contributions of FBOs to improved community health outcomes have been described.[5]

A development related to health programs offered by FBOs is the need for improving access to care for the 43 million nonelderly uninsured adults residing in the United States. It has been shown that uninsured individuals are more likely than those with insurance coverage to avoid seeking needed care, to have been hospitalized for a preventable condition, and to have been diagnosed with advanced-stage cancer.[6] Proposals for expanding health insurance coverage focus on increasing the role of government[7] and generally ignore the role played by nonfunded health care providers in providing access to care. Especially important for public health practitioners is whether faith-based health programs can, for example, provide predictable and measurable health benefits in the communities they serve.[8]

FBOs have a long history of independently and collaboratively[9] hosting health promotion programs in areas such as health education,[1,10] screening for and management of high blood pressure[11] and diabetes,[12] weight loss[13] and smoking cessation,[14] cancer prevention and awareness,[15–17] geriatric care,[18] nutritional guidance,[19] and mental health care.[20] However, little is known about the effectiveness of these programs. Nonfunded health programs are not part of an organized system of care and are sometimes considered "non-systems of care."[21] However, if such programs provide consistent access to specific types of care for specific individuals, they may actually be delivering predictable—but unmeasured—community health benefits.

A study was undertaken to review the health programs in FBOs and to examine their effectiveness. The Working Group on Human Needs and Faith-Based and Community Initiatives notes that the current vocabulary surrounding discussions of "faith-based" organizations tends to "confuse and divide."[22] The term FBO evokes images ranging from store-front churches, to the YMCA, to the local chapter of Habitat for Humanity. In the present article, the term FBO is used as a catch-all category referring to health programs designed, conducted, or supported by groups affiliated with or based in a nonsecular setting.

The National Congregations Study revealed that about 57% of US congregations participate in various social service delivery programs, including food and clothing, housing and homelessness, domestic violence, substance abuse, employment, and health programs.[23] In the present study, we examined the health activities of FBOs only or those activities specifically related to health promotion/disease prevention. Also, we examined the published literature on FBO health programs in an attempt to ascertain the effectiveness of these programs. Successful programs are likely to be overrepresented in such a review, which is consistent with our study intent: we were not concerned with presenting an exhaustive review of social service activities in FBOs;

rather, we intended this study as a first step in determining the possible contribution of health programs to maintaining or improving the health of individuals in the communities they serve.

Methods

Literature review and search strategies

We conducted a systematic qualitative review of health-related databases for the years 1990 through 2000.[24] This 10-year period was selected by consensus among the authors on the belief that a "faith and health movement"[25] occurred in the 1990s. Another reason we selected this period is that faith–health collaborations represent a rapidly developing phenomenon, and the results of a preliminary search indicated the existence of a large body of literature available during the period. The purpose of the review was to identify all published English-language research articles reporting the health activities of FBOs. Our search strategies were guided by a preliminary review of the literature, and the searches were conducted by one of the authors, who is a professional research librarian (L. W.).

We chose MEDLINE as our major database and, because there were no existing medical subject headings specific enough for our topic, we devised a comprehensive search strategy. Our strategy involved the use of a set of indexing terms related to health service delivery, such as health promotion, health education, counseling, and screening. These terms were combined with a second set of text words (e.g., parish, congregation, faith based, community church) describing where the health services might be delivered.

We performed supplemental searches of the HealthSTAR, CINAHL, and PsycINFO databases. In the case of HealthSTAR, we created and combined 3 groups of terms: health service terms, religion terms and phrases, and diagnosis and therapy terms. The CINAHL search consisted of identifying articles including one of 3 phrases—faith based, church based, or parish based—or either parish nursing or congregational nursing. We used 2 alternative strategies in the search of the PsycINFO database. The first focused on the phrases faith based and church based, since the phrase parish based was not useful in this database; the second focused on a group of religion terms and a separate group of community mental health service terms.

All articles (n = 386) meeting the search criteria were reviewed by 1 of the investigators (M.J.D.) for possible inclusion in the present study. Titles and abstracts were examined for consistency with our objective of identifying health programs involving FBOs. In cases in which abstracts were not available, determinations were made on the basis of title alone. If the title did not provide a clear indication of the article's content, the article was obtained before a determination was made regarding inclusion or exclusion. After evaluation of the search results, 106 articles[1–4,9–20,26–115] were identified for formal review.

The formal review consisted of reading an article to ensure that it addressed a specific, identifiable health program that could be linked to a specific health benefit. The following types of articles were excluded: articles discussing the existence of a program without describing its features, articles discussing a "healing ministry" without describing a specific program, and review articles describing a collection of programs without providing details about individual programs. In addition, articles were excluded when the church building was being used for a multisite program developed as part of a broader public health strategy (however, articles were included if the church or congregation was an active member of a communitywide health coalition). Once these articles were excluded, 53 articles remained.

Data gathering

Information was recorded about program features and outcomes, including location (city and state), scope (congregation, community, city, or region), number of congregations involved, target population (age and ethnicity), target conditions, and program objective (primary, secondary, or tertiary prevention). Objectives were coded as primary when the program was designed to increase awareness of disease, secondary when the goal was risk reduction, and tertiary if treatment was involved. When more than 1 type of prevention activity was involved, the objective of the majority of program activities was recorded. When a program qualified for more than 1 program scope area, the code for the largest geographic scope was entered.

Programs were categorized according to FBO level of involvement, whether program outcomes were measured, and number of participants. Almost all programs evaluated were based in a church or congregation, as opposed to an interfaith service organization, temple, or mosque, consistent with the finding of Chaves et al.[116] that only about 3.5% of all social services are delivered in non-Christian settings. Determining level of church involvement was essential since most analysts agree that collaboration is necessary for the success of faith-based health and community programs.[30,51,52,73] Church involvement was coded as "faith placed" if health professionals used the church to test an intervention and "faith based" if the program was part of the church's health ministry. Programs were coded as "collaborative" if they combined faith-placed and faith-based features.

In instances in which no clinical outcomes were reported, we used process measures. When only number of client contacts was reported, we did not include this information in our measurements because it was not related to possible health benefits. Finally, we recorded total number of participants, including experimental controls and, in the case of multiple-year programs, individuals participating in all years of the program. When program outcomes were reported, articles were evaluated by 2 investigators, and disputes over coding content were resolved through discussion.

In the following, we report descriptive statistics, including percentages and measures of central tendency and dispersion. We conducted all analyses using SPSS version 10.0. We used χ^2 tests of independence in examining relationships between categorical variables.

Results

Health programs were conducted in 30 distinct geographic locations, either counties or cities. Although most locations hosted 1 program, 5 cities accounted for approximately one third of the total number of programs: Chicago (n=6; 11.3%), Baltimore (n=4; 7.5%), Los Angeles (n=4; 7.5%), Cleveland (n=2; 3.8%), and Oakland (n=2; 3.8%). Programs were located in 23 different states, but almost half (n=26) were located in 5 states: California (n=8; 15.1%), Illinois (n=6; 11.3%), Maryland (n=5; 9.4%), Ohio (n=4; 7.5%), and Florida (n=3; 5.7%).

The majority of programs were directed at congregation members (60.4%) or the surrounding community (24.5%) (Table 1). Although more than 40% of the programs involved a single congregation, the median number of participating congregations was 3 (range=1–95), and the number of program participants ranged from 7 to 2519 (median=238). Most programs focused on primary prevention (50.9%), usually patient education, in the area of general health maintenance (24.5%), cardiovascular health (20.7%), or cancer (18.9%). Approximately one third of the programs did not target a specific population (32.1%); however, when a population was targeted, it tended to be African American (41.5%) and adult (43.4%). The over-whelming majority of programs did not involve a specific target in terms of gender (75.5%).

Faith-based programs developed as part of a congregation's health ministry accounted for the smallest percentage of programs (24.5%), while faith-placed programs, usually developed by health professionals outside of a congregation, accounted for the largest percentage (43.4%). Although more than one half of the programs (52.8%) reported outcome measurements, such reports were significantly related ($P \le .012$) to type of church involvement (Table 2). Faith-placed programs were significantly more likely to report outcome data (75%) than either faith-based (30.8%) or collaborative (37.5%) programs.

The characteristics and types of outcomes reported by programs with different levels of church involvement (n=28) are reported in Table 3. The "results" column indicates whether a study reported a process evaluation (n=8) or the effects of a program intervention (n=20). Among the 18 faith-placed programs reporting outcomes, only 11 (61%) reported the effects of a program intervention. Effects were measured via self-generated[33] or self-report[18,39,43,53,97,106] instruments or via biological measures.[12,13,84,112]

The areas addressed by the programs included heart disease (36.4%), weight/nutrition (18.2%), breast cancer (18.2%), prostate cancer (18.2%), and smoking cessation (9.0%). The programs focusing on these areas achieved

Table 1 Program features (n = 53).

Feature	Sample, No. (%)
Program scope	
Congregation	32 (60.4)
Community	13 (24.5)
Region	5 (9.4)
City	2 (3.8)
Not reported	1 (1.9)
Objective	
Primary prevention	27 (50.9)
Secondary prevention	13 (24.5)
Tertiary prevention	7 (13.2)
Other	5 (9.4)
Target population	
African American	22 (41.5)
Not specified	17 (32.5)
Low income	7 (13.2)
Hispanic	4 (7.5)
White	2 (3.8)
Other	1 (1.9)
Target conditions	
General health maintenance	13 (24.5)
Cardiovascular health	11 (20.7)
Cancers	10 (18.9)
Mental health	6 (11.3)
Other/not specified	6 (11.3)
Nutrition/weight control	4 (7.5)
Smoking	3 (5.7)
Faith involvement	
Faith placed	23 (43.4)
Faith based	13 (24.5)
Collaborative	16 (30.2)
Not specified	1 (1.9)
Outcomes measured	
Yes	28 (52.8)
No	25 (47.2)
Target age group	
Adult	23 (43.4)
Elderly	6 (11.3)
Not specified	24 (45.3)
Target gender	
Not specified	40 (75.5)
Female	10 (18.9)
Male	3 (5.7)
No. of participants	
7–46	9 (17.0)
55–187	9 (17.0)
238–668	9 (17.0)
743–2219	9 (17.0)
Not specified	17 (32.0)
Total	53 (100.0)

Table 2 Numbers of programs, by program type and published measurement of effects.

Program Type	Outcomes Not Reported, No. (%)	Outcomes Reported, No. (%)	Total, No. (%)
Faith placed	6 (25.0)	18 (75.0)	24 (100)
Faith based	9 (69.2)	4 (30.8)	13 (100)
Collaborative	10 (62.5)	6 (37.5)	16 (100)
Total	25 (47.5)	28 (52.8)	53 (100)

Note: Outcome differences are significant at the $P = .012$ level of significance.

statistically significant effects in terms of, respectively, reducing cholesterol and blood pressure levels, increasing fruit/vegetable consumption and reducing weight, increasing use of mammography and breast self-examination, increasing knowledge about prostate cancer, and increasing readiness to change regarding smoking cessation. The number of participants in these programs ranged from 30 to 2519 (median=133), and almost all of the programs (91%) were targeted at African Americans.

All 4 of the faith-based programs included in the sample reported intervention effects, and these programs addressed heart disease (25%), mental illness (50%), and asthma (25%). In both of the studies demonstrating significant effects, validated instruments showed decreased mental illness symptoms.[104,105] The number of participants was small, ranging from 7 to 46 (median=24).

Of the 6 collaborative programs, 5 (83.4%) reported program intervention effects on general health (40%), weight/nutrition (40%), and smoking cessation (20%). Outcomes were evaluated via self-report and biological measures,[18] validated instruments,[19] and biological measures.[13] Significant effects included improvements in overall health status, increases in fruit/vegetable consumption, and decreases in weight and blood pressure. These programs ranged in size from 30 to 966 participants (median=133), and the programs were almost exclusively (80%) directed toward African Americans.

Discussion

In this study, we reviewed FBO health programs and assessed their effectiveness. Our objective was to take a first step toward determining whether these types of programs can provide a measurable form of community-based care. The first conclusion offered by our review is that relatively little information exists on which to base assessments of the effectiveness of such programs. Although our literature search identified a substantial number of articles (n=386) possibly related to our study objective, fewer than 1 in 3 (n=106; 27.5%) were eligible for the review, and even fewer (n=53; 13.7%) actually discussed a specific program. Finally, only a small number of articles presented

Table 3 Program features and outcomes of programs at different levels of church involvement.

Study	No. Subjects	Program Scope	No. Churches	Ethnicity	Study Focus	Method	Result	Statistical Significance of Results
				Faith placed				
Wiist and Flack (1990)[112]	348	Congregation	1	African American	Heart (cholesterol)	Intervention	Decreased cholesterol	Significant
Holschneider et al. (1999)[64]	98	Congregation	1	Hispanic	Breast cancer	Screening	Process evaluation only	No statistics[a]
Fox et al. (1998)[58]	82	Community	1	Hispanic	Breast cancer	Screening	Process evaluation only	No statistics[a]
Duan et al. (2000)[16]	813	Congregation	30	Not specified	Breast cancer	Intervention	Increased/ maintained screening level	Significant
Flack and Wiist (1991)[56]	661	Congregation	6	African American	Heart (cholesterol)	Screening	Process evaluation only	No statistics[a]
Smith et al. (1997)[11]	97	Congregation	17	African American	Heart (blood pressure)	Intervention	Decreased blood pressure	Significant
Campbell et al. (1999)[39]	2519	Region	50	African American	Nutrition	Intervention	Increased fruit/ vegetable consumption	Significant
Voorhees et al. (1996)[106]	292	Community	21	African American	Smoking	Intervention	Increased readiness to change	Significant
Smith (1992)[97]	32	Congregation	3	African American	Heart	Intervention	Increased knowledge about hypertension	Significant
Wilson (2000)[10]	129	Congregation	3	Not specified	Heart	Screening	Process evaluation only	No statistics[a]

Study	N	Setting	No.	Population	Topic	Type	Outcome	Significance
Erwin et al. (1999)[53]	433	Community	11	African American	Breast cancer	Intervention	Increased breast self-examination	Significant
Collins (1997)[43]	30	Congregation	1	African American	Prostate cancer	Intervention	Increased knowledge	No statistics[a]
Huggins (1998)[65]	1200	Community	3	Hispanic	General health	Screening	Process evaluation only	No statistics[a]
Boehm et al. (1995)[33]	123	Congregation	.	African American	Prostate cancer	Intervention	Increased knowledge	Significant
Weinrich et al. (1998)[108]	743	Region	59	African American	Prostate cancer	Screening	Process evaluation only	No statistics[a]
Oexmann et al. (2000)[84]	133	Congregation	8	African American	Heart	Intervention	Decreased weight and blood pressure	Significant
McNabb et al. (1997)[12]	39	Congregation	3	African American	Weight	Intervention	Decreased weight and changed eating habits	Significant
Davis et al. (1994)[17]	1012	Congregation	24	Underserved (low income)	Cervical Cancer	Screening	Process evaluation only	No statistics[a]
Faith based								
Ruesch & Gilmore (1999)[93]	7	Congregation	1	White	Heart	Intervention	Increased knowledge of heart disease	No statistics
Toh & Tan (1997)[104]	46	Congregation	1	White	Mental illness	Intervention	Decreased symptoms and complaints	Significant

Table 3 (cont'd)

Study	No. Subjects	Program Scope	No. Churches	Ethnicity	Study Focus	Method	Result	Statistical Significance of Results
Toh et al. (1994)[105]	18	Congregation	1	Not specified	Mental illness	Intervention	Decreased symptoms and percentage complaints	Significant
Roque et al. (1999)[92]	30	Community	1	Underserved (low income)	Asthma	Intervention	Decreased hospital and emergency department visits	No statistics[a]
Collaborative								
Schorling et al. (1997)[14]	453	Region	14	African American	Smoking	Intervention	Found no change in quit rates	Nonsignificant
Turner et al. (1995)[15]	2212	Region	.	African American	Heart	Health promotion	Process evaluation only	...
Cowart et al. (1995)[18]	238	Congregation	4	African American	General health	Intervention	Increased overall health	Significant
Barnhart et al. (1998)[19]	30	Congregation	1	African American	Nutrition	Intervention	Increased fruit/ vegetable consumption	Significant
Kumanyika & Charleston (1992)[13]	187	Congregation	22	African American	Weight	Intervention	Decreased weight and blood pressure	Significant
Rydholm (1997)[94]	966	Congregation	20	Not specified	General health	Intervention	Cost savings/ costs averted	No statistics[a]

[a]Statistical analysis not reported or incomplete.

outcome measures (n=28; 7.25%) or outcome measures associated with a particular program intervention (n=20; 5.4%).

The data presented here nonetheless demonstrate that faith-based health programs can produce positive effects; for example, they can significantly increase knowledge of disease, improve screening behavior and readiness to change, and reduce the risk associated with disease and disease symptoms. According to the Bureau of Primary Health Care Faith Partnership Initiative, which seeks to facilitate partnerships between FBOs and health providers, there are 43 million uninsured citizens in the United States, it is not known how to meet the health-related needs of this group, there are more churches per capita in the United States than in any other country, and faith communities are involved in public health and community development issues related to social justice.[8] Our findings suggest a number of recommendations for future study if FBOs are to contribute to community health in the ways envisioned by the Faith Partnership Initiative.

Recommendation 1: Increase collaboration between FBOs and health professionals for the purpose of evaluating health activities and disseminating findings. Disproportionately more is known about the effectiveness of faith-placed programs than either faith-based or collaborative programs. In the present study, we found that 55% of the programs testing interventions were faith placed, 20% were faith based, and 25% were collaborative.

As many as 57% to 78% of congregations are involved in health activities.[23,117] By increasing collaboration between health professionals and faith-based groups, it may be possible to introduce evaluation strategies into programs and to disseminate the results to a wider audience. Researchers and other health professionals should consider developing user-friendly workshops and tools for use by individuals associated with FBOs that are accustomed to delivering but not evaluating health-related programs. Since FBOs and churches are familiar community-based institutions, they frequently succeed when outside health professionals cannot.[118] More thorough collaboration between researchers and FBOs will facilitate better understanding of the community on the part of these health professionals, contribute to building the credibility of their projects,[3,119] and, we hope, promote increased program evaluation.

Recommendation 2: Place more emphasis on effectiveness studies as opposed to efficacy studies. Efficacy studies test the effects of interventions regardless of their practical application, whereas effectiveness studies test interventions in a way that is sensitive to what is practical in the real world. Efficacy studies generally require a more sophisticated study design, a greater amount of funding, and a greater degree of commitment and control than is typically available in most community-based settings. Consequently, they may be difficult to replicate in most congregations, especially in a way that could reliably contribute to a community's health.

In the present study, 7 of the 15 intervention studies reporting significant findings involved either a quasi-experimental[53,112] or an experimental[12,16,39,104,106] design, and all but 1 of these interventions were classified as faith placed. We suggest the use of study designs that are concerned with the quality of the care delivery system as opposed to more sophisticated designs that may be beyond the expertise of local program planners and difficult to implement in their care setting. Continuous Quality Improvement efforts and "Plan–Do–Study–Act" cycles, with their emphasis on process of care, systematic methods, short cycles, and real-world application, offer more accessible and manageable approaches to evaluating programs in these community-based settings.[120,121]

Recommendation 3: Devote more attention to building relationships with the racially and ethnically diverse populations that increasingly characterize communities in the United States. When a target population was identified in the present study, it tended to be African American (41.5%), and most of the faith-placed intervention programs (91%) were directed toward African American populations. This finding is not surprising since, in a majority of African American communities, the church is considered the most important social institution[36] and is the key community agent linking the African American community to the wider society beyond the congregation.[51] In addition, African American churches can reach large numbers of individuals in the communities outside of their particular congregations[114] and can sponsor community activities for all of those in need.[73,103]

It is important to both continue and to expand the work that is currently being done in African American communities among the many successful and progressive faith–health partnerships. However, we must also recognize that there are significant needs in other racial and ethnic groups, especially Hispanics. Although non-Hispanic Whites represent approximately half of all uninsured individuals, African Americans and Hispanics, respectively, are twice as likely and 3 times as likely as non-Hispanic Whites to be uninsured.[122] As previously mentioned, uninsured individuals are more likely than those with insurance coverage (1) to forgo or postpone preventive care and skip recommended tests or treatments,[123] (2) to be hospitalized for conditions that can be treated in outpatient settings (e.g., uncontrolled diabetes), and (3) to be diagnosed with late-stage colorectal cancer, melanoma, breast cancer, and prostate cancer.[124] Given the types of health services offered through FBOs, increased collaboration between health professionals and FBOs serving Hispanic populations could potentially improve quality of life in this vulnerable group.

The present study and the recommendations offered help provide a better conceptualization and understanding of the extent of existing information, our need for more information, and possible directions for future collaboration between public health professionals and those providing health services through FBOs. Despite the different perspectives of these 2 groups, they tend to share a passionate commitment to improving the quality of life of vulnerable populations. If faith and health partnerships can help address the existing and expected health needs of vulnerable populations, more thorough information about their possible contribution is needed to make informed policy decisions. Only by increasing the evaluation component of faith-based programs and disseminating the information gained will it be possible to determine how these programs can contribute systematically to improving the health and quality of life of at-risk populations in our communities.

Contributors

M. J. DeHaven developed the idea, original conceptualization, and design for this study. I. B. Hunter contributed to developing the initial idea, performed reviews of the literature, and assisted with article preparation. L. Wilder developed the literature search strategies, performed the searches, and assisted with reviewing the literature. J. W. Walton and J. Berry assisted with the final review of the included studies, helped to reconcile appropriate categorization of programs, and reviewed final versions of the article.

Acknowledgments

We are grateful for the capable and timely assistance with article preparation provided by Shannon Lee, Division of Community Medicine, University of Texas Southwestern Medical Center at Dallas. We also thank Jan Rookstool for her assistance in study coordination.

Human Participant Protection

No protocol approval was needed for this study.

References

1. Hatch J., Derthick S. Empowering black churches for health promotion. *Health Values Achieving High Level Wellness.* 1992;16(5):3–9.
2. Sanders E. C. New insights and interventions: churches uniting to reach the African American community with health information. *J Health Care Poor Underserved.* 1997; 8:373–375.
3. Sutherland M., Hale C. D., Harris G. J. Community health promotion: the church as partner. *J Primary Prev.* 1995;16:201–217.
4. Chatters L. M., Levin J. S., Ellison C. G. Public health and health education in faith communities. *Health Educ Behav.* 1998;25:689–699.
5. Foege W. H., O'Connell U. *Healthy People 2000: A Role for America's Religious Communities.* Chicago, Ill: Park Ridge Center and Carter Center; 1990.
6. Schroeder S. A. Prospects for expanding health insurance coverage. *N Engl J Med.* 2001;344:847–852.
7. Feder J., Levitt L., O'Brien E., Rowland D. Covering the low-income uninsured: the case for expanding public programs. *Health Aff.* 2001;20:27–39.

8. Baird L. J. Spirituality and faith in health care delivery. *Community Health Center Manage.* 1999;33:24–26.

9. Thomas S. B., Quinn S. C., Billingsley A., Caldwell C. The characteristics of northern black churches with community health outreach programs. *Am J Public Health.* 1994;84:575–579.

10. Wilson L. C. Implementation and evaluation of church-based health fairs. *J Community Health Nurs.* 2000;17:39–48.

11. Smith E. D., Merritt S. L., Patel M. K. Church-based education: an outreach program for African Americans with hypertension. *Ethn Health.* 1997;2:243–253.

12. McNabb W., Quinn M., Kerver J., Cook S., Karrison T. The PATHWAYS church-based weight loss program for urban African-American women at risk for diabetes. *Diabetes Care.* 1997;20:1518–1523.

13. Kumanyika S. K., Charleston J. B. Lose weight and win: a church-based weight loss program for blood pressure control among black women. *Patient Educ Counseling* 1992;19:19–32.

14. Schorling J. B., Roach J., Siegel M., et al. A trial of church-based smoking cessation interventions for rural African Americans. *Prev Med.* 1997;26:92–101.

15. Earp J. A., Flax V. L. What lay health advisors do: an evaluation of advisors' activities. *Cancer Pract.* 1999;7:16–21.

16. Duan N., Fox S. A., Derose K. P., Carson S. Maintaining mammography adherence through telephone counseling in a church-based trial. *Am J Public Health.* 2000;90:1468–1471.

17. Davis D. T., Bustamante A., Brown C. P., et al. The urban church and cancer control: a source of social influence in minority communities. *Public Health Rep.* 1994;109:500–506.

18. Cowart M. E., Sutherland M., Harris G. J. Health promotion for older rural African Americans: implications for social and public policy. *J Appl Gerontol.* 1995;14:33–46.

19. Barnhart J. M., Mossavar-Rahmani Y., Nelson M., Raiford Y., Wylie-Rosett J. Innovations in practice: an innovative, culturally-sensitive dietary intervention to increase fruit and vegetable intake among African American women: a pilot study. *Top Clin Nutr.* 1998;13:63–71.

20. Jensen C. A., Flynn S., Cozza M. A., Karabin J. Including the ultimate: a spiritual focus treatment program in an inpatient psychiatric area of a hospital in partnership with a pastoral counseling center. *J Pastoral Care.* 1998;52:339–348.

21. Ferrer R. L. Within the system of no-system. *JAMA.* 2001;286:2513–2514.

22. Finding common ground: 29 recommendations of the Working Group on Human Needs and Faith-Based and Community Initiatives. Available at: http://www.working-group.org. Accessed January 10, 2002.

23. Chaves M., Tsitsos W. Congregations and social services: what they do, how they do it and with whom. *NonProfit Voluntary Sector Q.* 2001;30:660–683.

24. Cook D. J., Mulrow C. D., Haynes R. B. Systematic reviews: synthesis of best evidence for clinical decisions. *Ann Intern Med.* 1997;126:376–380.

25. *Engaging Faith Communities as Partners in Improving Community Health.* Atlanta, Ga: Centers for Disease Control and Prevention; 1999.

26. Abrums M. "Jesus will fix it after awhile": meanings and health. *Soc Sci Med.* 2000;50:89–105.

27. Parish nursing at St. Michael: when the congregation is 17,000 strong and growing. *Perspect Parish Nurs Pract.* 1998;1:3–6.

28. Atkins F. D. What should the church do about health? *J Christian Nurs.* 1997;14(1):29–31.

29. Bailey P. L. Social work practice with groups in the church context: a family life ministry model in an inner-city church. *Soc Work Groups.* 1993;16:55–67.

30. Baker E. A., Homan S., Schonhoff R., Kreuter M. Principles of practice for academic/practice/community research partnerships. *Am J Prev Med.* 1999;16 (suppl 3):93.

31. Baker S. HIV/AIDS, nurses, and the black church: a case study. *J Assoc Nurses AIDS Care.* 1999;10(5):71–79.

32. Boario M. T. Mercy model: church-based health care in the inner city. *J Christian Nurs.* 1993;10(1):20–22.

33. Boehm S., Coleman-Burns P., Schlenk E. A., Funnell M. M., Parzuchowski J., Powell I. J. Prostate cancer in African American men: increasing knowledge and self-efficacy. *J Community Health Nurs.* 1995;12:161–169.

34. Boland C. S. Parish nursing: addressing the significance of social support and spirituality for sustained health-promoting behaviors in the elderly. *J Holistic Nurs.* 1998;16:355–368.

35. Brown-Hunter M., Price L. K. The Good Neighbor Project: volunteerism and the elderly African-American patient with cancer. *Geriatr Nurs.* 1998;19:139–141.

36. Bronner Y. L. Session II wrap-up: community-based approaches and channels for controlling hypertension in blacks: barriers and opportunities. *J Natl Med Assoc.* 1995;87:652–655.

37. Brunner S. L. Collaborative efforts support poor elderly: a nursing center teams up with area churches to care for the elderly in their homes. *Health Prog.* 1994;75(7):46–48.

38. Burkhart L. Choosing the right outcome measurement system to capture parish-nursing practice. *Perspect Parish Nurs Pract.* Fall–Winter 1999:2.

39. Campbell M. K., Demark-Wahnefried W., Symons M., et al. Fruit and vegetable consumption and prevention of cancer: the Black Churches United for Better Health Project. *Am J Public Health.* 1999;89:1390–1396.

40. Canda E. R., Phaobtong T. Buddhism as a support system for Southeast Asian refugees. *Soc Work.* 1992;37:61–67.

41. Castro F. G., Elder J., Coe K., et al. Mobilizing churches for health promotion in Latino communities: Companeros en la Salud. *J Natl Cancer Inst Monogr.* 1995; 18:127–135.

42. Chase-Ziolek M., Striepe J. A comparison of urban versus rural experiences of nurses volunteering to promote health in churches. *Public Health Nurs.* 1999;16:270–279.

43. Collins M. Increasing prostate cancer awareness in African American men. *Oncol Nurs Forum.* 1997;24:91–95.

44. Cook C. Faith-based health needs assessment: implications for empowerment of the faith community. *J Health Care Poor Underserved.* 1997;8:300–301.

45. Delafield D. Southeast Christian Church Counseling Ministry: One church's model for ministering to those in need. *J Psychol Christianity.* 1997;16:148–153.

46. Demark-Wahnefried W., Hoben K. P., Hars V., Jennings J., Miller M. W., Mc-Clelland J. W. Utility of produce ratios to track fruit and vegetable consumption

in a rural community: church-based 5 a day intervention project. *Nutr Cancer.* 1999;33:213–217.

47. Denny M. S. Church-based geriatric care. *Nurs Adm Q.* 1990;14(2):64–67.

48. DeSchepper C. Healthier communities through parish nursing: a South Dakota system finds multiple ways to support parish nursing programs. *Health Prog.* 1999;80(4):56–58.

49. Dixon S. Parish nurse ministry improves health outcomes of low-income community. *Aspens Advisor Nurse Executives.* 1996;11(11):7–8.

50. Easton K. L., Andrews J. C. Nursing the soul: a team approach. *J Christian Nurs.* 1999; 16(3):26–29.

51. Eng E., Hatch J., Callan A. Institutionalizing social support through the church and into the community. *Health Educ Q.* 1985;12:81–92.

52. Eng E., Hatch J. W. Networking between agencies and black churches: the lay health advisor model. *Prev Hum Serv.* 1991;10:23–46.

53. Erwin D. O., Spatz T. S., Stotts R. C., Hollenberg J. A., Increasing mammography practice by African American women. *Cancer Pract.* 1999;7:78–85.

54. Ferdinand K. C. The Healthy Heart Community Prevention Project: a model for primary cardiovascular risk reduction in the African-American population. *J Natl Med Assoc.* 1995;87(suppl 8):638–641.

55. Ferdinand K. C. Lessons learned from the Healthy Heart Community Prevention Project in reaching the African American population. *J Health Care Poor Underserved.* 1997;8:366–371.

56. Flack J. M., Wiist W. H. Cardiovascular risk factor prevalence in African-American adult screenees for a church-based cholesterol education program: the Northeast Oklahoma City Cholesterol Education Program. *Ethn Dis.* 1991;1:78–90.

57. Ford M. E., Edwards G., Rodriguez J. L., Gibson R. C., Tilley B. C. An empowerment-centered, church-based asthma education program for African American adults. *Health Soc Work.* 1996;21:70–75.

58. Fox S. A., Stein J. A., Gonzalez R. E., Farrenkopf M., Dellinger A. A trial to increase mammography utilization among Los Angeles Hispanic women. *J Health Care Poor Underserved.* 1998;9:309–321.

59. Gerber J. C., Stewart D. L. Prevention and control of hypertension and diabetes in an underserved population through community outreach and disease management: a plan of action. *J Assoc Acad Minor Phys.* 1998;9(3):48–52.

60. Gunderson G. R. Religious congregations as factors in health outcomes. *J Med Assoc Ga.* 1998;87:296–298.

61. Harding D. J., Southern J. Using a community networking approach in a bereavement program. *Am J Hosp Palliat Care.* 1991;8(4):20–22.

62. Harper D. P. Angelical conjunction: religion, reason, and inoculation in Boston, 1721–1722. *Pharos Alpha Omega Alpha Honor Med Soc.* 2000;63:37–41.

63. Hirano D. Partnering to improve infant immunizations: the Arizona Partnership for Infant Immunization (TAPII). *Am J Prev Med.* 1998;14:22–25.

64. Holschneider C. H., Felix J. C., Satmary W., Johnson M. T., Sandweiss L. M., Montz F. J. A single-visit cervical carcinoma prevention program offered at an inner city church: a pilot project. *Cancer.* 1999;86:2659–2667.

65. Huggins D. Parish nursing: a community-based outreach program of care. *Orthop Nurs.* 1998;17(2):26–30.

66. Jackson A. L. Operation Sunday School—educating caring hearts to be healthy hearts. *Public Health Rep.* 1990;105:85–88.

67. Jackson R. S., Reddick B. The African American church and university partnerships: establishing lasting collaborations. *Health Educ Behav.* 1999;26:663–674.

68. Joel L. A. Parish nursing: as old as faith communities. *Am J Nurs.* 1998;98:7.

69. Johnson G. A. Recapturing a vision: lay counseling as pastoral care. *J Psychol Christianity.* 1997;16:132–138.

70. Kaufmann M. A. Wellness for people 65 years and better. *J Gerontol Nurs.* 1997;23(6):7–9.

71. Kiser M., Boario M., Hilton D. Transformation for health: a participatory empowerment education training model in the faith community. *J Health Educ.* 1995;26:361–365.

72. Kutter C. J., McDermott D. S. The role of the church in adolescent drug education. *J Drug Educ.* 1997;27:293–305.

73. Lasater T. M., Becker D. M., Hill M. N., Gans K. M. Synthesis of findings and issues from religious-based cardiovascular disease prevention trials. *Ann Epidemiol.* 1997;7(suppl 7):S46–S53.

74. Lashley M. E. Congregational care: reaching out to the elderly. *J Christian Nurs.* 1999;16(3):14–16.

75. Lenehan G. P. Free clinics and parish nursing offer unique rewards. *J Emerg Nurs.* 1998;24:3–4.

76. Lloyd J. J., McConnell P. R., Zahorik P. M. Collaborative health education training for African American health ministers and providers of community services. *Educ Gerontol.* 1994;20:256–276.

77. Lough M. A. An academic-community partnership: a model of service and education. *J Community Health Nurs.* 1999;16:137–149.

78. McDermott M. A., Solari-Twadell P. A., Matheus R. Promoting quality education for the parish nurse and parish nurse coordinator. *Nurs Health Care Perspect.* 1998;19:4–6.

79. McRae M. B., Carey P. M., Anderson-Scott R. Black churches as therapeutic systems: a group process perspective. *Health Educ Behav.* 1998;25:778–789.

80. McRae M. B., Thompson D. A., Cooper S. Black churches as therapeutic groups. *J Multicultural Counseling Dev.* 1999;27:207–220.

81. Morgan L. Faith meets health: religious congregation, outside agencies join to promote public health. *Healthweek (Texas).* 1999;4(18):15.

82. Mustoe K. J. The unbroken circle: parish nursing is becoming an important stage in the healthcare continuum. *Health Prog.* 1998;79(3):47–49.

83. Nelson B. J. Parish nursing: holistic care for the community. *Am J Nurs.* 2000;100(5):24.

84. Oexmann M. J., Thomas J. C., Taylor K. B., et al. Shortterm impact of a church-based approach to lifestyle change on cardiovascular risk in African Americans. *Ethn Dis.* 2000;10:17–23.

85. Ofili E., Igho-Pemu P., Bransford T. The prevention of cardiovascular disease in blacks. *Curr Opin Cardiol.* 1999;14:169–175.

86. Okwumabua J. O., Martin B., Clayton-Davis J., Pearson C. M. Stroke Belt Initiative: the Tennessee experience. *J Health Care Poor Underserved.* 1997;8:292–299.

87. Penner S. J., Galloway-Lee B. Parish nursing: opportunities in community health. *Home Care Provider.* 1997;2:244–249.

88. Phillipp M. L. Teaching the hungry to fish: group helps inner-city neighborhood help itself. *Health Prog.* 1997;78(4):52–53.

89. Porter E. J., Ganong L. H., Armer J. M. The church family and kin: an older rural black woman's support network and preferences for care providers. *Qual Health Res.* 2000;10:452–470.

90. Ransdell L. B. Church-based health promotion: an untapped resource for women 65 and older. *Am J Health Promotion.* 1995;9:333–336.

91. Riordan R. J., Simone D. Codependent Christians: some issues for church-based recovery groups. *J Psychol Theology.* 1993;21:158–164.

92. Roque F., Walker L., Herrod P., Pyzik T., Clapp W. The Lawndale Christian Health Center Asthma Education Program. *Chest.* 1999;116(suppl 1):201S–202S.

93. Ruesch A. C., Gilmore G. D. Developing and implementing a healthy heart program for women in a parish setting. *Holistic Nurs Pract.* 1999;13(4):9–18.

94. Rydholm L. Patient-focused care in parish nursing. *Holistic Nurs Pract.* 1997;11(3):47–60.

95. Schumann R. Parish nursing: a call to integrity. *J Christian Nurs.* 2000;17(1):22–23.

96. Schuster S. J. Wholistic care: healing a "sick" system. *Nurs Manage.* 1997;28(6):56–59.

97. Smith E. D. Hypertension management with church-based education: a pilot study. *J Natl Black Nurses Assoc.* 1992;6:19–28.

98. Solari-Twadell P. A. The caring congregation: a healing place. *J Christian Nurs.* 1997;14(1):4–9.

99. Stillman F. A., Bone L. R., Rand C., Levine D. M., Becker D. M. Heart, body, and soul: a church-based smoking-cessation program for urban African Americans. *Prev Med.* 1993;22:335–349.

100. Stoy D. B., Curtis R. C., Dameworth K. S., et al. The successful recruitment of elderly black subjects in a clinical trial: the CRISP experience. *J Natl Med Assoc.* 1995;87:280–287.

101. Stuchlak P. Toning the temple: a church-based health fair. *J Christian Nurs.* 1992;9(3):22–23.

102. Stuckey J. C. The church's response to Alzheimer's disease. *J Appl Gerontol.* 1998;17:25–37.

103. Taylor R. J., Ellison C. G., Chatters L. M., Levin J. S., Lincoln K. D. Mental health services in faith communities: the role of clergy in black churches. *Soc Work.* 2000;45:73–87.

104. Toh Y. M., Tan S. Y. The effectiveness of church-based lay counselors: a controlled outcome study. *J Psychol Christianity.* 1997;16:263–267.

105. Toh Y. M., Tan S. Y., Osburn C. D., Faber D. E. The evaluation of a church-based lay counseling program: some preliminary data. *J Psychol Christianity.* 1994;13:270–275.

106. Voorhees C. C., Stillman F. A., Swank R. T., Heagerty P. J., Levine D. M., Becker D. M. Heart, body, and soul: impact of church-based smoking cessation interventions on readiness to quit. *Prev Med.* 1996;25:277–285.

107. Wahking H. The problems and the glory in church related counseling. *J Psychol Christianity.* 1997;16:161–167.

108. S. P., Boyd M. D., Bradford D., Mbssa M. S., Weinrich M. Recruitment of African Americans into prostate cancer screening. *Cancer Pract.* 1998;6:23–30.

109. Weiss R. Serving the community: beyond medical care. *Health Prog.* 1992;73(9):60–62.

110. Wenzel D. R., Thomsen M. A multidenominational Christian counseling center. *J Psychol Christianity.* 1997;16:115–120.

111. Whisnant S. The parish nurse: tending to the spiritual side of health. *Holistic Nurs Pract.* 1999;14:84–86.

112. Wiist W. H., Flack J. M. A church-based cholesterol education program. *Public Health Rep.* 1990;105:381–388.

113. Williams D. R., Griffith E. E. H., Young J. L., Collins C., Dodson J. Structure and provision of services in black churches in New Haven, Connecticut. *Cultural Diversity Ethnic Minority Psychol.* 1999;5:118–133.

114. Winett R. A., Anderson E. S., Whiteley J. A., et al. Church-based health behavior programs: using social cognitive theory to formulate interventions for at-risk populations. *Appl Prev Psychol.* 1999;8:129–142.

115. Turner L. W., Sutherland M., Harris G. J., Barber M. Cardiovascular health promotion in North Florida African-American churches. *Health Values.* 1995;19(2):3–9.

116. Chaves M., Konieczny M. E., Kraig B., Barman E. The National Congregations Study: background, methods, and selected results. *J Sci Study Religion.* 1999;38:458–460.

117. Hilton D. Some models of church health ministry in the USA. Available at: http://www.interaccess.com/iphnet/hilton2txt.htm. Accessed July 19, 2000.

118. Public Health Service. *Churches as an Avenue to High Blood Pressure Control.* Washington, DC: US Dept of Health and Human Services; 1989.

119. Randall-David E. *Strategies for Working With Culturally Diverse Communities and Clients.* Bethesda, Md: Association for the Care of Children's Health; 1989.

120. Langley A. E., Maurana C. A., LeRoy G. L., et al. Developing a community academic health center: strategies and lessons learned. *J Interprofessional Care.* 1998;12:273–277.

121. Spernoff T., Miles P., Mathews B. Improving health care, part 5: applying the Dartmouth clinical improvement model to community health. *J Qual Improvement.* 1998;24:679–703.

122. Institute of Medicine. Coverage matters: insurance and health care. Available at: http://www.iom.edu/uninsured. Accessed September 15, 2001.

123. Henry J. Kaiser Foundation. Medicaid and the uninsured. Available at: http://www.kff.org/content/2002/142003/. Accessed January 5, 2002.

124. *Uninsured in America: A Chart Book.* Washington, DC: Kaiser Commission on Medicaid and the Uninsured; 2000.

91

GLOBAL HEALTH — THE GATES–BUFFETT EFFECT

Susan Okie

Source: *New England Journal of Medicine*, 355:11 (2006), 1084–8.

Standing before a giant AIDS ribbon, Bill and Melinda Gates greeted some 26,000 researchers and public health workers on the opening night of last month's conference hosted by the International AIDS Society in Toronto. Bill Gates's voice echoed through the stadium as he assured the conference delegates, "Melinda and I have made stopping AIDS the top priority of our foundation." The Gateses spoke in turn, revealing both their passion and their clear-eyed intellectual engagement. Bill Gates talked of the new optimism he senses in Africa with the increased availability of antiretroviral drugs, but he warned that without increased prevention efforts, the provision of long-term treatment for infected persons is "simply unsustainable." Melinda Gates spoke of the stigmas that limit efforts to control AIDS, noting that government officials in many countries refuse to accompany them when they meet with sex workers. The philanthropists promised to increase their foundation's funding for research on new prevention tools for women and called for expanded access to proven measures such as condoms, clean needles, and HIV testing. The demonstrators who had heckled previous speakers were silent; the Gateses were interrupted only by cheers.

In a world with many celebrities but few heroes, Bill Gates has attained heroic status by committing much of his enormous fortune to the advancement of global equity. He and his wife have targeted the causes of health disparities between rich and poor, and their foundation has become a driving force in international aid and in research on AIDS and other diseases. In June, the Bill and Melinda Gates Foundation's likely impact on global health was amplified when Warren Buffett, the world's second-richest man, announced plans to give most of his fortune to the foundation established by the richest one.

Buffett's gift, worth about $37 billion, will double the foundation's endowment from $29 billion to approximately $60 billion, making it by far the world's largest charitable foundation. The gift will also increase the foundation's annual giving from $1.36 billion last year to about $3 billion, or approximately $1 per year for every person in the poorer half of the world's population. By comparison, the World Bank estimates that total health-related aid to developing countries in 2004 (from governments, international organizations, and private sources) was about $12.7 billion (see graph).

If Gates donates more of his own fortune and if the value of Buffett's donated Berkshire Hathaway stock rises, the Gates Foundation's annual giving will increase further. Yet the projected cost of solving major health problems in the developing world is far higher than even the most optimistic projections for giving by Gates. In 2000, the United Nations adopted Millennium Development Goals to be achieved by 2015; they included substantially reducing child and maternal mortality, reversing the spread of HIV–AIDS and malaria, and reducing the prevalence of tuberculosis and associated mortality. It is estimated that to meet these health goals, international aid would have to increase by a factor of three to seven.[1]

Shortly after their marriage in 1994, Bill and Melinda Gates designated global health as the primary focus for their charitable giving and established

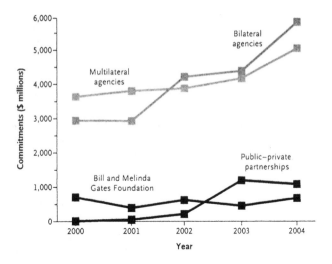

Development-Assistance Commitments to the Health Sector, 2000 to 2004.
"Bilateral agencies" include those in Australia, Austria, Belgium, Canada, Denmark, Finland, France, Germany, Greece, Ireland, Italy, Japan, Luxembourg, the Netherlands, New Zealand, Norway, Portugal, Spain, Sweden, Switzerland, the United Kingdom, and the United States (including the U.S. Agency for International Development). "Multilateral agencies" include United Nations agencies (the World Health Organization, the Joint Programme on HIV–AIDS, the Children's Fund, and the Population Fund), development banks (the World Bank, the Inter-American Development Bank, the Asian Development Bank, the African Development Bank, and the African Development Fund), and the European Union. "Public–private partnerships" include the Global Alliance for Vaccine and Immunization and the Global Fund to Fight AIDS, Tuberculosis, and Malaria. Data are from Catherine Michaud of the Harvard Initiative for Global Health, Cambridge, MA.

Key Health-Related Achievements of the Gates Foundation

An estimated 1.7 million deaths have been prevented through the work of the Global Alliance for Vaccines and Immunization (GAVI), which was formed in 2000 with the help of Gates funding and has received grants totaling $1.5 billion. About 90 million children have received hepatitis B vaccine, about 14 million have received *Haemophilus influenzae* type B and yellow fever vaccines, and about 21 million have benefited from expanded coverage with basic childhood vaccines. As a partnership of public and private organizations, governments, and pharmaceutical companies, GAVI also represents a successful model for alliances that the Gates Foundation is promoting in other areas.

An HIV–AIDS prevention initiative in India ($200 million) provides education, treatment for sexually transmitted diseases, condoms, and clean needles and syringes in six states with high rates of HIV infection. A national HIV–AIDS treatment program in Botswana ($50 million) is currently treating about 56,000 patients and has provided valuable lessons about scaling up HIV treatment. The foundation has also given $528 million for AIDS-vaccine research and $124 million for research on a microbicide to prevent sexual transmission of HIV. In August, it announced a 5–year, $500 million grant to the Global Fund to Fight AIDS, Tuberculosis, and Malaria, bringing its total contributions to the Global Fund to $650 million and its total funding for HIV–AIDS programs to about $2 billion.

Ten projects in malaria-vaccine development are being supported ($258 million) through the Malaria Vaccine Initiative of the international, nonprofit Program for Appropriate Technology in Health; one vaccine will soon be tested in a large phase 3 clinical trial in Africa. The first comprehensive national effort by a sub-Saharan African country to control malaria with the use of drugs, insecticide-treated bed nets, and other methods is being supported in Zambia ($35 million). The foundation is also supporting the development of better tuberculosis vaccines, including a genetically engineered, more immunogenic version of the bacille Calmette–Guérin (BCG) vaccine, which researchers hope to test soon in large clinical trials in Africa and India.

More than 20 million mothers and infants have received basic health services through $110 million in grants for Saving Newborn Lives (a Save the Children initiative).

the William H. Gates Foundation. By the end of 2005, the foundation (re-named in 1999) had awarded $10.2 billion in grants, about $6 billion of it for health-related projects. The mission of these grants can be summarized in three words: global health equity. The foundation holds that all human lives are of equal value, and the goal is to conquer diseases that dispropor-tionately afflict the world's poor, preventing them from reaching their full potential. "Until we reduce the burden on the poor so that there is no real gap between us and them," Gates said in 2005, "[global health] will always be our priority."[2]

Some of the earliest major grants of this foundation aimed to increase access to life-saving vaccines in developing countries. Other key targets have included HIV–AIDS, malaria, tuberculosis, malnutrition, acute diar-rheal and respiratory infections, tropical parasitic diseases, and maternal and child health. The foundation also mobilizes new resources for global health by promoting innovative financing mechanisms and product development and makes "focused investments . . . to achieve fundamental scientific break-throughs," as exemplified by $450 million in grants awarded last year to tackle 14 "grand challenges" in infectious disease, nutrition, and other fields. Recently, the foundation has begun to work on development issues that strongly influence health, such as clean water, sanitation, and girls' education.

The foundation has had several notable health-related achievements to date (see box), and some claim that the example set by Bill and Melinda Gates has been as important as the money they've donated. By calling atten-tion to global inequities, they have attracted funding from others and made it fashionable for the rich or famous to become involved in solving global problems. Buffett's move reflects that trend — and seems likely to intensify it. "The golden age of global health started when Bill and Melinda Gates put $27 billion into their foundation," says Jim Yong Kim, chief of the Division of Social Medicine and Health Inequalities at Brigham and Wom-en's Hospital in Boston. "They completely changed the sense of scale. It was the Gateses who really got us dreaming."

"I think people watch what the Gateses do and assume that if they're doing it, it's not only a smart humanitarian move, but a smart business move," said Helene Gayle, a former official at the Centers for Disease Control and Prevention (CDC) who spent 5 years at the Gates Foundation and now heads CARE. "They've put global health on the front burner like never before."

According to Gayle, a trip to Africa in the early 1990s opened the couple's eyes to the vast health disparities between rich and poor countries. Gates has credited William Foege, a former director of the CDC, with awakening him to the potential social impact of his money — particularly by suggesting that he read the 1993 World Development Report, which starkly quantified the toll of disease in developing countries. From infectious disease experts, the couple learned that an amazing number of lives could be saved for what seemed to them relatively small investments. "We really did think it was too shocking to be true," Bill Gates has said.[2]

Buffett, for his part, has long intended to give away most of his $44 billion fortune, but he only recently decided to do so while he is still alive. He also changed his mind about where to donate it, choosing the foundation established by Gates, his friend and bridge partner, rather than the Susan Thompson Buffett Foundation, named for his late wife. That shift reflects his business philosophy of investing in companies that have a track record, rather than reinventing the wheel. By serving on the board of the Gates Foundation, he will have some say in how the funds are spent, and he made his gift contingent on Bill or Melinda's remaining at the helm.

The doubling of the foundation's budget comes at a time of change in the leadership of its health program. Earlier this year, Tadataka (Tachi) Yamada was named president of the foundation's Global Health Program, replacing Richard Klausner. Yamada, a gastroenterologist and former chairman of internal medicine at the University of Michigan Medical School, previously headed research and development at GlaxoSmithKline, where he oversaw a budget of more than $4 billion and more than 15,000 employees. Although his staff at the foundation is much smaller — just over 100 employees — the Buffett gift offers unique opportunities both for tackling the health problems that are already being addressed and for broadening the foundation's mandate. Yamada, who had been on the job for only 10 weeks when I spoke with him, had been traveling to field sites and listening to ideas about how to spend the additional money.

"I project that we're going to be spending a little bit more than half [the foundation's annual awards] on global health," Yamada said. "My initial reaction is to do more of what we're doing — to do it more completely or better." The foundation has invested in the development of new vaccines, drugs, and diagnostic tests for malaria, tuberculosis, HIV, and other infections, he noted, and some of these products will soon be ready for manufacture, large-scale testing, or distribution, requiring additional resources.

Yamada mentioned two new areas that are likely to become foci of giving: health information and human-resource development. The improvement of health information systems could enable developing countries to quantify health problems, helping them to set spending priorities, improve health care delivery, and measure the effects of interventions. Yamada recently saw an impressive model program in Manhica, Mozambique, created in cooperation with Spanish epidemiologists. In the area of human resources, he said, the foundation is interested in worker-training projects that will improve health care delivery. "I'm not just talking about nurses and doctors; I'm talking about a broader array of health care workers with varying levels of education — down to community workers with very little," he said.

Some have urged the foundation to broaden its focus to include deadly noncommunicable diseases. Yamada said his program would like to become involved in efforts to reduce smoking and tobacco use in developing countries, perhaps by reinforcing initiatives for countries to sign the World Health Organization's Framework Convention on Tobacco Control, a treaty that will require signatories to increase taxes on tobacco products, ban sales to minors, regulate advertising, and take other measures.

When the Buffett gift was announced, some observers expressed concern that aid from other sources would decline because the Gates Foundation would be perceived as rich enough to solve the developing world's health problems. But experts say that the foundation's actions have consistently led to increased funding from others. "Without Bill Gates, we would never have had the Global Fund," said Kim. "And for sure, there would be no PEPFAR," the President's Emergency Plan for AIDS Relief.

In the area of malaria control, the size of the foundation's grants has enabled it to energize research and forge partnerships among academia, governments, and industry much more effectively than other institutions have, said Brian Greenwood, a professor at the London School of Hygiene and Tropical Medicine. Companies have been induced to develop drugs or vaccines for use in poor countries, because the foundation helps to pay the cost of development. "They have the potential to direct the overall pattern of what happens" in a field, Greenwood said. Critics have argued that such power to set the agenda has a downside. The foundation's grant making may not always reflect the priorities of recipients in developing countries, and its choices may influence the decisions of other funding agencies, potentially steering money away from basic science and toward product development. However, the Gates Foundation's wealth and independence allow it to take risks that could yield big payoffs. "Governments cannot afford to fail in the same way," noted Harvey V. Fineberg, president of the Institute of Medicine.

The history of the Global Alliance for Vaccines and Immunization (GAVI) illustrates both the dramatic progress that has been made and the continuing challenges. In the 1990s, childhood immunization rates with basic vaccines had stopped increasing in developing countries, and newer vaccines against diseases such as hepatitis B and *Haemophilus influenzae* type B were unavailable. Bill and Melinda Gates were attracted to a problem that might be attacked with money and technology; a $750 million Gates grant jump-started the alliance, and the foundation received a seat on GAVI's governing board. "Its intellectual input was critical," said Julian Lob-Levyt, president of GAVI. "I think the results-based nature of GAVI, which comes from Gates, is new in the development community."

GAVI now has almost $3.5 billion in commitments from governments and private sources, as well as $4 billion in long-term commitments to a new sister institution, the International Finance Facility for Immunization. In a financing innovation, pledges of future donations will be used to issue bonds on the financial market, allowing money to be spent up front to improve

delivery systems, purchase vaccines in larger quantities, and assure manufacturers of a stable long-term market. Although Lob-Levyt predicts that
financial incentives will attract new manufacturers and increase competition,
lowering prices, the high cost of some vaccines remains problematic. In many
countries, a weak health care infrastructure also represents a formidable
barrier, so GAVI and the Gates Foundation have shifted course to address
that underlying problem.

The Gates Foundation is still evolving, and its leaders acknowledge having
made mistakes. For example, some early grants did not cover operating
expenses for grantees; now they are included. The foundation staff underestimated the complexity of tasks such as delivering childhood vaccines in
developing countries and found that in some cases, 5 years of funding for
projects was not long enough to deliver results. Although the foundation is
known for its "lean" structure, some grantees said that current staff levels
are barely adequate to handle the existing workload, and Yamada said that it
will have to grow in order to double its spending. Choosing worthy recipients,
monitoring projects, and measuring their effects will be especially challenging. "For our largest grants, GAVI and the Global Fund, we know the results
that they've produced and they're pretty substantial," said Yamada. "For
others, it's harder to measure . . . [but] we're beginning to get some evidence."
In Botswana, for example, where the foundation supports a national HIV–AIDS
testing and treatment program, the prevalence of HIV infection among girls
15 to 19 years of age decreased by 22% between 2003 and 2005.

Perhaps the Gates Foundation's greatest influence derives from its assumption that intractable problems can be solved, given enough money and international cooperation. For example, as a condition of receiving $287 million
in grants for AIDS-vaccine research that were announced in July, 165
scientists in 19 countries will have to share their data in a central repository.
Yamada predicted that such collaboration will become more common in the
future, even in industry.

"We're trying to deal with very difficult problems that people are suffering
from in the developing world," he said. "The more information sharing there
is, the more patients will benefit."

Notes

1 Gottret P., Schieber G. Health financing revisited: a practitioner's guide. Washington,
   DC: World Bank, 2006.
2 Specter M. What money can buy. The New Yorker. October 24, 2005.

92

SOCIAL AND ENVIRONMENTAL RISK FACTORS IN THE EMERGENCE OF INFECTIOUS DISEASES

Robin A. Weiss and Anthony J. McMichael

Source: *Nature Medicine*, 10:12 (2004), S70–S76.

Fifty years ago, the age-old scourge of infectious disease was receding in the developed world in response to improved public health measures, while the advent of antibiotics, better vaccines, insecticides and improved surveillance held the promise of eradicating residual problems. By the late twentieth century, however, an increase in the emergence and reemergence of infectious diseases was evident in many parts of the world. This upturn looms as the fourth major transition in human–microbe relationships since the advent of agriculture around 10,000 years ago. About 30 new diseases have been identified, including Legionnaires' disease, human immunodeficiency virus (HIV)/acquired immune deficiency syndrome (AIDS), hepatitis C, bovine spongiform encephalopathy (BSE)/variant Creutzfeldt-Jakob disease (vCJD), Nipah virus, several viral hemorrhagic fevers and, most recently, severe acute respiratory syndrome (SARS) and avian influenza. The emergence of these diseases, and resurgence of old ones like tuberculosis and cholera, reflects various changes in human ecology: rural-to-urban migration resulting in high-density peri-urban slums; increasing long-distance mobility and trade; the social disruption of war and conflict; changes in personal behavior; and, increasingly, human-induced global changes, including widespread forest clearance and climate change. Political ignorance, denial and obduracy (as with HIV/AIDS) further compound the risks. The use and misuse of medical technology also pose risks, such as drug-resistant microbes and contaminated equipment or biological medicines. A better understanding of the evolving social dynamics of emerging infectious diseases ought to help us to anticipate and hopefully ameliorate current and future risks.

Popular writing on emerging infectious diseases resounds with dire warnings about the threat of modern 'plagues' and losing the 'war against microbes.' This adversarial language obscures the fact that most of the microbial world is either neutral toward, or supportive of, human well-being and survival. Indeed, we would not survive long without commensal microbes such as the beneficial strains of *Escherichia coli* in our gut. That aside, the study of emerging infections is more than a passing fad. The recent rate of identification of such infections, the impact of the SARS outbreak, the devastation caused by AIDS, and the ever-present threat of a new influenza pandemic indicate that we cannot control our disease destiny. Nor are emerging infections unique to humans; the Irish potato famine in 1845 and the English foot-and-mouth disease epidemic in 2001 underscore the consequences for human societies of disease emergence in crops and livestock.

Emerging infectious diseases in humans comprise the following: first, established diseases undergoing increased incidence or geographic spread, for example, Tuberculosis and Dengue fever; second, newly discovered infections causing known diseases, for example, hepatitis C and *Helicobacter pylori*; and third, newly emerged diseases, for example, HIV/AIDS and SARS.

This Perspective will discuss the human ecology of both the (apparently) new and re-emerging diseases.

The demography of infectious disease

Interest in infectious disease has itself recently re-emerged. In 1972, Burnet and White commented, "The most likely forecast about the future of infectious disease is that it will be very dull. There may be some wholly unexpected emergence of a new and dangerous infectious disease, but nothing of the sort has marked the past fifty years"[1]. Today, we may criticize the short-sightedness of our mentors' generation, yet in demographic terms they were essentially correct because the proportion of deaths from infectious disease has fallen throughout the twentieth century[2,3] (Figure 1).

Humankind currently faces neither apocalyptic extinction nor even a population reduction such as occurred in Europe during the Black Death of the fourteenth century. Rather, overpopulation in relation to environmental resources remains a more pressing problem in many developing countries, where poor economic and social conditions go hand-in-hand with infectious disease. In industrializing countries during the nineteenth century, a major reduction in enteric infections was achieved by separating drinking water from sewage—an environmental change that probably saved more lives than all the twentieth century vaccines and antibiotics together. Today, however, the growth of shanty towns without sanitation around the megalopolis cities of Asia, Africa and South America is recreating similar conditions, and in the past 40 years cholera has made a remarkable re-emergence through its longest ever (seventh) pandemic[4].

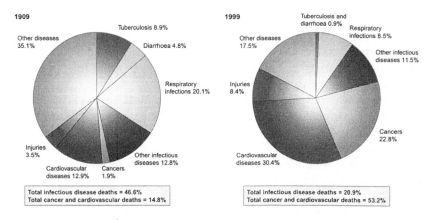

Figure 1 Proportions of total deaths from major cause-of-death categories, 1909 and 1999, in Chile[2]. This country illustrates the full transition from developing to developed status during the twentieth century.

In most countries, life expectancy has risen over the past 50 years[5] (Figure 2). The most important exception is those regions where HIV infection is rife. Moreover, during the past 15 years, falling living standards in some African countries and the breakdown of public health infrastructure in ex-Soviet nations has aided the re-emergence of transmissible diseases like tuberculosis[4,6]. Further, severe outbreaks such as the 1918–1919 influenza A pandemic temporarily reversed the decline of deaths caused by infectious disease.

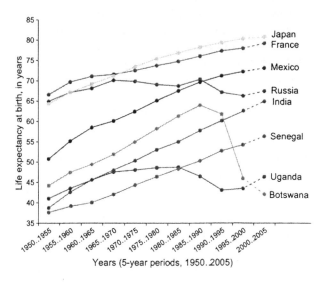

Figure 2 Changes in life expectancy at birth for both sexes in eight representative countries during the last 55 years[5].

The 50 million estimated deaths from that pandemic[7] represented about 2% of the global population at that time, and is twice as many as the cumulative AIDS mortality of the past 20 years. The next influenza pandemic may be just around the corner, and may spread even faster[8], if access to appropriate vaccines and drug treatment is not available[9,10].

For other newly emerging infections that make headlines, such as SARS, Ebola or vCJD, it is important to keep a sense of demographic proportion. Placing these emerging infections on a 'Richter' scale of human mortality (Box 1) shows that they elicit scarcely detectable minor tremors in numbers of fatalities—despite the fear they invoke. We do not know, however, which one might leap to the top of the scale like HIV has done; indeed, it may be a completely unknown agent, as the SARS coronavirus was two years ago. A major challenge is to predict which infection presages the next big quake, hopefully allowing preventive action.

Emerging infectious diseases, past and present

Like any other animal or plant species, humans have been prone to infection by pathogens throughout their evolutionary history. Such ancient infections by helminth and protozoan parasites, bacteria, fungi and viruses are endemic, eliciting a range of effects from a heavy burden of disease (*e.g.*, malaria) to being essentially commensal in immunocompetent hosts (*e.g.*, most types of herpesvirus and papilloma virus). Other infections depend on an animal reservoir for their maintenance; their infection of humans may be pathogenic, but it has little part in the evolving ecology of the microbe or parasite. An estimated 61% of the 1,415 species of infectious organisms known to be pathogenic in humans are transmitted by animals[11], for which the human represents a dead-end host. Occasionally, however, a zoonotic infection adapts to human-to-human transmission and diversifies away from its animal origin. Epidemic diseases are generally caused by infections that are directly transmissible between humans. HIV is a recent example of a long line of human infections initiated by a switch of host species, stretching back to the origins of measles and smallpox.

Free-living microbes may also find a human niche that suits their lifestyle, such as the lung for *Legionella pneumophila* and the gut for *Vibrio cholerae*. Legionnaires' disease, first recognized in Philadelphia in 1976, is the environmental equivalent of a zoonosis. It is seldom passed directly from person to person but it was human ingenuity in designing warm, aerated, humid 'artificial lungs' called air-conditioning systems that allowed the microbe to proliferate and become an opportunistic colonizer of the human lung. Cholera, which was unknown beyond the Ganges delta before it spread widely in Asia and the Middle East during the period 1815–1825, at around that time horizontally acquired a toxin gene and other factors in a genetic package that helped it to colonize the gut; the resultant diarrhea aids dispersal of the microbe[12,13].

Human society has undergone a series of major transitions that has affected our pattern of infectious disease acquisition and dissemination[4].

Box 1. Natural Weapons of Mass Destruction Placed on a 'Richter' Scale[52,53]

The values are approximate global death rates for the year 2003, taken from the World Health Organization (WHO) and other sources. HBV and HCV, hepatitis B and C viruses; RSV, respiratory syncytial virus; HPV, human papilloma viruses; vCJD, variant Creutzfeldt-Jakob disease.

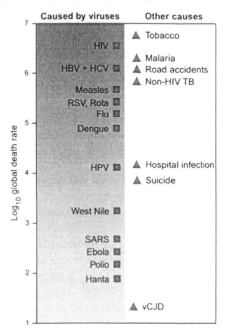

Two major, novel causes of mortality top the list: cigarette smoking and HIV infection; they emerged in the twentieth century and continue to increase in many developing countries. Among the chronic and re-emerging infections, malaria and tuberculosis are near the top, so it becomes apparent why there is a need for the Global Fund for Malaria, Tuberculosis and AIDS. Accidental injuries, particularly road deaths, continue to rise, with 85% occurring in developing countries[54]. Although 2003 was the year of the SARS outbreak[52,55], less than 1,000 people actually died as a result of SARS coronavirus infection despite the collateral damage to daily life, psychological well-being and economic activity in the affected cities.

This Richter scale represents a snapshot in time. Twenty years ago, HIV was three logs further down the scale, whereas polio was three logs higher. Fifty years ago, malaria was finally eradicated from Europe, where it had formerly been widespread, including in England (Shakespeare's 'ague'). Bacterial respiratory diseases used to have a more important role in human mortality and, despite concern over multi-resistance to antibiotics[40,56], the situation is considerably better than in the era before the advent of antibiotics. Common bacterial infections of childhood, such as diphtheria and whooping cough, have become rarities in the developed world, largely through vaccination. Viral diseases have similarly been reduced. Thanks to effective immunization policies of the WHO, smallpox was eradicated in 1977; polio and measles viruses, which have no animal reservoir, may soon be eliminated in the same way.

These transitions illustrate the interrelationship between environmental, social and behavioral influences on the emergence and subsequent spread of infectious disease. Some infections were acquired when our australopithecine ancestors left their arboreal habitat to live in the savannah. This ecological change included exposure to new species of mosquito and tick as vectors for infection. After the emergence of *Homo sapiens*, the eventual migration of neolithic hunter-gatherers out of Africa 50,000 to 100,000 years ago exposed them to new infections in distant regions.

The first major transition of prehistoric/early historic times gave rise to the epidemic, or 'crowd,' infections. This change must have started in the millennia following the advent of agriculture—from around 10,000 years ago—as agriculturally based society developed larger, denser populations. The domestication of livestock and the rich dividends available in human settlements to other animals (*e.g.*, rodents, dogs and various insects) provided further opportunities for pathogens to move between species. Sometimes such a pathogen (or a mutant strain thereof) would have been well suited to humans as a new host species, and, if human numbers were adequate, could therefore persist indefinitely as a human infection. Thus, measles emerged about 7,000 years ago, probably from rindepest of cattle, and diverged to become an exclusively human infection when population size and density became sufficient to maintain the virus without an animal reservoir. Similarly, smallpox became epidemic about 4,000 years ago, possibly evolving from camelpox, its closest phylogenetic relative.

The next two transitions were primarily to do with great extensions in the spread of infectious diseases, entering distant populations as 'new infections.' Thus, the second historical transition occurred in Classical times as large Eurasian civilizations came into commercial and military contact. They inadvertently exchanged their pools of infections, and vectors such as rats and fleas, across the Mediterranean basin, the Middle East, India and China. The plague of Athens in 430 BCE during the Peloponnesian war vividly described by Thucidides may represent the first report of typhus. This Rickettsial infection is transmitted from rats to humans and thence among louse-ridden humans. Typhus frequently accompanies human conflict and deprivation, as seen in a recent outbreak among Rwandan refugees in Burundi[14]. The Justinian plague of 542 CE devastated the eastern Mediterranean region and probably extended as far as China[15] like the Black Death 800 years later (and both are attributable to *Yersinia pestis*[16]).

The third historical transition accompanied the era of worldwide exploration and colonization by Europeans from circa 1500 CE onward. A contemporary account by one of Hernan Cortes' fellow conquistadors, Bernal Diaz, recalls that they might well have failed to overthrow the mighty Aztec empire had they not been aided by a raging epidemic. This was possibly a combination of smallpox and measles, both wholly unknown to the New World population. Curiously, the Columbian exchange was unidirectional regarding infectious diseases; the one contentious possible exception being syphilis. The New World is believed to have had substantially fewer human zoonotic infections[15,17], and vector-borne infections like Chagas' disease did not travel in the absence of an appropriate vector.

Two centuries later, Captain Cook unwittingly repeated the decimation of indigenous peoples through syphilis, measles and tuberculosis in many of the Pacific islands, whereas Lord Jeffrey Amherst deliberately attempted to spread smallpox among 'hostile' Native Americans, one of the better documented cases of germ warfare[18]. The transmission dynamics of infections in naive populations is markedly different from those in which the majority of adults are immune[19]. Onboard *The Beagle*, Charles Darwin observed with his customary acuity, "Wherever the European has trod, death seems to pursue the aboriginal . . . Most of the diseases have been introduced by ships and what renders this fact remarkable is that there might be no appearance of the disease among the crew which conveyed this destructive importation."

Today we are living through the fourth historical transition of globalization. Urbanization, dense and usually impoverished peri-urban settlements, social upheaval, air travel, long-distance trade, technological developments, land clearance and climate change all influence the risks of infectious disease emergence and spread. Although some of the apparent increase in infectious disease may be attributable to better diagnostic methods and surveillance, there seems little doubt that more incidents are occurring, and have the potential to spread more widely than 50 years ago, as outbreaks and spread of infections like Nipah virus and SARS would not have passed unnoticed.

Environment and emerging infectious diseases

As humans encroach further into previously uncultivated environments, new contacts between wild fauna and humans and their livestock increases the risk of cross-species infection[20]. This process will only diminish as wild species become rarer and eventually endangered, like the great apes today. An example of such contact followed the establishment of piggeries close to the tropical forest in northern Malaysia, where, in 1998, the Nipah virus first crossed over from fruit bats (flying foxes, *Pteropus* spp.) to pigs and thence to pig farmers[21]. Destruction of natural forest has also encouraged fruit bats to relocate nearer human habitation, like the large colony in the botanic gardens in the heart of Sydney. Indeed, in 1997, Hendra, a related paramyxovirus of Australian fruit bats[22], fatally infected a veterinarian examining a sick horse.

Rodents continue to be sources of re-emerging infections, as witnessed in the 1990s with hantaviruses in the United States. Rodent-borne hantavirus is prevalent in agricultural systems in South America and East Asia, in arid grasslands in North America and elsewhere. In mid-1993, an unexpected outbreak of acute, sometimes fatal, respiratory disease occurred in humans in the southwestern United States[23]. This 'hantavirus pulmonary syndrome' was caused by a previously unrecognized virus, maintained primarily within the native deer-mouse, and transmitted through excreta. The 1991–1992 El Niño event, with unseasonal heavy summer rains and a proliferation of piñon nuts, hugely amplified local rodent populations which led to the 1993 outbreak[23,24]. In South America, there have been several outbreaks of hantavirus and arenavirus infections linked to forest clearance and the growth of rodent populations in the new grasslands[4].

Habitat destruction is not the only cause of increased human infection, however. Dengue virus is extending its range and prevalence because its mosquito vector breeds rapidly in the urban environment[25]. In the United States, nature conservation and increased woodland in the eastern states has led to the emergence of Lyme disease. This disease is caused by a tick-borne spirochete and the presence of tick-infested deer near suburban homes leads to ticks residing on bushes adjacent to baseball diamonds and gardens.

Food-borne infections

Intensification of production of meat and meat products has led to new infections[26]. Most notorious is vCJD in the UK arising from consumption of contaminated food products of cattle affected by BSE[27]. BSE, or 'mad cow disease,' emerged in British cattle in 1986 because of industrialized cannibalism, whereby rendered neural tissue and bone meal from slaughtered cattle were recycled into cattle feed, as well as into pies and hamburgers for human consumption[28]. Originally, infectious prions from scrapie in sheep were the suspected source, but it now seems more likely that it arose from a bovine with sporadic prion disease. The extent of the human epidemic remains unclear. Although natural transmission is unsustainable ($R_0 < 1$ in both cattle and humans), there are concerns that vCJD might be transmissible through blood transfusions[29]. Without effective diagnostic tests for presymptomatic vCJD infection, this situation is extremely unfortunate.

Other recently emergent food-borne infections include *E. coli* O157:H7, which is harmless to cattle but toxic to humans, and *Salmonella enteriditis* in chickens. Better hygiene in abattoirs, butchers and domestic kitchens can greatly reduce the incidence of infection. In theory, closed and intensive farming of a single species should reduce the risk of cross-species infection. But it also allows large-scale epidemics to emerge, as seen recently for avian influenza strains in southeast Asia and the Netherlands[8,30].

Ancient dietary taboos, such as those of Hindus, Muslims and Jews regarding pork as unclean, doubtless had their roots in protection from infectious disease. Today, an increasing demand for consumption of exotic and wild animals raises new risks of infectious diseases such as SARS (Box 2).

Box 2. Bushmeat and Live Animal Markets

"If there is any conceivable way a germ can travel from one species to another, some microbe will find it," wrote William McNeill in his classic text Plagues and Peoples[15]. For millennia, small farmsteads accommodated mixed species living closely with humans—goats, pigs, cattle, ducks, geese, chickens and perhaps a water buffalo or a donkey—and exchanged infections. When species are raised separately but are sold together, the opportunity for cross-infection moves from the farm to the marketplace. The 1997 outbreak of avian influenza in Hong Kong occurred in mixed markets, where live chickens, quail and ducks were stacked together in close quarters with humans. The H5N1 virus that emerged may have been derived by recombination between those of different avian hosts[8]. After 1997, mixed species were separated into different areas of the markets. But this year's H5N1 virus is spreading among intensively reared chickens across southeast Asia.

The increasing predilection for meat of exotic species has exacerbated the risk of exposure to infections not previously encountered, and this situation probably triggered the SARS epidemic[55]. Although we are still not sure of the natural reservoir species of SARS coronavirus, the live markets and restaurants in Guangzbong sold small carnivores, and several species of civet cat, racoon dog and ferret badger captured in China, Laos, Vietnam and Thailand, were brought into close proximity[57]. Clearly, some of the palm civet cats were infected with SARS-related viruses, but it is less clear whether they represent the original source species. There is a danger in incriminating the wrong species; if the true reservoir resides in the rodent prey of these carnivores, then culling the predators may be counterproductive. Stopping the exotic meat trade altogether would seem to be a simple solution to prevent the reappearance of SARS, but once the taste for it has been established, that may prove no more practical than attempting to prohibit the tobacco trade.

In Africa, bushmeat also poses a serious problem for emerging infectious diseases, as well as for nature conservation. Sick animals may be more easily captured. For example, 21 human deaths owing to Ebola virus infection ensued from the butchering of a single chimpanzee[58]. HIV has crossed from chimpanzees to humans on at least three occasions, and a higher number of zoonotic events from sooty mangabeys are indicated for HIV-2 (ref. 32). Whether these cross-species infections arose from butchering the animals or from keeping them as pets is unknown, but a recent survey of primate hunters in Africa showed that they are susceptible, like handlers of primates in captivity, to infection (though not disease) from foamy retroviruses[59].

The escalating intercontinental trade in exotic pets can lead to unexpected infectious disease outbreaks. The United States has only recently imposed more stringent regulations and quarantine following cases of monkeypox in humans and in prairie dogs introduced by rodents imported from as pets[60].

Transmissibility and globalization

Changing patterns of human behavior and ecology affect two distinct steps in the emergence of new infectious disease. The first is an increased opportunity for animal-to-human infection to occur owing to greater exposure, which may be necessary but not sufficient to lead to the emergence of a new human infection. The second step is the opportunity for onward transmission once a person has become infected. For each novel epidemic, such as the 1918–1919 influenza pandemic or AIDS, there are probably thousands of failed transfers.

Some infections simply do not take in the new host. Innate host-specific restrictions on viral replication have recently become evident for primate lentiviruses[31], which may explain why certain species that harbor simian immunodeficiency virus, but not others more commonly in contact with humans, gave rise to HIV-1 and HIV-2. Even in the case of HIV-1, only one pedigree of three independent chimpanzee-to-human crossover events[32] has given rise to the AIDS pandemic, whereas the other two smolder as poorly transmissible infections.

Fatal pathogenesis is not necessarily coupled with infectiousness[12], which is evident for H5N1 avian influenza in humans[9]. But genetic reassortment between avian and human influenza viruses could easily give rise to a new, rapidly spreading strain[8]. A poorly infectious pathogen may not spread at all from the index case, as is usual with rabies, or may only infect close contacts and soon peter out, as seen with Lassa fever and Ebola virus. SARS nearly became self-sustaining but was brought under control. Some of the most insidious infections are those with long, silent incubation periods during which the person is infectious. These emerge surreptitiously so that when the new disease is eventually recognized, as AIDS was in 1981, the infection has already spread far beyond control.

Like the ships of centuries past, the speed of modern air travel works wonders for the dispersal of infectious diseases. SARS was eventually constrained by quarantine and strict adherence to infection control guidelines in hospitals, but not before it quickly traveled from Guangzhong to Hong Kong and on to Toronto. If Ebola broke out in a city with a busy international airport, it might also travel across continents in a similar manner. Brockmann[33] has modeled how rapidly such infections can move once they reach a major airport hub; closing the hubs becomes an immediate imperative. We cannot be sure what the initial vector was for the arrival of West Nile virus into North America in 1999: a migratory bird blown off course, an infected human with a valid air ticket or a stowaway mosquito on a similar flight. Whatever the means of entry and early colonization of crows in New York, it has taken less than four years to reach the Pacific coast[25]. Thus, West Nile virus has found a new reservoir in American birds, just as yellow fever virus reached New World primates 350 years earlier.

Social and economic conditions, behavioral changes and geopolitical instability

Microbes frequently capitalize on situations of ecological, biological and social disturbance. Biologically weakened and vulnerable populations—especially if also socially disordered and living in circumstances of privation, unhygienic conditions and close contact—are susceptible to microbial colonization. The severity of the bubonic plague (Black Death) in mid-fourteenth-century Europe seems to have reflected the nutritional and impoverishment consequences of several preceding decades of unusually cold and wet weather with crop failures compounding the incipient destabilization of the hierarchical feudal system.

Many of the rapid and marked changes in human social ecology in recent decades have altered the probabilities of infectious disease emergence and transmission. These changes include increases in population size and density, urbanization, persistent poverty (especially in the expanding peri-urban slums), the increased number and movement of political, economic and environmental refugees, conflict and warfare. Political ignorance, denial and obduracy often compound the risk of infectious disease transmission—as has been tragically observed with HIV/AIDS in parts of Africa, where widespread poverty, a culture of female disempowerment and political instability further exacerbate the problem[34,35]. But we have little understanding of why the prevalence of HIV infection varies so greatly between cities in sub-Saharan Africa[36].

The urban environment has only recently become the dominant human habitat. Urbanism typically leads to a breakdown in traditional family and social structures, and entails greater personal mobility and extended and changeable social networks. These features, along with access to modern contraception, have facilitated a diversity of sexual contacts and, hence, the spread of sexually transmitted diseases[37]. This risk is further amplified by the growth in sex tourism in today's internationally mobile world, which capitalizes on the desperation and ignorance of poverty, combined with exploitative behaviors, in developing countries. More generally, cities often function as highways for 'microbial traffic'[38]. Rapid urbanization boosts certain well established infectious diseases, such as childhood pneumonia, diarrhea, tuberculosis and dengue, and facilitates dissemination of various 'emerging' diseases—as occurred for SARS in the high-rise housing of Hong Kong. Crowded and dilapidated public housing can potentiate infectious disease transmission through drug abuse and sexually transmitted infections[39].

Nosocomial and iatrogenic infections

Technological advances in medicine and public health can also inadvertently promote the emergence and spread of infectious disease. It has become commonplace to quip that you go to the hospital at the peril of acquiring an intractable nosocomial infection such as methicillin-resistant *Staphylococcus aureus*[40], and such infections killed around 40 times as many people as SARS did in 2003 (Box 1). Multidrug-resistant tuberculosis has also become a major problem, and, paradoxically, regions with health programs that reduced wild-type tuberculosis strains can develop into 'hot zones' for multidrug-resistant tuberculosis[41].

By far the most effective medical vector of infectious disease has been the syringe and needle. Drucker *et al.*[42] have charted the massive increase in the use of injecting equipment over the past 100 years. Individuals with hemophilia treated with pooled clotting factors became almost universally infected with hepatitis B and C viruses before diagnostic screening tests were developed. Over 20% of such affected individuals also became infected with HIV[43], and more recently, transmission of West Nile virus by blood transfusion and by organ transplantation has been reported[44,45]. The use of contaminated needles among intravenous drug users has had similar consequences. Infectious diseases have also been amplified by the use of nonsterile medical injections in developing countries[42]. Egypt has the highest prevalence of hepatitis C infection in the world because of the use and reuse of syringes and needles in an earlier public health campaign to reduce bilharzia by medication given by injection. The transmission of CJD through contaminated surgical instruments is another example of iatrogenic spread of infection[29].

Biological medicines produced from animal-cell substrates present an inherent potential hazard for introducing new infections. Great care must be taken to ensure that live attenuated vaccines grown in animal cells or eggs are devoid of pathogens; for example, several early batches of live and inactivated polio vaccine unwittingly contained live SV40 virus, a polyoma virus of macaques. After SV40 was discovered in 1960, polio vaccine production shifted to virus propagation in primary kidney cells of African green monkeys. These cultures were free of SV40 but possibly contained SIVagm, a relative of HIV that fortunately does not infect humans[31]. The irony of the SV40 story is that the United States Food and Drug Administration prohibited the use of well known, permanent cell lines demonstrably free of adventitious infectious agents, for fear that such immortalized cells might exert oncogenic properties on the vaccine. There is no epidemiological evidence of increased tumor incidence in those populations who are known to have received SV40-contaminated polio vaccine. But there have been a number of recent claims of an association of SV40 DNA sequences in a variety of human malignancies[46], although these findings remain controversial[47].

The ultimate medical means of introducing animal viruses into humans is xenotransplantation. The implantation of animal cells or tissues into immunosuppressed individuals seems to be a perfectly designed way to encourage cross-species infection. It is astonishing that trials were started without much thought about the consequences for potentially emerging pathogens, for example, porcine retroviruses[48]. The generation of genetically modified knockout or transgenic animals to prevent hyperacute rejection of donor tissues may exacerbate the infection hazard[49,50]. Happily, there is no evidence so far of retrovirus infection in individuals who were exposed to living pig cells[50], and clinical xenotransplantation is now stringently regulated; so it seems all the more extraordinary that cellular therapies with fetal lamb cells and extracts continue to be practiced with impunity in alternative medicine clinics in Europe and the Far East.

Conclusions and prospects

Novel infectious diseases can emerge in any part of the world at any time. HIV and Ebola came out of Africa, avian influenza and SARS from China, Nipah virus from Malaysia, BSE/vCJD from the UK and hantavirus pulmonary syndrome from the Americas. It is difficult to predict what new disease will come next or where it will appear, but changing ecological conditions and novel human-animal contacts will be useful clues as to which horizons require scanning with most scrutiny. We must expect the unexpected.

As a codicil, another factor that needs to be taken into account is the potential impact of the HIV pandemic on the emergence of other infectious diseases[51]. We already know that persons with AIDS act as 'superspreaders' of tuberculosis, and we can only speculate what course the SARS outbreak might have taken had someone incubating the disease flown to Durban rather than Toronto[52]. People with AIDS may persistently harbor infections that would otherwise be transient, and this could hamper the eradication of measles and polio. Multivalent *Pneumococcus* vaccines are ineffective in HIV-infected people with CD4$^+$ lymphocyte levels below 200/µl, whereas live 'attenuated' vaccines such as vaccinia can cause virulent disease in the immunocompromised host. Immunodeficient persons living at high density could also be the seed-bed for microorganisms that are initially ill adapted to human infection to evolve into transmissible human pathogens. Thus, an infection from a zoonotic or environmental source—for example, the *Mycobacterium avium intracellulare* complex—could conceivably emerge as the tuberculosis of the twenty-first century, although direct transmission between individuals with AIDS of such opportunistic infections have not been documented so far.

We shall give Girolamo Frascatoro the last word on emerging and re-emerging infectious diseases by quoting from his treatise *De Contagione*, published almost 450 years ago, "There will come yet other new and unusual ailments in the course of time. And this disease [syphilis] will pass way, but it later will be born again and be seen by our descendents."

Acknowledgments

We are grateful to M. E. Chamberland, H. W. Jaffe and S. Leff for critically reading the manuscript.

Competing interests statement

The authors declare that they have no competing financial interests.

Notes

1 Burnet, F. M. & White, D. *Natural History of Infectious Disease* (Cambridge Univ. Press, Cambridge, 1972).
2 McMichael, A. J. *Human Frontiers, Environments and Disease. Past patterns, uncertain futures* (Cambridge Univ. Press, Cambridge, 2001).
3 Morens, D. M., Folkers, G. K. & Fauci, A. S. The challenge of emerging and re-emerging infectious diseases. *Nature* **430**, 242–249 (2004).
4 McMichael, A. J. Environmental and social influences on emerging infectious diseases: past, present and future. *Philos. Trans. R. Soc. Lond. B. Biol. Sci.* **359**, 1049–1058 (2004).
5 McMichael, A. J., McKee, M., Shkolnikov, V. & Valkonen, T. Mortality trends and setbacks: global convergence or divergence? *Lancet* **363**, 1155–1159 (2004).
6 Garrett, L. *Betrayal of Trust: the Collapse of Global Public Health* (Hyperion, New York, 2000).
7 Johnson, N. P. & Mueller, J. Updating the accounts: global mortality of the 1918–1920 "Spanish" influenza pandemic. *Bull. Hist. Med.* **76**, 105–115 (2002).
8 Webby, R., Hoffmann, E. & Webster, R. Molecular constraints to interspecies transmission of viral pathogens. *Nat. Med.* **10**, S77–S81 (2004).
9 Palese, P. Influenza: old and new threats. *Nat. Med.* **10**, S82–S87 (2004).
10 De Clercq, E. Antivirals and antiviral strategies. *Nat. Rev. Microbiol.* **2**, 704–720 (2004).
11 Taylor, L. H., Latham, S. M. & Woolhouse, M. E. Risk factors for human disease emergence. *Philos. Trans. R. Soc. Lond. B. Biol. Sci.* **356**, 983–939 (2001).
12 Weiss, R. A. Virulence and pathogenesis. *Trends Microbiol.* **10**, 314–317 (2002).
13 Speck, R. S. Cholera. in *The Cambridge World History of Human Disease* (ed. Kiple, K. F.) 642–647 (Cambridge Univ. Press, Cambridge, 1993).
14 Raoult, D. *et al.* Jail fever (epidemic typhus) outbreak in Burundi. *Emerg. Infect. Dis.* **3**, 357–360 (1997).
15 McNeill, W. H. *Plagues and Peoples* (Penguin, London, 1976).
16 Drancourt, M. *et al.* Genotyping, orientalis-like *Yersinia pestis*, and plague pandemics. *Emerg. Infect. Dis.* **10**, 1585–1592 (2004).
17 Diamond, J. *Guns, Germs and Steel. A Short History of Everybody for the Last 13,000 Years* (Jonathan Cape, London, 1997).
18 Duffy, J. Smallpox and the Indians in the American colonies. *Bull. Hist. Med.* **25**, 324–341 (1951).
19 Anderson, R. M. & May, R. M. *Infectious Diseases of Humans: Dynamics and Control* (Oxford Univ. Press, 1992).
20 Patz, J. A. *et al.* Unhealthy landscapes: Policy recommendations on land use change and infectious disease emergence. *Environ. Health. Perspect.* **112**, 1092–1098 (2004).
21 Chua, K. B. *et al.* Fatal encephalitis due to Nipah virus among pig-farmers in Malaysia. *Lancet* **354**, 1257–1259 (1999).
22 Halpin, K., Young, P. L., Field, H. & Mackenzie, J. S. Newly discovered viruses of flying foxes. *Vet. Microbiol.* **68**, 83–87 (1999).
23 Parmenter, R., Brunt, J., Moore, D. & Ernest, S. The hantavirus epidemic in the southwest: rodent population dynamics and the implications for transmission

of hantavirus-associated adult respiratory distress syndrome (HARDS) in the four corners region. *Sevilleta LTER Publ. (University of New Mexico)* **41**, 1–44 (1993).

24 Engelthaler, D. M. *et al.* Climatic and environmental patterns associated with hantavirus pulmonary syndrome, Four Corners region, United States. *Emerg. Infect. Dis.* **5**, 87–94 (1999).

25 MacKenzie, J. S., Gubler, D. J. & Petersen, L. R. Emerging flaviviruses: the spread and resurgence of Japanese encephalitis, West Nile and dengue viruses. *Nat. Med.* **10**, S98–S109 (2004).

26 Frenzen, F. D. Deaths due to unknown foodborne agents. *Emerg. Infect. Dis.* **10**, 1536–1543 (2004).

27 Will, R. G. *et al.* A new variant of Creutzfeldt-Jakob disease in the UK. *Lancet* **347**, 921–925(1996).

28 Schwartz, M. *How the Cows Turned Mad* (University of California Press, London, 2003).

29 Wilson, K. & Ricketts, M. N. Transfusion transmission of vCJD: a crisis avoided? *Lancet* **364**, 477–479 (2004).

30 Koopmans, M. *et al.* Transmission of H7N7 avian influenza A virus to human beings during a large outbreak in commercial poultry farms in the Netherlands. *Lancet* **363**, 587–593 (2004).

31 Lee, K. & KewalRamani, V. N. In defense of the cell: TRIM5α interception of mammalian retroviruses. *Proc. Natl. Acad. Sci. USA* **101**, 10496–10497 (2004).

32 Hahn, B. H., Shaw, G. M., De Cock, K. M. & Sharp, P. M. AIDS as a zoonosis: scientific and public health implications. *Science* **287**, 607–614 (2000).

33 Brockmann, D. Dynamics of epidemics spread across airline networks. in *SARS: A Case Study in Emerging Infections* (eds. McLean, A. R., May, R., Pattison, J. R. & Weiss, R. A.) (Oxford Univ. Press, Oxford, 2005).

34 Caldwell, J. C. Rethinking the African AIDS epidemic. *Popul. Dev. Rev.* **26**, 117–135 (2000).

35 Butler, C. HIV and AIDS, poverty, and causation. *Lancet* **356**, 1445–1446 (2000).

36 Auvert, B. *et al.* Ecological and individual level analysis of risk factors for HIV infection in four urban populations in sub-Saharan Africa with different levels of HIV infection. *AIDS* **15** Suppl 4, S15–S30 (2001).

37 Johnson, A. M. *et al.* Sexual behaviour in Britain: partnerships, practices, and HIV risk behaviours. *Lancet* **358**, 1835–1842 (2001).

38 Morse, S. S. Factors in the emergence of infectious diseases. *Emerg. Infect. Dis.* **1**, 7–15 (1995).

39 Cohen, A. Urban unfinished business. *Int. J. Environ. Health Res.* **13**, S29–S36 (2003).

40 Tiemersma, D. W. *et al.* Methicillin-resistant *Staphylococcus aureus* in Europe, 1999–2002. *Emerg. Infect. Dis.* **10**, 1627–1634 (2004).

41 Blower, S. M. & Chou, T. Modeling the emergence of the 'hot zones': tuberculosis and the amplification dynamics of drug resistance. *Nat. Med.* **10**, 1111–1116 (2004).

42 Drucker, E., Alcabes, P. G. & Marx, P. A. The injection century: massive unsterile injections and the emergence of human pathogens. *Lancet* **358**, 1989–1992 (2001).

43 Darby, S. C. *et al.* Mortality before and after HIV infection in the complete UK population of haemophiliacs. *Nature* **377**, 79–82 (1995).

44 Pealer, L. N. *et al.* Transmission of West Nile virus through blood transfusion in the United States in 2002. *N. Engl. J. Med.* **349**, 1236–1245 (2003).

45 Iwamoto, M. *et al.* Transmission of West Nile virus from an organ donor to four transplant recipients. *N. Engl. J. Med.* **348**, 2196–2203 (2003).

46 Butel, J. S. & Lednicky, J. A. Cell and molecular biology of simian virus 40: implications for human infections and disease. *J. Natl. Cancer. Inst.* **91**, 119–134 (1999).

47 zur Hausen, H. SV40 in human cancers—an endless tale? *Int. J. Cancer.* **107**, 687 (2003).

48 Patience, C., Takeuchi, Y. & Weiss, R. A. Infection of human cells by an endogenous retrovirus of pigs. *Nat. Med.* **3**, 282–286 (1997).

49 Weiss, R. A. Transgenic pigs and virus adaptation. *Nature* **391**, 327–328 (1998).

50 Magre, S. *et al.* Reduced sensitivity to human serum inactivation of enveloped viruses produced by pig cells transgenic for human CD55 or deficient for the galactosyl-α(1–3) galactosyl epitope. *J. Virol.* **78**, 5812–5819 (2004).

51 Weiss, R. A. Gulliver's travels in HIVland. *Nature* **410**, 963–967 (2001).

52 Weiss, R. A. & McLean, A. R. What have we learnt from SARS? *Philos. Trans. R. Soc. Lond. B. Biol. Sci.* **359**, 1137–1140 (2004).

53 Hale, P. *et al.* Mission now possible for AIDS fund. *Nature* **412**, 271–272 (2001).

54 Perel, P., McGuire, M., Eapen, K. & Ferraro, A. Research on preventing road traffic injuries in developing countries is needed. *BMJ* **328**, 895 (2004).

55 Peiris, J. S. M., Guan, Y. & Yuen, K. Y. Severe acute respiratory syndrome. *Nat. Med.* **10**, S88–S97 (2004).

56 Levy, S. B. & Marshall, B. Antimicrobial resistance worldwide: causes, challenges and responses. *Nat. Med.* **10**, S122–S129 (2004).

57 Bell, D., Roberton, S. & Hunter, P. R. Animal origins of SARS coronavirus: possible links with the international trade in small carnivores. *Philos. Trans. R. Soc. Lond. B. Biol. Sci.* **359**, 1107–1114 (2004).

58 Mahy, B. W. J. Zoonoses and haemorrhagic fever, in *Safety of Biological Products Prepared from Mammalian Cell Culture. Dev. Biol. Stand.* **93** (eds. Brown, F., Griffiths, E., Horaud, F. & Petricciani, J. C.) 31–36 (Karger, Basel, 1998).

59 Wolfe, N. D. *et al.* Naturally acquired simian retrovirus infections in central African hunters. *Lancet* **363**, 932–927 (2004).

60 Di Giulio, D. B. & Eckburg, P. B. Human monkeypox: an emerging zoonosis. *Lancet Infect. Dis.* **4**, 15–25 (2004).

93

TRAVEL AND THE EMERGENCE OF INFECTIOUS DISEASES

Mary E. Wilson

Source: *Emerging Infectious Diseases*, 1:2 (1995), 39–46.

Travel is a potent force in the emergence of disease. Migration of humans has been the pathway for disseminating infectious diseases throughout recorded history and will continue to shape the emergence, frequency, and spread of infections in geographic areas and populations. The current volume, speed, and reach of travel are unprecedented. The consequences of travel extend beyond the traveler to the population visited and the ecosystem. When they travel, humans carry their genetic makeup, immunologic sequelae of past infections, cultural preferences, customs, and behavioral patterns. Microbes, animals, and other biologic life also accompany them. Today's massive movement of humans and materials sets the stage for mixing diverse genetic pools at rates and in combinations previously unknown. Concomitant changes in the environment, climate, technology, land use, human behavior, and demographics converge to favor the emergence of infectious diseases caused by a broad range of organisms in humans, as well as in plants and animals.

Many factors contribute to the emergence of infectious diseases. Those frequently identified include microbial adaptation and change, human demographics and behavior, environmental changes, technology and economic development, breakdown in public health measures and surveillance, and international travel and commerce (1–4). This paper will examine the pivotal role of global travel and movement of biologic life in the emergence of infectious diseases. It will also examine the ways in which travel and movement are inextricably tied at multiple levels to other processes that influence the emergence of disease.

Travel is a potent force in disease emergence and spread (5). The current volume, speed, and reach of travel are unprecedented. The consequences of migration extend beyond the traveler to the population visited and the ecosystem (6). Travel and trade set the stage for mixing diverse genetic pools at rates and in combinations previously unknown. Massive movement and other concomitant changes in social, political, climatic, environmental, and technologic factors converge to favor the emergence of infectious diseases.

Disease emergence is complex. Often several events must occur simultaneously or sequentially for a disease to emerge or reemerge (Table 1) (6). Travel allows a potentially pathogenic microbe to be introduced into a new geographic area; however, to be established and cause disease a microbe must survive, proliferate, and find a way to enter a susceptible host. Any analysis of emergence must look at a dynamic process, a sequence of events, a milieu, or ecosystem.

Movement, changing patterns of resistance and vulnerability, and the emergence of infectious diseases also affect plants, animals, and insect vectors. Analysis of these species can hold important lessons about the dynamics of human disease.

To assess the impact of travel on disease emergence, it is necessary to consider the receptivity of a geographic area and its population to microbial introduction. Most introductions do not lead to disease. Organisms that survive primarily or entirely in the human host and are spread through sexual contact, droplet nuclei, and close physical contact can be readily carried to any part of the world. For example, AIDS, tuberculosis, measles, pertussis, diphtheria, and hepatitis B are easily carried by travelers and can spread in a new geographic area; however, populations protected by vaccines resist introduction. Organisms that have animal hosts, environmental limitations, arthropod vectors, or complicated life cycles become successively more difficult to "transplant" to another geographic area or population. Epidemics of dengue fever and yellow fever cannot appear in a geographic area unless

Table 1 Basic concepts in disease emergence.*

Emergence of infectious diseases is complex.

Infectious diseases are dynamic.

Most new infections are not caused by genuinely new pathogens.

Agents involved in new and reemergent infections cross taxonomic lines to include viruses, bacteria, fungi, protozoa, and helminths.

The concept of the microbe as *the* cause of disease is inadequate and incomplete.

Human activities are the most potent factors driving disease emergence.

Social, economic, political, climatic, technologic, and environmental factors shape disease patterns and influence emergence.

Understanding and responding to disease emergence require a global perspective, conceptually and geographically.

The current global situation favors disease emergence.

---

*Adapted from Wilson ME (6).

competent mosquito vectors are present. Schistosomiasis cannot spread in an environment unless a suitable snail intermediate host exists in that region. Organisms that survive only under carefully tuned local conditions are less likely to be successfully introduced. Even if an introduced parasite persists in a new geographic area, it does not necessarily cause human disease. In the United States, humans infected with *Taenia solium*, the parasite that causes cysticercosis, infrequently transmit the infection because sanitary disposal of feces, the source of the eggs, is generally available. In short, the likelihood of transmission involves many biological, social, and environmental variables.

Historical perspective

Human migration has been the main source of epidemics throughout recorded history. William McNeill (7), in his book *Plagues and Peoples*, describes the central role of infectious disease in the history of the world. Patterns of disease circulation have influenced the outcome of wars and have shaped the location, nature, and development of human societies.

Trade caravans, religious pilgrimages, and military maneuvers facilitated the spread of many diseases, including plague and smallpox. A map in Donald Hopkins' book, *Princes and Peasants: Smallpox in History* (8), traces the presumed spread of smallpox from Egypt or India, where it was first thought to have become adapted to humans sometime before 1000 B.C. Smallpox spread easily from person to person through close contact with respiratory discharges and, less commonly, through contact with skin lesions, linens, clothing, and other material in direct contact with the patient. Because patients remained infectious for about 3 weeks, many opportunities for transmission were available. Even in this century, until the 1970s, smallpox continued to cause epidemics. A pilgrim returning from Mecca was the source of a large outbreak in Yugoslavia in the early 1970s that resulted in 174 Yugoslav cases and 35 deaths (9). The pilgrim apparently contracted the infection in Baghdad while visiting a religious site. Because his symptoms were mild, he was never confined to bed and was able to continue his travels and return home.

For most of history, human populations were relatively isolated. Only in recent centuries has there been extensive contact between the flora and fauna of the Old and New Worlds. Schoolchildren hear the rhyme "Columbus sailed the ocean blue, in fourteen hundred ninety-two," but may learn little about the disaster brought upon the native populations of the Americas by the arriving explorers. By the end of the fifteenth century, measles, influenza, mumps, smallpox, tuberculosis, and other infections had become common in Europe. Explorers from the crowded urban centers of Europe brought infectious diseases to the New World (10), where isolated populations had evolved from a relatively small gene pool and had no previous experience with many infections (11). The first epidemics following the arrival of Europeans were often the most severe. By 1518 or 1519, smallpox appeared in Santo Domingo, where it killed one-third to half of the local population and spread to other areas of the Caribbean and the Americas (10). The population of central Mexico is estimated to have dropped by one-third in the single decade following contact with the Europeans.

Travel across the Atlantic Ocean transformed the flora and fauna of the New World as well. Some of the transported materials became important sources of food (plants), clothing, and transportation (animals). Other transfers were less welcome: Japanese beetles, Dutch elm disease, and chestnut tree fungus. A. W. Crosby, exploring these exchanges between the Old and the New Worlds, sounds a pessimistic note: "The Columbian exchange has left us with not a richer but a more impoverished genetic pool" (10).

The explorers also paid a price in loss of lives from disease. Philip Curtin (12) provides a quantitative study of "relocation costs," the excess illness and death among European soldiers in the nineteenth century when they lived or worked in the tropics. Until the most recent armed conflicts, infectious diseases claimed more lives than injuries during wars.

Plague holds a prominent place in history and remains with us today. A bacterial infection caused by *Yersinia pestis*, it is primarily an infection of rodents, spread by their fleas. Human infection is incidental to the maintenance of *Y. pestis* in animal reservoirs. Yet plague periodically has erupted in human populations, wreaking great devastation, killing millions and causing infection that can be spread directly from person to person by the respiratory route. Human population movement has been essential in the spread of plague and the dispersal of rodents and their fleas to new areas. For centuries plague spread along trade routes. It reached California by boat around the turn of this century, caused epidemic infection in San Francisco, and then spread to wildlife, where it persists today in a large enzootic focus.

Movement of people

Travel for business and pleasure constitutes a small fraction of total human movement (5,13). People migrating individually or in groups, may be immigrants, refugees, missionaries, merchant marines, students, temporary workers, pilgrims, or Peace Corps workers. Travel may involve short distances or the crossing of international borders. Its volume, however, is huge. In the early 1990s more than 500 million persons annually crossed international borders on commercial airplane flights (World Tourism Organization, Madrid, unpublished data). An estimated 70 million persons, mostly from developing countries, work either legally or illegally in other countries (14). Movement may be temporary or seasonal, as with nomadic populations and migrant workers who follow the crops. Military maneuvers worldwide employ and move huge populations. The consequences of armed conflict and political unrest displace millions. In the early 1990s, there were an estimated 20 million refugees and 30 million displaced persons worldwide (International Organization for Migration, personal communication).

Grubler and Nakicenovic estimated and plotted the average kilometers traveled daily for the French population over a 200-year period (1800–2000) and found that spatial mobility has increased more than 1000-fold (15). In the last 40 years, the size of Australia's population has doubled and the number of persons moving into and out of Australia has increased nearly 100-fold (16).

Although social, economic, and political factors push people from an area or draw them to another, environmental resources and their impact on food and water supplies are behind many conflicts leading to displacement of populations. Acute disasters, such as flooding, earthquakes, and hurricanes often force populations to seek shelter and sustenance in new lands. Chronic changes, such as drought, depletion of soil, and disappearance of fish from streams, lakes, and oceans, draw people to new territories, or, more frequently, to the fringes of large urban centers.

Another type of travel relevant to disease emergence is the shift of populations to urban areas. It is estimated that by the year 2010, 50% of the world's population will be living in urban areas. It is projected that by the year 2000, the world will comprise 24 "megacities"—sprawling metropolitan areas with populations exceeding 10 million (World Bank, UNDP, World Health Organization, unpublished data). These areas will have the population density to support persistence of some infections and contribute to the emergence of others. Many of these areas are located in tropical or subtropical regions, where the environment can support a diverse array of pathogens and vectors. Also developing are huge periurban slums, populated with persons from many geographic origins. Poor sanitation allows breeding of arthropod vectors, rodents, and other disease-carrying animals. Crowded conditions favor the spread of diseases that pass from person to person, including sexually transmitted infections. Travel between periurban slum areas and rural areas is common, paving the route for the transfer of microbes and disease. Transfer of resistance genes and genetic recombination may also occur in and spread from crowded environments of transients.

Acute disturbances, whether climatic or political, lead to interim living arrangements, such as refugee camps and temporary shelters, that provide ideal conditions for the emergence and spread of infections. Temporary living quarters often share similarities with periurban slums: crowding, inadequate sanitation, limited access to medical care, lack of clean water and food, dislocation, multiethnic composition, and inadequate barriers from vectors and animals. An example is the movement of 500,000–800,000 Rwandan refugees into Zaire in 1994. Almost 50,000 refugees died during the first month as epidemics of cholera and *Shigella dysenteriae* type 1 swept through the refugee camps (17).

Movement into a rural environment poses different risks and often places new rural populations in contact with pathogens that are in the soil and water or are carried by animals or arthropods (18). Some of these pathogens such as Guanarito (19) and Sabià viruses (20) in South America, were only recently recognized as capable of infecting humans.

Consequences of movement

Human migration favors the emergence of infectious diseases through many mechanisms. When people migrate, they carry their genetic makeup, their accumulated immunologic experience, and much more (Table 2). They may carry pathogens in or on their bodies and may also transport disease vectors, such as lice. Their technology (agricultural and industrial), methods for treating disease, cultural traditions, and behavioral patterns may influence their risk for infection in a new environment and their capacity to introduce disease into the new region. Their social standing and resources may affect their exposure to local infections and their access to adequate nutrition and treatment. People also change the environment in many ways when they travel or migrate—they plant, clear land, build, and consume. Travel is relevant in the emergence of disease if it changes an ecosystem. The following examples show the many ways in which migration can influence the emergence of disease in a new area.

1. Humans may carry a pathogen in a form that can be transmitted, then or later, directly or indirectly to another person. The pathogen may be silent (during the incubation period, chronic carriage, or latent infection) or clinically evident. Examples include hepatitis B virus, human immunodeficiency virus (HIV), *Mycobacterium tuberculosis, M. leprae, Salmonella typhi,* and other salmonella. Disease may be especially severe when a pathogen is introduced into a population that has no previous exposure to the infection. How long the consequences of migration persist varies with the specific infection. The two most critical characteristics are the duration of survival of the pathogen in a potentially infective form and its means of transmission.

2. Epidemic cholera in Africa spread along the West African coast and, when the disease moved inland, followed fishing and trading routes. Markets, funerals, refugee camps—events that involved migration of

Table 2 What is carried by humans into new regions?

Pathogens in or on body
Microbiologic flora
Vectors on body
Immunologic sequelae of past infections
Vulnerability to infections
Genetic makeup
Cultural preferences, customs, behavioral patterns, technology
Luggage and whatever it contains

---

persons and large gatherings with close contact—helped spread the infection. With El Tor cholera, asymptomatic and mild infections can outnumber severe disease by 100 to 1 (21), thus permitting those infected to continue to move and work.

3. Pilgrims carried an epidemic strain of group A *Neisseria meningitidis* from southern Asia to Mecca in 1987. Other pilgrims who became colonized with the epidemic strain introduced it into sub-Saharan Africa, where it caused a wave of epidemics in 1988 and 1989 (22).

4. Humans may carry a pathogen that can be transmitted only if conditions are permissive. This permissiveness can pertain to human behavior, the environment, or the presence of appropriate vectors or intermediate hosts. For example, the ease with which HIV spreads in a population depends on sexual practices, condom use, the number of sex partners, and intravenous drug use, among other factors. Malaria requires specific mosquito vectors (with access to susceptible humans) to spread to new geographic regions. Schistosomiasis can be introduced into a new region only if the appropriate snail host is present and if the eggs excreted (in urine or feces, from an infected person), reach the snails in an appropriate environment.

5. Humans may carry a strain of microbe that has an unusual resistance pattern or virulence genes. A multiple-drug-resistant strain of *Klebsiella pneumoniae* appears to have been transferred by an asymptomatic woman from a hospital in Bahrain to Oxford, where it caused outbreaks in two British hospitals (23). People also carry their background flora, in the intestinal tract, for example, which may contain plasmids and resistance genes that can interact with microbes in a new area. It is not just the classic pathogens that may be relevant to the emergence of a new disease but the individual traveler's total microbiologic "baggage."

6. Visitors to a region may lack immunity to locally endemic infections, such as hepatitis A and sand-fly fever. Visitors may suffer severe or different manifestations of infection or disease at an age when the local population is immune to it. Resettlement of populations into malaria-endemic regions can lead to a high death rate from falciparum malaria.

7. Kala-azar caused a deadly outbreak in remote villages in southern Sudan in 1994. The origin was thought to be the villagers' exposure to the sand-fly vector during migration to a food distribution center that had been established by a relief organization (24). The migration took a malnourished population from a nonendemic zone into the southern part of the kala-azar–endemic zone. Unfamiliarity with the disease and the poor nutritional status of the population probably contributed to a high death rate (24).

8. Behavioral patterns in a new region may place visitors at risk for infection, while the local population, possibly because of their knowledge of disease risks, may not be at risk. Behavior patterns may involve food

preparation (such as eating some foods raw), clothing (or lack of it), (for example, going barefooted), sleeping arrangements (sleeping on the ground or out of doors in an unscreened area), and contact with animals.

9. Susceptibility of a population may vary because of genetic differences. A microbe introduced into a new region may have a greater or lesser impact, depending on the host population. Genetic factors influence susceptibility to and expression of several infectious diseases. Although these interactions are not yet well defined for most infections, genetic factors influence infections caused by different classes of organisms, including cholera (25,26), parvovirus infection (27), malaria, and *Helicobacter pylori* infection (28).

To determine the consequences of travel both the traveler and the population visited must be considered. Migration may be in only one direction, though travel often involves returning to the point of origin, perhaps after the traveler has made many stops along the way. The changes in the various ecosystems as a consequence of the migration guide the emergence of diseases; any study that simply focuses on the traveler is too narrow.

The distance traversed is less important than the differences in biological life in different areas and differences in receptivity and vulnerability. In thinking about disease emergence, what matters is the potential of a disease to appear in a place, population, or extent not previously reported.

What is the long-term impact of migration and travel on human disease? Carriage of pathogens is only part of the influence on disease emergence. Introduced technology, farming methods, treatment and drugs, chemicals, and pesticides may have a far greater and longer impact on disease patterns in a region than the life of a person. Deforestation, building of dams, and opening of roads into previously inaccessible areas have all been associated with population movements and changes in distribution and frequency of a variety of infections in humans (such as malaria, schistosomiasis, Rift Valley fever, and sexually transmitted diseases).

Increasingly the vehicle of transportation is the site or even the source of outbreaks. During travel, people from diverse origins are enclosed in close proximity for a hours or days and then discharged to move on to many distant places. These temporary new habitats, jumbo jets or huge ocean liners, can be the sites for dissemination of the microbes (as happens, for example with *Legionella pneumophila* infections (29), foodborne infections, and cholera) or provide a milieu for person-to-person transmission (influenza, tuberculosis (30,31)).

Shipping and commerce

The biomass of humans constitutes only a fraction of the matter moved about the earth. Humans carry and send a huge volume of plants, animals and other materials all over the face of the globe. Much of this movement results from the planned transport of goods from one place to another, but some is an unintended consequence of shipping and travel. All has an impact on the juxtaposition of various species in different ecosystems. "Hitchhikers" include all manner of biologic life, both microscopic and macroscopic. Animals can carry potential human pathogens and vectors. The globalization of markets brings fresh fruits and vegetables to dinner tables thousands of miles from where they were grown, fertilized, and picked. Tunnels, bridges, and ferries form means to traverse natural barriers to species spread. The roads built to transport people often speed the movement of diseases from one area to another. Mass processing and wide distribution networks allow for the amplification and wide dissemination of potential human microbes.

Examples of introduced species include plants and animals—insects, microbes, and marine organisms.

1. Ships convey marine organisms on their hulls and in their ballast water. For example, 367 different species were identified in ballast water of ships traveling between Japan and Coos Bay, Oregon (32). Introductions have had devastating effects in some areas, for example such as the Black and Azov seas, where newly introduced jellyfishlike creatures called ctenophores have ruined local fishing (33).

2. *Vibrio cholerae* may have been introduced to South America by shipping (34). Researchers isolated the organism in samples of ballast, bilge, and sewage from 3 of 14 cargo ships docked at Gulf of Mexico ports. The ships had last ports of call in Brazil, Colombia, and Chile (35). *V. cholerae* O1, serotype Inaba, biotype El Tor, indistinguishable from the Latin American epidemic strain, was found in oysters and oyster-eating fish from closed oyster beds in Mobile Bay, Alabama (36). *V. cholerae* O139 has spread along waterways in Asia, although the people carried on the boats doubtless played a role (37,38).

3. *Aedes albopictus* was introduced into the United States inside used tires shipped from Asia (39,40). The mosquito's introduction causes concern because it is an aggressive biter, survives in both forest and suburban habitats, and appears to be a competent vector for several human pathogens. It has been associated with epidemic dengue fever transmission in Asia and is a competent laboratory vector of La Crosse, yellow fever, and other viruses (41). In Florida, 14 strains of eastern equine encephalitis virus have been isolated from *A. albopictus* (42). The mosquito is now established in at least 21 of the contiguous states in United States and in Hawaii.

4. The African anopheles mosquitoes arrived in Brazil in about 1929. This vector could breed under conditions other New World mosquitoes could not. Although the malaria parasite was already found in Brazil, this new vector expanded the range of transmission. An estimated 20,000 persons died of malaria before the introduced anopheles mosquitoes were eliminated.

705

5. It has been repeatedly demonstrated that mosquitoes are present—and survive—on international flights. In random searches of airplanes in London, mosquitoes were found on 12 of 67 airplanes from tropical countries (43). Arthropods can survive even more extreme environments. In one study, mosquitoes, house flies, and beetles placed in wheel bays of Boeing 747B aircraft survived flights of 6–9 hours with external temperatures of -42°C (43). Airplanes have also carried infective mosquitoes that caused human infection outside malaria-endemic areas (in Europe, for example).

6. Vehicles can transport vectors over land. *Glossina palpalis*, a vector for African trypanosomiasis (sleeping sickness), can fly up to 21 km but can be transported much longer distances on animals and in land vehicles.

7. Seven persons in Marburg, Germany, died after handling blood and tissues from African green monkeys from Uganda. The tissues contained an organism later named Marburg virus (44).

8. Exotic animals transported from their usual habitats are clustered in zoos; others are used in research laboratories where they have occasionally caused severe disease in humans. Two examples are B virus from primates (45) and hemorrhagic fever with renal syndrome from rodents (46).

9. The world trade and globalization of organs, tissues, blood, and blood products is growing. Researchers are considering animals as sources for tissues and organs for transplantation (47).

10. Plants may not directly cause human disease. But they can alter an ecosystem and facilitate the breeding of a vector for human disease. This can also displace traditional crops that provide essential nutrition. Vertical transmission of plant pathogens (and spread of plant diseases) can result from seed movement (48). Carriage of seeds into new areas can introduce plant pathogens.

11. Migration and altered environments have increased the so-called weedy species. These species migrate easily and have high rates of reproduction. If they lack local predators, they can displace other species and often upset local ecology.

Introduction of species into new areas

Introducing species into new geographic areas is not new, but the current volume and frequency of introductions are unprecedented. A pathogen's survival and spread in a new environment are determined by its basic reproductive rate, which is the average number of successful offspring a parasite can produce (49). To invade and establish itself in a host population, a parasitic species must have a basic reproductive rate exceeding one (49). The simplicity of this statement belies the complexity of circumstances that influence invasion and persistence. These circumstances encompass biological, social, and environmental factors.

As noted already, factors that can influence receptivity include climate and environmental conditions, sanitation, socioeconomic conditions (50), behavior, nutrition, and genetics. *V. cholerae* persists in an aquatic reservoir off the Gulf Coast of the United States, yet epidemic cholera has not been a problem in the United States. Where poverty and poor sanitation prevail, the presence of *V. cholerae* can be a source of endemic disease and periodic epidemics.

Disease emergence is often complex. An outbreak of malaria in San Diego, California, occurred when parasitemic migrant workers were employed in an area where mosquitoes capable of transmitting malaria had access to the workers and to a susceptible human population (51). Many conditions had to be met to allow transmission.

Migration may introduce parasites into an area where a different intermediate host or vector could change the incidence of disease. Cycling through a different host can lead to different transmission rates, different infectivity, and even different clinical expression. A parasite may be more successful in a new site because of a larger susceptible population or the absence of predators.

Confluence of events

Massive global travel is taking place simultaneously with many other processes that favor the emergence of disease. For example, the human population is more vulnerable because of aging, immunosuppression from medical treatment and disease (such as AIDS), the presence of prostheses (e.g., artificial heart valves and joints), exposure to chemicals and environmental pollutants that may act synergistically with microbes to increase the risk of diseases, increased poverty, crowding and stress, and increased exposure to UV radiation. Technologic changes, while providing many benefits, can also promote disease dissemination. Resistance of microbes and insects to antimicrobial drugs and pesticides interferes with the control of infections and allows transmission to continue. Changes in land use can alter the presence and abundance of vectors and intermediate hosts.

Microbes are enormously resilient and adaptable. They have short life spans, which allow rapid genetic change. Humans, by comparison, are slow to change genetically but can change their behavior. People move and construct barriers to prevent contact with microparasites, macroparasites, and the extremes of the environment. Technology fosters a perception of human invincibility but actually creates new vulnerabilities, as it enables us to go deeper, higher, and into more remote and hostile environments. Studies show that no place on earth is devoid of microbes. Their range and resiliency are truly phenomenal. Only a fraction of the existing microbes have been characterized. Travel and exploration provide a greater opportunity for humans to come into unsampled regions with these uncharacterized microbes.

Summary and conclusions

Global travel and the evolution of microbes will continue. New infections will continue to emerge, and known infections will change in distribution, severity and frequency. Travel will continue to be a potent factor in disease emergence. The current world circumstances juxtapose people, parasites, plants, animals, and chemicals in a way that precludes timely adaptation. The combination of movement at many levels and profound change in the physical environment can lead to unanticipated diseases spread by multiple channels. In many instances, the use of containment or quarantine is not feasible. Research and surveillance can map the global movement and evolution of microbes and guide interventions. Integration of knowledge and skills from many disciplines—the social, biological, and physical sciences—is needed. The focus should be system analysis and the ecosystem rather than a disease, microbe, or host.

References

1. Lederberg J., Shope R. E., Oaks S. C., Jr., eds. Emerging infections: microbial threats to health in the United States. Washington, D.C.: National Academy Press, 1992.
2. Centers for Disease Control and Prevention. Addressing emerging infectious disease threats: a prevention strategy for the United States. Atlanta: U.S. Department of Health and Human Services, 1994.
3. Wilson M. E., Levins R., Spielman A. Disease in evolution: global changes and emergence of infectious diseases. New York: New York Academy of Sciences, 1994;740.
4. Levins R., Awerbuch T., Brinkmann U., et al. The emergence of new diseases. American Scientist 1994;82:52–60.
5. Wilson M. E. A world guide to infections: diseases, distribution, diagnosis. New York: Oxford University Press, 1991.
6. Wilson M. E. Disease in evolution: introduction. In: Wilson M. E., Levins R., Spielman A., eds. Disease in evolution: global changes and emergence of infectious diseases. New York: New York Academy of Sciences, 1994;740:1–12.
7. McNeill W. H. Plagues and peoples. Garden City, N.Y.: Anchor Press/Doubleday, 1976.
8. Hopkins D. R. Princes and peasants: smallpox in history. Chicago: University of Chicago Press, 1983.
9. World Health Organization. Smallpox: Yugoslavia. Wkly Epidemiol Rec 1972;47:161–2.
10. Crosby A. W., Jr. The Columbian exchange. Westport, Conn. Greenwood Press, 1972:219.
11. Black F. L. Why did they die? Science 1992;258:1739–40.
12. Curtin P. D. Death by migration: Europe's encounter with the tropical world in the nineteenth century. Cambridge, U.K.: Cambridge University Press, 1989.

13. Bradley D. J. The scope of travel medicine: an introduction to the conference on international travel medicine. In: Steffen R., Lobel H. O., Haworth J., Bradley, eds. Travel Medicine. Berlin: Springer-Verlag, 1989:1–9.

14. Siem H., Bollini P., eds. Migration and health in the 1990s. International Migration 1992;30.

15. Grubler A., Nakicenovic N. Evolution of transport systems. Laxenburg, Vienna: ILASA, 1991.

16. Haggett P. Geographical aspects of the emergence of infectious diseases. Geogr Ann 1994;76 B(2):91–104.

17. Goma Epidemiology Group. Public health impact of Rwandan refugee crisis: what happened in Goma, Zaire, in July, 1994? Lancet 1995;345:339–44.

18. Meslin F.-X. Surveillance and control of emerging zoonoses. World Health Stat Q 1992;45:200–7.

19. Tesh R. B., Jahrling R., Salas R., Shope R. E. Description of Guanarito virus (Arenaviridae: *Arenavirus*), the etiologic agent of Venezuelan hemorrhagic fever. Am J Trop Med Hyg 1994;50:452–9.

20. Coimbra T. L. M., Nassar E. S., Burattini N. M., et al. A new arenavirus isolated from a fatal case of haemorrhagic fever in Brazil. Lancet 1994;343:391–2.

21. Glass R. I., Claeson M., Blake P. A., Waldman R. J., Pierce N. R. Cholera in Africa: lessons on transmission and control for Latin America. Lancet 1991;338:791–5.

22. Moore P. S., Reeves M. W., Schwartz B., Gellin B. G., Broome C. V. Intercontinental spread of an epidemic group A *Neisseria meningitidis* strain. Lancet 1989;2:260–3.

23. Cookson B., Johnson A. P., Azadian B., et al. International inter- and intra-hospital patient spread of a multiple antibiotic-resistant *Klebsiella pneumoniae*. J Infect Dis 1995;171:511–3.

24. Mercer A., Seaman J., Sondorp E. Kala azar in eastern Upper Nile Province, southern Sudan. Lancet 1995;345:187–8.

25. Glass R. I., Holmgren I., Haley C. E., et al. Predisposition to cholera of individuals with O blood group. Am J Epidemiol 1985;121:791–6.

26. Clemens J. D., Sack D. A., Harris J. R., et al. ABO blood groups and cholera: new observations on specificity of risk and modifications of vaccine efficacy. J Infect Dis 1989;159:770–3.

27. Brown K. E., Hibbs J. R., Gallinella G., et al. Resistance to parvovirus B19 infection due to lack of virus receptor (erythrocyte P antigen). N Engl J Med 1994;330:1192–6.

28. Boren T., Falk P., Roth K. A., Larson G., Normark S. Attachment of *Helicobacter pylori* to human gastric epithelium mediated by blood group antigens. Science 1993;292:1982–95.

29. Centers for Disease Control and Prevention. Update: outbreak of Legionnaires' disease associated with a cruise ship. MMWR 1994;43:574–5.

30. Driver D. R., Valway S. E., Morgan M., Onorato I. M., Castro K. G. Transmission of *Mycobacterium tuberculosis* associated with air travel. JAMA 1994;272:10311–35.

31. Centers for Disease Control and Prevention. Exposure of passengers and flight crew to *Mycobacterium tuberculosis* on commercial aircraft, 1992–1995. MMWR 1995;44:137–40.

32. Carlton J. T., Geller J. B. Ecological roulette: the global transport of nonindigenous marine organisms. Science 1993;261:78–82.

33. Travis J. Invader threatens Black, Azov Seas. Science 1993;262:1366–7.
34. World Health Organization. Cholera in the Americas. Wkly Epidemiol Rec. 1992;67:33–9.
35. McCarthy S. A., McPhearson R. M., Guarino A. M. Toxigenic *Vibrio cholerae* O1 and cargo ships entering Gulf of Mexico. Lancet 1992;339:624–5.
36. DePaola A., Capers G. M., Moters M. L., et al. Isolation of Latin American epidemic strain of *Vibrio cholerae* O1 from US Gulf Coast. Lancet 1992;339:624.
37. Ramamurthy T., Garg S., Sharma R., et al. Emergence of novel strain of *Vibrio cholerae* with epidemic potential in southern and eastern India. Lancet 1993;341:703–4.
38. Albert M. J., Siddique A. K., Islam M. S., et al. Large outbreak of clinical cholera due to *Vibrio cholerae* non-O1 in Bangladesh. Lancet 1993;341:704.
39. Reiter P., Sprenger D. The used tire trade: a mechanism for the worldwide dispersal of container-breeding mosquitoes. J Am Mosq Control Assoc 1987;3:494–501.
40. Craven R. B., Eliason D. A., Francy P., et al. Importation of *Aedes albopictus* and other exotic mosquito species into the United States in used tires from Asia. J Am Mosq Control Assoc 1988;4:138–42.
41. Moore C. G., Francy D. B., Eliason D. A., Monath T. P. *Aedes albopictus* in the United States: rapid spread of a potential disease vector. J Am Mosq Control Assoc 1988;4:356–61.
42. Mitchell C. J., Niebylski M. L., Smith G. C., et al. Isolation of eastern equine encephalitis virus from *Aedes albopictus* in Florida. Science 1992;257:526–7.
43. Russell R. C. Survival of insects in the wheel bays of a Boeing 747B aircraft on flights between tropical and temperate airports. Bull WHO 1987;65:659–62.
44. Martini G. A., Siegert R., eds. Marburg virus disease. Berlin:Springer-Verlag, 1971.
45. Weigler B. J., Hird D. W., Hilliard J. K., Lerche N. W., Roberts J. A., Scott L. M. Epidemiology of cercopithecine herpesvirus 1 (B virus) infection and shedding in a large breeding cohort of rhesus macaques. J Infect Dis 1993;167:257–63.
46. Desmyter J., LeDuc J. W., Johnson K. M., Brasseur F., Deckers C., van Ypersele de Strihou C. Laboratory rat-associated outbreak of haemorrhagic fever with renal syndrome due to Hantaan-like virus in Belgium. Lancet 1983;ii:1445–8.
47. Fishman J. A. Miniature swine as organ donors for man: strategies for prevention of xenotransplant-associated infections. Xenotransplantation 1994;1:47–57.
48. Anderson P. K., Morales F. J. The emergence of new plant diseases: the case of insect-transmitted plant viruses. In: Wilson M. E., Levins R., Spielman A., eds. Disease in evolution: global changes and emergence of infectious diseases. New York: New York Academy of Sciences, 1994;740:181–94.
49. Anderson R. M., May R. M. Infectious diseases of humans: dynamics and control. Oxford, U.K.: Oxford University Press, 1991.
50. Spence D. P. S., Hotchkiss J., Williams C. S. D., Davies P. D. O. Tuberculosis and poverty. Br Med J 1993;307:759–61.
51. Maldonado Y. A., Nahlen B. L., Roberto R. R., et al. Transmission of *Plasmodium vivax* malaria in San Diego County, California, 1986. Am J Trop Med Hyg 1990;42:3–9.

94

ENVIRONMENTAL AND SOCIAL INFLUENCES ON EMERGING INFECTIOUS DISEASES

Past, present and future

A. J. McMichael

Source: *Philosophical Transactions of the Royal Society of London B Biological Science*, 359:1447 (2004), 1049–58.

During the processes of human population dispersal around the world over the past 50 000–100 000 years, along with associated cultural evolution and inter-population contact and conflict, there have been several major transitions in the relationships of *Homo sapiens* with the natural world, animate and inanimate. Each of these transitions has resulted in the emergence of new or unfamiliar infectious diseases.

The three great historical transitions since the initial advent of agriculture and livestock herding, from *ca.* 10 000 years ago, occurred when: (i) early agrarian-based settlements enabled sylvatic enzootic microbes to make contact with *Homo sapiens*; (ii) early Eurasian civilizations (such as the Greek and Roman empires, China and south Asia) came into military and commercial contact, *ca.* 3000–2000 years ago, swapping their dominant infections; and (iii) European expansionism, over the past five centuries, caused the transoceanic spread of often lethal infectious diseases. This latter transition is best known in relation to the conquest of the Americas by Spanish *conquistadores*, when the inadvertent spread of measles, smallpox and influenza devastated the Amerindian populations.

Today, we are living through the fourth of these great transitional periods. The contemporary spread and increased lability of various infectious diseases, new and old, reflect the combined and increasingly widespread impacts of demographic, environmental, behavioural, technological and other rapid changes in human ecology. Modern clinical medicine has, via blood transfusion, organ transplantation, and the use of hypodermic syringes, created new opportunities for microbes. These have contributed to the rising iatrogenic problems of hepatitis C, HIV/AIDS and several other viral infections. Meanwhile, the injudicious use of antibiotics has been a rare instance of human action actually increasing 'biodiversity'.

Another aspect of this fourth transition is that modern hyper-hygienic living restricts microbial exposure in early life. This, in the 1950s, may have contributed to an epidemic of more serious, disabling, poliomyelitis, affecting older children than those affected in earlier, more endemic decades.

As with previous human–microbe transitions, a new equilibrial state may lie ahead. However, it certainly will not entail a world free of infectious diseases. Any mature, sustainable, human ecology must come to terms with both the need for, and the needs of, the microbial species that help to make up the interdependent system of life on Earth. Humans and microbes are not 'at war'; rather, both parties are engaged in amoral, self-interested, coevolutionary struggle. We need to understand better, and therefore anticipate, the dynamics of that process.

1. Introduction

Over the past decade, there has been renewed public and official concern about infectious disease as a major public health threat. Indeed, the concern has arisen against a background of some surprise.

After all, we modern citizens live in hygienic homes with sweet-smelling toilet bowls, we eat pressure-packed sterilized foods, and we are protected by a plethora of vaccinations and antibiotics. Surely germ-free Nirvana is near. Yet, recent experiences indicate otherwise. In the past quarter of a century we have encountered the emergence of Legionnaire's disease, Lyme disease, HIV/AIDS, Ebola virus, human 'mad cow disease', the Nipah virus, West Nile fever and SARS, as well as resurgent adversaries such as tuberculosis, cholera, dengue fever and malaria.

The public anxiety has been particularly evident within the media-driven culture of the USA. There has been much discussion there about the 'emergence and resurgence' of infectious diseases. Titles of some of the recent popular offerings by American authors, in this racy journalistic genre, include *The coming plague, The hot zone, Virus hunter* and *Secret agents: the menace of emerging infections.* In this popular discourse, military metaphors abound: we are under siege from microbes; germs are invaders; we brace for the next wave; we counter-attack with antibiotics. The word 'emerging' itself can have ominous overtones.

This perspective, inappropriately, implies malign microbial intent. This fundamentally misrepresents the aeons-old ecological struggle in which all microbes must engage for their survival.

It certainly appears that infectious disease agents *are* emerging, re-emerging, and spreading more freely in the modern world. In the words of the World Health Organization, written in 1996: 'During the past 20 years, at least 30 new diseases have emerged to threaten the health of hundreds of millions of people' (WHO 1996).

The ecological conditions for this appear propitious. Human mobility and long-distance trade have increased; ever-larger cities, often girded with slums, have become highways for microbial traffic; poverty perpetuates vulnerability to infectious disease; and sexual practices, drug injecting, intensified food production and much modern medical technology all create new opportunities for microbial opportunism. We have experienced recent food-poisoning outbreaks from, for example, listeria, *Escherichia coli* O157 and salmonella. We recognize the potential impacts on patterns of infectious disease of global climate change, massive land-use changes, biodiversity losses and other global environmental changes that characterize the contemporary world. Widespread antibiotic resistance, especially of staphylococci, streptococci and enterococci, has followed our ill-considered over-use of these wonder drugs.

Cholera provides an instructive example. The ancestral home of cholera was apparently the Ganges delta, in India, where epidemics of a cholera-like disease have been described over the past four centuries. During the past four decades, a major pandemic of cholera has occurred. This is the seventh pandemic since cholera, reinforced with its newly acquired toxin-producing genotype, first extended its range beyond south Asia in 1817. That initial spread occurred as a result of the Great Kumbh religious festival in the Upper Ganges, in which great numbers of pilgrims from all over India came to bathe in the sacred waters. Their subsequent dispersal, in association with British troop movements in the northwest frontier region, led to a cholera pandemic that spread from India to the Arabian peninsula and along the trade routes to Africa and the Mediterranean coast.

In the early 1830s, the faster-travelling steamboats enabled cholera to cross the Atlantic. The disease reached North America in 1832, arriving first in Montreal, New York and Philadelphia. In the United States, the disease spread rapidly around the coastline and inland via major rivers. Public hysteria, fanned by the flames of newly established newspapers, spread rapidly.

This seventh pandemic has reached further than ever before, affecting Asia, Europe, Africa, North America and Latin America. It began in 1961 and is by far the longest-lasting pandemic to date (Lee & Dodgson 2000; WHO 2003). The strain is the El Tor strain, which, in the mid-twentieth century, appeared to replace the more lethal classical biotype of the nineteenth-century pandemics. Nevertheless, the extraordinary scale of this pandemic seems unlikely to reflect, predominantly, the biology of the bacterium. Rather, the scale and persistence of the pandemic is thought largely to reflect the greatly increased volume of human movement between continents, the greater rapidity and distance of modern shipping-based trade, the escalation in nutrient enrichment of coastal and estuarine waters by phosphates and nitrates in run-off wastewater, and the proliferation of urban slums without access to safe drinking water. In other words, the world today has apparently become a more conducive culture medium for this infectious agent.

Cholera, however, is a well-established, familiar, disease. Our main interest, here, is in the appearance and spread of new infectious diseases, of 'emerging infections'. We should first clarify this word 'emerging', since its usage has been somewhat ambiguous. In 1992, the US Institute of Medicine defined 'emerging' as subsuming three things:

(i) established infectious diseases undergoing increased incidence,
(ii) newly discovered infections, and
(iii) newly evolving (newly occurring) infections.

In the wake of the dramatic outbreak and spread of SARS in 2003, our particular interest here is to understand the social, environmental and related factors that potentiate the appearance of a *new* infectious disease such as SARS. Such understanding should assist us in the anticipation of any such future risks as the configurations of human ecology—social, environmental, technological and behavioural—continue to change.

2. What else can we learn from emerging infections?

Of course, many new infectious diseases do not develop into serious public health problems (McMichael 2001; Patz & Confalonieri 2004). Some do little more than establish a toehold at the margins of human society. Others flicker sporadically. Some, such as the 'English Sweats' of the sixteenth century, may circulate for decades and then apparently disappear. In the meantime, we cannot know what the future trajectory of the new disease will be. Twenty years after the initial spread of HIV/AIDS we are aghast at the scale of the pandemic. Meanwhile, we can learn things from all such emerging infections. In particular, they widen our understanding of the ecology of infectious diseases, and of the often distinctive adaptation mechanisms that boost the pathogen's survival or spread.

The science of emerging infections used to be a lot simpler. In the words of the biblical Old Testament:

> The Lord shall smite thee with a consumption, and with a fever,
> and with an inflammation, and with an extreme burning.
> (Deuteronomy 28:22)

Indeed, when wrathful, the Lord was apparently partial to quite a bit of smiting. Strange and often fatal diseases were thus dispensed as Divine Retribution.

The Revelation of St John the Divine—part of the Apocrypha that follows the Christian bible's New Testament, and written in about AD 100—gives a colourful account of this category of disease. St John describes the Four

Horsemen of the Apocalypse, the fourth (pestilence, riding on a white horse) being the harbinger of near-certain death.

The four horsemen are instructive in another sense. They are: War, Conquest, Famine and Pestilence. Two millennia ago in the eastern Mediterranean region, these were the four main recurring scourges of human happiness, health and survival. As public health threats, they are all conceptualized in population-level terms. An individual may be starving or malnourished, but it is the population at large that undergoes famine. An individual may contract an infection, but it is pestilence that sweeps through the whole population. That is, these terms are attuned to the notion of population-based phenomena as determinants of health and survival. This is a perspective that is often missing in the modern, popular discussion of the determinants of health (Reiter & Sprenger 1987; McMichael 2002).

Contemporary discussion, therefore, needs to incorporate a clearer understanding of infectious disease within an ecological framework. It cannot be mere chance that there has been an upturn in the tempo of new and spreading infectious disease in recent decades. Therefore, can we clarify, and assess the relative roles of the environmental and social factors in infectious disease emergence?

Both those two adjectives should be treated liberally. 'Environmental' refers to the physical circumstances of contact between pathogen and human. Environments can change at the micro, meso and macro scales. 'Social' encompasses community-level and individual-level behaviours, contact networks, choices of technology, etc. 'Social' also embraces political and cultural circumstances, and the distribution of advantage and disadvantage of varying vulnerability.

3. The process of 'emergence'

The primary event—the 'environmental' event that initiates a new human infection—is a novel physical contact between potential pathogen and human. The infectious agent mostly derives from an animal source, though some derive from the soil. A particular requirement, usually, is that the potential pathogen is a mutated strain that fortuitously (for the microbe) has become better able to enter and survive in the human host.

This contact event may arise naturally. More usually, it appears that such contacts have come about because of some cultural, social, behavioural or technological change on the part of humans.

The subsequent spread of the 'new' infectious disease may depend on either environmental or social factors. These include the following:

(i)   demographic characteristics and processes, human mobility, etc.;
(ii) land use, other environmental changes, encroachment on new environments;
(iii) consumption behaviours (eating, drinking, and, more generally, culinary culture);

(iv)   other behaviours (sexual contacts, IV drug use, hospital procedures, etc.);
(v)   host condition (malnutrition, diabetes, immune status, etc.).

An example of an emerging disease that primarily reflects social–techno-logical change is hepatitis C. This previously unknown hepatitis virus was identified in 1989, and may have been quietly circulating in humans for a very long time. The advent of illicit intravenous drug use and of medical transfusion has allowed the wider spread and the recognition of this virus.

Meanwhile, the resurgence of previously well-established infectious diseases—such as cholera, malaria, tuberculosis and diphtheria (in 1990s Russia)—has been primarily attributable to changes in social conditions and behaviours. These include poverty, crowding and the weakening of public health infra-structure. Indeed, this is an old, continuing story. Epidemics have often accompanied periods of great social and demographic transition. Examples include the bubonic plague in fourteenth-century Europe, following the pri-vations and poverty of the feudal system under the stress of several decades of miserable weather and crop failures; the scourges of tuberculosis, smallpox and cholera in the squalid crowded cities of Dickens's nineteenth-century England; and the ravages of the Spanish influenza following the chaos of World War I.

Various environmental influences, both physical and ecological changes, also influence the resurgence of some of these infectious diseases. For example, the World Health Organization has recently estimated that *ca.* 6–7% of malaria in some parts of the world is attributable to the climate change that has occurred during the past quarter of a century (McMichael *et al.* 2004).

4. Historical transitions, past and present

During many millennia of human cultural evolution, dispersal around the world, and subsequent interpopulation contact and conflict, there have been several distinct transitions in human ecology and in interpopulation interac-tions that have profoundly changed the patterns of infectious disease in human populations. The main transitions have been as follows.

(i)   Prehistoric transition.
(ii)   Historic transitions:
   (1)   first (local), 5–10 000 years ago;
   (2)   second (continental), *ca.* 1–3000 years ago;
   (3)   third (intercontinental), from *ca.* AD 1500;
   (4)   today (global), fourth historical transition.

The prehistoric transition began, several million years ago, with the move from tree dwelling to savannah. This entailed changes in exposures to mosquito and tick species. Likewise, the growing reliance of early *Homo* species on meat eating, from *ca.* 2 Myr ago, and associated activities such as the use of animal skins and fur would have increased exposure to enzootic agents and their vectors (including lice). The subsequent radiation of these upright-walking hunter-gatherers into unfamiliar environments would have exposed them to various new parasites.

This early transition also illustrates the close interrelationship between the behavioural, social and environmental domains, as interacting influences on the emergence of infectious disease. Under evolutionary pressures, human behaviours slowly changed. The behavioural move to ground-dwelling upright-walking existence entailed various environmental changes. There were also consequent changes in social relationships, in family and tribal groupings, and in patterns of day-to-day interaction between these hunter-gatherer hominids. Clearly, it is likely to be misleading to attempt to make a clear-cut differentiation of environmental and social influences on emerging infectious diseases.

Following the early emergence of agriculture and livestock herding, which began *ca.* 10 000 years ago in the eastern Mediterranean, three great transitions in human–microbe relationships, occurring on an increasingly large scale, are readily recognizable. These have been well described by the historian William McNeill (McNeill 1976). These are referred to as 'historic' transitions in that they occurred after the advent of early writing, when recorded 'history' became possible.

(a) First historic transition

Early human settlements, from *ca.* 5000–10 000 years ago, enabled enzootic pathogens to enter *Homo sapiens* (Weiss 2001). Many mutant microbes, originating from husbanded animals and 'urban' pest species (rodents, flies, etc.) would, by chance, have made contact with members of the unfamiliar human species. Most such microbial contacts must have failed. However, some, just as with HIV/AIDS, the Nipah virus and SARS in recent times, would have survived and prospered. They were the progenitors of today's textbook infections: influenza, tuberculosis, leprosy, cholera, typhoid, smallpox, chicken pox, measles, malaria, schistosomiasis, and many others.

(b) Second historic transition

Early Eurasian civilizations, now large and powerful, came into military and commercial contact, *ca.* 1500–3000 years ago, swapping their dominant infections. Rome, China and the eastern Mediterranean swapped their germ pools, often with disastrous results—such as the Justinian Plague of AD 542 that devastated Constantinople and the Roman Empire. The historical record shows that China suffered a series of massive epidemics during these times (McNeill 1976).

Following this second great historical transition, a trans-Eurasian equilibration of infectious disease agents, European populations were becoming genetically and culturally attuned to many of these now endemic or recurring infectious diseases. Presumably, the same was true at the other end of Eurasia, in the ancient, vast civilization of China. Contact with the bubonic plague in Europe, however, had only been occasional, and the disaster of the Black Death in the mid-fourteenth century came at the end of this second transitional period.

(c) Third historic transition

The third transition resulted from European exploration and imperialism, beginning *ca.* AD 1500 and continuing over much of the past five centuries. This caused the trans-oceanic spread of often-lethal infectious diseases. The devastating impact of the repertoire of infections taken to the Americas by the Spanish *conquistadores* is well known. Similar processes occurred with European explorations of the Asia-Pacific region, with European settlement in Australia, and with the trans-Atlantic slave trade.

An interesting sidelight on this third transition comes from Charles Darwin's two-month visit to the east coast of Australia in 1836, en route home after his famous stopover in the Galapagos islands. In his journal Darwin (1839) writes, following his observations of diseases in Australian Aboriginals:

> Besides these several evident causes of destruction, there appears to be some more mysterious agency generally at work. Wherever the European has trod, death seems to pursue the aboriginal. We may look to the wide extent of the Americas, Polynesia, the Cape of Good Hope, and Australia, and we shall find the same result.

Darwin later continues:

> It is certainly a fact, which cannot be controverted, that most of the diseases that have raged in the islands during my residence there, have been introduced by ships; and what renders this fact remarkable is that there might be no appearance of the disease among the crew of the ship which conveyed this destructive importation.

Here, half a century before the elucidation of the germ theory, this great naturalist was once again making incisive observation and inference.

(d) Fourth historic transition

Today, we are living through the fourth great historical transition. This time the scale is global and changes are occurring on many fronts. The spread and increased lability of various infectious diseases, new and old, reflect the impacts of demographic, environmental, social, technological and other rapid changes in human ecology. Global climate change, one of the greatest of the human-induced global environmental changes now underway, will have diverse impacts upon the patterns of infectious disease occurrence.

The globalization of our economic activities and culture, the rapidity of distant contact, the spread and intensification of urbanization, and our increasing reliance on either intricate or massive technology, are reshaping the relations between humans and microbes. In particular, we are destabilizing ecosystems in ways that favour the proliferation of the *r* species—that is, those small opportunistic species that (in contrast to the larger *K* species such as ourselves) reproduce rapidly, invest in prodigious output rather than intensive parenting, and have mechanisms to efficiently disperse their offspring. Pathogens are typical *r* species, and they live today in a world of increasing opportunity.

Figure 1 makes a crude attempt to compare the relative importance of major categories of environmental and social factors to each of the four historical transitions. Note, however, that the relativities are more meaningful within each of the four transitions, rather than between the transitions. This is a rather inexact exercise, but it underscores how configurations of social and environmental influences change. It also shows the more intensive set of influences that apply in today's world.

5. Social and environmental influences on emerging infectious diseases: some examples

The following section provides some examples of emerging infectious diseases, considered under major categories of environmental and social influences, pertaining to patterns of travel, trade and land use.

(a) Travel and trade

Wherever we travel, unseen microbes accompany us. The plague bacterium, *Yersinia pestis*, accompanied Roman legions returning from the Middle East. In London in the mid-nineteenth century, John Snow noted that cholera epidemics followed major routes of commerce between Asia and Europe, appearing first at seaports when entering a new region. However, the speed, volume and reach of today's travel are unprecedented in human history, and offer multiple potential routes for microbial spread around the globe.

The African malaria vector mosquito *Anopheles gambiae* gained entry to Brazil in 1937. Apparently, the mosquito migrated from western Africa on the mail-boats that traversed the Atlantic in 3–4 days. In the ensuing years, this mosquito species spread along the Brazilian coastal region and inland, and caused up to 50 000 deaths. (Fortunately, an extraordinary eradication campaign, led by the American Fred Sopers, eliminated it in the early 1940s.)

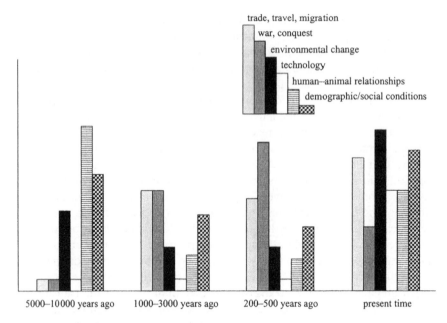

Figure 1 Indicative relative importance of various major environmental and social influences on infectious disease emergence, in each of the four major historical transitions (also see explanation in text.)

In today's globalizing economy, this story is often repeated. For example, a major mosquito vector for the dengue virus, *Aedes albopictus* (the 'Asian tiger mosquito'), has been spread widely in recent years, particularly via the unwitting intercontinental exportation of mosquito eggs in used car tyres into Africa and the Americas (Reiter & Sprenger 1987).

Neisseria meningitidis, a global pathogen, causes seasonal epidemics of meningitis in parts of Africa: the so-called 'meningitis belt'. The disease has spread more widely. Studies with molecular markers have shown, for example, how Muslim pilgrims that brought an epidemic strain of *N. meningitidis* from southern Asia to Mecca in 1987 then passed it on to pilgrims from sub-Saharan Africa, who subsequently initiated, back home, strain-specific epidemic outbreaks in 1988 and 1989. Studies of molecular markers traced the spread of this epidemic clone to several other countries (Moore *et al.* 1989).

The globalization of the food market has accentuated the movement of pathogens from one region to another. The commercial movement of foods, particularly fruits and vegetables, also redistributes microbial resistance genes along with the microbes. For example, an outbreak of cholera in Maryland, USA, was traced to imported contaminated frozen coconut milk (Taylor *et al.* 1993). Alfalfa sprouts grown from contaminated seed sent to a Dutch shipper caused outbreaks of infections with *Salmonella* species in both the USA and Finland (Mahon *et al.* 1997).

A primary drive that underlies migration is the urge to enter the cash economy, allied with the international demand for both skilled and unskilled workers in a globalizing marketplace. Rapid urbanization tends to boost old infectious diseases such as childhood pneumonia, diarrhoea, tuberculosis and dengue. It also facilitates the spread of various 'emerging' diseases; for example, high-rise housing creates new risks, as seen for SARS in Hong Kong. Such housing also increases family breakdown, drug abuse, sexually transmitted infections and HIV (Cohen 2003).

The disease West Nile virus, newly emergent in North America, further illustrates the impact of long-distance trade and travel. The disease originated in Africa, and occurs sporadically in the Middle East and parts of Europe. It was unknown in North America until it arrived in New York in 1999, via an infected mosquito on an aeroplane. Birds were affected first, humans later. There were apparently favourable conditions for the virus to survive and spread within New York City. They were as follows.

(i)   Early season rain and summer drought provided ideal conditions for *Culex* mosquitoes.
(ii)   July 1999 was the hottest July on record for New York City.
(iii) Suburban/urban ecosystems supported high numbers of select avian host and mosquito vector species adapted to those conditions.
(iv)   High populations of susceptible bird species existed, especially crows.
(v)   Suburban/urban ecosystems were conducive to close interaction of mosquitoes, birds and humans.

West Nile virus then spread rapidly across the United States, and has now established itself as an endemic virus, harboured by animals including birds and horses and transmitted via mosquitoes. There was a sharp increase in the number of human cases, involving most US states, during 2002–2003. In July 2003, Mexico declared a state of emergency when West Nile virus arrived in that country. The concern that the disease could spread more rapidly in Central and South America than in North America reflects the awareness that Latin American countries could be ideal breeding grounds, because of their warmer climate, large bird populations and year-round mosquitoes. Ecologists anticipate adverse impacts on domesticated horses and on the diverse animal and bird life in the tropics.

(b) Land use and environmental change

As Rene Dubos noted long ago, humans have always changed their environments (Dubos 1980). We are, in the words of the ecologists, 'patch disturbers'. The increasing scale of our intervention in the environment, both deliberately (e.g. land clearing, urbanization) and as collateral impact (e.g. global climate change, species extinctions), is inevitably accelerating the rate of emergence of new infectious diseases. The main human-induced environmental changes that affect infectious disease risk include: tropical deforestation; road building; irrigation; dam building; local/regional weather anomalies; intensified crop and animal production systems; urban sprawl; continued poor sanitation; and pollution of coastal zones.

A Working Group on Land Use Change and Infectious Disease Emergence, comprising several dozen scientists from around the world, met in 2002 and ranked the environmental factors, associated with land use, with most influence ('public health impact') on emerging diseases (Patz & Confalonieri 2004). The top 12 environmental changes, in descending order, were as follows:

(i)   agricultural development,
(ii)   urbanization,
(iii)   deforestation,
(iv)   population movement,
(v)   introduced species/pathogens,
(vi)   biodiversity loss,
(vii)   habitat fragmentation,
(viii) water and air pollution (including heightened respiratory susceptibility),
(ix)   road building,
(x)   impacts of HIV/AIDS,
(xi)   climatic changes, and
(xii)   hydrological changes, including dams.

Many natural systems—forests, drylands or cultivated systems—contain a distinct, exclusive set of infectious diseases. However, several major diseases, including malaria and dengue, occur across many ecosystems. Malaria is transmitted by 26 different species of anopheline mosquitoes, each of them dominant in particular habitats and locations. Because each species responds differently to a specified land use change, it is difficult to generalize the impact of ecosystem change effects across regions. Some other diseases such as yellow fever, however, can be transferred across ecosystems. The disease's natural, sylvatic, zoonotic cycle is between mosquitoes and monkeys high in forest canopies, but yellow fever can move into savannah, agricultural, and even urban areas in the wake of human economic activities such as logging or forest clearing.

6. Ecological disruptions

Next, some examples of emerging infectious diseases are considered in relation to six main ecological disruption situations. Each configuration of changes includes an aspect of land use (Patz & Confalonieri 2004). There is some overlap between these six categories, listed below, since they refer to changes in complex dynamic ecosystems:

(i)   altered habitat, with proliferation of reservoir or vector populations;
(ii)   biodiversity change and habitat fragmentation;
(iii)   ecosystem changes and loss of predators;
(iv)   intensified farming and animal husbandry;
(v)   niche invasion;
(vi)   host transfer.

(a) Altered habitat, with proliferation of reservoir or vector populations

Rodent-borne hantavirus occurs widely in agricultural systems, as in South America and east Asia, and in arid grasslands in North America and elsewhere. In mid-1993, an unexpected outbreak in humans occurred in the Four Corners region of southwest USA. The infection entailed acute respiratory distress, with high fatality. This 'hantavirus pulmonary syndrome' was traced to infection with a previously unrecognized virus, maintained primarily within the common native deermouse. Human infection occurs via contact in dried, wind-blown excretions of infected mice.

Apparently, the El Niño event of 1991–1992, with its unseasonally heavy summer rains, hugely boosted the local rodent populations, and potentiated the 1993 outbreak (Glass et al. 1995; Engelthaler et al. 1999). Populations of deermice were 10–15-fold higher than during the previous 20-year seasonal average (Parmenter et al. 1993).

(b) Biodiversity change and habitat fragmentation

Deforestation, with fragmentation of habitat, increases the 'edge effect', which then promotes pathogen–vector–host interaction. This process has contributed, in recent decades, to the emergence of the various viral haemorrhagic fevers in South America. These viral infections are caused by arenaviruses that have wild rodents as their natural hosts. They have been described especially in Argentina (Junin virus), Bolivia (Machupo virus) and Venezuela (Guanarito virus) (Maiztegui 1975; Simpson 1978; Salas et al. 1991).

These haemorrhagic fever infections typically occur in outbreaks ranging from a few dozen to thousands of cases. Outbreaks have mostly occurred in rural populations, when individuals become infected by contact with contaminated rodent excretions. Consider the example of the Machupo virus. The clearing of forested land in Bolivia in the early 1960s, which was accompanied by blanket spraying of DDT to control malaria mosquitoes, led, respectively, to infestation of cropland by *Calomys* mice and to the poisoning

723

of the rodents' usual predators (village cats). The consequent proliferation of mice and their viruses resulted in the appearance of a new viral fever, the Bolivian (Machupo) haemorrhagic fever, which killed around one-seventh of the local population.

The impact of forest clearance, with road building, ditch construction, and subsequent damming and irrigation, is known to have diverse impacts on anopheline mosquito species. Cleared land and the creation of ditches may enhance breeding opportunities for the preexisting local malaria-transmitting anopheline mosquitoes. By contrast, habitat destruction may eliminate some local mosquito species, perhaps thereby opening a niche for an invasive anopheline species (Povoa *et al.* 2001).

(c) Ecosystem changes, loss of predators and host species imbalance

Lyme disease illustrates this category of factor. This bacterial disease was first identified in the northeast USA in 1976 in the town of Old Lyme. The disease is spread by ixodic ticks that transmit the spirochaete *Borrelia burgdorferi*. The ticks normally feed on deer and white-footed mice, with the latter being the more competent viral host species.

Forest fragmentation has led to changes in biodiversity. This includes the loss of various predator species—wolves, foxes, raptors and others—and a resultant shift of ticks from the less to the more competent host species (as white-footed mice have become relatively more numerous, because of the reduced 'dilution' effect of biodiversity). These changes, along with middle-class suburban sprawl into woodlands, have all been interconnected in the occurrence of this disease (Glass *et al.* 1995; Schmidt & Ostfeld 2001).

(d) Intensified farming and animal husbandry

This category is well illustrated by the apparent interactions between avian viruses and humans in rural south China and environs. This interaction has been widely posited to underlie the emergence of new strains of influenza virus (perhaps with intervening passage through domesticated pigs). The influenza viruses are very unstable genetically, and are thus well adapted to evading host defences. Influenza viruses, when replicating in infected humans or animals, can undergo genetic rearrangement. For example, different subtypes of influenza A virus can swap genes, thereby producing a novel subtype with an altered antigenic profile, and this new subtype may on occasion be particularly virulent. This scrambling of genetic material, albeit usually minor, serves to ensure that animals and humans remain susceptible to the virus during each subsequent season. This enhances continuing survival prospects for the viruses.

(e) Niche invasion

The emergence of some infectious diseases results from a pathogen invading a new or recently vacated niche. A good example is the Nipah virus, which emerged as a human disease in Malaysia in 1999, causing over 100 deaths (Chua *et al.* 2000).

This highly pathogenic virus emerged from its natural reservoir host species (fruit bats) via domestic animal (pig) amplifier hosts. The ecological trigger appears to have been a complex series of human alterations to fruit bat habitat and agriculture in combination with a period of drought (Daszak *et al.* 2001; Chua *et al.* 2002). Three considerations are particularly relevant.

(i)   The virus does not appear to pass directly from bats to humans.
(ii) The fruit bat's habitat has been largely replaced in peninsular Malaysia by oil palm plantations.
(iii) Deforestation in adjacent Sumatra, coupled with a major El Niño-driven drought, led to significant seasonal air-pollution haze events that cover Malaysia. This reduced the flowering and fruiting of forest trees that are the natural food of fruit bats, thus impairing their food supply.

Thus, the Nipah virus outbreak in 1999 was associated with a marked decline in forest fruit production. This caused the encroachment of fruit bats (the key Nipah virus reservoir) into pig farms, where fruit plantations were also maintained. Infected pigs then passed on the viral infection to pig farmers (Chua *et al.* 2002).

(f) Host transfer

This, of course, is the old story of pathogens 'jumping ship'. The HIV/AIDS pandemic has reminded us of this ongoing risk, since it is clear that SIV mutants passed into humans some time during the twentieth century. Bushmeat hunting in Africa has led to other local emergence episodes (Patz & Wolfe 2002): for example, forest workers cutting up chimpanzee meat have become infected with Ebola virus (WHO 1996).

Cross-species transmission is, of course, bidirectional: it can also entail non-human primate species and other valuable wildlife coming into contact with human pathogens. For example, the parasitic disease, Giardia, was introduced to the Ugandan mountain gorilla by humans through ecotourism and conservation activities (Nizeyi *et al.* 1999). Non-human primates have acquired measles from ecotourists (Wallis & Lee 1999).

(g) Human-induced climate change

Many pathogens and their vectors are very sensitive to climatic conditions, particularly temperature, surface water and humidity. It has become

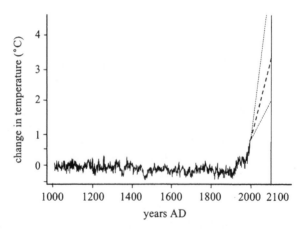

Figure 2 Reported variations in the Earth's average global surface temperature since AD 1000, supplemented by an estimated range of increases over the coming century (IPPC 2001) in response to recent and ongoing build-up of atmospheric greenhouse gas concentration. Note also the rapid rise in temperature of *ca.* 0.4°C since 1975. Hatched lines: approximate range of temperature increases estimated for the coming century by the IPCC (2001). Central estimate is 2–3°C .

increasingly certain not only that humans face anthropogenic climate change, because of the continuing excessive emission of greenhouse gases, but that the process has begun (see figure 2). In the words of a recent authoritative review: 'Modern climate change is dominated by human influences, which are now large enough to exceed the bounds of natural variability' (Karl & Trenberth 2003).

The frequency and geographical range of certain plant and animal infectious diseases has reportedly changed, at least partly in response to climate change, over recent years (Harvell *et al.* 2002). For human infectious diseases, the causal configuration is intrinsically more complex (entailing many more demographic, social and technological influences), and therefore it has proven difficult to attribute clear-cut impacts due to recent climate change. Nevertheless, some suggestive evidence exists for an influence of recent climate change upon cholera in Bangladesh, tick-borne encephalitis in Sweden, and malaria in parts of eastern Africa (Lindgren & Gustafson 2001; Patz *et al.* 2002; Rodo *et al.* 2002).

There has been considerable attention paid to how human diseases such as malaria and dengue fever will respond to the plausible range of global climate changes over the coming century. Various statistical and biologically based ('process') models have been brought to bear. However, much of the topic has not yet been broached. How will patterns of domestic and urban water use change in a warmer world? How will a change in climatic conditions, and associated changes in ecosystems, affect the probabilities of microbial mutation and successful speciation? What would be the infectious disease consequences of an increase in the tempo of extreme weather events and natural disasters?

With global climate change, we are beginning to change the conditions of life on Earth at the planetary scale. This is unprecedented. It will have diverse, mostly negative, consequences for biological systems everywhere and for dependent human societies.

(h) Dengue fever: a labile disease affected by urbanization, travel, trade and climate

Dengue is the most important vector-borne viral disease of humans. This disease has attained additional prominence recently, as one that is very likely to be affected by global climate change. Dengue is numerically the most important vector-borne viral disease of humans. Approximately 80 million cases are reported every year, of which *ca.* 20 000 die. Although dengue is primarily a tropical disease, it has extended in recent decades to countries with temperate climates. This reflects the increase in the number of imported cases, resulting from increased air travel, and the introduction of an exotic vector, *Aedes aegypti*, adapted to a cold climate (Kuno 1995).

This vector species, which breeds in water-containing sites typically found in the urban environment, has made extraordinary evolutionary adjustments to coexist with humans, having originated in forest Africa. The vector has followed humankind on its travels and migrations around the world (Monath 1994). It has attained further recent prominence as one of the main infectious diseases likely to be affected by global climate change throughout this century and beyond.

7. Concluding comments

Over the past two centuries, industrial and post-industrial changes in human ecology, rapid population growth and population movement have quickened. New infectious diseases emerged, even as some pathogens that have been around for a long time were eradicated or rendered insignificant. Nature is always trying out new genetic variants; ecological niches open and close; human society's defences wax and wane. Environmental and ecological change, local pollutants, the widespread loss of top predators, economic and social changes, and international travel, which drives a great movement of hosts, continue to change the profile of infectious disease occurrence, affecting pathogens across a wide taxonomic range of animals and plants.

Clearly, many factors, often interacting, can influence the emergence and re-emergence of infectious diseases. Thus, what is the relative importance of 'environmental' and 'social' factors?

The underlying initiating event, for a newly emergent disease, necessarily entails the entry into the human species, from an animal (broadly defined) source, of a normal zoonotic pathogen or of a fortuitous mutant pathogen. This event typically requires enhanced exposure of human subjects, and is best construed as an 'environmental' event. However, the particular environmental circumstance may be the result of some human behaviour or social practice, for example migration into a new environment, land clearance or climatic disturbance. Such 'environmental' events, or encounters, have underlain the recent emergence of new infectious disease such as HIV/AIDS, Lyme disease, the viral haemorrhagic fevers of South America, the Nipah virus and West Nile virus (within the USA).

The subsequent dissemination of these newly evolving or newly discovered infectious diseases within human populations then depends on a mix of environmental and social factors. Clearly, the disastrous spread of HIV/AIDS has had much to do with poverty, ignorance, prejudice and inept government. Similarly, urbanization, long-distance travel and freer sexual relations have all amplified the spread of many such diseases. Meanwhile, environmental mismanagement and change, whether agricultural land use, the damming of rivers, human-induced climate change or evaporative air-conditioning, can all contribute to amplification of spread.

Less relevant to today's discussion, the persistence or increase in familiar infectious diseases reflects particularly the widespread poverty, social disruption and the potent physical, economic and cultural forces of globalization. It is probably not a coincidence that the recent, longest-ever and widest-spread, pandemic of cholera, which has extended worldwide over four decades, has accompanied these aspects of the modern world. Malaria, tuberculosis and dengue fever have all increased their compass over the past 20 years, particularly within poorer communities or groups (Fineberg & Wilson 1996; Farmer 1999).

A little sadder and wiser, after this past quarter of a century, we are learning to think within an ecological framework—following a clue that Edward Jenner gave us just over two centuries ago: 'The deviation of man from the state in which he was originally placed by nature seems to have proved him a prolific source of diseases'.

We live in an increasingly globalized microbial world, a world that will continue to produce infectious disease surprises. We must think, anticipate, and act more in terms of ecological balance, and less in terms of ambush, warfare and arms race. Humans and microbes are not 'at war'. Rather, both parties are engaged in amoral, self-interested, coevolutionary struggle. We need to understand better, and therefore anticipate, the dynamics of that process. This has implications for environmental management, the alleviation of poverty as a generalized means of reducing susceptibility, the nurturing of social capital to ensure a stronger institutional base, the constraining of ecological folly arising from commercial pressures and consumerist drives, and, of course, the restitution of society's public health capacity and function.

Glossary

SARS: severe acute respiratory syndrome
WHO: World Health Organization

References

Chua, K. B. (and 21 others) 2000 Nipah virus: a recently emergent deadly paramyxo-virus. *Science* **288**, 1432–1435.

Chua, K., Chua, B. & Wang, C. 2002 Anthropogenic deforestation, El Niño and the emergence of Nipah virus in Malaysia. *Malay. J. Pathol.* **24**, 15–21.

Cohen, A. 2003 Urban unfinished business. *Int. J. Environ. Hlth Res.* **13**, S29–S36.

Darwin, C. R. 1839 Journal and remarks, 1832–1836. Quoted in F. W. Nicholas & J. M. Nicholas 2002 *Charles Darwin in Australia*, pp. 30–31. Cambridge University Press.

Daszak, P., Cunningham, A. A. & Hyatt, A. D. 2001 Anthropogenic environmental change and the emergence of infectious diseases in wildlife. *Acta Trop.* **78**, 103–116.

Dubos, R. 1980 *The wooing of Earth.* New York: Scribners.

Engelthaler, D. M. (and 11 others) 1999 Climatic and environmental patterns associated with hantavirus pulmonary syndrome, Four Corners region, United States. *Emerg. Infect. Dis.* **5**, 87–94.

Farmer, P. 1999 *Infections and inequalities. The modern plagues.* Berkeley, CA: University of California Press.

Fineberg, H. & Wilson, M. 1996 Social vulnerability and death by infection. *New Engl. J. Med.* **334**, 859–860.

Glass, G., Schwartz, B., Morgan, J. I., Johnson, D., Noy, P. & Israel, E. 1995 Environmental risk factors for Lyme disease identified with geographical information systems. *Am. J. Public Hlth* **85**, 944–948.

Harvell, C., Mitschell, C., Ward, J., Altizer, S., Dobson, A., Ostfeld, R. & Samuel, M. 2002 Climate warming and disease risks for terrestrial and marine biota. *Science* **296**, 2158–2162.

IPCC (Intergovernmental Panel on Climate Change) 2001 *Climate Change 2001: the scientific basis: contribution of Working Group 1 to the Third Assessment Report.* Cambridge University Press.

Karl, T. & Trenberth, K. 2003 Modern global climate change. *Science* **302**, 1719–1723.

Kuno, G. 1995 Review of the factors modulating dengue transmission. *Epidemiol. Rev.* **17**, 321–335.

Lee, K. & Dodgson, R. 2000 Globalisation and cholera: implications for global governance. *Global Governance 2000* **6**, 213–236.

Lindgren, E. & Gustafson, R. 2001 Tick-borne encephalitis in Sweden and climate change. *Lancet* **358**, 16–18.

McMichael, A. J. 2001 *Human frontiers, environments and disease: past patterns, uncertain futures.* Cambridge University Press.

McMichael, A. J. 2002 Population, environment, disease, and survival: past patterns, uncertain futures. *Lancet* **359**, 1145–1148.

McMichael, A. J. (and 11 others) 2004 Global climate change. In *Comparative quantification of health risks: global and regional burden of disease attributable to selected major risk factors* (ed. M. Ezzati, A. Lopez, A. Rodgers & C. Murray). Geneva: WHO. (In the press.)

McNeill, W. 1976 *Plagues and people*. Middlesex: Penguin.

Mahon, B. E. (and 11 others) 1997 An international outbreak of *Salmonella* infections caused by alfalfa sprouts grown from contaminated seeds. *J. Infect. Dis. USA* **91**, 2395–2400.

Maiztegui, J. I. 1975 Clinical and epidemiological patterns of Argentine haemorrhagic fever. *Bull. WHO* **52**, 567–575.

Monath, T. 1994 Dengue: the risk to developed and developing countries. *Proc. Natl Acad. Sci. USA* **91**, 2395–2400.

Moore, P., Reeves, M. W., Schwartz, B., Gellin, B. G. & Broome, C. V. 1989 Intercontinental spread of an epidemic group A *Neisseria meningitidis* strain. *Lancet* **2**, 260–263.

Nizeyi, J., Mwebe, A., Nanteza, M., Cranfield, G., Kalema, N. & Graczyk, T. 1999 *Cryptosporidium* sp. and *Giardia* sp. infections in mountain gorillas (*Gorilla gorilla beringei*) of the Bwindi Impenetrable National Park, Uganda. *J. Parasitol.* **85**, 1084–1088.

Parmenter, R., Brunt, J., Moore, D. & Ernest, S. 1993 The hantavirus epidemic in the southwest: rodent population dynamics and the implications for transmission of hantavirus-associated adult respiratory distress syndrome (HARDS) in the four corners region. *Sevilleta LTER Publ.* (University of New Mexico) **41**, 1–44.

Patz, J. & Confalonieri, U. 2004 Human health: infectious and parasitic diseases. In *Millennium ecosystem assessment: conditions and trends*. Washington, DC: Island Press. (In the press.)

Patz, J. & Wolfe, N. 2002 Global ecological change and human health. In *Conservation medicine: ecological health in practice* (ed. A. Aguirre, R. Ostfeld, G. Tabor, C. House & M. Pearl), pp. 167–181. Oxford University Press.

Patz, J., Hulme, M., Rosenzweig, C., Mitchell, T., Goldberg, R., Githeko, A., Lele, S., McMichael, A. & Le Sueur, D. 2002 Climate change: regional warming and malaria resurgence. *Nature* **420**, 627–628.

Povoa, M., Wirtz, R., Lacerda, R., Miles, M. & Warhurst, D. 2001 Malaria vectors in the municipality of Serra do Navio, State of Amapa, Amazon Region, Brazil. *Mem. Inst. Oswaldo Cruz* **96**, 179–184.

Reiter, P. & Sprenger, D. 1987 The used tire trade: a mechanism for the worldwide dispersal of container-breeding mosquitoes. *J. Am. Mosquito Control Assoc.* **3**, 494–501.

Rodo, X., Pascual, M., Fuchs, G. & Faruque, A. 2002 ENSO and cholera: a nonstationary link related to climate change? *Proc. Natl Acad. Sci. USA* **20**, 12 901–12 906.

Salas, R. (and 15 others) 1991 Venezuelan haemorrhagic fever. *Lancet* **338**, 1033–1036.

Schmidt, K. & Ostfeld, R. 2001 Biodiversity and the dilution effect in disease ecology. *Ecology* **82**, 609–619.

Simpson, D. 1978 Viral haemorrhagic fevers of man. *Bull. WHO* **56**, 819–832.

Taylor, J. L. (and 10 others) 1993 An outbreak of cholera in Maryland associated with imported commercial frozen fresh coconut milk. *J. Infect. Dis.* **167**, 1330–1335.

Wallis, J. & Lee, K. 1999 Primate conservation: the prevention of disease transmission. *Int. J. Primatol.* **20**, 803–826.

Weiss, R. A. 2001 The Leeuwenhoek Lecture 2001. Animal origins of human infectious disease. *Phil. Trans. R. Soc. Lond.* B **356**, 957–977. (DOI 10.1098/rstb.2001.0838.)

WHO 1996 *World Health Report 1996: fighting disease, fostering development*, p. 15. Geneva: WHO. See http://www.who.int/whr2001/2001/archives/1996/index.htm.

WHO 2003 *Global defence against the infectious disease threat*, pp. 74–79. Geneva: WHO.